Over-stating the Arab State

DATED – BUT STILL

ONE OF THE BEST –

HAPPY BIRTHDAY !

Brock

Over-stating the Arab State

Politics and Society in
the Middle East

NAZIH N. AYUBI

I.B.Tauris Publishers
LONDON · NEW YORK

Reprinted in 2001 by I.B. Tauris & Co Ltd
6 Salem Road, London W2 4BU
175 Fifth Avenue, New York NY 10010
www.ibtauris.com

In the United States of America and in Canada distributed by
St Martins Press, 175 Fifth Avenue, New York NY 10010

First published in 1995 by I.B. Tauris & Co Ltd. First reprinting in 1999

ISBN 1 85043 828 5

A full CIP record for this book is available from the British Library
A full CIP record for this book is available from the Library of Congress

Library of Congress catalog card: available

Typeset in Monotype Baskerville by Ewan Smith, London
Printed and bound in Great Britain by MPG Books Ltd, Bodmin

To Lindy, again

Contents

List of Tables

Preface and Acknowledgements

This is a book on the Arab (and more generally the Middle Eastern) state. It follows a broadly defined 'political economy' approach. While it gives particular weight to presenting the ways in which Arab authors themselves have analysed their own political affairs, it does lay the emphasis on broader conceptual and comparative perspectives, thus suggesting that Arab politics should no longer be perceived as being peculiarly and uniquely Arab.

The main argument of the book is that although most Arab states are 'hard' states, and indeed many of them are 'fierce' states, few of them are really 'strong' states. Although they have large bureaucracies, mighty armies and harsh prisons, they are lamentably feeble when it comes to collecting taxes, winning wars or forging a really 'hegemonic' power block or an ideology that can carry the state beyond the coercive and 'corporative' level and into the moral and intellectual sphere. The reasons why this has come about, and the detailed features and consequences of the process, represent the subject matter of this work.

Twelve Arab countries are given special attention in this book (Egypt, Syria, Iraq, Tunisia, Jordan, Saudi Arabia, Kuwait, the United Arab Emirates, Algeria, Yemen, Lebanon and Morocco). Of these, the first nine are used consistently throughout the work for comparative purposes, while the latter three are used more selectively. When the subject under discussion has warranted dealing with them, other Arab countries are brought in. From outside the Arab World, the cases of Turkey and Iran have also occasionally been invoked.

I have been working on the broad subject of this book, on and off, for the last ten years or so. Some of the original issues began to take shape as part of the preparation and teaching of a graduate seminar on the political economy of the Middle East, which I started at the University of California, Los Angeles (USA) and have continued to teach at the University of Exeter (UK). I have to thank my students on this course for their intelligent questions as well as for their sceptical looks at my continuing attempts to introduce non-politics and non-Middle East components into the course! Research for the book has been conducted over the years through the usual scholarly methods, supplemented by frequent visits – supported by a whole variety of excuses – to the Arab World (and Turkey).

My main concern has been to verify (at least for myself) that Middle Eastern issues may be 'specific' but that they are not particularly 'unique'. A lecturing tour to China and Japan in 1988/89, and repeated visits to these two countries in subsequent years, have helped me to confirm in my mind that 'culture' is significant but that it is not the over-arching variable that it is sometimes made out to be. The Japanese experiment is, of course, important for its own sake, but Japanese perspectives on the Middle East are particularly interesting because, as one Japanese scholar put it, this is a case of 'East looking at East'.

I had also suspected for quite some time that what one may loosely call the 'Latin American' school, especially in its post-dependency phase, was capable of offering many insights to the Middle East scholar, especially – but not only – when dealing with the more complex political economies such as those of Turkey, Egypt, Tunisia, etc. The literature on Latin America has indeed rewarded my curiosity, and a brief visit to Argentina and Brazil in 1991 gave me the opportunity to meet some of the Latin American scholars I had previously read – in particular Guillermo O'Donnell, whose strong influence on my analysis will be observed throughout much of this book.

The actual writing of the book was done mainly in 1992 and 1993. During the academic year 1991/92 I was a Jean Monnet Fellow at the European University Institute (EUI) in Florence. Although I was working there mainly on various aspects of European/Middle Eastern relations – work which is being published separately[1] – the city of Dante and Machiavelli provided a precious opportunity for further theoretical and comparative study and a splendid chance to reflect a little further on the significance of Antonio Gramsci, whose influence on my thinking will be obvious to the reader of this book. I would like to thank several people at the EUI but would single out on this occasion Susan Strange and Klaus Eder. During the academic year 1993/94 I was a Hallsworth Fellow in Political Economy at the University of Manchester. There, in a strong scholarly Department of Government with excellent and varied interests, I put my feet back on the ground and put my pen solidly to paper – and all but completed this work. Again, I am grateful to several people in Manchester, but would like in particular to mention Michael Moran and Geraint Parry.

As is to be expected, many people have helped me at one point or another while I was working on this book, usually by offering encouragement and support, by suggesting or providing some research material, or by commenting on earlier, related manuscript versions. I would like to thank in this respect John Waterbury, Ali H. Dessouki, Giacomo Luciani, Richard Chapman, Roger Owen, Sayyid Yasin, Richard Sklar, Bahgat Korany, Ray Hinnebusch, Fred Halliday, Aziz Al-Azmeh, Jean Leca, Samir Amin, Peter von Sivers, Hilmi Sha'rawi, Yves Schemeil, Muta' Safadi and Ilter Turan ... and I ask forgiveness of those whom I might have forgotten to mention. I was also supplied with research material by friends and colleagues at the Arab Organisation for

Administrative Sciences in Amman, the Arab Institute for Planning in Kuwait and the Centre for Political and Strategic Studies in Cairo.

Certain material in the book has appeared in different forms: parts of Chapter 7, in an earlier version, in the *Third World Quarterly*, Vol. 13, no. 1, 1992; parts of Chapter 9, in an earlier version, in G. Luciani, ed., *The Arab State* (London: Routledge, 1990); and parts of Chapter 11, in an earlier version, in *Arab Studies Quarterly*, Vol. 14, nos. 3–4, 1992. I acknowledge with thanks the permission of the publishers concerned for the use of this material.

Last but not least I would like to acknowledge the members of my own department at Exeter who have helped, directly or indirectly, and would single out for expression of my gratitude Michael Rush, a most decent and conscientious scholar whose enlightened policy (as head of department) on leaves of absence was in no small measure responsible for this work ever having been completed. I would also like to thank Paul Auchterlonie for an excellent library service and for his most competent indexing skills, and Sue Jackson for exceptionally efficient secretarial help.

I had been hoping that the more books one wrote, the easier the job would become – but how wrong I was. The magnitude of this particular undertaking, coinciding as it did with a time when the administrative and teaching burdens of British academics were multiplying alarmingly, made the last few months of work on this book particularly arduous. In this connection, a special debt of gratitude is due to my wife, Lindy, not only for the continuous help she has given in typing and editing but also for her patience and good humour during various tense moments. This book, once again, is dedicated to her.

The transliteration system used here is a simplified version of that adopted by the *International Journal of Middle Eastern Studies* (*IJMES*), except for words and names that have become familiar in their anglicised form (e.g. Quran, Nasser, Bourguiba, etc.).

Nazih N. Ayubi
Exeter, Summer 1994.

---

1. Nazih N. Ayubi, ed., *Distant Neighbours: the Political Economy of European/Middle Eastern Relations* (Reading, UK, Ithaca Press, 1994).

CHAPTER ONE

The Middle East and the State Debate: a Conceptual Framework

Why is it that even though they all call themselves Arabs, there are actually twenty disparate Arab 'states', all of which vary greatly in size and in resources and some of which are among the smallest in the world? Why is it that these 'states' engage so keenly in a multitude of attempts at political unification which always fail, one after the other? Why is it that although the rhetoric of politics in most Arab countries is based on broad or even universalist ideas such as nationalism or socialism, the actual 'ruling caste' is often very narrowly based and non-representative? Why is it that although they have large and expanding bureaucracies, armies and security forces, they fail to 'penetrate' the society in areas such as taxation and law enforcement? Why is it that these states appear to be so easily able to switch regional and international alliances (for example between the East and the West during the Cold War)? Why is it that they appear to be able overnight to launch complete reversals in domestic policy (say from socialism to economic liberalism and vice versa)?

These are some of the questions that have given rise to the idea of writing this comparative study on Arab politics.

The comparative method involves a synthesising exercise, both in general-isation and in specification (hence its vulnerability to criticism from both theoreticians and historians). Generalisation is mandatory, but it should not be so sweeping as to obliterate the distinct historical features of various 'cases'. Specification is also important, but it should not be so extreme as to turn every example into a 'special case' incapable of informing us beyond the contours of its own 'essence'. The book will attempt a certain balance between the two considerations. If there is a slight tilt, it may be in the direction of conceptualisation and generalisation since I am convinced that, whereas there is a reasonable number of good Middle Eastern country studies now available, comparative synthesising works (with few exceptions such as Hudson [1977], Bill and Leiden [1984], Bill and Springborg [1990], Richards and Waterbury

[1990], Owen [1992], and to some extent the Luciani volumes, culminating in Luciani [1990b]) are still lamentably lagging behind. Bromley's valuable book [1994], whose publication coincided with the completion of this book has a somewhat similar (political economy) approach to the present work, although it is different in scope and restricted to Western (although certainly not Orientalist) sources and debates.

In trying to deal with the subject I have been broadly informed by a 'political economy' approach without in fact overlooking the significance of 'political culture'. This was made possible by developing a simple, though in some ways unusual, conceptual framework, wherein concepts such as 'articulation', 'non-correspondence' and 'compensation' feature quite prominently. I believe that with the help of such concepts, 'political economy' and 'political culture' approaches can be reconciled and need no longer be regarded as inevitably contradictory. The writings of Arab authors about their own politics can thus cease to be mere statements of difference and signs of exoticness, and can be incorporated into a more universalist social science literature.

For this book aims at two apparently contradictory objectives. One is to place the Middle East (or more specifically the Arab World) within a theoretical and comparative framework that avoids the (Orientalist/Fundamentalist) claim of its utter peculiarity and uniqueness [see Halliday, 1993]. As one political scientist has rhetorically wondered, "Are Arab politics still Arab?" [Green, 1986]; and as another social scientist has conjectured, why should one always look for some peculiar reasons to explain things that take place in the Middle East? [Gilsenan, 1991].[1] The other objective is to rely as much as possible on literature produced by the Arab scholars themselves on their own societies and polities. The two objectives are not as contradictory as they may appear at first glance: our purpose is to show that although the Arab World and the Middle East region have their own *specificity* (I intentionally avoid speaking of 'authenticity') they are also – even when analysed by their own intellectuals – capable of being understood according to universal theoretical and 'social-scientific' categories.[2]

The coverage of this book proceeds in expanding circles. The 'core' is manifested by nine countries, covered in detail throughout the work, which have been selected to represent important 'categories' of Arab state (these are Egypt, Syria, Iraq, Saudi Arabia, Kuwait, the United Arab Emirates, Jordan, Tunisia and Algeria). Other Arab countries (e.g. Morocco, Lebanon, Yemen) are dealt with when the theme under discussion warrants tackling them as representative cases. From outside the Arab World, Turkey is referred to as being historically influential (through the Ottoman connection), as well as being an interesting comparative case (with regard to themes such as *étatisme*, populism, etc.). Iran is also referred to from time to time. The book is therefore based on a certain careful balance between case studies on the one hand, and comparisons and generalisations on the other.

In a certain sense this study is exploratory: attempting not so much to give a comprehensive coverage of any particular country or theme as to explore how they may be studied in the light of certain conceptual categories that do not stem either from a presumed socio-philosophical individualism (which has not yet established itself in the Middle East) or from an imagined (non-changing) cultural 'essence'.

The title of the book may perhaps warrant a little explanation. 'Over-stating' the Arab state is meant here to imply two theoretical concerns. The first aims at manifesting and explaining the remarkable expansion of the state in quantitative terms that has taken place during the last three to four decades, by way of expansion not only in state industrialisation and social welfare but also in public personnel, public organisations and public expenditures, etc. This process of expanding both the size of the state machine and the role of the state in the economy and society is what is usually described by the term *étatisme*. My use of the expression 'over-stating' in this context is analogous with the familiar word/concept 'overstaffing', and fairly akin to Hamza Alavi's [1979] concept of the 'over-developed state'. Very often, too, the Arab state is 'over-stated' in the sense of being over-stretched or over-extended; this is particularly true of populist regimes that try to pursue developmentalist *and* welfarist policies at the same time.

'Over-stating' the Arab state is also meant, ironically and by contrast, to imply that the real power, efficacy and significance of this state might have been overestimated. The Arab state is not a natural growth of its own socio-economic history or its own cultural and intellectual tradition. It is a 'fierce' state that has frequently to resort to raw coercion in order to preserve itself, but it is not a 'strong' state because (a) it lacks – to varying degrees of course – the 'infrastructural power' [Mann, 1986a] that enables states to penetrate society effectively through mechanisms such as taxation for example; and (b) it lacks ideological hegemony (in the Gramscian sense) that would enable it to forge a 'historic' social bloc that accepts the legitimacy of the ruling stratum.

Owing to the 'articulated' nature of the Middle Eastern social formations (a phenomenon that will be elaborated upon throughout the book), their politics tends also to assume an articulatory form, represented by various degrees and manifestations of 'corporatism'. This stems from the fact that in these societies neither 'philosophical individualism' nor social classes have developed well enough to allow for the emergence of politics as we see it in Western, capitalist societies. As with corporatism in general, Middle Eastern corporatism ranges between a more 'organic', solidaristic and communitarian strand at one end of the spectrum and a more organisational, interest-based and populist/mobilisational strand at the other. Saudi Arabia and other kin-based monarchies in the Gulf are illustrative of the first strand; Egypt and other sometime radical, populist republics are illustrative of the second.

Yet, and as G. O'Donnell [1977] has brilliantly observed, corporatism is not only 'statising' but also 'privatising'; i.e. it allows for special interests to make inroads for themselves within the state apparatus. The recent drive towards 'privatisation' as part of economic restructuring in the Middle East coincides with a broader re-examination of the state/civil society relationship. Within this re-examination, the public/private dichotomy is no longer only about ownership of the means of production but also about morality and social space, with the forces of political Islam declaring 'public' the sphere of morality, in order to fight back a state that has – perhaps for too long (and unsuccessfully) – declared 'public' the entire economic domain.

THE STATE DEBATE

Over the past decade or so, two apparently contradictory developments seem to have been taking place. Intellectually, political and social scientists have been busy 'bringing the state back in' as a major analytical concept (one which had apparently been eclipsed, mainly under the impact of American behaviouralism). In real political and economic life, however, there has been a great deal of talk about having 'less of the state' (*moins d'Etat*) and about 'getting the state off our backs'.

In the increasingly integrated world (market-wise and communications-wise) in which we live, the two developments (the intellectual and the politico-economic) have had an impact that extends far beyond their original birth place in the capitalist, advanced 'core' countries. And this has, of course, included the Middle East region.

Interest in the state and its role in the society and the economy started to grow among Arab intellectuals in the 1980s. The state had emerged in the Arab World at a time when Arab intellectuals were not really paying attention to its development – they were mostly preoccupied either with the 'Islamic *umma*' or with 'Arab nationalism', but not with the territorial bureaucratic state as such. With a few partial exceptions (notably Egypt, Morocco, Tunisia, Oman, Yemen and Turkey), the state – as a concept and as an institution – has been a recent introduction in the Middle East. Most Middle Eastern countries have, however, succeeded in preserving their newly established 'states', although not without cultural and social agony, while the state machines have themselves expanded most remarkably in size and in functional scope. It is only recently that this intellectual neglect of the state phenomenon has been partly ameliorated, and the contribution of authors in the Arabic language in this field is indeed worthy of review and critique – which we endeavour to do in this book.

Although most of the polities in the present-day world are usually described as 'states', the concept of the state that is familiar to political scientists cannot easily be isolated from the nationalist and organisational developments that took place in Europe in the period from the sixteenth to the twentieth century, or from the ideas of leading European thinkers such as Machiavelli, Bodin, Hobbes and Hegel.[3] The last, in particular, has been most influential and until Marx challenged several of his formulations in the nineteenth century, the Hegelian concept prevailed of the state as a moral expression of the triumph of unity over diversity, of the general over the specific, and of the public interest over the private [cf. Held, 1983: 1–58].

Marx, on the other hand, maintained that this was merely the state's concept of itself. In reality the state apparatus was a distinct entity that might be distinguished but could not be separated from the society at large. The state appears in two different capacities with Marx: either (as in the Communist Manifesto) it was an executive committee for the management of the collective affairs of the bourgeoisie, and as such a direct reflection of the interests of this class; or (as in the Eighteenth Brumaire of Louis Napoleon) it was an autonomous apparatus whose action ranged between balancing the existing interests in the society and promoting the 'parasitic' interests of the state personnel themselves [Draper, 1977]. There are therefore two potentially contradictory concepts of the state in Marx; one (instrumentalist, input-oriented) that sees the state as a reflection of the society, especially its class realities (Marxism Mark I); the other that sees it as a fairly autonomous body within the society capable of shaping events in it (Marxism Mark II) [cf. Badie and Birnbaum, 1983: 3–11].

Such a contradiction has opened the gate for debates among various Marxists as to the most pertinent way of conceptualising the state. In my view the leading figure in this debate was Antonio Gramsci. Given the influence of Gramsci's ideas on much of the analysis in this book, it may be in order at this stage very briefly to review his 'theory' on the state.

In many ways Gramsci filled in the gaps in Marx's theory of politics. His formulations part company with the conventional 'scientific' Marxist premise that the "base determines the form of consciousness", and establish instead the premise that the "base determines what forms of consciousness *are possible*" [Femia, 1975: 38]. According to Gramsci the state is "the entire complex of practical and theoretical activities with which the ruling class not only justifies and maintains its dominance, but manages to win the active consent of those over whom it rules" [Gramsci, 1971: 244].

It has of course been customary to speak of the state in terms of power ever since Botero's *Della Ragion di Stato* and in particular since Machiavelli's *Il Principe*. "That an impersonal structure of domination called the state is the core of politics is an idea so deeply embedded in our ways of thinking that any other conception of it appears counter-intuitive and implausible" [Viroli, 1992: 3, 126ff, 178, 281–5]. Even Weber's celebrated definition is based on power, albeit tempered power: "a state is a human community that (successfully) claims *the monopoly of the legitimate use of physical force* within a given territory" [in Gerth and Wright Mills, eds, 1970: 77–9; original emphasis]. Of course Weber's concept of domination as the basis of the state is tempered by his concept of 'legitimacy': "in principle, there are three inner justifications, hence basic *legitimations* of domination" – 'traditional', 'charismatic' and 'legal' [ibid.].

In Gramsci, 'domination' as a basic component of the state is also tempered, in this case by 'hegemony' – a concept far more comprehensive and less juridic than legitimacy. Of Greek origin, it is fortunate that *egemonia* also exists (most likely from the very same root) in classical and modern Arabic, as *haymana*. What is more, some shades of the same concept might have been anticipated in Ibn Khaldun's notion of *iltiham* (coalescence), which adds social integration and ideological cohesion ('a prophesy or a right doctrine'), to the overpowering physical capacity (*ghulb*) of the state. According to Ibn Khaldun in his *Muqaddima*: "Natural authority is derived from a group feeling (*'asabiyya*), [acquired] through the constant overwhelming of competing parties. However, the condition for the continuation of this authority is for the subservient parties to coalesce with the group that controls leadership" [quoted in Salamé, 1987: 208; compare also Qurban, 1984: 309–55].[4]

Gramsci develops the concept of hegemony from Marx and Lenin and makes it a seminal component of his concept of the state, a concept that he does *not* sharply contrast with civil society. He incorporates the apparatus of hegemony in the state, thereby expanding it beyond the Marxist-Leninist conception of the state as a coercive instrument of the bourgeoisie [Carnoy, 1984: 72ff]. Thus, according to Gramsci, "... the general notion of state includes elements which need to be referred back to the notion of civil society (in the sense that one might say that state = political society + civil society; in other words hegemony protected by the armour of coercion)" [Gramsci, 1971: 263]. As Martin Carnoy explains, Gramsci realised that the dominant class did not have to rely solely on the coercive power of the state or even its direct economic power to rule; rather, through its hegemony, expressed in the civil society *and* the state, the ruled could be persuaded to accept the system of beliefs of the ruling class and to share its social, cultural and moral values [Carnoy, 1984: 87]. A class becomes hegemonic in two ways: 'leading' and 'dominant'. "It leads the classes which are its allies, and dominates those which are its enemies" [Gramsci, 1971: 55–7, n. 5].

As Christine Buci-Glucksmann [1980] rightly illustrates, the concept of hegemony cannot be reduced to the Marxist notion of dominant ideology, or to the Weberian problematic of mechanisms of legitimacy that combine violence with ends of social integration. In the case of a successful hegemony, a class leads the whole of society forward:

> Its 'attraction' for the allied (and even enemy) classes is not passive but active. Not only does it not depend on simple mechanisms of administrative coercion, of constraint, but it is not even exhausted in the mechanisms of ideological imposition, ideological subjection (Althusser), or in legitimation by symbolic

violence (Bourdieu). Rather, from the moment hegemony becomes simply the backing for violence, or even worse, is only obtained by violence (the case of fascism, where 'consent is obtained only by the baton'), this hegemony is in fact no longer assured [Buci-Glucksmann, 1980: 56–8].

The Gramscian concept of hegemony is broader than the Weberian concept of legitimacy because it does not confine itself to the processes according to which political structures are accepted by the system's agents, but delves as well into the area of cultural and ideological consent, and emphasises the role of the state as *educator* [Gramsci, 1987: 187–8]. What Gramsci calls the 'gendarme-state' and the 'corporative-state' (i.e. the state in terms of its 'law and order' functions and the state in terms of its economic interests and functions) is simply a primitive and narrow, rather than a sophisticated, phase of state formation and development [cf. Buci-Glucksmann, 1980: 69ff, 89ff]. By contrast, Gramsci's concept of the 'integral state' or the 'state in its totality' (*lo stato integrale*) is not confined to the government but includes certain aspects of the civil society and is based on hegemony and leadership. The concept of the 'integral state' is thus often linked to that of the 'ethical state' or the state as educator – through the schools and the courts [ibid.: 127ff]. As Laclau and Mouffe put it, it is in the

movement from the 'political' to the 'intellectual and moral' plane, that the decisive transition takes place toward a concept of hegemony beyond 'class alliances'. For, whereas political leadership can be grounded upon a conjunctural coincidence of interests in which the participating sectors retain their separate identity, moral and intellectual leadership requires that an ensemble of 'ideas' and 'values' be shared by a number of sectors [Laclau and Mouffe, 1985: 66–7].

The contemporary state in the Middle East appears to correspond to the Gramscian categories of 'gendarme-state' and 'corporative-state'. Aspects of the 'police-state' in the Middle East are clear enough to most observers. As for the corporative aspects of the state, the following passage by C. Buci-Glucksmann would be relevant to the Middle East:

The economic-corporative phase of the state is necessarily longer ... the more 'gelatinous' and less developed civil society is. The state is then compelled to play a driving role in the social development, and this in the absence of earlier democratic traditions. When Gramsci writes how 'in Russia, the State was every-thing, civil society was primordial and gelatinous', it is necessary to add that precisely because this State was everything (authoritarian, tsarist), it could not be an integral state in the Gramscian sense. Class unification of an authoritarian and bureaucratic kind cannot be taken as a sign of strength ('expansiveness'), it is rather a sign of weakness [Buci-Glucksmann, 1980: 284ff].

Thus there is an inevitable 'productivist' phase, which may even lean towards a kind of 'statolatry' (i.e. an attitude of each particular social group towards *its own* state). But the transition from this to an integral state must take place by way of hegemony – or relationships at all levels of the society, from the factory through to the school, that aim at the creation of a new type and level of civilisation [Gramsci, 1987: 186–8]. To Gramsci the creation of an integral state with a leading or 'directive' class (*dirigente*) is equivalent to the creation of a *Weltanschauung* [Gramsci, 1971: 381]. Hegemony is achieved when this 'world-view' is diffused by agencies of ideological control and socialisation into every area of daily life to the extent that this prevailing consciousness is internalised by the broad masses to become part of their 'common sense' [Boggs, 1976: 39]. This is usually achieved through a dialectical interaction between the structure and the superstructure, between the objective and the subjective, manifested in the creation of a socio-political bloc, or, as Gramsci calls it, a historical bloc (*blocco storico*). This latter is "a *contingent*, socially constructed form of correspondence among the economic, political and ideological regions of social formation, [with an] anti-reductionist emphasis on the specificity of the 'national-popular' and the 'popular-democratic', in contradistinction to class demands and struggles" [Jessop, 1982: 209].

Gramsci's ideas on the state have been elaborated on or amplified by a number of thinkers including in particular Althusser and Poulantzas [cf. Carnoy, 1984: Ch. 4 and refs cited]. For our purposes the most useful idea to borrow from Althusser is his concept of the 'ideological apparatuses of the state'. Poulantzas is more complex, but his concept of the state as the most rational capitalist is not particularly pertinent for developing (pre-capitalist or early capitalist) countries (if indeed it is even appropriate for capitalist states). More useful for our purposes is his elaboration of the concept of the 'relative autonomy' of the state and his idea of the state as an arena for competition and struggle among the various 'class fractions' of the bourgeoisie [see, e.g., Poulantzas, 1971, and compare the critique by Miliband, 1983].

While benefiting from people like Poulantzas, I find that delving directly into Gramsci is often more rewarding. This is perhaps due to the fact that Gramsci had come originally from underdeveloped Sardinia and had lived in Italy at a period of (relatively) early capitalism combined for a while with Fascism (an atmosphere that is reminiscent of the situation in many semi-peripheral, and in some peripheral, countries today). In a certain sense, Gramsci may be regarded "as an original theoretician and a political strategist of 'uneven development'" [Laclau and Mouffe, 1985: 65–6]. His pertinence may also be attributable to his exceptional sensitivity to cultural issues (including the role of the intelligentsia), which are extremely important in the Middle East. Or is it perhaps due simply to the man's sheer intellectual genius and fecundity of thought? [cf. e.g., Davidson, 1977].

This is not to suggest that Gramsci's literature has been actually deployed for the purposes of studying Arab politics. While there is currently an un-deniable curiosity among Arab and Western scholars about the relevance of Gramsci to that part of the world [cf. e.g., Zureik, 1981; Al-Kanz, 1992; Davis,

1994; and most particularly Rashid et al., 1992], Gramscian concepts have not yet been systematically applied to the analysis and understanding of Arab politics in the way they have been applied to, for instance, Latin American politics.[5] Those in the Arab World who have attempted such an application have apparently found it delightfully rewarding:

> Gramsci's writings are texts with which you can enter into a dialogue, for they deal with issues that do concern us. Although they were written in Italy over half a century ago, the worries, aspirations and debates contained in them seem to be parallel to our own, to Arab and to international present-day concerns [Ghazul, 1992: 136].

Until quite recently, the prevalent concepts of politics (and of the state) that the Arabs tended to borrow from the West were first excessively formalistic, then, increasingly, excessively instrumentalist. An earlier concept of the state was heavily derived from the (continental European) 'constitutional law' school and its 'general theory of the state'. This was heavily indebted to the Hegelian concept of the state as an entity 'outside' the civil society and above it, which expressed more general and noble ideas pertaining to the public interest. To emphasise the separate and higher nature of the state the constitutionalists borrowed for it, from private law, the concept of a 'moral personality' (*shakhsiyya maʿnawiyya*): i.e. the state was thus an entity with a certain 'mind' and logic of its own that balanced in a dialectical way not only the considerations of specificity versus those of generality but also those of order versus those of change [cf. e.g., Burdeau, 1970: 103ff; Al-Badrawi, 1960: 61–3; Al-Jarf, 1960: 74ff].

This moral personality (the state) oversees the affairs of a specific 'people' on a specific 'territory', according to the principle of 'sovereignty'. This principle in turn has two manifestations: one external, connoting formal independence and equality *vis-à-vis* other states, the other internal, connoting the authority of the governor or of the government over its subjects. It was this internal aspect of sovereignty that Max Weber singled out as the most pertinent element in a sociological definition of the state: that it possesses the ultimate right to the legitimate use of force within the society [cf. Gerth and Wright Mills, 1970]. The fact that there was often a disparity between the legal equality of these subjects (citizens) *vis-à-vis* the state and the reality of their inequality (which was due to the division of the society into classes and to the protection given by the state to property rights) has not been part of the main concerns of traditional constitutional theory [cf. Poggi, 1978: 5ff, 94–5, 101–17].

More refined constitutional theory, however, contains, as a guarantee of the generality and objectivity of the state, a provision for the 'separation of powers' (by way of 'checks and balances' among the executive, legislative and judiciary functions) and a certain technique for restoring the (formally severed) connection between the state apparatus and the political society, which is elections [Miaille, 1982: 222–37].

Sociological concepts of the state (that of Max Weber included) had little currency in the Middle East, however. Weber remained basically identified with the legal-rational type of bureaucracy – most administrative and management experts in the Middle East (as we shall see in Chapter 9) accepted this concept with missionary zeal, many of them not realising that Weber had related this type of organisation rather closely to an (alien) 'protestant ethic' and that he had thus pronounced it to be rather remote from Muslim societies [cf. Turner, 1974].

Weberian social science reached the Arab World mainly in its modified American form. For the study of politics it was behaviouralism, structural-functionalism and systems theory which started to invade the scene from the 1960s on. Not unlike Marxism Mark I (i.e. the state is a reflection of the economic base as manifested in the class structure), what we may simplistically call 'American Political Science' also relied during this period on an instru-mentalist input-oriented approach. The difference was that whereas Marxism Mark I emphasised economic and socio-economic (class) inputs, American political science emphasised cultural and social-psychological inputs. Both neglected or overlooked the state as the major political actor, both under-estimated its relative autonomy, distinct identity and ability at times to shape society, and both were content simply to 'derive' the state either from economics or from culture.

Attempts to restore a sense of autonomy and prominence to 'the political' as represented by the state came first, and perhaps ironically, from the neo-Marxists, especially in the 1970s (e.g., Lukacs, Korsch, Poulantzas, Habermas, Offé, etc.] and was symbolically captured, among others, in the debate over the relative autonomy of the state, whereby the state does not 'reflect' but rather 'mediates' interests within society. During the 1980s and 1990s, Amer-ican political science came round to rediscovering the state and to 'bringing the state back in', although uncertainty has continued as to what exactly was meant by the 'state' [cf. Krasner, 1984; Evans, Rueschemeyer and Skocpol, eds, 1985].

THE STATE IN COMPARATIVE PERSPECTIVE

It is possible to conclude from what has been discussed so far that the 'state' is a phenomenon and a concept whose origins and precursors can be specified. Geographically and historically it is a European phenomenon that developed between the sixteenth and the twentieth centuries. Juridically, it is premised on the idea of law as general, impersonal rules. Organisationally, it is associated with unity, centralisation and functional differentiation (the so-called 'legal-rational type' with its bureaucracy and public servants). And economically, its rise has generally accompanied the development of capitalism and the rise of the bourgeoisie, including the need for extending and controlling the market, and for spreading and standardising the process of commodisation within it, so that it included human labour as well.

Although 'state' and 'society' are inseparable from each other in concrete terms, the two have often been contrasted with each other in conceptual terms. The state is often conceived as standing apart from, and above, society. A more useful idea, suggests Timothy Mitchell, is to regard the state as the 'structural effect' resulting from modern techniques of functional specification, organisational control and social surveillance that are exercised within society by institutions such as armies, bureaucracies and schools [Mitchell, 1991: 78–96]

But if this is indeed the case, to what extent can one speak of the state outside this just-mentioned geographical–historical–socio-economic context? For example, can one speak about states in the generic sense so that they may include, for example, pre-capitalist or non-European cases? [cf. Badie and Birnbaum, 1983: 42ff]. Peter Nettl, in a pioneering article, stated that this was possible and spoke about varying degrees of 'stateness' to be measured according to certain criteria that he enumerated. As such the concept is universal, although he thought that the developing countries had not, by the mid-1960s, adopted and internalised that tradition in an effective way [Nettl, 1968: 589–891].

Yet the state formula appears to have become truly globalised and one is justified in wondering, with the Turkish political scientist Ali Kazancigil, why it is adopted by all new states and why new formulas are not improvised, even in cases where the socio-historical prerequisites for a 'state' do not obtain and even when its nationalist/secularist concepts seem to contradict the native religio-political ethos so notably (as, he says, is the case with many 'Islamists')? Although part of the impact of the state concept may be attributed to its imposition by colonial powers, much of it is still due to cultural diffusion and to voluntary mimicry by the élites of non-Western countries [Kazancigil, 1986: 119–25].

But are these countries that mimic the European state formula 'real' states? Dumont [1986] suggests a link between the development of individualism as a cultural tradition and the emergence of the modern state, and although he does not appear to say it in so many words, he seems to imply that the two are somewhat correlated. Badie and Birnbaum are less sure about the economic (capitalist) prerequisites of the state but more emphatic about relating it to the development of a specific (European) set of cultural and religious values that date back to Roman law and to the Renaissance and are closely linked to the concept of secularisation. Such values are, in their view, incompatible with societies dominated by an organic religion (such as Islam or Hinduism); such latter societies are incapable of functioning according to the principles of 'differentiation' and 'autonomisation' of groups and organisations which are so fundamental for the Western state model – to enforce such a state model on such societies by 'exporting' it would only lead to the emergence of authoritarian trends within the political sphere [Badie and Birnbaum, 1983: 97–101, 135–6]. Their argument stems basically from the organic–contractual dichotomy used by many to contrast Eastern (including Middle Eastern) societies with Western ones [Nisbet, 1986: 79–80].

Jackson and Rosenberg [1985] indeed conclude that such 'states' are not real. At best they are quasi-states. They hold that one has to distinguish between a legal, juridic concept of the state and a sociological, 'empirical' concept of the state. Many countries in the Third World (especially in sub-Saharan Africa) are states in the first sense only, since the developmental pattern of the state phenomenon in the Third World has been the reverse of that pattern in Europe and the West. In the latter, 'states' developed as political, military and social entities first, and then endeavoured – through competition and war – to gain legal recognition of their existence. In Africa and much of the Third World the 'state' emerged first in its juridic sense, as part of a colonial legacy, before social and organisational factors sufficient to make of it a real state had developed. Not only this, but the 'legality' of these pre-mature states acts as a constraint on their development towards becoming real 'sociological' states because this legality gives a false impression of (and provides an artificial compensation for) the necessity of 'building' a real state on solid economic, administrative and cultural bases [see also Jackson, 1993].

Yet the problems of the post-colonial state are not simply attributable to its purely juridic 'pre-mature' nature. Part of the problem may be due to its 'lopsided' nature: to the fact that it is underdeveloped in certain respects but overdeveloped in others. This is an idea elaborated upon by Hamza Alavi [Alavi, 1979]. The state in the ex-colonial societies was not created by a national bourgeoisie but by a foreign colonial one which over-inflated the size of the bureaucratic machine, especially its military wing, to serve its own purposes in the colonies. As these purposes were generally separate from the main bulk of national interests, maintains Alavi, this state has developed a considerable amount of 'relative autonomy' vis-à-vis the native economic and social forces. And as a continuation of this colonial legacy, the military-bureaucratic oligarchy of the independent states has continued to play a mediating role among the competing demands of three owning classes: the landlords, the native capitalists and metropolitan capital. Inevitably this gave the state significant power in the economic as well as in the political affairs of the society. Alavi's thesis is indeed persuasive and potentially useful, but one has to be careful about its relevance for various cases. In the Middle East context it will not be very useful for states that have no clear and sustained 'colonial' past, or for post-colonial states which are not dominated by the military-bureaucratic oligarchy (as in the Gulf region, for example). It is generally true, however (as we shall see in Chapters 9 and 11) that bureaucracies are 'oversized' in the Middle East, both in relation to the society at large and in comparison to non-executive bodies of politics, and one can probably speak about an oversized (if not necessarily over-developed) state in the Middle East regardless of the colonial past of these states.

This exaggerated role of the state can more easily be related to the delayed capitalist development of most peripheral countries. The most powerful argument in this respect has been advanced by Alexander Gerschenkron [1962] who has illustrated that the later a country is in its economic development, the larger the role that the state is likely to play in trying to promote development [compare also B. Moore, 1969]. This is how *étatisme* has come to characterise the political economy of many countries in the South. Although some trace the historical origins of regulatory practices to Babylonian and Egyptian times, the term *étatisme* was first coined to describe the system of centralised administration and economic management instituted by Jean-Baptiste Colbert, the minister of finance and the controller-general under Louis XIV in seventeenth-century France (and by later regimes of centralised government and mercantilistic policies in France and elsewhere) [Chodak, 1989: 2–3, 96–100]. state policies that are highly interventionist and manipulative in the economic sphere are also sometimes described as *dirigiste*. *Dirigisme* is a practice that places "economics as the key area around which political battles are waged" and "views the state as a necessary and essentially benign agent of economic transformation" [Milanović, 1989: 64ff].

It is also worth noting that countries which obtained their independence before the Second World War – that is, before the consolidation of a global capitalist economy (such as in Latin America and the Balkans) – were more capable of developing a national bourgeoisie of sorts and of accumulating reasonable levels of domestic capital than were the countries that acquired their independence after the Second World War, as was the case with most Asian and African countries [Kazancigil, 1986: 131–7]. In these latter countries, one finds not only that the native capitalists are so dependent on the state for protection, subsidy and the provision of various services and products, but that the state also plays a more important role in the production process itself, especially with regard to controlling and disciplining the working classes by political (and sometimes violent) means [compare Aké, 1985]. Thus both the capitalist and the working classes are generally subservient in relation to their own 'peripheral' state, which explains, among other things, the crisis of democracy in most Middle Eastern countries (as we shall see in Chapter 11 and elsewhere).

But the subservience of the national bourgeoisie and of the working classes *vis-à-vis* their own state does not tell us the whole story about the nature of the peripheral state. Such a state cannot be understood with reference to its 'own' classes and social forces alone, because it is also governed by the requirements of what Mathias and Salama [1983] call the *Economie mondiale constituée* (the compound world economy), including in particular the needs of the national states of the core. This is an arena where the vagaries of the international division of labour confront the various attempts to modify this division. The peripheral state may thus be regarded as a bridge between the local society and the world system; it acts to spread trade relations and to preserve certain components of the international division of labour within its borders, using a mixture of legitimacy-building and violence-applying enforcement methods [Mathias and Salama, 1983: 35ff, 89-126]. Although the analysis of Mathias and Salama is still basically premised on a 'derivation' theory (i.e. that the state, although formally autonomised, can ultimately be traced to capital, via processes of commodification), it is certainly more sophisticated than the somewhat simpler formulation of Aké [1985: 105-7]. The derivation theory of the state has some proponents in the Arab World (e.g. Khalid al-Manubi of Tunisia) and although it can be useful at a certain rather general level it does not, in my view, offer a detailed analysis of the specific problems of states (in the plural) rather than of *the* state in the generic sense [for further studies and critiques of the state derivation theory see Clarke, 1991].

One is still in need of a theory that relates in detail the imperatives and requirements of the economy (domestic and global) to the potentialities and options of politics in a developing country. The best attempt in this vein, in my view, is the now quite influential one of Guillermo O'Donnell [1973, 1977]. The degree to which I have been influenced by O'Donnell's analysis will become clear in various parts of this book; it is sufficient to say here that his main contribution has been in trying to link the various stages in the development of certain economic strategies (mainly that of import-substitution industrialisation) with various changes in the nature of the state that are characterised by shifting socio-political coalitions (as represented, for example by populism, corporatism and bureaucratic-authoritarianism). Leonard Binder [1988] has lamented the fact that such an approach has not affected Middle Eastern studies – but recently it has started to exercise a certain influence [cf. e.g. Farah, 1985], and to good effect in my view. This present study in many ways continues along the same path.

Such an approach should consider not only the way in which the state's form and characteristics are modified under the impact of changing economic imperatives and socio-economic alliances, but also the way in which the state in many cases adjusts the economic imperatives and reshapes the socio-economic alliances. One need not regard the state only as a 'receiver' (i.e. along with what I have previously termed input-oriented approaches, whether economistic or behaviouralist). The state may 'reflect' (or 'represent', or 'condense', etc.) the social classes or may intermediate among them; but there are also cases, especially in the periphery, where the state manages to *create* its own classes.

Such a proposition is not completely novel, even within Marxist circles.

Obviously part of the debate over the so-called 'Asiatic mode of production' [cf. e.g. CERM, 1969] pertains to the possibilities of the emergence of classes from within state institutions or as a result of state action. There is no denying that a certain 'Orientalist' slant has characterised much of the Marxist debate with regard to non-European societies [cf. Turner, 1978]. Even our good friend Gramsci is not completely blameless in this respect. Yet there is still some validity left in the category of the Asiatic mode of production if one can overlook its ethno-culturalist connotations to concentrate instead on its geo-ecological and economic-historical dimensions. Thus for example, as Perry Anderson notes, no hereditary nobility similar to that of Europe was able to develop in the mediaeval Islamic empire, since individual private ownership did not exist as a principal *right* and because wealth and status were closely tied to connection with the state. In return the state also maintained tight control of the city, the market and the guilds, thus allowing little room for independent 'bourgeois' classes to emerge [cf. Anderson, 1979, esp. 361–77]. I accept such a description as being very generally true, and will leave a detailed discussion of the various implications to later chapters. For the moment we should keep in mind the proposition that, owing to its specific geo-historical background as well as its current heavy involvement in economic accumulation, the Middle Eastern state is not simply a reflection of the class reality of its society but very often a creator of such realities as well.

THE NON-INDIVIDUALISTIC PATH TO THE STATE

Thus far we have considered the socio-economic specificity of the Middle Eastern state, but what about its 'cultural' specificity? We have already referred to the views of some writers to the effect that the concept and institution of the state are exclusively European phenomena that are culturally incompatible with Muslim societies, due to the latter's 'organic' nature and to the weakness of individualist and secularist traditions within them. Even epistemologically, it is often said, the word state signifies different things in Arabic and in Latin. Scholars observe that the very linguistic origins of the word *state* in European languages and of the word *dawla* in Arabic actually imply opposite things: stability and continuity of position in the first; circulation and reversals of power and fortune in the second. We are also frequently told that it is the concept of the community (*umma*), especially in its religio-cultural sense, that is more important in the Islamic political tradition than any concept of the state or the political system [see, e.g., the discussion in Ayubi, 1991a: Ch. 1, also Ayubi, 1992c]. Although much of this is true, I would suggest that it may not be an Arab or an Islamic peculiarity and would like to argue in the next few pages that there are indeed potentially both non-individualistic and non-European paths to the state.

Part of the conceptual problem is related to the fact that when we speak of 'Western' political science we actually mean Anglo-Saxon and to some extent French political science (and in their 'liberal' strand at that); German sociological and historicist thinking, for example, tends on the whole to be absent. The problem is even more pronounced for Middle Eastern scholars because of their special colonial linguistic and cultural links with the English and French 'metropoles'. This is perhaps a pity, since there are several German ideas that have more affinity with certain Arabo-Islamic concepts and concerns than have some of the most prevalent English and French political ideas.

Historicist and romantic German thinking has always attached a special emphasis to the concept of the Community, *Gemeinschaft* (or *jama'a*; *umma* in Arabic), which they identified with the 'authentic' spiritual essence, *Geist* (or *ruh* in Arabic) of Germany in contradiction to the Renaissance philosophy of Napoleonic France. Through the ideas of such people as Sauvigny, Moser, Müller, Fichte and Mommsen the German Romantics were able to relate the concept of the Community to the concept of the state (via the concept of the Nation), so that the state came to be regarded as the fullest and noblest expression of the Community. In certain ways they generalised the moral principles of the village or the guild to include the entire nation, and they coloured their concept of freedom not by individualism but by a distinctive collective aura derived from the concept of loyalty, on the assumption that the strength of the group and the freedom of the individual always went hand in hand [cf. Black, 1984: 196–202; Dumont, 1986: 74–5, 114–17, 134–59, 260–61]. Another branch of the German tradition, deriving its antecedents from Herder and Beseler, was to see in language and law the most supreme expression of the nation. This was to reach its apogee in Gierke and Tönnies, who tried in the late nineteenth and early twentieth centuries to enliven the concept of a collective personality based on brotherhood and solidarity [Black, 1984: 210ff]. Such concepts and concerns of German and other European Romantic, Historicist and Conservative thought are strikingly akin to many of the concepts and concerns predominant in Arab and Islamic political thinking.[6]

More specifically, "we have a Romantic notion of history which is familiar in modern history – from Herder and his patrimony in Germany, to ideas current in the Risorgimento, to the organicist, racist conservatism of Gustave Le Bon. All these are widely attested to in the history of modern Arab thought" [Al-Azmeh, 1993: 28]. From the early stages of 'reformist' Arab thought under the encounter with modern European ideas in the nineteenth century, the two main intellectual leaders, Jamal al-Din al-Afghani (1839–97) and Muhammad 'Abduh (1849–1905) had inclined towards a 'vitalist', 'organismic' concept of the body-politic, that invites comparison with Herder's romanticism and his emphasis on *Bildung*, and with Spencer's social-Darwinism [ibid.: 44–5, 81]. Their theory of the 'tight bond' (*al-'urwa al-wuthqa*) "is very decidedly anti-Enlightenment – both in its tenor and its content, and has been implicitly or explicitly embraced by all revivalist movements." It adopts an organicist and vitalist paradigm of the polity according to which a body-politic in which the various parts are not related by a purposeful 'unity' resembles a body in distemper. Ideas of 'political organisms' were prevalent in the Middle East at the time under the influence of Spencer, and were shared even by secular Arab thinkers such as Shibli Shumayyil.[7] Another comparison that can be made is with Herder's vitalist Romanticism, which is detectable in Young Ottoman thought and apparent in the 'solidaristic corporatism' of the Turkish nationalist Zia Gökalp and in the ideas of the Pan-Arab Ba'thists and of the Syrian Social-Nationalists [ibid.: 82–7].

The Pan-Arabists (as we shall see in Chapter 4) were particularly fond of people such as Nietzsche, Spengler and Bergson. The neo-Islamists inherit parts of that influence, usually adding to it a certain "naturalization of history" (e.g. *din al-fitra*) that Aziz al-Azmeh finds analogous to the National-Socialist cult of nature [1993: 30]. Another connection might be found in the fascistoid Frenchman Alexis Carrel (d. 1944), who seems to have influenced such important Islamic thinkers as Abul-Hasan Nadwi, Sayyid Qutb and 'Ali Shari'ati [cf. Al-Sayyid, 1988: 349; Hanafi, 1986: 44–5; Al-Azmeh, 1993: 30; but see most particularly Choueiri, 1990: 140–49].

The influence of such concepts is also starting to find its way into the works of contemporary Arab political scientists as well. A good case in point is to be found in the writings of Hamid Rabi' (d. 1989), an influential Egyptian political scientist who taught also in Iraq, Syria, Saudi Arabia and elsewhere in the Arab World. Influenced in particular by German and Italian Historicist schools (he studied and lived in Italy for many years), he is a kind of 'cultural nationalist' with a distinct Islamic inclination. Rabi' is openly anti-Enlightenment. In his view the 'nation-state' in its European form was mainly a reaction to the Catholic model, attaching first place to rights of the individual, aiming at creating a direct unmediated relationship between the citizen and the state, forcing the Church to retire into its own cocoon, and thus expelling all non-political agencies from the relationship and ending up by adulating the state in the name of individual rights [Rabi', 1980: 15–16]. This model is not suitable for the Arab countries, for which Rabi' suggests an inspiration from the Islamic model by way of a certain revival of the 'cultural heritage' (*turath*) to be guided by a distinct 'political function' (*wazifa siyasiyya*). He finds the German national school worthy of consideration in this respect, and admires the way the German thinkers, when faced with the humiliation of the French conquest, delved into their own Teutonic heritage in search of cultural and civilisational roots that raised the Germans' awareness of their national distinctiveness and 'authenticity' [ibid.: 21].

Any attempt to create an Egyptian or Arab national self-awareness has, likewise, to search in older Islamic sources for aspects of distinctiveness and authenticity. Rabi' endeavours to undertake some of this task himself, and abstracts a number of features from what he calls the Islamic political paradigm that should inspire the contemporary quest for national authenticity:

> The cultural heritage (*turath*) is the means to self-recognition. The national Self is one and indivisible. It is the expression of a fixed continuity, in spite of some diverse manifestations on the individual and collective levels. Self-recognition cannot spring up except from the past. Just as a tree may not be complete without a multiplicity of branches, its ability to survive will obtain only as to the depth to which its roots can reach [ibid.: 218].

The Islamic model, he maintains, has its aspects of political vitality that can inspire contemporary politics. Although it has not known the idea of 'voting', or of representative councils, institutionalised political opposition, or guarantees for the political liberties of the individual, it has its own concepts and dynamics for political equilibrium. These concepts include moderation, consensus and compromise, and those dynamics include balance and mutual control between the caliph, the *'ulama'* and the judges [ibid.: 46–51, 133–49]. The Islamic polity is not a state in the European sense (i.e. territorially defined) but an organised politico-religious community (*umma*). The purpose of the *umma* is spreading the message (*da'wa*) and the function of power and authority (*sulta*) is to act as the instrument for achieving such a cultural/civilisational mission (*risala hadariyya*). The Islamic 'state' is therefore a 'doctrinal' state (*'aqa'idiyya*) with a distinct communicational function (*wazifa ittisaliyya*) based on the merger of ethical principles with political ideals, and on the non-separation of private life and public life. The state is closely linked to culture/civilisation (*hadara*), and the Islamic *hadara* is distinctively militant (*kifahiyya*), based on group loyalty within and on civilisational encounter outside [ibid., 1980: 154–67].

That concept, states Rabi', is different from the state concept as it developed with the nation-state in Europe. In the latter the idea of the civilisational function of the state has declined in favour of a purely 'political' function (notwithstanding the 'ideological' conflict that characterised the Cold War). The Islamic state, by contrast, followed in the tradition of the Greek and Roman civilisations where the state and the 'civilisational will' (*al-irada al-hadariyya*) were at one. The civilisational function of the Islamic state revolves around *al-da'wa* (the 'call'), and politics is about securing the environment that enables the individual to realise his Islamic idealism. That state is also universalistic in its appeal. The European state since Machiavelli, and in particular since the French Revolution, has become too abstract and too isolated from society and culture; its "concept of the state is void of any moral or cultural existence" [287–8]. By contrast the Islamic state is the expression of a certain ethical ideal: Islam presents a certain ideal, if not a specific political model [289–93]. The modern Arab national state should in turn be an instrument for sustaining a permanent link between the past, the present and the future. For the nation (*al-umma*) is not based on racial unity but on a unity of perception, language and civilisation, and the ideal of this community is not overwhelmingly economic but moral and ethical [Rabi', 1985: 46–7].

Rabi''s improvisation is important, first because he is one of very few Arab *political scientists* who wrote on the Islamic state, and second because, unlike most other 'modern' scholars, he did not try to interpret the Islamic state according to the French-constitutional or the American-behavioural school. Instead, Rabi' is an idealist (it is often impossible to draw a distinction in his writing between the 'was' for the idealised Islamic polity and the 'ought' for the desired Arab state), he is avowedly anti-Enlightenment, hostile to the French Revolution and openly inspired by German and Italian historicist/ romantic ideas. He rejects the concept of state autonomy and the attempt to confine the state's function to the political domain. For him the French Revolution represents "a dangerous decline for many political concepts and perceptions. If it has released political forces and realised the concept of national politics, it has at the same time sowed the seeds for racialism and national chauvinism, and drained the political vocation of any civilisational essence" [Rabi', 1983: 268–93, 288]. By contrast Rabi' finds the tenets of the German historicist school more capable of capturing the essence of the Islamic (and hence the Arab) state, and his writings are replete with sympathetic references to people such as Sauvigny, Fichte and Mommsen. It is also possible to trace in his writings echoes of the concept of the ethical state (*lo stato etico*) as espoused by such writers as Croce, Gentile and ultimately of course, Hegel [cf. Bellamy, 1987: 8 *et passim*]. He calls for a politically driven revival of the *turath*, and he even attributes the success of contemporary political Zionism to its having been inspired by the historical German school on the one hand and by the Abbasid and Fatimid Islamic literature on *da'wa* on the other: "the Zionist call has been able to find, via the Islamic *turath*, a starting point from which to address the world of the twentieth century ... and to achieve ... this success that could not have been anticipated by the most optimistic of analysts" [Rabi', 1980: 192–5]. The message is clear: the contemporary Arabs should do the same if they really want their own effective (and therefore by definition authentic) state that is modern but also faithful to the cultural values of their historical community.

One possible device for linking the concept of the community to that of the state (of which there are also some shades in Rabi''s writings) is through the concept of corporatism: i.e. that of various corps that act (or are utilised) as intermediaries between the community and the state. Because it is a 'bridging' concept (of intermediation), corporatism has always tended to tilt either towards the community (in the more culturalistic, romantic strands of corporatism) *or* towards the state (in the more organisational, authoritarian strands of corporatism) – hence, incidentally, the methodological elusiveness of the concept of corporatism, in spite of its extreme importance. Corporatist thought, originating in Germany, France and Belgium, has exercised important influences in Southern Europe, Latin America and the Middle East. It has influenced Arab legal thinking via the highly regarded scholarship of dean Léon Duguit, who taught at Bordeaux and Cairo;[8] Arab political thinking via the influential writings of the early Harold Laski and of G.D.H. Cole and the guild socialists; and Arab sociological thinking via the penetrating impact of the Durkheim school [cf. e.g. Al-Jarf, 1960: 74 *et passim*; Saif al-Dawla, 1991: 60–78; Nasr, 1963: Part 2; Al-Naqib, 1985: 8–9; Mitchell, 1988: 119–27]. There is also a more recent revival of certain corporatist themes, especially among the writers that I label 'cultural Islamists' (e.g. 'Adil Husain, Tariq al-Bishri or Galal Amin, etc.), whom we shall be referring to elsewhere in this work. My own use of the concept of corporatism in this book is not meant by way of recommending its possible ideological or 'moral' tenets as a solidaristic concept, but by way of regarding it as a useful analytical tool for understanding a whole range of devices for organising and managing state/society relations [my concept is therefore quite close to that of G. O'Donnell in 1977].[9]

Most of the non-individualist approaches to the state that I have just surveyed were intellectually suppressed in recent decades (because of their presumed affinity with Fascism), and thus it is currently rather hard to imagine how the concept of the state can be separated in reality from its liberal Western intellectual correlates of individualism, contractualism, secularism, differentiation, and so forth. Fortunately, however, the emergence of Japan as a leading world state, followed in recent years by a number of East Asian 'economic tigers', has now made it possible to see real, prosperous and in some senses strong states with antecedents that are distinctly different from those associated with the French and the English models.

Thus, for example, in a critique of Western modernisation theory, the Japanese political scientist K. Mushakoji [1985] draws attention to the fact that Western political scientists are often incapable of even posing the same questions about political development that their Japanese colleagues may be able to ask with the Japanese experience in mind: for example, what is the role of family and village groups in the formation of modern institutions in Japan? What are the traditional origins of the Japanese state including the ancient state institutions of China? What is the 'cosmology' that envelopes and governs the work of political and administrative institutions? It is suggested by some that collective sharing of power is more important in the Japanese tradition than individual struggle over power. Others point to the fact that the Japanese perception of rationality is distinctly different from its Western counterpart. Others say that decisions in Japan 'emerge' and are not 'taken': they are not based on a selection from among clear alternatives but on an adjustment among various options and views [see also from a Marxist perspective Taguchi and Kato, 1985].

We are not interested here in the details of these various propositions, only in the correct suggestion by Mushakoji that there are different possible 'principles of polity-formation' among which Japan represents but one non-Western manifestation. And the significance of some recent Arab attempts at re-discovering Japan [e.g. A. Abdel-Malek, 1981, 1983; Husain, 1985; Rashad, 1984] lies not in the fact that Japan necessarily represents a relevant example for the Arab World to emulate, but rather in that it illustrates the 'conceptual' possibility of economic and political development according to a non-European model of the polity and the state.

THE ARABS AND THE ISSUE OF THE STATE

Although the concept of the state is, as we have seen, a European one, the daily 'reality' of the state is now a fact that encompasses twenty-odd Arab countries and at least half-a-dozen more 'Middle Eastern' ones. This 'state' has in the main come to the Middle East as an 'imported commodity', partly under colonial pressure and partly under the influence of imitation and mimicry [cf. Ben Achour, 1980]. It is noteworthy, however, that Arab thought in the nineteenth and twentieth centuries has concerned itself with various concepts of unity and integration except for that of the state. The subject matter of this integration has varied, ranging from a religio-moral 'tight bond' (al-'urwa al-wuthqa) in Afghani and 'Abduh, to a linguistic-cultural bond for most theoreticians of Arab nationalism (Zaki Arsuzi, Michel 'Aflaq, Sati' al-Husri, etc.). Both the Arabist and the Islamist movements have undervalued the issue of the state, and have tended to regard matters of borders, populations, rights, markets, and so on, as rather artificial or superficial details [Sharara, 1980: 61–83].

Until the beginning of the nineteenth century Muslims had thought of politics in terms of the *umma* (a term originally connoting any ethnic or religious community but eventually becoming nearly synonymous with the universal Islamic Community) and of *khilafa* or *sultan* (i.e. government or rule of respectively a more religious or a more political character). A concept of the 'state' that may link these two previous categories of analysis (i.e. the community and the government) was not to develop until later on. The term *dawla* (used today to denote 'state' in the European sense) existed in the Quran and was indeed used by mediaeval Muslim authors. However, in its verbal form, the word had originally meant 'to turn, rotate or alternate'. In the Abbasid (and subsequent) periods it often conveyed the sense of fortunes, vicissitudes or ups and downs (e.g. *dālat dawlatuhu* = his days have passed). Gradually the word came to mean dynasty and then, very recently, 'state'. Rifa'a Rafi' Al-Tahtawi [1801–73] had already paved the way for a territorial rather than a purely communal concept of the polity when he emphasised the idea of *watan* (*patrie*; *vaterland*; *rodina*). None the less he could not break away completely from the (religious) *umma* concept, nor did he call for a 'national state' in the secular European sense. According to Bernard Lewis the first time that the term *dawla* (*devlet*) appears in its modern meaning of state, as distinct from dynasty and from government, is in a Turkish memorandum of about 1837 [Lewis, 1988].

Islamic thinkers were, however, in no hurry to espouse this new concept of the state. Afghani and 'Abduh were still speaking of the Islamic *umma* and its 'tight bond' (*al-'urwa al-wuthqa*) and of the Islamic ruler and his good conduct. 'Abd al-Rahman al-Kawakibi (1854–1902) went a step further by talking about the Islamic league (*al-jami'a al-islamiyya*) as a religious bond, while using the term *umma* not in an exclusively religious but sometimes in an ethnic sense, and using the term *al-watan* when he spoke of what united Muslim with non-Muslim Arabs. He also distinguished between the politics and administration of religion (*al-din*) and the politics and the administration of the 'kingdom' (*al-mulk*), saying that in the history of Islam the two had united only during the Rashidun era and the era of 'Umar ibn 'Abd al-'Aziz [Nassar, 1986].

Although the Arabs have been concerned since the nineteenth century with the 'manifestations of power', they seem to have paid little attention to its social, economic and intellectual foundations within the state [Salamé, ed., 1987]. The Arabs moved fairly rapidly in adopting the structural features of the state and the bureaucracy (in the European style) but they were rather slow in internalising the concept of the state itself, or the 'ethics' of public service and the attitudes of collective action [Bonné, 1973: 17–19; Umlil, 1985; Al-Jamal, 1984: 365–8]. Nor were they particularly impressed by the concept of 'freedom' (which Western thinkers closely relate to the development of the modern state), when they learned of it in the European literature. For Khair al-Din of Tunisia, 'liberty' still came second in importance after the conventionally crucial 'justice' (*'adl*) in explaining the basis of Europe's strength and prosperity. Tahtawi also likened liberty to justice, in order to bring it closer to the Arab conception. Certain Christian Arabs (especially those exposed to Protestant influences), and Ahmad Lutfi al-Sayyid (who adopted a liberal nineteenth-century concept of freedom) were, according to Albert Hourani, rather exceptional in their interest in freedom [Hourani, 1970: 90, 101, 173–4, 248].

Much of the writing of 'Abdallah Al-'Arawi (Laroui) on the state, which counts among the best by any Arab writer, revolves around a similar theme: that the Arab state is all body and muscle but with little spirit and mind and with no theory of liberty. A brief review of Laroui's ideas may therefore be in order here. Laroui starts with the conventional Arabic concept of *dawla* (connoting turns and rotations with regard to power and riches), and comments that as such, this type of state must ultimately be based on usurpation and coercion: forever subject to the threat of a stronger contender and always removed from the domain of moral values (except in the case of the 'unreal'

Islamic utopia) [Al-'Arawi, 1981: 116, 125]. This contrasts with the 'European' (mainly Hegelian/Weberian) concept of the state, adopted by Laroui, which sees in the state a totality of instruments aimed at the rationalisation of society – a rationalisation (the Marxists further maintain) that was historically tied to the practices of the bourgeoisie [ibid.: 72–4].

As for the 'actual' modern Arab states, Laroui sees in them the outcome of two processes: a natural evolution of the despotic Sultanic state (based on oppression and arbitrariness); and a reform process that has changed some of the higher administrative arrangements and borrowed from the West the modern means of transport and communication (and some improvements in agriculture and trade). This reformist process was historically initiated in the *tanzimat* (organisations and arrangements) which were introduced in their first phase by the Turkish Sultan in order to consolidate his own authority internally and externally, and were then pushed ahead in a second phase by the European colonialists in order to expand the imperial market and weaken the native leadership, while cultivating the loyalty of newer social élites [ibid.: 129–33].

However, Laroui believes that the *tanzimat* and the other organisational reforms that followed were not successful in transforming the attitude of the Arab individual towards political authority; they failed to entice him into regarding the contemporary (nationalist) state as a manifestation of a general will or of public ethics. The reasons for this are multiple. The 'foreignness' of the apparatus of power and administration has prevented the state from permeating the society. Thus the 'legal rule' was never combined with a 'moral conscience', nor has the emotional bond with the community or with the nation been identified with a political association (the state). The state machine was reformed, and a technocracy of sorts was allowed to function, bringing economic improvements to most people, but the state remained 'alien' in relation to society, and the nationalist movement and the Arab intellectuals remained attached to Utopia, and a long way away from accepting the reality of the state or dealing objectively with it [ibid.: 138–54]. The Islamic jurists continued to be attached to the concepts of the *umma* and the caliphate. But the newer concept of Arab nationalism has not helped either, Laroui believes, because it pinned its allegiance to a Pan-Arabist ideal, thus depriving the territorial state of a badly needed measure of legitimacy [ibid.: 156–71].

One finds in consequence, maintains Laroui, that the contemporary Arab state is obsessed with power and strength, and it may indeed be strong in terms of its 'body'. But (and here he echoes Gramsci) the violence of this state is in reality an indication of its weakness and fragility: the (coercive) apparatus may be powerful but the state as a whole is weak because it lacks rationality and because it lacks the necessary moral, ideological and educational supports [Al-'Arawi, 1981: 146–58, 168].

How can all this be explained? Laroui considers that the problem of the

Arab state can be attributed mainly to the fact that it has never been associated, in its emergence and development, with the idea of *liberty* (in its Western
sense). Liberty (*huriyya*) in Islamic thought has a psychological/metaphysical
meaning, whereas in Western thought it carries mainly a political and social
meaning. And whereas Western liberal thought has linked the concept of
liberty to the concept of law (and therefore to the state), the signs and symbols
of freedom in Islamic society are usually extra-statal or anti-statal, e.g. nomadism, tribalism, sufism. Thus there is mutual exclusivity between the concept of
liberty and the concept of the state in traditional Arabo-Islamic society: the
more extended the concept of the state, the narrower the scope for freedom
[Al-'Arawi, 1983: 11–86].

What about modern Arab society then? If anything it fares even worse
with regard to freedom, Laroui finds. In the traditional society there was
more of an equilibrium of sorts between the state and Society: nomadism pre-
dated the state and represented the freedom of origins, the tribe preserved a
certain degree of freedom of action within the state, and Sufism represented
an outlet whereby the individual could opt to be completely outside the
domain of the Sultan. The polity was characterised by absolute despotism,
but the scope of the 'political' was limited – the political society was not
synonymous with Arab society at large: the individual could resist the political
through a group to which he belonged, or he could withdraw from it completely to live on his own and for himself. In the eighteenth and nineteenth
centuries an important transformation (i.e. the *tanzimat*) took place, leading to
an expansion of the scope of the state and a contraction of the horizons of the
'non-state'. The autonomous group appeared to be a threat that should be
suppressed before the colonialists could exploit it for their own purposes, and
the autonomous individual seemed to resemble an enemy that should be
subjugated. Like the traditional state, the new one remained concentrated
and authoritarian, but its domain has expanded tremendously at the expense
of the freedom of the group and of the individual [Al-'Arawi, 1983: 29–36,
107].

The analysis in this book will, in many ways, follow on from the point at
which Laroui had arrived. There is little purpose in anticipating the entire
story in advance, but it may be in order at this juncture to sketch an outline
of the main argument and conceptual framework of this study.

SCHEMATIC ARGUMENT AND CONCEPTUAL
FRAMEWORK

The argument of this book can be roughly condensed and encapsulated in the
following few pages. The Middle East has historically possessed modes of
production that were mainly tributary in nature. Such a predominance of
'control-based' modes of production has often constrained the process of

accumulation but it has certainly increased the importance of the political factor.

In modern times, the tributary modes of production have been articulated with the encroaching capitalist mode of production (especially in its 'exchange' manifestations). With few exceptions, the outcome has often been the emergence of a basically 'circulationist' type of system whereby the ruling caste is fairly autonomous from the production process and the social classes, but often excessively dependent on the outside world.

The class nature of such a society manifests a dispersed, fluid class map with classes excessively dependent on the state (or on the outside world) and with many intermediate strata, *couches moyennes*, in existence. Several of these contend with each other for social and economic prominence but without any of them being structurally capable of assuming class hegemony within the society.

Owing to the lack of class hegemony, politics in such a society is not characterised by an orderly process of aggregating demands but by acts of capturing the state and acts of resisting the state. Once in power the ruling caste usually has no intention of giving it up, but the techniques of maintaining power vary from case to case – although there are two important types. In situations where the preservation and enhancement of the privileges of the group that captured the state would require preserving the status quo (without necessarily rejecting economic growth or artificial modernisation), the ruling caste would strive to co-opt other groups, in a 'consociational' manner if possible. This situation is true of the oil-exporting countries of Arabia and the Gulf.

In situations where the promotion of the interests of the group/fraction that captured the state would require changing the status quo via acts of social engineering (e.g. developmentalism or so-called socialism, etc.), the political techniques would include both political co-optation and political isolation (*'azl siyasi*). Formulas of an artificial corporatist nature are more likely in such a situation, with the heavy hand of the state either tightly controlling the various corps that belong to the ruling coalition or alliance (*tahaluf*), or sometimes replacing certain corps altogether and simulating others in their stead in the state's own image.

The political pattern is also governed by the 'logic' and the episodes of the economic strategy that the ruling caste finds itself obliged/tempted to follow. In general, expansionary phases are conducive to socially and politically inclusive practices, whereas contractionist phases are more conducive to socially and politically exclusive practices. This principle seems to apply to all cases, although its manifestations may vary between examples where the expansion is based on externally derived rent (as in the oil-exporting countries) and examples where the expansion had been based on domestically derived sources (as was the case, at least partly, in the 'developmentalist' states).

There is no hegemonic ideology involving all classes and groups in such a state; developmentalism is too vague a concept to be considered as such and in most cases it remains confined to the technocratic and 'intellectual' fractions. There may, however, be bursts of nationalistic fervour, charismatic arousal or populist jubilation – but this is hardly ideology. In the regional/external sphere, there is a wavering between an emotional attachment to utopian pan-ideologies (such as Arabism or Islamism) on the one hand, and on the other, an inarticulate, untheorised identification with the territorial state, often closely tied to the pursuits (and the claimed achievements) of the techno-bureaucratic élites. Whereas the more conservative systems have managed to internalise certain elements of an Islamic ideology into the ideological apparatus of the state (by co-opting, rather than simply controlling, the Islamic clerics), the more 'radical' modernising systems have seen their marginalised groups adopting political Islam as a counter-hegemonic ideology in recent years.

A few brief notes about our conceptual framework may now be in order. Obviously I cannot clarify all concepts in detail at this point, but the main purpose is to show how they relate to each other. Each concept will be elaborated upon in its own appropriate context. Concepts that appear in single quotation marks, but especially those that are italicised, represent especially important conceptual devices in our analysis. Sometimes I distinguish between 'principles' and 'methods': the first are hypothetical (and often diagnostic) concepts; the latter are strategy-oriented (or prescriptive) concepts.

The concept of 'articulation'

Our analysis starts from the concept of 'modes of production', with the intention of correlating it gradually with 'modes of coercion' and 'modes of persuasion'. The start from modes of production is necessary to remind ourselves that we are not looking at bourgeois capitalist societies with elaborate class structures, differentiated social roles and advanced 'contractual' traditions. Not only that, but the lineages of contemporary modes of production are different in the Middle East: for example, the 'feudalist' antecedents of the 'modern' period are very often missing, and in their stead there are various tributary modes based on irrigated agriculture, pastoralism, long-distance trade, and so forth. All such 'histories' have had a tremendous impact on the social formation and on the 'political culture' in the region.

Not only can a great deal be learnt by remembering that the antecedents of the contemporary modes of production were very different in the Middle East from those in, say, Europe, but a lot can also be gleaned by bearing in mind the operation of two principles: (a) that modes of production in the Middle East are often not singular and uni-dimensional but rather are *articulated* (i.e. two or more modes can often coexist and interlink); and (b) that in many Middle Eastern social formations there is little *correspondence* among the various 'instances' or manifestations of structural power in society [for an attempt to apply the concepts of 'articulation' and 'non-correspondence' to Arab historical material see Sharara, 1977: esp. 151–66].

Here a little elaboration may be worthwhile. Power in society manifests itself structurally in three types of modalities: modes of production, modes of coercion and modes of persuasion. In conventional Marxist theory these modes were placed at different levels and endowed with different degrees of autonomy. The economic 'instance' (i.e., the mode of production) was considered the base, whereas the 'politico-legal' and the 'ideological' instances (modes of coercion and persuasion) were described as superstructure. Many classical Marxists did not believe in any degree of functional autonomy of the political from the economic – i.e. they believed in direct economic determinism. Others believed in some functional autonomy and in economic determinism 'in the final analysis'. In general, however, there has been agreement that there was a very strong tendency towards 'correspondence' among the 'three' instances: the economic, the political and the ideological. In such analyses there is either a crude instrumentalism that does not allow for any independence of the state from the capitalists, or else a conception of the state as the ideal collective capitalist that organises particular capitals and class fractions for their own common interests or for the interest of capital in general.

Others, however, could allow for a higher level of autonomy for '*the political*' (i.e. the state). One particularly known conjuncture is when the equilibrium among class forces permits the emergence of an autonomous state (the so-called Bonapartism, a category which has been used in the study of some Middle Eastern regimes, such as that of Nasser). This was still regarded, however, as an exceptional or abnormal situation, often leading to stagnation or to catastrophe (as in Fascism). Less often, but more appropriate for our purposes, such situations are analysed in terms of the overall weakness of class forces (whether or not they are in equilibrium). If class forces are generally weak, a situation typical of most pre-capitalist or newly capitalist societies, then the state may enjoy a high degree of independence from capitalists most of the time. If the classes are economically and/or politically weak, that would allow for an independent state (such as in Tsarism, Sultanism, bureaucratic-authoritarianism, etc.). Or else hegemony could be organised by the intellectuals, in a contingent way, via specific *supra-class discourses* (which is in reality an aspect of articulation) [cf. Jessop, 1990].

Articulation may therefore take the form of linkages not only among various modes of production, but also among (non-corresponding) 'instances' of structural power. Thus it would be possible to imagine in a particular society an articulation between, for example, certain economic and technical elements of the capitalist mode of production and certain social and cultural elements of pre-capitalist (e.g. feudalist, even slavery) modes of coercion and persuasion.

Japan has been the outstanding case, but most Fascist regimes and many bureaucratic-authoritarian ones manifest similar articulations. The *method* of articulation, on the other hand, focuses on hegemonic practices, general strategies or *articulating discourses* which meld the different institutional systems together, typically via the state and/or a national-populist ideology. Laclau and Mouffe [1985: 105ff] define articulation as such: "We will call *articulation* any practice establishing a relation among elements such that their identity is modified as a result of the articulatory practice."[10]

Not all instances, however, can articulate with all other instances, at all times. Articulation is contingent on certain conditions and circumstances, and *contingency* is not another word for voluntarism (although it may involve structural or strategic selectivity). Articulations are more likely in situations where no one mode of production or no one class has emerged to dominate, and also at 'transitional' stages where a certain mode of production or a certain class loses its supremacy without another having yet taken its place. Articulating discourses (i.e. ideologies) are contingent both in the sense of depending on social conjunctures and in the sense of being flexible and adaptable and able to change meanings and political character in different circumstances [Halliday and Alavi, eds, Introduction in 1988: 5–7].

It is only in such a way that one may properly comprehend the phenomenon of patronage and clientelism in 'transitional' societies while avoiding the trap of attributing it all to the 'essence' of their cultures, or that one can understand, for example, a term such as 'political tribalism' [Al-Naqib, 1987] with regard to states in Arabia and the Gulf. Such a term suggests that some of the coercive and/or persuasive aspects of the 'lineage mode of production' may continue to survive even when the economic (e.g. pastoral) base of such a mode might have declined or even disappeared. In contemporary Arabia, an export-based rentier economy is articulated in very interesting ways with tribal and other community-based solidarities, animosities and compromises, as we shall see in detail later on.

The concept of articulation can also explain why a discourse like that of the Islamists does not seem to carry much by way of a clear class content. Being essentially an anti-state discourse it often manages to *interpellate* (i.e. to 'call', entreat or persuade by pleading) different, or even contradictory, classes and forces (e.g. the proletarianised intelligentsia and the prosperous traditional and/or 'new' merchants), which may eventually form a *power bloc* united in its opposition to the state: to its managerial failure and its cultural alterity [cf. Ayubi, 1991a].

The concept of *interpellation* (which has Gramscian and Althusserian antecedents) connotes the articulated (or, more pejoratively, the eclectic) discursive process that has been constructed in such a way that it literally *appeals* to people from different classes and groups who all feel they are being addressed or 'called' by it. It is therefore an ideological mechanism through which subjects are endowed with specific identities, interests and social positions. It is usually involved in the construction of 'historic blocs' and in most populist discourses [Laclau, 1979; Jessop, 1991]. Nationalist and religious discourses have a strong 'interpellatory' potential because they represent cases whereby the same symbolic code can attract disparate social constituencies.

Another related feature can be brought in at this point: culture cannot be treated simply as a 'reflection' of the economic base, and this is particularly so if one is to follow an 'articulation' approach. Culture changes much more slowly than the economy. It is influenced not only by the mode of production but also by many geographically and historically contingent factors, such as the natural resource endowment, the ecological environment, encounters with other civilisations, the spread of a particular religion, being colonised or not, by whom, and for how long, etc. We may describe all such factors as a *conjuncture.*

It is a distinct advantage of the articulation method that it would enable us to conceive of a situation where the 'technical' arrangements most typical of a particular mode of production may be articulated with the cultural (and the political) aspects more typical of another mode (and therefore possibly of another 'age'). Thus tribalism may be expressed socially and politically even though its economic base may have weakened or disappeared. Even slavery was still known in Arabia until recently, and quasi-slavery relations are still to be observed today. The bureaucratic centralised traditions of a 'hydraulic' society may persist even when irrigated agriculture ceases to be the source of livelihood for the majority of the population and even when land and other economic resources are no longer exclusively owned by the state.

There are other extremely important implications for the principles of 'articulation' and 'non-correspondence': one is that they enable us to see that the class map in such a society is often likely to be variegated and fluid, thus not allowing for the emergence of a hegemonic social class. Another is that this state of affairs may give rise, according to the *'principle of compensation'* (or *asynchrony*),[11] to a situation whereby the 'political' (the state) is likely to assume primacy within the social formation, by way of compensating for the absence (or the weakness) of a leading entrepreneurial class or a hegemonic national bourgeoisie. In other words, "the political sphere can be linked to the social sphere not in the sense of a representation but rather in the sense of a compensation: political forms do not reflect what is social, *they complete it*" [cf. Vergopoulos, 1990: 142, 154, original emphasis].

Another advantage of the concepts of articulation and non-correspondence is that they are likely to help in anticipating certain possible developments. They would seem to suggest, for example, that there is no direct, immediate, and necessary relationship between, for instance, the recent drive towards economic liberalisation on the one hand and prospects for political liberalisation on the other: economic 'openings' and privatisations can indeed be articulated with political authoritarianism (as will be elaborated upon in Chapters 10 and 11).

Yet in spite of their importance, the principles of articulation and noncorrespondence have not been as frequently utilised as they could have been in analysing politics in the periphery, where 'transition' appears to be quite a long-term process. 'Transitional' episodes are of course the most difficult to analyse, but they are also the most interesting to study. Curiously, it was a public administration man, Fred Riggs [1964] who came near enough to applying such a concept (under the banner of the 'prismatic society') quite early on in the 1960s, although in relation to administration rather than to politics or the state. The concept was then more directly applied to society and politics by a number of political economists dealing with peripheral countries in the 1970s and 1980s, as we shall see later in the book.

Defining the 'state'

So what exactly is this 'state' about which we are constantly speaking? Obviously it is our key concept in this study, and eventually all the shades of meaning which the term suggests should become clear. Yet some simplified working definitions may be needed at this stage. In one such definition, the state can be said to be an abstract construct that connotes the ensemble of institutions and personnel that possess the exclusive right to public power (or to the legitimate use of force) within a certain territorial society. But such a definition is a narrow one because it overlooks several things about the functions of the state, one of which is that it acts as a bridge and a linkage point between the economic system on the one hand and the cultural system on the other – that is, the state guarantees the conditions conducive to the processes of (capital) production and reproduction, and the state oversees the process of the authoritative allocation of values in society. Let us elaborate a little upon this preliminary definition.

First, the 'state' is a juridic abstraction. It connotes exclusive authority (sovereignty): domestically over a certain territory with its inhabitants, and externally, *vis-à-vis* similarly defined units (i.e. other states). The real substance of this authority is actual power exercised within the society through government; and *vis-à-vis* the foreign 'others', if necessary through war. This legal abstraction is therefore a formal expression of power relationships.

The origins and bases of many power relationships in modern, complex societies are, however, derived from economic relationships pertaining to property rights or control over the means of production. The state normally plays a crucial role, either in setting the conditions that enable certain types of economic relationships to take place and to reproduce themselves, or, more immediately, in directly controlling the means of production and fixing most of the economic relationships in a more authoritative way.

Behind the state's control of the conditions and/or of the resources themselves, it is usually possible to detect a certain normative pattern: an ideological
underpinning, an ethical code, or a cultural vocation that inspires the state
either in a declared (conscious) or in an undeclared (unconscious) manner.[12]
The study of states therefore has to deal with the following:

— the extent to which the state is legally and juridically abstracted so that it
   appears to be, for example, fairly distinct from the individuals who rule
   and from their personal whims;
— the features of the structure and institutional build-up of the state, especially
   the bureaucracy and the army, or, in other words, its 'body and muscle';
— the ways and modalities according to which the state goes about its exercising of power over the society, or, in other words, the functioning of the
   state;
— the types of class and group interests that the state action tends to favour
   or disfavour, relatively speaking, and the extent to which such class and
   group interests may be represented within the ruling élite itself. Also the
   types of social patterns and economic relations that state action (as represented by public policies, for example) tends to induce or to reproduce
   within the society;
— the types of normative assumptions (cultural, ethical, ideological, etc.) that
   seem (in a declared or undeclared manner) to lie behind state action: for
   example, its concepts of the 'self' and the 'other', and its 'allocations' of
   the major political values of freedom, equality, justice, and so on.

Although it is not always easy in less-developed countries, where (as for
example in 'Sultanism') the rulers and the state are often so thoroughly en-
tangled with each other, the distinction should always be kept in mind between
government, régime and *state*:

> Regimes are more permanent forms of political organization than specific govern-
> ments, but they are typically less permanent than the state. The state, by contrast,
> is a (normally) more permanent structure of domination and coordination in-
> cluding a coercive apparatus and the means to administer a society and extract
> resources from it [Fishman, 1990: 428].

One aspect of the primacy of 'the political' in developing countries manifests itself in the state's 'intervention' in the economic sphere, not only as
animateur, planner and coordinator but also as producer and manager – this
is what is usually termed *étatisme*. This 'intervention' carries with it two political
outcomes: (1) that the state becomes powerful, because it now controls both
the system of authority and the system of wealth; and (2) that the 'legitimacy'
of the regime and of the state in general (since the duration of a certain
government or regime is not known in advance, the two actually overlap in
the Arab World) will become closely tied to its *achievement* and *performance* in

the economic field. This often transmits politics and its language into a language of economics, management (and technocracy). An economic crisis thus becomes a crisis for the state, which will often try to find financial solutions for the difficulties without readily conceding its economic (and thus political) control.

We also deal in this book with the economic and the managerial sphere (including the bureaucracy and the public sector) for other important reasons, including: (a) to illustrate that economic and managerial matters have their *own* politics, even though they are often presented as a (more useful) alternative to politics; (b) to show that part of the failure in economic and managerial spheres is due to their assumed technicality; and (c) to illustrate that although controlling the economy augments the state's power, it also increases its vulnerability, since all economic problems and failings are bound to be blamed on the state, thus detracting from its legitimacy.

It will be noticed that although I sometimes use the term 'legitimacy' in this work, I do obviously prefer the concept of *hegemony*. The concept of hegemony is superior to that of legitimacy in that it includes, but also surpasses, the latter. In addition, hegemony is not as closely tied to the specific mechanisms of political representation and participation (which are too closely tied to Western/capitalist pluralistic and parliamentary democracy) as legitimacy seems to be. It may also be easier to analyse the concept of hegemony within the conditions of developing countries. All definitions of legitimacy are based on a *belief*, and this has to be quantitatively measured through certain technical devices (attitude surveys, opinion polls, etc.) whose free application is not permitted in Arab countries. It should also be noted that not all definitions of legitimacy emphasise the elements of achievement and performance or consider the legitimacy of the socio-economic system, even though these are particularly important in defining the concept of legitimacy in most developing countries. Legitimacy in the Middle East is closely intertwined with an evaluation of the performance of the state both as a producer (the public sector) and as a distributor (social welfare), and considerations of 'sufficiency' and 'justice' play a far more important role as components of the concept of legitimacy than they do in advanced capitalist countries.

Furthermore, whereas the use of the legitimacy concept requires us continuously to make a careful distinction between feelings towards the political institutions and those towards the regime and its incumbents [cf. e.g. Gurr, 1970: 183–92 and refs cited], the concept of hegemony is far more closely associated with the *state* (which forms our main category of analysis), while being at the same time more sensitive to social and economic factors (which in turn suits our political economy approach). Since hegemony is both social and ideological, it allows more scope for the study of coalitions and alliances among classes and groups (i.e. 'socio-historic blocs'). Indeed, I find the *inclusionary/exclusionary* scales improvised by authors inspired by the Gramscian concept of hegemony (e.g. O'Donnell, Stepan, Mouzelis, etc.) far more efficacious in dealing with a Middle Eastern politics that lacks devices such as voting, elections, parties, etc. In this vein, a concept like '*incorporation*' assumes great relevance, and so do terms such as *fronts, coalitions, charters, pacts,* and so forth.

The concept of inclusion/exclusion is more useful than the restricted concepts of representation and participation because it implies both socio-economic *and* political involvement (the first being particularly important for many developing societies). It also allows the 'principle of compensation' to apply, in the sense that in the short- to medium-run a higher level of socio-economic inclusion may distract from/compensate for political participation. In the longer run, however, the more comprehensive the socio-economic inclusion, the more certain that claims/demands for political participation will emerge (Iran under Muhammad Reza Shah is a good case in point here).

Corporatism

The mention of inclusion/exclusion represents a good opportunity to say a few words about another key concept of this book, that of corporatism. For the purposes of this work, I define *corporatism* rather broadly. It is a political concept which, along with the organisational arrangements that it inspires, is premised neither on the supremacy of the individual nor on the supremacy of class. In societies where theoretical individualism is weak and where classes are embryonic, neither the conventional liberal nor the conventional Marxist paradigms seem to be able to capture the realities of the situation. There are no free elections or even opinion polls that would allow us to assume that national politics represents in some way an aggregate of the ideas and interests of the individual citizens. Nor are there long-term, well-established and self-conscious classes that either have superordinated within the society in a 'hegemonic' way or that have, alternatively, taken over power by force and established, for example, a 'dictatorship of the proletariat'.

What tends to be there, by contrast, is a situation that invokes a political vocabulary which appears to reify a 'collectivity' (the 'community' – variously defined – and/or the state) and a whole range of activities that seem to locate much of the political function with clientelistic networks (thus the importance, among others, of 'patronage') and/or within nominally formal organisations (thus the importance, among others, of 'bureaucratic politics'). We seem therefore to be having *groups* (some of them more 'primordially' solidaristic and some more socio-economic in nature), and we have the state. Then we have a whole variety of 'arrangements' (some more abrupt and cruel than others) for sorting out the relationship between the groups and the state. Some of these arrangements are collaborative and inclusionary: tribal confederations, national fronts, populist coalitions, ethnic consociations, etc.; while some are more conflictual and exclusionary: subordination, encapsulation and segmentary 'capture' of the state apparatus, etc.

I attribute such manifestations less to an imagined cultural continuity (e.g. an 'organic' conception of society in Islam) and more to the articulated, and often transitory, nature of the modes of production in developing countries (a point repeatedly elaborated upon elsewhere in this work). Yet such manifestations are very much there, even though they are often missed in analyses that are exclusively premised on a presumed individual-derived or class-derived politics. While individualism and classes are both growing in the Middle East, an analysis that concentrates on them to the neglect of group/state relationships (both conflictual and collaborative) will certainly be missing a great deal about political realities in that region. Politics in capitalist, liberal societies can be understood – as we have already suggested – with reference to two main categories of actors: individuals and classes. Individualism establishes the rights and the 'dignity' of the 'nuclearised' free individual who is released from all primordial 'bonds' and who is then presumed to enter into all kinds of social relationships by his/her own free will and in a contractual fashion. This type of relationship also governs the individual's connection with the state, through mechanisms such as voting, elections and representation. Classes are social groups that join together individuals who, generally speaking, occupy similar positions with regard to the means of production and the relations of production in society. Through their collective action they are presumed to influence strategic decision-making in society, including decisions that emanate from the state.

It should follow from these definitions that neither individualism nor class analysis will – if used exclusively – provide a very useful paradigm when one is dealing with a society where neither the historic-intellectual prerequisites for individualism nor the socio-economic bases for a clearly differentiated class structure are present. In much of the Third World the individual, even though he has often been forced out of his primary group, has not yet enjoyed the protection of individualism as a juridic-intellectual concept, nor has he been accommodated within a clearly differentiated class structure. Thus we have a state of flux whereby the human being is partly nuclearised but not fully individualised; he is partly a member of his primary group and partly a member of an emerging class structure. The 'state' in such a situation cannot be 'derived' or deduced either from the presumably 'contractual' relationship that binds the individual to the government in liberal theory, or from the presumed class domination that is supposed to give the state its character in Marxist theory. The outcome of such a fluid situation is either open 'praetorianism', i.e. politics being the *immediate* rather than the potential or ultimate application of violence, or, alternatively, situations in which politics represents a continuous search for intermediaries that can bind the individual and the groups to the state.

'Intermediary' politics features not only individuals and classes, but also – and sometimes primarily – groups. These groups in turn may include primary, solidarity-type groupings (*Gemeinschaft*) or functional, interest-type groupings (*Gesellschaft*). Individuals, groups and classes may be linked through various mechanisms (e.g. patronage, clientelism, proportionality, etc.), and through various 'organisational' modalities (chambers, networks, '*shillas*', etc.). The relative importance of the various groups varies from one society to another depending on a society's level of socio-economic differentiation and its social and cultural history.

In short, I adopt a broad concept of corporatism, similar to that of G. O'Donnell [1977], in which it is regarded as a set of relationships between state and society, between the public and the private. Although this approach does not stem from the belief that corporatism is the necessary organisational outcome of certain political cultures, it has to be sensitive to any aspects of cultural specificity that may be of significance within the social history of any particular country or region. And there is little doubt in this respect that the Arabo-Islamic cultural tradition has its own distinctive features with regard to state/society and public/private relationships.

As happened in some other parts of the world, Middle Eastern experimentation with corporatism could afford to follow basically 'inclusionary' practices during their early (mainly *populist*) phases. This was helped, in the short run, by the ability of the 'relatively autonomous' state to expand national industry, public employment and social services. The relative autonomy of the state, as well as its ability to disburse largesse, were both made possible through the acquisition by the state of significant financial resources by way of nationalising private enterprises (foreign and local) or through the receipt of considerable external payments (oil revenues, foreign aid, etc.). *Etatisme* and bureaucratisation represented some of the obvious correlates of such a state of affairs.

But the increasing reliance on 'un-earned' income, invoking the description of many Arab countries as rentier (or semi-rentier) states, has rendered the state vulnerable to several (mainly external) forces over which it had little control. This, combined with the growing financial burdens of welfarist policies has led to the escalation of a 'fiscal crisis of the state', that left the state panting both for cash and for legitimacy. Such developments (supported by important globalisation pressures) started, in turn, to usher the exhausted state in the direction of economic *privatisation* and a certain degree of political *pluralisation* – a story that will be recounted in detail in the rest of this book.

NOTES

1. "I have been asked a thousand times for the deep cultural explanation of all sorts of profound differences between 'us and them'. Now, as that dubious creature, a Middle East specialist ... I have virtually a vested interest in talking about historical and sociological specificities. They certainly exist. But on nearly all occasions the answers have actually seemed to me *not* to require

any special insight into unique cultural peculiarities. Rather, they appear to demand a relatively straightforward attempt at a political reading of the situation rather than the citing of some supposed mental or cultural condition" [Gilsenan, 1991: 30–31].

2. The specificity of the Middle East derives from a number of factors including most particularly: (1) the arid zone ecology with its important economic and social consequences; (2) the predominance of Islam as a religion and a way of life; (3) the proximity to Europe and the special sensitivities and vulnerabilities caused by this; and (4) the crucial role (economic, social and political) played by oil in the last two decades, especially but not exclusively in the oil-exporting countries of the region.

3. It is not exactly clear when the transformation was achieved of the semantics of *status, estate* and *Stand* into those of *state, état, stato, estado, Staat,* etc. Even Hobbes still used 'state' as synonymous with *civitas* and Commonwealth, and handled it according to the old metaphor of the body [cf. Luhman, 1990: 129–35].

4. This is somewhat similar to Ibn Khaldun's distinction, with regard to the formation of the political community, between two types of influence, or *wazi'*: an 'external/objective' type based on coercive disincentives, and an 'internal/subjective' type based on (religious) motivation ['Abd al-Salam, 1985: 88–96; Al-Jabiri, 1982a: 472–3]. This is the nearest that one comes in the traditional literature to a distinction between 'incentives' and 'motivation'. The word *wazi'* is almost impossible to translate – the use of the English word 'influence' here is very approximate.

5. Peter Gran [1987: 92] finds that "While the Arabs have yet to produce a Gramsci, the questions which Gramsci raised in the 1920s are now quite freely raised in the *Ahali* newspaper in Cairo, in Jumblatist circles in Lebanon, in the Islamic Left of the Ayatollah Muhammad Baqir al-Sadr and Hasan Hanafi, and in academic writings, represented here by an essay by Elia Zureik." Traces of a Gramscian influence on some Arab writers in recent years have been observed by Labib [1992a: 64ff].

6. The influence of conservative European thought on Arab and Muslim writers and scholars continues to be a very poorly researched area, as Western and Arab writers on the subject have tended to emphasise (and often to celebrate) the impact of liberal (and to some extent socialist) ideas on Arab and Middle Eastern thinking [cf. e.g. Hourani, 1970; 'Awad, 1969–86; Al-Ansari, 1980; a partial exception is R. Khuri, 1983]. Conservative (including organicist) concepts and ideas present in Arab political discourse were always assumed, not necessarily correctly, to have an 'Islamic' or 'Oriental' genealogy.

7. According to Alfred Stepan, the 'organic state' tradition is not confined to Hegel and the German writers but considerably pre-dates them. It pertains to a normative vision of the political community in which the component parts of society harmoniously combine to enable the full development of the human potential. This corpus of political thought runs through Aristotle, Roman law, mediaeval natural law and into contemporary Catholic social philosophy, and is still very alive as a philosophical and structural influence, especially in southern Europe and Latin America [Stepan, 1978: 26–7]. Similar concepts, likening society to the human body or to a 'tight building' (*bunyan marsus*) and calling for the solidaristic integration of its members (*takaful*), are quite familiar in Islamic writings.

8. Léon Duguit was a colleague of the major corporatist sociologist Emile Durkheim (1858–1917) at the University of Bordeaux and is regarded as one of the leading minor theorists of corporatism [Black, 1984: 220–23]. He is usually classified as a 'social functionalist' whose top political values were social solidarity and social function [Brecht, 1959: 304]. Not only did Duguit teach and enjoy a tremendous intellectual influence in Egypt, but in 1927 he also drafted the curriculum and regulations of the Faculty of Law of Cairo University – the model for such faculties in the Arab World. He was critical of the concept of the sovereignty of the nation or the people and advised an emphasis on social responsibility, legal controls and collective interests [Gourdon, 1989: 563 n.52; Saif al-Dawla, 1991: 60–78]. It is often assumed that the influential law schools (and by extension the law profession) in the Middle East must have been bastions of liberalism, but this is not exactly the case as the content of the courses was often anti-individualist and

opposed to concepts of 'sovereignty' of the 'nation' or of the 'people'. For specific examples from Egypt see 'I. Saif al-Dawla, 1984: 603–8.

9. The terms *corporativismo*, *Korporativismus*, etc., which tend to imply a doctrine or ideology, have had unfortunate etymological associations in the inter-war period. "The more inventive Italians and Germans rather quickly resolved the issue by dropping out the 'iv' and referring to *corporatismo* and *Korporatismus* as Anglo-Saxon-imposed neologisms conveniently purged of their discredited past associations" [Schmitter, 1985: 59]. For the uncertain attempts to render the term into Arabic, see Chapter 5, n. 6.

10. Laclau and Mouffe [1985: 103ff.] proceed further than I would in this analysis by giving "the structured totality resulting from the articulatory practice" the name: *discourse*. I would prefer to distinguish, at least analytically, between the socio-political bloc on the one hand and political discourse on the other. I would therefore agree that the practice of articulation consists *among other things* "in the construction of nodal points which partially fix meaning" [ibid.: 112–13]. I also agree that "the general field of the emergence of hegemony is that of articulatory practices" [ibid.: 134ff].

11. The notion of *asynchrony* is also employed in the writings of O. Ianni, T. di Tella, G. O'Donnell, J. Nun, A. Touraine and others.

12. The concept of the state as a 'normative order' concentrates on the symbolic attributes of the state as a unifying force for the entire community. Its implications range from a highly idealist 'total' form as in Hegel and in the Croce/Gentile doctrine of *lo stato etico* (as well as with many of the modern Islamists such as Mawdudi and Qutb), to a more micro-level practical concern with ethics in specific state apparatuses. Anthony Black [1988: 113–21; 156–7] contrasts the liberal view of the state with what he calls the *civic view*, according to which the state has a substantive purpose all of its own, namely to promote the good life and justice in society. What characterises the liberal view is that it starts and ends with the individual. The liberal state is, in more than one sense, a *Rechtstaat* (legal-constitutional state), whereby the public sphere (*res publica*) exists solely to enable persons to pursue their own ends, and where a clear distinction is made between crime and sin. The 'civic state' by contrast aims to ensure that its inhabitants lead a good moral life and regards *moeurs* and beliefs as its direct concern. Gramsci often uses the terms 'ethical state', 'cultural state' and 'educator state', but is obviously more inclined towards the latter: "Every State is ethical in as much as one of its most important functions is to raise the great mass of the population to a particular cultural and moral level" [in Buci-Glucksmann, 1980: 127, 301]. We take this concept on board in this book, supplemented by David Easton's 'allocative' (and therefore political-economy amenable) formulation about politics being the "authoritative allocation of values" in society [Easton, 1953: 130]. On the possible 'highest values' that may be adopted by the state see Brecht [1959: Ch. 8], and for a further discussion see Black [1988: 98ff].

CHAPTER TWO

Modes of Production and the Origins of the Arabo-Islamic State

Power in society has three structural dimensions: economic, political and cultural/ideological. Without accepting N.G. Runciman's evolutionary theory of 'competitive selection', I find his terminology for describing the sources of power quite satisfactory; power is about access to, or control of (a) means of production; (b) means of coercion; and (c) means of persuasion [Runciman, 1989: 12ff – the order of the two last having been reversed by me]. In this work, 'Modes of production' represent the core of my analytical category of political economy; modes of coercion are synthesised and condensed in the political sphere by the state; modes of persuasion are represented by ideology/culture – in the Middle East it can be argued that 'Islam' forms a major ingredient of this.

Runciman argues that "the history of any chosen society has ... to be narrated as an evolving range of alternative modes of the distribution of power within an evolving set of constraints" [Runciman, 1989: 40]. The problem with the keyword 'alternative' in this passage is the impression it gives that sources of power represent autonomous spheres, fairly isolated from each other, whereas what need to be studied are the interrelationships and the overlapping among the three sources. Furthermore, his idea of 'competitive selection' of the practices by which roles are defined in societies and by societies gives his analysis, in my view, too much of a voluntarist character.

I am more inclined to the structuralist view that sees most forms of power as being, in the majority of cases and in the final analysis, rooted in the economic base and, more specifically, in the modes of production. The terms 'in most cases' and 'in the final analysis' are meant to constrain any sense of mechanistic determinism by implying that the modes of production do point in the direction of a whole range of possible political and ideological options, which may be followed by societies – in specific historical conjunctures – through processes of intellectual consciousness and social struggle. Moreover,

the relationship between the 'infrastructure' and the 'superstructure' is reciprocal: although in most cases modes of coercion and modes of persuasion
are most obviously shaped by modes of production, the state may also create
its own classes (and not simply represent existing ones), and may very often
transcend its main sphere of coercion into the spheres of persuasion and of
production. Ideology and culture, too, frequently acquire a certain autonomy
which enables them to transcend the socio-historical context from which they
would have risen in the first place – this is particularly true with religion
which, furthermore, seems to satisfy a very real psychological need in many
human beings.

MODES OF PRODUCTION AND SOCIAL FORMATIONS

A little elaboration on some of these concepts may be useful at this point. A
mode of production is an abstract construct; a theoretical concept or 'ideal
type' that is never to be found in reality in its 'full' or 'pure' form. It is simply
a synthesised and abstracted version of some previous knowledge, which has
the potential to be used for describing, analysing and comparing specific situations. Our working definition of modes of production includes two ingredients: (a) 'forces of production' or the methodology, techniques and means by
which human beings exploit nature and produce goods; and (b) 'relations of
production' characterising in particular the patterns of organising the labour
processes, the ownership and control of the means of production, and the
distribution of economic surplus.

A mode of production is therefore a combination of the 'labour processes'
by which man extracts his means of existence from nature and the social
patterns that determine access to and control over resources and means of
production as well as determining the division and organisation of labour
tasks, and the forms of product distribution or 'circulation' [cf. Godelier, 1978:
85ff]. In short, a mode of production is defined essentially by certain forms of
appropriation of resources, of means of production and of product. Godelier
has made an interesting contribution by arguing that in pre-capitalist societies
the various social processes are not all neatly differentiated and autonomous
from each other. Thus, for example, in some societies relationships of kinship
serve as relations of production, emerging naturally from within the society
itself. In such a society the distinction between 'infrastructure' (economic base)
and superstructure (politics/culture) is not a distinction between institutions,
but a distinction between functions within the same institution. In other cases,
religion or politics may function in a natural internal way as a "relation of
production" (e.g. distributing labour processes among various religious groups
or according to a citizen/non-citizen criterion). Therefore the distinction between infrastructure and superstructure is a distinction not mainly between

institutions or 'instances', but between functions. It is only in certain societies, particularly in a capitalist society, that this distinction between functions comes to coincide with a distinction between institutions. Godelier is aware, however, that we must still look for the reasons why kinship or religion may in a particular context function as a 'production relation' and hence dominate a certain social formation [Godelier, 1978: 87–90].

A 'social formation' is a broader category describing the real system that presumably emerges from and clusters around a specific mode of production (or a number of 'articulated' modes, as we shall see), including the class con-figuration and other organisations and associations to which such a mode may give rise. 'Class' here can be simply, and initially, viewed as the key 'mediator' between modes of production and human action [cf. Foster-Carter, 1978: 77]. Social formation is equivalent to the 'society-as-a-whole', or to the social system in its interrelated and interlocking economic, political and cultural/ideological aspects, that make the system function and maintain (reproduce) itself. Thus whereas modes of production are abstract theoretical constructs, social forma-tions are concrete historical entities that can be specified by name, place and date in our analysis [cf. Taylor, 1979: 106ff and refs cited].

In theory, there is no limitation to the number of modes of production that one may think of, and indeed Marx himself referred on occasions to some modes (e.g. the 'Asiatic' or the 'Germanic' modes of production; the nomadic mode of production which he did not incorporate into his famous linear succession of stages: communalism, slavery, feudalism and capitalism. Other Marxist thinkers, notably Trotsky, although mainly bound by the 'stages' perspective, laid emphasis on the role of the state in certain non-West European societies, in promoting development and modernisation at certain historical junctures [cf. Brewer, 1980: 261–2]. It should also be observed that although each mode of production gives rise to a characteristic conjunction that embodies its dynamic and reproduces the conditions for its proliferation, each mode tends also to create its own characteristic fissures and oppositions [Wolf, 1982: 386].

We suggest that in dealing with the Middle East, two modes of production in particular will have to be added to Marx's conventional set: the lineage (kin-ordered) mode of production and the bureaucratic mode of production (otherwise called the 'Asiatic', the 'Oriental', the 'hydraulic' or the 'etatist' mode of production). Furthermore, the various suggested 'stages' should not be viewed in a unilinear, uni-directional manner. Pierre-Philippe Rey has made an important contribution by suggesting that a social formation may contain more than one mode of production. Such a process of interaction or articu-lation of modes of production takes so long that transition is often the normal state of affairs [cf. Brewer, 1980: 182ff]. This concept will prove to be of considerable value in the understanding of much about the historical develop-ment of social formations in the Arab-Islamic world.

The concept of articulation will also prove extremely important in explaining the process (from the nineteenth century on) of incorporating the Arab World – mainly through 'colonialism' – into the world capitalist system. Capitalism neither evolved mechanically from the modes of production that preceded it in the Arab World, nor did it completely dissolve these modes. As in many other societies, it sometimes coexisted with such modes and sometimes even buttressed and prolonged certain of their aspects [cf. Foster-Carter, 1978: 51ff]. Rey has illustrated the way in which the 'lineage mode of production' in Africa (which is similar to but not identical with nomadic tribalism in Arabia) was articulated with the capitalist mode of production following the colonisation of the continent [Dupré and Rey, 1980: 141ff]. In the Gulf, certain elements of the nomadic mode of production were articulated with the capitalist mode, and in Egypt certain elements of the 'Asiatic' mode of production were likewise incorporated. Indeed, as happened in Latin America, it was precisely the impact of an external market and/or colonial power which intensified – or even instigated – a partly feudal, partly capitalist type of *latifundia* agriculture in Egypt, Algeria, Iraq and parts of Syria.

Capitalism, however, is the first mode of production that is global in scope: it now envelops practically the entire world – with its exchange system (relations of production), if not its mode of production [compare Wolpe, Introduction, 1980: 36–9]. Thus whereas various modes of production may be articulated with each other in countries of the periphery, and as certain sectors within these are in turn articulated with capitalism in the 'core' countries, the World System is now, on the whole, one big market subject to the capitalist relations of production and laws of exchange. A third level of analysis will therefore have to be added – thus: mode of production > social formation > world system.

Furthermore, if one accepts the concept of 'articulation' in relation to modes of production, the question may be posed in a similar manner in relation to manifestations of the superstructure; i.e. the state or ideology [compare Foster-Carter, 1978: 73]. Rey has in fact suggested, without much elaboration, that there are certain 'modes of domination' that correspond to certain types of economic activity in neo-colonial situations [Dupré and Rey, 1980: 158–9]. Other writers have also loosely suggested that certain 'composite' types of ideology may be characteristic of post-colonial societies. I shall myself try to illustrate later on that articulated modes of production tend often to give rise, politically, to corporatist practices and, ideologically, to eclectic formulations.

THE ANCIENT NEAR-EASTERN STATE AND THE 'ASIATIC MODE OF PRODUCTION'

The idea of the existence of a distinct 'Oriental mode of production' is not entirely new. Adam Smith classed China with Ancient Egypt and Indostan, making the point that the government in these societies paid much attention to the canal system. The idea of 'Oriental society' was put forward some years later, by James Mill and also John Stuart Mill [for further details see Ayubi 1980: Chs. 1 and 2].

Karl Marx was familiar with such writers and when he wrote about an 'Asiatic mode of production', he expanded their hints into a theory that is both historical and sociological, a theory that was unfortunately never formulated in a systematic fashion, but has to be pieced together from his published and unpublished writings [Lichtheim, 1963: 100]. In explaining the phenomenon, Marx states that:

> Climate and territorial conditions, especially in the vast tracts of desert extending from the Sahara through Arabia, Persia, India and Tartory, to the most elevated Asiatic highlands, constituted artificial irrigation by canals and waterworks the basis of Oriental agriculture ... This prime necessity of an economical and common use of water, which in the Occident drove private enterprise to voluntary association as in Flanders and Italy, necessitated in the Orient, where civilisation was too low [sic] and the territorial extent too vast to call into life voluntary association, the interference of the centralised power of government. Hence an economical function developed upon all Asiatic governments, the function of providing public works [Lichtheim, 1963: 90].

Oriental society as Marx understood it was nevertheless something more complex than a system of canals. It had to do, on the one hand, with centralised – i.e. despotic – regulation of the basic economic functions and, on the other, with the prevalence of a self-sufficient village economy. Marx traced this peculiar character of Oriental society to the absence of private ownership in land, and related this to the overriding role of the central government by suggesting that under the 'Asiatic system' the state was the 'real landlord': "the State is here the supreme landlord. Sovereignty here consists in the ownership of land concentrated on a national scale. Conversely, no private ownership of land exists, although there is both private and common possession and use of land" [Marx, quoted in Lichtheim, 1963: 95].

These two basic characteristics of 'Asiatic society' – state control over the producer and the absence of private property in land – are presumably related to the strategic role of the central government in administering the irrigation network through an integrated system of public works. But one important question still arises about the way this complex interrelationship comes about.

Following what is basically a Marxist argument, Wittfogel attempted to develop the theory of 'Oriental despotism', influenced not only by Marx but also by Weber [Wittfogel, 1957: 38off]. To be sure, Weber himself observed that in China, India and Egypt ("the countries with the earliest development of bureaucracy" as he called them), bureaucratisation was usually based on irrigation [Weber, 1947: 288ff]. While to Weber these were largely 'patrimonial bureaucrats', Wittfogel saw in them a reminder of the nineteenth-century concept of bureaucracy: a glance at them "recalls the original meaning of the term bureaucracy, 'rule through bureaus'. The power of the agro-managerial regime was indeed closely interlinked with the 'bureaucratic' control which the government exerted over its subjects" [Wittfogel, 1957: 50].

Wittfogel argues that 'hydraulic societies' lend themselves to some form of an 'Oriental despotism', which quite often takes the shape of a bureaucratic state (*Beamtenstaat*) [Wittfogel, 1957: 309]. What he attempted to do was

> to analyse the patterns of class in a society whose leaders are the holders of despotic state power and not private owners and entrepreneurs. This procedure, in addition to modifying the notion of what constitutes a ruling class, leads to a new evaluation of such phenomenon as landlordism, gentry and guild. It explains why, in a hydraulic society, there exists a *bureaucratic* landlordism, a *bureaucratic* capitalism, and a *bureaucratic* gentry. It explains why in such a society the professional organisation, although sharing certain features with the guilds of Medieval Europe, were societally quite unlike them. It also explains why in such a society supreme autocratic leadership is the rule [Wittfogel, 1957: 4].

Wittfogel's theory suggests a number of themes with regard to hydraulic societies. It argues that the hydraulic economy is basically 'managerial' and 'political' in nature. It also explains how the 'state' is stronger than 'society', and relates this to the great amount of organisational power it enjoys, both in internal affairs (e.g. irrigation, flood control, construction, etc.), and in external affairs (i.e. warfare and defence). Furthermore, it reveals how, as a result, private property is usually very weak in such societies, and how the state is further strengthened by attaching to itself the country's dominant religion.

The overall picture is that of a system of total power (despotic), one that lacks almost any independent centres of constitutional or societal checks. The government is characterised by 'absolutism' and 'autocracy'. The individual is subject to 'total terror, total submission, total loneliness'. The class structure is unique, and the 'total ruling class' is a 'monopoly bureaucracy'.

Wittfogel attempted what Marx did not, which was to relate the 'Asiatic mode of production' to a general theory of bureaucracy. He attempted to incorporate in his theory three elements: a technical one of large-scale irrigation works, an 'organisational' one of bureaucracy and centralism, and an 'attitudinal' one of tyranny and terror. As such, his theory may be useful, at least as an 'ideal type', for analysing societies that contain these three elements. Otherwise the theory does not help [Abrahamian, 1974: 8–9].

In its most general sense, it seems that a variety of the 'Asiatic mode of production' would apply, though not without reservations, to most societies where water is the scarcest and the most needed of their resources, and where irrigation (in this case almost a synonym for organisation), is the major method of securing it. These material elements will gradually tend to reflect themselves on the whole political culture and will produce the socio-political aspects of 'Oriental despotism' (e.g. centralism, hierarchy, authoritarianism, submission, etc.). Passing through a period of conflicts and balances between centralisation and decentralisation, such cultural traits will usually take a longer time to fade away, even if the material elements lose partly or totally their central importance. Oriental despotism is therefore the result of both the objective material conditions and their reflection on the socio-political culture. The product is quite distinct: if in other polities the bureaucracy is just one component of society, in 'pure' hydraulic systems the whole society seems to function like a big bureaucracy.

The idea of a 'hydraulic society' as being a 'total bureaucracy' has not only been a subject of debate in Marxist and pseudo-Marxist circles but has also attracted the attention of some non-Marxist and anti-Marxist writers. However, it is the extremely broad usages of the category of the 'Asiatic mode of production', both historically and geographically, that have caused many commentators to be critical of the concept. We agree with Perry Anderson that one cannot jumble together Imperial Rome, Tsarist Russia, Hopi Arizona, Sung China, Chaggan East Africa, Mamluk Egypt, Inca Peru, Ottoman Turkey and Sumerian Mesopotamia – not to speak of Byzantium or Babylonia, Persia or Hawaii [Anderson, 1979: 487]. If it is to be of useful analytical value, every possible attempt has to be made to make it more precise and to narrow down its applicability. Attempts to use the concept for analysing tribal or semi-tribal social formations (based on kin relationships, communal rural property and cohesively self-sufficient villages) are not, in our view, as successful. Yves Lacoste, for example, has observed that in both the tribal or village communities of North Africa and in the 'hydraulic societies' of Egypt, Mesopotamia and Andalusia (Muslim Spain), private ownership of land was absent or weak. The relations of production in these two types are similar even though they characterise two different modes of production – the similarity in this case being mainly derived from the dissimilarity of both from the conventional slave, feudal or capitalist modes [Lacoste, 1984: 5ff, 26ff]. If the overall mode of production is taken into account, one can then understand the different political outcomes of the two modes: a centralised state of an agrarian base in Egypt, whereas in North Africa "the 'State' was in a sense a confederation of tribes allied to a sovereign", in structure based on 'military democracy' and international trade [Lacoste, 1984: 29–33].

Given such likely confusions, we would rather retain for the notion of the 'Asiatic mode of production' its original emphasis on a powerful centralised state, frequently dealing in hydraulic agriculture and public works, and involved in 'generalised slavery', i.e. labour drafts levied from the rural populations by a superior bureaucratic power [Anderson, 1979: 485–6]. For one thing, our knowledge of the historical 'village communities' is scantier and far less accurate than our knowledge of the 'hydraulic state'. Second, the concept would be a poor one indeed if it merely functioned as a generic residual category for non-European development (or lack of it). However, we do not agree with Anderson that the concept should be 'buried' altogether [cf. ibid.:

485–9]. If it is used mainly as an 'ideal type' in the methodological Weberian sense, against which real historical developments may be measured and compared, it could indeed have a useful conceptual function.

Part of the hostility towards the concept of the Asiatic mode of production can be attributed to the inclination of many Marxists to shy away from recognising the geographical or technological determinants of social structure. This is probably an over-compensation for the exaggerated theses of Montesquieu and the legacy of the Enlightenment. But as Anderson suggests, "no truly materialist history can put geographical conditions into silent parentheses, as simply external to modes of production". After all, Marx himself emphasised the natural environment as an irreducible prior constituent of any economy [Anderson, 1979: 546]. Another cause for the lack of sympathy, especially among Marxists as well as 'nationalists', towards the concept of the Asiatic mode of production is its apparent attribution of a 'stagnant' or 'stationary' character to Eastern societies. Of course, this is not entirely true, historically speaking, for prosperity and advancement had characterised many periods of Eastern history.

There is no doubt, however, that the concept of the Asiatic mode of production has its own internal contradictions: i.e. between the centralising state power that appropriates directly part of the labour that it dominates, and the communal and social forces that push for more decentralisation and private property, and in the general direction of autonomous class formation. The difficulty is that in the Asiatic mode of production the state not only appropriates surplus labour from the society (which feudal systems also do), but further plays a crucial role in the reproduction of the prerequisites for production itself. In this way the state's role in the process of production contributes to the reproduction of the Asiatic mode itself [Taylor, 1979: 178].

Taylor suggests that within the Asiatic mode of production, the reproduction of the determinant relation of production is ultimately ensured through the determinancy of the "ideological instance" [Taylor, 1979: 183]. In order that the state can extract surplus labour in the form of tribute, in order that it can own and control the distribution of the surplus product, the intervention of ideology is required, since it is, above all else, within ideology that the right of the state to the surplus labour produced is defined and legitimised:

> The State, whose apparatus is controlled by the monarch and his family, exercises its right to the surplus via genealogy and tradition, usually expressed ... in religious and philosophical ideologies, embodied in particular rituals and practices exercised through the political power of the State ... Surplus labour is extracted because the monarch has an 'ideological right' to it, a right accepted by the communities and expressed in religion, art, literature and so on, throughout the social formation. It is this, of course, which produces the very fetishism of the ideological instance within the Asiatic mode that Marx repeatedly refers to [Taylor, 1979: 182].

The dynamics of this mode result directly from the determinancy of the ideological, and the subsequent power of the state. Taylor argues that, as opposed to other modes of production such as the feudal or the capitalist, "the dynamics of the Asiatic mode establish no real possibility for laying a basis for a transition to the dominance of a new mode of production". The "determinancy of the ideological", embodied in the actions of the state, places severe restrictions on the processes of capital accumulation, the private owner-ship of land or capital and, of course, on any separation of direct producers from their means of production (except for occasional seasonal or cyclical labour in the state 'factories' or mines). By its total control over these pro-cesses, the state prevents these possibilities – any of which could establish the likelihood for a basis from which a transition to another mode of production could begin to develop – from being reproduced. This restriction of transitional tendencies appears to be maintained in the histories of social formations dominated by the Asiatic mode, despite the very 'dramatic' changes that characterise their political history. State power is repeatedly seized by one dynasty, only to be defeated and replaced by another invading dynasty, in a highly discontinuous process. Yet, despite this political discontinuity, the nature of the relations between village and state is continually perpetuated [Taylor, 1979: 183–5].

These are obviously the features of the 'pure' form of the Asiatic mode of production. But in reality the state does not remain perpetually powerful and totalitarian, and the system does not remain continuously closed. When the state weakens, its own officials are likely to indulge in an exercise of amassing their own private wealth, and sometimes property. The local peripheries are also likely to establish more autonomy for themselves or to come under the domination of nomadic tribes. If the state is tempted to involve itself, either directly or through control over the merchants, in the area of foreign trade, this opens the way for all kinds of potential influences and may make the state itself too dependent on external factors which it cannot easily control.

Last and by no means least, the state may lose its monopoly over the 'ideological instance' that ensures its hegemony over society. Religion is never completely and exclusively absorbed into the dominant ideology: the 'believing' masses may eventually develop their own versions of the 'right religion' or the 'right faith', and religiously coloured protest movements may emerge, ex-pressing a different set of social interests, in opposition to state power and 'official' religion [cf. Bertrand, 1979]. There are illustrations of all such develop-ments throughout much of the social history of the Middle Eastern counties, as we will see in detail further on.

I have argued elsewhere [Ayubi, 1980] that the category of the Asiatic mode of production can furnish not only a useful tool of analysis for the understanding of various stages of Egypt's development (e.g. the 'Old King-dom', Muhammad 'Ali, 'Abd al-Nasser), but also a much longer-term *leitmotif* that colours its political culture in general.

More recently, there has been much debate as to the historical relationship between irrigated agriculture and the emergence of the state. An important issue that is often raised is that not all types of irrigated agriculture require centralised, rather than local, organisation. Michael Mann has produced one of the fullest recent discussions on the relationship between irrigation and the state. He argues generally that the correlation between irrigation and despotism is spurious [Mann, 1986b: 94]. He does, however, regard it as "obvious" that "irrigation agriculture was decisive in generating civilization, stratification and the State in Egypt" [ibid.: 108]. However, in his analysis the power of the state is less attributable to the distributive aspect of the irrigation process and more related to "geographical control over the Nilotic communications infrastructure" [ibid.: 112], and to what he calls the "caging" effect, the growth of focused, inescapably intense, centralised social relations [ibid.: 86]: "in ancient Egypt, where virtually no one could live outside the Nile Valley, the barrier became almost absolute, and so did the identity of 'Egyptian'" [ibid.: 92].

The recent revival of the debate over the Asiatic mode of production has spread beyond the traditional concern with Egypt, and some writers have been testing the applicability of the concept with regard, for example, to the other two ancient civilisations that have had a strong impact on the development of the Islamic state: Persia and Byzantium. Irrigation was indeed important from the time of Ancient Mesopotamia, interacting with its region and environment to give rise both to quasi-private property and to the state [Mann, 1986b: 78–93]. However, because the Euphrates and the Tigris were to a large extent uncontrollable, irrigation was precarious enough to "break existing social organization as often as extend it", and the social form that emerged was the city-state, exerting control over only a limited length and lateral flow of the river [ibid.: 94–8].

Although hydraulic works were important to the Sassanid and the Byzantine states they were never as comprehensive or as centralised as their Ancient Egyptian counterparts, and although there were in both strong tendencies towards the public ownership of land (or at least ownership by higher state officials), neither of these represented a 'pure' case of the Asiatic mode of production. For in the case of Persia, the tribal element and the decentralising forces were always strong, while in the case of Byzantium, semi-feudal formations were strong and some traces of the slavery tradition were always there. There is no doubt, however, that the type of 'feudalism' that might have existed in these two states was different in character from most of subsequent European feudalisms and that the two systems were much more 'bureaucratic' as well as autocratic in nature [cf. Lambton, 1980; Al-Rayyis, 1985: 25–84; Mumjian, 1981: 76–9]. Later on, in Islamic polemics, Pharaoh of Egypt, Chosroe of Persia and Caesar of Byzantium would become the symbolic epitome of political despotism (this was the rhetoric; in reality these three were the cultural, political and organisational traditions from which the Muslims borrowed the most).[1]

Once the application of the concept of the Asiatic mode of production is extended historically over a long span of time, it tends understandably to face fiercer criticisms, because one would appear in such a case to be talking more about historical legacy and about political culture than about a technically defined Mode of Production. Even so, this is precisely what several Egyptian writers, Marxists included, feel tempted to do about their own country, Egypt. Anwar Abdel-Malek, for example, maintains that there is a certain 'specificity' of Egypt, represented in particular by the fact that "the tendency to unity, to centralism, to concentration, to pyramidal hierarchy spares no domain" [A. Abdel-Malek, 1979: 353-4]. The outcome of all the relations involved is a highly bureaucratised society, where everything is hierarchical and where the state has a crucial role to play in all aspects of social life. To control the public bureaucracy, then, is to control everything, including in particular the sources of wealth: the dominant class is a political (namely bureaucratic) rather than an economic one. As Fu'ad Mursi, a leading Egyptian Marxist says, "The state in Egypt, centralism in Egypt, bureaucracy in Egypt have origins of deep impact on the Egyptian character. In all human societies, wealth is usually the source of power, in Egypt it is power that is usually the source of wealth" [Mursi, 1969: 36].

What use can we make of the concept of the Asiatic mode of production in comparative analysis, especially of Middle Eastern social formations? It seems to me that if the Asiatic mode of production is used as an 'ideal-type', that is, as a 'pure' abstracted category of comparison, it can retain a certain analytical value. Even a well-established concept such as feudalism has multiple manifestations, within the European continent alone, without this necessarily making it a useless category of analysis. The hydraulic origins of the Asiatic mode of production may sometimes be empirically difficult to trace, but a concept such as the 'social contract', presumed by many to be behind the formation of modern European states, is even more difficult to pin down empirically.

Two main – and often related – factors seem to impart to the Asiatic mode of production its specific character: absence, or weakness, of private land-ownership, and the powerful role of the state. These two elements do not have to be confined to hydraulic societies based on macro-management of irrigation systems (although these may represent a 'purer' form of the category). They apply in the broader sense to a whole range of ecosystems and social for-mations that are control-based. Macro-hydraulic systems are a variety of these, but a mercantile system that is so dependent on the control of trade routes may be another. Nor does the Asiatic mode of production have to be regarded as an exclusivist closed system. In the Middle East in particular, hydraulic systems, whether of the macro- or of the micro-type, have never been far removed from the 'nomadic factor', and even Egypt, historically the most obvious macro-hydraulic system, was considerably affected by nomadic infiltrations and influences. The concept of articulation of modes of production would be useful here, where the emphasis would be on examining the inter-relationships among various modes: hydraulic and nomadic, and – later on – mercantile and iqta'i (Eastern, bureaucratic-feudalist).

All these modes are mainly control-based (or 'tributary', as Samir Amin calls them), and this is in our view the historically distinct character of the 'Eastern' modes, a feature that might have been difficult for many Marxists of the conventional 'economistic' school to accept. For although economics and politics are inextricably linked in such modes as in all others, it is politics that tends often to have a stronger impact on economics in the Middle East, rather than the other way round.

EARLY ISLAMIC ARABIA AND THE NOMADIC/ CONQUESTAL MODE OF PRODUCTION

The 'Asiatic mode of production' – inasmuch as it applies to the Middle East or parts thereof – cannot be understood, as we have just suggested, without taking account of another mode of production that was never very far away from any Arab society, the hydraulic or agricultural ones included: that is, the 'nomadic' kin-ordered mode of production. Even Engels, who originally related the specificity of Oriental political history to the lack of private land ownership (which he thought might be attributed in turn to climatic and geographical factors) was later to pay attention also to the factor of perpetual struggle between nomadism and sedentarism. Not only was the mode of production in Eastern societies constrained in its development, and often unable even to reach the feudalistic stage, but it was also subject to repeated attacks from the nomads who were both poorer and more belligerent as well as envious of the relative riches of the settled communities. The nomads' repeated encroach-ments, combined with the poorly developed mode of production of their neighbouring agrarian societies, had made the alterations in political power often repetitive rather than cumulative, in that most new individuals or groups taking over power had kept the economic conditions and the social formations as they had been previously, rather than introducing a new economic and social system [cf. Al-Tawati, c. 1985: 33–49].

One wonders whether Engels had ever read Ibn Khaldun, for as is known, the conflict between badu (nomads) and hadar (urbanites) is indeed a major category in the latter's analysis. The nomads despise agriculture and crafts and are disinclined to engage in them (the Arabic word for a 'craft' or 'profession' is derived from the same root as 'humiliation', imtihan), but they are at the same time tempted by the riches of the settled lands and inclined to take them over and control their producers "by the points of their spears" [cf. Baali and Al-Wardi, 1981: 103]. A cyclical pattern is then often set in motion: a militant nomadic wave relying on strength derived from their 'group solidarity' ('asabiyya) takes over power, but in due course this ruling élite is tempered and softened by the luxury of settled urban life, leading to its weakening and decay, which in turn paves the way for a fresh wave of nomads whose group solidarity is still strong and who are eager to take over power ... and thus the cycle continues.

'Ali Al-Wardi holds that conflict between badawa (nomadism) and hadara (urbanity; civilisation) characterises the entire social history of the Arab World, and it is possible, he maintains, to classify the Arab countries according to this conflict into three categories: countries where hadara and badawa exist side by side (most Arab countries); the countries where badawa is more dominant (such as in the Arabian Peninsula); and then those where hadara is more dominant (such as in Egypt) [cf. Baali and Al-Wardi, 1981]. Even the Egyptian society is subject, in his view, to such repetitive cycles under the impact of this perennial conflict, and indeed the bedouin customs (mores) have left their permanent imprint on the society of Upper Egypt in particular. Several other Arab writers have also affirmed the long-lasting impact of tribal values and attitudes on most Arab societies [cf. Barakat, 1984: 45–8, 65–78 and refs cited].

'Abid Al-Jabiri finds Ibn Khaldun's theory interestingly indicative of a certain mode of production that he calls a 'conquestal mode of production' or a 'military mode of production'. The term 'production' here is obviously only figurative, for this is basically a consumerist or circulationist, not a producer, type of civilisation. Wealth in such a society is mostly derived from the acquisition of ready 'goodies'. The superstructures in such a society are in no substantial way related to the infrastructure: political power is not derived from the relations of production but from a sense of group solidarity leading to domination and to the acquisition of privilege and ready wealth. Al-Jabiri believes that Ibn Khaldun's observation can be generalised to most phases of the history of the Islamic state: monies are collected to be distributed among the fighters and the officials for consumption but not for investment. The 'conquestal' economy in short is based on "wealth accruing to the state, via statist methods, to be spent by the statesmen" [Al-Jabiri, 1982a: 404–31].

In such a kind of political economy, the 'booty' (al-ghanima) takes pride of place: it is the source of income (which may by extension be tributary), it reflects itself on distribution (which is based on donation), and it promotes a certain 'rentier mentality' which is averse to production and to the work ethic [Al-Jabiri, 1990: 49–50, 112ff]. According to Al-Jabiri too, this Khaldunian analysis has a certain contemporary significance to the Arab World and may be regarded as "headings for a reality that we live, but dare not speak about" [Al-Jabiri, 1982b: 464ff].

Nomadism is, of course, basically an 'ecological' phenomenon that corresponds to the natural and geographical conditions of certain types of environment. It is based on small primary units that normally start with the family and end up with the 'tribe'. The 'means of production' in a tribal society are simple: the switching of pasture land and the shifting of animal herds. Physical mobility is needed to link the two. Relations of production are also often quite simple: ownership of the land is communal, ownership of the herds is individual or familial. It seems that Marx himself had, in the *Grundrisse*, considered nomadic pastoralism to form a distinct mode of production, based on the collective property of immobile wealth (land) and individual property of mobile wealth (herds) [cf. Anderson, 1974: 217–22]. Although pastoral nomadism is the main form, especially in arid zone desert regions, other types of nomadism also exist, e.g. in hunting or fishing and pearl-diving, or in seasonal agriculture and in palm groves [Al-Fawwal, 1983: 297–305]. Middle Eastern nomadism (*badawa*) has three levels or degrees depending on the extent to which the community is immersed in desert life: camel herders are the most nomadic, followed by sheep herders, and then semi-sedentary nomads who practise some cultivation on a seasonal shifting basis, or in the vicinity of oases, wells and small valleys.

A nomadic community has not only to be sensitively tuned to nature and its changes, but has also to be critically alert to the movements of other nomadic communities that are trying to use the same limited resource base. The vital rule of social organisation is absolute internal solidarity and absolute external antagonism. The major organisational unit is the tribe (*qabila*) which includes smaller descending layers of *'ashira* (clan), *humula* (sub-clan) and *bait* or *'a'ila* (extended family). There are controversies among specialists as to the definition of 'tribe', basically over whether the main defining criterion is organisational/political or cultural/linguistic [cf. Eickelman, 1981: 65ff; Tapper, Introduction, 1983; Tapper, 1991: 51ff]. In the Arab World, however, tribal units that are ethnically or culturally distinct (except by dialect) are rarer than, say, in Iran or Afghanistan, and the tribe is better understood as a mode of social organisation based on a presumed (and constantly re-affirmed or re-defined) idea of common ancestry. The key distinctions by descent and by affinity are symbolised as ties of blood and flesh: *damm* (blood), *rahm* (womb), *jilda* (skin); and as ties of parts of the body: *batn* (belly), *fakhdh* (thigh), etc. Tribalism, however, belongs more closely to the '*social imaginaire*' than it does to the 'facts' of genetics. Thus, for example, Arabian tribalism was to become politically consolidated and consecrated (and in some cases 'invented') after the Islamic conquest of new lands, due to the way the troops were recruited, housed and remunerated via the 'donations register' (*diwan al-'ata'*) established by 'Umar ibn al-Khattab [Al-Jabiri, 1990: 156ff].

The tribe has for a long period of time represented an alternative to the state in its modern sense; however, it is mistaken, in our view, to define the tribe by its opposition to the state – many tribes are indeed very much 'interested' in the state, and 'political tribalism' can indeed exist, but, as will be elaborated upon below, everything depends on the specific historical conjunctures.

In a nomadic society the individual's entity and identity can only be understood in relation to his tribe and in contrast with that of the others. To ensure
internal cohesiveness, practices such as cousin-marriage may be followed. To
ensure the idea of collective belonging and responsibility, the concept of
'solidarity vendetta' (tha'r) is reinforced – the whole tribe, and not only its
individual members, is responsible for any criminal act by one of its members.
The practice of tha'r is also intended to re-establish the order of status and
balance among the various tribes as much as it is meant to consolidate the
internal cohesion of the tribe itself [Mahjub, c. 1975: 153–6]. Customary rules
govern not only extended lineage relationships in the tribal space, but underlie
many economic and political relationships among (and within) tribes. They
elaborate on the selection and responsibility of tribal leaders and on the levels
of commitments and duties, individual and collective, decided by sex, by status
and by wealth, etc. [ibid.: 181–5]. Within the tribe, loyalty is not to 'place' but
to 'time' (the presumed ancestral lineage), while penal law is strict and firm,
aiming not only to punish the criminal but to compensate the victim; in the
absence of permanent specialised institutions, it can be tempting to break the
rules and penalties have thus to be severe in order to ensure compliance
[Sabir and Mulaika, 1986: 135–8].

Ultimately, however, the position of a tribe vis-à-vis the other tribes (and of
course in relation to the settled and sedentary communities) is established and
maintained by the sword (an instrument so important that it has countless
synonyms in Arabic). The importance of war for the survival of the tribe is
presumably behind the male-dominance and the low esteem accorded to the
status of women in tribal societies. Conquests and wars are common among
nomads, not only over immediate water and pasture resources, but by way of
establishing a certain ranking order among the tribes and, of course, over the
settled communities, whereby the stronger tribes would collect a khuwwa (a
'status' tax enforced on the militarily weaker units).

Tribal alliances (confederacies) are known, of course, especially in times of
common threats, but these are shifting, temporary arrangements that do not
even have a specific Arabic term to describe them in the same exact way that
the tribe and its sub-divisions are described [Sharara, 1981a: 20–23]. The
striking of alliances and confederacies (including the arrangement of tribal
intermarriages) is the function of the tribal chief (shaikh) whose chivalry and
generosity, as well as his intelligence and cunning, must be well established so
that he emerges as the 'first among equals', who is in reality more equal than
others. If he is seen to have failed he is replaced by another close relative –
this is a means not only of ensuring the survival of the tribe but also a certain
degree of 'rotation of office' [Dahir, 1986: 34–5].

However, the definition of the relationships between the tribe and its hierarchical sub-divisions (e.g. batn, fakhdh, humula, fasila, etc.) remains quite fluid
and mercurial in spite of the presumed consanguinity. The relationships vary

in strength and weakness, and may even descend to the level of inner fighting, depending on a variety of ecological changes or on pressures and influences emanating from the surrounding communities and states. *Batn* and *fakhdh* are basically 'political' extensions of the tribal gathering – the *fakhdh* is indeed the main form of tribal solidarity, with distinct political, 'semi-statal' functions: the protection of wells and pastures, the collection of *khuwwa* and the decision on family disputes, pursuit of vendettas, protection of strangers, or the declaration of war and peace [Sharara, 1981a: 23–4, and refs cited].

There is a fundamental irony that characterises the role of leadership within the tribal set-up, for although the chief is a major factor in the cohesion of his tribe and the main instrument in establishing its system of alliances, the immutability and permanence of his position would wreck the whole ecological system on which tribalism is based, with its requirements of constant alertness and mobility both in relation to the pastoral base, and also to the surrounding urban and agricultural centres and their linking routes. For it would be a mistake to define nomadism simply in terms of its base activity of pastoralism; nomadism cannot be properly understood as a social formation without relating it to interlocking urban and agrarian centres and to interlacing commercial routes. The city has always received the 'human surplus' of the desert, and for all the disdain with which the nomads regard the city dwellers, the city has always been part and parcel of the reality of their life. Historical as well as ethnographic evidence confirm that non-pastoral products have always been an important part of the diet of pastoralists, and that activities associated with acquiring them have figured largely in their annual cycle and division of labour. No major increases in productivity comparable to those of arable farming were possible because the means of production was not soil, but herds which essentially permitted only quantitative augmentation rather than qualitative improvement [Foran, 1988: 359–60]. This has made interaction with the interlocking and/or surrounding agrarian and urban centres a must for the continued survival of most nomadic societies.

It is for such reasons that we should not identify the mode of production under examination simply with pastoralism. The term 'lineage mode of production' used by Rey [quoted in Brewer, 1980], Taylor [1979] and others is broader and thus more appropriate. This is also close enough to the term 'kin-ordered mode of production' used by Eric Wolf [1982: 88ff].

According to Wolf, kinship can be regarded as a particular way of establishing rights in people, and thus laying claim to shares of social labour. Most kinship-ordered modes allocate people differentially to positions of power (depending on sex, age and relationships, etc.) and establish a genealogical range of mobilisable allies. "The terminology of marriage and filiation is thus used to convey information about differential capacities to mobilize labor for work and support" [ibid.: 91–3].

As we have seen, there are always oscillations of rise and decline as leaders who are made effective in the redistribution of goods and the building of alliances gain at the expense of less apt contenders. But this is precisely "the Achilles' heel of the kinship mode, one of its diagnostic points of stress. For as a chief or other leader draws a following through judicious management of alliances and redistributive action, he reaches a limit that can only be surpassed by breaking through the bounds of the kinship order" [Wolf, 1982: 94]. The ability of the kin-ordered mode to regenerate itself is probably due to the fact that oppositions which are usually played out are particulate, the conjunction of a particular elder with a particular junior or a particular lineage at a particular time and place, not the general opposition of elder and junior as classes – i.e. the mode contains its oppositions by particularising conflicts and tensions. Witness for example the endless family feuds that characterised Arabian society until very recently.

Yet conflict resolution may encounter an ultimate structural limit when it accumulates to a point exceeding the mode's capacity to cope with it. Groups will then break up and disintegrate, a process which often represents a needed source of change, and which is more likely to happen under pressures from societies in the tributary and capitalist modes. The tendencies towards in-equalities in function are greatly enhanced when kin-ordered groups enter into relationships with tributary and capitalist societies. Such relationships afford opportunities for the seizure and transfer of surpluses beyond those available with the kin-ordered mode. This is why chiefs have proved to be notorious collaborators with European traders, bounty hunters, colonial ad-ministrators and oil excavators. Connection with the Europeans offered access to arms and valuables, or to money, land and property, and hence to a following not necessarily encumbered by the strict requirements of the kinship relationship [cf. Wolf, 1982: 95–6].

To what extent can the concept of the 'lineage mode of production' help in understanding historical Arabian politics. To start with, the nomadic social formations obtaining in Arabia in the seventh century represented the basic model which, infused with the mobilisational impact of the new Islamic message, was greatly extended and recast in many ways to produce the main features of the first Arab-Islamic state in history. Here again, the most im-portant feature is not the presumably autonomous tribes, but the way in which they intermesh with cities and agrarian communities, and in particular the way in which they control the trade (and military) routes that join all these components together.

The tribal society of Arabia about a century or so before Islam was by no means a simple one of autonomous, egalitarian tribes. It had known poverty and wealth, and had witnessed chiefly authority based on some degree of ownership and/or on elements of control over the means of production. Markets existed both for the interchange of goods and of ideas (through poetry in particular), and in Hijaz and especially around Mecca a commercial semi-aristocracy (mainly Quraishi) was involved in local and medium-distance trade, and was capable of possessing herds and slaves, of controlling large expanses of pasture land and of owning some agricultural land (in Ta'if, Yathrib and elsewhere) as well as money represented by currencies of the surrounding empires. In the sixth century, the commercial importance of Mecca grew as a centre for much of the Eastern, and not only the Arabian, trade. A northern tribal federation (al-'ilaf) was formed to protect the Meccan trade and to secure its routes, extending into Iraq, the Gulf, Yemen, Ethiopia and Syria [Baydun, 1983: 54–82].

Politically, the concept of al-mala' of Mecca represented an association of the dominant trading chieftanships which also kept 'African' guards to protect their houses as well as the Ka'ba, used both as a religious sanctuary and as a money store. The nadwa represented the location where these leaders took all decisions pertaining to their civil affairs as well as to war and peace, according to patterns broadly reflecting their relative economic wealth and social prestige. All these manifestations could be taken collectively to indicate the emergence of an embryonic state form in the late Jahili period [Muruwwa I, 1981: 212–37; Baydun, 1983: 87–99].

Islam then came in the seventh century to represent a homogenising and unifying influence, forging most of Arabia – through the nucleus of Quraish and the Meccan communities – into a more integrated society subject to one law, the new Islamic shari'a. The unifying process was not comprehensive and fixed, however, as evidenced by the ridda (apostasy) wars that followed the death of Prophet Muhammad. Pushing outside Arabia was then to represent an effective vehicle for forging unity inside. In the traditional society, confrontations with the other tribes (mainly through conquest) was the way to ensure the internal solidarity of the tribe; this time it was the extended 'Arabian' tribe that was involved in conquest against the territories and dynasties surrounding Arabia. Conquest has now acquired not only some more tempting 'economic' objectives but in the religious name of jihad also a godly mission to fulfil, while in the process establishing a higher level of social (and national) integration. The nomadic tribal formations, so explicitly condemned by the Quran, are not in fact dissolved but are merged in a higher integrative level in the name of the Islamic umma, which is in reality – at least initially – basically all Islamised Arab tribes of the Peninsula. By extending the 'conflict' outside Arabia a certain element of cohesion and integration is imparted for the first time to all the inhabitants of Arabia – who are no longer merely members of this or the other tribe but who are basically 'Arabs' fighting the cause of the new religion.

It would be mistaken, however, to argue the reductionist case that the early Arab-Islamic state was simply the outcome of the commercial interests of Quraish needing to ensure its direct control over trade routes by creating a unified state, for the unification process did not spring from commercial Mecca but from agricultural Madina, and the Islamic conquests had in any case meant the decline of Quraish as a commercial class and its transformation into a warrior and ruling class [cf. Baydun, 1983: 363–8]. Nor was the concept of *tawhid* in Islam ('unification', i.e. monotheism) simply an ideological (theological) formula for ensuring the political integration of society (for political unity can coexist with polytheism, and monotheism does not guarantee political unity) [Asad, 1980: 116–31].

Yet it would be equally naive to deny any economic incentive on the part of the Islamic conquests. It is certainly telling that the Islamic conquests had started in the same year in which the *ridda* (apostasy) movements were put down (these movements having had, in addition to the religious, some socioeconomic dimensions that were represented by conflicts over the payment of *zakat* and *kharaj*, and over the relations between Quraish and the Hijazis on the one hand and the other Arabian tribes on the other) [Isma'il I, 1980: 52–4]. These conquests included some rich lands based on complex hydraulic systems, which represented both a tempting target and a difficult organisational/ financial task for the Arabians to deal with.

Several classical Arab writers, including Al-Baladhiri and Al-Tabari, wrote on the economic promise of the conquests. Al-Baladhiri, for example, refers to a letter from Abu-Bakr to the Arabs calling them for *jihad* and "tempting them by the booty of the Romans – whereupon the calculating and the greedy raced to Mecca from all parts". Al-Tabari also refers to a speech by Khalid ibn al-Walid in which he is tempting the Arabs to the land of the Persians and Romans (*ajam* and *rum*) by saying, "By God, had not jihad for the Almighty obliged us to it, and had it been solely for the sake of our livelihood, then opinion would (still) have been to attack that countryside and to get hold of it for ourselves and to drive away hunger and poverty" [Salim, 1983: 180–85].

It was thus possible for the first time in the history of Arabia to establish, through external conquest, a unified Arab state. Whereas the earlier attempts in Kinda and elsewhere had failed to build up a stable state or to forge a unified sense of Arabism, it was this attempt that pushed into the 'green belt' surrounding Arabia which managed to do so.

The origins of the Islamic state, as Waddah Sharara has eloquently illustrated, can be traced back to a process of 'Islamisation' of the traditional conquest (*ghazw*) practice, and more specifically to an Islamisation of the rules of 'distribution' following war [Sharara, 1981a: 125–42]. There are several indicators of the 'economic' dimensions of the conquests. First, there were the immediate spoils of war, distributed initially according to traditional nomadic rules and then increasingly according to Islamic rules (as we will see). Secondly, the conquerors did not insist on the full Islamisation of the populations of the conquered lands. This was particularly true of countries whose inhabitants did not resist the Islamic accord (*sulh*) on offer. Given that the Byzantine and Persian rulers of Egypt and Syria had exploited the indigenous populations of peasants and artisans and that the Byzantines had also persecuted the native Eastern Christian churches, these populations offered a fairly welcoming hand to their Muslim conquerors in the routing of their previous masters. They were in turn treated by the Muslim rulers as *dhimmis* (protected 'people of the book'). *Dhimmis* who chose to remain in their previous religion (Christians, Jews) were charged the *jizya* tax. The category of *dhimmis* was then expanded to include Sabaeans and Magi in order to increase the income. Some Arab rulers in fact refrained from encouraging mass conversions to Islam, or even specified certain annual quotas for conversion, to avoid the immediate decline in income from *jizya* – a large income indeed, amounting in the time of 'Umar to some 14 million golden dinars from Egypt and around 10 million silver dirhams from Iraq alone. Further, if a non-Muslim peasant converted to Islam he continued to pay a *kharaj* tax (unless he moved to the city – which was not always permitted – in which case he would pay *zakat*); the income was too good to lose, even if the objective of Islamisation was not achieved – a situation which was only changed under 'Umar ibn 'Abd al-'Aziz. The proselytising of Islam was not therefore the only concern of the conquerors. If anything, one can detect a certain 'national' factor at work. Not only were the Eastern Christians of the conquered lands accorded their religious freedom under their native clergy, and many of them employed as administrators and accountants, but some Christian Arab tribes were, under 'Umar, exempt from paying the *jizya* and were even included – as Arabs, not Muslims – in the Islamic army of conquest, at a time when non-Arab Muslims were not accepted in the conquering forces [Muruwwa I, 1981: 409–23].

Distribution of the spoils of war was at first equitable among Arabs regardless of differences; it then became increasingly based on a system of gradation. Abu Bakr, the first caliph, related the distribution directly to internal considerations of the Arabian society by adopting the (nomadic) principle of equal shares of the booty. With 'Umar, however, gradation in compensation was introduced according to Islamic 'seniority' (how long in Islam and whether the crucial battle of Badr had been attended or not) as well as relationship to the Prophet (which is clearly a mixed nomadic/Islamic criterion). He thus moved from egalitarian warrior nomadism to a more stratified, settled Islam [Sharara, 1981a: 163].

Furthermore, 'Umar made the grant to the fighters annual, after accumulating the money, and not occasional with each conquestal collection: "for if you divided it (the land) among those who are at present, nothing will remain to those who will succeed them" [Al-Rayyis, 1985: 107–8]. 'Umar had therefore departed from the nomadic norm of immediate distribution and resorted to deferment, thus separating the booty from the disbursements. The leader is now no longer in charge of immediate, full distribution, but of accumulation and storage. This is now a 'political calculus' although still tied to a military base. Political leadership assumes a treasurer function, but it cannot achieve this without still gripping the reins of war [Sharara, 1981a: 170]. It prevents inner fighting by excluding land and its peasants from the spoils, by expanding in more territories and accumulating more for storage, and by establishing grades and strata within the same *umma* in proportion to a hierarchy of participation in Islamic wars. Political leadership is thus the treasurer of war and the overseer of its rent; it is also the agency that shapes the community into a certain order of distinctions (i.e. into strata).

But war does not only bring money; it also brings people: 'people of the grain' (*ahl al-habba*) or 'people of the water' (*ahl al-miyah*), otherwise called by the conquerors: 'a substance for Muslims' (*maddatu 'l-muslimin*) or workers, peasants, heads, skulls, necks, etc. All such terms make conquered peoples fully equal within one class, whereas it has already established strata among Muslims. War did not lead to the killing, or otherwise to the Islamisation of all Christians, Jews and others in the new lands – these people had instead to be incorporated. This process was based on two elements, a legal one where land left to its owners and tillers could not subsequently be taken over by the Muslim rulers, and an economic one based on the collection of tribute.

The *dhimmi* neighbourhoods became an integral, though distinct, element of the community – both in lands where they formed a majority and within metropolitan cities. But, as Waddah Sharara explains, their presence had to be void of any obvious cultural manifestation of difference, and they were relegated to a defeated and lowly rank that maintained them merely as the 'necks' and 'arms', i.e. as the source of tribute. *Jizya* and *kharaj* were thus a continuation of war by other means; the conquered is defined by production, just as the conqueror is distinguished by distribution [Sharara, 1981a: 177]. Although it is customary, it is nevertheless inaccurate to describe *jizya* as a 'poll tax' and *kharaj* as a 'land tax', since neither of them was really a tax in the technical sense, but was a tribute in the sense of being a politico-military levy enforced by the politically and socially superior on the politically and socially inferior [Sa'd, 1988: 103–9]. This is the basis of the tributary mode of production which by this time had become characteristic of the entire Islamic state. Tribute was of course known within the nomadic society of Arabia as a levy imposed on weaker tribes; by now it had turned into the basis of a whole social formation, and was applied most specifically to the agrarian sector, creating a series of what Peter Gran terms "agrarian tributary states" [Gran, 1980: 522].

The Islamic state did not initially involve itself in the process of production, but confined itself mainly to the process of distribution and circulation, a practice that had its early origins in the nomadic mode of production. In the latter, production was the function of the 'other' (the lowly one at that): slaves, minorities and people of 'doubtful' tribal origin. In the early Arab-Islamic state there was also an ethno-religious division of labour whereby the further away one was from Arabism and Islam, the closer was the link to a production function; the nearer one was to Arabism and Islam, the closer to a control and circulation function. The Muslim Arabs were more interested in the functions of war, rule and organisation than they were in the functions of crafts or agriculture. The Muslim conquerors initially, and for a long time, lived in newly built garrison camps or cities (*amsar*), outside the main economic and social centres of the conquered lands, which were planned and organised according to a tribe-by-tribe pattern (e.g. Basra and Kufa in Iraq, Fustat in Egypt, Qairawan in Tunisia). The Islamic idea was closely identified at that stage with an urban-oriented concept of the community (*jama'a*) away from the rough desert and from the discordant nomads (reversion to nomadism was almost tantamount to apostasy) and towards a more centralised polity (only after emigration to the *amsar* would an Arabian be entitled to share in the *fay'* – payment) [Baydun, 1983: 132–5; Al-Duri, 1984: 47–52].

The early Islamic economy was basically a tax economy, and even till considerably later, most classical works on the economy consisted of treatises on varieties of tax and the times and methods of their extraction. Another significant practice pertains to currency. Abu Bakr and 'Umar had kept the foreign currencies of their conquered lands, including the Byzantine dinars with crosses and the Persian dirhams with fire temples. Even when they started to mint coins they continued to reproduce foreign ones with an Arabic inscription of the name of God or the Prophet and a sign saying 'approved' or 'accepted' added to them [Salim, 1983: 204–6]. It was all indicative of the 'externality' of the sources of income and a certain reluctance to involve the Islamic state organically into the economies of the conquered lands.[2]

'Umar (d. 644) was of course the leader credited with the greatest role in laying down the foundations of an Arab-Islamic state that transcended Arabia. His state was highly and personally centralised, some would say too centralised [cf. Tabliyya, 1985: 65–9]. The foundations included a professional army with a supporting rudimentary bureaucracy (*diwan*), a legal code based in the shari'a and on 'Umar's own improvisations (*ijtihad*) in interpreting it, and an extensive taxation and financial system to deal with the huge ensuing resources [Baydun, 1983: 141–3]. The economic base of this state was represented by agricultural land, still mainly owned by the indigenous inhabitants, and by cities – old and new – where both the indigenous artisans and the Meccan merchants were in action.

The rule of 'Uthman (a Quraishi 'aristocrat' who followed 'Umar) saw the beginnings of important social and political changes. Many of the governors whom he sent to the *amsar* were Umayyads by tribal lineage who started to build up their own wealth through exaggerated taxation and some confiscating of land. A new semi-feudalism, if still very political in character, was creeping into the social formation. Resentment emerged not only among the exploited masses but also among the various political factions (*ahzab*) in Madina which were kept away from the politico-economic game by 'Uthman and his entourage. Thus in AD 656 delegations from Egypt and Iraq came to Mecca for the pilgrimage, bringing with them their grievances against their local rulers, and asking 'Uthman either to limit the injustices committed by his men, or to go. His refusal to abdicate was to give rise to the serious socio-religious upheaval known as the 'great strife' (al-fitna al-kubra) which ended with the murder of 'Uthman, and the accusation that 'Ali was behind the killing. The 'war of the camel' erupted, and 'Ali's candidacy for the caliphate, which was objectively and formally obvious, became the subject of great controversy – even resistance – especially from the Umayyad aristocracy who were then ruling in Syria under Mu'awiya and in close alliance with local commercial, bureaucratic and communal interests. As 'Ali had been proposed for the caliphate by many Muslims, he removed Mu'awiya from his position as Emir of Syria, which action prompted the latter to launch the war of Siffin where the Syrian and the Iraqi armies confronted one another. And it was in Siffin that the khawarij (Kharijites) emerged; they were a radical political faction who espoused an egalitarian message discreetly enshrined in their theological call that "there is no sovereignty but to God".

'Ali was trapped by the irony of fate. As an individual he was a man of integrity and espoused the ideals of right and justice – which would have endeared him to the dispossessed and disappointed. As a member of the Hashemite tribal solidarity, however, he was regarded by his kith and kin as an appropriate tool for defending their vested political interests vis-à-vis not only the Ummayads but also the disgruntled social groups. 'Ali eventually ended by encountering enmity from both the Mu'awiya (Syrian aristocracy) side and the 'popular' (Kharijite) side [cf. Muruwwa I, 1981: 435–43]. His murder by one of these Kharijites in 661 ended the era of the Four Rightly Guided (Rashidun) Caliphs. Yet the theological question of 'Ali's 'divine' right to the leadership (which is held as a matter of belief by the Shi'is) did not die with him and continues to be a lively issue even to this day.

This brief historical account should be sufficient to give one an idea as to how the characteristics of the lineage mode of production coloured the early experience of the Arabo-Islamic state. As we have already seen, the lineage mode of production is transformed via two possible mechanisms. Historically, Arab nomadism (and other Middle Eastern nomadisms such as that of the Berbers, Turks, Mongols, etc.) was weakened through a process of urbanisation (e.g. as with the first Islamic state; the North African states of Ibn Khaldun; the Saudi state, etc.). Nomadism can also be weakened, as we shall see later, through a process of 'pinning down' to agricultural land (e.g. the late Abbasid, the late Ottoman, and the Colonial eras). These are also precisely the processes that transform tribe into state, because they divide the population into a class of surplus producers and a class of surplus takers. Such a transformation requires mechanisms of domination to ensure that surpluses are transferred on a predictable basis from one class to another. This cannot be secured without the development of an apparatus of coercion to maintain the basic division into classes and to defend the resulting structure against external attack: namely the state [Wolf, 1982: 99].

THE UMAYYADS AND THE LINEAGE/*IQTA'I* SYMBIOSIS

The Umayyad dynasty was established in Damascus by Mu'awiya in AD 660, even though 'Ali was confirmed by his supporters as Caliph in the same year. Mu'awiya established a new state based on an alliance between the Kalbi Arab tribes (as opposed to the Qaysis) and the semi-feudalist and the 'official' élite of Syria. This state was to last for just under a century, and was governed according to hereditary dynastic rules, signifying thus the abandonment of the formal method of consultation and selection of the ruler that had been more or less followed for nominating the first four caliphs. Mu'awiya was aware of this change in the nature of government, since he described himself as 'the first of the Arab-Muslim kings'.

The social formation under the Umayyads was a semi-feudal one, resting on an agrarian tributary mode of production. Although the land belonged in theory to the Islamic state, the old feudal lords continued to utilise it with help from the old official and organisational (security) class [Al-Rayyis, 1985: 179ff], but under tighter state control and with parts of the land going increasingly to elements of the Umayyad dynasty and their Kalbi Arab allies who, in addition, monopolised the military function.

The bureaucracy was developed by separating the *diwan* into five different departments: the army, taxation, correspondence, registry and posts [Husaini, c. 1958: 166–71]. The language of the diwans continued, however, to be Greek in Syria, Persian in Iraq and Coptic in Egypt, and the circulating currencies continued to be foreign, until the era of 'Abd al-Malik ibn Marwan and Al-Walid ibn al-Malik, who systematised and Arabised the administrative system and ran frequent land surveys. Some important legal and tax reforms were introduced and significant improvements were made in agriculture and irrigation, which in turn helped artisan industry and the expansion of trade (including the building of a navy) [Dallu, 1985: 112ff].

However, while it remained in theory public land, the expanding ownership of the land among members of the military and official ruling class increasingly involved the growing exploitation of the peasants, especially non-Arabs, and impeded the development of the means of production in agriculture. Mu'awiya's attitude was telling. He was reported as saying, "I have seen these red elements increasing (meaning non-Arabs within the state) ... and I dread that they will ambush the Arabs and the power. I have decided to kill part of them, and to spare another part to run the market and construct the roads." [Ibn 'Abd Rabbih, quoted in Tizini, 1981: 178].

Mu'awiya died in 680 and his son Yazid succeeded him to the 'throne' of the caliphate; the Shi'a (supporters of 'Ali) were outraged, especially as they learned that Al-Husain, their third Imam in Mecca, had refused to recognise this succession. The drama of their unequal battle with the Umayyad army and their crushing defeat in Karbala' in the same year provided a deeply felt source for their collective memory and cognitive system from that time onwards. Apart from the 'issue of principle' involved, there were also several forces opposed, because of their own interests, to a permanent shift of the caliphate from Arabia to Syria. As the Umayyads one by one served their term of office, they had also to deal with the opposition forces represented by the Khawarij and the Shi'a, who, although appearing to be debating some religious issues, were in reality successful in attracting many of the disaffected groups and communities that suffered from growing exploitation and injustice. Slave revolts, ethnic revolts and class revolts also occurred and were crushed during the era of 'Abd al-Malik ibn Marwan and Al-Walid ibn 'Abd al-Malik. But the two main challenges which continued for many generations and which also had an ideology to support their social and political action were the Khawarij and the Shi'a.

THE ABBASIDS AND THE *IQTA'I*/MERCANTILE SYMBIOSIS

The oppressive and exploitative policies of the Umayyads, especially towards non-Arab groups and the peasant communities, resulted in a number of ethnic and peasant revolts in various parts of the empire, and in the emergence of the *shu'ubiyya* movement ('nationalistic' tendencies among the non-Arab communities) which, together with the inner fighting among the various 'Arab' factions, led eventually to the demise of the Umayyad dynasty and their centralised state in AD 750. In what amounts to a veritable *blocco storico* [Al-Jabiri, 1990: 329–31], the Abbasids took over, with help from the popular masses (mainly composed of peasants and slaves as well as urban folk), the non-Arab communities, and the Shi'a and the Khawarij, who were also opposed to the centralised state.

The Abbasid dynasty (c. AD 750 to c. 1258) made much political capital of their Quraishi lineage and set about constructing a prosperous state, by developing the economy, improving the hydraulic system and reclaiming more land, and also by improving the tax and financial system.

The state bureaucracy was greatly expanded, by adding to the five central departments already initiated by the Umayyads several others such as for accounting (audit), for justice (*al-mazalim*), for land and for court affairs [Husaini, c. 1958: 293–307]. The ministerial post (*wazir*, vizir) was also introduced for the first time as the function became necessary with the growing complexity of the tasks of government. A sophisticated system for police, prisons and security was also introduced.

Extensive trade networks were developed internally and with the rest of the world (even reaching Russia and Scandinavia), resulting also in artisan and industrial development, and benefiting from the scientific renaissance of that age (in chemistry, biology, astronomy, medicine, mathematics, mechanics and so on). Industries in sugar, glass, paper, textiles, carpets, chemicals and metals all flourished. A commodity and monetary economy was developed, controlled again by the state, since mercantile activities were not yet autonomous from the interests of state élites and military leaders.

The centralisation of the state, however, could not always be guaranteed, and local emirs, often exploiting nationalistic feelings and socio-economic grievances in their regions, were always attempting to enforce their own autonomy. Various revolts occurred, for example from 816 to 838 involving Persians, Turks, Kurds and Azeris as well as Arabs, protesting against high taxation or asking for increased autonomy. From 833 to 861, wars with the revolting communities and regions were almost continuous. Some territories eventually established their own dynasties where the economy had prospered on a small scale, such as in Tulunid Egypt and Umayyad Spain, but the parcelling out of the empire eventually meant, by the eleventh and twelfth centuries, a shrinking of the market and limitations on commodity circulation and the freedom of trade.

The emerging mercantile class was soon to decline after a vigorous and promising start, its demise resulting from its symbiotic ties with the state, and from the shrinkage in the market caused by the secession of the peripheries. The social formation was reverting to semi-feudal modes, and the large-scale industry was reverting to home crafts and village artisanship. Even agriculture was reverting to small-scale private farming.

Some of the revolts against the state were very distinctively socio-economic in nature, most notably the Zanj, the Qarmatian and the Babiki revolutions in the ninth century [Muruwwa II, 1981: 11–23]. They were partly a result of the growing duality of the nature of the state, which was still 'Oriental' (despotically controlled) in the centre and increasingly semi-feudal in the periphery. The peasants and the artisans were now having to provide economic surplus both for the central treasury and for the local emirs. Abu Yusuf's elaborate description of the cruel methods that should *not* be used to extract tribute is indicative that such methods were widely practised in Abbasid times: "No man should be beaten for tribute money, or be made to stand on one leg – for I have heard that they stretch people due for tribute in the sun, beat them severely, and hang clay storage jars on them, and chain them thus preventing them from prayers. This is too much before God and grotesque in Islam" [Al-Rayyis, 1985: 422–7].

Starting with the Caliph al-Mu'tasim, the Abbasids resorted to assembling military forces from among Turkic ethnicities, in an attempt to cope with the rebellious peripheries. New groups had to be found that were relatively 'autonomous' from society and loyal only to their political master, and these were used in an attempt to enforce unity on the society. But before long it was these 'mercenary' ethnic armies that interfered with the running of state affairs, that imposed their will on rulers, and that eventually took over power for themselves, thereby signalling the end of the Abbasid dynasty. As the state lost its grip over the economy and its declining productive forces, it became increasingly unable financially and organisationally to sustain centralised power over a unified imperial market. The state was being attacked both by the persecuted and exploited communities and by the regional leaderships, while the ethnic armies were gnawing away at the very core of the state.

The state was also being ideologically challenged. Ironically the socio-political conflict among nationalities within the Abbasid state was accompanied by cultural and intellectual interaction among them. The Islamic state was opened up to the cultural traditions of the various communities, which were in their turn accessible not only to the ancient cultures of the Near East but also to those of Greece and India. The new capital Baghdad, built in 862, was home to numerous translations from Syriac, Persian, Greek and many other languages, and many theological and philosophical debates were to emerge. Part of this intellectual endeavour was aimed, at most times indirectly, at the state itself. Whereas the Abbasid dynasty was making considerable capital out of its descent from the Prophet, and using the jurists to establish a case for its rule based on the *Shari'a*, the emergence and development of Arab-Islamic philosophy was at least in part a counter-reaction to this move. Its emphasis on 'man' and humanity was in some ways an attempt to undermine the ideology of the Abbasids as deputies of God on Earth [compare Muruwwa II, 1981: 193ff].

The caliph did in fact live and move within two distinct entourages: an external, public one of jurists and clerics, and an internal, private one of cohorts, concubines and clowns. Linking the two circles through the caliph there was then a political clique of profiteers and allies of interest [Muruwwa II, 1981: 197–8]. The legitimisation game did work as long as the caliph, although not just (and therefore not fulfilling his internal *shar'i* obligations towards the community), was at least carrying on with his external duties of *da'wa* (propagation of the faith through conquests or *jihad*) and as long as he ensured the workings of the economy and the unity of the administration (which the Abbasid caliphs more or less did down to the caliph Al-Mutawakkil in the nineth century). When the external conquest petered out, when the economy was neglected (including in particular its hydraulic base and its taxation system), and the central administration started to disintegrate under pressure from the periphery, the legitimacy of the caliph started to be seriously shaken. For not only the justice of government, but even the ideal unity of the *umma* (Islamic community) was now at stake.

It was at this juncture that the jurists' attempts at conserving the concept of the unity of *umma*, as well as the social and intellectual attempts to oppose the state were both to proliferate. Thus there were the social rebellions alluded to earlier. There were also the *sufi* (mystic) orders. Originally these were devotional movements of social withdrawal aiming basically to conceal themselves from the ruler and his social order. Increasingly they acquired a theoretical dimension. If the ruler by being likened to God was, according to official theory, so different and so separate from ordinary mortals, then by developing a theory that man could reach God, indeed be united with him, these movements were actually challenging the political as well as the theological foundation of the concept of 'one-ness' (*tawhid*) [cf. Muruwwa II, 1981: 200ff]. Through their emphasis on the concept of *'irfan* (gnosticism), the sufis were actually challenging the main intellectual device employed by the jurists to establish the authority of the caliph, *vis-à-vis* the concept of *bayan* (i.e. the divine truth to be gleaned from linguistic and textual analysis of the Quran and Sunna). Soon, too, the intellectuals were to engage in philosophical debates which, by emphasising the methodology of *burhan* (evidence) were also to represent a kind of 'counter-ideology' that challenged the juristic premises on which the caliphate was hinged [these categories are from Al-Jabiri, 1985].

Muruwwa maintains that the emphasis of the intellectual schools on the issue of man and humanity was an attempt at developing a counter-ideology opposed to the state ideology, by implying man's worth and effectiveness in the universe (the sufis), or by arguing man's ability to understand the world through logical thought (the *kalam* and philosophy scholars). These movements had their social motive too in challenging the vested interests and unmasking the false premises of the 'Establishment'. The fact that most such thinkers were of a relatively underprivileged background (either from the ethnic minorities or from families of relatively humble artisans and merchants) and that most of their attempts corresponded with times of important social change can be taken to indicate a certain social orientation [Muruwwa II, 1981: 289ff]. These intellectual movements were not completely successful, however, in standing up to the official ideology; since the state was still in control of tremendous economic and intellectual resources, the public was still attached to the categories of religious thinking, and the thinkers were unable to liberate themselves completely from the mainly theological orientation of the discourse – for to do so would have exposed them to oppression from the authorities and to indifference from the public, under accusations of infidelity and blasphemy.

THE OTTOMANS AND THE MILITARY/*IQTA'I* SYMBIOSIS

Few Arab accounts of the history of the Arabo-Islamic state pay any attention at all to the Ottoman period, although it continued for nearly four hundred years from its beginnings in the sixteenth century, though it embraced most of the Arab World with few exceptions such as Morocco, and even though, too, it was an era that left a most noticeable impact on many Arab countries in the specific domain of state traditions. The Arab nationalist orientation (whether of the 'territorial' type as in Egypt or of the more Pan-Arabist type as that of the Ba'th) has tended – perhaps because of some Western influence as well – to regard the entire Ottoman episode, including the earlier, more prosperous phase, as a period of decline and decay (*inhitat*) that is not worth much attention [Abou-el-Haj, 1982: 185–201; Haarmann, 1988: 175–96].

This is rather a pity, for the Ottoman era included some praiseworthy manifestations of a remarkable skill in organisation and administration, and some very interesting innovations in the area of statesmanship that included, among others, the elaboration of a dynamic system of socio-cultural pluralism. The Ottoman period is also important in telling us much about the political traditions of most Arab countries: as Albert Hourani remarks, "many of the things Middle Eastern countries have in common can be explained by their having been ruled for so long by the Ottomans; many of the things which differentiate them can be explained by the different ways in which they emerged from the Ottoman empire" [Hourani, 1981: 17].

The Ottoman empire originated as a *ghazi* (conqueror) state, in the same manner in which other dynasties were founded in the Middle East by nomadic warriors. It was installed in Anatolia in the fourteenth century, on the heels of the Seljuks and other Turkic dynasties that had overrun the region since the eleventh century. In the fifteenth century the Ottomans occupied Constantinople and the Balkans, and in the sixteenth century they took over most parts of the Arab World. In a familiar pattern, when the Ottoman administration proper was first established in Anatolia, all agricultural lands passed into the ownership of the state, although some of them were later assigned as fiefs (*timars*) to certain cavalrymen in return for tax collection on behalf of the state. Thus the "economic bedrock of the Osmanli despotism was the virtually complete absence of private property in land". It followed that there could be no stable, hereditary nobility within the empire, because there was no security of property which could found it. "Wealth and honour were effectively co-terminous with the state, and rank was simply a function of positions held with it." The *timars* were not inheritable; indeed, at the access of every new sultan, their holders were systematically reshuffled in order to prevent them from becoming entrenched on their land. Any nuclei of a local or provincial landowning class were eliminated by the Turks, thus precluding the development of an indigenous feudal aristocracy [Anderson, 1979: 366–74].

The same pattern applied to the urban centres. The Ottoman state reinforced its authority over the artisan guilds and their Sufi brotherhoods. The cities were deprived of any corporate or municipal autonomy and were, in a typically 'Sultanic' fashion, considered part of the empirical domain. The crafts were carefully supervised by the state, and commodity supplies and prices were frequently regulated by the Sultan, thus curtailing any potential development of an autonomous mercantile or industrial bourgeoisie [cf. Anderson, 1979: 374–76].

In the Arab provinces of the Ottoman Empire, the Turkish authority introduced a badly needed sense of order after a long period of instability that had resulted from frequent Mamluk in-fighting in Egypt and the Levant. However the Turks did not really destroy the Mamluk set-up – rather, they incorporated it in their own state, and reinforced its system of 'military feudalism' (*iqta' harbi*) which was run by the Mamluk *multazims* (tax officials). They subsequently also recognised the special semi-feudal entities of certain tribal/confessional solidarities in Greater Syria, namely that of Mount Lebanon [Makhzum, 1986: 9ff, 117ff]. By institutionalising 'military feudalism', the Ottomans were not introducing a new system but rather were spreading and organising practices that were already in existence. The Buwaihids (AD 932–1055) had first introduced the practice of assigning land instead of paying salaries to their military leaders. The Seljuks (AD 1038–1194, then in Turkey to 1307) then spread the system in many parts of the Muslim world. The Ayyubids and particularly the Mamluks (AD 1250–1517) then consolidated the system in Egypt and the Arab East. Similar arrangements also existed in North Africa. When the Ottomans took over those Arab territories, they incorporated the Mamluks into their own state. In several Arab countries a Mamluk 'parallel' hierarchy continued to exist, often side by side with a smaller but formally more authoritative Ottoman hierarchy [cf. Shaw, 1962].

The Mamluk Sultans used to reallocate land among their amirs and lieutenants at each accession to power, and also at random intervals throughout a new "inspection of the military" [Tarkhan, 1968: 63–82]. The periodic reallocation of land (*rok*) in Egypt and Syria served as a useful administrative and financial control device and also as a means of checking any likely growth or entrenchment of the power of the amirs. It reinforced the authority of the state *vis-à-vis* its officials and constrained the inclination to regard the *iqta'* as being in any way permanent or hereditary. The old Seljuk practice of assigning lands widely scattered from each other was also carried out for the same purpose [Tarkhan, 1968: 95–108]. The system was therefore based on 'utilisation' rights and not on 'ownership' rights (as in the European tradition). Most *iqta'*s went to 'people of the sword' or to the Mamluk military, as well as to some 'Arab', Kurdish and Turkmen leaders with strong local *asabiyyas*. A certain number were assigned to those 'people of the pen' (clerics and clerks) who were closely associated with the governors, but only a few went to professional merchants and craftsmen [Tarkhan, 1968: 145–74]. But whatever the background of these *muqta'*s (i.e. people in charge of agricultural land), they remained as mere employees in a very personally centralised government, and it is that which most distinguishes this system from European feudalism [ibid.: 265].

This was therefore the type of 'feudalism' that the Ottomans maintained when they took over the Arab countries. Thus the assignment of a tract of land to a person under the Ottomans did not imply his ownership of it, but merely delegated him to collecting its taxes and other tributes that were due to the Ottoman Sultan while expecting him to maintain order and to be ready to supply the Ottoman ruler (Pasha) or the local provincial Ottoman governor (*Wali*) with men, both military and civilian, in times of need [al-Shinnawi I, 1980: 49–183]. The Wali, of course, had his own assistants, officials and accountants, as well as his own *diwan* run by Turkish officials and Arab scribes, and he also had access to various regular and non-regular troops from various ethnic backgrounds [al-Zain, 1977: 18–40]. But these existed side by side – and very often overlapped – with the Mamluk set-up. In the meantime, many of the administrative functions pertaining to the religious minorities were left to their own clergy, and several of the control functions over foreign merchants, craftsmen's guilds and urban neighbourhoods were delegated to their own special leaders (*shaikhs*) who mediated between the state and their own communities [Raymond, 1974: 12–43].

The Ottoman theory of the state seems to have been derived, in its initial phase, from a 'secularist' Turkic concept of supreme law (*yasa*), that the benevolent ruler, guided by the principles of 'necessity' and 'reason', would enforce through a set of practices and commands (*orf-i-sultani*) [Heper, 1985: 21–6]. Called *adab*, this was a continuation of a certain strand in the later Arab-Islamic political tradition that was oriented more towards statesmanship than towards *shari'a*. Although the state was centred around the person of the sultan, the ruler was expected to listen to his advisers and jurists, and the administrators were expected to act according to a certain set of values and norms.

A main pillar of the Ottomans' power was their own army units as well as the other military forces in the provinces on which they could call (e.g. the Mamluks). The Ottoman *devshirme* and the Mamluk forces alike were formed mainly of white 'slaves'. This practice of using military persons exogenous to the population that they are subduing is an old 'Muslim' tradition that dates back to the Abbasid period, as we have already seen. It represents an extreme case of asserting the 'autonomy of the state' (or of the ruler) *vis-à-vis* its own society, and seems to have no equivalent in European feudalism. It is, in fact, structurally linked to the economic base of state autonomy: the lack of private landownership.

> Once all landed property was a prerogative of the Porte, it ceased to be degrading to be the human property of the Sultan: 'slavery' was no longer defined by opposition to 'liberty', but by proximity of access to the Imperial Command, a necessarily ambiguous vicinity that involved complete heteronomy and immense privilege and power [Anderson, 1979: 367–8].

The *'ulama'* had the same relationship with the ruler as in the typical Sunni context: they were often appointed and dismissed by him, and although they could in theory oppose his policies, in practice they seldom did so. For the ruler treated the state as his own household, and the state officials, the senior 'ulama' included, were part of his personal entourage, an 'extension' of the ruler into society. But the Ottoman Empire was not simply a 'family state': it was also, and in a complex way, a Turkish state, an Islamic state, and a universal state [Hourani, 1981: 7–10]. The ruling group was 'Turkish', but higher offices were open – at least in theory – to all Muslims, the Arabs among them strongly represented in the religious and juridic hierarchy; the military ('askar) were often drawn from men of Christian, Balkan or Caucasian origin, and the religious leaders of the non-Muslim communities were actually 'civil heads' whose decisions and orders had the force of the government to back them up [Hourani, 1981: 10–12].

By adopting a community-based, quasi-consociationalist political formula, the Ottomans were acknowledging the pluralistic nature of the society, while seeking to subordinate the smaller communities – whether tribal, ethnic or religious, whether villages, urban quarters or guilds/orders – to the hegemony of the larger religious and cultural community: i.e. the Sunni community ruling the state [cf. Karpat, 1988: 39].

With the inclusion, in the fifteenth century, of large non-Turkic and non-Muslim communities into the empire, the state became distinctly pluralistic; during the second half of the century the *millet* system was evolved as a formula for dealing with this socio-cultural reality. A Christian Orthodox *millet* (under the Greek Patriarch), an Armenian *millet* (to include all Eastern Christians), and a Jewish *millet* were successively established, with legal status and an institutional network for religious, social and educational affairs. They also had subdivisions which followed ethnic or confessional lines and which gained a higher degree of self-autonomy over time (reaching nine in number by the end of the nineteenth century). Although such an arrangement bound these communities tightly to their own church hierarchy and clergy, it secured their allegiance to the state as Osmanli subjects [Karpat, 1988: 39–45]. Ironically, although the Ottoman Muslims did not view themselves in 'sectarian' terms but regarded themselves as followers of *the* religion, the concept of *millet* was gradually changing its connotations in ways that enabled the Muslim Turks to apply that term to themselves. Towards the end of the nineteenth century, the term *millet* denoted "mainly a narrow confessional group, in which ethnicity was given added weight, rather than a broad communal entity in which religion and authority were amalgamated, but with religion having the greatest weight and being determinative of identity" [Karpat, 1988: 46–53]. Gradually the Turks were to adopt the term *millet*, with a strongly ethnic connotation, to describe their own nation as well, though admittedly this was only achieved after the Ottomans had used Islam to develop a culturally homogeneous community in Turkey.

A similar process of 'decentralisation' was also taking place within the economy and the administration during the second half of the Ottoman era.

The empire was becoming too large to manage and relations of production in agriculture and in the artisan/industrial sectors were undergoing important changes, due to domestic and also to international factors. When the economic surplus accruing directly to the state began to decline, the state was prepared gradually to sacrifice its hitherto high degree of autonomy by conceding various powers to the military élite and to the tax farmers. The military were now able to marry before recruitment, and they were no longer prohibited from engaging in their own trade or industry. The tax farmers in charge of small parcels of land (*shifliks*) were now able to expand their own economic and social interests in the countryside and to seek recognition of them by the ruler in their capacity as local notables (*a'yan*). The Lands Law of 1858 gave recognition to private landownership, and the Tapu Law of 1861 provided for its registration and taxation. New types of familial and social conflicts were to result from such changes [Hanna, 1987: 27–9]. Eventually some of the ascending notables were to seek an implicit alliance with certain government officials, enabling them both to deceive the state and to exploit the peasants still further.

The local notables of the Arab provinces did not all come from similar social backgrounds: in addition to the military of local garrisons, they included learned scholars and jurists, as well as people with local (sometimes tribal or confessional) power bases. However, Albert Hourani has argued that, regardless of their social background, they tended to act politically in much the same way: enjoying formal access to the governor's *diwan* on the one hand but forming a broad coalition of local forces on the other. Thus the notables acted as a focus for local forces and were able at the same time to oppose the government or else oblige it to act through them [Hourani, 1981: 42–62]. The nature of the dominant group within the leadership of the groupings of the notables and the extent to which they could collectively influence the Ottoman government varied from one provincial centre to another, giving the subsequent development in each province its specific features and characteristics. But the general move was unmistakeably in the direction of more autonomy being acquired by the 'intermediary' groupings at the periphery, at the expense of the central government in Istanbul.

It was in the context of the weakening of the central power of the state that the Sultans sought, by the turn of the eighteenth century, to strengthen their claims to absolute authority by increasingly underscoring their religious role as the spiritual leaders (caliphs) of the community while increasingly relegating administration as such to a more autonomous – though still traditional – bureaucracy of viziers, civil servants and diplomats [Heper, 1985: 31–6]. Subsequently, and throughout the nineteenth century, the Ottoman rulers, in an attempt to face up not only to the growing internal difficulties but also to external challenges, were to introduce the series of legal and administrative measures that culminated in the Tanzimat (organisational reforms) of 1839– 76. These measures, aimed at rationalising the bureaucracy, were only partly the result of growth in domestic legal learning and administrative experience. Nor were they really representative of a genuine drive for 'democratisation'; in the main they were attempts at strengthening the government while appearing to make it more representative. They were meant both to appease the European powers (encroaching ever more vigorously – economically and politically – on the Ottoman Empire), and to make the government better able to keep them at bay.

If they involved a certain measure of decentralisation, it was for the precise purpose of directly maintaining state control of the subjects, over the heads of the local notables, "i.e., an effort to re-create, in a revived form, the traditional ideal of the centre, that there should be no intermediaries of any sort between the State and its subjects" [Heper, 1985: 37–40]. This involved also a reassertion of control over the state-owned (*miri*) land which, over the centuries, had passed by one means or another out of the hands of the state. This was not expected to be particularly difficult to achieve, since the local notables had not established solid bases of really autonomous power and most of them were still closely linked to the existing political network. The Tanzimat had in reality meant shifting the balance more in favour of the civil bureaucrats of the central administration, now claiming to act in the name of the state and in the light of 'modern principles' of law and administration [Heper, 1985: 40–47].

At around the same time, a similar process was taking place in two provinces that had by then gained a fair amount of autonomy from the High Porte – Egypt under Muhammad 'Ali and Tunisia under Khair al-Din were aiming equally at transferring the ideology of the 'rule of law' to their countries with the intention of modernising administrative and other organisations. In the Arab East, activity among the Arabs was centred more around the field of educational and cultural '*risorgimento*' (*nahda*) as this region was still part of the Ottoman Empire, in a more direct sense.

It is conceivable that the reforms of the Tanzimat period in the Ottoman Empire (including the Arab East) and the similar reforms in Egypt and Tunisia, if carried to their logical conclusion, could/would have destroyed the independent power of the notables and the mode of political action such power made possible [Hourani, 1981: 51ff]. But the reforms could not be carried out completely given the nature of absolute personal rule, the contradictory influences of the growing European encroachment, and the opposition of the notables to the centralising orientation of the reforms. The European 'presence' was soon to become the major concern of the Egyptians and the North Africans. In the Arab East, however, Ottoman influences continued for a longer period, as did the role of the notables as a landowning-bureaucratic élite mediating between the central Ottoman authority and the provincial social forces, up to and even beyond the end of the Ottoman rule [Khoury, 1983b].

THE ARTICULATION OF MODES OF PRODUCTION IN THE HISTORICAL ARABO-ISLAMIC STATE

We have seen that during most stages of development of the Arab state, there was not one dominant mode of production prevailing in the society but a set of 'articulated' modes, some more important than others at certain times or in certain regions.

In the Rashidun era it was mainly the 'conquestal' streak of the nomadic mode of production, invigorated by a new mobilisational and integrationalist ideology: Islam. The state's attitude towards conquered land at that period was rather confused, for whereas it refused to make over land to the Arab conquerors and preserved an ethnic division of labour (Arabs = army; conquered peoples = agriculture) it had sometimes, especially under 'Uthman, encouraged a strengthening of the native semi-feudal aristocracies with whom it was easier to strike alliances. It was therefore understandable that the revolt against 'Uthman came mainly from among the farmers and the smaller land-owners in Iraq and Egypt, or 'people of the water' (*ahl al-miyah*) as 'A'isha was to describe the supporters of 'Ali [cf. Isma'il I, 1980: 58–9].

In the Umayyad era the tribal framework enveloping the conquered territories remained, but it now acquired an extended Arab – though by no means all-Arab – character (remember the Kalbi/Qaysi antagonism). This patriarchal-tribal system is then increasingly articulated with elements of the ancient hydraulic mode of production, represented in particular by the state's role in repairing and improving the irrigation networks both in the systemic (overall) hydraulic settings (such as in Egypt) and in the sub-systemic hydraulic systems such as in Syria and Mesopotamia [compare Isma'il I: 1980: 54]. The new state élite gradually integrates itself with the older official and semi-feudalistic élites, the inheritors of the Sassanian, Byzantine and Pharaonic traditions. A smaller commercial sector and tiny slavery sector were also there, articulated with the other components of the complex system, but any further growth in the commercial sector was constrained.

In the Abbasid era, the Islamic rather than the Arab symbolic character of the state is emphasised. The 'bureaucratic' feudalism of the Umayyad period increasingly acquired some 'purer' feudalistic characteristics as patterns of landownership became increasingly less controlled by the central state. The mercantile sector grew fast, *almost* imparting its hegemonic character to the whole system and leading among other things to a stimulation of artisanal, industrial and technological activities, and to the emergence of a distinct 'cosmopolitan' intelligentsia of scientists and literati, many of whom were of relatively humble background [Isma'il I, 1980: 154]. Slavery, although still limited, became more economic rather than being simply domestic in nature. However, this new mercantile bourgeoisie did not quite make it as a hegemonic socio-political force. The reasons for this are multiple but most important among them are two: (i) the continued symbiotic relationship between the merchants and the state; and (ii) the continuation, sometimes even the flourishing, of feudalistic production and social relations, rather than their decline, under the impact of growth in the mercantile sector (with some of the merchants re-investing their capital in land acquisition).

A closer examination of the development of *iqta'* (Islamic-type bureaucratic feudalism) and of the mercantile sector may now be in order.

Iqta'

The tradition of public ownership of land is an ancient one in the Middle East, promoted in many cases by the organisational requirements of securing agricultural and economic life in an arid environment. 'Umar, the second caliph, was to take a historic decision (contrary in fact to both nomadic and 'Islamic' rules governing conquest) when he decided that land in the conquered territories (Iraq, Egypt and Syria) would not be distributed among the fighters but would be kept intact with its owners (peasants and semi-feudal farmers and officials), in return for a land tax that would then be distributed among the Arab soldiers by way of 'salaries'. Water resources were also to remain as public property [Al-Duri, 1982: 51]. This did not prevent some private ownership of land, especially of tracts that were handed to certain Muslims as a gift (*iqta'*), especially lands whose owners had deserted them, or land that was barren and unworkable. Now the most significant feature of this decision is that it reinforced the 'Asiatic' principle of public ownership and strengthened the state sector by making it the extractor of the agricultural surplus and the disburser of it in the form of 'salaries' for 'public' soldiers and officials. In other words, taxes (*kharaj*) became from the beginning the main point of contact between state and society in the Islamic dominion. *Zakat*, a community-based type of solidarity gift-tax, was also important initially, but it was gradually taken out of the organisational and financial concerns of the state. Even when land ownership was permitted, the early Muslims rejected the system of *muzara'a* (crop-sharing whereby the owner rents the land to its tiller in return for a certain share – half or a third – of the crop). This limited the prospects of private, capitalist-type, investment in land on any large scale.

Kharaj was therefore the foundation of the political economy of the Islamic state. It was indeed no accident that the earliest *political* treatise in Islamic writing was the introduction of the book on *kharaj* commissioned by Harun al-Rashid from Abu Yusuf, and that *kharaj* subsequently became an important concern of the administrative treatises written by various scribes working for the state (e.g. Ibn Ja'far, Al-Sawli, etc.) [Shalaq, 1988: 131–2].

The (nomadic) concept of booty (*ghanima*) was gradually turned into an (Islamic) concept of income derived from public property (*fay'*). Historians have also distinguished between lands conquered by force (*'unwa*) whose ownership was theoretically supposed to shift to the conquerors, and lands opened by 'accord' or without resistance from their inhabitants (*sulh*) which were to be left to their owners. In practice, however, there was not a great deal of difference. 'Umar's non-distribution of Iraq's land, even though it was conquered by force, was regarded as a tradition (*sunna*) to be followed. All land was considered a collective resource for the Muslims (the state), although some segments of it were offered to individuals either by right of utilisation (*al-manfa'a*) or by right of ownership (*al-raqaba*). *Kharaj* had to be extracted from all land, however, and land tax was to be distinguished from *jizya* (the poll-tax on non-Muslims) and *sadaqa* (crop or production tax). At most times, *kharaj* continued to be the main source of income for the state [Shalaq, 1988: 132–44], especially as the numbers of non-Muslims dwindled with conversion.

Private landownership was not completely prohibited, as we have said, and in fact increasingly there were pressures from military and administrative personnel to buy land or be given it, not to speak of land deserted by its owners, which in theory fell to the ownership of the caliph to be used for the benefit of the state but which was gradually granted or sold by him to others. The state had always had an interest, however, in keeping such grants and sales limited, for land on completely private ownership had no *kharaj* attached to it; its owners paid only *zakat*.

This system of mainly public ownership (combined with *kharaj* in return for using the land) in addition to some full private ownership in certain cases, continued to be the pattern more or less until the tenth century, the time of the ageing and decline of the Abbasid state. The Buwaihids entering Baghdad in the middle of that century eventually attached *kharaj* to a certain 'security payment' (*daman*) to be received from the tax collectors in advance, in return for their right to keep for themselves any further agricultural surplus they could extract. A new intermediary stratum between the farmers and the state thus emerged, increasingly representative of the mercenary military groups that were being employed by the state from that stage onwards. This was the beginning of the so-called 'military feudalism' (*al-iqta' al-harbi*), which was subsequently spread by other nomadic or semi-nomadic armies such as the Seljuks, the Zankis, the Ayyubids and the Mamluks, and which was eventually reinforced and 'institutionalised' by the Ottomans [Al-Duri, 1982: 85–145].

Military feudalism involved commitment by the officers (*iltizam*) to supply the state with *kharaj* in return for their non-hereditary right to exploit (*istighlal*) the land as compensation for receiving no salary from the state. In reality this was a kind of *de facto* crop-sharing arrangement between the peasants on the one hand and the officers/the state on the other. This system, although different from its predecessor in obvious ways remained distinctly 'Oriental' in character: the state was still the legal owner, and the *multazims* were basically government employees, who were not able to consolidate their private owner-ship (ownership was not always for life, and land was intentionally scattered to prevent concentration), nor pass on the land through inheritance to their sons, who themselves were not even permitted to follow a military career. Admittedly there were many variations (as indeed there were with European feudalism), and the *étatiste* character of that mode of production was more pronounced in territories with stronger state traditions such as in Egypt under the Ayyubids, where even the *muqta's* (those given land) remained strictly subject to the administration and where the state continued its close supervision of all services. However, this system had nowhere led to the emergence of a hereditary landed class, nor did the *muqta's* (given the urban orientation of the Islamic society) reside on this land or have a close relationship with their peasants, as was the general pattern in European feudalism. The nature of the *muqta's'* role is not really decided, as in the 'typical' European feudalist system, by their relationship with their serfs (peasants) but mainly by their relationship to the state [Shalaq, 1988: 168–73].

The mercantile sector

We have seen how important trade has been throughout most stages of Arabo-Islamic history. Samir Amin would go further by characterising the entire Islamic 'formation' (civilisation) as predominantly 'mercantile': in fact from pre-Islamic Arabia all the way and all over the entire Arab-Islamic empire (with the partial exception of Egypt) to the period of Turkic and Ottoman domination (when in his view it becomes more feudalistic) [cf. Amin, 1978: 13–23, 93–102]. This, I consider, is rather too sweeping, and even Amin in his discussion of the articulation between the agrarian and the mercantile sectors of the Arab-Islamic tributary mode of production does not sound quite confident as to whether the flourishing of trade was merely the consequence of progress in agriculture or whether, on the contrary, advance in agriculture was induced by a growth in commercial prosperity, in which case the mercantile relations would have exercised a domination over the whole system [Amin, 1978: 94–5]. Although he is more inclined to the latter view and does present a good case in its favour, the historical evidence, as he admits, is not yet sufficiently detailed and accurate to establish the causation pattern with any certainty. I would most definitely agree, however, that the mercantile mode of production was the dominant one during the Abbasid period, especially in its early phase. During the second Abbasid phase and the subsequent Turkic-Ottoman eras, the *iqta'i* mode was becoming increasingly predominant.

The availability under the Islamic empire of one big market, the eventual minting of an Islamic currency, and the improvement of routes and the encouragement of foreign trade led to a prosperous economic life, especially in the Abbasid era. But there were still many constraints: exports were rather limited, although payment and credit cheques were known, no autonomous banking or financial institutions existed on a large scale, and little was reinvested in crafts and industries. The market was also smaller than it appeared to be since it catered mainly for the luxury consumption needs of the small privileged classes, mostly revolving around the state [Dallu, 1985: 258ff]. Most important probably was the continued state control over commerce. Although this provided the merchants (*tujjar*) with a certain element of security and 'protection' it did constrain their activities, as they were repeatedly forced to lend money to the state which interfered in various economic fields and fixed the price of currency. More specifically, the entrenched and semi-hereditary bureaucratic class preferred to engage itself almost directly in many commercial activities, rather than to encourage the activities of an autonomous commercial class. The state was unable to reconcile the often opposing interests of the officials and the merchants [Ismail I, 1980: 89–91, 104–5].

There were of course several commercial and artisan guilds in the cities, especially the newer more 'economically' conceived ones such as Baghdad, with prosperous markets and hotels and with various economic activities taking place in them. But even here the heavy hand of the state was always felt through the *muhtasib* (the market controller or inspector) and other state functionaries. The *muhtasib* was responsible for checking the availability and quality of goods, price levels and the authenticity of currencies, the accuracy of scales and weights and the appropriateness of prescriptions and drugs, the cleanliness of shops, mosques and public baths, as well as the general atmosphere of public order and moral conduct in the markets [Ziyada, 1962: 37ff].

A few passages on the Islamic 'guilds' (*asnaf*) may be useful here, not only for their importance to the overall mercantile formations within the state, but also for their political significance as part of the broadly 'corporatist' character of the Islamic state. As has been alluded to, the Arab bedouin had traditionally looked at the pursuits of peasants and artisans with contempt, and a largely ethnic division of labour was thus maintained in the new Arabo-Islamic state for a considerable time. However, with the decline in conquests and in the recruitment of Arabs into the army, growing numbers of Arabs started to move into the productive sectors. Yet nearly two centuries after the *hijra*, Al-Shibani and Al-Mawardi were to give the following descending 'social' ranking to the sources of earning (*wujuh al-kasb*): "Command (*imara*), commerce, industry and Agriculture" [in Al-Sayyid, 1984: 82–3].

The emergence of the 'guilds' (*asnaf*, sing. *sinf*) is still shrouded in ambiguity, and there is disagreement over whether their early beginnings were more closely associated with certain religious sects (e.g. the Isma'ilis, the Qarmatians, or the Sufis) or with certain segments of what we may identify in modern terminology as the urban 'lumpenproletariat' (e.g. *al-zu'r*, or *al-harafish*). Most of the available literature is less clear about the origins of the *asnaf* than it is about their relationship to the state [Al-Sayyid, 1984: 85–111]. Whatever the case may be, it appears that the *asnaf* ended up acting as a convenient vehicle of control by the state over professional and social activities in the city. The shaikh of each *sinf* had to record the personnel involved in each activity and was responsible for their conduct within and outside the profession, and it was through such records that the state extracted its taxes and fees from the guilds through the *muhtasib* or the *qadi* (judge). The guilds were even sometimes used to recruit men for military and civilian works for the state. Internally, the guilds attended to vocational training in a craft, to production and quality control, and to storage and hygiene. They were run according to a simple hierarchy of expertise and authority (*shaikh, naqib, ustaz, sani', sabiy*, etc.), and had their own rituals for initiation and for other civil and religious ceremonies. Their functions also included guarding and protecting their shops, markets and alleyways at times when unrest threatened. The *muhtasib* held extensive powers over the guilds on behalf of the state. He checked weights and measures, quality and hygiene and sometimes specified quantities to be produced, and could also pass and enforce certain penalties. Mainly, of course, he extracted taxes and fees, and although the price of products was generally left to 'supply and demand', the state did often interfere to change prices or to break a certain monopoly [Ziyada, 1962].

The guilds were probably the last aspect of the political economy of the Islamic state to die out and disappear, as they more or less survived – in one attenuated form or another – until the nineteenth century: at this point the encroaching of modern commercial and industrial capitalism brought about through European colonialism signalled their final demise, although traces of their quarters remain and are still to be seen in many Middle Eastern cities to this day.

Articulations

There can be little doubt from the previous survey that the mercantile sector had been extremely crucial in the make-up of the historical Islamic state. Maxime Rodinson has put forward the most detailed case illustrating how the mediaeval Islamic merchants had nearly 'made it' into capitalism, failing only narrowly to do so [Rodinson, 1978: esp. Ch. 5]. An irony of the Islamic mercantile bourgeoisie of particular relevance to us is that although it owed much of its emergence and prosperity to the state, which built the cities, extended the trade routes and represented with its various élites the main buyers and consumers, that bourgeoisie also acquired its fragility and vulnerability from its dependency on the state: its organic relationships with the state sectors were closer than they were with the producers (agricultural and industrial). When the state weakened, not only did the market shrink and the trade routes contract, but parts of the economy were to become almost completely autonomous since a process of 're-nomadisation' of the armed forces (on multi-ethnic lines) was eventually to lead to the disintegration of the Islamic Empire. For the later Abbasid rulers had had to rely increasingly on fresh recruitment from among the semi-nomadic Turkic peoples of Central Asia, as well as other peripheral semi-nomadic forces of Middle Eastern, African and even European (Balkan and Caucasian) backgrounds, to impose order on the ageing empire. A revival in the commercial and military activities of China in the east and Byzantium in the west had also seriously constrained the extensive trade networks of the commercial bourgeoisie. Other European powers were also encroaching on the Mediterranean Sea.

Internally, the halt in military conquests had meant higher levels of extraction of the domestic economic surplus to meet the growing needs of the state, the army and the political élites, which further exhausted the productive social forces. Corruption grew among the officials, who often appropriated money directly for themselves, and from time to time the rulers would arrest and torture their own officials and confiscate their huge 'savings' [al-Rayyis, 1985: 458–64]. The ensuing economic recession led to growing social revolts against the state in which elements of the commercial bourgeoisie sometimes participated. The re-nomadisation of the armed forces was soon to lead to their growing power and independence in the periphery, where they found it more convenient to reinvigorate the semi-feudalistic modes of production which had never given way completely to the urban/commercial modes that were closely tied to the central state. From the ninth century a 'retrieved feudalism' started to creep back into the periphery – through the semi-nomadic armies – whereas some of the remnants of the Arab 'asabiyya (by now almost completely deprived of its traditional military functions) were in the process of reverting to their original bedouin state [Ismail II, 1980: 10–21].

However, the 'retrieved feudalism' was still 'Eastern' in character, and quite distinct from its European counterpart (itself by no means consistent in nature). The revival of the semi-feudalist mode was so sweeping that not only did it attract fractions of the bureaucracy and the clergy to acquire land, but it even tempted the commercial bourgeoisie in that direction: hence we see the growth of 'merchants' feudalism' (iqta' al-tujjar) in Iraq, in Egypt, Morocco and Andalusia, as the merchants were often repaid for the loans they made to the military regimes with land allocations [Ismail II, 1980: 34–9; Al-Duri, 1982: 85ff].

This military feudalism, however, had a devastating impact on the economy as it tended to neglect the hydraulic systems and to over-tax the direct producers, especially the peasants, thus constraining any possible development of the forces of production in agriculture, and leading as a consequence to a weakening of the trading activities and even of industry itself. Merchants had indeed been relegated, from the eleventh century on, to secondary status by the ascendant military, who invested directly in land, commerce and the crafts and who organised the state to their own advantage [Rodinson, 1981: 164–7].

From the caliphate of Al-Mutawakkil (AD 847–861) to the Buwayhid (Buyid) conquest (AD 932–1062), the influence of the Turkic soldiers grew fast, with their interference in politics and in the appointment of caliphs, until they had dominated Iraq, Egypt and Syria and established their own dynasties. Rural and urban resistance movements eventually emerged, sometimes under religious banners such as the Isma'ilis, and sometimes in the form of urban bandits (e.g. *futuwwa* movements), and sometimes as social revolutions (the Zanj, the Qarmatians, etc.). Such movements paved the way for the emergence of another commercial renaissance in the fourth century AH (tenth century AD), accompanied by a renaissance of non-conformist religious and intellectual schools. This was again attributed to a revival of trade and naval strength as the Chinese and Slavic pressures eased in the East (for dynastic reasons), and as the pressures from Byzantium eased in the West (following their rift with the Italian cities). The Mediterranean became virtually an 'Islamic lake' following a fierce struggle with the Byzantines and the West Europeans. Regional dynasties, such as the Fatimids in Egypt and the Umayyads in Andalusia, enhanced their status and extended their trade. The Muslim states, although no longer united in one polity, had now regained their control over trade routes between East and West, North and South. Many of the new dynasties, such as the Fatimids in Morocco, Egypt and Syria, and the Buwayhids in their later stage in Iraq, tended to suppress the practice of military feudalism in favour of tighter state control of the land, giving only utilisation, not ownership, rights in return for some income to the state and an undertaking by the 'owner' to look after irrigation and construction. Agriculture and the hydraulic system improved greatly, and so did administration, with the development of elaborate *diwans* and financial procedures. In Egypt extensive irrigation works were undertaken, and at Aswan a 'high dam' was in the process of being erected, while in Andalusia an elaborate network of covered canals was constructed and a special hydraulic agency was formed (*wikalat al-saqiyya*) [Ismail II, 1980: 144–54]. Industry also flourished, with encouragement from and sometimes participation by the state, especially in textiles, carpets, glass, ceramics, leather and furniture, etc., reinvigorating commercial exchange and creating new markets. All this was to lead to urban prosperity and advanced construction and architecture.

The rise, prosperity and decline of the Buwayhids in Iraq, the Fatimids in Egypt and the Umayyads in Andalusia all at very similar periods must have some historical significance. It possibly points to the importance of the articulation of external and internal forces in the making of an Arab (Middle Eastern) state. Hydraulic development, internally, and active trade externally, seem to be the pillars of the political economy of a Middle Eastern state. Mahmud Isma'il posits the theory (in which he would concur with Samir Amin) that all three states deteriorated when their control of maritime trade routes waned as a result of the growing strength of the Byzantines, the Italians and the Normans. The decline in financial resources derived from trade led to neglect of hydraulic and agricultural (and consequently industrial) activities, driving the state to harsher appropriation of surplus (through taxes) from the domestic producers (farmers, artisans, local merchants, etc.), and to growing social discontent, for the suppression of which mercenary armies were subsequently again hired. These, in their turn, moved against the state whenever it failed to pay their salaries, whereupon the state increasingly paid them in the form of land allocations. This further weakened the state and impoverished the economy and led to further disintegration, making it easier for foreign forces (e.g. the Mongols, the Crusaders) to encroach. In all cases, the state was to be overtaken by such semi-nomadic military forces: Seljuks in Iraq, Turks and Kurds in Egypt, and Berbers in Andalusia [Ismail II, 1980: 235–48].

Tributary modes

Taking account of such historical developments, Samir Amin has improvised a certain conceptual schema that is capable, among other things, of admitting many of the useful analytical aspects of the Asiatic mode of production but without condoning the assumption about the utter uniqueness of the East [cf. S. Amin, 1974: 137ff, 359ff; 1976: 13ff; 1978: Chs. 1, 2 and 5; 1985: 78ff]. Amin distinguishes between all pre-capitalist modes of production on the one hand, and the capitalist mode of production (which is the only global mode) on the other. He regards all pre-capitalist modes as being basically 'tributary' in nature.[3] Feudalism was the more backward form of the tributary mode of production whereas its more advanced form was the *étatiste* variant (being elaborate, tight, and more integrated). According to Amin the limited change and development (the so-called 'stationariness') in the East was the result not of the stagnation of its mode of production historically speaking, but of the early advancement and sophistication of that mode. European feudalism was by contrast less advanced but more flexible, and was therefore more capable of proceeding with the kind of qualitative change that made modern capitalism possible.

The tributary mode of production, maintains Amin, was more integrated in the Muslim world than it was in its 'peripheral' (i.e. European feudalist) version in more than one sphere. On the level of the infrastructure, there existed an *étatiste* ruling class and the surplus was centralised through the state (whereas the surplus was divided and the state was weak in feudalism). On the level of the superstructure, there existed a strong unified ideology which was of a total nature. With regard to dialectical relationships between the two levels, the relationship was closer and the correspondence greater in the *étatiste* variant, leading eventually to a certain rigidity and lack of flexibility that delayed further transformations. Contrary to the theory of 'Oriental Despotism' this integrated variant corresponded to a higher, not a lower, level of development in the forces of production. Furthermore, ideology in the integrated tributary form functioned in the pre-capitalist society as does 'commodity fetishism' in capitalism: as an ideology not only for the ruling class but for the society at large. It was therefore a strong and hard ideology that directed the forces of production in a certain way and helped in the re-production of society.

Thus, for example, in Egypt the state historically was so dominant over the society and in such a manner that the peasants were left without the margin of freedom that would have enabled them to improve agricultural techniques or to resist economic exploitation, as happened in Europe. In the Egyptian case the peasant had to confront the centralised state directly. Nor did the strength of the state permit the emergence of a free class of traders in auto-nomous cities, as occurred in Europe. Furthermore, says Amin, the crucial importance of the state made most foreign conquerors content themselves with dominating the state machine itself without having to penetrate the society socially and culturally in ways that might have prompted further change. The limited development and transformation in Egypt's case was therefore the price she paid historically for her advanced, rather than backward, mode of production.

Although Samir Amin's theory remains largely hypothetical, it does repres-ent an important contribution. It refuses to condone exaggeration in attributing utter uniqueness (and the inevitable 'stationariness') to Oriental society, without overlooking the distinctive features of this society, including in particular the political and ideological centrality of the integrated state. However, by refrain-ing from discussing the details of the Asiatic mode of production theory, Amin ends up being unable to explain (but simply taking for granted) the reasons why the state is so centralised and so crucial in Egypt and other Muslim/ Eastern societies.

Whether or not we agree fully with Amin's conclusions, there is little doubt about the value of his category of 'tributary modes of production' for the purposes of comparative analysis. It is also interesting that although Amin was the one who gave currency to the concept, a Japanese historian (Jiro Hayakawa) and a Romanian historian (Ion Banu) seem to have used it earlier as an equivalent to the Asiatic mode of production – interesting because these two societies lie outside the 'European Core' that gave rise to generalisations about feudalism [cf. Wolf, 1982: 402; CERM, 1969]. The installation of 'feudal-ism' as a separate mode merely converts a relatively short period of European history into a type-case against which all other 'feudal-like' phenomena should be measured. By contrast, to count feudalism as one possible variety of a larger 'tributary' type would open the door for broader and more fruitful comparisons.

Eric Wolf [1982: 80ff] explains that in the tributary mode of production, social labour is organised for the transformation of nature primarily through the exercise of power and domination – i.e. through a political process. It is possible to envisage two polar situations: one in which power is concentrated in the hands of a ruling élite standing at the apex of the power system. Here the ruling élite of surplus-takers will be strongest when it controls some strategic element in the process of production, such as waterworks, and some strategic element of coercion, such as a strong standing army. Conversely the central power will be weak and local power holders will be strong, where strategic elements of production as well as means of coercion are in the hands of local surplus-takers. In broad terms, the two situations correspond to the Marxist concepts of the 'Asiatic mode of production' and the 'feudal mode of production': one is usually ascribed to Europe and the other to the East. Basically, however, we are dealing with variable outcomes of the competition between classes of non-producers for power at the top. To the extent that these variable outcomes are all anchored in mechanisms exerting 'other than economic pressure', they exhibit a family resemblance to each other, which is best covered by a common term: the 'tributary mode of production'. This is all the more so as strongly centralised 'Asiatic' states frequently break down into political oligopolies resembling feudalism, and feudalistic local power holders often yield to more centralised power over time: as Wolf remarks, "To reify the weak phases of the Sassanian, Byzantine or T'ang Chinese states into a feudal-like mode of production, and the strong phases of these same states into an Asiatic mode, wrongly separates into two different modes of production oscillations within the continuum of single mode" [1982: 81–2].

In contrast to the kin-ordered mode, both the tributary and the capitalist modes divide populations into a class of surplus producers and a class of surplus takers. Both require mechanisms of domination to ensure that surpluses are transferred on a predictable basis from one class to the other. This cannot be secured without the development of an apparatus of coercion to maintain the basic division into classes and to defend the resulting structure against external attack. Both the tributary and the capitalist modes are marked by the development and the installation of such an apparatus, namely the state. One difference is that in the case of the tributary mode, the mode itself is constituted by the mechanisms of domination that extract tribute from the producers by "other than economic pressure". Politics in a tributary state also affects the concentration and distribution of tribute among contending categories of surplus takers [Wolf, 1982: 99].

POLITICS AND IDEOLOGY IN THE HISTORICAL ARABO-ISLAMIC STATE

We have seen that the commercial class was so tied to the state that it lacked functional autonomy. It had to support the state or remain vulnerable to all kinds of environmental and political risks. Little economic accumulation was possible, no class hegemony was feasible politically, and no ideological debate could survive outside the domain of 'state matters'. A hierarchy of social strata (*tabaqat*), headed by the *khassa* (the élite or 'special ones') did exist in the society and people were conscious of its existence [Rodinson, 1981: 157–8]. But of course the close symbiosis with the state and subservience to the ruler, and the dominant ideology of peaceful coexistence and harmony advocated by the jurists had often constrained the emergence of high levels of class consciousness [compare Al-Jabiri, 1990: 331–46].

If rebellion occurred it was from the peasant folk or from the urban masses (*'amma* or *'awam*) and lumpenproletarian vagabonds (*'ayyarun*; *zu'ran*, etc.) [Duri, 1982: 76–84]. Such groups which form a component of the contemporary concept of the popular masses were regarded with the utmost contempt by the traditional writers, who treated all subjects of the sultan as a 'flock' (*ra'iyya*), whose only virtue lay in their utter obedience to him [Arkoun, 1990: 116; Al-'Allam, 1994: 17ff]. The commercial class was neither in power nor in the vanguard of popular opposition, for it was not strong enough to enforce its character on government nor well enough integrated with the domestic forces of production to form their political and ideological vanguard. The state was further strengthened by its control over land and specifically over its rent. This not only rendered peasant revolts extremely difficult (because the revolt would be against the state, and not against a local feudal lord), but it also prevented the commercial class from investing in the development of agriculture.

A further constraint to the commercial and financial class's potential for playing any important ideological and political role was that a significant number of its members were from the religious minorities and, increasingly, from foreign communities and could not therefore (for religious and juridical reasons) play an effective political role at the time. So vulnerable was the commercial bourgeoisie – due to its dual dependence on foreign trade and on the state – that it never managed to take over the reins of the state or to accelerate and expand the process of capitalist transformation [cf. Ismail II, 1980: 245–63].

Such socio-economic factors, indicative of the state's supremacy over society, would also explain why it was that the conservative, textual 'Sunni ideology' elaborated upon, in defence of the state, by the official élite of jurists was eventually to reign supreme, at the expense of the more 'liberal' and 'radical' ideologies of the Shi'is or the Kharijites, and over the 'rational' discourses of the *mu'tazilites*. Conversely it would also explain the recurrence of mystic tendencies that represented an attempt at 'escaping from the state' and the lasting popularity of Al-Ghazali's valedictory thoughts about religion and politics.

Like all hegemonic ideologies, Sunni Islam has often induced the consent of the ruled – its power in this case was multiplied due to the 'divine' nature of the ideology. Gramsci did indeed recognise the importance of religion (especially Catholicism), as part of ideological/cultural hegemony [cf. Boggs,

1976: 42–4]. Owing to the intellectual and juridic articulations of the Muslim *'ulama'*, Sunni Islam was turned into a hegemonic ideology, not only legitimising government but imparting, through education, a certain element of cultural order and consistency to the society at large [compare Al-'Azma, 1992: 47–72]. As Gramsci explained, for hegemony to assert itself successfully it must operate in a dualistic manner: as a 'general conception of life' for the masses, and as a 'scholastic programme' or set of principles which is advanced by a sector of the intellectuals [Boggs, 1976: 39]. Sunni Islam was developed as a moral and intellectual system not only inspired by God's will but also shaped and adjusted throughout Islamic history by the world-view of the dominant strata, and with the *'ulama'* and the educational system inducing the masses to consent to such an ideology.

Thus the Islamic state has had its 'apparatus of hegemony', represented by various institutions, schools, intellectuals, agents, and of course the 'mosque'. The role of jurists was particularly important in the case of the Islamic state; like all theorists of law, the essential role of their jurisprudence was to fix the legitimacy of power and to emphasise the legal obligation to obey it.

The Islamic state was, in Gramsci's terms, an 'educator': urging, inciting, soliciting and 'punishing' [Gramsci, 1971: 247]. The dominant individuals, groups and strata did not have to rely solely on the coercive power of the state or on their economic wealth – through ideological/cultural hegemony the ruled could be persuaded to accept the system of values and beliefs most conducive to the interests of the privileged groups.

Yet there is little doubt that the apparatus of hegemony of the Islamic state was more incorporated by the state than it was absorbed by the civil society. This has always been a problem for the Islamic state, one that we may describe as a problem of 'incomplete hegemony': a hegemony that is more ideological than it is social. We have already hinted at some of the causes that prevented the merchants from assuming sufficient socio-political supremacy to enable them to join the 'special class' (*al-khassa*, or the 'patricians) that circulated around the Caliph and the Court. In addition, the juridic theory of the Sunni *'ulama'*, although not completely deaf to the merchants' inclinations, was far more 'statist' in its orientation than it was mercantile or even 'social' in the broader sense.

By the same token, however, resistance to state power has had to rely to a large extent on man's thought and consciousness. The arena of ideas was thus the primary ground for the struggle between the dominant and the subordinate classes and groups in the Islamic state. In problematic situations, the *'ulama'*, who enjoyed a degree of relative autonomy, had sometimes sided with the subordinate classes against the state (e.g. Ahmad ibn Hanbal in the *mihna*). In major crises of the society or of the state, and especially as the rulers resorted to coercive force alone and lost their ability to inspire acquiescence, important segments of the masses became detached from their traditional ideology – a (religious) counter-ideology, or consciousness, was in the making, which eventually 'surrounded' the state (e.g. Shi'ism or Kharijism) or simply gnawed away quietly at the fabric of the state's hegemonic ideology (e.g. Sufism).

NOTES

1. Aspects of that 'borrowing' (and adaptation) have been detailed by Crone and Cook in their controversial book *Hagarism* [1977]. The overall orientation of their 'theory' is rather disparaging, however, and does not, so far, seem to have been corroborated by other scholars.

2. Incidentally, these foreign currency names are still used in many Arab countries, especially in the Gulf, where even now with their huge oil sales, they still prefer to receive the payments in a foreign currency – the dollar – indicating yet again the "externality" of their sources of income.

3. T.J. Byres [1985: 14] claims that in spite of assertions to the contrary, the 'tributary mode of production' bears more than a passing resemblance to the much-maligned notion of the 'Asiatic mode of production'. What Samir Amin has done, according to him, is to "re-formulate it – without village autarky and communality, and with classes – and present it in a watered down version. Are we not witnessing the Asiatic mode being sneaked in through the back door?"

CHAPTER THREE

State Formation in the Modern Era: the Colonial/Indigenous Mix

No proper understanding of the nature and characteristics of the contemporary Middle Eastern state can be obtained without reference to the colonial legacy in the region. The title of this chapter is meant to suggest, however, that the existing territorial Arab states have not been manufactured purely by colonialism. As should have been apparent from our analysis in other parts of this work, cultural and/or economic nuclei or embryos for 'states' existed in various parts of the Arab World, most notably Egypt, Morocco, and Oman, and also, though to a lesser extent, in other parts of North Africa, Southern Arabia (Yemen) and possibly too in parts of Syria (especially Mount Lebanon) [compare Harik, 1987: 19ff]. However, the colonial era was most instrumental in drawing up boundaries in roughly their present form, in redirecting economic relations away from the Middle East and towards Europe and additionally, at least in the case of geographical Syria and the Gulf region, in defining – often very artificially – the units that were to be singled out as distinct states. Be this as it may, and regardless of the form taken by European rule, "the end result was the same: the institutionalization and consolidation of territorial states in the image of the European pattern" [Korany, 1987: 47ff].

THE EUROPEAN ENCROACHMENT

The European capitalist encroachment on the Arab World of course precedes the actual colonial occupation and/or rule of most countries. It emerged first in the form of a process, stretching from the sixteenth to the nineteenth century, of 'incorporating' the Ottoman Empire into the capitalist world economy [cf. Wallerstein et al., in Islamoglu-Inan, 1987: 88–97]. Foreign merchants and financiers gained, as the European powers won, important legal and taxation exemptions for their subjects and for their non-Muslim clients under the Capitulations.

The reforms, initiated by the Turks, the Egyptians, the Tunisians and others in the period from 1800 to 1850 (often known as the *tanzimat*), were in large measure an attempt at 'defensive modernisation' as a way of keeping the European encroachment at bay. Bureaucratic centralisation, registration of land ownership, the building of new armies and modern educational systems, and the attempt to reassert the control of government over the economy and to maximise tax revenues, were the main aspects of such reforms [see also Al-'Azma, 1992: Ch. 2]. Ironically, however,

> the major effect of the reforms was entirely the opposite of what was originally intended. Instead of making these states more independent of Britain, France and Russia, they made them more dependent, instead of allowing them to control the process of European economic penetration it made the whole process of penetration a great deal more easy. [Owen, 1981: 57–8].

The ever-increasing need not only for European expertise but also for European trade and finance eventually led to serious financial and economic difficulties everywhere as well as to Ottoman and Egyptian bankruptcy, while Egypt's indebtedness actually brought British occupation to the country. In the process, the Ottoman, Egyptian (and Iranian) economies were in fact 'de-industrialised': the imposition by the European powers of commercial treaties whose tariff and duty arrangements favoured the foreign trader rather than the native producer and merchant gave European merchants and financiers ready access to Middle Eastern markets and a lasting influence on their economic and ultimately their political affairs [cf. Issawi, 1982]. Of course certain issues will always remain controversial. For example, was the decline of Muhammad 'Ali's industrialisation programme in the nineteenth century caused basically by domestic difficulties which sooner or later would have led to the closure of the factories, or was it basically attributable to the imposition on Egypt of the terms of the Anglo-Turkish commercial convention of 1838 (which banned all monopolies and preserved a low tariff of 5 per cent on Ottoman imports) and of the Treaty of London (which limited the size of the army to 18,000 men)?[1]

Be this as it may, there is little doubt that agricultural output was expanded in many territories in response to European demand, sometimes on the basis of the existing means and methods of production but in other cases through a substantial injection of capital and technology (e.g. in cotton, citrus, vineyards and wheat), often with government intervention. However, the growth of agricultural exports and of industrial imports was not necessarily accompanied by the total extinction of local handicrafts, since in most parts of the Middle East the artisans showed themselves to be remarkably tenacious by adopting new techniques when necessary and discovering or even creating new markets for their products. Thus, for example, there were more textile weavers in the major Syrian towns at the end of the nineteenth century than there were at the beginning [Owen, 1981: 287–9]. And whereas several of the traditional crafts declined, a growing segment of the artisan class became involved in 'servicing' workshops that supported the increasingly modern machinery and technology (mechanics, electricians, vehicle and equipment repairs, etc.).

The establishment of an 'open economy' based on free external trade and private land ownership, which was often initiated by the local rulers, was consolidated and expanded by the colonial powers. Roger Owen maintains that it was the local states themselves that performed certain key roles such as the introduction and enforcement of low tariffs and new systems of commercial law, long before European political intervention was organised on a regular basis. The rulers of such states were also easily persuaded of the need to borrow large sums of money to improve infrastructures or simply to purchase expensive European goods like weapons and machines. "It was only when foreign-imposed economic arrangements seemed directly threatened by the movement of popular revolt – as in Egypt – that there was a direct imposition of colonial control" [Owen, 1981: 289].

The British occupation of Egypt in 1882 was ostensibly intended to be 'temporary', but as it happened it lasted in one form or another for some seventy years and was to be the cornerstone of British colonial supremacy throughout the Near East from the end of the First World War to the 1950s [cf. Monroe, 1963]. This, combined with the colonising of Aden after 1839, with tutelage over the Gulf Shaikhdoms from 1853 onwards and with an 'Anglo-Egyptian' condominium in the Sudan from 1899, made Britain the most supreme European power in the region.

Nor did France stand idly by. In 1830 it took over Algeria, defeated the 'Abd al-Qadir uprising and proceeded to colonise the land as a settler appendage to France. From there it invaded Tunisia in 1881 and made it a French protectorate, and in 1912 it subjected Morocco to the same fate (while around the same time Italy was invading Libya, with considerable resistance from the local populace).

Tunisia was too close to Europe and to French Algeria to be left alone. Only four years after the fall of the great 'moderniser' Khair al-Din, the French expeditionary forces moved on from Algeria into Tunisia, which was now in a state of upheaval. The establishment in Tunisia in 1881 of the French Protectorate accelerated and consolidated the process of state formation that had begun in the pre-colonial era [Anderson, 1986: 114ff, 137ff]. In the economic sphere, colonial policy involved an acceleration of the process of commercialisation of agriculture and the development of a real estate market, which – as in Algeria "provided an auspicious context for European colonisation and eventually led to European control of the most fertile lands in the realm. Population growth and dispossession of Tunisian agriculturalists and pastoralists created an agricultural proletariat, landless wage-labourers who were at the mercy of the market and dependent on their landlords or other patrons" [Anderson, 1986: 137]. By the 1920s Europeans held between 14 and 18 per cent of the productive land in Tunisia, including large tracts of the most fertile terrain in the north. But more important than the absolute acreage was the disruption of Tunisian agriculture that this restructuring entailed.

In terms of institutions, the French colonial era consolidated the Tunisian state through a near monopoly of the use of force, and extended the policing and recruitment powers of the central government. The central administration became more elaborate and differentiated, and was better equipped to interfere in the daily economic and political lives of the subjects. Socially, tribal affiliation lost much of its political significance, but was transforming itself into new styles of patron–client ties that would eventually provide the principal organisational structure of the nationalist movement [Anderson, 1986: 155–7].

In the meantime, France continued her special cultural and commercial relationship with the Catholics of the Levant, mainly in Lebanon, whereas Britain continued her commercial and economic relations with the Near East in general. Formal dominance of the Mashriq was relatively belated:

> In the Fertile Crescent the nineteenth century Eastern game was played for smaller stakes by lesser players. France championed native Catholics; Russia supported the Orthodox; and Britain – finding no native Protestants – settled for the Druze ... The rest of the area, as a provincial hinterland, was spared the fate of Egypt, blessed and cursed by its strategic position and the Suez Canal, or of Tunisia, too close to Europe and to French Algeria. In retrospect, the Fertile Crescent, Lebanon aside, probably remained free of direct European control until after the First World War because a short route to India via Aleppo to the Euphrates and thence down to the Persian Gulf was never developed. Instead, the Suez Canal was dug [Brown, 1984: 94].

However, Anglo-French imperialist rivalry could not help but eventually encroach on such territories, if only for strategic purposes, and thus the period from 1918 to 1923 witnessed a "remaking of the Near East" [Yapp, 1987: 322–51] along new border lines, with the 'mandate' of Syria and Lebanon going to France, and that of Iraq, Palestine and the 'residual' territory of Transjordan going to Britain.

In terms of political style, British colonialism had the reputation of emphasising economic concerns and relying as much as possible on indirect rule, whereas French colonialism was felt to emphasise cultural links and a *mission civilisatrice*, and to prefer a policy of direct rule. In reality, however, both types of colonialism were equally interested in maximising economic gain from their administered territories, and they were both equally proud of their own culture and contemptuous of Arab-Islamic culture. Both were equally interested in what Timothy Mitchell [1988] calls the "enframing" of the societies they ruled, in subjecting them to a kind of order and discipline that made managing them and 'understanding' them possible, the political power itself being quite discreet and not fully definable:

> The reorganisation of towns and the laying out of new colonial quarters, every regulation of economic or social practice, the construction of the country's new system of irrigation canals ... the building of barracks, police stations and classrooms, the completion of a system of railways – this pervasive process of 'order' must be understood as more than mere improvement or 'reform'. Such projects were all undertaken as an enframing, and hence had the effect of re-presenting a realm of the conceptual, conjuring up for the first time the prior abstractions of progress, reason, law, discipline, history, colonial authority and order [Mitchell, 1988: 179].

The older French 'culturalist' theory of *assimilation* was applied most vigorously in Algeria and to an extent in Tunisia, with the intent of turning Muslims into French citizens and of incorporating their economy and society into that of France. In Morocco and Syria, the newer theory of *association* was applied, whereby the colonial policy was – at least in theory – to be developed mainly along native, rather than European, lines. This formula put a premium on the "subtle exploitation of the strengths and weaknesses of native society" and on respect for local religion, customs and law, rule through native institutions, and economic (though not necessarily industrial) development [Khoury, 1987: 55–6]. It was basically therefore a 'semi-corporatist' formula applied from a position of dominance. The system, improvised by the French colonial officer Marshall Lyautey, rested on a hand-picked élite corps of French native affairs officers with knowledge of Arabic and of Islam, and of local culture and customs, who would then recognise and exploit the political, social and ethnic divisions of the country they ruled (e.g. the Arab–Berber split in Morocco; the religio-ethnic mosaic in Syria). Traditional urban and tribal elements would be co-opted for that function, with reward, to be used against hostile leaders and groups. The colonial army was to be employed as a coercive force only when other methods of persuasion had failed.

Concerning Syria, not only did the French sever Lebanon from Greater Syria but they also put Syria proper through several legal and territorial permutations in a bid to keep the country from uniting politically: they created the separate states of Damascus and Aleppo and divided other provinces and districts (e.g. the 'Alawite state, Jabal Druze). The second major strategy was to isolate the nationalist movement by pitting rural areas against the more politically conscious and hostile urban nationalist centres, via a change in the rules of landownership which was the basis of the urban political leadership's wealth and power [Khoury, 1987: 58–60]. The French also played on the various religious and sectarian divisions of Syria, including the use of ethnically based military forces. The 'Alawite 'separation' policy is a good case in point. The French made good use of the fact that "although the Alawites were internally divided, when they were threatened with domination by a more powerful urban absentee Sunni landowning class which supported unity with Damascus, they responded as a 'sect-class'". The French thus formally incorporated Latakia and Tartus into a single territory which was administered separately from the rest of Syria, and they weakened the economic base of the Sunni latifundia and promoted certain 'Alawite tribal leaders. The numerous divisions and redivisions of Syria by French rule over a quarter of a century obstructed the development of a unified administrative élite in the country. Denied the opportunity to acquire and assimilate experience in governance, factionalism and inefficiency intensified, and the nationalist leaders were to carry a certain degree of administrative incompetence with them into the era of independence [Khoury, 1987: 520–21, 622].

A COLONIAL MODE OF PRODUCTION?

Once they occupied the position of formal authority, the colonial powers, British and French, pushed ahead further and faster, with all the 'economic liberalisation' policies that they had previously persuaded and/or pressurised the Arab countries to adopt. In addition to the fact that they stood to profit economically from such policies, such an orientation encouraged the development of a kind of 'local oligarchy' that they could rely on in 'ordering' these societies. Thus although the British at some point encouraged the Egyptian small farmer, the end result of their total policies was an economy for which cotton represented 92 per cent of the total value of exports, and where 13,000 landlords owned nearly half the cultivated land [Owen, 1969: 307; Vatikiotis, 1968: 241]. Likewise in Jordan, although British officials were originally sympathetic to the small farmers and initiated programmes for supporting them, they soon found it easier and more convenient to condone a policy of land privatisation that mainly benefited the influential tribal shaikhs [Robins, 1988: Ch. 7].

The extent to which colonial powers were intentionally and ardently hostile to local industrialisation in the countries which they ruled is not clear, but there can be little doubt that their policy of expanding and legalising the private holding of land by officials and shaikhs meant, at least initially, that little of the surplus was reinvested in industry or even in agricultural development. In any case, the great increase in sea-borne trade with Europe was bound to involve a fundamental restructuring of the economies, especially when the production of cash crops needed to be expanded. The sector that enjoyed the most rapid growth, and tended to act as a focus for entrepreneurial efforts and local capital resources, was that of trade with Europe, and associated activities such as infrastructural development and the construction of buildings in the major port cities. In consequence, greater socio-economic benefit tended to go to groups that were "able to insert themselves into the chain of commerce and credit which linked Middle Eastern peasant with European manufacturer and consumer" [Owen, 1981: 290–92]. This sort of link began initially in the commercial field, later took on a financial dimension, and finally acquired a political aspect. 'Reform' attempts by local élites

> only exposed new weaknesses which increased dependence rather than reduced it. In these circumstances it proved difficult to resist foreign pressure for economic and financial concessions, the more so as they could often be presented in terms of the wide area in which the interests of Europe and local rulers seemed to coincide, whether in terms of improving security, increasing agricultural production or placing entire populations within the domain of a single system of commercial and criminal law [Owen, 1981: 292–3].

Although they did not always act directly in correspondence with European economic interests, nor had they the power to enforce particular policies in every part of their territories, the dominant élites passed through a process of formation that was bound to impose its limitations on, and to impart its characteristics to, these native classes. This was by no means the European type of bourgeoisie generated by a capitalist mode of production, but was a specific type of class that was characteristic of dependent or peripheral capitalism. The old modes of production, and the classes that corresponded to them, were maintained under colonial rule, although they were subjected to the general laws of capitalist accumulation and reproduction. Alongside this, the new capitalist sectors eventually produced their own bourgeoisie and proletariat. But the development of this bourgeoisie was closely linked to the 'logic' of its integration into the 'colonial' (i.e. dependent–capitalist) mode of production and the world capitalist system, and confined to certain sectors and roles assigned to it by the emerging international division of labour.

Samir Amin observes that this new class should not be confused with the traditional pre-imperialist mercantile class, despite certain links between them. This new class found itself in a contradictory situation: while it was created by Western capitalism, its further development was also constrained by Western capitalism. Confined initially to agriculture and mining, this bourgeoisie on the whole "remained a mere potentiality" [Amin, 1978: 25–6].

In agriculture, the landlord class was promoted in those societies where it existed, such as Egypt, and was created by way of 'latifundist' colonialism in countries where it had not existed before, such as Iraq; and these transformations took place as a result of the integration of agricultural production into the capitalist market in order to satisfy the demand for exports and, usually later, to meet domestic needs. Such classes gradually lost their semi-feudal and tribal characteristics and became increasingly subordinated to the laws of agrarian capitalism. Thus this new agrarian bourgeoisie had complex characteristics, "half capitalist, half pre-capitalist" [Amin, 1978: 28]. This class also initiated some investments in non-agricultural fields so that by the Second

World War, it was no longer possible to speak of a new industrial bourgeoisie opposed to an old land-holding aristocracy: "we are talking about a fusion between the two sections of the same class". This was most typical in Egypt: the native bourgeoisie began to grow under British occupation; at first agrarian it then became agro-capitalist and even industrial [Amin, 1978: 29–35; Al-Disuqi, 1975]. In other parts of the Arab World the landed aristocracy was largely created by colonial rule during the 1920s, such as in Iraq, Sudan and Morocco, where private ownership of land was assigned to members of the traditional chiefly classes (as was done with the Zamindars in India). This class was quick to submit to the interests of the foreign Occupation after receiving guarantees that its privileges would be maintained.

The urban 'Third Estate' (as Amin terms it), consisting of the traditional classes of clerks, artisans and what was left of the old merchants, and its rural equivalent, composed of village notables, reacted quite differently. As heirs to the popular tradition, they were more aware of the challenges to native culture, and as traditional producers they were more sensitive to the harmful effects of imported merchandise. This Third Estate was liquidated by the colonialists, first politically and then economically, and the generation of petty bureaucrats that replaced it was, with few exceptions, quick to accept foreign domination. Even the nationalist Wafd Party in Egypt was to join in the collaboration game.

In the Mashriq, Ottoman domination had preserved the unity of the region but did not provide a sufficient guarantee against imperialist penetration through trade and finance. Syria's integration into the world capitalist system was much slower than that of Egypt or the Maghrib, as the region was unsuited to a developed export agriculture. The process only really began during the French Mandate and, in addition to some cotton cultivation, took place mainly in the field of trade and finance. As we have seen earlier, from the late nineteenth century a fairly homogeneous landholding-bureaucratic élite began to take shape and was able to mediate, with a fair degree of effectiveness, between the central authority and the provincial forces. These 'notables', who were mainly Sunni-Muslim and who were identified most closely with the ascendant idea of nationalism, managed for a brief period after the end of Ottoman rule to become the rulers of modern Syria, thus imparting a remarkable degree of continuity to the exercise of local political power in that country.

However, the notables were interested basically in a 'restorative' type of nationalism, that would ultimately lead to the gradual phasing out of the French Mandate and leave them comfortably in power [Khoury, 1987]. By the end of the 1920s, a National Bloc representing such groups had emerged which was able to direct popular discontent towards the presence of foreign rule and away from local power structures. Yet nationalist politics, by their very nature, required the mobilisation of new forces associated with modern institutions and activities, and new forms of political association were actually encouraged, especially between the towns and the countryside and between different ethno-religious groups. But the National Bloc had its own limits. During the Mandate, most traditional Nationalist leaders failed to go beyond their narrow 'city bases', and a majority of them rejected the concept of Arab unity, in spite of its considerable popular appeal. Arabist sentiments were originally stimulated in Syria as a result, after 1908, of the Young Turk policies of centralisation and Turkification, from which the Arab élites stood to lose. The Pan-Arabist movement in Syria was also given a special meaning and vigour (surpassing its equivalent in most other Arab countries) because 'geographical' Syria had been artificially divided by the Anglo-French mandates in defiance of actual demographic, cultural and commercial ties. By the time of independence, the notables were finding their power base eroded by the rise of a group of merchants and landowning entrepreneurs who challenged the politics of the traditional urban leadership previously associated with the landowning-bureaucratic classes and with the National Bloc.

As Philip Khoury [1987] illustrates, new political movements emerged during the 1930s in response to the gradual socio-economic and cultural changes that were taking place beneath the political surface. The most important and the most representative of these organisations was the League of National Action; the League was the 'ideological parent' of the Ba'th Party, the movement which eventually toppled the commercial and landowning élite from power to become the most influential organisation in the contemporary history of Syria. Khoury's analysis also indicates the lasting impact of French attempts during the 1920s and 1930s to sponsor minoritarian and rural forces as an opposing counterbalance to the Sunni urban traditional leadership, and offers a detailed explanation of how the apparent continuity in the styles of exercising power was gradually undermined through factors such as the loosening of family ties, the spread of modern education and new ideologies, the establishing of modern institutions and the reorientation of the Syrian economy.

Not until the 1950s were plans devised by the urban bourgeoisie to attend to agriculture and to develop the Gezira region of Syria through the utilisation of modern capitalist methods: "agricultural growth, an urban victory" wrote Rizqallah Hilan [in Amin, 1978: 40]. This development was also to be supported by a few light industries related to agriculture (textiles, food processing), but by 1955 the process had run out of steam, and Syria was forced to start along a new path, that of state capitalism. To achieve this end, the new élites made particular use of the Syrian army which, for a number of historical and social reasons, has always tended to include a disproportionately high representation of Alawites, Druzes and rural Sunnis. Ba'thism, with its secularist, egalitarian orientation, was a useful ideological tool for such unprivileged minoritarian and provincial groups, and by using the army as their main political tool, an alliance of these groups was finally able to "break apart the

economic and social foundations of the old regime's power", and to replace it
with a new way of playing politics [Khoury, 1987: 628–30].

In Iraq, the irrigated zones have historically fluctuated in size by a factor
of about 1 to 10. The irrigation works carried out under the Mandate were to
play a decisive role in the constitution of a new latifundist agrarian bourgeoisie,
since 90 per cent of the lands were distributed to a thousand chiefs of semi-
nomadic tribes, while the exploitation of oil helped to enhance the value of
land [Amin, 1978: 40–41, 93]. In the last year of the monarchy (1958), the
families that owned more than 30,000 *dunums* of land and who, in effect,
formed the nucleus of Iraqi landlordism, were forty-nine in number and owned
between them about 16.8 per cent of all privately held agricultural land, usually
of the richest quality. Twenty-two of these families belonged to the tribal
shaikhly order, twelve to the stratum of Sadah or claimants of descent from
the Prophet, and eleven to the mercantile class. They accounted respectively
for 51 per cent, 31 per cent and 12.3 per cent of the area just mentioned. Thus
it is clear that during the monarchical period and until 1958, the tribal shaikhs
formed the most important segment of the small landed class that dominated
the greater number of peasants in Iraq [Batatu, 1978: 57–152]. Batatu further
observes an

apparent direct correlation between political quiescence and big shaikhdoms:
with few exceptions, the big landed shaikhs and *begs*, or to be more historically
accurate, the shaikhs and *begs* that became big landowners under the monarchy,
had provided a shaikhly anchor for British policy during and after the years of
the British occupation, taking no part in the Iraqi uprising of 1920 or in the
subsequent movement against the 'Mandate'. They also had no share in the
tribal rebellions of 1935–1937 [Batatu, 1978: 82].

In addition to the old 'aristocracy' of officials, the ex-Sharifian officers and
the Muslim merchants, this new landed class had come to form the socio-
political backbone of monarchical Iraq. And, as in Egypt, the new bourgeoisie
was openly collaborationist with the colonial power, leaving the task of the
nationalist struggle – mainly initiated by the Ahali Group – to the intelligentsia
and the urban masses, and eventually to the army officers.

From 1920 to 1948 European colonialism reigned supreme in the whole
Arab region. In Egypt, Syria and Iraq, the agrarian and latifundist sections of
the bourgeoisie, reinforced and made wealthy in the wake of colonialism,
were secure in their position. Such opposition as existed remained merely as
a weak, 'intelligentist' opposition without any real class base of its own, torn
between its dissatisfaction with conditions in its country and its attraction to
the pro-colonial national bourgeoisie [Amin, 1978: 47]. Given the intelligentsia's lack of 'economic' means with which to effect a change in political
and social life, it was perhaps understandable that it was the army officers
who, possessing 'physical' means that were capable of breaking the stalemate,

eventually intervened in politics with the declared intention of finding a solution to the escalating problems of stalled development and mounting social discontent, problems that had affected several segments of the petty bourgeoisie.

Although it is sorely needed, no imperial history of the Arab World is yet available; nor can we embark on the writing of such a history in the present context. But however undesirable the practice may be, it is necessary here to make a few generalisations on the nature of the mode of production and state formation under colonialism.

First, unlike Rey and Alavi [cf. Brewer, 1980: 270–72], I do not favour defining the mode of production emerging under foreign rule as a 'colonial mode of production', although this characterisation has been adopted by the occasional Arab writer, notably Mahdi 'Amil [1987: 55ff] who speaks of an articulation of modes of production within which colonial relations of production predominate. The economic activity of the colonial powers took various forms, depending on the nature of the colony and on the stage of development of capitalism, both internationally and at the level of the metropolitan state, at the time the colony was occupied: thus, for example, plantations in North Africa, agro-capitalism in Egypt, latifundia in Iraq, trade and finance in Syria/Lebanon, and mining in the Gulf. The extra-economic methods to which the colonialists may have resorted (such as the *corvée* in Egypt for the digging of the Suez Canal and some other public works) are by no means confined to colonialism but apply to all situations where the 'political instance' is paramount.

Under colonialism, the process of incorporating the Arab World into the capitalist world system was being completed [cf. Amin, 1982a], but this by necessity was a peripheral, dependent type of capitalism in the sense that, in the main, its logic emanated not from domestic forces and classes, but from classes and forces of the metropole. On the whole, pre-capitalist modes of production were not destroyed by the colonial powers, but rather were subjugated to the requirements of capitalist accumulation. As P.P. Rey comments, extending his observation to the post-colonial era as well,

> many well-intentioned European observers believe that the capitalist states of the West could, from a technical point of view, have an interest in supporting the development of an efficient modern bureaucracy as against the tribalist bureaucracy. They forget one thing, that capitalism is not interested in the *technical* aspect of development (production of use values), but in the social aspect (development of capitalist relations of production and above all the extraction of surplus value [in Brewer, 1980: 197].

The pre-capitalist modes were only challenged if they stood obviously in the way of colonial plans, for instance in plantation areas. In fact they were preserved as much as possible, especially in agriculture as a cheap guarantee for the reproduction of the labour force itself. Clashes did take place, however, if such 'enclaves' of pre-capitalist social formations embarked directly on resisting the colonial presence, as occurred with tribal formations in practically all Northern African countries.

Although there were several colonial officers who always remained doctrinally opposed to the capitalist development, and especially the industrialisation, of the colonies, and others who believed that non-European societies would never be capable of going beyond agriculture, and although the pre-capitalist formations were often hostile, and even resistant, to capitalist transformation (sometimes simply because it was colonial and 'foreign'), we still think that the main determinant has been the logic of capitalist development in the metropole itself; hence, the attitude of the 'core' countries towards capitalist development in the periphery has tended to go through various phases.

In the first phase the metropole supported modernised agricultural production (plantations or agro-capitalism) if there was a good export potential; industrial development was denied even if local forces asked, and were ready, for it (e.g. Egypt under Cromer). At a later stage (i.e. from the late 1930s and the 1940s), light industries, especially those that were agriculturally based such as textiles and food processing, were allowed by the metropolitan countries. Until the 1950s, however, metropolitan countries would not support heavy industry even in the formally independent ex-colonies – this was still the reserved territory of the core. Countries like Egypt and India were having to assemble their iron and steel complexes piecemeal from German, Russian and other suppliers. One may comment in passing, that in the current phase of post-industrial capitalist development, a Third World country can buy steel works at any time – for now the name of the game is 'information technology'. Capitalism therefore is inclined to expand everywhere; indeed it is historically the first mode of production that is basically universal. This expansion is most obvious everywhere in the field of capitalist relations of *exchange*. When it comes to the capitalist mode of *production*, the picture is more complex because it depends on historical and social conditions both in core and in peripheral countries (as we shall see elsewhere).[2]

However, it remains true that practically all colonial powers have had to resort in a big way to extra-economic means (such as military and political coercion) in order to pave the way for the penetration of commercial and eventually capitalist relations. They also needed a strong military and security machine to confront any possible resistance, and here Hamza Alavi's thesis of the over-developed state is indeed helpful [Alavi, 1979]. The over-developed state is basically a 'bureaucratic state' (usually with a strong military wing) that encroaches rather heavily on civil society. It is interesting to observe that the organisational phase of capitalism and the corresponding political phase of the bureaucratic state, which tended to appear in the core at the later stages of capitalist development, appear in the periphery at the very early stages of capitalist transformation. Be this as it may, there is in any case much to suggest that the tradition of a 'bureaucratic state', with its 'relative autonomy' from social groups and its claim for balancing forces, was perhaps one of the most important political legacies from the colonial era [compare Tlemcani, 1986].

On the other hand, in examining the post-colonial state, it is very important not to confine oneself simply to attempts at analysing the texts of economic treaties between the new state and the ex-metropole, or at examining the statutes and counting the personnel of the administrative organs inherited from the colonial era. The phenomenon is far more complex than this. As Foucault and his followers explain, one should not only consider the privileges of sovereign power and its right to decide life and death, nor should one look only at the legal and institutional manifestations of power: it is the multiplicity of its relations that should be examined. Sovereignty of the state, the form of law, or the units of domination, are only the 'terminal forms' that power takes on. What matters more are the discreet power relations of ceaseless struggles and confrontations or of transformations and reverses, as well as the relations of mutual reinforcement or disjunction among the relations. The various social hegemonies, the formulations of law, and the state apparatus, come in the final instance to be the institutional crystallisation of these more complex relations [Foucault, 1984]. In the colonial situation, not only the economy but also the whole society and 'mind' is 'enframed' in the colonial mould, whereby power penetrates everywhere but becomes at the same time more and more unnoticeable. Eventually Arabs even started to think of themselves in terms of 'Orientalist' concepts about the Oriental national character, the position of women in Islam, or the power of custom and superstition in the East, and Orientalist themes steadily penetrated the writings of Arabs about themselves [Mitchell, 1988: 168ff].

Also of relevance to our concerns in this book is the cultural dualism that tended to characterise the Arab World following its imperialist encounter with the West. Whereas the bureaucrats started to speak the language of legalism and rationality and the intelligentsia, educated in the European style, began to speak the language of modernity and secularism, the 'Third Estates' of small merchants, traditional artisans and minor functionaries, as well as the traditionally educated clerics and clerks, continued to speak a different, Islam-ically coloured, language. In terms of their nationalist, anti-colonialist attitudes, it is difficult to distinguish as clearly between the two socio-cultural com-munities: several elements from within the first group refused to collaborate with the colonialists, whereas some of the 'ulama's and the sufis collaborated with, or acquiesced to, colonial interests. Yet the first group was definitely organically more tied to the colonial legacy and tended to act accordingly in the political and economic as well as in the cultural spheres.

This was a partial cause behind the fact that, shortly after independence, the military officers in a number of Arab countries were to take over power, with the intention of severing most of the subservient political and economic ties with the ex-colonial powers. However, although the military were seemingly rejecting Westernisation, they were in fact accepting its main underlying tenets under the banner of modernisation, and although they were not keen on the legalist aspect of the modern state, they were over-zealous with respect to its bureaucratic aspect. They were, after all, trained in Western-style military academies and working in one of the most typically bureaucratic of all organisations (hierarchical, specialised and control based). Even when such officers adopted 'socialist' terminology and opted for cooperation with the communist countries, they were still, culturally speaking, within the same camp, pursuing basically the same goals: 'progress', premised on the concept that 'man' can control his destiny.

STATE FORMATION IN EGYPT

It is sometimes suggested that Egypt is the only 'real' state in the Arab World. In the generic geo-political sense of the word, Egypt is one of the oldest 'states' on earth, dating back about 5,000 years from the time when Menas unified the Delta and Upper Egypt under one central authority that was eventually to make the best possible use of the country's 'hydraulic' and agricultural potential. As the Pharaohs' power declined, the country's rule became more dynastic than 'bureaucratic' in nature, and this was certainly the case during an exceedingly long period under dynastic rulers of various foreign origins.

In the juridic, basically modern European sense of the 'state' – as a territorial entity based externally on sovereignty and internally on legal institutions and a unified market – the history of the 'modern state' in Egypt is usually identified with the reign of Muhammad 'Ali, who came to power in 1805. Not only did he build a national army but he also constructed an extensive industrial network and an impressive educational system. Under Muhammad 'Ali a daring attempt to build up (state) capitalism was launched, and the early intimations of a concept of citizenship (or at least of nationality) were to emerge. The experiment had its internal contradictions and faced several external threats, and was eventually to falter during the mid-nineteenth century, ultimately paving the way for the British occupation of Egypt in 1882.

We have already discussed (in Chapter 2) the concept of the Asiatic Mode of Production and its possible relevance to the study of Egypt. The concept (and ideas similar to it) has gained sympathy among various Egyptian writers. Egyptian politics and state formation were related to the country's 'hydraulic' background, by the renowned educator Rifa'a Rafi' Al-Tahtawi in the mid-nineteenth century, and by people such as the historical geographer Jamal

Hamdan and the political sociologist Anwar Abdel-Malek in the mid-twentieth century. In spite of various criticisms, the theory has engaged several contemporary scholars in its favour, including Kamal Al-Munufi, Ikram Badr Al-Din, 'Adil Husain and, most particularly, Ahmad Sadiq Sa'd [see in particular 1981]. Even a dedicated orthodox Marxist such as Fu'ad Mursi was tempted to suggest that whereas in other societies ownership and wealth are normally the way to power and the state, the movement is usually reversed in Egypt, owing to the specifically "bureaucratic character of the Egyptian state across the ages" [cf. Ayubi, 1989b: 25–39 and refs cited].

The emergence of the 'modern state' in Egypt is usually traced to the coming to power of Muhammad 'Ali in 1805. More broadly, the story of the modern state can be regarded in some ways as the political and institutional expression of an articulation between the Asiatic mode of production and the capitalist mode of production, characterised by a rapid move towards the superiority of the latter.

The 'pure' Asiatic mode of production is distinguished by semi-communal processes of production and organisation in the village on the one hand, and a supreme collective represented by the state apparatus (which encompasses the owners) on the other. The state extracts the economic surplus in the form of a tribute and uses part of it in maintaining the agricultural and the infrastructural base of the economy. The Ottoman system in Egypt (following its conquest in 1517), was a 'hybrid' possessing, in addition to its 'Asiatic' features, a significant mercantile sector and a semi-feudal component.

With Muhammad 'Ali's arrival, the move towards a capitalist mode of production began, although in a problematic way. State centralisation, typical of the purer examples of the Asiatic mode of production, was enforced, while the semi-communal organisations of the countryside, as well as the artisan and commercial guilds and the Sufi orders, the bedouin solidarities and the social organisations of the minority religious *milla*s were all dissolved [Sa'd, 1981: 231–347]. The Egyptian path towards capitalism, as represented by Muhammad 'Ali's experiment, was therefore *étatiste* and took the form of state capitalism, yet many of the methods that were used to develop the economy remained distinctively 'oriental'.

Such a characterisation of the nature of the Egyptian formation and the Egyptian state during and following the Muhammad 'Ali era remains quite controversial however: was Muhammad 'Ali's experiment at heart an attempt to resecure the tributary (Oriental) mode, or was it in reality an attempt to build up industrial capitalism, albeit via the state? And in terms of its outcome: was the main product of Muhammad 'Ali's experiment the emergence of a certain variety of agricultural feudalism (or was it an 'agricultural capitalism') in Egypt; or was the main product in fact the introduction of a commercial and 'comprador' capitalism'? [see on these debates Ayubi, 1989b].

Most analysts agree that the mode of production up to the beginning of the nineteenth century was based on semi-communal village units combined with state ownership of the land (although the historical information on the second aspect is far more abundant than on the former). During the 'purer' episodes, the production surplus was appropriated by the central state in the form of 'tribute' (under a variety of technical and legal categories), and the labour surplus was absorbed in the form of a *corvée*. Such a system does not, by its very nature, allow for the crystallisation and development of class contradictions, and depending on historical contingencies, it was open to a variety of class formations.

When Muhammad 'Ali assumed power, the tributary form was not pure or complete because the *iltizam* (tax farming) system as well as the *waqf* (religious endowments) systems had allowed a certain part of the agricultural surplus to trickle from the state to the semi-feudal intermediaries. These could possibly, in due course, have allowed for the emergence of a new social class whose privileges might have clashed with the power of the central state. Was Muhammad 'Ali's economic policy therefore aimed at restoring the Asiatic or tributary mode in its pure form by re-tightening the grip of the state over the economic resources of society? It was long after Muhammad 'Ali's assumption of power that he abolished the *iltizam* completely and imposed direct and increasing taxes to be paid by the peasants to the state. In the meantime, he continued to confiscate all lands including those of *rizq*, *wisiyya* and *awqaf*. Mahmud 'Awda finds in this a revival of the Asiatic, tributary mode in its pure form, since all confiscated lands were then registered as being in the use of the village (*hiyaza*), and the rural community became responsible in a direct way for paying the taxes to the state without intermediaries, but without being allowed to *own* the land either individually or collectively [cf. 'Awda, 1979]. A similar situation could be said to have obtained in industry. As Muhammad 'Ali proceeded to introduce many new industries designed in the European style, he simultaneously exerted every effort to destroy industries or crafts remaining from the Mamluk period, forbade native looms, and abolished the yarn and textile guilds, compelling their members to join his factories by force, and establishing a special *diwan* to enforce the centralisation of the textiles industry into the hands of the state – thus restoring the 'Oriental' system in its pure form that considers the crafts and the artisans to be mere appendages to the ruler [cf. Baer, 1964: 11ff].

Samir Amin, on the other hand, is not inclined to make much of the 'Oriental' features of Muhammad 'Ali's experiment. To him, this experiment was an attempt to build capitalism within the available conditions and possibilities obtaining at the time, an attempt that represented, historically, a repetition on a larger scale of the attempt by 'Ali Bey al-Kabir to build mercantilist capitalism in the eighteenth century. If Muhammad 'Ali failed, the reason was not, in Amin's view, that he was too Oriental but that in a certain sense he was not Oriental enough in his political choices. Rather than cooperating with the native mercantile elements of Egyptian craftsmen and merchants he chose to ally himself with a foreign mercantile bourgeoisie of Europeans, Jews and Christian Levantines. This was a dilemma that confronted other countries attempting the transition towards capitalism (e.g. Italy, Russia and the Balkans) and, according to Amin, success has always occurred in the cases where a 'nationalist line' has been chosen [Amin, 1985: 125–31]. The reason behind this choice in Muhammad 'Ali's case was, in Amin's view, political, for Muhammad 'Ali thought that the foreign bourgeoisie would not challenge his absolute rule, whereas to rely on an emerging Egyptian bourgeoisie (whom he had used to rid the country of the Ottomans/Mamluks and to resist the British when they attempted to land at Alexandria in 1807) would have required him to concede a certain degree of power in their favour. Indeed he followed a similar approach with regard to the modernisation of the state and the army, by relying on foreign experts and avoiding the nascent Egyptian bourgeoisie. Not only this, but Muhammad 'Ali in some ways reversed the intellectual renaissance that had started in the eighteenth century under the *hadith* school of Shaikh Hasan al-'Attar by excluding its followers in favour of the *kalam* school, at that time rigid and scholastic in outlook [cf. Gran, 1979].

Thus Muhammad 'Ali, once difficulties began to confront him, was unable to call on the help of a native bourgeoisie but had instead to rely increasingly on a 'bureaucratic aristocracy' which needed repeatedly to be bribed with parcels of land for private ownership – a policy that distracted him from his original project of state capitalism.

Following Muhammad 'Ali's defeat in 1840 and with continuing and growing imperialist pressures, this state of affairs persisted, reaching its peak, under Isma'il, when a class of rural aristocrats made up of large landowners turned virtually all of the countryside into a large cotton-field for the satisfaction of the needs of the British textile industry. The Egyptian capitalist formation was becoming increasingly 'peripheral' and dependent [cf. 'Abd al-Hakim, 1986: Part II].

Although it has been a familiar pattern, especially in the political literature of the 1952 revolution, to characterise the Egyptian formation from the time of Isma'il onwards as feudal, there is a growing trend among social scientists to prefer the category of an 'agricultural capitalism'. Such an agricultural capitalism has been articulated with some remaining 'tributary' pockets and with the beginnings of modern commercial capitalism. Indications of the tributary pockets were to be seen, for example, in the continued arbitrariness of taxes under Isma'il where there were no fixed times for taxes but whenever the government needed more money the burden was distributed over the rural counties and each *umda* (mayor) was ordered to collect his village's share. A manifestation of the modern commercial capitalism can be observed in the activities of the European and 'minoritarian' entrepreneurs and in the experiment during the 1930s of Banque Misr, which was initially financed by the

Egyptian agricultural capitalists before it increasingly allied itself with foreign 'comprador' capitalism [cf. Davis, 1983; Tignor, 1984].

One of the few analysts explicitly to use the concept of articulation is Mahmud 'Awda. He identifies the Egyptian formation in the second half of the nineteenth and the first half of the twentieth century as a variety of peripheral capitalism that is witnessing an articulation between a number of pre-capitalist modes (some being pseudo-tributary and some semi-feudal) which intersect at different points with a modern economic sector, whether in the area of intensive cropping agriculture or in commercial, financial and industrial activities ['Awda, 1979: 133–9].

There were aspects of 'articulation' in the political sphere too, under Muhammad 'Ali. On the one hand, the state machine was unified and standardised and new ministries (diwans) were established one after another and systematised in 1837 for revenues, war, sea, schools, commerce, factories, etc. The diwans were reorganised into European-style ministries under Isma'il in 1878 [Rizq, 1975: 9–11 et passim] and administrative provincial systems were introduced with state officials running them. The army was 'nativised', unified and subjected to the political authority, new secularist laws were issued and new secularist schools were introduced, and the taxation system was standardised.

Yet several 'Oriental' features continued: above all Muhammad 'Ali's personalistic, despotic style, the corporal punishment of 'negligent' peasants by state officials and the corporal punishment of negligent state officials by the Pasha and his men, the allocation of some non-taxable state lands to members of the royal dynasty or to higher officers and officials, and the continuation of – even expansion in – the corvée.

Thus the partial disentanglement between the state apparatus and the owning class (whose beginnings, emerging under Muhammad 'Ali, ushered in the route towards a capitalist society) was in many cases achieved via counteractive 'oriental' means, since it was the extended royal family, its entourage of Turko-Circassian officers and officials and its patronised allies of merchants of various Mediterranean ethnicities which were to form the nucleus of the new owning and business classes.

There is little doubt, politically speaking, that Muhammad 'Ali was the 'builder of the modern Egyptian state' in the sense of ensuring for the country a high degree of autonomy vis-à-vis the Ottoman Sultan (even indeed conquering parts of the Sultan's lands in Syria, Arabia, Sudan, Crete and part of Anatolia), and in the sense of giving rise to the idea of Egyptian-ness through the institution of the state [Al-Rafi'i, 1982: 561–2; Marsot, 1984: 262–4ff; Al-Bishri, 1980: 9]. In achieving this, Muhammad 'Ali had ridden the popular wave against the Ottoman/Mamluk rule that reached its peak in 1794–95, thus igniting the revolt which the Napoleonic expedition (1798–1801) tried unsuccessfully to exploit. Arriving in Egypt as an Ottoman officer in the same year (1794/5), Muhammad 'Ali managed to acquire authority on the basis of support from the 'ulama', the notables and the merchants against the Ottoman *wali*. This rebellion against the Ottoman viceroy resulted in a popular and pseudo-democratic act when the two popular leaders 'Umar Makram and 'Abdallah al-Sharqawi bestowed the Wali's mantle on Muhammad 'Ali in the official court. Muhammad 'Ali was selected as a *wali* in 1805 "under our own conditions", as the act of investiture affirmed ['Awad, 1969: 75, 119–23].

Muhammad 'Ali's methods in constructing the 'modern state' were a mixture of European-style organisational patterns and 'Oriental' practices. Although a modern-looking bureaucracy was built, Muhammad 'Ali's style of addressing his officials in formal correspondence was despotic and insulting ('swine' was one of the favoured epithets for officials who were found wanting!). If he inspected some of the state farms or factories and found what he considered was evidence of negligence by one of his high officials he would instruct that the offender be "beaten by a hundred strokes on his behind with the thick stick and exiled; if he returns he is to be crucified". The *Siyasat-nameh* law of 1837 was clear in stating that "public employees, senior and junior, will duly be given a disciplinary punishment if they fail to follow the laws and regulations, or if they do something that is contrary to human honour or to the *condition of servitude* (to the ruler)" [Al-Harawi, 1963: 268–74, my emphasis].

Despite the fact that Muhammad 'Ali's policies undoubtedly sowed the institutional seeds for the idea of 'Egyptian-ness', "the Egyptianness of Muhammad 'Ali's regime had its serious limitations". Although the army was greatly expanded and manned by peasants, its leadership remained largely confined to the Turco-Circassian ethnicities. And although industry was constructed and commerce was eventually extended, the Pasha relied heavily on European technocrats for the first and on minoritarian Mediterranean ethnicities for the second [Al-Bishri, 1980: 11; 'Awad, 1969: 92–4; Landes, 1985: 27–80; Barakat, 1982: 42–5].

Muhammad 'Ali thus gradually turned his back on the native bourgeois and popular forces that had brought him to power, preferring instead to rely on the familiar Turco-Circassian élite for matters related to the army and administration and on the European bourgeoisie for matters of commerce and transportation. Once the Pasha's monopoly system had been forcibly broken by the 1838 Anglo-Turkish treaty, we find him opening up the Egyptian economy increasingly to the world market and its privileges and to European import/export and finance houses with his contracts – a situation that reached dangerous levels and had many repercussions under his successors 'Abbas and Isma'il and that led eventually, among other factors, to the British occupation of Egypt in 1882 [Girgis, 1958: 36–48].

The defeat of Muhammad 'Ali's attempt at building an industrialised state in Egypt was to lead to the emergence of a typical case of a lop-sided economy centred around the production and export of cotton as a mono-crop [Farah, 1985: 49–61]. The expansion in irrigation, transport and communication projects made necessary by this type of specialisation was one of the main causes leading to the financial crisis that occurred under Isma'il (1863–79), and it was this crisis that made it easier for the capitalist powers of Europe, under the guise of supervising the repayment of the public debt, to force Egypt into handing over to European officers a great many of the sovereignty functions of the Egyptian state. This intervention was one of the main reasons behind the rise of the nationalist 'Urabi movement in 1881 which, in its turn, was the main event that prompted the British to move in and occupy the country in the following year.

The export-oriented mono-crop economy was consolidated under the British, creating with it some important social changes, of which the most significant was the emergence of a proper landowning class. This class was eventually to form the solid social base of a political system premised on a limited degree of constitutional government. The state increasingly represented the interests of such a 'landed aristocracy' by undertaking the major part of investment in irrigation and the agricultural infrastructure. In addition, the state also undertook to attend to a modern system of education (an activity that the British administration had done its best – not wholly successfully – to curtail). This allowed for the establishment of a fairly compact bureaucracy that was, legally and organisationally, relatively stable. This bureaucracy was, in turn, the base for the branching out of a 'new middle class' of officials and officers, professionals and technocrats, as well as of a small but intellectually and politically active intelligentsia.

The first major crisis to be faced by this export-oriented system followed Europe's great recessionary financial crisis in 1906–7. The repercussions of this crisis led to a substantial recession and to a serious deterioration in Egypt, and the after-effects, which continued to be felt more or less up to the eruption of the First World War, corresponded to the mainly middle-class agitation against the British that culminated in the 1919 revolution.

Although the main sources of support for the 1919 revolution were urban (the intelligentsia, the officials and clerks, etc.), some agricultural élites lent their support, hoping for a relatively more nationally based economic policy that could protect their interests from the vagaries and excesses of the world market. This nationalist symbiosis was also made possible because the native commercial and industrial capitalism had actually developed from within the agricultural aristocracy, representing a pattern of 'diversifying' investment rather than a basic contradiction in interests between two opposing classes [Al-Disuqi, 1981: 27 ff].

According to Louis 'Awad, the fact that Egyptian industry had emerged as part of a state capitalist project under Muhammad 'Ali, and its reliance on officials and officers who eventually turned to agricultural ownership, in the same way as the industrial workers were to turn to the services, meant that for a long time these two classes lacked any distinguishing features as autonomous classes. In his view, the result was a delay in the spread of ideas of democracy and political rights. The Egyptian bourgeoisie was not the real catalyst for democracy as was the case in Europe, but democracy was buttressed by the class of middle landowners and especially their professional offspring ['Awad, 1980, I: 353-4].

The state machine constructed by Muhammad 'Ali was reformulated by the British and the Khedive. The latter was made the formal head of the state and other leading politicians were selected to assist him from among the *dhawat* (well-off) class of Turco-Circassian background, through which the British dominated the workings of the top bureaucracy and especially its sensitive sectors such as finance, public works and agriculture, as well as the army and the police.

Increasingly, more and more positions within the bureaucracy were to be assumed by Egyptians. The official class had by now been unified linguistically and culturally (by absorbing the Turkish minority and including growing numbers of Copts). At the same time, the British had consolidated and regulated the system of private landownership that had started in an *ad hoc* way under Muhammad 'Ali. This landowning class was eventually to beget not only the higher official but also, in due course, the professional strata, of lawyers, accountants, doctors, etc. [cf. Al-Disuqi, 1975; Ramadan, 1981; Abdel-Malek, 1968; Berque, 1972]. The 'new' social classes sought to express their nationalism economically as well, through the formation of the Banque Misr economic conglomeration – but this nascent branch of the bourgeoisie was increasingly allying itself with 'Egyptianised-foreigner' (*mutamassir*) and foreign business communities, and subjecting itself to the caprices of the world capitalist market [Davis, 1983].

In such an environment, a limited degree of political pluralism was to emerge, as represented for example by the creation of political parties [cf. Rizq, 1977; Hilal, 1977; Al-Bishri, 1983; Ramadan, 1981; Vatikiotis, 1969; Deeb, 1979; Ayubi, 1989b]. The oldest of these was the Nationalist Party, established in 1907 under the popular leadership of Mustafa Kamil, although it was later to become a minority party obsessed with power. The party that exercised the most influence in Egyptian political life, however, was the Wafd. Formed in 1918 to negotiate with the British over independence, it played an important role in leading the 1919 nationalist revolution, and was instrumental in forging an impressive sense of unity between Muslims and Christians, and in developing a truly secularist concept of citizenship [Al-Bishri, 1980: 135-47; Ramadan, 1981: 39-40; Al-Fiqi, 1985]. The revolution led eventually to the formal independence of Egypt as a monarchy (with some important areas withheld) in 1922 and the promulgation in 1923 of a constitution largely modelled on that of Switzerland.

The Wafd had a relatively broad social base of support represented by the intelligentsia, civil servants and clerks, professionals, merchants and some workers and farmers. It played an important role in opposing both the presence of the British and the power of the Palace, and when in power, introduced a number of significant reforms in the field of education and employment, and extended useful projects in such areas as credit facilities and social services. Yet the Wafd was too weak to challenge the British openly; indeed it accepted British support against the Palace in making its return to power in 1942. For its part, the Palace had its own supportive parties (such as Al-Ittihad, formed in 1925, and Al-Sha'b formed in 1930), which took a certain role in forming coalition governments and, more generally, in playing the political games of manoeuvre that were being conducted the whole time among the British, the Wafd and the Palace. However, the Wafd was increasingly becoming more attuned to the interests of a landowning class that was continuing to extend its activities into commerce and to ally itself with new industrialists who had close links with international capital. The Wafd thus represented a kind of 'unfulfilled promise', nor could it ever hold on to power to the same extent that, for example, the Congress party in India had done – it was outside government for longer than it was inside.

The Wafd was not organisationally solid either: it suffered several splits and breakaway groups, some of which were fairly detrimental to its overall popularity (such offshoots gave rise to the Liberal Constitutionalists in 1922, which represented the conservative wing of the Wafd and supported the landowners and the bourgeois classes; to the Sa'dist Assembly in 1938, composed of elements that were out of favour with Nahhas; and to the Wafdist Bloc in 1942, in which supporters of Makram 'Ubaid were involved). It remained heavily dependent on the personal leadership of Sa'd Zaghlul, Mustafa al-Nahhas and, to some extent, Makram 'Ubaid, and it indulged in a system of bureaucratic 'spoils' to reward its supporters whenever it came to power.

The gradual decline in the popular representativeness of the Wafd and the apparent impossibility of ameliorating political and social matters increased the growing importance of extra-parliamentary political organisations, namely the pseudo-Fascist Misr al-Fatat (1923), the religious and 'fundamentalist' Muslim Brothers (1927), and the small Marxist organisations (including initially the Communist Party in 1922 but subsequently several others, the most notable of which was HADETU – the Democratic Movement for National Liberation, 1947) [for details see Al-Bishri, 1983; Vatikiotis, 1969].

Such extra-parliamentary political and intellectual trends revolved around three important influences: Islamist, populist and *étatiste*. The 1952 revolution (ushered in by the Free Officers' military coup) represented in many respects a blend of the latter two, without being hostile to the first of these influences. Thus the 1952 revolution 'interpellated' a following from among various classes and orientations. Its alliance with the Islamists was, however, severed in 1954;

and the conflict between the populist and the *étatiste* components of its strategy
was to plague its fortunes for many decades to come.

STATE FORMATION IN THE LEVANT

The 'mosaic' image of the Middle East is out of favour nowadays, having
come to be regarded rather as an Orientalist distortion (and/or Zionist wishful
thinking) [cf. Turner, 1978: Ch. 3]. But if this image has any validity at all,
then it must be the Levant, or the Arab East – Al-Mashriq – where it can be
applied with the least difficulty. Even the pan-Arabist Centre for Arab Unity
Studies, while preparing for its large research project on the future of Society
and state, gave serious consideration to the use of the term 'the mosaic state'
(*al-dawla al-fusaifisa'iyya*) to describe the ethnically and religiously plural polities
of the Arab East [cf. Ibrahim, *mimeo*, 1984: 43–6].

If the Levantine region is taken as a whole, the mosaic image is not an
accurate one. The majority of the population is Sunni Arab. Historically
Sunnism, the state, and the city went hand in hand: the non-Sunni Muslim
sects had not reconciled themselves to the state and continued to have their
own distinct 'political economies' and 'cultural spaces'. The non-Muslim
religious minorities – although more prepared to adjust themselves to the
logic of the state – were increasingly enjoying separate social and cultural
lives under the *milla* (*millet*) system [cf. Al-Khuri, 1988]. Yet this 'state' with
which the Sunni Arab majority had been associated was the 'Islamic' state
whose last symbolic head was the Ottoman Caliph/Sultan. When the caliphate
was abolished in Turkey in 1924, the predominantly Sunni-Arab notables of
the Mashriq were disconcerted, as they were not psychologically prepared for
the event. Territorially divided under European colonialism, it was often the
rurally based and ethnically minoritarian groups that were eventually to
become more capable of acting upon the new, changing realities which were
to follow the formal independence of these countries inside their 'artificially'
created borders.

State formation in the Arab East, therefore, was not the outcome of an
integrative social process emanating 'from within', but was largely the result
of a disintegrative political process imposed 'from without'. Waddah Sharara
is accordingly absolutely correct in implying that the state model more appropriate for understanding the Mashriq is not the French (Napoleonic) state
model, but rather the Austrian (Metternich) state model [Sharara, 1981b: 309–
40 ff]. The Ottoman Empire was indeed an Austrian-type state which, if
anything, was even more heterogeneous and disparate than its prototype, and
its legacy in the Arab East is of a very distinct nature.

In the 'Napoleonic' model, the state comes forth out of an organic, internal
process of social and cultural integration, subsequently moving towards political centralisation, legal standardisation, equality of citizenship, and sovereignty

for the people. It thus emerges as a relatively autonomous entity that represents (and harmonises) the entire society, not only the victorious bourgeoisie. In the Austrian model, by contrast, the state is merely an arbiter among conflicting groups. It does not integrate or harmonise, but simply tries to neutralise classes, nationalities and ethnicities. This is done not in an 'organic' way that leads to the emergence of a 'nation', but through the instruments of central rule such as the army and the bureaucracy. The state rulers through pacifying the communities or balancing them (turning them) against each other. In a passage that is strongly suggestive of Lebanon, Sharara maintains that such an Austrian state can only result in

> a confinement of the bourgeoisie to one nationality rather than the others ... the multiplication of exploitation; a correspondence between civil war and external war; [and] a deep cultural disjunction so that the culture of the dominant side joins up with the superior European currents, whereas the culture of the dependent sides retreats into the cocoon of a historical and linguistic heritage whose prime function is to proclaim its difference [Sharara, 1981b: 342–4].

The Levantine state thus excludes important parts of the social experience of its society, not by transforming them into a more homogenous and 'transparent' political space but by coercively separating and isolating them; by abridging society into the state. The state is thus 'anti-society': it isolates the society, then sits in the social emptiness and dominates [Sharara, 1981b: 104–12]. As the inheritor of the 'Asiatic' tradition of autonomous, juxtapositional communities, the contemporary Mashriqi state is also based not on integrated, but rather on parallel, social entities. Government itself is based on blocs and alliances that join together groups which retain all their specific characteristics as they move to power, and indeed transmit these characteristics to that power. There is no social unification but an 'external' assembly that cannot hide the continued marginality of the ruling groups [ibid.: 227–9]. The group in power has no structural autonomy from the society but continues, while in government, to represent in a 'literal' sense the society from which it derives; its assumption of rule does not take the group out of its particularity but rather sustains this peculiarity by feeding/supplying it with the resources of central government. Nor would such a group permit any degree of opposition, however partial, for the alternative to its dominance is not rule under a different programme but rule under an alternative group which will take over power and do the same thing.

If one considers the situation historically it is possible therefore to say that the Ottoman state was an exaggerated and distinct example of the 'Austrian state model'. In as much as it was meant to represent an Islamic state, it had acted for the largely urban Sunni notables of the Arab East as the focal point for their political allegiance. Although they might have been less privileged than ethnic Turks in the centre, the Ottoman state had guaranteed the suprem-

acy of the Sunni Muslim Arabs over other communities within the Mashriq.
The fall of the Ottoman Caliphate, combined with the European colonial
division of the Arab East has left most of the urban Sunni Arab notables
confused and perplexed. Rural and minoritarian communities were apparently
more agile at perceiving the changes and at making the best social and political
use of them. As Ghassan Salama puts it:

> Whereas most of the body-politic in the Near East, which was largely urban,
> had been slow to understand what had happened to it with the fall of the
> Ottoman Empire, rural groups that had previously been isolated from the prac-
> tice of politics knew how to benefit from the emergence of the modern States in
> order to climb the social ladder and to strengthen their political position to enable
> them subsequently to take over the State. These communities have had to learn
> quickly that the partition of the Arab East into a number of entities was not
> casual, and that the return of the Ottoman or any other unifying state was not
> realistically on the horizon under the existing international order. They have
> also understood that the city is the gate to power, so they have entered it for
> education and enrichment (via the modern tools of integration created by the
> State: especially the school, the barracks and the administration, followed by the
> parties). They have not however entered the cities as mere individuals, but rather
> have preserved their previous loyalties – without making them obvious... And
> they competed over the leading role ... until the most suitable or ambitious
> among them was to reach power [Salama, 1987a: 23].

Once they reach power these groups want to run the state like an obedient,
efficient machine, but – and here Salama agrees with Sharara – one of their
main tasks is usually "to hide the identity of he who drives it" [ibid.: 24].

Another distinctive feature of state formation in the Arab East is the more
obviously arbitrary nature of its current borders, resulting as they did from
acts of conflict, competition and bargaining between Britain and France and
between these two on the one hand and the fading Ottoman state on the
other. This is probably responsible for the fact that the Pan-Arabist doctrine
has emerged and thrived in this region and that there is a distinctive Levantine
(*shami*) perception of Arab nationalism that is far more suspicious of the existing
territorial state than in, say, Egypt or North Africa.

What is the background to the existing states of the Arab East?

Iraq

The concept of Iraq is a relatively new one, although it does of course have
weighty historical antecedents. Mesopotamia was sometimes a distinct entity
(e.g. in the Sumerian era 3500–2500 BC) and it certainly had a long political
history in one shape or another under the Akkadians, Assyrians, Babylonians,
and of course the Arabs (from AD 637 but especially after AD 749, when
Baghdad became the capital of the Islamic Caliphate). The territorial integrity

of the country has always been under threat, however, and strong influences/ pressures from its powerful Persian neighbours have always been a constant source of anxiety in pre- as well as post-Islamic times. Controversial too has been the modern inclusion of the Mosul region: although its capital Ninevah was the centre of the Assyrian state, Mosul has had strong links with, and has been claimed by, both the Turks and the Syrians. The nearest precedent to modern Iraq is perhaps the region ruled by the Georgian Mamluks (1749 - 1831) within the Ottoman Empire.

The current territory of the state, shaped, as some modern Iraqis comment, in the form of a long palm tree, was in many ways the result of an agreement in interest between the British and the rulers of Iraq, at a time of British competition with France (which dominated Syria), dissolution of the Ottoman Empire, and vagueness over the likely future of Iran. Britain wanted a formally autonomous but politically affiliated country, a situation which was sanctioned by the treaty of 1922 between the two countries, appointing as its head the Arabian prince Faisal, whose Syrian days were numbered because of France's intervention. State-building was accelerated via two main mechanisms: the largely urban Sunni élite (administrative and military) became involved in the process of institution-building and absentee landownership, and the British strengthened the petroleum capabilities of Iraq, both technically and organisationally, and also vis-à-vis the oil companies. The Hashemite monarchy and its supporters continued, however, to walk a tightrope between their British allies on the one hand, and the increasingly anti-colonial forces among the Iraqi population on the other [Salama, 1987a: 31-6]. The social formation too was increasingly finding its base not in pastoralism and trade, but in land ownership (introduced after 1914 through the British consolidating land titles for shaikhs and aghas) [cf. Batatu, 1982: 87ff], and more and more in oil rent. The perspective became ever more inward-looking and, in spite of some claims for regional secession (especially in the 1920s) and various tribal uprisings against the forcible transformations in the mode of production (especially in the 1930s), the political rhetoric was becoming progressively more concerned with one Iraqi people and one Iraqi state, although reference to 'Arab brotherhood' was sometimes to be heard.

When the monarchy was abolished and the republic declared in 1958, more talk about Arab nationalism was often heard, but the new military leader, Qasim, was able to keep the Pan-Arabist tide – advancing in the form of Egypt's union with Syria as the United Arab Republic in 1958-61 – at bay. Nor did the 'Arifs or their successors in power go for unity with other Arab countries in spite of the negotiations with Egypt and Syria for that purpose in 1963. Even the presumably Pan-Arabist Ba'thists also preserved the Iraqi identity and resorted to a symbolism that contained a mixture of Ancient Mesopotamian and Arab nationalist elements. Saddam Husain carried the line further, using both the Mesopotamian era of Nebuchadnezzar and the

Islamic battle of Qadisiyya as connective symbolic reference points in his nationalist discourse.

The ethnically pluralistic composition of the population has continued, however, to represent a sign of fragility and a source of apprehension. Not only did the (non-Arab) Kurds of the north represent a sizeable portion (some 20 per cent) of the total population, but the Arab population of Iraq was also religiously divided by sect, which thus rendered the Sunni-Arab community a definite minority within the country.

The Sunni-Shi'i dichotomy has been geographical (the former in the middle and north, the latter in the south), but it also overlapped until the inter-war period with class divisions [cf. Ayubi, 1992c and refs cited]. Thus the most influential landlords of the province of Basrah were Sunnis while the cultivators of their palm groves were overwhelmingly Shi'i. Sunnis were also highly represented among the affluent landowners or merchants of all other southern areas except for the Shi'i holy cities of Najaf and Karbala. In Baghdad too, where the two sects enjoyed almost numerical parity, the socially dominant families were, with some exceptions, Sunni. And in the Iraqi army of the 1930s the officers were Sunni but the rank and file was mostly Shi'i [Batatu, 1982: 44–5]. The Shi'i south had for a long time been more culturally and economically tied to Iran, whereas the Sunni north had been more culturally and economically tied to Syria and Turkey. From the inter-war period, and especially after the Second World War, the Shi'is went through a period of accelerated social mobility, not least in the matter of wealth which they managed to accumulate through commerce. The Sunnis, however, continued to be more preponderant in holding state offices, both civilian and military [Batatu, 1982: 47–9].

The conventional view on the position of the Shi'is in Iraq maintains that the traditional supremacy of the Sunnis, inherited from Ottoman and pre-Ottoman times, has been continued in independent Iraq, royal and republican. Because the Shi'is were politically disenfranchised, runs the conventional argument, they have come to represent on the whole an 'oppositional' community. While Sunnis have identified with Arab nationalism (the other Arab states being predominantly Sunni), those Shi'is who have adopted modern political ideologies have tended towards leftist orientations, notably the Communist Party. Yet as Sami Zubaida rightly illustrates, the political organisations of the Shi'is are diverse, and this diversity is as much the product of political institutions and processes and of class and economic factors as it is of communal solidarity [Zubaida, 1989: 63ff]. Under the monarchy, southern Shi'i shaikh-landlords were a predominant part of the political establishment. Different factions of the 'ulama' had different associates: peasants and merchants, conservatives and progressives, domestic patrons and foreign agencies. In due course, Nasserism and Ba'thism did attract many Shi'is. Equally, at various points in its history, the Communist Party included many Sunni Arabs in its leadership. The presence of the Shi'is was notable, but their numerical representation was no higher, and was perhaps even a little lower, than their representation in the population at large. The remarkable fact about Iraqi Shi'is is the extent to which they have been predominant in politics generally: rather than saying that they have a propensity towards communism, it would be more accurate to say that they have a propensity for politics. And the directions in which this propensity is expressed change often, with yet another shift occurring after the Iranian revolution which has politicised the Iraqi Shi'is even further [Zubaida, 1989: 63–6; cf. also Al-Shaikh, 1988a: 60–67].

It is also important to note that the recent 'politicisation' of Shi'is under the impact of the Iranian revolution has taken different forms, depending on the distinct political conjunctures pertaining in various Arab countries. The contrast between Iraq and Lebanon is illustrative in this regard, refuting as it does the claim that communal entities have a permanent, essentialist character. In spite of their exclusion from authority and in spite of the opportunity for rebellion provided for them by the prolonged Iran–Iraq war (the majority of the soldiers being Shi'is), the Iraqi Shi'is have not opted for a purely 'Shi'i' solution (e.g. through secession or segregation), or even for a separate political organisation for their community: exclusively Shi'i political parties have always been weak, from the Nahda party in the 1920s to the Da'wa party in the 1980s. The Shi'a of Lebanon, on the other hand, have either accepted the 'confessional' framework of Lebanon and tried to enlarge their share within its confines *as a community* (Amal), or else have rebelled against the entire territorial-state paradigm and declared their identification with the Islamic revolution of Iran, claiming that religion has no geography (Hizbullah) [Salama, 1987a: 85–98].

This newly-acquired sense of Iraqi unity had certainly withstood the challenge of the Iran–Iraq war, in spite of the majority of the Iraqi soldiers belonging to the same sect as that of the leaders of the Islamic revolution in Iran. By the end of the war, however, there were fewer Shi'is in prominent political positions than before it. In fact, it was mainly the 1990/91 crisis with the devastating destruction of the country's infrastructure and the imposition of embargoes and security zones on Iraq that seems to have revived a distinct sense of ethnicity and of the Sunni–Shi'i divide in the land.

Geographic Syria and its successors

'Natural Syria', 'Greater Syria' or *Bilad al-Sham* was the area affected most by the disintegration of the Ottoman Empire and the European colonial scramble over territory and influence in the Near East. At the beginning of the nineteenth century this region was organised into four Ottoman provinces, each embracing a major city: Damascus (including Transjordan and eastern Palestine), Aleppo (including Alexandretta), Tripoli, and Acre (later, in 1887–

88, Jerusalem became the centre of a new Sanjaq and Beirut was made a separate *wilaya*). These provinces were unified briefly, for less than a decade, under the Egyptian rule of Ibrahim Pasha, before the Ottomans' return in 1841.

The dismemberment of Greater Syria was mainly the outcome of colonial policies. The Sykes–Picot Agreement of 1916 between Britain and France separated Lebanon, Jordan and Palestine from it, and the Balfour Declaration of 1917 ushered in the formal Judaisation of the latter. Not only this, but these 'countries' were now ruled by different (quarrelling) colonial powers. The State of Syria as it is known today is in some ways no more than a 'residual state' of whatever was left of the previous 'natural Syria' after many of the peripheral areas had gone their own way [Salama, 1987a: 59ff].

Nowhere was this 'artificiality' of entities more obvious than in the case of Transjordan, a 'corridor' country without a distinct history, or focal point, or even a native royal family. Given the poverty of resources of the new kingdom, Britain was not only its creator and the protector of its king, but to a large extent its financier and the commander of its armed forces. Increasingly, however, the king had reluctantly to accept that provincial Amman was not a stop on the way to greater Syria. Borders to the east (with Syria) and to the south (with the Hijaz) became more fixed. Also, as in Iraq, a social base for the state was being formed by (a) promoting the private ownership of land and creating thus both a 'landed aristocracy' of the ex-tribal shaikhs and a settled semi-agricultural community of ex-nomads that was pinned down to the land; and (b) promoting an indigenous élite of officials and dignitaries to replace the 'multi'-Arab élite that surrounded the Hashemite kings when they first arrived [Robins, 1988]. Tribals represented a particularly important component in the formation of the army [Jureidini and McLaurin, 1984]. However, the process of Jordanisation could not ultimately be as thorough as that of Iraq-isation: Syrian merchants continued to be prominent in Amman's marketplace for several decades, and the West Bank of the Jordan (Eastern Palestine) was to be annexed after the 1948 war (resulting in the creation of Israel), thus bringing in a large farming community with an important élite of merchants and 'intellectuals'. The West Bank was subsequently occupied by Israel in 1967, but many Palestinians departed to live in Jordan, thus forming nearly half its population. Since then the Jordanian state has continued to be vulnerable since most Palestinians did not accept it as 'home', while many Israelis wanted to turn it into the (only) state for the Palestinians.

The separation of a distinct Lebanese state was equally arbitrary but perhaps less artificial. Mount Lebanon, a small geographic zone that was gradually extended to include all Maronite and Druze areas, was converted by France into a greater Lebanon in 1920, through the annexation of the (mainly Sunni and Shi'i) coastal towns, Jabal 'Amil and the Biqa' Valley according to a system of deliberate privilege for the Maronite Christians. From the beginning therefore the political entity and the governmental system (or else the state and the Regime) were considered inseparable [compare Salama, 1987a: 53].

Historically Mount Lebanon has indeed had a distinct cultural history and a distinct 'political economy' of its own. Some maintain that social organisation in Mount Lebanon between the sixteenth and nineteenth centuries was exceptional within the Levant in being remarkably similar to a European-type 'feudal' system [cf. Dubar and Nasr, 1976: Ch. 2 and refs cited]. In addition, the Maronites were almost unique among the non-Muslim religious minorities in the Middle East in their resistance to the *dhimmi* status, an attitude that eventually culminated in their refusal to join the *millet* council organised by the Ottomans in the nineteenth century. Such an attitude, derived as it is from their distinctive history as well as their collective mythology, makes them different from other religious minorities – to the extent that Fu'ad Khuri classifies them, functionally speaking, among the sects (*tawa'if*) and not among the minorities (*aqaliyyat*) [Al-Khuri, 1988: 13, 109]. Like sects, the Maronites have historically inhabited the mountain and developed their own semi-autonomous 'political economy'. Their sense of distinctiveness has been reinforced by the fact that they probably originated as a tribe rather than as a Church. Indeed their bishops were conventionally representatives of the sub-lineages of the tribes and not of various geographic parishes, as is the case with other churches, Eastern and Western [Salama, 1987a: 109, n.28 and ref. cited].

Although the Maronites emerged as one of the Eastern Churches, they started to establish contacts with Rome from AD 1215, thus eventually becoming followers of the Catholic Papacy, although still culturally and organisationally distinct. Their conception of the self is premised on a vision of a long history of struggle against all odds, in which the distinct religious rite (established by St Maron) always converges with images about a glorious Phoenician past. The myth particularly emphasises a collective emigration to Mount Lebanon from various parts of Syria and Iraq under persecution from the year AD 671 onwards. The stress is always on distinctiveness, perseverance and resistance to assimilation. Their later association with the Catholic Church during the time of the Crusades helped in reorganising the church and in strengthening the monastic orders, which have since played a major role in developing the distinct 'Maronite ideology' [cf. Harik, 1987: 31–3; also Harik, 1968].

The distinctive Maronite personality was stressed through an extensive school network as well as a relatively prosperous political economy of intensive agriculture and silk production. This 'economic base' was instrumental in giving rise to the Ma'ni and the Shihabi emirates from the seventeenth to the nineteenth century, and in enabling the Maronites to maintain a high degree of autonomy under the Ottomans and later of course under the French. This opening to the West, facilitated by the Vatican connection, the spread of education and publishing, and their extensive migration throughout the world since the mid-nineteenth century, has reinforced their self-image of their Phoenician, trading origins. Thus the sense of being Maronite and the sense of being Lebanese have developed hand in hand, the whole time strengthening each other – Lebanon is claimed to be the Biblical paradise of Eden, Noah "is Lebanese", Christ "came to Lebanon" to spread Christianity to the World, and the Cedar of Lebanon is the "Cedar of God" [Al-Khuri, 1988: 202–8, and refs cited].

According to Ghassan Salama, the term 'Mount Lebanon' did not have the same political connotation that it has today until the end of the eighteenth century, whereas 'Lebanon' as a political concept did not surface until the creation in 1861 of a Lebanese *mutasarrifiyya* (province) under Ottoman sovereignty, that was accepted by France, Britain, Russia, Austria and Prussia. It goes without saying, however, that Lebanese nationalists such as those of the pseudo-Fascist Kata'ib party (Phalange Libanaise) would prefer to trace the roots of an autonomous Lebanese identity much deeper into history. The whole issue was only to come into consideration again under the impact of the Syrian national movement against the French when, in 1937, the nationalists asked for Lebanon 'to be treated like Syria' in the event of independence.

In the meantime, most of the Sunni notables of Tripoli and the North were becoming increasingly reconciled to the new entity, especially as they were in reality let down by the Syrian National Bloc. From the 1940s on, they would increasingly benefit from the expanding Lebanese market, by calling in part on their family and commercial ties with Syria. Many of them (and many of the equally urban Greek Orthodox Christians) were to be attracted to the ideas and the political parties of Arab nationalism, and most supported the United Arab Republic of Egypt/Syria in 1958. Others, however, remained attached to a concept of a 'natural Syria', as for example in the case of the Syrian National Social Party, and would call for a unified Fertile Crescent (with the addition, sometimes, of Cyprus as its star!).

The Syria that we know today is in some sense a 'residual entity'; it is the Syria of what is left after all such acts of dismemberment. Even then there were still calls to be heard, both native and colonial, for dividing what is left of Syria even further: for example into Damascene, Aleppan, Druze and Alawite regions. The main Sunni trend, however, as expressed in the Arab Independence Party, the Syrian Union Party and the National Bloc, was for unity and against division. Other political parties opted for a pan-Arabist position: e.g. the League of National Action, the Arab Ba'th Party, and the Arab Nationalist Party.

The mainstream nationalist élite had developed new economic and professional interests within its new, compact entity, and had also come to understand that the price of ending the French mandate and acquiring Syrian independence was to accept the existing new borders. By way of reaction, however, many Syrians later tried to compensate for the failure of Syrian unity, and rushed into a more comprehensive concept of the 'Arab Nation' through "escaping forwards in a process of Utopia-making" [Salama, 1987a: 61–3].

However, the main practical objective after independence, and given the challenges all around Syria (Alexandretta lost to Turkey, Israel strengthening, Jordan surviving and Lebanon enriching), was not about how to restore unity but about how to preserve what was left of Syria intact.

STATE FORMATION IN NORTH AFRICA

The origins of state formation in North Africa can historically be traced back to the emergence of power centres capable of enforcing their authority on the adjacent rural centres and tribal confederations, a process the cyclical background of which was well described by Ibn Khaldun.

It has been suggested that from quite early on (i.e. from the eighth to the tenth centuries and beyond) the process had produced three distinct hubs for governmental networks, one in the middle that corresponded to the Tahirt imamate (today's Algeria), another in the East that corresponded to the Fatimid state (Zaidiyya and Hamadiyya – today's Tunisia) and a third associated with the Mohads' empire corresponding to today's Morocco [cf. Jaghlul, 1987: 209ff]. The two latter regions have usually had a distinct governmental capital for most of the time (Al-Qayrawan and Fez respectively). Early state formation was characterised by concentric circles. First there was *bilad al-makhzan*, literally terrain belonging to the Treasury (i.e. the state). Surrounding this nucleus there was usually an intermediate circle inhabited by tribes which were subject to the central authority via some local leaders appointed or confirmed by the centre, and from which taxes were extracted. A third peripheral area, with ambiguous boundaries, was then inhabited by other tribes that were not subject to the state's authority, which indeed often threatened the power of the centre and from time to time even grabbed power from the existing rulers to establish another dynasty – this unruly terrain was traditionally known as the 'loose country' (*bilad al-sibah*).

As we have observed about the tribal mode of production, it is not only the conflictual relations between nomad and town that should be emphasised but also the functional cultural and economic interrelationships that bind the whole system together. For all it was tenuous and shifting, there was a certain element of equilibrium there, that was induced by a sense of cultural and to some extent social unity, and heightened at certain times by external threats. Thus while the élite changed and alternated, some political 'centre' was usually there. This 'centre', according to 'Abd al-Baqi al-Hirmasi [1987: Ch. 1], was capable of moving towards a more stable state form in the nineteenth century, when it could recruit a regular army instead of relying on the separate tribes, and when the aspects of power were pinned down through land ownership and administrative institutions, a process that was further strengthened by colonial rule. This traditional polity, however, was never based on a 'feudal' pattern in the European, or Japanese sense. For even though the *makhzan* tribes were increasingly allotted certain lands in return for their military services to the state, there was no fixed hierarchical pattern, nor acknowledged rights for the populace. Thus the rise of intermediary leaderships was not a sign of the emergence of a feudal society but rather signified the process of forcible unification by the *makhzan* who recruited the local leaders mainly as individuals at the expense of their tribal base. This last process proved to be more successful in Morocco and Tunisia than it was in Algeria where the colonial impact was earlier and more profound. But all three countries were of course eventually to fall under the full yoke of French colonial rule.

Lisa Anderson argues along similar lines and observes that state formation in societies where kinship was a prominent mode of social organisation often initially entails the creation of a peasantry [Anderson, 1986: 28ff]. Such a process of 'peasantisation' draws the rural population into closer supervision by the state, via patrons who act as intermediaries between the two. The 'clients' become more easily exploited and more dependent than they had been before the extension of the bureaucratic state apparatus. This process produces a class of rural power-holders, whose access to the agricultural surplus of the peasantry makes them among the most important allies of the élite that controls the state. This class of rural power-holders is in large measure a creature of the state and therefore bears little resemblance to the independent landed aristocracy of pre-capitalist Europe. It is allied to the state from the outset and indeed the ability of the patrons to reward and coerce their clients through intervention with the state authorities depends very much upon the stability of the bureaucracy [ibid.: 29–30]. Eventually powerful tribal leaders and rural patrons are identified and transformed into government functionaries, thus further consolidating the state bureaucracy (*al-makhzan*) at the expense of the open, loose terrain (*al-siba*).

A new pattern of authority emerged during the eighteenth century when the Ottomans recognised the establishment of relatively stable local political dynasties in the countries of the Maghrib, apart from Morocco. A principal cause of dispute between the Ottomans and local governments was the activities of the Barbary corsairs who operated out of Maghribi ports. One of the results of limiting corsair activity effectively reduced the incomes of the Maghribi states, thereby bringing about a financial crisis, especially in Algeria [Yapp, 1987: 158–9].

The details of the process of dealing with their fiscal difficulties varied from one country to another [Al-Hirmasi, 1987: Ch. 1]. Thus in Algeria the state's revenues from agriculture were limited, and so it increased general taxes and its monopoly on trade and struck contracts with foreign companies to exploit the country's mineral resources. In Tunisia the economic situation was not much better and here too the government endeavoured to monopolise trade, but the state also indulged in important reforms in administration, the army and education, with significant foreign 'assistance'. In Morocco, where the rulers always strove to stand in the face of external interference, fiscal reforms also became necessary and by 1901 the Sultan had to change the previous *shari'a*-based taxation system into a unified one in order to improve the budget. This revised system included the local notables for the first time, which resulted in revolts, and the Sultan was obliged to ask the French to rescue his throne.

Under colonialism the processes favoured were for more power for the state within borders more or less defined by the dynastic polities of the sixteenth and seventeenth centuries and for less tribal 'segmentation' among the population [Al-Hirmasi, 1987: 23ff], except that in the case of Algeria the whole indigenous demographic structure was more or less to be destroyed.

Tunisia

Given the decay of its tribal solidarities and the weakness of its intermediary (shaikhly) leaderships, Tunisia was perhaps the most integrated and centralised of the Maghrib countries. This, in addition to a higher exposure to external influences, not only European but also Ottoman and Egyptian, had paved the way for the important reforms that were eventually introduced in the nineteenth century by Khair al-Din and that were aimed largely at rationalising the state apparatus [Al-Hirmasi, 1987: 31ff]. Tunisia also had a distinct and compact political history for a considerable length of time. The Husaini dynasty had become established as *beys* in 1710 (and continued to rule until 1957). Early in the nineteenth century, under Ahmad Bey al-Husaini, a modernising, centralising attempt similar to that of Muhammad 'Ali in Egypt was undertaken but with only very limited success. The state continued with the policy of pacifying the tribal areas and co-opting the heads of towns and tribes [Al-Nayfar, 1992: 32–6]. Under Ahmad's successors, Tunis slid deeper into economic trouble, suffered a rebellion in 1864, went bankrupt in 1869 and was obliged to accept British, French and Italian representatives to superintend the state finances. Under European pressure too, the country was to issue constitutional reforms in 1857 and 1861 and to promulgate the "first Constitution in the Near East" [Yapp, 1987: 160]. The country was occupied by France in 1881 and there were significant attempts at reform by Khair al-Din. French administration was strong, with a distinct programme for economic development and modernisation involving the establishment of a fairly large number of settlers [Yapp, 1987: 245–6].

In general French policies under the protectorate system had worked to strengthen the state. A standing army was completed, the administration was modernised and rationalised, and agriculture was developed on a more

rigorously legalised system of land ownership. Under French control the Tunisian state consolidated its near monopoly of the use of force and extended the
central government's policing and recruitment powers. The central administration became more elaborate and the government endeavoured to create and
protect a real estate market, thus making it clear that state formation was
consistent with commercialisation of the economy [Anderson, 1986: 141–57].
State formation entailed 'peasantisation'. The rural élite was "a creation and
creature of the bureaucratic state, which claimed it both as an ally and, more
importantly, as a subordinate". The Tunisian case thus illustrates the "significance of the existence of the bureaucratic State in creating, rather than simply
reflecting, social structures" [ibid.: 277–9].

The Tunisian national movement was eventually to attach itself strictly to
its territorial state. Its leadership, which quite unmistakeably went to the Neo-
Destour party (formed in 1920), managed gradually to shift political eminence
away from the big urban families (baladi) and increasingly in favour of a new
élite of bureaucrats, teachers and professionals. These were mostly of petty
bourgeois background, had a mainly European, but also some traditional,
education, and hailed from an urban and small town environment [cf. Larif-
Beatrix, 1987: 129–41; Al-Hirmasi, 1987: 39–76]. Their concept of the state
was heavily influenced by the French model.[3] Their post-independence polity
was based on a fairly mobilisational system, led by the party and the 'boss',
that managed to incorporate the trade unions and many other organisations,
and which continued and consolidated the process of state-building in Tunisia
under the hegemony of the one dominant party.

Morocco

In the case of Morocco, a political community has existed for over 800 years
even if the borders of the state remained fluid for centuries and the capital
city changed depending on the changing weight of various regions and various
networks of external relations. Even to this day the borders of Morocco are
perhaps the most 'controversial' in North Africa [Shafir, 1988: 35–43]. This
was the country of the makhzan/siba dichotomy par excellence, and territories
changed their status from time to time and especially after the death of each
monarch, when a more widespread siba (insolence or dissidence) customarily
took place. Under the still ruling 'Alawi dynasty which emerged in the seventeenth century (and which is thus one of the oldest in the world) the institution
of the sultanate was given more substance around the core territories of
Meknes, Fez and Marrakesh and was expanded by the Sultan Mawlai Isma'il
(1672–1727). The makhzan was centred around armed forces based on four
major tribes, and the white-slave battalions were replaced with black-slave
ones.

The legitimacy of the dynasty has been based on the twin pillars of claimed

Sharifian ancestry (Arabian origin related to Prophet Muhammad via his daughter Fatima and his cousin 'Ali) and of 'uterine' relationships to people of the land through the custom of the monarch always marrying a Berber wife. The Sharifian Sultanate is thus based on a synthesis of religious authority and 'blessing' (baraka) combined with blood or racial bonds (jus sanguinus) [Darif, 1988]. This combination gives the monarch, as symbol of the state, the appearance of neutrality from and superiority over the 'asabiyya of any single tribe or the potency of any local saint in a remote regional zawiya [Agnush, 1987].[4] The 'Alawid monarchy is also steeped in rituals and 'sacred performances', many of them blood-related, thus entrenching the definition of rule within the definition of life and ultimate hope. For a long time this made for a 'strong nation' but 'weak apparatus' – which was, however, compensated for under French colonial rule (formalised in 1912) that kept the Sultan but trimmed his power and enlarged the administrative institutions around him. According to M. Combs-Schilling: "For centuries, the monarchy had been replete with meaning but weak in apparatus; the French colonial government had been replete with apparatus but weak in meaning. Post-colonial Morocco combined them" [Combs-Schilling, 1989: xii, 292 et passim].

From the 1930s the makhzan maintained fairly cooperative relations with the main branch of the independence movement represented by Al-Istiqlal party, which was founded in the 1930s by the mildly Islamic 'Allal al-Fasi. King Muhammad V refused to go along with all French demands and was certainly opposed to the Berber Decree (al-Zahir al-Barbari) of 1930 which tried to exclude the Berbers from the application of Islamically based national laws. The French decision to deport Muhammad in 1953 was equally ill advised and turned him into a national hero who triumphantly returned to his independent country in 1956. From then on the king would cooperate with Al-Istiqlal but without giving it a monopoly of nationalist representation, while consolidating his direct alliance with the rural notables. He gradually merged the institutions of the traditional makhzan with modern European-style administrative institutions [cf. BuRaqiyya, 1991]. While maintaining a fair degree of autonomy for (tribal) local community leaders and their 'teams', new territorially and economically based local units were designed and a modern cabinet, headed by a prime minister, was established.

By allowing internal divisions within the Istiqlal party to work their way within the party while marginalising (but not actually prohibiting) all political parties emanating from the independence movement, the state was reformulated into a mix of monarchical and traditional, pre-capitalist social structures that permitted only a small margin of movement for 'modern'-type organisations such as parties, unions and associations [Al-Zaghal, 1992: 456–8]. The king is of course the constitutional monarch, but over and above that he is the Commander of the Faithful (amir al-mu'minin), and the Arbiter among the state's groups and institutions. He is not subject to the law, he may 'intervene' with any political function, and whatever political rights do exist are only his gift. As he stated when addressing the parliamentary deputies in 1963: "I shall bestow upon you part of the powers that have been with the ruling family for twelve centuries ... I have made the Constitution by my very hands, and it has not given the deputies any powers, only obligations" [cf. Darif, 1991: 203–12]. By relying on three distinct sources of legitimacy, the monarchy seems to have achieved a fair degree of hegemony, and a distinct ability to keep conflict within the system and to handle most counter-legitimacies by manipulating them or, if necessary, incorporating them [ibid.: 215–17].

In this mix the army remains the only odd organisation and possible challenger for the Moroccan *makhzan*. Indeed it was the army from which, in the early 1970s, at least two attempted coups came and from which King Hasan II was miraculously saved (with Godly *baraka*). According to some accounts the monarchy has been gaining in legitimacy during the 1980s, partly because of the king's careful balancing and counter-balancing of domestic policy and partly because of his firm stand over the Western Sahara issue and because of his carefully calculated reputation as a good host of Pan-Arab functions and a good arbiter in inter-Arab disputes. Both images are adding to the development of a distinct Moroccan identity centring around the existing Moroccan state.

Algeria

The dynamics of state formation in Algeria are quite different. Prior to the French expedition of 1830 and the annexation in 1848, the country was not highly centralised: it was ruled by a *dey* and three *beys*, supported by Janissary forces, and with tribal chiefs still enjoying considerable autonomy. Resistance to the occupation was widespread, including the major revolt by 'Abd al-Qadir, the effect of which was somewhat reduced by his arrest but which continued in Kabylie until 1857 with a further important eruption in 1871. Algeria rapidly became a typical case of settler-colonialism, ultimately with a million Europeans implanted and many lands confiscated and farmers dispossessed. The impact of French culture and institutions was overwhelming, but attempts to assimilate the Algerians were unsuccessful and the authorities instead encouraged various Algerian notables, chiefs and functionaries to work as *adjoints indigènes* (native associates or assistants) alongside the European officials.

Algerian nationalist resistance picked up again in the 1920s, and acquired organisational forms in the urban centres in the early 1950s, until the Front de Libération Nationale (FLN) declared full revolution in November 1954 and then constituted itself into a government in September 1958. Although the FLN had relied heavily on rural resistance, its leadership was falling increasingly into the hands of the petty bourgeoisie who, while giving it a populist character, concentrated on the creation of military and administrative organs within the movement [Tlemcani, 1986: 48–65].

These two groups, the 'native associates' and the FLN apparatchiks, came eventually to form the nucleus of the bureaucratic state bourgeoisie that set about the process of state-building after independence in 1962 [cf. Entelis, 1982: 92–132]. Although socialist objectives were declared and self-management (*autogestion*) was adopted in the farms and factories of the liberated Algeria, a counter trend was moving in the direction of a "re-activation of the colonial administration" [Tlemcani, 1986: 89–105]. Administrative institutions replicated from the French model were retained with minor changes. Personnel were rushed to France for training and the number of functionaries in the bureaucracy grew by about 30 per cent per annum during the initial years after independence [Chaliand, 1964].

Self-management was facing serious problems even under the first president, Ahmad Bin Bella. But with the advent of Boumedienne in 1965, the switch to large-scale industrial public projects (*industries industrialisantes*) was stepped up and "the process of statization was swiftly and rigorously accelerated." If the war of national liberation has been the main catalyst in the process of 'nation-building' in Algeria, a country that has always lacked a socio-political core, the industrial policy of 'strategic poles of growth' embodied in the concept of *industries industrialisantes* was meant to be the main pillar not only for preserving national independence and enhancing economic development but also for furthering the process of 'state-building' itself [cf. Bennoune, 1988].

In taking over the colonial apparatus in 1962 the Algerian 'intermediary classes' speedily transformed themselves into a new class as they achieved political, administrative, economic and above all military control over the civil society. Yet, as Tlemcani maintains, this 'social bloc' has not been able to achieve a position of hegemony (in the Gramscian sense), due to the lack of a 'cultural cement' that would bind the fragmented social forces together [Tlemcani, 1986: 189ff]. As the memory of the national liberation struggle faded away among a demographically young population, the 'socialistic' slogans were not matched by the reality of a just, integrated society, and 'political Islam' came eventually to haunt the bureau-technocratic élite and its military guarantors – when they were least expecting it.

STATE FORMATION IN ARABIA AND THE GULF

It is quite familiar to think of the countries of Arabia and the Gulf as 'tribal states' [cf. e.g. Korany, 1991: 456ff, 484ff]. This description, however, should be taken only as a simplifying generalisation, because the older quasi-stately traditions in the region have often tended to have a religious as well as a tribal dimension.

This is true, historically, of Oman and Yemen, and is partly true, more recently, of the case of 'Saudi Arabia'. Historically speaking, whenever the solidarity of sect coincided with the solidarity of tribe, the group was more often capable of achieving an element of political autonomy. Thus, the settlement of a Kharijite branch (the Ibadis) in Oman in the eighth century AD gave the country the distinct political character which it has retained ever since. The settlement of a certain Shi'i branch (the Zuyud) in Northern and Eastern Yemen in the ninth century century AD has also given that country a certain distinct political personality. In modern times, the appearance of new religious sects or movements that are tribally supported has also been influential in imparting a certain political character to a certain country, as was the case with the Wahhabis in Arabia in the eighteenth century [cf. Al-Khuri, 1988: 53–65; Harik, 1987: 25–30].

The importance of studying tribalism in Arabia and the Gulf is not only warranted by the significant demographic and economic weight that nomads still represent in some of these countries, but because of its at once surviving, but changing, social and political significance. As we have previously indicated, study of the interrelationships between the nomadic and the agricultural and commercial communities represents a major key to understanding many of the historical and political developments of several parts of the Arab World [see also Eickelman, 1981: 63–83 and refs cited]. More specifically, it can be argued that the cultural and socio-political characteristics of tribalism (as a socio-cultural phenomenon) outlive the 'ecological' requirements of pastoral nomadism as a 'means of production' and as a mechanism of natural survival, and penetrate the value system and social organisations of a number of Arab societies, especially in Arabia and the Gulf. As also maintained earlier, a successful understanding of the move from tribe to state in Arabia and the Gulf will have to place nomadism within its surrounding context of commercial, cultural and political relationships.

Even in the heart of Najd, the most 'desert-y' part of the Arabian desert, towns did exist, not to speak of the cities that were to be found at the 'periphery' of Arabia where the desert meets the settled regions in Syria, Mesopotamia and Egypt. The bedouins have always exchanged their meat, wool, dates and butter for other necessities and luxuries that come not only from the surrounding regions but also from far away places in Asia and Africa (such as grains, spices, fabrics, crafts and so on). The bedouin vis-à-vis the city is a consumer, but he is also an 'intermediary' between these cities and the caravan routes that lead everywhere. He is the self-appointed protector of trade and pilgrimage passages in return for the receipt of an enforced protection tax (khuwwa). Ten important urban centres were thus developed in Arabia, between Riyad and Ha'il, linking the peninsula to Damascus and beyond, and indeed this axis has been the domicile of those bedouin political formations, or 'tribute states' as Henry Rosenfeld calls them [in Eickelman,

1981: 67], that showed some stability; the Rawla emirate, the Ibn Rashid emirate, and most recently, the Saudi Arabian kingdom. A functional link had existed whereby the trade route provided an economic surplus to the tribal groupings which in turn constrained haphazard aggression and offered 'protection' instead [Sharara, 1981a: 35–44].

Conventional studies on nomadism in the Arab World have traditionally concentrated on the anthropological description of tribes as presumably segmentary and 'isolated' social units, or have, more recently, predicted and/ or described their encapsulation and demise under the impact of growing modernisation and of the encroaching forces of the nation-state and its vehement efforts at sedentarisation [cf. e.g. Sabir and Mulaika, 1986: 29–41]. Such approaches have tended to overlook (a) the web of relationships that has always interwoven pastoralism with other socio-economic activities – especially commercial and military – in the surrounding social space; and (b) the way tribalism as a 'state of mind', as a set of values, and as a pattern of social organisation, may outlive its main 'natural ecology' functions and survive and even penetrate the new and presumably 'modern' structures brought into being by the forces of modernisation, bureaucratisation and state-building.

In other words, tribe and state have not always been, nor do they necessarily need to be, in contradiction with each other as conventional wisdom has tended to suggest. Ernest Gellner has argued that tribes may or may not be cultural units, but that they certainly are political ones. According to him a tribe is "a local mutual-aid association", whose members jointly help maintain order internally and defend the unit externally. To him, arid-zone tribalism is a technique of order-maintenance. It is a political solution to a political problem. It is "an alternative to the State". Tribalism is based on 'nesting': "the tribe resembles the tribal 'confederation' of which it is a part, but it also resembles the 'clans' into which it is divided, and so forth." The 'nesting' process may be further expanded through various "devices for incorporating individuals and groups without the benefit of the appropriate ancestry" [Gellner, 1983: 436–48]. Now, it is possible to argue that even though the original 'environmental' requirements of order maintenance and self-defence have changed in ways that no longer warrant the tribal 'technique', the political patterns acquired through the tribal experience may still survive and function [compare M.J. Al-Ansari in Al-Hayat, 6 April 1993]. For example, the careful observer of contemporary Arab societies cannot fail to see how 'mutual aid', 'nesting' and 'differential incorporation' are practised on a large scale. Indeed, the amalgamation and partial transformation of the tribal 'base' has often been an important component of the process of state-building, and a good illustration of how the principles of 'articulation' and 'non-correspondence' work in reality. Thus "the process of transition from tribe to state may not mean the demise of the previous tribal foundations, but rather a broadening of them". In the conditions of Arabia, and as Mas'ud Dahir acidly puts it, the movement has been from "pastoral nomadism to petroleum tribalism" [Dahir, 1968: 15–51].

Khaldun Al-Naqib [1987: 21–2] considers that this is the main difference between the ethnographic study of tribes as kin units on the local level, and the sociological study of tribes and tribal alliances viewed as units in the overall socio-political organisation of the Arabian society, which is characterised by what he calls 'political tribalism' as an underpinning 'general mentality'. According to Al-Naqib, the 'natural state' economy of Arabia and the Gulf could not have sustained itself for so many centuries simply on pastoralism and conquest. Rather, he maintains, mercantile activity within a very extensive network of routes, cities and ports was the main source of generating economic surplus. This was a specific type of commercial activity (*al-mudaraba*), characterised by the high cost of the enforced payment (*itawa*) given by the merchants in return for the protection of their trade on land and sea (sometimes avoiding the costs and fees for transportation), which eventually formed part of the final price. These 'protection levies' were part of a redistributive process that involved political agents such as the tribal shaikhs or sultans. Al-Naqib even suggests that the familiar rotation of tribal élites in the traditional nomadic society was correlated not only to the fluctuations of income derived by various shaikhs from the activities of conquest and the imposition of *khuwwa*, but also to the income that they obtained through the provision of 'protection services' and through dues acquired from trade in general. The victory of the BuSaids over the Ya'ariba in Oman, the emergence of the Qawasim and 'Utub in the Gulf, the appearance and predominance of Al Sa'ud over the Khawalid in Ihsa' and over Al-Rashid in Northern Najd, the emergence of the Sultans of Lahaj in Aden, and the cyclical flourishing or decline of the Shamar and 'Anza tribal groupings (Al-Muntafiq, Al-Dafir, Al-Rawla) in the Syrian and Iraqi deserts may all – according to him be viewed within such a perspective of tribal élite circulation. More generally, the ruling families in cities and ports have usually been in a position of confrontation with the merchants, fishermen and craftsmen (sometimes using tribal militias such as the *fidawiya*, etc. against the other social forces). This fulfilled two contradictory functions: to secure protection for trade, always linking it with the tribal interior, and to subjugate the urban population to the absolute power of the tribal families [Al-Naqib, 1987: 29–39].

Al-Naqib also notes that the natural state economy, although challenged from the sixteenth century by expanding Portuguese military power, lasted more or less until the mid-nineteenth century when British imperialism succeeded in removing other European powers from, and imposed its commercial monopoly over, the Indian Ocean. Traditional (*mudaraba*) trade was then turned into commercial agency work, protection treaties were imposed on the ruling families, and Gulfian commercial fleets were eventually to decline almost to extinction. Politically, the imperialist domination led to a shift in relative social-political influence from the coastal trading towns to the tribal land interior, although the capitalist penetration itself did not go deep into the hinterland until after the First World War and the discovery of oil in large quantities [Al-Naqib, 1987: 55–90].

It was within this conjuncture of economic, political and strategic factors that the modern 'states' of Arabia and the Gulf were to emerge. In the coming pages, a brief analysis of this process is presented.

The Saudi state

The first Saudi-Wahhabi state emerged in the eighteenth century around the territorial nucleus that was centred on towns and stations along the crucial Riyad-Ha'il axis, related loosely to trade routes and to pilgrim caravans. It was based on a combination of the military force of Muhammad Ibn Sa'ud, the amir of Dar'iyya, and the spiritual influence of Muhammad Ibn 'Abd Al-Wahhab, the puritan Hanbalite Shaikh. The social bases of this movement, through which most of Arabia was unified for the first time since the Prophet Muhammad, are not properly understood. But through this bond, an integrationist, centralising process was somehow initiated, in the name of supporting the uniate religion over discordant nomadism. As one of the chroniclers of the fighting was to remark: "many tribal Arabians (*'urban min al-qaba'il*) were defeated, and the 'Muslims' gained much booty" [in Sharara, 1981a: 77]. The theological concept of *tawhid* (monism) was thus given a political function by a refusal of all variety in interpretation and by a rejection of all intermediaries between the original message and the existing moment and place. Cultural Wahhabism thus had a crucial role to play in the society by paving the way for the state [Sharara, 1981a: 75–83].

However, by extending its influence not only to urban Hijaz but also to southern Iraq and to the Red Sea lanes, many 'neighbours' were alerted to the potential danger of the movement, and Muhammad 'Ali's Egypt, with support from the Ottoman Sultanates, the British Empire and the Shi'ite centres around the Gulf, inflicted a severe defeat on the emerging power, and a rival tribe, Al-Rashid, subsequently replaced Al Sa'ud even in their own territories.

Half a century later, the Saudi-Wahhabi state was to re-form itself through a similar process of tribal conquest and 'pacification'. Instrumental in this process was the role played by the Ikhwan in their migratory camps (*hujar*, sing.: *hujra* or *hijra*). These were neo-Wahhabi agricultural/military colonies gathering outside their normal bedouin domicile for a process of training and organisation as well as political acculturation. They were really the main force in defining the new bedouin-state and in creating it in Arabia, in the name of Islam. Starting with an occupation of Riyad in 1902, 'Abd al-'Aziz Al-Sa'ud (Ibn Saud) continued to conquer town by town, ending with Taif and Mecca in 1924 and Medina and Jidda in 1925. The new unified state was declared under the name of Saudi Arabia in 1932. Thus the control of these towns and the trading and pilgrimage routes that link them together and also connect them to the nearby agricultural oases was to represent (together with the usual conquest booty) a reasonable economic base and a source of 'economic surplus' for the emerging state [Sharara, 1981a: 49–57]. It was also during this process that Arabian lands which were 80 per cent controlled directly by the tribes, were confiscated from the defeated tribes and turned into 'state' lands. Only a limited percentage of the cultivated lands in the peripheral areas that were not originally part of the Saudi 'core' remained in private ownership [Salama, 1980: 113–14].

Yet neither the spoils derived from conquest, nor the surplus extracted from agriculture could alone support a state in Arabia; only the city could: the city is always the factor that lures nomadism into the state. This was achieved by establishing one tribal leadership above all, a certain enforced order, by collecting on a 'centralised' basis new types of 'commercial' taxes, and by preventing further fighting and 'conquest' among the tribes. The nomads might have played a crucial role initiating the process of mobilising for unification; but it was the cities and townsmen which in the final analysis provided the support, the leadership and the main source of economic (commercial) surplus [Sharara, 1981a: 49–62]. The move from tribe to state established a magnified role for leadership, under new types of relationship whereby the shaikhs acted increasingly as 'intermediaries' between their (slowly disintegrating) tribes on the one hand and the 'central' state/tribe on the other. The emphasis on the role of the city also expands the role of religion as a unifying and urban-coloured factor of cohesion over the presumably chaotic nomadic inclinations.

We can thus see that the original formation of the Saudi state was in the main an endogenous affair: it involved the expansion by the Al Sa'ud masters of the Dar'iyya oasis into most of the lands of Arabia (including Hijaz) in the period from 1765 to 1803. This expansion was to be severely challenged by the Egyptians (and others) several times but was then re-formed during the early decades of the twentieth century, this time with some help from the British. From then on the Saudi entity was no longer fully autonomous although of course the country was never formally colonised. British subsidies and military personnel were sent to the Saudi king; however, he continually sought for a larger scope for independence, eventually bringing in the Americans to prospect for oil (and to counterbalance the British), and often encroached on British spheres of influence in the surrounding countries under British rule or Mandate [Salama, 1980: 34ff].

To consolidate their role the Saudis resorted to various methods, including the age-old practice of tribal alliance-through-marriage to expand the 'social base' of the ruling clique. They also turned several nomadic groups into military forces under their command. They re-absorbed the remaining groups of the defeated Ikhwan by re-confirming the alliance with the Al-Shaikh family, and by incorporating the *'ulama'* into the state machine. This was quite an intricate process. Although the *'ulama'* had issued a *fatwa* in 1926 which indicated a certain sympathy with several of the demands of the Ikhwan, they also issued the most crucial opinion, which was that the pronouncement of *jihad* (war) was the responsibility of the *imam* (leader) alone. The *'ulama'* had thus expressed a certain degree of 'relative autonomy', although politically speaking their *fatwa* was to work to Ibn Sa'ud's advantage. When the Ikhwan decided to resist by force, the *'ulama'* were brought one step closer to the government, being finally submerged – after the final defeat of the Ikhwan – into the newly established state machine which removed many of their traditional functions and entrusted them, as employees of the state, with tasks that were related only to religious, ethical, educational and judicial matters [Al-Yasini, 1987: 59–77]. The Saudis thus increasingly turned the tribal-religious alliance of the eighteenth century into more and more of a straightforward tribal alliance [Dahir, 1986: 283ff].

For their part, religious sources maintain that up till 1915 'Abd al-Aziz Ibn Sa'ud had no particular religious inclinations. From 1915 to the late 1920s he had contained the Ikhwan religious movement and adopted its slogans, in order to succeed in his military war against tribes refusing to pay him allegiance. From 1930 – the date he defeated the Ikhwan – Saudi rule increasingly revealed its tribal-royalist, rather than its religious, character [e.g. Al-Qahtani, 1985: 9ff]. There is disagreement with regard to the origins of the Ikhwan movement (which became known first around 1914 as a revival of the *Salafi* puritanical doctrine of the eighteenth-century thinker Ibn 'Abd al-Wahhab); was it an independent movement or was it instigated by Ibn Sa'ud himself? It is clear, however, that the latter had coopted the movement and relied on it heavily for establishing his rule, to the extent of 'ordering' all Najdis to join it in 1916 [Al-Qahtani, 1985: 40–57]. Ibn Sa'ud needed a religious rationale for his military expansion, understanding very well that nomads could not be subjugated for long by force or by money. He therefore opted for containing the movement, and not, as Ibn Jalwi had recommended, for combating it, until he had exhausted its potential use for giving a religious impetus to his conquest; at which point he crushed the active leadership of the Ikhwan while co-opting the *'ulama'* on to his side. In fact most *'ulama'*, having dispersed their 'natural' following, had little alternative but to accept Saudi tutelage in the hope that they could influence future policies through the state machine.

Following the birth of the Saudi state in a region increasingly dominated by the requirements of international trade and of oil extraction, and strategically controlled by British interests, the Saudis were more and more inclined to repress their Wahhabi allies (especially in the major confrontation of 1929/30) and to ameliorate their position *vis-à-vis* the British. The latter were themselves equally interested in containing the Wahhabis whose points of influence extended into territories dominated by the British: Iraq, Jordan and the Gulf. Because the Saudis were suppressing a major human base of their power (the Wahhabi Ikhwan) they had to rely increasingly on the British. The *hujar* (the military–agrarian settlements) where the Ikhwan were being trained were dismantled, their arms and possessions confiscated, and their particularly rebellious members were forced to merge among other tribes.

The causes for the confrontation between the Saudis and the Ikhwan were multiple. The Ikhwan were resentful that Ibn Sa'ud had put a stop to the practice of tribal tributes being enforced on the weaker tribes (*khuwwa*) and that he had instead forced the Najdis to pay not only Islamic alms-tax (*zakat*) but also commercial, non-religious taxes (*mukus*) [cf. Helms, 1981: 151–73]. They were also opposed to many of the 'modernising' measures that Ibn Sa'ud had accepted, such as the introduction of cars, telephones and telegraph, etc. The Ikhwan tribes had further resisted the emerging 'territorial' concept which not only confined each tribe to a particular space but also prevented them from grazing their herds in the territories of neighbouring countries and from raiding them occasionally for booty. These countries were almost all under British Mandate or rule, and 'Abd al-'Aziz had come to realise that it was in his interest to establish an 'understanding' with the British in relation to fixed borders as well as other matters. Indeed, it would be with the help of the British that Ibn Sa'ud was finally to defeat the Ikhwan and establish full authority over his re-unified state [cf. Helms, 1981: 250–72].

Thus, at last, through the city, the tribe was turned into a state, the *'asabiyya* into a *mulk*. Increasingly:

> this new state, supported by the English, was being established on foundations of a capitalist character, linked to foreign capital. Confrontation was inevitable between a mode of production moving towards capitalism, and the nomadic mode with its tribal system. The Saudi family was seeking to benefit from the oil funds in modern projects, whereas its nomadic masses, especially the Ikhwan, were brought up to values and traditions that are as far as can be from capitalist relations [Dahir: 1986: 283–4].

Resistance to the Al-Sa'ud family was indeed fierce and one of the leaders, Faisal al-Duwish, was nearly successful in removing the Saudis, had it not been for the British forces bombing the Bedouins' gatherings. According to Mas'ud Dahir, there is strong documentary evidence as to the close connection between the Saudi project for the establishment of a state and the British interests which supported them against the Ikhwan masses [Dahir, 1986: 276–91].

From now on, almost forced sedentarisation would be imposed on most of the remaining nomads to accelerate the move towards a 'modern-looking' society that would not obstruct the expansion in trade and in oil activities.

The nomads under the leadership of their shaikhs were now needed for the purposes of protecting the oil installations, pipelines and ports. The nomads had to be 'pinned down' to such activities, and to the tending of agriculture around the oases. The pacification of the bedouin was also necessary for the safety of the growing network of railways and surface roads that was now linking all parts of Arabia. Even within the emerging 'economic' sector the new 'companies' were often formed according to a closed tribal base. The tribal shaikhs were handsomely rewarded in financial terms for rendering such services to the 'state', which was in its turn adjusting the society to the requirements of a peripheral capitalist mode of production [compare Dahir, 1986: 291–301].[5]

Subsequently, the main process of state formation was a function of the "institutionalisation of power – without losing it" [Salama, 1980: 56 ff]. The incorporation of Hijaz after the defeat of the Hashemites in 1925–26 posed some problems given the relative commercial and administrative superiority of the Hijazis over the Najdis. Ibn Sa'ud appointed his son Faisal as deputy in Hijaz while keeping the laws and organisations there intact. In 1932 the entire land was united (Najd, Hijaz, al-Ihsa', Asir) and the administrative experience of the Hijaz was extended to the rest of the kingdom, with governors and new institutions in all provinces of the country.

Administration in Saudi Arabia remained quite personalistic in nature, however, so that although a Ministry of Finance was established in 1932 (together with one for Foreign Affairs), it was difficult, even until the end of the 1950s to distinguish between the public treasury and the King's private purse.[6] The number of ministries increased successively, but the more serious institutionalisation was a function of two factors: the death in 1953 of the charismatic builder of the state, Ibn Sa'ud; and the expansion in oil extraction in the late 1940s and early 1950s [Salama, 1980: 59–61]. Then a cabinet was formed in 1953 to attempt a routinisation of the charismatic power of Ibn Sa'ud and to utilise the funds accruing from oil. However, the 'familial' nature of the ruling élite remained quite obvious, with the royal family always controlling the most important ministries (based on their own internal familial order and their proximity to Ibn Sa'ud), together with some representation from the Al-Shaikh family. Furthermore the administrative organs, both the central but particularly the provincial, tended to acquire a semi-private character and to be regarded as natural fiefs for certain branches of the royal family and as the personal exclusive domain of their heads. Many ministers communicated directly with the king, especially from the more important 'shaikhly' families, many of them also acquiring other academic and technocratic titles [Salama, 1980: 62–73].

Thus it can be seen that, in the Saudi process of integration, both kinship and bureaucratisation were utilised. If the introduction of regulations and institutions appeared for a while to sever the precious familial or tribal relationships, patronage was soon introduced to bridge the gaps. At the summit of the patronage pyramid there was the core network of the main Saudi 'clan-class' that controlled all the strategic functions, ministries and provinces (e.g. Interior, Defence, Foreign Affairs, Petroleum, etc.). The descending pyramid structure then extended into a status network of patron–client relationships, while towards the bottom, much of the 'productive base' acquired a certain 'externality' to the whole system, being assigned mainly to foreigners and members of out-groups [cf. Sharara, 1981a: 130–54]. The Saudi society has thus in a sense been unified *by* the state – but it also remains, in a sense, only unified *into* the state, as the society continues to be quite diffracted and dispersed [ibid.: 208–9], a subject that will be dealt with later in the book.

The Gulf states

As we have seen, the British had already been flexing their muscles around the Gulf, economically and militarily, since the eighteenth century. By 1820 they had defeated the influential Qawasim clan of Ras al-Khaimah and en-forced a 'trucial' system on them as well as on the shaikhs of Ajman, Umm al-Qaiwain, Abu Dhabi, Dubai and Bahrain. Each of these signed a separate 'General Treaty of Peace' with the British government, on the one hand signalling their capitulation to British power, while on the other hand con-stituting "the genesis of the Gulf States as separate political units". The 'truce' between the Gulf entities was renewed several times until 1853 when a Per-petual Maritime Truce was signed, and the shaikhs undertook to bring an end to all hostilities. Kuwait and Qatar joined the other Gulf states in the 'treaty relationship' with Britain in 1899 and 1916 respectively. Such politico-strategic arrangements secured British maritime and trade interests in the area (which was of course on the route to India), and later guaranteed for Britain exclusive oil concessions in the region according to various treaties that were signed between 1913 and 1922 [Zahlan, 1989: 7–11].

Politically speaking, the combined effect of the relationship with Britain and the opening up of the region by the oil companies had a powerful impact on the position of the local ruler:

> He signed the treaties, and he was personally responsible for the application of all their clauses. The British authorities – whether the political resident, the political agent or the senior officer of the Persian Gulf Division – dealt with him alone. The Treaty system strengthened his position and assured the continuity of his influence. With time, it became a guarantee. Most important, it contributed to the institutionalization of his position [Zahlan, 1989: 19–20].

One outcome of such 'fixing' of certain families permanently in power was to destroy any link that might have existed between the circulation of tribal élites and the local and regional commercial and economic cycles in the 'traditional' society of the 'natural' economy [Al-Naqib: 1987: 95ff]. Put differently, the 'state' was separated from its socio-economic base and given a specifically political/strategic underpinning within newly defined, 'rigid' and often artificial borders which restricted the tribes' traditional movement (that formerly had taken place for economic as well as 'political' reasons). The conventional right of 'exit' was thus to all intents and purposes blocked, with serious political implications to follow. The new borders were basically the boundaries within which these small city-states were to acquire their formal independence: starting with Kuwait in 1961 and ending with the countries of the lower Gulf (Bahrain, Qatar and the United Arab Emirates) in 1971. Unlike their larger neighbour-kingdom, Saudi Arabia, these were all extremely small city-states, or as some other Arabs sarcastically call them 'oil-field-states' or even 'oil-well-states' (al-dawla al-bi'r). They can hardly believe that they are real states and every one of them insists on incorporating the word 'state' formally into the very formal name of the country (e.g. Dawlat al-Kuwait, Dawlat al-Imarat al-'Arabiyya al-Muttahida, etc.) – just for good measure! [cf. Rida, 1992: 13].

From now on the tribal leadership would have supremacy over the merchant classes, not only because the former had acquired political power, but also because of the decline in the merchants' fortunes following the Western economic penetration in and around the region. In a process similar to that which occurred with the 'ulama' in Saudi Arabia, the merchant families were reincorporated during the 'petroleum era' into the new 'states' of the Gulf in a different, and more subservient capacity as commercial agents and importers of commodities from the capitalist world.

The 'petroleum era', although signalled in the 1930s, did not develop fully until the Second World War – then, of course, following the Arab–Israeli war of 1973, it reached its zenith, its effect being finally to transform the Gulf economies from pastoral/mercantile into export-mineral-based economies with a dominant rentier character. Such a type of economy has also had its political and ideological corollaries, as we shall see in subsequent parts of this book.

NOTES

1. Whatever the case with Muhammad 'Ali's strategy might have been, one cannot help but ponder, with Roger Owen, the fact that "perhaps for the first time in history, a ruler well-embarked on a programme of import substitution had discovered that such policies often lead to an increase rather than a reduction in the need for imports" [Owen, 1981: 75–6].

2. It should be clear from this that the economies of the periphery have become very closely tied to the world capitalist order, whose features and arrangements have been mainly formulated by the core capitalist countries. Society/state relations in a peripheral country cannot therefore be deduced from a simple examination of the relationship of the native government to its economy and social classes – the world capitalist system is an important element in defining the Third World state.

3. Ironically, the knowledge of many Tunisian intellectuals even of their own Maghribi culture and society is often derived from French sources. This is manifested, for example, in the Arabic writing of two renowned Tunisian political scientists about *bilad al-sibah*. It has been spelt once beginning with a *ṣad* and once ending with an *alif* (whereas it is in fact: *sin, ya, ba, ha*) – thus perhaps revealing the European sources of their knowledge of these 'native' concepts! [cf. Al-Hirmasi, 1987: 26–7; Zaghal, 1992: 440.]

4. Moroccan society appears to meet the social anthropological category of a 'ingesting' rather than a 'disgorging' society – i.e. it conquers the 'other' by absorbing rather than by expelling him. The term is in fact used literally, and when the Moroccan Sultan succeeds in subduing dissident tribes or communities he is said to have "eaten" them [Darif, 1988: 184].

5. Trying to keep his distance as much as possible from the British, 'Abd al-Aziz Ibn Sa'ud chose to give the most extensive oil concessions to the Americans, with whom he formed the Californian Arabian Standard Oil Company (ARAMCO) in 1933, as well as important military facilities in Dhahran and elsewhere. ARAMCO virtually ruled the country for many years [cf. Al-Shaikh, 1988a], and enforced on it a serious type of economic and technological dependency that was to last even into the years of the 'oil boom' – as we shall see in due course.

6. According to Donald Cole [1975], tribal people such as Al Murrah distinguish between two aspects of the modern Saudi Arabian state – the *dawla*, by which they mean the modern bureaucracy, and the *hukuma*, or the Rulers, by which they mean the members of the Al Sa'ud royal family and a few other religio-political families [p. 109].

CHAPTER FOUR

The Arab State: Territorial or Pan-Arabist?

The shift from the 'Household of Islam' (*Dar al-Islam*) to the contemporary territorial states has not been an easy one in the Arab World. In the Mashriq in particular, where it involved conflict between two Muslim peoples – the Arabs and the Turks – it had to be intellectually mediated via the idea of Pan-Arabism, all the more so since the Arab population of the Levant had also included significant and influential numbers of Christians.

Due to the long historical influence of the idea of the *umma* as a unified religio-political community, the Arabs have not been conventionally sympathetic to any concept of the body-politic that bases itself on land or territory (*tarf, nasiya, nitaq* or even *watan*). When the polity did not go hand in hand with the community of belief (i.e. when the basis of rule was not *shari'a* but force) the *dawla* could be defined by its initiators (i.e. the dynasty) but still not by its region or territory. Even when, in the sixteenth century, there were three major Muslim states ruling in Turkey, Egypt and Persia, their rulers always gave themselves (universal) Islamic titles and it was only their enemies or competitors who contemptuously identified them as the Sultans of their territorial states [cf. Kawtharani, 1988: 33–41].

It is sometimes argued (e.g. by Abdallah Laroui, Waddah Sharara, etc.) that this attachment to the concept of community, Islamic and then subsequently Arabist, has been behind the limited evolution of the national territorial state in the Arab World because it has deprived this latter of popular legitimacy. Although this may be partly true, it does not explain the whole story behind the weakness of the national territorial state. Furthermore, the ideology of Pan-Arabism in the Mashriq has had some concrete social and political factors behind its emergence. Its failure to achieve its main goal of Arab unity and its degeneration into a device for interstate manoeuvre have also had, as we shall argue, some concrete social and political factors behind them. Once Pan-Arabism had exhausted the 'oppositional phase' of defining the 'self' *contra* the 'other' (a task achieved with the end of Turkish and European rule), it lacked a broad enough and strong enough socio-political 'historic bloc' that was both intent on, and capable of dealing with, the 'constructive phase' of unifying the inter-Arab markets and building a comprehensive inter-Arab institutional structure. In comparative perspective, one may be able to draw some hints from European cases [cf. Hroch, 1985; Puhle, 1992]. The emergence of cultural nationalism tends to correspond with the ascendance of the urban intelligentsia – this phase has taken place in the Arab countries. The transition to political nationalism and, in particular, the quest for a nation-state tends to correspond with the emergence of an 'industrial revolution' and the organisation of a working-class movement. In the Arab World, the latter has either not taken place or, as we shall see, was directed by the state and not, as in the familiar European cases, by the bourgeoisie. But before we proceed any further with the argument, let us first review the development of Pan-Arabism as an ideology and discourse, with particular reference to its conception of the state.

THE PAN-ARABIST IDEOLOGY

Although it had several intellectual and political precursors in the nineteenth century, Pan-Arabism is basically a twentieth-century doctrine that developed in conjunction with the breakdown of the Ottoman Empire and the encroachment of Western colonialism.[1] One may count among the possible nineteenth-century precursors the Wahhabi movement that contributed to the unification of most of Arabia, Muhammad 'Ali's extension of the domain of the Egyptian state into the Levant, and the emergence of various clubs and societies in Greater Syria that had proto-nationalist objectives or activities.

As with many other nationalist movements [cf. Hroch, 1985; Hobsbawm, 1990], Arabism emerged first among a small circle of the intelligentsia (school-teachers, journalists and 'aspiring subaltern officials') and was mainly concerned with cultural matters, especially the revival and renovation of the Arabic language and its literature. Several of the pioneering contributions in this respect came from Christian teachers and writers in Syria/Lebanon, such as Nasif al-Yaziji (1800–71) and Butrus al-Bustani (1819–83), although a Muslim from Egypt, Shaikh Hasan al-Marsafi (d. 1890) perhaps already had a clearer concept of language as the basis for a nation [cf. Nassar, 1986: 223ff].

Although the linguistic conception of nationalism has remained the most dominant in all Pan-Arabist ideas, it has always acquired additional shades from one thinker to another.[2] Some analysts regard the Syrian 'Abd al-Rahman al-Kawakibi (1849–1902) as "the first true intellectual precursor of modern secular Pan-Arabism" [Haim, 1974: 27ff]. He was the earliest unreservedly to declare himself as a champion of the Arabs against the Turks and called for a purely spiritual Caliphate, although he was still attached to the conventional goal of Islamic renaissance [Nassar, 1986: 58ff]. For some, Arabism as a basically linguistic concept was mixed with an ethnic, often anti-Turkish, slant, such as, for example, in the writings of Najib 'Azuri (d. 1916), 'Abd al-Ghani al-'Arisi (1889–1916), Salah al-Din al-Qasimi (1887–1916), or 'Umar Fakhuri (1895–1946) [for a detailed anthology see Haim, 1974]. Not unexpectedly, such writers were influenced by the European ideas of nationalism circulating at the time, particularly those of the French Gustav Le Bon and the German Theodor Mommsen.

It should be noted at this point that although secular-nationalist concepts had emerged first among the Christian intellectuals they were not confined to them for long. Nor were all secularist Christians anti-Ottoman, or all anti-Ottoman Christians necessarily Arab Nationalists. Much of the anti-Turkish sentiment was not anti-Ottoman as such but emerged as a reaction to the Turkification policies promoted by the Young Turks and as a quest for cultural equality, possibly within the Ottoman formula itself [for details see Al-'Azma, 1992]. Such nationalist sentiments were expressed most forcefully, but still in a confused manner, in the First Arab Congress of 1913, organised by Arab students in Europe to demand equal political rights for the Arabs within the Ottoman state. Because Arabism was perceived basically in contrast to 'Turkism' within the Ottoman state the Arabs were then conceived of as the inhabitants of Greater Syria and Iraq (in addition to Arabia itself).

This 'cultural nationalism' of the intellectuals could not, however, link up with any ascending social class (e.g. a bourgeoisie) that would have championed its cause. In spite of the reforms of Muhammad 'Ali and his son Ibrahim between 1831 and 1940 and the Tanzimat reforms that followed, "Syria was by no means a bourgeois society, but a semi-feudal one with some incipient bourgeois features". As Bassam Tibi explains [1981: 88–90], the undeveloped bourgeoisie and the petty-bourgeois writers were unable to lead a revolt against the Ottoman Empire by themselves. They allied themselves with the 'feudal' masters of the Arabian peninsula at the time, the Hashimite dynasty, and entrusted them with leading the 'Arab revolt'. Sharif Husain of Mecca, the head of the dynasty, agreed to lead the movement under assurances from his close allies, the British, that they would support it and guarantee the 'liberation of the Arabs' of Asia within an independent Arab kingdom under Husain's headship. This promise proved to be a tactical manoeuvre, since Britain and France had, with the connivance of Russia, already concluded the Sykes–Picot Agreement in 1916, in which they had distributed the Arab territories potentially liberated from the Turks among themselves. This Western 'betrayal' had paved the way to formalised 'colonial' British and French presence (under the title of the Mandate) in the Arab East (Mashriq) and opened the door – among other things – for Zionist settlement in Palestine (under the Balfour Declaration of 1917).

It was this colonial encroachment on the Arab East, combined with the accelerating demise of the Ottoman state, which contributed more than anything to the politicisation of Arab nationalist ideas there. Furthermore, whereas the pre-colonial cultural nationalism of the Western-educated intellectual was usually liberal in outlook and aspired to emulate Western constitutional and democratic practices, with the diffusion of colonial domination the West was now the oppressor, and the increasingly anti-Western nationalism was becoming also less liberal and more authoritarian/totalitarian in its general outlook. As Bassam Tibi explains:

> Arab nationalism, once francophile and partly anglophile, changed with the British and French colonisation of the area and became anti-British and anti-French, and germanophile ... Furthermore, the germanophilia was narrow and one-sided. The German ideology absorbed by the Arab intellectuals at this time was confined to a set of nationalist ideas which had gained particular currency during the period of the Napoleonic wars. These ideas carried notions of romantic irrationalism and a hatred of the French to extremes. They excluded from consideration the philosophers influenced by the Enlightenment, such as Lessing, Kant, Hegel and others, on the grounds of what was considered to be their universalism. They were particularly attracted by the notion of the 'Volk' as defined by German Romanticism, which they proceeded to apply to the 'Arab Nation' [Tibi, 1981: 91–93].[3]

A major example of such an intellectual transformation is Sati' Al-Husri (1882–1968) himself – the most influential theoretician of Arab nationalism, who gave the predominant linguistic concept of Arabism more of a 'historical' dimension. Of Syrian origin he lived during his early formative years, and then worked, in Ottoman Turkey, witnessing the demise of this empire and the rise of Turkish and non-Turkish nationalities within it [cf. Cleveland, 1971]. He worked subsequently in Iraq and Egypt, and allocated a great deal of his efforts to winning the minds and hearts of the Egyptian intelligentsia for the idea of Arabism. A dominant theme in Al-Husri's writing is that there is little freedom to be enjoyed by the individual outside the nation:

> The national interests which may sometimes require a man to sacrifice his life, must perforce entail in some cases the sacrifice of his freedom ... He who refuses totally to extinguish [yufni] himself within the nation to which he belongs might in some cases find himself lost to an alien nation that may one day conquer his fatherland. This is why I say continuously and without hesitation that patriotism and nationalism come before and above all ... even above and before freedom [quoted in Haim, 1974: 90].

Having studied in France, Switzerland and Belgium, Al-Husri seems to have been attracted in his younger days by the ideas of Rousseau and Renan, and by the 'French idea of the Nation', but subsequently he became more influenced by the German philosophers such as Herder and Fichte (and

Schönerer and Arndt), and by the idea of the organic nation-state. The main German political thinkers (from Herder to Plessner) have always made a distinction between 'state' and 'nation', where the latter is seen in cultural terms, while the 'state' is seen as a mechanical and legal construction that is external to the nation. Al-Husri praised German Romanticism for having brought about the idea of the nation as distinct from the state, well before the French or the British did. He then fused the German concept of the nation with the Arabic concept of 'group solidarity' (*asabiyya*) which he derived from Ibn Khaldun, and proceeded to develop his own 'pure' theory of nationalism [Tibi, 1981: 100–115].

Renan's concept of a *nationalité élective* was severely criticised by Al-Husri. His idea of free will that makes of the nation 'a daily plebiscite' would not have helped Al-Husri in his attempt to prove the actual existence of a unitary Arab nation. He was concerned to illustrate that the Arab people who lived in a number of separate states were actually one nation that should be united in a single state. Instead, Al-Husri could draw a historical parallel between divided Germany before 1871 and the fragmented Arab World extending from the Persian Gulf to the Atlantic Ocean. According to him, the Arabs long for an 'Arab 1871' but, as Bassam Tibi adds, "How this is to be achieved is a matter of indifference". For Al-Husri does not consider in specific terms how to apply the French or the German concept to the concrete Arab situation, but tries simply to adduce a general proof that the German concept is superior [Tibi, 1981: 101, 124–5].

In his obsession to prove the nation, Al-Husri has certainly overlooked the state and its foundations (apart from the 'population' as defined by its language), whether geographic or socio-economic. He is categorical that the 'state' can never be a factor in forming the nation and employs many historical examples to prove his point [Nassar, 1986: 276–92]. But if, as he keeps repeating, the nation is not contingent on the state, if it precedes the state and continues even after it has lost its own state or after it has been divided among several states, then why, one wonders, are 'nations' constantly striving to create their own states? Territorial continuity is not important except in the likely event of affecting linguistic unity in the long run. The formation of the state contributes to the development of the nation only inasmuch as it unifies the language. Nor are common economic interests (although generally important) particularly pertinent in the formation of a nation: for they unify in some cases and disperse in others and they always vary among different individuals, groups and regions.

> Economics plays a very important role in the life of nations, but its role does not include the 'formation of the nation'. Economics may strengthen the nation, but it does not create it. It is no different in this respect from what concerns the State. For the State, as is known to everyone, may strengthen the nation or even take it to the peak of power, but it never creates it [Al-Husri, 1984/85: 278].

The Historico-Linguistic concept of nationalism was given political life in two main manifestations, one represented by the emergence of the Ba'th Party in the Arab East (in the 1940s) and the other by the emergence (in the 1950s) of Nasser's leadership in Egypt. By emphasising the idea of Arab *unification*, both orientations have implicitly considered the state indispensable to the self-realisation of any nation (still linguistically defined) – although as we shall see this consideration has remained only implicit and void of any detailed or practical implications.

Although one of the sources of the Ba'th ideology may be found in the metaphysical-linguistic ideas of the 'Alawite Syrian Zaki al-Arsuzi, there is no doubt that its main ideologue has been Michel 'Aflaq (1910–89). A Christian Damascene, he formed the Arab Ba'th (Rebirth) group in 1943, with a Muslim colleague Salah al-Bitar and a group of the Syrian intelligentsia who had all studied at the Sorbonne. During their studies in Paris they were influenced by the ideas of philosophers such as Nietzsche, Fichte, Hegel, Schilling and Bergson [Hanna: 1987: 84ff]. In 1947 this group joined ranks with Al-Ihya' al-'Arabi (Arab Revival), led by Arsuzi, and were eventually joined by the Arab Socialist Party of Akram al-Hawrani in 1952 to form the organisation known to this day by the name of the Arab Ba'th Socialist Party (and active in most countries of the Mashriq).

'Aflaq's conceptualisation of Arab nationalism remained foggy, if distinctively romantic. When once asked by some youngsters to define it he answered:

> Love, young people, comes before anything else; first comes love, then the definition will follow: ... a tolerant spirituality that will open its heart and will shade with its wings all those who shared with the Arabs their history, who lived for generations in the atmosphere of their language and culture until they became Arab in thought and in sentiment ['Aflaq, 1970: 118].

From this and from other writings of 'Aflaq it becomes clear that it is always language that specifies the sense of Arabness, although other factors may be added here and there: sometimes ethnic origin, but only as a remote history – for contemporary Arabism is not racial; sometimes Islam, which is held in high esteem by 'Aflaq – but basically as a cultural heritage and not as a belief system; and sometimes common history – although this translates more immediately in the contemporary period into "a unity of suffering and hopes" and a desire for a unified destiny.

From quite early on 'Aflaq had been sensitive to social issues (which tended to be overlooked by Al-Husri), and came increasingly to use a socialistic idiom in his pronouncements. Like Husri, however, 'Aflaq conceived of the individual only as part of the national community. Within the Arab nation the individual will be culturally fulfilled and socially prosperous. The Arab nation will foster a distinct 'Arab socialism' which is as much spiritual as it is socio-economic. Eric Rouleau suggests that in his attempt to blend socialism with nationalism

'Aflaq might have derived the theoretical basis for such a synthesis (during his time in Paris in 1937) from Grosclaude's French translation of Alfred Rosenberg's book on the 'Myth of the Twentieth Century'. A colleague of 'Aflaq's who taught at the University of Damascus found him full of admiration for Rosenberg and Hitler. He thought at the time that, by contrast with the communist countries, Germany was more successful in achieving a synthesis between nationalism and socialism. Furthermore when power in Iraq was seized by pro-German nationalists in the coup of Rashid 'Ali al-Gilani, 'Aflaq formed a committee which assured the new regime of its full support [Rouleau, 1967: 57].

Although the idea of the state is implied in most of 'Aflaq's pronouncements, it is basically the idea of the *party* that takes precedence. Not only is the formation of the Pan-Arabist party a measure of the conscious and productive existence of the Arab nation but the party is, more specifically, the nation in miniature: "we represent the whole of the nation which is still slumbering in [a state of] self-denial of its own reality, and forgetfulness of its own identity" ['Aflaq, 1970: 80]. As a political party the Ba'th has, of course, succeeded more than any other Pan-Arabist party in reaching power – often via alliances with the military in coups d'état – and in staying there for relatively long periods of time, including in today's Syria and Iraq. To this day it entertains the theoretical concept of being organised on two levels: one pan-Arab (called 'national') and one territorial (or *qutri* in Arabic; i.e. based on a single country). The Ba'th was also behind the one and only experiment in actual unification among Arab countries in the post-independence period, that of the United Arab Republic between Syria and Egypt from 1958 to 1961, under the charismatic leadership of Nasser.

Another significant but less influential Pan-Arabist organisation was Harkat al-Qawmiyyun al-'Arab (the Arab Nationalists' Movement – ANM). This time the nucleus was a group of Palestinian youth studying at the American University of Beirut (Lebanon) shortly after the Arabs' disastrous defeat in the Palestine war of 1948 which resulted in the creation of the State of Israel. A Christian Arab nationalist, Constantin Zuraiq, immediately wrote an influential monograph describing the event as nothing less than a total catastrophe (*nakba*). The Arabs had little hope of confronting the more advanced and powerful Zionist state, he reasoned, except by dedicated and well-disciplined political organisation for which the Palestinian issue should act as the catalyst. Zuraiq's appeal fell on receptive ears and a group of his students at the American University of Beirut headed by a medical student, George Habash, responded with zeal to his call and started organising a group of enthusiasts (initially under the name al-'Urwa) from 1948. The ANM remains poorly researched (the main source being Kazziha [1975]) but there are only two particular aspects that will concern us here. First is the close way in which it allied itself with Nasser's leadership up to the Six Day War of 1967, which deprived it of a great deal of autonomy, and left it with little leeway within Egypt itself.[4]

Secondly there is the devastating impact on the movement of the 1967 defeat, which led simultaneously to its radicalisation in a Marxist direction and to its fracturing into smaller groups. The diagnosis was that there was no longer any hope of achieving the liberation of Palestine through collective action by the Arab states since these states were dominated either by decadent 'feudal' classes or by hesitant petty bourgeoisies whose interests lay neither in Arab unity nor in the liberation of Palestine. Some of these splinter groups became country-based (thus reducing the Pan-Arabist potential of the movement): among them, the most significant was the Organisation of Lebanese Socialists in Lebanon; the most politically successful as a ruling government was the National Liberation Front in South Yemen from 1967 to 1990; and the most influential as an opposition movement was the liberal-nationalist group led by Ahmad al-Khatib in Kuwait. Other groups split over ideological matters, the most notable example being the division within the left of the Palestinian resistance movement between the more populist wing led by George Habash (known as the Popular Front for the Liberation of Palestine) and the more Marxist-oriented wing (known for short as the Democratic Front for the Liberation of Palestine).

But if both the Ba'th Party and the Arab Nationalists sought Egypt's encouragement and Nasser's leadership in their endeavour to achieve Arab unity, what in fact were the Pan-Arabist credentials of Egypt and of Nasser? Egypt was, of course, the largest and most culturally and strategically influential Arab state. But Egypt had been virtually autonomous from the Ottoman Empire since the early nineteenth century, had already established a modern-looking state under Muhammad 'Ali, and had constructed a secularist concept of citizenship revolving in particular around the 1919 revolution and the popular Wafd party [cf. Al-Bishri, 1980]. Egypt already had its own concept of nationalism in which the 'nation' (*umma*) was Egyptian, not Arab [cf. e.g., Ahmed, 1960; Hourani, 1970: chs. 8 and 9; 'Awad, 1978]. Space does not permit any lingering among the intricacies of this process of intellectual and political transformation but suffice it to say in this respect that during the inter-war period Egypt underwent a process of 'political Arabisation' [cf. Al-Ansari, 1980: 134–51; Coury, 1982; Gershoni, 1981]. As with most of the Arab World, including for the first time the hitherto 'secluded' Maghrib countries (Tunisia, Algeria and Morocco), the most important 'Arabiser' was the military triumph of the Zionist settler project in Palestine and the defeat of the Arab armies in 1948 – except that in the case of Egypt the threat of Israel was, geographically, more immediate.[5]

The Arabist line was to receive political sanctioning in Egypt when Nasser, the leader of the 1952 revolution gradually, and by extension, subsumed the concept of Egyptian nationalism into a broader one of Arab nationalism.

Prior to 1956 there seem to have been in his pronouncements two concepts for the nation: one Egyptian and one Arab. The overwhelming support that Egypt received from all over the Arab World in 1956 during the Suez crisis and the tripartite aggression by Britain, France and Israel, was the main catalyst. From then on the terminology used was often that of the 'Arab nation' and the 'Egyptian people', both implied in a political, secularist sense [cf. Nasr, 1981].

Nasser of course was a soldier and politician and not an ideologue, and the conceptual structure of his Arabism was quite simple. Arabism started in his thinking as the most immediate and important 'circle' in which Egypt had to function (in addition to the African and the Islamic circles). From the beginning, therefore, Arabism had a political character, but this was both culturally and 'strategically' premised: culturally in terms of a common language and shared history; and strategically in terms of a 'common struggle' against colonialism and for liberation and progress. Nasser's Arabism was also political in the sense that it implied that the real test (the real meaning) for Arab nationalism was in fact Arab unity – i.e. a political unification of the Arab countries. This political unification was, however, relegated following the failure in 1961 of Egypt's unity with Syria, to a third order of priority after 'liberation' and 'socialism'. From then on, the existence of the 'nation' was presumed to derive from its linguistic-historic reality, whereas political unification in one state was made contingent on a number of socio-economic and political requisites that were unlikely to materialise in the immediate future [Nassar, 1986: 326–35].

PAN-ARABISM AND THE 'STATE'

Nasser's perception of Arab nationalism was distinctively political, yet it remained surprisingly vague about the issues pertaining to the nature and the form of the state. It was left to non-Egyptian intellectuals, such as Nadim al-Bitar, to spell out the implications of a Nasserist perspective on Arab nationalism with regard to the issue of the state.[6] Al-Bitar is certainly more sophisticated: he distinguishes between national existence and national identity and is daring enough to reverse the conventional link in Arabist thinking by suggesting that the decisive variable in forming nations might, instead of language, be the 'political factor' which can blend with other factors specific to each situation to form a nation: "languages have not made a national history. National histories are the ones that make languages." The historical pattern, he suggests, is that of moving from the 'political' to the 'cultural', not the other way around. If the Arabs are to be united then the beginning of wisdom should not be simply to believe in the inevitability of unity and to propagate its cause with missionary zeal but to learn from historical experience the 'laws and trends' that govern the unification process.

Another of Al-Bitar's important ideas, reflecting his attachment to the Nasserist experience, is that of the necessity of a base-territory (*iqlim qa'ida*) around which all unification efforts and processes are to circle: "the higher the degree of division, the more important is the 'base' as a pole around which to interact". Such a territory that is well qualified to lead the process of Arab unification, in all Al-Bitar's works, is of course Egypt – except at a late stage when he starts to hint at the possibility that Iraq might be able to go in that direction, were it to unite with other countries in Arabia and the Gulf (one wonders whether Saddam Husain has read these pages!).

In general, most Arabic writings on the 'nation' that relate the concept most directly to that of the 'state' tend to come from authors who hail from countries, such as Egypt or Tunisia, which possess a stronger sense of their own political community derived in no small measure from relatively early (nineteenth century) efforts at the modernisation and secularisation of their state machines (e.g. Muhammad 'Ali in Egypt and Khair al-Din in Tunisia, and their respective 'theoreticians': Rifa'a al-Tahtawi and Ibn Abi al-Diyaf).[6] Thus for example the leading Egyptian literary critic Louis 'Awad was to write that

> sophisticated nationalism has not emerged except in relation to patriotism, or indeed in relation to the central state, whereby the rules of law and institutions replaces the ruler's whims, customs and traditions, and where the people turn from 'subjects' into 'citizens' ... Thus we cannot speak today about an 'Arab Nation' or the 'Arab Fatherland' until the political borders are removed and a unified central state is established, a sovereign state with one constitution and unified laws ... a matter which is currently a mere hope and dream.

According to 'Awad, therefore, the concept of the nation is closely related to that of the state, and – for preference – to that of citizenship. It follows from this that whereas the concept of the Egyptian nation is close enough to a historical reality, the concept of the Arab nation cannot be anything but a political myth ['Awad, 1978: 163–6, also 130–32].

A similar line of argument is to be found in the writing of the Tunisian educator Al-Bashir bin Salama, who also speaks openly of a Tunisian nation. This he establishes on the grounds that "we live today in the era of national-ities, of 'patriotic solidarity'", *'asabiyyat al-watan* (i.e. country-based group feeling), and that the Tunisians do possess a distinct Tunisian character/personality (*shakhsiyya Tunisiyya*), whose distinctiveness is not impeded by the fact that Tunisians share a bond of language with other Arabic speakers [cf. Nassar, 1986: 498–502].

The salience of the state as a formative factor for the nation is also detected by the Lebanese philosopher Kamal al-Haj, except that in this case it appears to be correlated to his rationalisation of the multi-ethnic Lebanese state. He is clear that 'nationalism' is not simply 'nationalist feeling', but that the realisation of this feeling lies in what complements it, i.e. in politics. He is rather exceptional, in the Arab context, in drawing a distinction between the concepts of the nation and nationalism (*umma*) on the one hand, and the concept of nationality (what he calls *qawmiyya*, although the legalists usually call it *jinsiyya*) on the other: "nationality is a political existence, and political existence is nationality ... [Thus] I say that there is a Lebanese nationality, not a Lebanese nation, and there is an Arab nation but not an Arab nationality." For al-Haj it is the state alone that can preserve the components of nationalism and enable the individual to experience freedom. It is only the state which can be sovereign at home while keeping the community free from the domination of other communities[7] [cf. Nassar, 1986: 495–7].

Another component which has been rather weak in Pan-Arabist thinking is that pertaining to socio-economic factors; until, that is, the Arabists were forced by the 'oil boom' of the mid-1970s to acknowledge the extreme economic divisions of the Arab World not only by classes but also by countries. The contribution of the contemporary Iraqi social historian 'Abd al-'Aziz al-Duri is quite valuable in this respect. Especially distinct is the way in which he implies that the emergence of an 'Arab Nation', although closely tied to the unity of language, was in many ways moulded through a unified – or at least similar – socio-economic historical pattern [cf. e.g. Al-Duri, 1984].

The Egyptian political economist Samir Amin has also contributed to the debate with an important monograph [Amin, 1978], in which he suggests that Arab unity, when it existed (presumably as the core of the Arabo-Islamic empire), was the "historical product of the mercantile integration of the Arab World, as carried out by a class of merchant-warriors". With the decline of Arab trade, national disintegration set in, a process that was accentuated by the subsequent integration through colonialism of the Arab countries into the world capitalist system. Imperialist domination transposed the Arab sentiment of unity to a different level, that of a struggle against a common enemy. But this sentiment was unable to translate itself into a concrete union, because none of the dominant Arab classes of the 'imperialist era' (the comprador and the latifundist bourgeoisies, followed then by the state bourgeoisie) were capable of, or interested in, bringing such a unification about. In short, therefore, the problem with modern and contemporary Pan-Arabist ideas is that they have lacked a championing class that would find in the creation of a unified Arab state a realisation of its own class interests. Amin's thesis is vindicated by recent developments: state bourgeoisies, even when ruling in the name of Pan-Arabism (a device that enhances domestic legitimacy and can be used to chastise competitive neighbours),[8] are bound to strengthen the state apparatuses of the new countries they dominate rather than to encourage their merger into a larger entity.

The degree to which the Pan-Arabist idea has influenced the existing territorial states varies from one case to another and may, at least initially, be detected by examining the various constitutions or even sometimes the very name of the state. With regard to the concept of the nation, various constitutions in the mid-1960s, George Jabbur has found the following:

> There are 13 Arab constitutions that describe the nation as being the 'Arab nation' without any other different clear description; there are three constitutions that relate the 'nation' openly to their respective 'territory' thus using the term the 'Lebanese nation', the 'Tunisian nation' and the 'Somali nation'; there are four constitutions that remain silent with regard to the matter, which are those of Morocco, Mauritania, Algeria and the Sudan, with some hinting in the latter two constitutions to the effect that the 'nation' in question is most likely an 'Algerian nation' and a 'Sudanese nation' respectively [Jabbur, 1976: 113].

Even the very name of the state can be significant. Thus, for example, one has at one end of the spectrum the case of Syria, where the adjective 'Syrian' comes in the name (in its Arabic form) only as a qualifying appendage to the word 'Arab'. The population of the Syrian state is described as 'the Arab people in Syria'. In the case of Egypt, on the other hand, the name Egypt comes first (in Arabic again), and is then qualified by the adjective 'Arab'. At the other end of the spectrum there are those states that do not use the word 'Arab' in any capacity at all, except perhaps to describe the official language (e.g. Morocco) or who may use another description in the name of the state, such as 'Islamic' (e.g. Mauritania), or for that matter 'Popular' (e.g. Algeria, Libya and ex-South Yemen). Then of course there are the small, oil-rich Gulf 'statelets' that insist, just for good measure, on including the word 'state' itself in their official names: e.g. the State of Kuwait, the State of Bahrain, the State of the United Arab Emirates [for details cf. Al-Sa'igh, 1980].

From the start, Pan-Arabism has been a reactive, rather than a pro-active doctrine, forever trying to respond to a perceived challenge from the 'Other': first the Turkification policies of the late Ottoman Empire, then the division and domination enforced by the colonial powers, and then the settler-colonisation imposed by the Zionist state on the centre of the 'Arab Fatherland', thus separating its Asian from its African wing. The conceptual tenets and points of emphasis in the doctrine have been frequently adjusted in an attempt to cope with the changing challenges and the perceived threats. However, the doctrine of Pan-Arabism has remained, from its inception to the present time, basically language-centred and rather reluctant to take adequate account of other factors. Although the slogan of 'unity' has been invoked by most Arab nationalists, Arabism remains closer to a concept of a *Kulturnation*, and has not been pushed far enough in the direction of a *Staatsnation*: Arabism forms a cultural community and an emotional bond that can be invoked in the political arena, although it has not been able to modify the practice of state sovereignty in any significant way.[9]

The only political association among Arab countries is the League of Arab

States, i.e. an organisation of sovereign, independent *states*, historically encouraged by the 'colonialist' British rather than by any Arabist zealots [cf. Gomaa, 1977]. Even the English translation of the word *Jami'a*, as League, is too strong. And although some subsequent documents started to speak in semi-Pan-Arabist terms this was mainly indicative of how "governments came to manipulate sincere pan-Arabist feelings to their advantage, quietly becoming experts in mixing isolationalist policies with a pan-Arabist vocabulary" [Salamé, 1988: 259–64].

Pan-Arabism is an extremely belated doctrine of national unification which confronts serious, real problems, not the least of which is the general Western and Zionist hostility to what it stands for (for reasons that cannot be elaborated upon in the limited space available). Its death warrant has been signed several times, most notably by Fouad Ajami [cf. Ajami, 1978/79, 1982, and for further discussion and a rebuttal, Farah, ed., 1987]. It is still quite influential, however, among many segments of the intelligentsia in most Arab countries [cf. Ibrahim, 1980], even though in recent years it has had to concede plenty of ground to a potentially (although not necessarily) competitive doctrine, that of 'Islamic fundamentalism'.[10]

Although the failure of Arab nationalism hitherto in realising its unification objectives cannot simply be attributed, as it is by Elie Kedourie [e.g., 1985, 1970], to its European derivation or to its logical inconsistency or to the opportunistic inclinations of some of its leading proponents [cf. Davis-Willard, 1978], there is little doubt that the 'Theory of Arab Nationalism' itself is not entirely flawless. As an 'imagined community' [cf. Anderson, 1983], the 'Arab Nation' is not really clearly perceived (witness for example the flimsy basis on which Somalia and Djibouti are considered 'Arab' and are admitted to the League of Arab States). Even its 'myth of origins' in time, space and ancestry [cf. Smith, 1991: Chs. 1 and 2] is not adequately defined.[11] It also remains excessively 'romantic', and it has only recently started to pay adequate attention to the importance of social and economic variables (including the huge wealth disparities among Arab countries), and to the crucial issue of the state (contrast this, for example, with the Zionist ideology, one of whose earliest manifestoes was a book on the Jewish state). If the odd Pan-Arabist radio station (such as Sawt al-'Arab – Voice of the Arabs – of the Nasserist period) could at some stage stimulate the ideological imagination of the average Arab to think of his/her 'nation' as extending from the '(Persian) Gulf to the (Atlantic) Ocean' (*min al-khalij ila al-muhit*), then his social '*imaginaire*' was always more tied to daily livelihood experiences (in education, employment, transport and communication, military conscription, etc.) which limited his symbolic horizons to a more specifically territorial state [cf. Zubaida, 1989].[12]

Arab nationalism continues to be characterised by a kind of 'identity-mania': the eternal question is forever: 'who are we?' and very rarely 'what are we going to do?', and how can we do it?[13] One Moroccan scholar [Bin

'Abd al-'Ali, 1992] has recently described this 'mania' most succinctly. A certain degree of self-searching is needed, especially in times of weakness and challenge, when issues of 'identity', 'authenticity' and 'specificity' acquire a particular pertinence. What he finds remarkable, however, is the long halt by contemporary Arab thinkers at this point, where nothing appears to matter as much as issues of the 'self' and the 'roots' and the 'heritage'. The Arab World witnesses, according to him, what amounts to "a pathological obsession with this set of related issues, and especially that of identity". What is more, this search for identity is only manifested at a static level of reaction and emotion. It is not the outcome of an actual engagement in a real act of constructing the self through interaction with the other, but is a purely theoretical issue, concerned merely with "displaying ourselves to the other" in endless, repetitive "letters of introduction".

But what might be the underlying reason for this obsession with identity and cultural issues and this inefficiency with regard to actual integration and institution-building, and could this have anything to do with the absence of 'a championing social class'?

At one level of analysis, it is possible to argue that 'Arabism' has never in reality been more than a linguistic bond, void of any sociological substance. As one writer has sardonically expressed it, "the Arabs are a phonetic phenomenon" (Al-'Arab zahira sawtiyya) [Al-Qasimi, 1977]. In spite of the noise, however, Arabism did not take any distinct shape in the socio-economic sphere. Muhammad Jabir al-Ansari [1994] has recently come up with an interesting theory to explain this. The Arabs, he suggests, have interacted very little with each other. This was due, ecologically, to the extensive desert tracts that cover much of their territory and separate the regions from each other. Historically, it was due to the nature of their tributary system of 'bureaucratic-feudalism' (iqta') which created a centrifugal arrangement pulling all the resources to, and establishing all the contacts with, the capital city. Not only did the regions become impoverished as a result but they were never allowed to establish any elaborate infrastructures or institutional setups of their own, nor to interact directly (i.e. horizontally) with each other. According to al-Ansari, the contemporary territorial states in the Arab World may be acting, functionally speaking, as a delayed 'feudal' stage (in the European sense) setting about, as they are, to build the infrastructure and to fill in the demographic and constructional voids within and between the Arab countries. He concludes from this that if Arab unity is to be achieved one day, it is more likely to be through a strengthening, rather than through a negation, of the territorial states in the Arab World.

Also missing, in what is perhaps a related point, has been the presence of a championing class whose own specific interests coincide with the prospects of a larger unified market and integrated state. Samir Amin has suggested that, historically, the Arabo-Islamic 'state' was only united at the period when the merchant class that was engaged in long-distance trade had come near enough to forming a dominant class [Amin, 1978]. The thesis is persuasive, although some reservations may be expressed: mainly that the commercial class was neither autonomous enough nor sufficiently steady and 'continuous' to form a hegemonic class because it was at most times vulnerable to, and dependent on, the politico/military élite. The commercial class continued to exist in social terms but its economic and political weight became even more reduced when long-distance trade became less important (under European competition) during the Ottoman era, although inter-Ottoman trade was large enough to support a reasonable merchant class [cf. Al-Naqib, 1986: Ch. 11, n. 20].

With the penetration of European commercial interests into the Ottoman Empire, some of the traditional inter-Ottoman trade started to be drawn away outside the empire, directed and dominated by European interests. This process was given a politico-strategic dimension when the Arab East was divided under the mandate of the two leading colonial European powers: Britain and France. For example, the trade routes that linked Aleppo to Mosul and Istanbul and those that linked Damascus to Jerusalem and Nablus had to be severed. It was not surprising therefore that the growing ideas of Arab nationalism found their greatest appeal at that time among the urban merchants (and their educated sons) as they experienced the artificial (i.e. political and military) separation and curtailment of their traditional markets [cf. Khoury, 1983b, 1987; Qazziha, 1979]. Incidentally, a similar pattern was to be observed in Sudan, where a large proportion of the Unionists who were in favour of integration with Egypt were from among people who had commercial and/or educational links with Egypt. However, the Pan-Arabist commercial/intellectual élite in the Levant was never strong enough to be able to cut through the newly imposed economic and political borders. Nor was Egyptian capital, represented by Banque Misr, able to hold its own in its attempt to go Pan-Arabist and to invest in the Arab East in the inter-war period, given that it had to succumb to foreign capital even in its own home country [cf. Davis, 1983]. The excessive emphasis in early Pan-Arabist thought on cultural and moral matters to the exclusion of any solid economic or strategic vision (related for example to the form and nature of the hoped-for United Arab State) may be regarded either as a partial cause for the eventual faltering of the Pan-Arabist ideology, or it may be regarded as an inevitable outcome – since the economic and political domain appeared at the time to be so far out of reach.

Formal independence itself was achieved by the 'traditional' nationalist élite that had its social roots in landownership, commerce and the conventional bureaucracy. But not long after independence, this class was removed from power by army officers representing the interests of an ascending 'new middle class' of professionals and technocrats. One such movement, the Egyptian Free Officers, was to adopt the Pan-Arab principles that had first emerged in the Mashriq. Yet it was not the commercial bourgeoisie which had championed the cause of Arab unity in this case but the Egyptian state, with its relatively well-established traditions and relatively well-advanced capabilities. This task was made easier thanks to the charismatic leadership of Nasser and to his 'political' victory in Suez. But when Egypt and Syria were united, from 1958 to 1961, there was a serious incongruency of expectations. Among other things, the traditionally important commercial bourgeoisie of Syria was still economically and politically active, unlike its counterpart in Egypt where an emerging public sector and a ban on political parties had increased the state's control.

The Syrian business bourgeoisie, proud of its commercial skills and traditions, had hoped to prosper within the much larger Egyptian market, and indeed many Syrian merchants moved to Egypt, where a whole marketplace (in Alexandria) was called after them. However, the Syrian merchants were disappointed to find not only that the Egyptian market was not as wide open to them as they had anticipated, but also that the Egyptian state sector was in addition starting to 'crowd them out' of their own Syrian home market [cf. Ayubi, 1989b]. Their fears were confirmed when a major collection of 'socialist' nationalisation measures was issued in July 1961 for application in both regions of the United Arab Republic. And to make things worse, the commercially important Syrian borders with Jordan, Saudi Arabia and Iraq were also closed. Political parties and interest associations were dissolved, thus making any venting of the bourgeoisie's grievances almost impossible [cf. Hilal, 1980: 67–72]. Big Syrian business, allied with certain disgruntled Ba'th party personnel, soon rallied behind a military coup d'état that effected Syria's secession from the UAR.

Paradoxically, from that point onwards, the commercial bourgeoisie that at an earlier stage had harboured much of the Arabist sentiment, found itself widely categorised in the political rhetoric of the 1960s as an enemy of Arab nationalism. Nasser pushed his nationalisation programme much further in Egypt, declaring that it was a way of disarming the anti-revolutionary *and* anti-unionist capitalists. When the Ba'thists regained power in Syria in 1963– 1966 they came down very hard on the commercial bourgeoisie, partly to 'atone' – so to speak – for their party's sin of having joined the bourgeoisie in its anti-union strike in 1961. From then on an Arab cold war developed between the so-called Arab 'radicals' and Arab 'reactionaries'; with the latter believed to be pro-capitalism and anti-unity [cf. Kerr, 1971]. Both Ba'thists and Nasserists had 'Freedom, Socialism and Unity' (albeit differently ordered) as their tripartite slogan. To fight the anti-unionists now also meant fighting the commercial bourgeoisie. And to counter the commercial bourgeoisie, the state was now expanding the size and scope of its activities in the economic sphere, and building up a very extensive and dominant public sector.

Yet the more entrenched the machine of the territorial state became, the less likely it was that Arab integration would take place. Particularly ironic was the fact that in some cases the formal Pan-Arabist ideology adopted by a certain regime would be manipulated in such a way as to ensure in reality the consolidation of the territorial state *vis-à-vis* its neighbours who may equally espouse, in theory, the same Arabist ideals. The antagonistic relations since the late 1960s between an Iraq and a Syria both ruled by a certain branch of the Ba'th party is of course the most outstanding example [see Kienle, 1990]. For the new military and technocratic élites of the independent states had by now pinned most of their interests and most of their aspirations on the existing territorial state and its expanding economic sector rather than on the illusory Pan-Arabist state. These countries were busy issuing development plans that restructured their own territorial-state economies but that made no provision for possible complementarity of investments among the various Arab economies. The public sector, which was built at least partly as a component of radical Pan-Arabism, ended up by being in some ways a barrier to Arab unification. Not only did the interests of the new élites develop around the territorial state and its extensive administrative and economic machine, but the division of the Arab World into so-called 'socialist' and anti-socialist or non-socialist countries was used to justify the lack of progress towards economic integration. As a slogan of the 1960s declared, unity of objectives, *wahdat al-hadaf* (i.e. socialism), was more important than the unity of ranks, *wahdat al-saff* (i.e. a unified Arab structure). The oil boom of the 1970s could only add a financial edge to such a dichotomy, as the socialist states were more often poor countries while the rich countries were more often headed by 'conservative' dynasties.

THE REGIONAL/FUNCTIONAL APPROACH

As opposed to the ideological/political comprehensive approach preached by the Ba'thists, the Nasserists and the Arab Nationalists, the more limited regional/functional approach to integration was given a try in the early 1980s through the formation of the Gulf Cooperation Council (GCC). This approach is almost the exact opposite of the overall, overnight unitary-state approach, which used to be favoured by most Pan-Arabists, and which is often described by critics as the 'Prussian model' because it over-emphasises the role of a 'pivotal-territory' in overwhelming others into accepting unification [cf. Al-Jabiri's "Comments" in Hanafi and Al-Jabiri, 1990: Ch. 4; Bilqaziz, 1991: 42ff].

Although only a 'regional' organisation and not a federal or confederal state, the GCC represents an illustration that Arab integration *can* take place once the concrete conditions are right: in this case geographic contiguity, common strategic concerns and a similar socio-economic outlook. And even though initially it was criticised by many as a mere '*club des riches*' and as an anti-Arabist arrangement, most have come to realise since that the regional approach to Arab integration, while not without problems, is probably the most likely way to achieve any degree of success.

The establishing of the Gulf Cooperation Council in 1981 was a significant development since it represented, among other things, the first inter-state regional organisation to have been formed in the Arab World since the establishment of the League of Arab States itself, and because, with the partial exception of the Arab Maghrib Union formed in 1989, it remains the most effective attempt to reach some sort of inter-Arab – although not all-Arab – integration.

Behind the setting-up of the GCC – which includes Saudi Arabia, Kuwait, the United Arab Emirates, Qatar, Bahrain and Oman – were two kinds of concerns: security and economic. With Egypt busy at the time with the details of her separate peace with Israel, with Iran's Islamic revolution generally gaining the upper hand militarily over Iraq and encroaching on the smaller Gulf states, with the Soviets in Afghanistan apparently to stay, and with the controversial US Rapid Deployment Forces (RDF) at the ready, the Gulf states were understandably becoming increasingly apprehensive over their strategic vulnerability. At the same time they were concerned about their developmental prospects and about their economic future in the post-petroleum era. Fluctuations in oil prices and the utilisation of surplus funds worried them, as did their almost unavoidable dependency on the West in terms of trade and technology and their dependence on other parts of the Third World in terms of manpower requirements.[14] The need to pull together could therefore hardly be overlooked, especially in view of the demographic smallness and relative wealth of these countries, which factors, when combined, added tremendously to their fragility and vulnerability.

During the 1970s, encouraged by the similarity in their economic and political systems, and by a sense of sharing in certain common problems, the countries of Arabia and the Gulf began to develop ways and means of working together. Several treaties were ratified for the coordination of economic, financial, monetary, commercial, industrial and customs systems, with the aim especially of encouraging the movement of capital and personnel among them, although many such agreements in the 1970s were bilateral rather than multilateral. Another area of cooperation was in joint ventures, including a project for a dry dock, a company for petroleum investments, the Gulf International Bank, the Arab Navigation Company, and so on. There were also various negotiations for amalgamating airlines and other land and sea transport organisations, accompanied by other steps towards solving some of the outstanding border conflicts between the Gulf states and by increased cooperation in the field of intelligence [Kuwait, Ministry of Finance, 1986].

Such cooperative efforts gathered momentum from the mid-1970s and led to the formation of several integrative institutions [Nye, 1978]. In June 1975, for example, four of the smaller Gulf states decided to take steps towards unifying their currencies and creating a common Gulf dinar as a move in the direction of complete monetary union, and some countries agreed to make their respective currencies legal tender in each of the others. The subject was considered several times subsequently but the time was judged not yet ripe for such a measure. The Gulf International Bank was also created in 1975 with equal subscriptions of capital from the six countries that later formed the GCC, as an international merchant bank whose principal goal was to finance and expand Gulf trade; Iraq later participated in the bank's capital. An Arab Investment Group (AIG) was established in 1974 for investing capital in the development of Arab resources in the seven signatory states (five of which were Gulfian plus Egypt and the Sudan). An Arab Gulf Organisation for Industrial Consultancy (AGOIC) was set up in 1976 between the six states that later became the GCC and Iraq, to coordinate the planning of industrial projects in the area and to devise a regional development plan. The United Arab Shipping Company was formed in 1976, financed by shares from five of the subsequent founders of the GCC (Kuwait, Saudi Arabia, the UAE, Qatar and Bahrain), plus Iraq, and became a functioning joint venture. An Association of Gulf Ports was also created by an agreement signed in 1976 by the six GCC founder countries and Iraq. Gulf Air, formed in the mid-1970s, became the successful national airline for Bahrain, Qatar, the UAE and Oman, and while Saudi Arabia did not favour a full merger of its own airline Saudia, joint operations were set up with Gulf Air. From the 1980s increased competition prompted recommendations for greater cooperation and standardisation among all Gulf airlines [*Saudi Report*, 1 November 1982]. Several projects to link the Gulf states in a communications network were also established: a Gulf News Agency opened in 1978 (including Saudi Arabia, Kuwait, the UAE, Qatar, Bahrain and Iraq), and there was also coordination in television and in telecommunications.

These various developments culminated in the announcement in May 1981 of the formation of the Gulf Cooperation Council, whose stated aims were to consolidate relations between the Gulf states, not only in economic and other 'functional' areas but also in strategic and security-related matters. To achieve its objectives it was organised into a number of units: (a) a Supreme Council, meeting annually, whose members include the heads of the six member states and whose presidency is run on a rotating basis. Attached to the Supreme Council is the 'Conflict Resolution Commission'; (b) a Ministerial Council composed of the six foreign ministers, meeting twice a year or more, plus other groups of ministers meeting in a number of specialised committees (of which there were around twelve in 1985), including committees for Social and Economic Planning, Economic and Trade Cooperation, Financial and Monetary Cooperation, Industrial Cooperation, Petroleum Affairs, Transport and Communications, and Social and Cultural Services; (c) an expanding secretariat in Riyadh, with a secretary-general as well as deputy secretaries responsible for economic, political and other affairs [cf. Anthony, 1982; Qatar News Agency, 1981, 1982; Al-Khalij, special suppl., 2 November 1986].

A supplementary collective security agreement and a unified economic agreement were also signed by the GCC members in 1981 and arrangements were later made for the removal of customs duties on agricultural, mineral and industrial products in their movement among the six countries. An Industrial Cooperation Committee was formed with the aim – among others – of encouraging the use of such products when produced by government projects. The Arab Gulf Organisation for Industrial Consultancy provided information and research for this and for other projects. Other initiatives included the inauguration of an all-Gulf University (based in Bahrain) and the creation of a Gulf Investment Corporation (capital $2 billion) jointly funded by the six member states [see Al-Sharq al-Awsat, 11 February 1982; Saudi Report, 11 October and 2 November 1982 and 28 June 1983].

In addition there are collective security arrangements among GCC members that cover most security-related matters, both internal and external, and there are also bilateral agreements for 'single cooperation' between Saudi Arabia and respectively Bahrain, Qatar, the Emirates and Oman [Al-Sharq al-Awsat, 24–25 February 1982]. Such collective arrangements included the formation in 1984 of a joint military force with an air defence system and a unified military command and were aimed ultimately at the creation of a regional arms manufacturing facility – the Gulf Arms Manufacturing Authority (capital over $8 billion) with headquarters in Riyadh that would partly replace the Arab Arms Manufacturing Authority (this latter organisation was based in Egypt although largely financed by the Gulf countries, but was dissolved after Camp David) [Saudi Arabia Yearbook 1980–1981: 49].

It was also the intention of the six members of the GCC to harmonise their economic policies, including policies on oil pricing and production, since between them they account for over half of OPEC's production. Their relative ability (especially that of Saudi Arabia and Kuwait) to lower their production levels without their economic programmes suffering seriously as a result gives them an added advantage over many of the more economically 'needy' oil producers. If OPEC is ever to succeed in becoming a cartel, the process will almost certainly have to start with the GCC countries.

Major industrial and other projects were another area in which the GCC members intended to coordinate their economic policies. There was an obvious need for coordinating projects in the fields of petrochemicals and fertilisers, cement, steel and metallics, and so on, in order to avoid waste and duplication, and establishing joint ventures among member countries was found to be one of the most effective ways of achieving this: thus the Saudi-Kuwaiti-Bahraini Petrochemicals Company, the Saudi-Kuwaiti Cement Company and the Saudi-Kuwaiti Pharmaceutical Company. Another method was to turn some new projects into all-GCC projects, as with the decision by the Yanbu' industrialisation authority to sell 70 per cent of the project's shares to citizens of all GCC states [*Saudi Arabia Yearbook 1980–1981*: 52], while in the opposite direction, Saudi Arabia took a 20 per cent stake in Aluminium Bahrain. Arrangements of this sort would be further consolidated by the GCC countries arranging to buy their requirements jointly and indeed it was announced that the six intended to pay for at least 50 per cent of their medical requirements together until all their purchases of medicine were made jointly, a procedure that would save them at least 30 per cent of the cost [*Saudi Report*, 4 October 1982].

The GCC members also sought to coordinate their growing banking and finance activities which represented something of a success story although the potential for uneasy competition did certainly exist. Arab-led banks (mainly from the Gulf) accounted in the mid-1980s for around 27 per cent of the total world loan market [*Saudi Report*, 23 August 1982], an achievement that could be maintained and consolidated only if proper coordination was sustained among the three main banking centres of the Gulf: Bahrain, with its large offshore banking sector set up mainly as a channel for funds to and from Saudi Arabia; Kuwait, in effect the investment centre for the region; and the UAE, with a number of flourishing small-scale commercial banks. It was also recognised that the GCC would benefit greatly from coordinating their transport and communications systems, from rationalising their education programmes (especially the competition for building new universities), and from harmonising their cultural policies.

Shortly after the setting-up of the GCC the mood among the Gulf élites regarding the future of the Council was enthusiastic and optimistic, and indeed the Saudi Minister of Finance and Economy predicted that in another year or so the members of the GCC would become a unified economic group similar to the European Economic Community (EEC) [*Arab Perspectives*, Vol. 3, 1982: 31]. Another Saudi source quoted, presumably with approval, a report in a respectable American newspaper which suggested that "In its own low-key way, the six-member Gulf Cooperation Council (GCC) is really the only 'Arab unity' plan that looks as if it will go the distance ... The GCC ... is maturing from a fledgling common market for the Gulf nations into what could well become a mini-NATO" [*Saudi Report*, 8 November 1982].

Certainly the GCC's approach to such unity tended – as with the European Common Market – to be piecemeal and functional, rather than comprehensive and ideological in the way that had characterised most integration thinking among the Arabs in the 1950s and 1960s. Interestingly too, there were signs of renewed interest in developing links between the GCC Six and what were at the time the EEC Ten, especially in the area of technical cooperation and information exchange [cf. *Arabia*, no. 12, August 1982: 46]. Indeed, Abdallah Bishara, the GCC's first secretary-general, contrasted the functional 'cooperation' approach of the GCC with what he called the 'Syrian School' in

Arab unity, characterised by 'vigour and daring'. He noted that by comparison the GCC avoided too much 'theorisation' on the one hand and excessive institutionalisation on the other, because it was neither a federation nor a confederation but was simply a 'cooperation council' based on agreement and consensus, with every state maintaining the right "to be exempted from applying decisions approved by the other states if its own circumstances would not so permit" [Bishara, 1985: 29].

Even so, and notwithstanding the initial mood of optimism that greeted its appearance, one may wonder whether the GCC will continue as a viable functional union, and whether the cooperative and integrative relations between the six countries are likely to deepen through any sort of 'ramification' or 'spill-over effect'? It is not an easy question to answer. To begin with, owing to the similarity of the economic structures of these countries and due to their trade dependence *vis-à-vis* the industrialised countries, trade amongst them is negligible – only Kuwait and Bahrain, in both cases because they re-export goods, seem to have any trade worth noting with other Gulf countries. With the partial exception of Oman, the economic structures of all GCC members are so similar in their one-dimensionality that in a way this limits real opportunities for complementarity. Above all, these countries depend to a very large extent on foreign markets to generate revenues through exports. In 1976, for example, the ratio of exports to GDP was 87.1 per cent in the case of Saudi Arabia and 78.4 per cent in the case of Kuwait, and was even higher in the case of the UAE and Qatar. Moreover, with the export dependency of the Gulf states centring round their one main export commodity – oil – we find that in 1977 oil represented 96.2 per cent of the value of all Saudi Arabia's exports, 76 per cent of the value of Kuwait's exports, 96 per cent of the value of the exports of the Emirates, and 98 per cent of the exports of Qatar [Ayubi, 1982b, and refs quoted]. Oil revenues thus accounted – and indeed still account – for a particularly high percentage of state revenues in all countries of the GCC.

A further problematic factor relates to the history of personal, tribal and territorial conflicts among the GCC countries, many of which have still not been permanently settled [Al-Rumaihi, 1980: 73–95]. It was believed that such conflicts were behind the fact that when the United Arab Emirates was formed in 1971 only seven of the nine Gulf shaikhdoms could be included, since Bahrain and Qatar insisted on staying out. Even this smaller union remained rather fragile and not long ago trembled under the impact of a quarrel between its two larger members, Abu Dhabi and Dubai, a disagreement that happily was solved successfully. In the spring of 1982 the two shaikhdoms that remained outside the Emirates were seriously reviving an old territorial conflict over the island of Hawar, and Saudi Arabia, the predominant force in the Gulf, who had previously managed to resolve the more complex conflict between itself and Abu Dhabi over the Buraimi Oasis, did not seem able to mediate a rapid solution. The GCC at large was no more successful in this respect [cf. *Al-Mustaqbal*, 3 April 1982: 32–5], than it was in solving the subsequent border conflicts between Bahrain and Qatar and between Saudi Arabia and Qatar.

The predominant role of Saudi Arabia within the GCC is something of a controversial subject. By far the largest country within the Council in terms of territory, population and resources, Saudi Arabia is also, and in consequence, the most prestigious and influential member both regionally and internationally. The Saudi role in the Gulf has tended to take the form of two functions: the conciliator and the financier [see Ahmad, 1979, esp. Part II]. Although relations with Kuwait in the pre-Second World War period tended to be characterised by an element of competition and restlessness, they improved greatly from the latter half of the 1960s, and border relations with Kuwait and other Gulf countries started to advance a good part of the way towards settlement when the Buraimi conflict, among other disputes, was solved. Indeed Saudi Arabia turned into one of the main backers of the formation of the UAE in 1970–71, and this new federated state subsequently became a main supporter of Saudi regional diplomacy as well as a supporter of Saudi policies within OPEC. The Saudis also used "financial aid as a lubricant for inter-state unity" [Nye, 1978: 13], by, for example, bearing the entire cost of $1 billion for the causeway linking them to Bahrain, by offering loans to Oman for various purposes, and so on.

Might the predominant Saudi role in the GCC make it easier to provide the union with the sustained cohesive leadership that is usually needed by endeavours such as this?; would the other members ever assemble together to counterbalance the Saudi weight?; or would they – especially the élites of countries like Kuwait and Bahrain – find it unacceptable to be allowed only an auxiliary role in comparison with that of the Saudis? These are important questions that cannot yet be given a full answer.

What can be reported with a fair degree of confidence at this stage is that the GCC does indeed have its problems. It has been criticised for being more concerned with security, especially domestic political security, than with development [cf. Al-Nafisi, 1982; Al-Majid, 1986: 30ff]; not that it is particularly efficient even with regard to security. The draft internal security agreement of 1982 was signed by only five of the six members (even though the countries are believed to exchange intelligence) and the Gulf Rapid Deployment Force, created in 1984 and based at Hafr al-Batin in Saudi Arabia, is not subject to a unified command. It has been basically symbolic except for the brief episode of the Iraq/Kuwait crisis, and proposals for expanding it after the crisis were not pursued. Economically, not all aspects of the Unified Economic Agreement have been implemented, even though trade among members is reported to have risen, monetary policy is reported to be more closely coordinated, and the number of joint ventures is reported to have increased. Free movement of citizens across borders of the member states is not complete, customs and tariffs are disparate and investment projects remain basically parallel and thus competitive, rather than complementary.

Yet although the GCC is indeed riddled with problems it still counts, relatively speaking, as one of the most concretely successful attempts at Arab integration. The other two cases usually quoted are the United Arab Emirates, a 'confederal' state of small principalities that is not without problems (see references to it in Chapters 3 and 7), and the Yemen, a once promising model whose integrity could not, however, be maintained except by military force (see the section on Yemen in Chapter 11).

The GCC experiment has in a sense been emulated in the Arab Co-operation Council and the Arab Maghrib Union, both formed in 1989. The first (formed amongst Egypt, Iraq, Jordan and North Yemen) withered away under the pressures of the Gulf crisis of 1990/1991; the second is still alive, albeit rather shakily, under the combined impact of common worries over marginalisation by the European Union and limited scope for integration among the basically non-complementary economies of its member states.

THE 'MISSING BOURGEOISIE' AND THE FUTURE OF ARAB UNITY

The collapse of the Soviet Union and of Yugoslavia as political units in the early 1990s makes it quite tempting for one to arrive at the sweeping conclusion that, unlike bourgeois capitalism which forged national unity in Britain, France and elsewhere, state capitalism is incapable of forging national integration. Yet let us concentrate for the purposes of this exercise on the case of the Arab World, where one can suggest with a fair degree of confidence that Arab Unity and state capitalism (so-called socialism) were by necessity contradictory to each other. The Iraqi writer 'Ali al-Sarraf explains this contradiction:

> It is clear that, for pure economic-structural reasons, national unification and socialism were two opposites that could never meet ... For whereas socialism, as the public ownership of the means of production, consecrates itself to domestic self-sufficiency and may develop direct relations with the outside world, national integration is based on a unification of the whole national (i.e. Pan-Arabist) market that would negate territorially-defined self-sufficiency ... Nor could the 'socialist' state act as a capitalist one in lieu of the absent bourgeoisie, because whereas [the leadership of] State capitalism gives precedence to its political interests and to the process of spending (which is the source of its power), the leadership of class-based capitalism gives priority to its economic interests and to production (which is the source of its strength and influence) [Al-Sarraf, 1992: summarised and edited by the present author].

In the 1970s the oil boom caused both a weakening in the 'socialist' orientation of the so-called 'radical' states and a tremendous growth in the public sectors of the so-called 'conservative' oil-exporting countries. The differential between the rich and the poor Arab states reached a peak at this stage. In 1972 the countries that now form the Gulf Cooperation Council (GCC) hosted 7 per cent of all Arab population and possessed 26 per cent of all Arab GNP. A decade later, the GCC countries hosted 8 per cent of all Arab population but possessed 52 per cent of all Arab GNP [Al-Nasrawi, 1990: 30–31]. This development has implied, among other things, a change in the regional balance against the countries with leading public sectors and in favour of the countries that formally adhere to the ideals of a 'free market economy'. The financial polarisation between the rich and the poor states is likely to have hampered the prospects of unity between these states as states (why should a Kuwaiti or an Emirati voluntarily agree to share his wealth with millions of Egyptians and Yemenis!). But this polarisation does not by itself explain the dearth of *private* Arab investment in other Arab countries. The explanation for this lies largely elsewhere, in factors such as the continuing bureaucratic complications in the potential recipient countries and the lack of investment and entre- preneurial experience in the potential sending countries.

The 1970s and early 1980s, however, witnessed an interesting and potentially integrationist phenomenon. In addition to an unprecedented increase in labour migration among the Arab countries, an extensive network of inter-Arab 'functional' and professional organisations began to proliferate, run by a growing élite of Arab technocrats [cf. Kerr and Yassin, 1982; Luciani and Salame, 1988; Ayubi, 1984b; etc.]. Some hoped that an Arabist organisational and developmentalist concept might emerge as the technocrats from various countries started to look at 'Arab' issues in their totality and in terms of their potential complementarity. But this emerging inter-Arab bureaucracy was not large, permanent or stable enough, nor was it adequately autonomous *vis-à-vis* various Arab states (especially the donor oil-exporting ones) for its technocrats to be able to act as a 'championing class' for Arab integration. As one writer put it, "interaction is not integration" [Green, 1986].

The 1980s ushered in the beginning of the liberalisation and privatisation trend in most parts of the Arab World (for details see Chapter 10). Although the development of domestic business bourgeoisies (especially in the field of industry) has not so far been particularly impressive, relatively sizeable private sectors do now exist where they scarcely did two decades ago, and it would be useful to consider briefly both their concrete 'integrationist' contribution so far, as well as their potential contribution in this respect, in light of our previous discussion concerning the 'historical' role of the bourgeoisie in achieving national unification.

To start with, it is perhaps worth remembering that the oil boom did not stimulate inter-Arab trade in any impressive way. In the period from 1980 to 1986 this represented a mere 8.3 per cent of all exports and a mere 6.7 per cent of all imports, and was mostly confined to a limited number of Arab states [Arab Monetary Fund, 1989, 1990]. It is not clear what percentages the private sector was responsible for, but they are unlikely to have been large. In terms of private capital movements, most went outside the Arab World, although certain amounts were deposited in places like Beirut, Kuwait and Bahrain. A series of conferences linking Arab financiers with technocrats and experts on joint ventures was started in 1982, and met in places such as Ta'if, Casablanca and Kuwait. However, inter-Arab private investment continued to be largely confined to a few activities such as real estate and tourism (and more recently some marginal commodities), and to a few countries such as Sudan, Tunisia, Morocco and Mauritania. In 1985 the entire value of inter-Arab private capital investment did not exceed $327 million [Al-Himsi, 1990: 811–14].

Following the oil boom, Arab joint ventures grew to reach, during the second half of the 1980s, some 830 in number and about $36 billion in total capital value. Of these, 391 projects, at a capital value of $21.4 billion, were exclusively Arab, and 439 projects, at a capital value of $14.3 billion, were Arab/international. Of the exclusively Arab projects, 39 per cent were located within the countries of the GCC (59.5 per cent of total capital), 0.3 per cent of the projects (9.5 per cent of the capital) were in the countries of the Mashriq, 28.1 per cent of projects (15.4 per cent of capital) were in countries of the Nile Valley and Horn of Africa, and 8.8 per cent of projects (13.5 per cent of capital) were in countries of the Maghrib. The main fields in which such joint ventures function are financial investments ($14.5 billion) and the manufacturing industries ($11 billion), followed by transport and communication ($3.6 billion), agriculture ($2.3 billion), and extracting industries ($2.1 billion). Of all the joint ventures (exclusively Arab plus Arab/international), 271 projects ($17.4 billion capital) were subscribed by public sectors, and 286 projects ($7.6 billion capital) by private business, while 273 projects ($10.7 billion capital) were mixed (public/private) projects [Al-Himsi, 1990: 818–20; Barqawi, 1988: 33–47].

As a regional sub-division, members of the Gulf Cooperation Council have gone further than other sub-regional units (i.e. the Maghrib and the Arab Cooperation Council) in encouraging investment by citizens of any one member country into any one of the other member states. In 1988 a total of 263 intra-GCC joint ventures were identified. However, the private sector joint ventures did not account for more than 35 per cent of the total capital invested in non-financial joint-venture enterprises (mainly in transportation services, construction materials, petrochemicals, trading and engineering). While nationals from various GCC member companies benefited from the floating of some of SABIC's shares in 1987, further steps are being taken to identify "regionally privatisable public or mixed enterprises in the GCC member states. These enterprises may include such giant enterprises as SABIC, PETROMIN, the grain silos of Saudi Arabia, telecommunications, sea- and air-ports, airlines, electricity generation, water desalination, and similar public-owned enterprises in the GCC members states" [Khatrawi, 1989: 183–201]. Yet even within the GCC and in spite of the shared outlook and the common fears, citizens were quick to observe that they could purchase property in a fellow member country only for private residence and not for investment purposes, whereas it could be bought for investment purposes more or less freely in 'foreign', Western European and North American countries [cf. *Al-Majalla*, no. 619, 18 December 1991: 15, also 26–46].

As can be seen, inter-Arab joint ventures are still small in size and, judging by their activities and locations, also limited in impact. Which of the two main sectors (the public and the private) is more effective in terms of the integration process is difficult to determine, although some believe that the private sector is more efficient in siphoning out Arab capital towards foreign markets (both from the oil-exporting countries such as Kuwait, and the labour-exporting countries such as Egypt). Private Arab investments abroad were estimated at about $400 billion in 1989 of which 80 per cent was in the form of savings and deposits in Western markets and no more than 10 per cent was in the form of credits and indirect contributions within the Arab World [Federation of Arab Banks, cited in *Al-Hawadith*, No. 1834, 27 December 1991: 34]. One can of course quote the names of a handful of successful inter-Arab entrepreneurs (e.g. Rafiq al-Hariri in Lebanon, Bin Mahfuz and Salih Kamil in Saudi Arabia, and 'U. Ahmad 'Uthman in Egypt, etc.). More generally, however, it is true that domestic 'push' factors and international 'pull' factors have combined to induce Arab private capital to move abroad, and to accept for itself a passive, if apparently secure, place within the globalised finance markets. One can, of course, add the indirect and largely unintended 'integration' that sometimes takes place via foreign contractors or via international organisations. Account should also be taken of the fact that the major part of inter-Arab manpower movements are subject to private contracts and their personnel do accumulate private funds that may be invested within an Arab context. Even so, the overall impact of inter-Arab private activity is still rather modest in its totality [Zalzala, 'Comment', in Al-Nasrawi et al., 1990: 844–51].

But if the size and the impact of private inter-Arab investment were to grow in the foreseeable future, would it be likely to contribute to an enhancement of the Pan-Arabist integration potential? At least one Arab economist is certain that capitalists are more likely to be Pan-Arabist (because of their interest in larger markets) than are the ruling élites of the territorial states who would lose many of their privileges in a unified country. He even contends that "the march of Arab economic integration would perhaps have accelerated, had the governments originally not interfered in economic life to the degree that they did" [Jalal, 'Discussions', in Al-Nasrawi et al., 1990: 363, 856–7].

Perhaps he is right. For the future, however, it is hard to imagine how private Arab capital would voluntarily go 'Arabist' after it has already opted to go 'globalist'. It may well be that the common class interests of the 'international corporate bourgeoisie' [Sklar, 1976] will prove to be more potent than the presumed Arab sentiments and regional interests of Arab capital.[15]

NOTES

1. The term 'Pan-Arabism' has no equivalent in the Arabic language. It is normally to be inferred from those who use terms such as *al-umma al-'arabiyya* (the Arab 'nation'), *al-qawmiyya al-'arabiyya* (Arab nationalism), and *al-watan al-'arabi* (the Arab Fatherland). Such concepts are often contrasted with the concepts of *wataniyya* ('patriotism' – i.e. attachment to one's 'country', *patrie*, rather then to one's 'people', *Volk*) and – more pejoratively – with the concepts of *iqlimi* and *qutri* (territorial/provincial; country-based).

2. Parts of the analysis in this section have appeared in N. Ayubi, "Pan Arabism", in M. Foley, ed., 1994. They are being used here with permission from the publishers, and with thanks to them.

3. The term used to specify this Arab 'nation' was the old Arabic word *umma*, which denotes a community defined either in an ethnic or else in a religious sense – a confusion that has not been completely sorted out to this day.

4. The Arab Nationalists' Movement had Egyptian sympathisers within the Youth Organisation and the Vanguard Organisation (both élite organs within the official Arab Socialist Union) but they were usually ousted under the accusation of adhering to divergent ideologies [cf. 'Isa, 1986; Salim, 1982].

5. The *ideology* of Arab nationalism has remained basically a *mashriqi* preserve and has not significantly penetrated political ideas in the Maghrib, where preference seems to be for the concept of the territorial state [cf. Al-Hirmasi, 1987; Al-Jabiri, 1989: Ch. 4]. Morocco was never part of the Ottoman Empire and Algeria and Tunisia lost their connections with the Ottomans in 1830 and 1912 respectively. Unlike in the Mashriq (and Egypt), where the presence of sizeable native Christian minorities had imposed the secular-nationalist issue on the political agenda at an early stage, the main divide in the Maghrib was that between the 'Arabs' and the 'Berbers', and Islam (not Arabism) was more convenient as a unifying national bond. The French annexation of Algeria and attempts at cultural assimilation in Tunisia and Morocco encouraged that orientation by normally categorising Algerians (and other North Africans) simply as Muslims – since their nationality was meant of course to be French, not Arab. The help received by the Algerian revolution from Egypt and Syria in the 1950s and 1960s, and the relocation of the headquarters of the League of Arab States to Tunisia in the 1970s have, among other things, helped in the 'political Arabisation' of the Maghrib. The exceptionally strong popular support for Iraq and condemnation for the Western 'role' in the Gulf crisis of 1990/91 provided ample proof that at least Pan-Arabist sentiments are alive and well in the Maghrib.

6. Unfortunately the writings of Nadim Al-Bitar are less influential than they might have been, perhaps because most of them were published after the death of Nasser, the possible 'Bismarck' of the Arabs, and following the rise in the regional power of the generally anti-Pan-Arabist oil-rich Gulf states. Nor are his writings analysed by Arab writers as frequently as one might have anticipated – an important exception being Nasif Nassar [1986: 335–58] on whom I have mainly depended in writing these passages on Al-Bitar.

7. The Gulf crisis of 1990/91 precipitated by Iraq's invasion of Kuwait has in some ways confirmed the 'sanctity' in the Arab World of the territorial state which, however small, had to be protected by resorting to the assistance not only of fellow Arab states but also of a basically Western alliance. The crisis has had intellectual repercussions too. Thus for example, one finds that Muhammad Al-Rumaihi, a Kuwaiti scholar and writer who was previously fairly sympathetic to Pan-Arabism, now writes to the effect that Arab unity is a great, unachievable myth and that the main theme for the coming period "is to accept that we are distinct Arab *States*, as a prelude

to accepting that we are distinct *nations* that happen to be Arabic-speaking" [*Al-'Arabi*, no. 10, 1991: 10, no. 1, 1992: 16].

8. The most notable case of such rivalry is of course that of the two varieties of Ba'thism ruling in Syria and in Iraq [cf. Kienle, 1990].

9. This distinction was made by Friedrich Meinecke in the early twentieth century, and is found useful by Anthony Smith [1991: 8–9].

10. For a thesis on the affinities between Arab nationalism and Islamic fundamentalism see A. Al-Azmeh [1988]. For further elaboration on the relationship between nationalism and Islam in the Arab World, see Centre for Arab Unity Studies (CAUS) [1981], and Bezirgan [1978/79].

11. The point of reference is sometimes *jahili* (i.e. pre-Islamic Arabian), sometimes Islamic, on the grounds that it was Islam that unified Arabia and initiated the large and civilised Arab-Islamic state, and sometimes 'Semitic' as manifested in attempts at classifying several Ancient Near Eastern civilisations (Chaldean, Assyrian, Akkadian, Phoenician, etc.) as being 'Arab'.

12. The French term *'l'imaginaire social'* connotes the set of images and symbols (partly based on 'historical memory') through which the society recognises itself and defines its norms and values; it implies a cognitive construct of collective 'self-identification' that guides social action.

13. The Germans and the Japanese, among others, have also of course dwelt upon the issue of identity and authenticity, but in the two cases the discourse of identity was closely entwined both with an interest in state-building and an action-oriented concern about improved 'performance'. To put it differently, whereas the Arabs have stuck to an 'identity of origin', the Japanese have combined this with an 'identity of role': the first digs for an essentialist identity to be derived from a historical myth, while the second constructs a relational identity to be acquired through a projection into the future.

14. 'Dependency' is more critical than 'dependence' and lends itself to higher levels of fragility and vulnerability. Dependence may be defined as an 'actor-to-actor' relationship (i.e. Britain relies/ depends on India for rice imports). Dependency is a broader, structural category and may be defined as an 'actor-to-environment' relationship (e.g. Senegal is in a dependency situation *vis-à-vis* the world capitalist market). For concepts and comparisons see Keohane and Nye, 1977: 9–13 *et passim*; Caporaso, 1978: esp. 19ff. For Gulfian analyses of the dependency of GCC countries, see Al-Nafisi, 1982; and Al-Majid, 1986.

15. Globalisation implies that capitalist relations of *exchange* envelope practically the whole world and that the capitalist mode of *production* strives to penetrate the whole world. The capitalist mode of production is hegemonic but in many societies it is articulated with other (pre-capitalist or non-capitalist) modes. This situation of internationalisation plus articulation means that globally there are two class systems which interlock in complex ways: (1) a class system of states stratified according to average GDP (mainly rich North vs. poor South, with OPEC as an exception and the NICs as a quasi-exception or a 'middle class'); and (2) an international class system of individuals and groups, stratified by their own wealth, investments and interests, regardless of their country of origin – this includes some people from the South (especially but not exclusively from OPEC countries) who may qualify to be members of the 'international corporate bourgeoisie'. The potential conflict of allegiance must be particularly tricky for members of the international corporate bourgeoisie who are citizens of 'proletarian nations'.

CHAPTER FIVE

The Sociology of Articulated Modes: Community, Class and Polity

There is widespread agreement in the literature about the failure of Arab regimes to sustain their legitimacy in the context of the modern nation-state [cf. in particular Hudson, 1977]. In the heavily Weberian-influenced political science of today, the failure has been attributed to the 'patrimonial' nature of the Middle Eastern state [cf. e.g. Turner, 1974; Badie, 1986]. The patrimonial state is fairly advanced in terms of its staffs and administrative units, but it is still, in terms of its ethos, tied to the 'political' factor in general, and to the person of the absolute ruler and to the realm of prerogative and favouritism surrounding him, in particular. Various writers have traced this patrimonialism to various cultural roots in the Middle East but more especially to the nature of Islam. Elia Zureik was pioneering[1] in asking the question differently:

> To draw upon Gramsci's discussion of hegemony ... we raise the following question: could it be that the failure of Arab regimes to sustain their legitimacy in the context of the modern nation-state is due to their inability to adapt the long-standing system of 'direct' rule of government to the more indirect method of 'hegemony' (the twin concepts in Gramsci's scheme of domination) which is more suited to achieve class domination in the contemporary differentiated nation-state? [Zureik, 1981: 240]

Following on from such a question, we set out in this chapter to trace some of the social bases of politics in the Middle East with a view to understanding the relationship between 'community', 'class' and 'polity', and with particular emphasis on the movement from 'clientelism' to 'corporatism'.

POLITICAL CULTURE OR POLITICAL ECONOMY?

Related to the foregoing question there is another debate that ponders the reasons for this inability to transfer direct domination into hegemonic power:

whereas some would maintain that the reasons are cultural, others would tend to relate them more closely to the nature of the modes of production and to the resulting configuration of social forces.

Historically speaking, one may single out for special attention the dearth of institutions and the 'unincorporated' nature of most groups in the historic Middle Eastern city, with the result that the power of the 'state' was more despotic (i.e. direct and personalised) than infrastructural (i.e. organisational and institutional), and that most politics had to be conducted through informal networks. In Mamluk and Ottoman times these networks were managed by the 'notables' (a'yan) who acted as intermediaries between al-khassa (the 'special ones'; the ruler and his entourage; the élite), and al-'amma (the 'public'; the commoners or the plebs). The 'ulama' as a group and the awqaf (religious endowments) as an institution also played a certain intermediary role [cf. Kawtharani, 1988; 'Imara, 1993]. But the guilds and the professions (tawa'if, asnaf) had remained vulnerable to government interference, and neither the city nor its smaller organisations could draw upon any concept of juridic or corporate 'personality' to counteract the Islamic doctrine of 'oneness' (tawhid) and the principle of unmediated relationship between man and God [cf. Moore, 1974; Hourani, 1970; Lapidus, 1984; R. Al-Sayyid, 1984a].

Although informal networks had played a certain integrative or at least stabilising role, as did the neighbourhood solidarities (in haras; mahallas; hawmas, etc.) in several Arab cities, the outcomes were not always predictable. The urban marginals (al-harafish) proliferated and both the marginalised youth gangs (al-shuttar; al-'ayyarun; al-zu'r) as well as the neighbourhood toughs (al-futuwwa; more recently: al-qabadayat in Turkey, Syria and Lebanon, lutis in Iran and al-fidawiyya in the Gulf) could easily lapse into extortion or larceny and other manifestations of 'social banditry' [cf. Hobsbawm, 1959: Ch. 2; Al-Naqib, 1986: Ch. 11; Farahat, 1987: 99–112]. Indeed the clientist networks themselves could become destabilising, as local leaders would mobilise their respective constituencies against each other or against the government. Patron–client networks could not in any case guarantee stability in the cities because the lower classes included a population that was not normally part of the clientelist system of control, or whose integration into the clientelist structure was tenuous at best – a population described in the most contemptuous terms in the classical Arabic chronicles: al-awbash (the riffraff); al-ghawgha' (the trouble-makers); al-suqa (the rabble of the marketplace), etc. [cf. Denoeux, 1993: Chs. 3 and 4 and refs cited; also Farahat, 1987]. The most important features of urban protest movements in the traditional Middle East, however, have been their informal organisation and their defensive nature. Urban collective action in the traditional Middle East was usually distinctively reactive. Its purpose was not to advance new claims, but to resist the perceived or real new claims of others: the state, foreign powers, or members of the religious minorities. By the same token these movements were essentially past-oriented – they were against real or perceived challenges to situations sanctioned by tradition and, especially, by religion [Denoeux, 1993: Ch. 6].

How can this historical heritage, which has certainly lent itself to a despotic, authoritarian tradition, be explained: in terms of political culture? or in terms of political economy?

One of the most interesting examples of the culturalist approach is represented by Hisham Sharabi's theory of neo-patriarchy [1987]. He traces the origins of Arab authoritarianism to the old tribal formation with its survivalist, blind sense of group loyalty. He labels contemporary Arab society neo-patri-archal: in it the individual has no individuality: he/she is lost if he breaks with the family, the tribe or the sect. The modern state is not only incapable of replacing such primary groups for him but is also usually regarded by the individual as a source of oppression and persecution. The individual's sense of morality is collectivist and applies only within his primary group but not in the larger society.[2] Thus, although the Arab child, like, for example, the Japanese child, is brought up upon the values of loyalty and solidarity, the Arab, unlike his Japanese counterpart, tends to keep these values confined within the smaller community rather than to extend them to the wider society. In some sense, he remains a 'child', obeying and complying only when authority is physically present about him, and when the superior is closely supervising him [Sharabi, 1987: 45–54].

Fu'ad al-Khuri observes in the Arab a combination of personal loneliness, an inclination towards communal solidarity and a disposition for manoeuvre and manipulation. He relates these mental traits to a typically 'Arab' worldview that sees human existence in terms of disparate sets of tents and not in terms of a pyramidal or hierarchical order [Al-Khuri, 1993: 8ff]. In a somewhat similar vein, but adding a certain psychological touch, 'Ali Zai'ur maintains that in order for the Arab to get over his anxiety, resulting from fast social change, he is always seeking security in solidarity-type relationships rather than in rational-type organisations [Zai'ur, 1982: 19–22]. Lacking in self-esteem, the Arab is on a continuous quest for a hero or a 'charismatic leader' who will deliver him and rectify all wrongs. The leader then "presents himself as the big patriarch and head of the large family and addresses his folk with words such as *my* dear people, *my* dear children" [ibid.: 180ff, 210]. This style fits well with the pattern of hierarchical and authoritarian family upbringing: the modern relationship of the citizen to the state is similar tò the child's traditional relationship with the father: he punishes but one can expect him to provide everything. The image of a cruel/compassionate father is matched by an image of a 'benevolent despot' in politics [Sharabi, 1987: 215–16].

It would be easy in such a type of society, maintains Sharabi, for the basically primordial concept of 'loyalty' to lend itself to the emergence of complex, but flexible, patronage networks. Patronage and clientelism are practices that integrate the individual vertically into social life on the basis of conformity, of accepting the legitimacy of the status quo and becoming trained to its rules of conduct.[3] Sharabi suggests that accepting patronage is often a matter of life and death in such a situation, since resorting to the state and its laws is not normally effective or sufficient in the neo-patriarchal society. The relationships in such a society remain mainly personalistic and cannot be established on a legal, contractual or 'rationalistic' basis. The Ottoman reforms from the mid-nineteenth century on, and the colonial and semi-colonial rule that followed them, he maintains, have only led to the concentration of land and power even more securely in the hands of the tribal and traditional leaderships, thus merely resulting in a legal modernisation of the same patriarchal structures [Sharabi, 1987: 55–62]. Consequently he views the contemporary Arab state as a mixture of patriarchal, patronage arrangements and ex-colonial bureaucratic organisations. Being patriarchal, the discourse of the state is really more of a monologue that aims not at information but at subjugation. Even its concept of the nation (umma) is not much more than an extension of the family image: hierarchical and apportionate in essence [ibid.: 71–2, 83–4, 121].

This brief selection of some of the contributions by Arab critics towards understanding their own political culture will have to suffice. While many of these descriptions may be accurate and most of them are certainly fascinating, the important point to emphasise, from my point of view, is that such traits which have rather old historical origins do not survive in exactly the same old form – they are adjusted by and intertwined with other influences, as various modes of production articulate with each other and as social formations go through uncertain transitional periods. For example, patronage networks represent the way in which primordial loyalties (familialism, tribalism, sectarianism, etc.) are transposed into a modernising semi-capitalist society: family, tribe, sect or village are no longer the individual's entire world in the semi-urbanised, semi-industrialised modern city, but they are still found necessary if not for the individual's functional survival, then at least for his emotional consolation [on some of the possible emotional rewards of patronage see Black, 1988]. Nor is it all simply a matter of time and development – culture does count and it is conceivable, for instance, that although the family will always weaken with industrial capitalism, it will nevertheless remain relatively more important in certain industrial countries than in others.

Many of the characteristics of the Arab 'personality' that are often quoted as aspects of a distinct political culture [cf. Yasin, 1983: 117–60, 210–12 and refs cited; see also Ju'ait, 1984: 175ff] in reality represent mechanisms through which a personality socialised to the requirements of an 'older' mode of production and an 'older' type of social organisation can be adjusted; such a personality struggles to survive in a different type of environment that is usually larger and more mobile, often urban and bureaucratised. Thus the 'floating aggression' noted by some observers is characteristic of the move from enclosed nomadic or mountain environments to wider social environments. Attitudes would tend to be dualistic in such a transitory situation. For example, people will be very polite and courteous towards those whom they know (giving them precedence when entering buildings, rooms, etc.) and extremely competitive and rude towards people they do not know (getting on to a bus or driving a vehicle in the street). While personal acquaintance inspires a sense of generosity and grace, impersonal encounter inspires anxiety, insecurity and hence aggressiveness. Hypocrisy, also noted by a number of observers, is characteristic of the relatively early insertion into authority-based organisations, such as the bureaucracy. In the absence of long-established traditions of professionalism and meritocracy, hypocrisy is a known – if pathological – instrument of exchange in organisations: I give you praise, compliance and (apparent) loyalty and you, using the allocative jurisdictions at your disposal, will give me a higher share of the organisational rewards. City and market expansion, the increasing dominance of the capitalist mode of production, growth in the size of the state machine and the emergence and political activation of new social strata, all lead to a shift from oligarchic/traditional to state/bureaucratic forms of patronage. Several empirical studies have shown that the entrance of the urban middle and lower classes into politics is perfectly compatible with the continuation, albeit adjusted, of vertical clientelistic forms of organisation in many peripheral and semi-peripheral formations [Mouzelis, 1986: 76ff].

In short, therefore, although patronage and clientelism have a long history and an elaborate vocabulary in the Middle East [cf. Leca and Schemeil, 1983] they are not the inevitable outcome of certain essential and permanent cultural traits.[4] They are in reality behavioural correlates to articulated modes of production and attitudinal accompaniments of a stage of transition that requires a higher degree of intermediation between the rural and the urban, between the local and the central, between the private and the public. The study of patron–client relationships, cliques, cronies and informal networks, in which Robert Springborg has particularly excelled [e.g. 1974, 1982], can be useful and they are indeed very interesting. Their validity will be constrained however if they are viewed as being exclusively culturally specific, rather than socially and politically contingent. It is also worth noticing that such an approach has not been utilised (or favoured) by the Arab scholars themselves [cf. M.K. Al-Sayyid, 1991: 381ff], except with regard to the study of small specific groupings [but see the excellent 'political' study by Aklimandus, 1988, which, he says, was inspired by his experience in a sports club], or else with regard to studying the unique case of Lebanon [cf. Khalaf, 1987], where clientelism had, up to the early 1970s, acted as a mainstream device for the entire system, albeit at the expense of developing a civic conscience or an autonomous state.

But even in this most special of cases, a political economy approach such as that ably followed by Michael Johnson [1986] can bring insight into understanding the Lebanese 'state' and its sectarian and informal politics in their capacity as correlates of a specific type of social formation and mode of production that characterises an incomplete capitalism with a less-than-mature class structure; a situation that was ripe for turning sectarianism and 'inter-mediation' into a useful resource in an increasingly acute socio-economic competition. Such an approach was partly anticipated by Mahdi 'Amil [1979], who viewed the Lebanese state in terms of a 'financial caste' allying itself with the forces of 'political feudalism'. These latter engaged in pre-capitalist relations of production, and practised politics via a system of fiefs and sects. The state in turn 'reproduced' the sects in a political form by consecrating the role of confessional representation in all state institutions.

The 'political factor' is also important in making clientelism significant and quasi-structural. The establishment of controls from the top over governmental and societal resources, and the anxiety from below to find a place in the complex vertical links of political power, yield "a variety of structures familiar enough to observers, but difficult to place within the pluralist or class approach to politics" [Chalmers, 1977: 33]. Clientelism has been commonly used to describe informal ties in which services (and some goods) are exchanged between people of unequal status. These are sometimes so important that they constitute the only links which hold together combinations of political forces that otherwise participate in major confrontations. As a pattern of vertical dependency, clientelism may lend itself, in certain situations, to a transformation in the direction of loose and conservatively inclined varieties of corporatism [ibid.: 34–5]. At the same time, clientelistic networks may also function as policy circles or at least as 'policy tribes'. *Shillas* and other types of cliques and informal networks should not be regarded as a Middle Eastern peculiarity: we know increasingly more about their presence in countries such as Italy, Japan and even the United States of America [cf. e.g. La Palombara, 1963; Farnsworth, 1989; Lindberg et al. in Campbell et al., eds, 1991].

It is this analytical shift, however, from micro- to macro-politics that repres-ents the most challenging conceptual difficulty with clientelism. Given the intellectual history of a concept drawn from anthropology and applied without much theoretical adjustment to complex political systems, it is not surprising that the concept loses much of its explanatory power as one moves from inter-personal relationships to clientelistic structures (i.e. corporate clientelism) at the local or national level [Graziano, 1983: 426ff; Leca and Schemeil, 1983: 458ff].

But before we proceed further, let us consider first how dependent and clientist groupings have developed historically in the modern Middle East.

SOCIAL CORRELATES OF ARTICULATED MODES

We have seen that the colonial era had resulted in the incorporation of the Arab World into the capitalist world system, and in the consolidation of an (internally) 'bureaucratic' state and an (externally) 'territorial' state. As has already been mentioned, this incorporation into the world capitalist system did not necessarily mean that the capitalist mode of production predominated over all other modes; rather it was an articulation of various modes, with the capitalist mode increasingly gaining the upper hand. Furthermore, capitalist *relations* (especially exchange) have tended to penetrate faster and more thoroughly than did the capitalist division of labour within the production process.

Imperialist penetration in the periphery tends to restrict development except in cases where this is considered crucial for industrial capitalist reproduction, where the sectors concerned do not effectively compete with imported commodities, or where they provide a means for strengthening the industrial capitalist state's control over the Third World formation. An economy of multiple, imbalanced sectors emerges as a result. In addition, of course, the continuing reproduction of non-capitalist modes of production and/or divisions of labour seriously limits the ability of capitalist production to penetrate certain sectors during and after the colonial period [Taylor, 1979: 220ff, 223ff]. Labour in Third World formations may thus be concomitantly related to two different systems of production. This is obvious, for example, in seasonal agricultural labour where the costs of maintaining the agricultural workers outside season is met by production in the agricultural-household sector. Much the same applies for labour migration to the cities during the non-productive agricultural seasons (traditionally, for example, *Sa'idis* from Upper Egypt to various cities). The *muhasasa* or *muzara'a* (crop-sharing) system familiar in several Arab and Muslim countries is also a compound one that includes elements of 'tribute' as well as elements of rent and wage.

The artisan sector, as we have seen, is both extended and restricted by capitalist penetration of the non-capitalist social formation. Artisanal activity may grow in the area of servicing imported foreign machinery or in the area of exportable and touristic artefacts, whereas it would shrink in other areas under competition from imported mass-produced commodities. Relations of production even in the 'modern' parts of the sector (such as metal works or car mechanics) may keep for an extensive period some characteristics of the old guild system. The contemporary *usta* may still be seen eating with his apprentices from the same bowl, or else disciplining them with a stick!

John Taylor observes that the coexistence of modes of production in Third World formations greatly enhances the role of the merchant or trader [Taylor, 1979: 226]. This, incidentally, may explain why the merchants have always been so important throughout most stages of Muslim history – precisely because the modes of production in any one place at any one time have often been multiple and 'articulated'. In modern times, the expansion of the home market, the export of agricultural commodities and the distribution of imported goods all provide a basis for a rapid increase in the 'circulation function' and for an economic strengthening of the role of members of the merchant class, who essentially act as 'linkmen' between modes of production or divisions of labour (for example, buying from a tribe or a village to sell to a merchant in the city or to an exporting trader in the ports or abroad). They may even act as 'linkmen' between the state sector and the private sector, for example by supplying government organisations with agricultural produce, raw materials, furniture and equipment, etc., or by 're-selling' products of public enterprises to other public or private buyers.

Another factor influencing the character of the social formation is the nature and characteristics of international capitalism at the particular historical juncture in which it encroached on any individual Arab country. As we have seen, most Arab countries were incorporated into the world capitalist system via colonialism. Some, such as Egypt and North Africa, were incorporated during the nineteenth century at the stage of expanding monopoly capitalism and were subjected to capitalist relations by way of commercial capital and the import and export of commodities. The introduction of semi-feudal, capitalist agriculture (and acceleration of the move towards private land-ownership to make this possible) was an important aspect of this episode. Other countries, such as in the Mashriq (Levant), were dominated politically by the colonial powers at the stage of hegemonic capitalism when the export of capital had become more important than the export of commodities, and when the 'political factor', via state institutions, had become more obvious in the relationship between the metropole and dependencies, than the economic. However, by the end of the Second World War, when they were starting to gain their political independence, all the Arab countries had already been incorporated in the world capitalist system, in terms of production, exchange and cultural relations.

Just as, historically, the emergence of the modern state has been very much tied to the development of capitalism, likewise the extension of the state system to the rest of the world cannot, in many respects, be separated from the expansion of capitalism on a world level. Put differently, it is possible to argue that the appearance and expansion of the modern state was a "necessary corollary of the distribution of tasks resulting from the new international division of labour" that accompanied the consolidation of capitalism. On their part, the nationalist leaderships that acquired formal independence for most Arab countries were tempted by the idea that modern state-building was a sign of progress: its rationality, industrialisation and urbanity were taken to signify the move towards modernity [cf. Etienne, 1987: 85–100].

Considered on a world level, one must conclude that the Arab countries are part of a global capitalist system. Immanuel Wallerstein (in agreement with Samir Amin) argues that capitalism is the first mode of production that is global in scope. It has created a single division of labour, comprising multiple cultural systems, multiple political entities and even different modes of surplus appropriation [Wallerstein, 1974; cf. also Dale 1984]. From a global perspective, one has thus to conclude that the capitalist mode of production is at least 'enframing' (if not actually penetrating) the Arab states. Some would then hasten to qualify this as being dependent-capitalism, peripheral-capitalism or (in some cases) semi-peripheral capitalism. Aspects of the dependency, marginality and vulnerability of Arab states within the world system are looked at elsewhere in this book.

Domestically, and over the years since independence, the capitalist sector in the various Arab states (whether foreign or domestic) has been articulated in different forms and in varying proportions with the following modes of production: (a) pre-capitalist modes of production, such as pastoral-nomadism in some countries and semi-feudal/semi-commercial agriculture in others; and (b) a state-capitalist mode of production, which began to emerge in a certain proportion or another in practically all Arab countries regardless of their declared ideologies. One important variant of the Third World state-capitalist mode is related to the control of export minerals (petroleum in the Gulf and North Africa and phosphates in Morocco and Jordan); another variant, which applies in many Arab countries, is related to nationalised or newly created industries. It is possible to argue that, in a certain sense, most countries in the Arab World have increasingly developed into cases of 'dependent state capitalism'.

Given such articulations, the extraction of surplus tends to be effected through a mixture of purely economic and extra-economic (e.g. familial, tribal, political) methods. However, the capitalist mode of production continues increasingly to gain the upper hand. The cultural and institutional processes through which this is achieved are usually called 'modernisation', and are pursued by both the so-called 'radical' and the so-called 'traditional' regimes. Following their independence, several Arab countries tried to improve their status within the international division of labour and to establish an economic 'base' for their independence. Interestingly, most of these countries have resorted to one of the newest technical devices of capitalism: the large corporation. The so-called radical or socialist regimes managed to do this in the 1960s through the nationalisations of foreign and local firms, and several of the conservative states found it possible as a result of the oil bonanza. Thus the public economic sector became a reality of life in the Arab World, regardless of the official ideological utterances. Some may want to speak about 'state socialism' and others about 'state capitalism' in different Arab countries. However, given that state capitalism and state socialism are, as Henri Lefebvre puts it, "two species of one genre", there is much to recommend using one appellation for the two; namely the "statist mode of production, *le mode de production étatique*" [Lefebvre, 1978].

The predominance of the 'political' and the cruciality of the state is in some ways a function of the lack of class hegemony in society, which is, in turn, closely related to the articulated nature of the modes of production. The state here comes to fulfil a compensatory function and to enforce a certain kind of formal unity on a body that is not socially homogeneous or balanced. In many Arab societies the élite of the 'notables' – the landowners and merchants – had developed near enough to the point of forming such a hegemonic class. Yet the impact of such social groups on state action was still seriously constrained by many factors. First there was the 'colonial' administration which was, on the whole, far more sensitive towards its own social forces and political constituencies in the metropole than towards any domestic social forces, the notables included. Admittedly, both the British and the French had enhanced the status of the landowning classes (and had in some instances – such as Iraq, Jordan – even created them), and they were on the whole more attentive to their interests than to those of other classes. However, their metropole-inspired policies often prompted the colonial administrators into actions that were in some ways counter to the main interests of the landowners. The British administration in Egypt was prepared every so often to issue laws that were more favourable to the cultivator than to the landowner. The French administration in Syria was in reality undermining the interests of the traditional notables in its heavy reliance on rural minoritarian groups for recruitment in the military and security apparatuses. And in many cases the apparent affluence of the native merchant simply disguised the constraints on his real power, since many of the important commercial and financial activities in a number of Arab countries were dominated by foreign nationals and by members of the 'commercial minorities' (Greeks, Armenians, Jews, etc.) whose ties were often closer to the metropole than they were to the local societies. Such a situation existed in one form or another in Egypt, North Africa, Sudan, Yemen, the Gulf and elsewhere, and although a similar 'cosmopolitan' commercial community did not exist to the same extent in Syria, Westernised Christian minorities played a role that was similar, functionally speaking, to that of the foreign communities in other countries (some of their members often enjoying 'honorary' European legal status). The failure of the Banque Misr group in Egypt in the 1930s and 1940s to accumulate and to invest commercial and industrial capital independently from the European and the *mutamassir* (resident foreigner) capital is an excellent illustration of such a constraint [cf. Davis, 1983].

In short, therefore, the landowning/commercial social forces had nearly 'made it' as a hegemonic social class in many Arab societies; but not quite. By the same token, a proletariat, or a modern, organised native working class, did not really exist except in Egypt [for further details and pertinent theoretical queries see Al-Naqib, 1986]. The encroachment of European manufactures on Arab markets left a suffocated artisan sector in a few parts of the Arab World, that sometimes continued to function well into the twentieth century according to mediaeval guild patterns. Similar patterns sometimes obtained in the emerging small (modern) workshops for electric and motor repairs. Even in Egypt, because most business owners and a sizeable percentage of all industrial technicians, foremen and senior workers were foreigners, the Egyptian proletariat had gradually developed a collective consciousness that was more outspokenly 'nationalist'-oriented in tone than it was class-oriented [cf. Beinin and Lockman, 1987]. The first workers' trade unions and the first Marxist movements to be formed in Egypt were, significantly, organised by foreign or *mutamassir* workers and intellectuals.

The fluid class situation in Arab societies had prevented the emergence of a dominant social class with a hegemonic social ideology that would be internally accepted by the majority as expressing the 'natural' state of affairs of the society. The only way to influence policies was actually to assume direct control of the state machine. In some cases where there was much at stake (e.g. in the oil-rich Gulf states) the process of holding and maintaining control over the state machine (however small that was) was helped and later in some ways 'guaranteed' by foreign powers. In other cases indigenous forces were more actively at play without of course negating the role of external factors.

In addition to relying on the landowners and the traditional 'notables', colonial rule had needed, in order to maintain itself, the services of other types of personnel, albeit in small numbers: soldiers, officials and teachers. In response, indigenous expansion in these categories in the face of colonial opposition or restriction was eventually to develop into a 'nationalistic' target in its own right, notwithstanding the fact that training for such occupations was conducted according to European methods, in European-style institutions. In a number of Arab countries, personnel from such a 'new middle class' (especially army officers) were eventually to grab power from the hands of the previous regimes (generally representing the landowning/commercial alliances) which were often entrusted with the functions of government during the process of 'decolonisation'. Accused of not being sufficiently patriotic or modernistic, such regimes were changed, during the 1950s and 1960s in Egypt, Iraq, Syria, Yemen, Sudan, Libya, and so on. In Algeria, a similar type of regime came to power in the wake of independence.

A CLOSER LOOK AT SOCIAL CLASSES

Before we consider an outline of the class map in the Arab World, however, let us define briefly what we mean by social classes. Classes are not simply layers or strata in a hierarchical system of differentiation, but are social entities defined by the relationship of their members to the means of production. This basically Marxist concept has been given a 'power' slant by Max Weber and his followers (that is, concerning the ability to influence and/or control the behaviour of others). It should also be kept in mind, especially with regard to 'circulationist economies' (which abound in the Middle East), that classes may be more easily identifiable by their consumption patterns than they are in relation to the means of production (of which very little takes place in the oil-exporting countries, for example). A class is both 'a category of similarly situated individuals' *and* under suitable social conditions, 'a cultural and political agency'. Structures of income differentiation are not classes, however, and, as such, are not of great concern to the political scientist: only when they start to engage in political organisation (however rudimentary) do they become a subject of interest for the political scientist. This distinction has its origins in Marx, who defines a class *in itself* by a position in the organisation of production that may be occupied by a mass of distinct individuals. This class, however, becomes a class *for itself* only when these individuals, and later groups, become aware of the existence of a community of interests among them.

Both the Marxist and the Weberian paradigms were tried for the study of Middle Eastern societies (for example by R. Gallisot and D. Ben Ali for the former; A.E. Hermassi and C.H. Moore for the latter), but being basically Western paradigms pertaining to capitalist societies, none of them has been found to be fully satisfactory [cf. Zaghal, 1982/83: 7–25]. In pre-capitalist societies as well as in societies with articulated modes of production, one may find, first, that modes of production are very closely intertwined with modes of coercion and secondly – which is often related to the previous and which is particularly pronounced in the case of the Middle East – that modes of 'distribution' or of 'circulation' are just as important, if not more so, than modes of production.

One outcome of the articulated nature of modes of production in Middle Eastern societies is the variegated and fluid nature of their class structure. Very often aspects of horizontal stratification (i.e. classes, élites, etc.) are intermeshed in such societies with aspects of vertical differentiation (e.g. tribe, sect, ethnie, etc.) [cf. Bill and Leiden, 1984: Chs. 3 and 4; Esman and Rabinovich, 1988]. An analysis of the complexities and intricacies of such economic and social articulations would therefore prove most crucial for understanding the politics of Arab societies. Such a study has by its very nature to be country-specific, but a certain degree of aggregation and generalisation will have to be introduced in our analysis here if the comparative purposes of our endeavour are to be achieved.

An early perceptive study by James Bill [1972] had already suggested that class structure in the Middle East was particularly elastic:

> This resiliency has been intimately related to intra-class group patterns as well as to inter-class relationships and mobility processes ... Although Middle Eastern class relationships have been marked by strong reciprocal power patterns, the classes always relate to one another in a generally permanent imbalance ... One effect of [the] related group-class tension is the increased permeability of class lines. This is best explained in terms of two principles: (1) the overlapping

membership that characterizes inter-class groups; and (2) the high rate of inter-class personal mobility. These two characteristics are interrelated since over-lapping membership facilitates mobility and vice versa [Bill, 1972: 429–31].

Now, keeping the fluid nature of the class structure in mind, what have been the most pertinent changes in the class map during the last half century or so? The most important general observation is that in most Arab societies the position of the landed aristocracy and of the traditional merchants had seen a relative (or at least a tentative) decline. In the meantime the *salariat* has grown in a big way in practically all societies, and so have several 'proletaroid' sectors. The industrial proletariat has grown rather slowly, whereas the merchants and contractors have fluctuated with the changes in economic policies.

A particularly significant development has been the growth in the size, diversity and importance of the intermediate strata. Intermediate class formations are products of the historical process of development of the capitalist mode of production, for pre-capitalist modes do not form intermediate elements to any appreciable degree (remember the *khassa/'amma* dichotomy in traditional Muslim society). Gramsci made a crucial contribution to the study of such intermediate strata, especially on the occasion of his notes on the role of the 'intellectual' and the Southern Question. Particularly interesting is his contrast between the 'old type' and the 'new type' intellectual: how the first type, an eloquent person more typical of the South, is identified more closely with state employment and with commerce, whereas the second type is identified more closely with industry, construction and technical organisation [cf. Buci-Glucksmann, 1980: 19–38].

Available surveys and studies about the contemporary Arab World seem to point out to the special importance of two functionally distinct but socially proximate groups: the petite bourgeoisie and the intermediate strata (*couches moyennes*) [cf. Batatu, 1978; Longuenesse, 1979, 1987; Ahmad, 1985]. The intermediate strata are numerically larger in most Arab countries than the industrial proletariat. The industrial working class represents no more than a sixth or a fifth of the labour force in most of the semi-industrialised countries of the Arab World (e.g., some 13 per cent in Jordan, 14 per cent in Egypt, 15 per cent in Syria, and 20 per cent in Tunisia, by the end of the 1970s). By contrast, estimates of the intermediate strata put them in some cases at between 45 and 60 per cent of the entire labour force [cf. 'Abd al-Fadil, 1988: Ch. 4 and refs cited].

The political importance of the intermediate strata derives not only from their size and relative weight but also from their high social mobility and from the symbiotic links that tie them, in spite of distinct functional and social outlooks, to the petite bourgeoisie in the conventional sense (craftsmen, shopkeepers, money-lenders, etc.). Within this broad range of the petite bourgeoisie, there is little doubt that the 'new middle class' or the 'bureau-technocratic bourgeoisie' (of army officers, managers, administrators, university professors and technocrats) has been the most significant in the period from the 1950s to the 1970s (even though their claim to prominence has been challenged since the 1980s; ideologically by the Islamic movements and organisationally by the new business groups). As in the rest of the Third World, activities of the state have been primary sources of the formation of intermediate class categories. The overdevelopment of the peripheral state was in part a compensation for the presence of weak classes of local capitalists or even their virtual non-existence. In such conditions,

> States assume entrepreneurial functions, giving birth to technocratic, managerial and technical groupings that do not owe their existence to private property. The bloating of the public bureaucracy is also due to systems of clientelism ... most of which are modern patronage systems, not carryovers of traditional ways [Johnson, 1985: 14–15].

The state in developing societies attempts to manage, contain and repress – within the state apparatuses – the conflicts and struggles emanating from the social distress that accompanies development. And as local bourgeoisies are only incipiently formed, the intermediate strata come to achieve an inordinate importance as a social base of state power and to occupy a strategic field in the economy and politics of their countries [Johnson, 1985: 16–17]. As Aijaz Ahmad argues, the intermediate classes in peripheral countries do aspire to hegemony, trying to count on their powerful presence within apparatuses of the state:

> It is through the agency of the State that the personnel drawn from these classes strives to dominate the whole of civil society as such. On the ideological level, this is expressed in a certain fetishization of the State, and the creation of a whole range of disparate and mutually contradictory ideologies – e.g. Western-style developmentalism, the 'socialism' of the radical-nationalists with its emphasis on 'nationalizations', the ethno-religious fascism of the Khomeini variety – which are none the less united in viewing the state as the principal agency of social transformation [Ahmad, 1985: 44–5].

The proliferation of intermediate strata should not be taken, however, as a manifestation of a Middle Eastern peculiarity or 'cultural exceptionalism'. Gramsci had already noticed a similar situation in other peripheral Eastern and Southern European countries in his time: "In the typical peripheral countries ... a broad spectrum of intermediate classes stretches between the proletariat and capitalism: classes which seek to carry on ... policies of their own, with ideologies which influence broad strata of the proletariat, but which particularly affect the peasant masses" [Gramsci, 1978: 409].

Thus the relative weakness of the polar classes (i.e. the bourgeoisie and the proletariat) and the enhanced significance, by contrast, of the intermediate classes in the Middle East is not a function of their cultural peculiarity but of the historical conjuncture:

> The crux of the matter is that the social formations we are discussing here are, by and large, transitional in character, where capitalism is dominant but not universal and where a variety of non-capitalist forms exist not only alongside capitalism, occupying their own effective space, but also intertwined with the capitalist mode itself, with profound effects on the social relations of capitalist production per se. The balance of class powers, and hence the modalities of class struggle in such peripheral formations, have characteristics that correspond to this transitional character of the systems of production. Likewise the genealogy of the capitalist state in the periphery ought also to be studied not so much on the theoretico-abstract level of the capitalist mode of production as such, but in relation, fundamentally, to the specific modalities of transition as it has unfolded in the actual histories of these formations [Ahmad, 1985: 46–7].

This kind of analysis has several implications. One is that the composition and balance of class forces in the periphery provides a wide social space for the hegemonic projects of the intermediate classes (that seek to dominate over all other classes). Another is that the intermediate classes seek to establish their dominance over civil society mainly by monopolising the apparatuses of the state itself. The disproportionate power of what Marx and Engels used to call 'the governing caste' comes from the fact that the peripheral state arose, as a rule, prior to the formation of the bourgeoisie as a politically dominant class and that the state is the principal agency through which the dominance of the capitalist mode is established; not only does this state act as the largest entrepreneur but it is also planning and reorganising every sector of the economy [ibid.: 47–9].

Also politically significant in the Middle East is the fact that the industrial proletariat is not only outnumbered by the middle strata but also by the pseudo-proletariat, the sub-proletariat, and the lumpenproletariat. The political folklore of the region has produced some colourful terms to describe segments of these social groups, such as the *shammasa* (those always hanging about in the sun) in Sudan, or the *hittistes* (those always leaning against a wall) in Algeria! These groups have not received the analytical attention they deserve [Gran, 1987: 77ff], and the few good studies available are on Iran rather than the Arab World. These 'masses' are difficult to categorise in class terms. They are 'little people' (*popolo minuto*) reminiscent of Eric Hobsbawm's descriptions of the *lazzari* of Naples in the late eighteenth century. [The words *lazzari* and *lazzaroni* sound to me suspiciously like an Italian rendering in the plural of the Arabic word *al-az'ar*, plural *al-zu'r* or *al-zu'ran*, mentioned above.] They include shop workers, stevedores and fishermen, journeymen and minor artisans, vendors and servants and 'Jacks of all trades'. In some cases they may include more marginal (and colourful!) types such as dancers and musicians, monkey trainers and snake charmers, jugglers and clowns, fortune-tellers and drug-pushers, not to mention female and male prostitutes, pimps and racketeers [see Hobsbawm, 1959: 110ff; Johnson, 1986: 18; Farahat, 1987: 102].

These groups are called in Italy by the picturesque name of *morti di fame* (literally, though not actually, 'starveling' – for which there are Egyptian-Arabic equivalents). Gramsci has commented on their heterogeneous *déclassé* nature and their voluntarist but often subversive political character. They dislike 'gentlemen' and officialdom but their 'generic' hatred "cannot be taken as evidence of class consciousness – merely as the first glimmer of such consciousness" [Gramsci, 1971: 202–3, 272–5]. Such types have recently played a prominent role in several 'bread riots' and sectarian disturbances in the Middle East. The significance of these social groups and fragments is reflected in the fact that spontaneous, street politics become every so often more important than organised, institutional politics: thus food riots, violent demonstrations and challenging 'mass prayers' are a distinct feature of current Arab politics that can bring together elements of the middle strata and elements of the proletaroid groups.

The picture is further complicated by the often articulated nature of the modes of production and of social and political relations in the countryside as well. The debate between historians and sociologists continues over whether the Muslim world and the East in general have practised 'feudalism' in any way that approximates to the European sense – the debate is not merely a matter of academic concern for these specialists but carries with it crucial significance for the political scientist [cf. e.g. Byres and Mukhia, 1985; Butshit, 1989: 98–109; Al-Ansari, 1994]. One factor that emerges out of the specialised controversies is that one should be aware of both ownership rights (*milkiyya*) as well as *hiyaza* and *intifa'* (approximately leasehold and tenancy respectively), and the various complex combinations of them. Whereas certain modes of agricultural organisation, such as the *'izba* in Egypt, may carry features of a transitional stage from semi-feudal to capitalist modes of production, there are almost everywhere in the Arab World ways whereby pre-capitalist (familial and small peasant) patterns of production are articulated with the increasingly dominant capitalist mode of production [cf. 'Abd al-Fadil, 1988: 70ff; Glavanis and Glavanis, 1983; Seddon, 1986].

There are various political implications for the complex nature of production and class relationships in the countryside. One is that agrarian reforms for redistributing agricultural land, which have been popular in many Arab countries, may succeed in weakening the power base of the landowning classes. Yet this may not automatically mean a commensurate increase in the power of the peasantry which often becomes encapsulated by the state bureaucracy. Nor does it necessarily mean the end of the rural bourgeoisie; quite the reverse. The middle farmers are often well connected to government networks and better able to diversify and to utilise modern technologies so that they end up doing quite well out of the overall exercise. It is an exaggeration with little evidence that suggests, as did Binder [1978], that such a middle stratum had in the case of Egypt formed the main political support for the Nasserist regime. But it is true that in Egypt, Syria, Tunisia (as in other Middle Eastern countries such as Turkey), the agricultural entrepreneurs have been flexible and efficient enough to be among the earliest social groups to benefit from economic liberalisation and indeed to start building 'privatising' channels within the state apparatus.

Just as the proletariat in Arab societies is small and structurally weak, so also – and logically – is the bourgeoisie. To start with, the commercial and business bourgeoisie (inasmuch as it was not 'foreign' or of an openly 'comprador' nature) was originally too closely linked to the landowning class and therefore lacked an independent, innovative perspective [cf. e.g. Al-Disuqi, 1981; Batatu, 1978]. The Iraqi historian Kazim Habib summarised the situation rather succinctly, as follows:

> [The bourgeoisie] had faced two types of pre-capitalist relations: one type included paternalistic relations associated with nomadism, pastoralism, and subsistence agriculture and semi-feudal relations with distinct Asian characteristics; the other was commercial capitalist relations emanating from the outside and the new Arab bourgeoisie was to depend from the beginning on the protection of the foreign bourgeoisie ... The reliance on two disparate allies the foreign bourgeoisie and the [indigenous] landowners and the coexistence with two qualitatively different (although equally exploitative) modes of production had given the Arab bourgeoisie its distinguishing features – some of which one may detect to this very day [Habib, 1991: 91].

This is basically the argument of the lack of entrepreneurship, or 'the missing middle class', that tends to regard the Middle East as a peculiar area in this respect. But one should not carry this type of analysis to extremes. As Bryan Turner [1984] has convincingly argued, such an 'entrepreneurial' British route to industrialisation was not followed in the case of France, Germany or Italy, not to mention Russia, Japan and Southern Europe. Turner finds Rodinson's criticism of the Weberian tradition in this connection irrelevant. Rodinson [1978] demonstrated most pointedly the important role played by the merchants within the Islamic empire, but Turner's argument is that merchants will not always develop into capitalists. He contends that Britain remains the really unique case, and that the Middle East is not as historically peculiar as is widely believed. The important differences between North European societies and the Middle East are to be found in the very different conditions which are inevitably posed for 'late developers'. As he says: " 'late developers' will be typically forced to solve the problem of accumulation not through external colonies, but through their own agricultural and pre-capitalist sectors." The solution does not lie in the behaviour of risk-taking entrepreneurs but may take "some form of state management, usually state capitalism" [Turner, 1984: 61–2].

And this is indeed what happened at a subsequent period, when the state started to act as the main planner, producer and distributor. The landowning class was curtailed and industry (nationalised and newly created) was almost monopolised by the state. The private business bourgeoisie, insofar as it was allowed to exist, became subservient to the state and to the requirements of state capitalism. When it was not a straightforward 'brokerage' bourgeoisie (*simsariyya*)[5] of deals and commissions, it was at best a contractors' bourgeoisie (*muqawalat*) [cf. e.g. Khafaji, 1983: Ch. 3; Ghunaim, 1986: Table 52 and 350ff; Al-Maliki, 1989].

The picture was further complicated in recent years by the spill-overs of the 'oil boom', especially in the labour-exporting countries of the Arab World. New 'capitalised segments' have emerged among bureaucrats, workers and peasants, thus diluting their own self-perception of their class identity while separating them, financially and in terms of potential political action, from their fellow (co-classist) members of the same basic class [cf. Al-Sa'ati, 1985; Sabagh, 1988; 'Abd al-Fadil, 1988: 185–8].

Not only was the bourgeoisie structurally weak and socially ineffectual (hence the emotional term 'the parasitic bourgeoisie'), but – which is particularly important politically speaking – it has also as a consequence lacked hegemony over the society [cf. e.g. Lazreq, 1976: 28ff]. One aspect of the structural weakness of the bourgeoisie is manifested by the fact that in many Arab societies, economic stratification is still in some ways articulated with communal (tribal, religious, ethnic) differentiation [cf. e.g. Khuri, 1988; Dubar and Nasr, 1976]. This structural weakness obliges the bourgeoisie to function either as an appendage to its own state or as an agent to multinational capital, or both [cf. e.g. Al-Maliki, 1989: 6ff; Batatu, 1983].

The articulated nature of modes of production and of social relations, and the lack of class hegemony carry with them important political implications. For one thing, the technical weakness of the production base as such, and the articulated class/power relationships mean that one should consider not only aspects of 'exploitation' and potential 'class struggles', but also the inclusion/ exclusion scale, the marginalisation of certain social groups, and the potential protestations that may result from such a situation. Marginalisation is an important phenomenon in many Third World countries not only because of the large size of the lumpenproletariat but also because of the dangerously growing unemployment (or underemployment) of the educated. Marginality is an important concept here because it deals with the lack (or limited nature) of participation not only in the political but also in the socio-economic sphere. It implies a limited (and distorted) degree of insertion into the productive system (e.g. unemployment, underemployment), as well as a limited (and distorted) degree of insertion into the consumption system and into the cultural system [cf. Germani, 1980: 6–7, 49–64]. As I have illustrated elsewhere, marginalisation is a potent breeder of protest movements, such as that of

'Political Islam', and it often leads to confrontation with the state over contested public space [cf. Ayubi, 1991a: esp. Chs. 7, 8, 10].

The lack of class hegemony and the articulated nature of modes of production and of social relations also carry with them important implications with regard to ideology. Ideology in such a society is often a blueprint or a declaration of intent (either by a governing group or by an opposition group) and not an overall view of the world that develops gradually as a process of growing consensus. (It is perhaps telling that in the Arab World the word 'ideology' is always understood in the former and hardly ever in the latter sense.) Political power is often acutely contested because the subject of disagreement is not who is assuming government now but the very rules of the political game itself. Lacking real ideological hegemony the ruling castes often resort to eclecticism in an attempt to appeal to as many symbols and groups as possible. Eclecticism has been condemned by many political and cultural analysts in the Arab World as one of the causes behind the poor performance of Arab politics [e.g. Abdallah Laroui, Kamal 'Abd al-Latif, Jabir al-Ansari, 'Aziz Al-Azma, and several others]. Every political discourse is, of course, to some extent eclectic: what can be criticised about Arab ideologies is basically the non-organic juxtaposition of disparate or discordant ideas that at the end fails to get the society moving politically. Potentially hegemonic discourse is the one, however epistemologically disparate, that succeeds in 'interpellating' several social classes and groups. And it is this variety, apart from a few brief 'populist' bursts, that has been lacking in the Arab World.

The lack of class and ideological hegemony also explains the relative ease with which Arab governments seem to be able to reverse their political positions domestically and internationally: yesterday's ardent socialists are today's dedicated liberalists; yesterday's Soviet satellites are today's American allies; yesterday's enemies of Israel are today's negotiators with its leaders. As certain classes are often in a state of flux and transition, and as the entire class map is quite fluid and uncertain, it is familiar enough to come across individuals or even entire social strata that switch and reverse their ideological and political allegiance practically overnight. This variety of voluntarism has been colourfully labelled 'political nomadism' by Gramsci. As Gramsci explains, this is caused by a combination of factors; namely, the traditional a-politicism and passivity of the popular masses, the existence of sizable lumpenproletariat and other déclassés segments, and the presence of a fairly large 'rural-type' middle- and petit-bourgeoisie that "produces a large number of dissatisfied intellectuals – hence ready 'volunteers' for any enterprise (even the most bizarre) which is vaguely 'subversive'; to the Right or to the Left." [Gramsci, 1971: 202–5, 272–5]. Such an analysis is confirmed in the case of the Middle East as we observe for example that it has been from amongst roughly the same following that supported secular-nationalist and socialist politics in the 1950s and 1960s that the political Islamists of the 1970s and 1980s have emerged [cf. Ayubi, 1991a: esp. Chs. 7 and 10].

CORPORATISM AND STATE–SOCIETY RELATIONS

It is not true, as modernisation theorists claim, that political integration and state-building can only take place through the eradication of 'traditional' solidarities and intermediary linkages. Bernard Schaffer has elaborated this point in an excellent but insufficiently known essay [1974] in which he argues that integration should not necessarily be seen as an escape from history and myth, from a sense of friends, allies and enemies, and towards inevitable secularisation, equity and institution-building. Integration may involve processes such as tutelage, incorporation, institutional manipulation, and cooption as well as reconciliation. Many kinds of state–group relationships can exist within integration, which may be achieved not by surrendering 'traditional' (kin or spatial) relationships, but in fact by employing them. A certain degree of communalism, 'segmented pluralism', clientelism and patronage, as well as 'populism' may all work as integrative devices. There is no reason to assume that integration can and must only mean bureaucratisation. The two forms can go hand in hand: patronage and bureaucratic linkages are not necessarily alternatives – bureaucratic linkages may need to be supplemented.

To be sure, writes Schaffer,

> if integration had to mean less use of intermediaries (including patron–client relationships) it would indeed be unlikely to occur in many societies ...

> Integration can include ghettoes and apathetics as well as revolt and opposition. It can be organised through hierarchies and intermediaries as well as through political and administrative penetration ...

> Many solidarities survive and are reinforced. Some of these communal solidarities make very large claims, indeed approaching the level of political autonomy. Integration occurs just at the point at which these claims are managed, somehow or other ...

> The number of situations in which what we are looking at is the development of open, limited republican constitutionalism is in fact so small as to be exceptional ... Integration has to include an extraordinary variety of practices: millets, pales, ghettoes, intermediaries (patrons and brokers, with bureaucratisation), stranger-traders, myths, communal separation (... in the Lebanese Parliament). It may employ but goes far beyond proportional representation and single transferable votes. But even these ploys themselves are sometimes regarded as barely proper [Schaffer, 1974].

This discussion brings us quite close to the subject of corporatism/consociationalism. A likely political corollary of articulated modes of production and variegated class maps is often represented by corporatism [cf. Schmitter's classic overview, 1974]. In organisational terms, this is a more 'advanced' form than the patronage and clientelism discussed earlier on, and may indeed develop via a process of 'firming up' of clientelistic patronage systems [Marin, 1987: 59–60]. Claiming to be a collaborative form of political action, corporatism is premised on the proposition that it is not possible and/or desirable to establish the absolute political and ideological dominance of one class or group in society.[6] In corporatism generally, individuals and classes do not interact with the state directly, but through intermediaries. Historically, corporatist thought has perceived of two main strands: (I) community- (or group-) centred corporatism, and (II) state- (or organisation-) centred corporatism.

The traditional-authoritarian systems in the Arab World usually carry many of the features of type I corporatism. The often-called bureaucratic-authoritarian systems usually carry many of the features of type II corporatism. This is merely an analytical simplification, since type I systems may indeed use some 'organisational' methods and type II systems may use some 'group' methods in mobilising support, as we shall see in detail later on.

I should make one point clear at this juncture. In experimenting with a corporatist approach to the study of certain aspects of Middle Eastern politics, I am not basing my approach on any assumption that corporatism emanates from certain essential cultural features of Arab or Muslim societies. Although such cultural influences cannot be ruled out completely, corporatism is far more intimately related to the articulation of modes of production than it is to any 'eternal' cultural traits pertaining, for example, to the idea of an 'organic' society. In other words, culture can tell us quite a few things, but not the whole story, nor even the major part of the story. [On the usage of the term 'corporatism' that emphasises the cultural or psychological, rather than the structural or functional aspects, see Williamson, 1989: 23ff.]

Corporatism is not an easy concept to define as it may contain all sorts of shades of meaning [see Schmitter, 1974]. Corporatism may be variously understood as a (basically solidaristic) social and political ideology; as a type of political regime with certain distinct strategies (of interest intermediation); or as an explanatory and interpretive method (of studying state–society relations) [compare Chalmers, 1985: 56–79]. My major concern in this book is with the second, and particularly the third connotation of the term, although some reference to the first meaning will be made when it happens to be the sense in which it is meant by other writers (especially 'Islamic' ones).

As I have already stated, I do not subscribe to the theory that relates corporatism firmly to certain cultural zones – i.e. the so-called 'organic' cultures such as Islam and Catholicism [compare Stepan, 1978: 60–61]. I would only suggest that societies with such cultures may be better endowed with an elaborate cultural repertoire that can more readily evoke such (solidaristic, collaborative) images and symbols once the objective, historical and socio-economic conditions have made a corporatist political 'moment' more likely.

I shall start first with a few notes on corporatism as an intellectual tradition. A major assumption of corporatism (as an ideology or intellectual tradition) is that society is not composed primarily of individuals or groups that operate in an open, market-like relationship with each other or that function according to an imaginary 'social contract'; rather, societies are perceived of as being composed of bodies of people – *corps* – which, because their members share distinct tasks, roles and activities, possess a *natural* internal solidarity which is somehow more fundamental than membership of the state or market-place. Part of the confusion over corporatism's exact connotation derives from the fact that the *corps*, which represent the historical and conceptual antecedents of corporatism in Europe, could be either vocationally-based or solidarity-based [cf. Black, 1988: 48–52, 131, 203]. The same overlap pertained in the Arab World, where the word *tawa'if* had meant historically either trade/craft guilds and/or religious/sectarian communities. The corporatist idea rests traditionally on a conception of solidarity and mutual help (*takaful*) and a conception of apportionate justice (*'adl*) that are inherently social or group-based rather than individualistic. The social groups themselves develop, historically, in a contingent fashion, but usually in some order of hierarchy, and hierarchy usually operates within the *corps* or the communities and groups as well [compare Cerny, 1987: 3–5]. This is indeed the same tradition that Alfred Stepan calls "the organic-statist vision" which has in its "moral center ... not the individual taken by himself but rather the political community whose perfection allows the individual members to fulfill themselves" [Stepan, 1978: 30].

Such European ideas all have parallels and counterparts in mediaeval Islamic political thought. Some of them were reconstructed by the Muslim Brothers, especially in the 1940s and 1950s [cf. Ayubi, 1991a]. A new wave of proto-corporatist themes has crept up again, during the 1980s, into the writings of a number of Egyptian authors that I loosely call the 'cultural Islamists'. More specifically, there also exists a small faction of writers which some label the 'neo-salafis', most notable among whom are Tariq al-Bishri, 'Adil Husain and to some extent Galal Amin, and quasi-corporatist themes figure increasingly in their writings. Each of these three used to be quite sympathetic to the left (indeed Husain was a Marxist activist who was imprisoned on that account), but they seem to have become more attracted in recent years to a utopian community-centred corporatist formula which remains nationalist – even populist – but with strong Islamist overtones.[7]

There is also a small group of Western scholars starting to look at the Middle East in somewhat similar light. These include mainly Robert Bianchi [1984 and 1989] but also people such as Louis Cantori [e.g. 1986] who is inclined to equate corporatism with conservatism, collective morality and group solidarity, and Peter von Sivers [1988] who suggests a more diverse scheme involving small and medium enterprises, trade unions, Islamic associations and other 'moral communities' (families, clans, sects, etc.).

Corporatism/consociationalism does of course have a history within the

Islamic political tradition represented in particular by the *milla* as a religious community and the *sinf* as a vocational association. Orientalists and other students of the Middle East are not in agreement as to how much real autonomy such associations, or even the all-important cities and quarters (*amsar, harat*) themselves might have had: were they genuine fraternities and solidarities, or were they mainly organisms emanating from the administrative apparatus of the state? There is little doubt, however, that with the passage of time, a tension had grown between the original simple egalitarian image of the Islamic *umma* and the government's increased need for more defined and fairly stable social bases to organise production, control diversity and secure support for the state.

As the society became more complex and especially in times of transition from one mode of production to another and/or the articulation of several modes, the Islamic state in general and the Ottoman state in particular were more inclined towards a system of hierarchically ordered, interdependent elements, even though the diversity had often resulted from the weakness of state penetration at the periphery of the 'imperial' society more than it had from a genuine state desire for a diversified society [cf. Mardin, 1973 and 1969]. The closest that the Ottoman state had come to a corporatist formula, however, was in the relatively late stage of the eighteenth and nineteenth centuries when modes of production were articulated in a most complex way that gave rise to a whole variety of economic, social and ethno-cultural interests. Even when the Ottoman state tried in the early nineteenth century to reinforce a sense of centralisation as part of its 'defensive modernisation', local interests were so powerful that they put up strong resistance to the state's attempt to encroach on their traditional status and newly acquired privileges. They were now, however, having to cope with a new generation of secularist modernising bureaucrats; these were emerging with a stern centralising French-style concept of the national interest which was intolerant of the social mosaic and intermediary associations over which they ruled [Mardin, 1973: 175ff].

This conflictual process eventually gave rise to the emergence of an ideology of 'corporatist nationalism' espoused by Ziya Gökalp, described by him as 'solidarism' (*tesanütçülük*), and very similar to syndicalism in its tenets. In due course this was in turn to give rise to Mustafa Kemal's 'populist corporatism', which was increasingly to acquire more and more of an *étatiste* economic policy, trying to impose administrative order on the newly emerging socio-economic interests and structures [Bianchi, 1984: 92–3, 100–107]. The legacy of such conflicts and developments is something that the Turkish state has had to grapple with until the present time.

Similar if weaker trends were manifesting themselves in the Arab countries. As the Ottoman Empire was disintegrating, and British and French hegemony was stretching over the Middle East, popular revolts took place in various parts of the Arab World: the anti-Ottoman 'Great Arab Revolution' in 1916, followed by the popular revolutions in Egypt in 1919 and in Syria and Iraq in 1920. These 'revolutions' brought the local landowners and merchants to political power or active opposition for the first time since the tenth to eleventh centuries. But rather than lead to a pluralist democratic transformation, this had resulted in an eventual semi-corporatist formula of power sharing among the landowners, merchants and politicians/bureaucrats. The formula also included openly corporatist/consociationalist representations of religious, ethnic and tribal *communities* in the state institutions (and often in the radical opposition parties as well). Thus for example Kurds were heavily represented in the early Iraqi army, as were various religious minorities in the Syrian army, and there were also stipulations for the representation of 'tribes' in Iraqi and Syrian institutions [Al-Naqib, 1991: 92ff].

In a 'second phase' of Arab politics in the post-Second World War period, community-centred incorporation continued as a favoured formula in 'tribal' societies (and in the religio-tribal case of Lebanon), whereas in the countries where a coalition of the 'new middle class' had managed to remove the older coalition of landlords/merchants, more of a state-centred form of corporatism was eventually to emerge.

As a political strategy, corporatism is premised on a 'collaborative' rather than a 'conflictual' approach. The argument is usually based on the proposition that social and political outcomes cannot and/or should not be decided by conflictual means. As such, corporatism is probably more typical of transitional or 'articulatory' periods during which class hegemony is not possible. Its current revival in the 'core' countries of the world probably corresponds to the emergence of new articulations created by the post-industrial phase of capitalism, characterised as it is by decline in the conventional manufacturing sectors (i.e. those based on the industrial proletariat), combined with fast development in the services and the technology and information sectors (which are dependent on scientists and managers).

The problem with neo-corporatism as an analytical paradigm for analysing modern societies has been with the attempt to locate and to specify the 'bodies' (*corps*) which are the main components of any corporatist analysis and/or their precise mode of interaction. In a capitalist society the usual bodies or forces identified are capital, labour and the state. Neo-Keynesianism, the Welfare State, technocracy, indicative planning and labour-management co-ordination are all examples of corporatist practices aiming at intermediation among various interests with a view to ensuring cross-class compliance with the social and political outcomes envisaged or achieved. Different types of collaborative action (clientelist, consociational, corporatist, etc.) emerge from the relationship between the state and the various groups reflecting several social processes of a quasi-political, non-market kind [Cerny, 1987: 27–8; Carnoy, 1984: 39ff, 249–50].

Some view corporatism as merely a political sub-system, opposite to pluralism, that is based on a process of 'interest intermediation' via the state. Philippe Schmitter's most often-quoted definition emphasises this relationship:

> Corporatism can be defined as a system of interest representation in which the constituent units are organized into a limited number of singular compulsory, non-competitive, hierarchically ordered and functionally differentiated categories, recognised or licensed (if not created) by the State and granted a deliberate representational monopoly within their respective categories in exchange for absolving certain controls on their selection of leaders and articulation of demands and supports [Schmitter, 1974: 93–4].

As implied in this definition, "all models of neo-corporatism have at least some *étatiste* bias: it is always 'the state' which is conceptualized as the most privileged and crucial actor in the neo-corporatist game; interlocutor, arbiter, addressee, silent reference point, implementing agency, regulatory force, mastermind, ultimate guarantee" [Marin, 1987: 57].

One of the weaknesses of the 'economistic', technocratic approach to corporatism derives from its failure to relate corporatism to changes in the mode of production. Thus it often ends up by assuming that the corporatist state is neutral and independent from classes, which become submerged in their constituent, non-competitive, interest-oriented organisations. Such a position would not help, either, in understanding the socio-economic reasons that may give rise to corporatism. For it is most likely the conjuncture of certain socio-economic factors that is particularly instrumental in giving rise to corporatist formulae in certain societies at certain moments in time. Transitional phases witnessing a complex articulation of modes of production, and the social formations and cultural formulations that go with such articulations, are likely to represent a particularly appropriate environment for the emergence of corporatist formulae. Situations of 'late development' and attempts at 'catching up' with earlier industrialisers and modernisers seem to be conducive to the encouragement of a corporatist trend, either in its more populist, or in its more etatist variety.

The orientation of such corporatism may vary, however. Conservative corporatism (possibly Fascism) may represent an attempt to restore the 'nostalgic' presumed harmony of society that was shattered through abrupt industrialisation, by placing the process under control (often of the established interests) and by excluding the possibility of working-class demands getting out of hand.

Mobilisational corporatism may, on the other hand, emerge as part of a nationalist and social revolution in an attempt to launch a concerted effort by the various 'nationalist' and popular classes for accelerated development 'under the leadership of the state'. Corporatist formulae give the appearance of avoiding disastrous conflicts and, particularly in their populist strain, appear to strike an "ideological synthesis of traditionalism and modernism" [Stewart, 1969: 191–3]. They claim an ability for problem solving without sacrificing the 'identity' of the society and the 'authenticity' of its culture. This variety of corporatism appears to be a convenient formula for élites wishing to initiate modernisation and/or industrialisation, while controlling its form and direction. Populist-corporatism often gives rise to Bonapartist formulae, such as in Peronism for example [Canovan, 1981: 137ff]. Nasserism is the best-known example of this formula in the Arab World. In countries with strong state traditions such regimes are likely to acquire important *dirigiste* or *étatiste* features.

I regard corporatism mainly as a particular set of questions pertaining to state–society relations. I tend to think that corporatism is a likely outcome of a situation characterised by an articulation of modes of production and/or by a fluid and overlapping social configuration. Transitional phases in general and periods where late capitalism coincides with early welfarism in particular would seem to lend themselves to corporatist arrangements. Basic to all corporatist formulas, although of course to varying degrees, is a major role attributed to the state in directing the economy and in manipulating social groups. I agree with O'Donnell that corporatism is both 'bifrontal' and 'segmentary'. Corporatism is 'bifrontal' in the sense of being both 'statising' and 'privatising': the first process consists of the conquest and subordination by the state of organisations of civil society; the second entails the opening of institutional areas of the state to the representation of organised interests of civil society. Corporatism is also 'segmentary': its actual functioning and social impacts differ systematically according to cleavages largely determined by social class. Thus for example, in the variety of corporatism that is typical of a bureaucratic-authoritarian regime, the "main link established with the popular sector is one of control" and penetration by the state. At the same time the state exercises control over the dominant sectors by less direct and much less coercive methods than those applied to the popular sector [O'Donnell, 1977: 48–50].

It must be obvious from these brief notes that corporatism has so many manifestations that it is necessary to sort out the various categories before any significant use can be made of it as an analytic paradigm. Schmitter has already distinguished between 'state' corporatism and 'societal' corporatism. The state-dominated version is currently associated with authoritarianism and with dependent developing countries. The 'societal' form has tended to develop in more advanced capitalist societies. The first variety is coercively and abruptly imposed from above, often in the context of delayed dependent capitalist development and incipient, disorganised pluralism. The second (often termed neo-corporatism) is said to evolve more gradually from below in the context of advanced welfare state capitalism and highly developed, organisationally consolidated pluralism [Schmitter, 1974: 93ff; Chalmers, 1985; 59–61]. It would be useful, however, to provide a more differentiated conceptualisation of corporatism by identifying additional varieties of each generic type, including intermediate or hybrid varieties that may contain elements of both state corporatism and societal corporatism [Bianchi, 1984: 377ff]. Furthermore, there may be grounds, when studying certain societies, for resurrecting the more traditional notion of corporatism circling around communities of 'natural' internal solidarity (*Gemeinschaft*). This, it may be recalled, is a concept that has an affinity with Ibn Khaldun's '*asabiyya*, and could be rewardingly applied to societies where the 'lineage mode of production' (and/or its social and political relationships) still exerts a distinct impact on the society. Thus it may be useful to introduce a third category in addition to state-centred corporatism and society-centred corporatism: that of community-centred corporatism (whether based on the *qabila*, the *milla* or whatever).

Although not elaborating on the theoretical nuances and the specific applications of such a concept of corporatism, Khaldun al-Naqib is pioneering in trying to apply it to modern and contemporary societies of the Arab East. Al-Naqib has observed that in the Levant, especially in the 1930s and 1940s, religious, ethnic and tribal communities were represented in a 'corporatist' manner in state institutions, including parliaments, armies and political parties of both the government and the opposition [Al-Naqib, 1991: 92ff]. Partial communal incorporation is indeed still practised in some Arab countries (such as, for example, the Christians in Egypt and in Jordan), whereas Lebanon illustrates the most extreme case whereby community-centred corporatism (i.e. consociationalism) has represented the basic formula for the entire political system (at least until its collapse in 1975).

The consociational problematique concerns "the relations between subcultures that may intensely hate each other [and] are almost fully segregated at the social and organizational level." They tend to have (fully or partly) *internally* differentiated social structures. Consociationalism takes place between their tightly-knit élite sets, and is characterised by "elite predominance over a politically *deferential* and organizationally *encapsulated* following" [Scholten, 1987: 2–4]. The consociationalist approach (i.e. a grand coalition based on high internal autonomy, proportionality of representation and mutual veto) has been conventionally applied to countries such as Holland, Belgium, Switzerland, etc., and some suggest that its 'problem context' applies to many new states within the Third World [cf. Lijphart 1977].

Lebanon represents the main Middle Eastern example (in some senses a 'stretching' of the Ottoman *millet* formula to its extreme possible limits) and one of the most significant cases on the international level. Over fifteen years of civil war have destroyed many things Lebanese, but not their basic consociational formula which has only been ameliorated, rather than abandoned, in Al-Ta'if's agreement of 1991. The 'principle of proportionality' has been extensively applied in Lebanon. According to the unwritten National Pact of 1943, the highest governmental offices are reserved for the largest communities. The president is to be a Maronite Christian, the prime minister a Sunni

Muslim, the speaker of the House of Deputies a Shi'i Muslim, and the deputy speaker and the deputy prime minister Greek Orthodox Christians. Cabinet portfolios are also carefully distributed along 'confessional' lines among the country's sixteen or so 'recognised' Christian and Muslim sects, and so are top civil service positions. Proportionality is also written into the electoral law, each sect being allocated a certain number of representatives in the Chamber of Deputies ostensibly according to its numerical strength within the population. Within each constituency, the sectarian composition decides the number of deputies representing each sect. They are elected by the entire constituency and not only by members of their own sect. Thus candidates belonging to each main sect compete against each other, not against the 'other' religion, and no community fights in order to maximise the number of its representatives at the expense of the others [cf. Hudson, 1968; Suleiman, 1967; Harik, 1982: 224–35; Nordlinger, 1972: 22–4]. The formula does have its problems, as it consecrates and solidifies the sectarian divisions rather than downplaying them in favour of integration. The end result is an extremely weak state, too embedded in its social environment to enjoy any degree of autonomy. The consecration of the sectarian identity also encourages groups to seek external allies among co-religionists or sympathetic circles outside the country, thus making the country so sensitive to regional and international developments that it is almost a country 'without an interior'. This latter seems to have been one of the main causes behind the prolonged civil war. Yet the formula does not seem to have lost the support of most Lebanese, even after the long tragedy of death and destruction. Not only that, but there has certainly been some mild sympathy expressed towards this approach in general by various Arab writers in recent years [cf. e.g. Al-Ghabra, 1988; Salama, 1987b: 99ff; Masarra, 1986; Ibrahim, 1992: 231ff].

It should be possible to note the striking affinity and similarity between consociational and corporatist arrangements and to suggest a juxtaposition of the two categories for analytical purposes. There is a common preoccupation with crisis management and social stability, with the governability of divided societies through collaboration of antagonistic forces [Marin, 1987: 47–8]. Some of the familiar cases of corporatism (e.g. Austria, Turkey) have had a history of consociationalism, thus confirming the possible affinity between the two formulae. Taken together, as Ilja Scholten suggests, "the corporatist and consociational mode of analysis may give direction to the generation of new studies on the complexities of the relationship between State institutions, associational collectivities, and civil society on the one hand, and economic policies and developments on the other hand" [Scholten, 1987: 31].

We need therefore to distinguish between two major types of corporatism, of which the second has two distinct varieties, as follows:

1. State-centred corporatism. Although the state is basic to all corporatist

formulas, in state-corporatism there is little doubt that the state is supreme, almost managing to oblige all other groups to accept its 'rules of the game', and often re-creating certain strategic groupings that are in the state's own image (i.e. 'simulating' intermediary associations). This form is perhaps more likely to emerge among 'late industrialisers' that try to achieve capital-ist transformations via the state, often invoking nationalist sentiments and usually relying on a solid techno-bureaucracy. Politically, it tends to exclude the traditional land-holding classes and to strike a 'national alliance' be-tween a number of 'popular' classes, none of which seems to have hegemony over the society by itself. Peronism and Nasserism represent good cases in point. Tunisia, Algeria, Iraq and Syria represent, to one degree or another, approximations or imitations of this type.

2. Group-centred corporatism. Although the state is still important here, it cannot (or would not) enforce its supremacy over a 'silent void' to be represented by civil society. Depending on the nature of the groups that would not allow the state to have the show all to itself one can distinguish between two varieties: (a) one in which the groupings are mainly of the primordial, solidarity type (*Gemeinschaft*), which we term community-centred corporatism, and (b) another in which the groupings are mainly of the associational interest-representational type (*Gesellschaft*), which we term society-centred corporatism.

Community-centred corporatism tends to emerge in conditions of early *modernisation* and represents an attempt to involve pre-capitalist social groupings in an integrationist endeavour that is not yet going through vigorous capitalist transformation. During such a stage, classes in the modern sense are still 'in the making', or they have acquired certain structural features (classes 'in themselves') but not yet the consciousness to act politically (as classes 'for themselves'), since they are not yet neatly differentiated, or sufficiently separ-ated from primordial ties. Ottoman Turkey in the eighteenth and nineteenth centuries, and the contemporary Arabian countries, are illustrations of this type. Lebanon is a historically peculiar case.

The practice of tribal confederations in its more 'modern' forms in the contemporary Gulf states has puzzled the Arab analysts: Al-Naqib [1987] proposed a corporatist label; Diyab [1988] thought a consociationalist label would be more accurate. They have struggled with the conceptualisation – it may be more appropriate to describe it as community-based corporatism, with some consociational undertones.

In some situations one group (not always the majority) dominates and applies a policy of 'differential incorporation' to other groups; this applies to countries of Arabia and the Gulf and can also be observed in some countries of the Arab Levant. I would class arrangements of ethnic superordination/ subordination [compare Lustick, 1979: 325–44] and even some cases of 'enforced consociationalism' as examples of differential group incorporation [M.G. Smith, 1986]. Consociationalism should not therefore be contrasted with 'control' (as Ian Lustick does) as it is actually one possible technique of domination and control, based on manipulation and often anti-democratic methods.[8]

Society-centred corporatism is more typical of conditions of late *industrialisation* combined with an early emergence of the welfare state [cf. Cerny, 1987: 24–5]. This combination does not seem to be strongly conducive to a situation (as in early capitalist societies) of confrontation between a working class with a long militant history and a state that is taken to be the 'committee for managing the common affairs of the bourgeoisie'. The state's direct involvement in development and welfare, and the workers' preparedness to cooperate, or at least to come to terms, with management and capital are characteristics of society-centred corporatist regimes. Sweden and Austria are usually quoted as the most representative cases of society-based corporatism. It is less clear, however, whether such a situation is more typical, as Leo Panitch suggests, of 'good times' when growth and prosperity may temporarily obscure the deepening social contradictions of highly developed capitalism, or as Gerhard Lehmbruch suggests, of 'hard times' when corporatist arrangements are initially regarded as unconventional responses to crisis situations but then gradually become a routine technique of conflict resolution [cf. Bianchi, 1984: 396].

A similar sort of question may be asked as to whether the 'structural exhaustion' of state corporatism may be conducive to the emergence of a certain variety of societal corporatism. As suggested by Marin [1987] one path towards the emergence of societal corporatism may take the form of an *étatiste* system, loosening up and moving towards a type of private interest government. G. O'Donnell [1979] has observed that the repeated but unsuccessful efforts, by exhausted state corporatism, to implement austerity programmes necessary for the deepening of industrialisation, and to de-emphasise their earlier populist distributive policies, have weakened the already heterogeneous coalitions pertaining in such countries. The state's authority has been seriously weakened as a result of such attempts, giving rise to divergent social demands and to an atmosphere of 'mass praetorianism' that often sets the state "dancing to the beat of civil society". O'Donnell has further suggested that the weakening state may have no alternative in such circumstances but to succumb to the calls for 'democracy' under the incessant pressures from various segments in the society. Although one should not hurry to issue the death warrant of the authoritarian state in countries such as Turkey and Egypt, there are important indications in these two countries (and in others in the Arab World) that such an analysis should be taken seriously.

This approach that we are suggesting may be able to benefit in part from David Apter's typology of 'nondemocratic representation' [Apter, 1987: 132ff]. Our state-centred corporatist systems are similar to his bureaucratic systems, and he does explicitly count the Kemalist and the Nasserist regimes as examples. Our community-centred corporatist systems are similar to his reconciliation system, with a kinship base and a certain 'theocratic' touch ("based on proprietary and memorial rights and local and reciprocal allegiances, [and] held together through lines of unstable kinship"). These types of systems respond differently to growing pluralism and 'embourgeoisement'. Bureaucratic systems respond by manipulating interest group representation and functional representation, and restricting popular representation. Reconciliation systems respond to pluralism and 'embourgeoisement' by "oligarchical manipulations, corruption and the use of economic advantage to restrict popular representation and to expand interest group representation with functional representation subordinate to interest group representation" [ibid.: 132–4].

Although quite distinct, these categories of corporatism enlisted above (i.e. I, IIa and IIb) should not be regarded as mutually exclusive. This is particularly true of Third World countries with their articulated modes of production and overlapping social and cultural settings. This distinction is therefore only schematic, as many states try to incorporate both socio-cultural, communal groups (sects, tribes, etc.) as well as socio-economic, functional groups (syndicates, merchants, etc.). Thus, whereas in Egypt it is mainly the functional groups that have been incorporated, there have been semi-consociational improvisations with regard to the Copts. And although the formula in the United Arab Emirates is essentially consociational, it pays (as in Kuwait) special attention to the incorporation of merchants as a socio-economic group. The epitome of the composite consociational/corporatist formula is probably reached in Yemen. There it includes the armed forces, the tribes (some of them Royalist) as well as the intelligentsia. Another point that needs to be pondered and that should not be ruled out of hand is whether certain cultures, because of their specific historical experience with communal-type corporatism may be inclined at a later stage to have a certain propensity to (or temptation towards) state-corporatism or societal-corporatism. In their own different ways, Austria and Turkey may be illustrative of this idea.

We now proceed to a closer look at manifestations of these varieties of corporatism within the Arab World.

NOTES

1. Even earlier 'Abdallah al-'Arawi [Laroui] had praised Gramsci's rediscovery of the autonomy of politics, analysed in the context of Machiavelli (to whom Gramsci had returned after a long detour by way of the German school of history, Bismarck and Croce). Al-'Arawi then wonders "Cannot the Arabs of today, by taking the same long detour, encounter it [i.e. the autonomy of politics] in the form expressed or symbolised by the trio Ibn Baja–Ibn Khaldun–Ibn Taimiya?" [Laroui, 1976: 105].

2. With a great deal of simplification, it could be suggested that the morality of the Arab is 'externalist' rather than 'internalist' and is collectively rather than individually referenced. Shame

is more relevant than guilt. The concept of conscience is relatively new. In my training of Arab managers and administrators I often find it difficult to explain to them 'internalist' concepts such as 'motivation' (they would understand 'incentive'), or 'commitment' (they would understand 'loyalty').

3. Although patronage and clientelistic practices are commonplace in the Middle East, each specific one of them known by a certain word, there is no commonly accepted collective noun in Arabic for clientelism or patronage in general. Some of the words used in different countries are: *taba'iyya*; *zibana*; *muwala*; *ma'iyya*; *istitba'*; *istizlam*, etc.

4. According to Samuel Huntington, the political culture of most modernising societies is "marked by suspicion, jealousy and latent and actual hostility towards everyone who is not a member of the family ... These characteristics are found in many cultures, their most extensive manifestation being in the Arab World and in Latin America" [Huntington, 1971: 28].

5. This term was first used by the Kuwaiti sociologist Muhammad al-Rumaihi.

6. Part of the ambiguity about corporatism is reflected in the fact that no satisfactory Arabic (or Turkish) translation has yet been found for the term 'corporatism'. It has been given so many disparate Arabic translations including *ta'adudiyya* (S. Ibrahim), *mu'assasatiyya* (N.R. Farah), *ittihadatiyya* (U. Gh. Harb), and I have sometimes translated it as *sharikatiyya* and sometimes as *talahumiyya* [Ayubi, 1989b; 1992a]. If one wanted to coin a new term by way of extending some conventional 'Islamic' concepts, I would suggest *takafuliyya* (from *takaful* – i.e. mutual aid) for the more moral/solidaristic strand of corporatism and *asnafiyya* (from *asnaf* – i.e. crafts and guilds) for the more organisational/intermediary strand. None of these is capable of conveying the moral/solidaristic as well as the organisational/intermediary connotations of the term *at the same time*.

7. According to Tariq al-Bishri, for example, the Ottoman *tanzimat* as well as Muhammad 'Ali's reforms were useful in developing modern bureaucracies, but harmful in terms of eroding the autonomy, status and significance of the various associations (*tawa'if; hay'at*) that used to counterbalance and constrain the ruler's despotism. These Western-inspired reforms had thus helped to centralise the authority of government, but had led to the collapse of 'plurality' in society, in its traditional sense, scattered people into nuclear individuals and hit all solidaristic and corporate (*jami'iyya*) links in the name of rationality and modernity [Al-Bishri, 1989: 86–9].

8. For an interesting attempt to use the superordinate/subordinate model for analysis of the Israeli–Palestinian situation, see Dumper [1994].

CHAPTER SIX

The Political System of Articulated Forms: the Radical, Populist Republics

The radical, so-called 'socialist', or 'revolutionary' (*thawri*) Arab regimes represent a distinct combination of *étatiste* and welfarist policies. Their once-familiar description as 'socialist' might have suited the needs of domestic élites and the vocabulary of the Cold War in the 1960s and 1970s, but I would prefer to describe them as populist-corporatist regimes. Most of them are still worthy of the 'radical' description, however, in view of the fact that they did embark on serious strategies of 'social engineering' that did produce important mobilisational and redistributional changes in the society. Several of them were indeed examples of what Gramsci calls 'passive revolution' i.e. radical transformations in the society imposed from above rather than initiated and achieved from below [cf. Buci-Glucksmann, 1980: 314–17].

Let me first explain why I think that the socialist description of these regimes is less accurate than describing them as populist-corporatist.

SOCIALISM OR *ETATISME*

A familiar concept of socialism suggests defining it as "an ideology and a structure of institutional practices derived from it, which treats *the State* as the key agency of direct economic planning and management and therefore attempts to reallocate resources according to priorities established by the state, rather than through the alternative mechanisms provided by the market" [Clapham, 1992: 13ff]. I suggest, for the sake of accurate analysis, that the 'ideology' and the 'structure' should be disentangled from each other, because socialism as an ideology never contemplated the state as *the producer*. Moralist socialism emphasised equity; Marxist socialism emphasised the 'withering away' of the state', as harmony between forces and relations of production was to be restored. It follows, from the above-mentioned definition of socialism, that people are attracted first to the ideology, then 'a structure of institutional practices *derived from it*' is subsequently adopted which places the state at the central point. It should follow, by contrast, that if the ideology is accepted *subsequent to* the exercise of practices that place the state at the centre, any talk about socialism must be rather inaccurate (that is because the 'structure of institutional practices' is supposed to be *derived from* the 'ideology', and not the other way round).

If one looks more specifically at some of the regimes that were often described as socialist, for example in Egypt, Syria, Iraq, etc., it will become clear that rather than a socialist ideology inspiring their institutional arrangements, it was actually their political and institutional pursuits (the quest for national independence and for state-building) that eventually led them to a semblance of socialism.

This chapter suggests that, as has been the case in some other parts of the Third World, the main concerns of the radical Arab states have been political: 'Seek ye first the *political* kingdom' (Nkrumah) applies to the main radical Arab models – Nasserism, Ba'thism and Bourguibism – and even to an extent Algeria (national liberation); socialism was a later addendum [cf. Ayubi, 1978]. It is not sound to call a system socialist simply because its leaders happen, at a particular political juncture, to raise socialist banners and to use socialist terminology. We do not accept so readily the appellation 'democratic' that many of the command regimes attribute to themselves, so why are we so easily prepared to accept a 'socialist' designation of a regime simply because it is called so by its leaders?

I would distinguish between three aspects of socialism and would be prepared to describe a certain system as socialist if and when it incorporates the three aspects:

1. socialism as an *ideology*, generally aspiring to a broadly based popular control of and participation in the economic and political affairs of society, according to a broadly egalitarian principle;
2. socialism, as described 'ideologically' in (1) can on the whole be put into practice only via a political and social *movement* involving classes, groups and individuals that see in the realisation of (1) the nearest approximation to their aspirations;
3. socialism as a *structure* has no ready-made theory, especially in the field of economics. Communes, cooperatives, 'autogestion' and other formulas have been experimented with, and even a concept of 'market socialism' has been innovated. The association of socialism with the state as producer is incidental – it was a Leninist-Stalinist improvisation. It was never part of socialism as an idea or part of socialism as a movement. This explains why Henri Lefebvre regards 'state socialism' and 'state capitalism' as "two species of the same genre" of the 'statist mode of production' (*le mode de*

production étatique) [Lefebvre, 1978]. Such an association has become a characteristic of Soviet model regimes and their imitations, but socialism can be
perceived of without etatism, and etatism is not confined to socialism; for
example, the 'Zaibatsu' in Japan and the 'Chaebol' in Korea [compare S.
Amin, 1986].

Certain one-time 'radical' Arab regimes were often described as socialist –
mainly Egypt, Syria, Iraq and Algeria, but sometimes also Tunisia, Sudan,
Libya, etc. I would suggest that although such regimes have used socialist
slogans, applied social policies and adopted institutional arrangements reminiscent of the Soviet-style East European regimes, it would be misleading to
describe these 'radical' Arab regimes as socialist. According to my criteria for
a socialist system (above) I would suggest the following:

— in terms of criterion (1), socialism was not, historically, the initial concept
from which the various practices have followed, nor was it development of
other concepts and practices. Socialism has crept, gradually and piecemeal,
into the ideologies of such regimes, juxtaposed on to other more important
'nationalistic' or 'modernising' concepts. 'Socialism' has developed partly
as an extension of the nationalist concerns into economic spheres (the so-
called 'comprehensive national independence'), and partly as a mechanism
for mass mobilisation and political control, for the benefit of ruling élites
that *did not* initially take power (often via coups d'état) with the intention of
'applying socialism'. The term 'socialist' was a later adjective that was
eventually added to Egypt's Ittihad (Union), to the Arab Ba'th Party that
ruled in Syria and Iraq, and to the New Destour Party that ruled in Tunisia.
— in terms of criterion (2), and as just suggested, 'socialism' did not come to
power by way of a political movement intent on putting socialist ideals into
practice. Socialism did not come about through a political party formed
before assuming power along a socialist platform, or through a mass or
revolutionary movement with clear popular and egalitarian orientations.
The norm was a military coup or a 'palace coup', and although this sometimes proceeded to build up a single political organisation that eventually
adopted some 'socialistic' objectives, this was done from a position of
authority and was often aimed at installing 'socialism without socialists', as
a familiar Arab phrase describes it. The socialist components were also
gradually added up in an eclectic way, often as a response to a perceived
external or internal *political* challenge. In Egypt, for example, the first single
organisation was a military revolutionary command, then a Liberation Rally
was formed, then a National Union, and lastly – over ten years after the
1952 coup – an Arab Socialist Union was organised.
— in terms of criterion (3), arrangements similar to those followed in Soviet-
style regimes were increasingly adopted, especially with regard to economic

planning, public enterprise and centralised organisation. These were mainly adopted, however, as *technical* devices deemed more effective for achieving the tasks of accelerated growth, 'rational' decision-making and political control.

This is a group of practices that is better termed *étatiste* than socialist. It is similar to what Gramsci calls the 'corporative state'. To be sure, public policies were becoming increasingly 'social-welfarist' and even to a considerable extent egalitarian (e.g. agrarian reforms, expansion in education, social services and subsidised basic commodities), but this was basically a function of the 'populist' types of alliances that were so necessary at the time in order to confront the old oligarchies and to face up to external challenges. According to Ernesto Laclau it is such antagonism towards the 'power bloc' that renders a particular discourse 'populist' in character [Laclau, 1979: 143–98].

So, in short, these regimes were basically applying a distinct combination of *étatiste* and welfarist (i.e. populist) policies. We will argue later in the chapter that in order to achieve this combination, these regimes had experimented with a variety of semi-corporatist formulae. We will also set out to show, here and in following chapters, that as the problems of these regimes escalated they lost many of their populist characteristics and resorted to relatively more elaborate corporatist arrangements. Populism was then taken over by the Islamists and oriented in different directions – but this is, of course, a different story.

Let us now look briefly at the conjunctures in which a large public economic sector was to emerge, and a distinct *étatiste* policy was to be followed in a number of 'radical' Arab states – let us, in other words, look at what Gramsci calls the "phase of economic-corporate primitivism" in the development of the state [in Buci-Glucksmann, 1980: 283].

In Egypt the 'socialist transformation' (1961–63) had followed, historically and logically, the confrontation with imperialism in Suez in 1956, and the adoption of the first five-year plan for 1959/60–1964/65. Socialism was not a blueprint to be followed but a line of thinking and orientation of policy that developed through trial and error from the time agrarian reforms were introduced, shortly after the 1952 coup d'état [the authorities that confirm this thesis are so many that there is no point in enumerating them; but see in the meantime Ayubi, 1980: Ch. 3]. By the end of the Nasserist period, the public sector had dominated all economic activities, except agriculture and retail trade. In 1970/71 it accounted for 74 per cent of industrial production, 46.1 per cent of all production, 90 per cent of investments and 35.2 per cent of GDP. In spite of the abandonment of 'socialism' after Nasser (in fact the policy shift had started under Nasser, following the defeat of 1967), the public sector still accounted for 68 per cent of industrial production in 1979, for 37.1 per cent of total production in 1981/82, for 77 per cent of all investments in

1979, and for 27 per cent of GDP in 1981/82. In spite of the adoption of an economic open door policy since 1974, and the growth of the role of the private sector in the field of commerce and finance, the state still owns most mining and metallic works (except in oil where foreign capital is important), 60 per cent of manufacturing industries, most public transportation and communication, the leading construction firms, and an important portion of the banking and insurance sector [Abdel-Rahman and Abu Ali, 1989]. The privatisation policies announced in 1987 did not change the picture to any great extent, except in the tourism and hotels sector.

In Syria the first 'socialist' measures were introduced politically and from above during the brief union with Egypt (1958–61) when land reforms and nationalisation of foreign companies and some major domestic companies took place. This orientation was resumed when the Ba'th party took over power from 1963. From 1964 to 1966 important nationalisations were implemented, and a second, but this time a centralised, plan was introduced (1966–70) according to which 95 per cent of industrial investments were assigned to the state. These measures were inspired, among other things, by the Egyptian example and the need to prove that the Ba'th was no less revolutionary than Nasser. In addition, as the Egypt–Syria union which had been initiated by the Ba'th was brought to an end by an alliance of army officers and wealthy merchants, it was natural for the Ba'thists, on coming back to power, to want to eradicate the socio-economic bases of their potential opponents among the old oligarchy and the commercial bourgeoisie.

Five-year plans continued, with the public sector contributing 69.7 per cent of all investments in the second plan, 80.6 per cent in the third, 82.7 per cent in the fourth, and 79.6 per cent in the fifth plan [Hilan, 1989]. In reality, however, it seems that the actual contribution of the public sector in total investment was lower, ranging in general between 57 per cent and 77 per cent of the total, and accounting in 1981/82 for some 62 per cent of total investments. From the early 1980s no further expansion in industry was to take place, and indeed overall public sector investments were to decline owing to the lack of finance. A sixth development plan (1986–90) could not be issued, and the general policy has tended towards an encouragement of private and joint capital, especially in agriculture, food industries and tourism. A number of joint companies started to appear, with the state contributing no more than 25 per cent of the total capital, and they were given various exemptions and privileges and excused from several public sector regulations and foreign currency restrictions. Yet in spite of the political shifts, the share of the private sector in total investments has been fairly stable: 41 per cent in 1973 and 43 per cent in 1987 [Hilan, 1989 and refs cited].

In Iraq the economic role of the state was to grow following the 1958 anti-monarchy coup, and the initiation of a number of industrial projects in co-operation with the Soviet Union. The private sector remained dominant, however, contributing some 78 per cent of the national income and about 71 per cent of net domestic product (excluding oil) in 1960. It was only in 1964 that the government "surprised everybody by issuing the Socialist decrees", according to which the major industrial and commercial firms as well as all banks and insurance companies were nationalised [Al-Sayyid 'Ali, 1989 and refs cited]. A major motivation behind the nationalisation seems to have been the 'political' consideration of needing to make the Iraqi economic system as similar as possible to that of Egypt and Syria in order to facilitate the projected union of the three countries which was being negotiated at that stage.

With the arrival of the Ba'th party into power in 1968, an intensification of the 'socialist' policies was to take place. This was partly motivated by the need to pull the rug from beneath the feet of the Communist Party, which had a considerable class and ideological following in Iraq. As happened to a lesser extent in Syria and Egypt, the military regimes were trying to undermine the popular sources of support for the leftist movements by appearing to outbid the latter's programmes on nationalisation, industrialisation and social services. Such Ba'thist policies in Iraq eventually led, in addition to industry, to all foreign trade and most of domestic trade being placed in the hands of the state. As a result, the state had by the early 1980s come to dominate the national economy and the various economic sectors: in 1981 it contributed 60.3 per cent of GNP (compared to 24.5 per cent in 1968) and was responsible for 56.8 per cent of all industrial production (and 97.7 per cent of capital formation in industry), 52.3 per cent of all trade and commercial activities (and 90.3 per cent of capital formation in these fields), and 49.4 per cent of all agricultural production [Al-Ba'th Party (1982) quoted in Al-Sayyid 'Ali, 1989].

I am not suggesting that the leaders of the populist-corporatist Arab regimes were dedicated capitalists in devious disguise – many of them must have taken their socialistic terminology quite seriously. By the same token the anguish of those whose property was 'Egyptianised', nationalised or simply confiscated (musadara) must have been very real. But the loss of the possessions of such people should not be taken as a testimony for the 'socialism' of those who dispossessed them: property was taken away sometimes for 'nationalistic' reasons, sometimes for 'political-security' reasons, and sometimes for reasons of sheer personal greed or primordial vengeance. I admit that very few leaders of the populist-corporatist regimes were straightforward laissez-faire capitalists; but neither were they really devoted socialists. What was particularly clear about their regimes was the forces to which they were opposed: the old oligarchy and the old-style colonialism; beyond that their alliances and their orientations were subject to a great deal of contingent change.

The land reforms initiated by such regimes had various objectives in addition to the most often declared ones of social justice. Above all, their main political objective was to eliminate the power base of the large landlord as a politically influential force, an objective which was effectively achieved in the countries that launched significant land reforms. In addition, agrarian reforms were often seen as part of an overall developmental strategy that aimed at releasing capital from agriculture and towards industry. Land reform was often, as Richards and Waterbury described it, the "handmaiden of state-led industrialization strategy", although quite often the delivery was not fully successful, as these policies have tended not only to redirect the agricultural surplus but also to squeeze the already impoverished rural population, thus ultimately running counter to the requirements of expanding the domestic consumer market [cf. Richards and Waterbury, 1990: 149–52].

Such regimes were never particularly anti-capitalist: to start with they always encouraged domestic capital, and – following a brief period of striving for 'economic independence' via import-substitution – they frequently ended by indulging in joint ventures with international capital. They were basically technocrats interested in modernisation through industrialisation, rather than ideologues or militants striving to install the rule of the working classes. They needed certain political alliances and a certain measure of political control to carry them through – these have sometimes warranted a socialistic terminology and the adoption of certain techniques of the sort applied in the former Soviet Union, Yugoslavia or even China. At the grass roots, for example in the localities and within the 'affiliated associations' such as the youth organisations, the socialist rhetoric was sometimes taken more seriously than it was meant to be – the outcome was always intervention to put an end to such 'leftist excesses' (e.g. the dissolution of the 'Propagators' Organisation' and the gradual phasing out of the Youth Organisation in Egypt in the mid-1960s).

In order to deal effectively with the Soviet Union and its satellites, which had become major trade partners of the radical Arab regimes (mainly for Cold War strategic, rather than ideological, reasons), these regimes found it sometimes useful to create organisations parallel or similar to their Soviet or East European counterparts. The Soviet Union ascribed to these regimes some undeserved socialist credentials [cf. refs in Ayubi, 1980: Ch. 3; Waterbury, 1988; Halliday, 1989: Ch. 4]. In an early appreciation of the idea of the 'relative autonomy of the state', some Soviet scholars developed the concept of the 'non-capitalist path to development' (or to Socialism). Some 'national-democratic' regimes were felt to be capable of transforming their societies to socialism without necessarily exhausting the stage of capitalism, and without a proletarian revolution, but rather by the gradual movement – via the state – towards socialism in alliance with the major socialist powers [cf. 'Aziz, 1983]. When the Egyptians expelled their Soviet advisers in 1972 (as did Numairi in Sudan and Barri in Somalia) and Egypt's 'socialist' policies were being reversed under Sadat, it must have confirmed in some Soviet minds the concept of the 'relative autonomy of the state' (or at least of the ruler!) although it must have shattered their illusions about the non-Socialist road to socialism. Only from the late 1970s did Soviet observers become more at ease in applying to such regimes terms like 'populism' and 'state capitalism', or describing their ruling élites as members of a 'bureaucratic bourgeoisie' [cf. e.g. Primakov, 1985; Khoros, 1986].

There were also, no doubt, some similarities with Soviet-type or peoples democracy-type regimes, but most of these sprang from the strong importance attached to planning and sometimes from the dual nature of the command system (party/bureaucracy). For example, Leninist organisational concepts were frequently applied, and the practice of *nomenklatura* (*tasmiya*) has been well known, especially with regard to 'sensitive' and/or lucrative positions. As with other systems of state socialism/state capitalism there was both centralisation of economic power and its unification, in one locus of decision, with political power. Political and economic power are fused into a single state power, and 'citizenship' and 'livelihood' are integrated "so that the subject's whole existence shall be ruled by one and the same command–obedience relation, with no separate public and private spheres, no divided loyalties, no countervailing centres of power, no sanctuaries and nowhere to go" [de Jasay, 1985: 253].

Particularly important, however, is the emphasis laid on legitimisation of rule in the light of goals rather than in light of procedures or of achievements, or rather treating noble goals, correct procedures and real achievements as one and the same thing. "Tasks and 'campaigns' (to conquer new heights or stamp out evils) replace legal frames as the language of the state" [Di Palma, 1991: 55–7]. Strictly, the success of performance is less relevant than the truth of tasks: thus leaders such as Nasser can fail in defending their national soil at war (1967) but are still forgiven and can continue in power. Inauguration of new factories, dams, highways and so on is more important in the formal propaganda than their efficient functioning. After all, and as happens in several Arab countries, the economic statistics can be massaged for the annual statements, advanced missiles can be simulated in empty metal shells for the military parades, and dying crops can be sprayed with green paint just before the leaders pass by! [cf. e.g. Al-Naku', 1991: 6off]

The dynamics of populism

The politics of such countries lay somewhere in between what would define authoritarian regimes and what would define totalitarian systems. Their affairs revolved, but in varying degrees from case to case, around three poles: the President, the army and the party. So that what we had was a combination of a boss-state (*état-raïs*), a security-state (to include aspects of the police-state or *dawlat al-mukhabarat*) and a party-state (*partitocrazia*) that dominates over most associations in society.[1] The civil bureaucracy is directed and controlled by all three. The mobilisation of the people within this system is partly charismatic (via the boss), partly ideological/political (via the party) and partly organisational (via the bureaucracy and sometimes the army). The frequency (often excessive) of 'popular referenda' gives the impression of a 'plebiscitic' – rather than an institutional – democracy. As 'Iyad Bin 'Ashur describes it, with special reference to Nasser's Egypt and Bourguiba's Tunisia:

> The relationship between the *ra'is* and the people is a direct one: immediate, emotional, marvellous, almost 'bodily'. It forms the backbone of the political system, in a situation where political organisations are no more than tools for mobilisation and recruitment for the sake of a plebiscitic, populist democracy (*bay'iyya Ghifariyya*) The discourse in this democracy is addressed at the 'people', in the sense of the needy, the badly-off in terms of money or culture. It is a political discourse full of wishes, promises, and appeals to the joy of life, to progress and equality [Bin 'Ashur, 1990: 59].

The Boss is extremely crucial and is usually a 'presidential monarch' in the sense that he enjoys constitutional or *de facto* life tenure of office. With the exception of Lebanon in its pre-civil war days, the Arab World has yet to produce its Nyerere, who would leave the presidential office voluntarily – not at death or on the heels of a coup d'état. As of this writing (1993), Asad has been president of Syria for twenty-three years, Saddam president of Iraq for thirteen years, and Mubarak of Egypt was starting a third presidential term (the first having started in 1980). Bourguiba was the president, or as he preferred to call himself '*al-mujahid al-akbar*' (*le combattant suprême*) for three decades. A president in an Arab radical populist country not only heads the state for a long time but enjoys a great deal of political power – *l'état, c'est presque lui*. When asked about the nature of his country's political system Bourguiba was not atypical in asking, in some surprise: "What system? I *am* the system" [Moore, 1970: 95].

The relative power of the other organisations varies from regime to regime and sometimes from period to period. Thus in Nasser's Egypt the role of the army and the bureaucracy were most important, in Algeria the army and the party, in Syria the party, the army and the security-machine, in Iraq the party and the security-machine, and in Tunisia the party and the bureaucracy.

No further detailed description of the political systems of these countries will follow since, out of all aspects of Arab politics, political systems have received the most attention by other authors and are already well covered in the literature. Rather we will continue to follow their regimes and their power coalitions or blocs as indicative of the nature of their states. We have already described these regimes and coalitions as populist: what exactly do we mean by this?

The Arabic words *sha'b* and *sha'bi* have connotations similar to the Latin American *el pueblo* and *lo popular*, which are not captured by the English words 'people' and 'popular'. Unlike for example in citizen/citizenry, the word *sha'b* has no individualised, singular form and has always to be a collective noun.

Another favourite political category is that of *al-jamahir* (the masses), whose singular form is also a collective noun (*al-jumhur – la foule* or the crowd)! As O'Donnell explains, "el pueblo and lo popular involve a 'we' that is a carrier of demands for substantive justice which form the basis for the obligation of the state toward the less favoured segments of the population" [O'Donnell, 1979: 288–9]. As a very popular song (*ehna esh-sha'b*) in Nasser's Egypt used to say: "We are the people, the people are Us."

However, the term populism (Turkish *halkçilik*; Arabic *sha'bawiyya*) is not an easy one to define and its connotations vary quite widely; so let us first indicate what we do *not* mean by populism in this work. First, we do not have in mind the concept of populism as an intellectual idealisation of the agrarian/artisanal society, either in its Russian Narodnik version [cf. Khoros, 1986] or in its modern 'small is beautiful' version [cf. Kitching, 1989: Ch. 2]. As we can see from their *étatiste* policies, the radical Arab regimes have laid great emphasis on industrialisation and most of them have been if not anti-rural then certainly strongly pro-urban. Like most Latin American populisms, Arab populist regimes formulated their discourse and built their coalitions in contradistinction to an oligarchic power bloc made up of (domestic, 'minoritarian' and foreign) commercial-urban and landed-rural classes. This distinguishes Arab populism from, for example, contemporary Turkish populism whose discourse and coalitions are defined in contradistinction to an etatist, bureaucratic power bloc [Sunar, 1993].

Populism should also be distinguished from Fascism, although the two are not completely unrelated, especially with regard to the use of theatrical trappings in order to "replace institutional forms of integration with a purely emotional sense of unity" [O'Sullivan, 1983: 98–101]. Populism is predominantly a middle-class movement that mobilises the lower classes, especially the urban poor, and entices them into politics, whereas Fascism is a movement that enjoys some upper-class support and aims at de-politicising the lower, especially the working, classes and pushing them out of politics.

Although populism (especially if regarded mainly as a discourse) is not necessarily confined to a certain type of socio-economic system or to a certain level of political development, as witness, for example, the success of Thatcherism, it does seem to have a particular affinity with transitional politics and with the early, easy phase of an economic policy based on import-substitution industrialisation [cf. Germani, 1978: Chs. 3 and 4, 151, 235ff]. Fast industrial *expansion* at such a stage allows both the proletariat and the technocracy to benefit *at the same time*, thus creating the political conditions conducive to an inclusionary coalition. Expanded industrialisation is accompanied at the same time by 'welfare state' services – and the 'welfare state' is by definition 'inclusionary' [Luhmann, 1990: 34ff]. In classifying Khomeini as a populist (a classification I quite agree with), Ervand Abrahamian maintains that populist movements inevitably emphasise the importance not of economic-social revolution but of cultural, national and political reconstruction [Abrahamian, 1991: 102–19]. This generalisation may be particularly influenced by the case of the 'Islamic revolution' in Iran but cannot as easily be applied to the Egyptian, Algerian or other Arab cases where populism has had a very important economic-social dimension.

My understanding of populism is much closer to the dominant trend within what one may call the 'Latin American school', and one of the earliest definitions here, that of Torcuato Di Tella, remains – to my mind – one of the most useful (especially as he includes 'Nasserism' among his examples). According to him, populism is:

> [a] political movement which enjoys the support of the mass of the urban working class and/or peasantry but which does not result from the autonomous organizational power of either of these two sectors. It is also supported by non-working class sectors upholding an anti-status quo ideology [Di Tella, 1965: 47].

In populism there is therefore an amorphous coalition between the urban popular classes and a predominantly middle-class leadership that is intent on changing the status quo. There are many reasons that may motivate the leadership to seek such a change in the status quo: including status incongruities within their own ranks (which are often caused by 'premature bureaucratisation') combined with a strong sense of national injustice and/or delayed development for the society at large. Although populist movements do not emanate from the common people, they mobilise and often manipulate them [Canovan, 1981: 139–43]. According to Di Tella, "the incongruent groups (generally of above average status) and the mobilized, disposable masses complement each other. Their social situations are different, but what they have in common is a passionate hatred of the *status quo*" [Di Tella, 1965: 50].

Because populist movements are more united by what they are against than what they are for, and because they aim at including and mobilising as many social sectors as possible, they are usually quite renowned for their eclecticism. Most typically, as we have gleaned from our discussion of the socialist claims of Arab populist regimes, they would develop "a pseudo ideology, *ex-post-facto*. Ideology is flexible, opportunist and continually subject to changes in political strategy" [Van Niekerk, 1974: 34]. As they have no overall world view according to which they want to re-socialise the individual, their systems tend to be more authoritarian than totalitarian [Germani, 1978: 10–11]. The purpose of the populist regime's 'inclusionary' policies is to underpin their power and to increase the autonomy of the state. Towards that end, populist regimes in the Arab World, like their counterparts in Latin America, had sought "not only to mobilize a broad popular base but also to control that base, and structure the relationships of its support groups to the state". As populist regimes offered material as well as symbolic gratification to their supporters, they also:

sought to fashion centrally controlled organizational structures to link their support groups directly into the state structures. The bulk of these organizations were formed on sectoral and functional criteria, thereby fragmenting support groups into parallel primary organizational structures joined at the top by interlocking sectoral élites [Malloy, 1977: 12–14].

The preference of the Arab populist regimes for a corporatist solution to the pressures of fast socio-political change was seldom stated explicitly (with partial exceptions in the Nasserist and Bourguibist cases), but there is little doubt that they all (with the exception of Qadhafi's Libya) manifested a clear predilection for corporatist organisational principles, even though the actual success of their organisational efforts has varied considerably from case to case. As dedicated 'modernisers' intent on accelerated industrialisation and fascinated by technologism [cf. Laroui, 1976: 104, 160], the leaders of these regimes strove to assimilate politics into economics and to call on the energies of the workers and on the expertise of the technocrats while keeping the potential political demands of such classes and groups in check. Or, as David Apter puts it:

> populism is used to support functional representation ... The tendency is to move downward through the restratification of the public into corporate functional groupings relevant to development and system-maintenance. Not class, but *corporate* grouping, is characteristic: hence, a kind of 'corporate representation' in primary stage modernizing, mobilization systems is seen as the means of reconciling populism with functional expertise [Apter, 1987: 148–9].

This tendency towards corporatist arrangements did not spring from essential cultural traits or elaborate ideological orientations but from the specific requirements of their populist policies. I can safely quote O'Donnell's words about Latin America here to express what I would like to say about the 'radical' Arab republics:

> Populism was also corporatist. The social incorporation and political activation it permitted and in its early movements, fomented, were carefully controlled, especially by the imposition of vertical relationships subordinating the unions to the state. Among other things, quite a few of these unions were created by the populist rulers, who reserved the right to grant or deprive them of recognition, to supervise the handling of their funds, to influence the selection of their leaders, and to decide upon the right of representation before the state and the employers ... This corporatism was not a new type of state or society, but rather a new way of 'organizing' the popular sector by means of its subordinate association with the populist state, which facilitated its controlled social incorporation and political activation in a period of rapid urbanization and industrialization [O'Donnell, 1977: 67–8].

Arab populisms, like many others, manifest themselves in the symbolic as well as in the socio-economic (welfare-distributionalist) spheres. In symbolic manifestations of populism, the values and ways of life of the common man are glorified and native wit greatly appreciated. The long speeches (typical, for example, of Nasser, Bourguiba, Qasim, etc.) in which the boss reverts to colloquialisms, cracks jokes and makes fun of the 'enemies of the people', are typical, and their discourse was usually highly 'interpellatory'. As populists often try to square the circle by bestowing social welfare and financial largesse to all social classes at the same time, their language is often coloured by a (misguided) optimism derived from their claim that they can always surmount all difficulties and outwit all adversaries, local and foreign. Some analysts have related this kind of posture to a familiar urban stereotype known as the *fahlawi* personality.[2]

Because Egypt's (and most other Arab republics') experimentation with corporatism has coincided with a populist phase (and often with the leader's charisma) the organisational sophistication of their corporatist arrangements could not exceed a certain prescribed level without upsetting the populist character of the regime and threatening to unravel its coalition. The populist coalition was basically 'distributive' and it had therefore mainly incorporated its component classes and groups *economically* while excluding them *politically*. This is similar to what Niklas Luhmann [1990: 148] calls 'passive' rather than 'active' inclusion. As C.H. Moore explained with special reference to the engineers, the heroes of Nasser's technocracy:

> Though he probably never read Durkheim's *De la division du travail social*, Nasser's praxis fulfilled to the point of contradiction its theoretical implications of profes-sionalisation and corporatism.[3] On the one hand, his policies of rapid industrial-ization and concomitant recruitment of managers gave the engineering profession a prestige that it had not achieved since the time of Imhotep's pyramids. On the other hand, his authoritarian revolution encouraged professional syndicates to resemble a political base that would control the enthusiasm of the new middle class. Using the syndicates this way, he undermined and almost destroyed them in the mid 1960s, and by this time the sultanic tendencies of his regime dimin-ished the chances of any genuine reform of the profession. [1980: 42].

Rather than consolidate itself institutionally, Nasser's corporatism continued to rely quite heavily on personal networks of patron–client relationships. Even 'corporations' were too 'dangerous' politically to entertain. As Ilkay Sunar succinctly puts it, one outcome of the absence of an organised civil-society access to the state was:

> the emergence of particularist strategies of influence that fragmented the State into bureaucratic factions, clientelist networks and personalist cliques. Nasser, as the occasion warranted, sided with one or the other, played them against each other, or condemned them as 'power centers' and viewed them with suspicion and disdain ... The Nasserist dilemma was how to forge a support coalition without getting organisationally entangled with the popular sectors. The solution was to form a coalition that would mobilise the popular sectors ideologically and include them economically but exclude them politically. The strategy, in other

words, was to uphold state autonomy by keeping the masses unorganised. [Sunar, 1993: 15–16, 29–31].

CORPORATIST DEVICES: MACRO AND MICRO

Politically speaking, the populist coalition (*tahaluf*) of Nasserism, which was broadly emulated in other countries such as Syria, Iraq, Yemen and Sudan,[4] was organised, on the macro level,[5] in a corporatist (or rather 'incorporative') formula known as the 'alliance of the working forces of the people' (sometimes the stronger word *talahum*, coalescence, was used instead of alliance or co-alition). Groups incorporated included workers, peasants, soldiers, the intel-ligentsia and the national bourgeoisie.[6] Arab populism was no different from other populisms in this respect: it "acknowledges the existence of social classes, but puts the emphasis on the need for and the possibility of making the class interests coincide by means of cooperation and national solidarity, in light of the challenge of progress" [Van Niekerk, 1974: 38]. Such regimes have often resorted to *trasformismo* [cf. Gramsci, 1971: 58], or the creation from above of coalitions between different factions, by 'transforming' erstwhile opponents into allies through the use or abuse of government patronage; turning an opponent into a supporter by bribery and corruption [Bellamy, 1987: 5, 172–3]. This is roughly the same process as the so-called *el turno* in Spanish.

The constituent components of the 'included' socio-political categories in Egypt were defined, in a corporatist fashion, according to official, and mainly functional, categories since a certain numerical balance had to be kept among the various social classifications (with a minimum of 50 per cent of seats in all representative bodies going to workers/peasants). Thus in December 1961 a National Congress for Popular Forces was formed by election and was eventu-ally to endorse the National Charter of 1962 and its popular alliance formula. This congress was meant to represent popular 'interests' as measured socio-economically, but mainly on the basis of their contribution to GNP, and it was composed as follows: 375 to represent peasants, 300 to represent workers, 105 to represent 'national capitalism' (commerce and industry), 100 to represent public functionaries, 105 to represent members of professional unions, and 105 to represent university lecturers and students [Saif al-Dawla, 1983: 60–61]. According to the constitutional jurist, 'Ismat Saif al-Dawla [1991: 194ff], the system was based on 'representation of interests' which did not complement the system of deputies (and delegation) but was in fact contradictory to it. A great deal of time was spent in the 1960s in defining the 'people' (and its 'enemies'), as well as its various social 'forces', especially the workers and the peasants, for the purposes of representation.

Within the ruling political party or political organisation, there has always also been an attempt at balancing and counter-balancing various pseudo-ideological trends, cliques and groupings within the confines of the overall prescribed 'ideology'. This was clear, for example, in the attempt in Nasser's Egypt, to form a 'vanguard organ' or a proper, disciplined (and initially selective) political party within the looser, open-for-all Arab Socialist Union (ASU). This 'vanguard' party-within-the-party was initiated in 1963 using in its formation a combination of conspirational and semi-corporatist methods in a meeting to which Nasser had invited 'Ali Sabri (an air force officer and trusted organiser with reputed Soviet sympathies), Muhammad Hasanain Haykal (a 'modernist' journalist and confidant of Nasser's), Ahmad Fu'ad (a long-trusted Marxist) and Sami Sharaf (the President's chef de cabinet) [cf. Salim, 1982]. The idea was to aim for something similar to the Communist League within the Yugoslav Socialist Union. Each member of this nucleus team was to recruit a cell of ten trustees in secret, after clearing their names with Nasser and with the security organs. The idea was to form an 'iron organisation' of trusted people with socialist and/or nationalist inclinations. When hearing of it, Field Marshal 'Amir also asked one of his lieutenants to form a few branches within the armed forces.

A secretariat for the vanguard organ was formed of thirteen officials and writers, headed by Sha'rawi Jum'a, the Interior Minister, which set out to recruit and organise the organ on a functional and economic basis, subsidised by a geographical basis (i.e. ministries, universities, mass organisations, the media, etc.). However, patron–client relationships remained extremely import-ant, and so was the power struggle between top figures and 'orientations': Nasser the charismatic versus 'Amir the military patron; 'Ali Sabri the 'leftist' versus Zakariyya Muhyi al-Din the 'rightist', and so on.

Even within the presumed 'left' there was a great deal of competition and conflict: the official, Soviet-inclined, left headed by 'Ali Sabri, the sometime prime minister and ASU secretary-general, was not completely comfortable with the ex-HADETU[7] cadres working as individuals within the vanguard, and was at odds with the other Marxist organisations that did not dissolve themselves. Sabri's faction was also jealous of the socialist/nationalist group centred around the Thought and Propagation Secretariat headed by the nationalist officer, Kamal Rif'at, the Du'at teams of 'militant ideologues' in the countryside under the ex-military police officer Muhammad Nusair, and *Al-Ishtiraki*, the official organ of the ASU, edited by the Coptic, Arab-Nationalist writer Sami Dawud. Even Field Marshal 'Amir was starting to claim for himself some 'socialist' credentials. He imposed a kind of tutelage on the leftist-leaning *Al-Jumhuriyya* newspaper, championed a Higher Com-mission for the Liquidation of Feudalism and merged it into the ASU, while trying to contain and marginalise the ASU's Youth Organisation, where some Marxist and radical Arab-nationalist tendencies and some criticism for the privileges of the 'stratiocracy' were beginning to emerge [cf. e.g. Al-Hakim et al., 1975; 'Isa, 1986; Muhyi al-Din, 1992; Beinin, 1987]. Looking at all these trends one can see how Nasserism, true to its populist and semi-corporatist inclinations, had had some 'Seven Veils', as Louis 'Awad put it ['Awad, 1975].

Trade unions were 'functional' (organised by activity and specialisation), and were required to belong to a general federation that is incorporated into the state via its subsidiary affiliation to the Arab Socialist Union, and often through the general secretary of the federation also acting as Minister of Labour and Manpower. Robert Bianchi [1989] maintains that "the corporatization of the Union signified the consummation of an important 'gentlemen's agreement' between Nasser and noncommunist labor leaders after a full decade of mutual suspicion and frustrating bargaining", and that "Egypt's new labor law was a landmark piece of corporatist legislation that was strikingly similar to the labor code of the Brazilian Estado Novo" [78–80]. The state corporatist structure under Nasser put the Trade Unions Federation in a strictly supportive position towards government policies, and continually manipulated the corporatist union structure itself [Pripstein-Posusney, 1992]. Ellis Goldberg [1992 and refs cited] suggests that what Nasser called 'socialism' and what contemporary political scientists call 'corporatism' "might be best seen as a large socio-economic compromise centering on market closure mediated through the state" [154]. The formula was sometimes described as a variety of 'political trade unionism' [cf. e.g. Abu 'Alam, 1968], in other words, 'syndicalism' – a doctrine that has several affinities with corporatism.

The Islamic religious establishment (and its 'clerics') was incorporated into the Egyptian state via the Ministry of Awqaf and Religious Affairs and through the 'nationalisation' and partial secularisation of Al-Azhar University. The Coptic religious community was also incorporated: the selection of the Coptic Patriarch had to be confirmed by the President, and the Patriarch counted as a state official with a distinct jurisdiction domestically and with diplomatic status abroad. A number of Copts (up to ten) were included in the parliament by presidential appointment [for details see 'Awda, 1988: 89ff]. The Nasserist regime had been strong enough not to need to share power with other political parties (even with these assuming a subservient role), although individuals from among the Muslim Brothers, Young Egypt, the Nationalist Party and a number of Marxist parties were co-opted at various stages.

Other similar regimes (e.g. Ba'thist Syria and Iraq) have allowed a token representation of other 'nationalist' (especially Pan-Arabist) and 'progressive' (including Communist) parties as components of a symbolic 'national front' [cf. e.g. Hinnebusch, 1990: 145, 202; Heine, 1993: 44–6]. The pattern here is reminiscent of what the Colliers call "pre-emptive co-optation" [Collier and Collier, 1977, 1979].

In Tunisia the 'special relationship' was always with the trade union federation (UGTT), which was used by the Bourguiba regime as a major corporatist device. The alliance dates to the colonial period when, owing to the relatively large settler community, discrimination against Tunisian workers had made trade union demands take on nationalist, and hence political, overtones. The alliance which Bourguiba had struck with the UGTT in the summer of 1955 was of decisive importance in his power struggle with Bin Yusif [Ruf, 1984: 104], and from that time on the UGTT, initially under the leadership of Ahmad Bin Salih, did not cease to offer its support to the 'constitutional socialism' launched by Bourguiba and the single Destourian party. This 'socialism' was premised on a populist-corporatist concept of solidarism (*tadamuniyya*) or the unity of all social classes and categories, in the framework of the nation, in order to achieve their common objectives [M.S. Al-Hirmasi, 1990: 42ff].

The organisational instruments utilised towards achieving this goal were the UGTT in industry and the cooperatives in agriculture. The trade union movement had gained some handsome organisational and social welfare benefits in return for its collaboration but it had also become 'encapsulated' by the state. In 1977 the UGTT signed a social charter (*al-mithaq al-ijtima'i*) with the government, based on a special partnership (*shiraka*) between labour and capital under state intermediation [M.S. Al-Hirmasi, 1990: 120ff]. In the meantime, and in the absence of competing political parties up to the early 1980s, the UGTT had also harboured a certain fringe of opposition to the regime, expressing its views in Marxist or in Arabist terms. Such views could be contained or constrained, and 'excesses' were harshly dealt with as in the 1978 arrests and detentions. The objective was to reduce the workers' social and political struggle to the minimum possible, while increasingly transforming their federation into a junior partner of the ruling Destourian Party [ibid.: 133ff]. The 'national front' formula was therefore a prelude to re-adjusting the alliance in a way that enabled the political élite to incorporate and contain the labour movement and to shape it to the purposes of state capitalism, especially after 1963. In 1969 Habib 'Ashur was appointed secretary general of the UGTT and in 1977 a social progress Charter (SPC) reconfirmed the collaboration between capital and labour as a policy of the UGTT, in close cooperation with the party in government.

However, from the mid-1970s relations began to come under considerable pressure because of the escalating economic troubles and the emergence of a union left within the UGTT that resisted, among other things, the freeze on wages required by the SPC. Strikes increased (reaching 452 in number in 1977) and culminated in a general national strike in January 1978 that was put down by calling in the armed forces. This confrontation and the 'food riots' of 1983–84 ushered in a new era in defining a somewhat condensed role within the state for the UGTT, necessitated by the requirements of re-structuring the economy in more 'liberal' directions that impelled a more 'bureaucratic-authoritarian' attitude towards labour. The state finally disposed of Habib 'Ashur and his group, and deprived the federation, which was vigorously reshuffled and reorganised, of its share of public sector employee payments.

On the micro level, semi-corporatist arrangements were also resorted to in the economic sphere, whereby employers/managers, workers and the government/party were represented on the boards of directors of public enterprises. In Egypt, workers in the early 1960s were represented on the management boards of all public companies by two members who were later increased to four. Within each firm they also formed their own trade union committee and were represented by at least 50 per cent of the membership of the ASU Committee of the concerned 'productive unit' [cf. Ayubi, 1980: 452 and refs cited]. In Algeria the system of workers' self-management (*auto-gestion*) which emerged on the heels of the departure of the Colons was subsequently replaced within the public enterprises (*sociétés nationales*) by a system of joint technocratic/ workers' management, under the organisational *tutelle* of the government bureaucracy [cf. Clegg, 1971; Osterkamp 1982]. In Syria an ambitious attempt at workers' management in 1964 was also discarded in favour of a milder form of workers' joint participation with professional management in public enterprises [cf. Hinnebusch, 1986: 97–9; Perthes, 1992b: 18].

In extreme cases of state corporatism, some Arab regimes have managed not only to reconstitute existing associations and organisations and to consolidate the position of pliable unionists over their more radical rivals, but they have sometimes resorted to what one may call 'the politics of simulation', whereby the state re-creates certain intermediary organisations and associations from above in its own image, sometimes with the intent of creating an organisational and political vacuum that others may not fill [cf. Williamson, 1989: 39]. Z. Bauman [1982: 136ff] describes corporatism as 'simulated politics' and that is precisely what several Arab regimes have endeavoured to do. In such a situation of simulated politics, 'state autonomy' or perhaps more accurately the leaders' autonomy (think of Nasser, Bourguiba, Asad or Saddam) appears to be so great that almost any policy may be declared, cancelled or reversed at almost any time. Although simulated politics can last for a while, very often the eventual result is, in the short run, the pulling of politics inside the state machinery itself (hence 'bureaucratic politics'), and, in the longer run, the pushing of politics out of the legal, institutionalised arena and into the society at large (in the form of protest politics, such as with the Islamic movements, for example).

The current crisis of such populist-corporatist regimes is attributable to the fact that, given the international situation as well as their own domestic and regional policies, these regimes were no longer able to reconcile the *étatiste* and the welfarist components of their public policies. Although corporatism and populism can be coupled for a period, they represent different aspects of state/society relations that should be distinguished from each other (as in the 'dual-state thesis' developed by A. Cawson and P. Saunders and corroborated by P. Williamson [1989: 65–6, 124–9]). Whereas the corporatist mode of interest representation is mainly associated with the politics of production (socioeconomic) populism is more associated with the politics of consumption. It may not be possible to reconcile the two in the longer run. Iliya Harik [1992:

2ff] describes such a state as a 'patron-state' (the Turkish term *devlet baba* – the paternal, fatherly state – may be even stronger): it is "a business entrepreneur and a provider at one and the same time, and in the Middle East the development in that direction occurred shortly after independence".

Under stress, as I have argued elsewhere [Ayubi, 1989a; 1990a], such regimes have been prepared to jettison the welfarist (i.e. pseudo-socialist) functions of the state, rather than its *étatiste* (control-based) functions. But the problem was not as simple as that, for these states have also suffered from multiple, mutually-reinforcing gaps: a 'differentiation-integration gap', a 'demands-delivery gap', and a 'mobilisation-institutionalisation gap' [cf. O'Donnell, 1973: 76–80]. Egypt may be cited here as an illustrative case in point [cf. Ayubi 1991b: Ch. 12]. Nasserist Egypt was both '*étatiste*' and 'populist'. The regime had tried to manage both growth and welfare, production and distribution. In an adaptation of a dictum by Anatole France – 'Le Socialisme, c'est la bonté et la justice' – Nasser defined Arab socialism as being *kifaya* (sufficiency) and '*adl* (equity). The contradiction between the two strands in the make-up of the Egyptian state reached its peak after the end of the first five-year plan (1960–65), and the adoption of a second plan was not possible due to the decline in domestic and foreign financial resources, and then – more dramatically – to the aftermath of the June 1967 war [compare Cooper, 1982; Hinnebusch, 1985].

As with most other populist regimes relying economically on a policy of import-substitution and politically on the state bureaucracy, the Nasserist regime had come to face a crisis in the late 1960s, a crisis that was not only caused in this case by the technical limitations of the import-substitution strategy but that was aggravated politically by the 1967 war and its aftermath. The Nasserist state was reluctant in demanding immediate social sacrifices from the major social classes in order to continue with the regime's developmental projects [Waterbury, 1983]. The state bourgeoisie then split into two wings; one in favour of private capital and economic liberalism, the other in favour of strengthening state capitalism and maintaining public controls.

The Sadat leadership came to favour the first wing, and the main thrust of the open door policy was indeed characterised by an apparent retrenchment of the economic role of the state and an opening up to private capital – foreign and domestic – as well as a political *rapprochement* with the West. Yet that policy orientation has not, for reasons that will be dealt with later, produced in the Egyptian case outcomes similar to those that it produced in other cases (such as Brazil and Argentina) where it did help with the promotion of industrialisation, although at the high cost of rising social tension.

ARAB POPULISMS IN COMPARATIVE PERSPECTIVE

How do the corporatist practices of the populist Arab regimes compare with corporatism in other parts of the world?

State-centred corporatism is an 'integrated' variety of corporatism wherein the corporations are not viewed as the bearers of private interests, nor as mediators between the individual and the state, but are in effect 'state agents' [cf. Black, 1985: 667]. state corporatism has been a known phenomenon in modern times in Latin Europe and Latin America. Within the Middle East, Turkey presents the most familiar case [cf. Bianchi, 1984; Keyder, 1987], but there has recently been growing interest in applying varieties of this paradigm to the study of Egypt and to a lesser extent to the study of a few other countries such as Syria, Iraq, Tunisia and Sudan. Most of these cases would fit the category that Philip Cerny calls 'pseudo-corporatism' or 'patchwork state corporatism', based on a high level of political 'patronage' and 'state-imposed solidarism' [Cerny, 1990: 169–70]. Although not using the term corporatism as such, I have illustrated [Ayubi, 1980] the collaborative nature of the Nasserist political formula of 'alliance of popular forces' and explained the way in which it relied not only on a strong and expanding state apparatus, but also on the 'bureaucratisation' of political and associational life (the 'political party', the trade unions, the professional syndicates, the Islamic 'clergy', etc.). C.H. Moore built upon some of his earlier studies to provide such an analysis of the role of Egypt's technocratic community within the political system [Moore, 1980]. John Waterbury applied a somewhat similar approach to an analysis of the growing crisis of Nasserist *étatisme* and the complex transition to an open door policy under Sadat [Waterbury, 1983].

Egyptian political scientists are also becoming distinctly attracted to corporatism as an analytical device. Mustafa Kamil Al-Sayyid has produced an important study on the role of interest groups within the Egyptian political system under both Nasser and Sadat [M.K. Al-Sayyid, 1983]. According to him, the workers' and professionals' unions were 'organised' or formalised interest groups, the religious establishment (Muslim and Coptic) and the student body were semi-formalised, whereas some segments of the urban masses remained unorganised. Ahmad Faris 'Abd al-Mun'im produced a similar study of workers' and professionals' unions, using more openly the language of the corporatist paradigm especially in its 'state corporatism' variant ['Abd al-Mun'im in Hilal, ed., 1983: 241–318]. Amany Qandil concentrated more specifically on the impact of interest groups and business associations on Egypt's economic policies [Qandil, 1988]. From a political economy perspective Nadia Ramsis Farah has in part used the concept of populist corporatism to analyse the crisis of development and political transformation in Egypt under Nasser and Sadat [Farah, 1985]. Usama al-Ghazali Harb has also applied a similar approach, and given the term 'corporatism' an interesting Arabic translation [Al-Ghazali Harb, 1987].

From a historical perspective, Beinin and Lockman [1987] have argued that the Egyptian workers' movement has been subjected to 'corporatist' designs and practices more or less since its inception. They illustrated persuasively that the organisations and the struggles of the working class have had a significant influence on the course of Egyptian social and political history and on shaping the country's economic and political development, especially during the 1940s and 1950s. The fact that after the 1952 'revolution' a significant section of the trade union leadership acquiesced to incorporation into the state apparatus is very telling of the nature of the Egyptian working class movement as it had by then developed. The movement was strong enough to prompt the new regime into offering the workers some concrete economic gains. Yet the workers' movement was too weak to resist the rising political tide: in the absence of a strong and widespread ideological commitment to the political independence of the labour movement, most workers and their trade union leaders accepted the government's control, particularly once the regime had made good its economic and political promises, including in particular the struggle for national independence – which had been intertwined for so long with the specifically working-class objectives of the labour movement. As the authors succinctly remark, "In this sense the Egyptian working class was 'disorganized' as a historical actor by the partial success of its struggles up to 1954." The new regime would eventually follow with a policy towards the working class informed by the same 'corporatist' conception of Egyptian society shared by most of the postwar political forces.

The most elaborate application of a corporatist paradigm is perhaps that of Robert Bianchi [1989], although his model is much closer to the concept of group politics and interest intermediation, and is therefore more appropriate to the post-Nasserist era. According to Bianchi the current "multiplicity and competitiveness of actors in the Egyptian economy point to the need to disaggregate conventional categories such as the 'state sector', 'foreign capital' and the 'private sector' so that attention can be focused on divisions and rivalries within these groups instead of assuming a tendency toward greater collaboration between them" [p. 14]. He regards Guillermo O'Donnell's distinction between 'populist (inclusionary) authoritarianism' and 'bureaucratic (exclusionary) authoritarianism' as "an indispensable starting point for examining the evolution of authoritarian rule in Egypt" [p. 26]. His very detailed analysis of what he classifies as the corporatist sectors (i.e. the professional syndicates), the corporatised sectors (i.e. the labour unions and agricultural cooperatives) and the 'hybrid sectors' (i.e. the businessmen's associations and religious groupings) under Sadat and Mubarak leads him, however, to conclude that attempted corporatism in Egypt has proved to be 'unruly', leading to unstable and self-defeating outcomes [p. 250ff].

Although we view corporatism in this work mainly in structural terms, corporatist experiences should always be situated in their historical context. This in turn makes comparative analysis quite rewarding. It is observed that state corporatism tends to emerge in situations of 'late' industrialisation and development. This state may thus assume a leading *dirigiste* economic role, not only as a regulator of economic affairs but also as a direct entrepreneur. Following the historical model of Japan, some have described this as the model of the 'developmental state' which represents the most concentrated form of statist corporatism, whereas the most diffuse form of statist corporation is found in many Third World societies [Cerny, 1990: 168–70]. If there is already within the society a powerful community of entrepreneurs that is anxious enough for industrialisation but which is not confident enough to function under competitive conditions and is furthermore apprehensive of working-class radicalism, then the outcome is often of a 'Fascist' character. If, on the other hand, neither a powerful entrepreneurial community nor a threatening working class exists, the outcome is more often of a 'populist' character. Thus, in spite of the authoritarian colouring of both, Fascist corporatism and populist corporatism draw on quite a different constituency and have quite different historical functions. Fascist movements are fundamental attempts by middle classes, who feel threatened by working class movements, to push their social inferiors back out of the political arena. Populism on the other hand is a way of mobilising the lower classes and bringing them into politics more or less for the first time [cf. Canovan, 1981: 147–8; also Ionescu and Gellner, 1969].

Populist corporatism is therefore distinctly mobilisational, unleashing social forces through various policies of economic development and modernisation. The main political dilemma for such regimes, however, is finding the appropriate institutional arrangements that could provide the leadership with greater support from these forces, while ensuring at the same time greater control over them. As G. O'Donnell [1973, 1977] has argued, populist corporatism, in its earlier stages, represents a device for promoting controlled lower class activation, and for incorporating their groupings as subordinate partners in a multi-class coalition, with a view to ending the traditional domination of rural oligarchies and accelerating the development of national industry, via import-substitution strategies. At this phase populist policies include, in order to win the support of the lower classes, a wide range of economic benefits and social services. As import-substitution programmes tend to work fairly successfully in their earlier stages, the regimes tend to be more co-optative than coercive in their policies. Lower class groups are activated politically and rewarded economically, in return for their losing part of their actual or potential organisational autonomy and being incorporated in, and subordinated to, the state.

However, import-substitution strategies which are fairly easy to implement at the beginning (especially when combined with extensive nationalisations and accompanied by a reasonable amount of foreign 'aid', as in Egypt's case), eventually start to face difficulties. Technically, it transpires that for such policies to be sustained and deepened, expensive intermediary and capital goods have to be imported, resulting in chronic balance of payment difficulties and escalating foreign indebtedness. The state then attempts to adopt austerity policies by restricting the earlier welfare benefits offered to the lower classes in the populist phase, but it does not always succeed. In the process, social conflict escalates, creating new divisions in the heterogeneous populist coalition, as the relatively powerful lower class groups continue to express demands that are perceived as excessive by 'economic reformers', local and foreign. Such conflicts appear to weaken the state, without removing the technical and financial bottlenecks. The whole process is accelerated and exaggerated if the state is also perceived to have been wanting politically, as happened, for example, to Egypt and Syria when they were defeated in the 1967 Arab–Israeli war. The 'crisis of socialism' in such countries should thus better be described as the crisis of the populist corporate regime and its import-substitution economic policies.

Thus one finds that the *étatiste* economic policies of corporatist regimes require – in the existing conditions of late, dependent capitalist development – a raising of the level of domestic capital accumulation if the country is to deepen its industrialisation policies by expanding in intermediate and capital goods and going for some export-oriented industrialisation. Such policies, however, come into open contradiction with the social and political benefits acquired by the popular classes during the populist phase. Local investors and prospective international investors would call for a higher degree of certainty and stability for investments. This is done by deactivating lower class groupings and excluding them from new 'coalition shifts' which would emphasise the role of the local technocratic and entrepreneurial élites and/or a policy of joint ventures with international capital. This stage is, according to O'Donnell, characterised by a 'social impasse', resulting in a 'hegemonic crisis' whereby no single class or sector is capable of achieving stable domination. This gives rise to coalitions that are too weak to impose their own policy preferences, but strong enough to prevent other coalitions from imposing theirs [cf. also, in relation to Turkey, Bianchi, 1984: 381–98]. According to O'Donnell this phase of corporatism is, however, more likely to become bureaucratic-authoritarianism in nature, based as it is on exclusivist and coercing strategies, with regard to the lower classes in particular.

While accepting some of the 'Latin American' paradigm as being relevant to Egypt's case (especially those connecting state corporatism with crises arising at various stages in dependent capitalist development and during major attempts either to co-opt or to smash organisations of the working class), Robert Bianchi maintains that

> Apart from Turkey and the Philippines, there are very few prospective Argentinas or Chiles in the Middle East and Asia. In most other Third World countries, industrialization is less advanced and privately controlled, modern class structures are less crystallized and rigidified, and foreign economic commitments are less stable and irreversible. Accordingly, state corporatism appears to be more of a choice and initiative of fairly autonomous élites than a necessary or reluctant

response to forces beyond their control. Indeed, it may be the notion of the 'autonomy of the state' – so celebrated in both the neo-Marxian and neo-conservative writings that currently dominate the field of political development, and trivialised in earlier liberal writings – that is at the heart of the matter [Bianchi, 1989: 221–2].

O'Donnell's generalisations should also be qualified on some other accounts. Faced with the dilemma of choosing between development and welfare, the ruling élites may opt for maintaining the second rather than pushing for the first, in order not to wreck the base of their political survival in the short run. This may be made relatively easier if some reasonable sources of foreign or rentier-type revenues are made available to the state, as happened to countries like Egypt and Syria, with aid from Arab and foreign states and with remittances from their workers employed in the oil-exporting countries. In the meantime, the regime may be able to continue with at least some inclusionary corporatist strategies, somewhat adjusting the nature of the corporatist co-alition. Thus, for example, Sadat had initiated certain inclusionary strategies for forces and groups such as women, the Islamists, the Copts and even, ironically, the Marxists (the only two Marxists to be appointed as cabinet ministers in modern Egypt were under Sadat), while at the same time applying exclusionary strategies to forces and groups such as the workers and the Nasserists. It can therefore be said that state corporatist policies may simul-taneously be inclusionary and exclusionary. This may be among the various groups, as we have seen, and/or within each group, as the state intervenes to ensure a favourable outcome within the various organisations (e.g. the Arab Socialist Union in Sadat's Egypt) without purging the organisation as a whole [compare Collier and Collier, 1977].

Thus we can see that one possible development of populist corporatism, which is an increasingly coercive, military-bureaucratic regime intent on deepening the industrialisation process, did not take place in Egypt due, among other things, to a weakening in the political clout of the state (with the 1967 defeat) shortly to be followed by the availability (after the 1973 war) of external revenue capable of relieving the state from the task of undoing its populist (welfare) policies speedily and abruptly.

A somewhat different development of the crisis in populist corporatism is possible. As the state seems to be structurally exhausted under the impact of its eroded political hegemony and its growing fiscal difficulties, the civil society may be able to gain some room for manoeuvre, first by challenging some conventional symbols of state power and discipline (e.g. disregard for the police; riots and strikes, etc.) and then increasingly by organising or reviving alternative interest associations applying pressure on the state. The state's inability to continue with industrialisation without heavy external borrowing implies depriving the state of the use of development as a means for further incorporating important fractions of the popular and working classes into the developmental project of the dominant classes. It also implies a reduction in the state's clout and prestige as a result of its deepening dependency on international capital. This in turn undermines mass identification with the authoritarian state as the "carrier of national culture" [Carnoy, 1984: 205].

Although reluctant about renouncing its authoritarian practices, the state becomes increasingly fragile due to its limited scope for expanding its social base. Interest-centred groupings (e.g. merchants, businessmen) as well as culture-centred groupings (e.g. religious societies and organisations) become increasingly vocal and the authoritarian state may ultimately have to succumb to the 'nostalgia for democracy': "The issue of democracy is of course the Achilles heel of this system of domination. By proposing a limited form of democracy such systems do not express the gracious concession of a triumphant power, as much as reveal their intrinsic weakness" [O'Donnell, 1979: 314–17]. Such 'democratisation' proposals have surfaced most obviously in Egypt and Algeria, but also to a lesser extent in Tunisia, Syria and other countries. What tends to take place in reality is an act of 'political exchange' (*scambio politico* as the Italians call it) whereby "the State gives up part of its decision-making authority to interest groups in exchange for these groups guaranteeing their members' adherence to the decisions reached" [cf. Schmitter, 1985: 35–6; Bull, 1992: 263 and refs cited in each]. Given such trends it is possible that the situation – at least with regard to Egypt – may eventually develop, as happened in Turkey, in the direction of a qualified type of 'societal corporatism' where, however, the state would continue to play the role of the "leading architect of associational representation" [Bianchi, 1984: 377].

Of the groupings that increased their power as a result of the structural exhaustion of the state in Egypt, two stand out as possible coalescent allies or partners in a new conservative corporate formula: namely the Islamic movements, and the native commercial bourgeoisie (once functioning under the label of 'money utilisation companies' [see Ayubi, 1991a: Ch. 8]. Regardless of the various legalist, technical and moralist objections voiced against the so-called 'Islamic business' sector, it is perhaps reasonable to regard it as a manifestation of a certain 'awakening' of the civil society, in an attempt partly to make up for the failure of the formal banking and financial institutions and partly to confront the omnipotent state, sometimes by 'seducing' its own economic, administrative and 'ideological' institutions [cf. Al-Ghazali Harb, 1988; 'Abd al-Fadil, 1989: Ch. 3]. One writer has gone so far as to suggest that the emergence of the money utilisation companies has been "the first and biggest attempt since the 1952 [coup] to achieve the autonomy of the civil society of the 'people' and the 'subjects', and to create a 'popular capitalism'" in the land. If the authorities were soon to suppress and persecute such companies, this was precisely because their economic activities had reached levels that could not be tolerated by a 'totalitarian state' [Kishk, 1989: 42ff, 139ff].

Under the slightest pressure or at the slightest temptation, the radical Arab regimes were capable of turning their backs on the socialist slogans that they had advocated a few years earlier, and of overseeing the implementation of economic liberalisation and privatisation programmes as a public policy by themselves (for a brief survey see Chapter 10). There were no socialist forces ('popular' or 'bureaucratic') intent on resisting the regimes' plans for reversing many of the previous social policies [cf. Waterbury, 1988]. As we have just pointed out, contemporary struggles in such countries do not engage labour against capital: rather they engage the civil society against the state.

The *étatiste* policies of the radical regimes have, perhaps inevitably, paved the way for the installing of capitalism in their specific countries [cf., e.g., Said, 1982; Khafaji, 1983; Hafiz Mahmud, 1989]. State capitalism created a bureaucratic bourgeoisie which, when it came to the point, was not averse to renewing alliances with international capital. As Alexander Gerschenkron had anticipated more than three decades ago, "capitalist industrialization under the auspices of socialist ideology may be, after all, less surprising a phenomenon than would appear at first sight" [1962: 25]. Under the current conditions of globalisation, both of the production process and of the labour market, capitalist external alliances seem more useful to the state bourgeoisie than domestic populist coalitions. However, a few welfarist policies, more typical of the earlier, populist strain in the make-up of these regimes, arose to cloud the horizon and to stand in the way of capitalist transformation. Such welfare-type policies had therefore to be discarded, sometimes at a certain political cost; but this was merely an adjustment within the same system, and not a reversal of a 'socialist' commitment – which never really existed.

NOTES

1. The use of the word *ra'is* and its vernacular renderings (e.g. *rayyes*) to describe the president in various Arab countries connotes both deference and affection. The term *l'état-ra'is* in this form is due to Pierre Mirel [1982: 242ff]. *Dawlat al-amn* is the proper term for the security-state. *Dawlat al-mukhabarat* (the secret-services state) is a term used popularly to imply the security state/the police state. This variety of coercive state is both a militarised state and a police state and its origins may lie in a national liberation struggle, in a revolution and/or in a military coup [compare Gurr, 1989: 49–65]. For a haunting description of the workings of the most notorious Arab security-state see Samir al-Khalil's *Republic of Fear* [1991]. *Partitocrazia* is a term used in Italy to describe the system of privilege and spoils that benefits the cadres of a political party that is in power.

2. The colloquial term *fahlawi* comes from a word that implies a clownish clever/foolish type of person. The idea was first put out by the Egyptian anthropologist Hamid 'Ammar and was later corroborated by the Syrian philosopher Sadiq Jalal al-'Azm – so its applicability is presumably not confined to one Arab sub-culture. The detailed outlines of the profile are interesting in themselves but cannot be elaborated upon in this context. Basically, however, the term applies to a rather opportunistic personality that combines native wit, a distinct sense of humour and a 'know-it-all', 'can-fix-it-all' image that enables the individual to reach his objective even by cutting corners, by whatever means possible. Basically he is a person who does not accept reality but is unable to change it; he goes round it – hides deficiencies and failures and strives to *appear* clever and

successful. He is inclined initially to be extremely enthusiastic and energetic; he then loses interest, lacking perseverance and being exercised only by actions that bring quick and flashy results rather than in action requiring long, organised, cumulative effort. Failure, when it becomes impossible to conceal, is always blamed on someone else ['Ammar, 1964; Al-'Azm, 1969]. Al-'Azm's formulation is particularly significant because he relates that personality to the sphere of politics and illustrates how many Arab officials are unable to relate bad news to their superiors and how many politicians are likewise unable to admit defeat or failure – in both cases the attitude is normally to claim that the worst has *not* happened, to cover up all deficiencies or even to claim achievement and success where it never took place. Such characteristics identified with the *fahlawi* personality have recently been confirmed by a number of distinguished experts in psychiatry and sociology in Egypt, including Samia al-Sa'ati, 'Adil Shafiq and Yusri 'Abd al-Muhsin [cf. *Al-Ra'y al-'Amm,* special supplement, Summer, 1987: 8–12]. The *fahlawi* personality-profile is particularly typical of fast mobility situations, where promotion may not necessarily be solidly based on educational attainment or entrepreneurial achievement. It represents an opportunistic type that is specifically urban and more typically lower-middle-class (hailing either from its commercial or from its bureaucratic wing). It is traditional at heart but very upwardly mobile (and hence its mercurial flexibility and the inclination to blame all failures on somebody else) [compare Yasin, 1983: 180–83 and refs cited].

   3. The sources of Nasser's corporatism have not been systematically investigated. Durkheim's ideas have indeed been influential within Egyptian social science, as were Duguit's ideas within Egyptian legal thinking, but no direct impact of either can be easily traced. More important perhaps were the ideas of Subhi Wahida, the secretary-general of the Egyptian Chamber of Industry. Both he and his predecessor, Isaac Levy, were exposed to Italian corporatist influence [Bianchi, 1989: 69–76]. His analysis [cf. Wahida, 1950], laying emphasis on a blend of nationalism, industrialisation and social dynamics, was appreciated by Free Officers and socialist intellectuals alike [cf. Abdel-Malek, 1968: 42–3]. From a practical point of view, Nasser is said to have been interested in the models of Salazar and of Peron, and particularly attracted to Tito's experiment – which represent different varieties of corporatism.

   4. In Sudan under Numairi, the formula of the 'alliance of the working forces of the people' was adopted in the Sudan Socialist Union. Other pseudo-corporatist formulae were also known in the Sudan including the practice of setting aside certain parliamentary seats for the university graduates and the 'new forces' (including the trade unions). Representatives of trade unions (workers but particularly professionals) were directly incorporated in cabinets at various points, including the periods following the October 1964 'revolution' and the April 1985 popular uprising. The idea seems popular and keeps recurring in Sudanese political life, although some, especially among the Islamists, condemn it as a kind of 'professional tribalism'. In addition, pragmatic attempts at reviving the system of 'native administration' (through tribal chiefs and councils of elders) have been made by different Sudanese governments since the mid-1980s [cf. e.g. Kumair, 1989; Elhussein, 1991].

   5. For a distinction between macro-corporatism and meso- and micro-corporatisms, see Cawson, 1986: Chs. 5 and 6.

   6. The use of the term 'incorporative' (as Mouzelis does in 1986: xvi–xvii, 205ff) is preferable here because it implies more of a (manipulative) method and technique than it implies a doctrine or ideology. Unlike in many European countries where active and massive participation by relatively autonomous class organisations took place, in the Middle East the new middle and 'popular' classes are brought into the political arena in a more dependent/vertical manner.

   7. HADETU was the Arabic acronym for the Democratic Movement for National Liberation, a Marxist organisation headed among others by the Italian-Egyptian Henri Curiel, which had close relations with some of the Free Officers, such as Yusuf Siddiq and Khalid Muhyi al-Din, with Ahmad Fu'ad being the main liaison person with direct access to Nasser. The movement had helped in printing and distributing the literature of the Free Officers shortly before the 1952 revolution and cooperated directly with the then Colonel Nasser, who was known to them at the

time under the *nom de guerre* of Comrade Maurice. It was unique among the Marxist organisations in supporting the Free Officers movement when it came to power. Such a position was perhaps influenced by Curiel's ideas on the desirability of a national-democratic or a national-popular line and the importance of building a multi-class front to assume the struggle for full national liberation. The idea is somewhat reminiscent of Gramsci's concept of the *nazionale-popolare*, and one wonders to what extent Curiel might have been influenced by Gramsci. True to character, Nasser had also kept close contacts with the Muslim Brothers during more or less the same period, and even swore their oath of allegiance with hand on the Quran and the pistol [cf. Muhyi al-Din, 1992: 45ff, 87ff et passim].

CHAPTER SEVEN

The Political System of Articulated Forms: the Conservative, Kin-ordered Monarchies

Monarchies characterised by various degrees of 'conservatism' exist in different parts of the Arab World.[1] This chapter is intended, however, to tackle mainly the Gulf region, where most of the Arab monarchies are concentrated, even though some comparative references to Morocco and Jordan may be made from time to time.

We have already hinted that Arabian Gulf societies are among the most 'articulated' in the world, combining as they do a whole range of modes of production and of socio-economic cultures extending all the way from simple pastoral nomadism to ultra-modern petroleum and other industries. Owing to the articulated nature of their social formations, the institutional logic of the Gulf states is to a large extent centred around acts of reconciliation between the requirements of oil-exportation on the one hand and those of communal order on the other. Put crudely, the state's function is to reproduce patriarchy, tribalism and ethnic domination in ways that are as compatible as possible with the preservation of an oil-exporting economy and the circulation of its revenues.

RENTIER ECONOMIES, RENTIER STATES

The political economy of Saudi Arabia and the Gulf states represents an obvious – if somewhat peculiar – case of what is sometimes called 'the export enclave syndrome', displaying most of the economic distortions that result from such heavy reliance on exportation [cf. Alnasrawi, 1979]. Not only are Saudi Arabia and the Gulf states heavily reliant on exportation, but they are also extremely dependent on just one main export commodity. Oil revenues represent a particularly high percentage of state revenue. The non-depletable (i.e. the 'non-oily') part of GDP is very small in proportion [cf. p. 156 and

p. 254, n.8]. It goes without saying that in such circumstances any disruption in oil production, distribution and/or consumption will be disastrous, not only for the development but also for the very survival of these countries.

It is not difficult to observe that, notwithstanding villas, limousines and couturier fashions, the socio-economic development of Saudi Arabia and the Gulf states is nearly as 'constrained' and 'distorted' as that of any other one-export-based economy. There have, of course, been attempts to build up industry: steel, fertilisers, cement and petrochemicals, and the superficially impressive projects at Yanbu' and Jubail, etc. But in addition to being limited in number, the industries do not seem to establish linkages with the economy at large, nor do they help these countries to integrate themselves economically with the rest of the Arab region [cf. Malone, 1981: 27; Duwaidar, 1978: 29–32]. Many sectors of the population of these countries continue to harbour certain 'traditional' attitudes towards work, 'mobility', 'achievement' and so on that are not considered compatible with a 'modern' or at least a dynamic type of society [cf. Palmer, Alghofaily and Alnimir, 1984]. Such attitudes, as well as structural dependency relationships with the capitalist world, were at least partly responsible for the consolidation in Arabia and the Gulf of a newly emergent 'lumpenbourgeoisie' [Ibrahim, 1982: Ch. 2, sections 2 and 3]. This 'class', embracing shaikhs, traders, officials and middlemen, hastened to concentrate its investment endeavours in the area of commercial and real-estate activities that include the notorious *kafil* and *muhawwil* practices (whereby the work is normally done by 'foreigners' – who are not allowed to own or manage certain types of business – while a large share of the returns goes to their local 'sponsor'). The oil boom made such practices easier and more tempting, but they are not at all conducive to the promotion of dynamic entrepreneurial habits and productive development endeavours. As such, oil money plays a peculiar role in most of these countries since, while it has led to social mobility among various segments of the society, it also consolidates the role of the traditional élites who have the right to allocate most of the society's financial resources [Al-Rumaihi, 1975: 53–4ff].

It should again be remembered that in these countries the economic role of the state is extremely large and powerful, in spite of all the anti-socialist rhetoric of the governing élites. The Saudi development plans extolled the virtues of 'free enterprise', and advisers to the Saudis assured observers that the government's rapidly growing role in the economy was "viewed as only a temporary evil" [Crane, 1978: 65]. Some saw the economy as basically *laissez-faire*, dominated by the public sector because of the country's huge oil revenues, so that the Saudi government in effect became the senior partner in a system of 'Islamic state capitalism' [Long, 1976: 56]. However, the state has continued to play the major role in resource allocation through its control of oil as the major source of income in the society, with the government sector being responsible for as much as two thirds of GDP (as expenditures).

But what exactly is the nature of the modes of production in the Gulf states? There is no doubt that the Gulf economies are currently part of the world capitalist system. It is rather difficult, however, for a number of combined reasons, to speak about a capitalist mode of *production* in these states. To start with there is very little production as such (though much distribution and circulation) taking place in these countries. The term 'oil-producing countries' is very misleading for oil is not produced in any technical sense (nor is its price really related to its production cost). Oil is excavated, then it is exported. Recently, the 'ethnic' division of labour, typical of nomadic society, has been articulated with the capitalist relations of exchange that predominate today. Thus the 'production function' in relation to oil activities is mainly assigned to expatriates from the 'First World', and many of the services, as well as most secondary types of production activities (construction, car and machinery repairs, electric works, carpentry, crafts, etc., are assigned to expatriates from the Third World. The production function remains, therefore, fairly 'external' to the society and to the state.

Although policies of 'economic diversification' have often been advocated and to some extent tried, such policies are not without political costs and risks. A move in the direction of 'industrial deepening' (as in Saudi Arabia's Jubail and Yanbu' and other giant and less giant projects) is certainly diversifying, but it could eventually result in more pronounced class differentiation and political consciousness that might ultimately challenge the very basis of the system. A move towards 'financial deepening' (as in the case of Kuwait's extensive international investments in the late 1980s) [cf. e.g. Rida, 1992: 64–5] enables the state to 'export the class conflict', but it also increases the economy's sensitivity and vulnerability [compare Aarts, Eisenloeffel and Termeulen, 1991: 212–14]. Kuwait represented a rather extreme instance of 'financial deepening'. With exceptionally limited industrial or agricultural potential, the society used its tremendous oil revenues and called upon its long commercial traditions to invest heavily in financial instruments. The financial deepening had obviously gone to some extremes, leading to dangerous crashes in the Suk al-Manakh crisis, but the overall result was an oil-exporting country that was by the end of the 1980s gaining more income from financial investments than from petroleum exports. The process was apparently so 'deep' that even when the country was swallowed up by Iraq in August 1990 its financial 'tail' continued to wag, with extended investment being planned in several Western countries.

The relations of production themselves are not typically capitalist: the (mainly foreign) labour force is not free-floating at all, but is subject to various legal and political restrictions and to a number of pre-capitalist practices. A foreign worker can only enter the country on the authorisation of a native sponsor (*kafil*) who is legally responsible for the worker's conduct, who normally takes away the individual's passport by way of a guarantee, and who has to report to the authorities (and possibly hand over the foreign worker) if he no longer requires his/her services. Saudi newspapers, for example, are full of advertisements referring to foreign workers who have 'deserted' their employers and warning other prospective employers against using the services of the absconders.

Such types of 'patronage' systems are possibly derived, at least in part, from the traditional practices of the pearling industry and from other pre-petroleum modes and relations of production, with their exploitative and despotic characteristics [cf. Al-Rumaihi, 1983: 14–32]. In the pearling industry, the ship owner/boss (*nukhadha*) was responsible for the conduct of his team, including the payment of fines on their behalf (which he would subsequently 'retrieve' from them in his own way!) [Mahjub, c.1975: 111–13]. It can be argued that every native Gulfian employer has now become such a *nukhadha* in relation to his expatriate workers. Indeed to some observers the relationship smacks of semi-slavery – Fred Halliday has labelled it the "new slavery" [Halliday, 1974: 431ff], and Mas'ud Dahir reminds us that slavery existed in some parts of the Peninsula until the inter-war period and possibly beyond [Dahir, 1986: 376–7]. Capitalism has not, therefore, subjected all relations of production in the Gulf to its particular logic. What it has done is to subject the region to its relations of exchange, both internally and externally. The end result is a 'hybrid' type of society with several modes of production and several economic, social and cultural patterns articulated with each other [cf. Al-Rumaihi, 1983: 290–308].

Particularly significant is the fact that in contrast to the continued 'externality' of the 'production function' in these societies, we find that the states of the region are, domestically speaking, deeply involved in a 'distribution', 'circulation' or 'allocation' function. The concept of the 'rentier state' has been used in recent years to describe such a situation. The idea was first suggested in relation to Iran by Hossein Mahdavi [1970: 428–67]. A rentier group or class may exist in any society, a class that derives its income from land, mines or any 'gift of nature' (such as location, climate, etc.). For a particular country to possess a rentier economy, rent should be predominant among its sources of income, and this rent should be in the main externally derived, since pure internal rent represents little more than a situation of domestic payments transfer [Beblawi in Beblawi and Luciani, 1987: 51ff].

If the majority of the population of a certain country is engaged in the utilisation and distribution of the rent, then one can justifiably speak of a rentier country or society. It is to be expected that a kind of 'rentier mentality' would also prevail in such a society. Individuals can live well without having to commit themselves to any strict 'work ethic', nor does any distinction need to be made between income 'received' and income 'earned'. An 'easy come, easy go' attitude may inspire both individual and public spending – it is indeed a 'bonanza time' for all to enjoy [cf. Halliday, 1974: 47ff, 453ff]. A *rentier state* obtains if most of the previously described rent happens to accrue to the government of a particular society, not to its individuals. In order to be influential and to impart its character on the whole society, one would assume that the rent is of such proportional magnitude as to enable the state (a) to do away with the need for much (if any) taxation to be extracted from the citizens, and (b) to be able in fact itself to allocate and distribute (and therefore to circulate socially) large amounts of money that influence the employment, the livelihood and the welfare of the majority of the members of that society.

A rentier state therefore is based on a circulation-type economy [Chatelus in Beblawi and Luciani, 1987] or an allocation-type economy [Luciani in Beblawi and Luciani, 1987] where the state machine is the main engine of this circulation or allocation function *vis-à-vis* the various economic sectors and social groups. Various political outcomes may result from such a situation: the following are some of the important ones concerning the Gulf states;

a. Given that the rent is externally derived, the receipt and expenditure of that income by the state makes of it an intermediary between the world capitalist order on the one hand and its own economy and society on the other.
b. Given the crucial importance of the circulation (rather than the production) function in society, "getting access to the rent circuit is a greater pre-occupation than reaching productive efficiency" [Chatelus in Beblawi and Luciani, 1987: 111].
c. Given the abundance of welfare services and facilities that are offered by such an *état providence*, a certain dependence may be promoted in the citizen whereby he will be disinclined to act economically or politically on his own behalf, let alone seriously to criticise or to challenge the state. This type of consumerism means that even though people "may be earning relatively high incomes, [they are] dependent in the final instance upon a government that supplies them with a wide coverage of paternalistic protection" [Pike, 1974: 185–6].
d. Given the high level of financial independence enjoyed by the state, it tends as a result to possess a high degree of 'relative autonomy' from the specific interests of various classes in society. This will enable the ruling élites not only to switch and to reverse public policies if the need arises but also, if they choose to do so, to select their allies and to change their political allegiances with relative flexibility.
e. The state's relatively high degree of autonomy may even enable it to create new classes and/or to dismantle and reassemble existing ones.

How does the state create or reconstitute classes in the Gulf countries? This is achieved through devices such as (i) general public expenditure; (ii) employment in the large bureaucracy; and (iii) specific public policies such as those pertaining to economic subsidies and land allocation. 'Land allocation' or 'land acquisition' is a policy (which is still extensive, private land ownership being a relatively new practice in the region) whereby parcels of state lands are distributed or 'sold' at a symbolic price to (often selected) citizens, to be subsequently repurchased by the state (for public works) at a much higher price. It is an important allocative and distributive mechanism which is usually referred to only in passing [cf. e.g. on Saudi Arabia, Hajrah, 1982: 31–5, 230ff, 252ff] and has not received the research attention it deserves, with the partial exception of Ghanim Al-Najjar [1984] on Kuwait. With detailed statistical evidence, Al-Najjar illustrates how the land acquisition policy, which was initiated in Kuwait in the early 1950s, has served a multiplicity of functions: to establish cohesion within the princely family and to provide its members with entrées into the business sector; to tie the traditional merchant class to the growing organisational web of the new state; to benefit a sizeable group of bureaucrats and speculators; while at the same time imparting a certain sense of citizenship, as all Kuwaitis hoped that they would eventually own a piece, however small, of their own emerging country. In the UAE, every citizen is reportedly 'entitled' to three plots of land for housing, planting, and for business activities.

To these devices contributing to the creation or reconstitution of classes should be added what one may call a certain 'tolerated level of corruption'. Corruption is of course both an emotive word and a relative concept. In this case we mean a whole range of practices starting from overlooking the combination of a public post with a business interest (even when this is nominally prohibited by law) and the sanctioning or toleration of receiving so-called 'commissions', and ending with various 'white-collar crimes' of business and financial fraud; manipulation of tenders, customs dodging, false registration of lands and buildings, and a whole long list enumerated by the Kuwaiti sociologist Fahd Al-Thaqib [1985: 65–73].

The whole process is 'statising', in the sense of creating new wants that are closely linked to new dependencies on the state for their satisfaction. But the process is also 'privatising'. Until recently, the prince's purse and the principality's purse were one and the same thing, and even up to the present, it is not easy to distinguish the two from each other. Just as the *état providence* is also an *état famille*, the *raison d'état* is not easily distinguishable from the *raison de famille*. Indeed, as the financial resources of the state expanded in the boom years, so too did the social solidarity within, and the political stature of, the ruling family and a whole network of families and tribes connected to it, as we shall see later on.[2] The situation comes in some respects near enough to what the concept of 'private government' describes:

> A private interest government exists where a non-State association [in this case the princely family network – NA] allocates goods, services or status that are monopolistic in nature and indispensable for members [in this case oil rents]; it

is therefore capable of affecting and potentially controlling their behaviour, and does so with the specific encouragement, licence or subsidization of the State, thus imposing certain public standards and responsibilities on the behaviour of the association [Schmitter, 1985: 47 and refs cited].

As Ghassan Salame [1984] has illustrated with regard to the situation in the mid-1980s, the general trend in the Gulf countries has been to concentrate the highly political positions in the government in the hands of members of the royal family. This is quite a recent phenomenon and its implications have to be carefully studied both for power distribution within the family and for the family's place in the society at large. Foreign relations are obviously a domain reserved exclusively for the family. Like King Faisal of Saudi Arabia, Sultan Qabus of Oman is his own Foreign Minister, while in Kuwait and Qatar this position is held by the Emir's brother. In Bahrain the post is held by a first cousin, in the UAE by the representative of Shaikh Hamani. The same rule has been applied to defence matters, with the portfolio in the Sultanate of Oman held by the Sultan himself, in Saudi Arabia by the King's full brother, and in Kuwait by a Salem. In Bahrain, Qatar and the UAE there is an obvious trend to nominate the Emir's eldest son and Crown Prince as Minister of Defence. The interior portfolio is another exclusive area. The Emir's full brother is in charge in Kuwait, as is also the case in Saudi Arabia, while in Qatar, Bahrain and Oman other members of the ruling family hold the portfolio. Apart from these four very political positions, the number of princes to be found in government is also striking, with the Head of State often seeming to be surrounded mainly by his brothers, sons, cousins and nephews in the Council of Ministers. In Kuwait the government included six princes of the Al Sabah family among its sixteen members (constituting 40 per cent), who held important portfolios such as foreign affairs, information, interior defence, oil, justice, and legal and administrative affairs. In Saudi Arabia, nine out of twenty-nine members of the Council of Ministers (31 per cent) are also leading members of the Royal Family. In Qatar the ratio is the highest, with eleven out of eighteen full ministers (61 per cent), followed by seven out of sixteen in Bahrain. In spite of their specific circumstances the same trend can be observed in Oman and the UAE where, outside the Council of Ministers, the directing of higher committees, as well as the top positions in the army, in the security forces and in the governing of provinces have been given to members of the ruling families. A still more recent trend has been to name younger, educated princes as ambassadors.

POLITICS AND IDEOLOGY: THE KINSHIP/RELIGION SYMBIOSIS

In all countries of the Arabian Peninsula (with the exception of Yemen) the state is ruled by a 'traditional', tribal leadership. The titles may vary –

kingdom, sultanate, emirate, etc. – but the essence is always hereditary and patriarchal. Not only the headship of states but also most sensitive ministerial portfolios in these countries are held by the ruling families and their entourages. There are also significant variations in the level of social and political control. Bahrain is usually regarded as the most socially liberal (with a number of women working, relatively open entertainment, etc.), while Kuwait is (or was) usually regarded, comparatively speaking, as the most open politically (with the parliament – admittedly covering only a small proportion of the people of Kuwait – reconvening, and with a reasonably liberal press, etc.). On the other hand, Oman has the reputation for being the most oppressive politically, while Saudi Arabia is said to be the most repressive socially. However, it would still be reasonable to say that all these countries are generally conservative, in both their political and social outlooks (a more favoured term, especially with strategists, is the rather elusive and often misleading word 'moderate').

E.R. Peterson [1977] has shown how these 'states' are formed around a nucleus of a ruling family that controls the political leadership and the military forces and the major ministerial portfolios. "Complementing the family élite is a second élite composed of the shaikhly clans from other major tribes in the state. Their allegiance is secured through subsidies, intermarriages and government posts" (and franchises for foreign products). In several states, representatives from the major tribes and merchant families have been allocated seats in consultative assemblies [306–7]. The semi-corporatist, semi-consociationalist aspects of such formulae should be quite recognizable [for further details see Peterson, 1988].

In the case of Saudi Arabia, the vast Royal Family has historically allied itself, as we have seen, with the puritanical Hanbalite *Wahhabi* movement, and has developed a fairly cohesive, if quite narrow, political élite [cf. Wenner, 1975: 157–91]. Religion is used in Saudi Arabia as a main tool for social control and political legitimisation through institutions like the *shar'i* (religious) courts, the Organisation for the Enforcement of Good and the Prevention of Evil (established in 1929), and the moral police (*mutawwi'*) system [Piscatori in Esposito, 1980]. The political system is quite centralised, with the influential members of the Royal Family, and to a lesser extent the Council of Ministers, being the main policy-making force. The country has no written constitution or legal political parties, and though there have been recurring promises for a *majlis shura* (consultative council) since the early 1960s, no such council has been created until 1993, nor have promises for a truly decentralised system of local government (*muqata'at*) been realised. The Saudi regime is not cruelly repressive, however, even when compared to a number of ostensibly more 'democratic' regimes in the Middle East. Since the 1970s execution, torture or detention for political reasons seem to have been fairly infrequent. The relative socio-political quiescence in Saudi Arabia and the Gulf during the 1970s and

1980s – though partly related to the decline in Egypt's stature – was due mainly to the increase in oil revenues and to the distribution of a portion of these revenues among a larger section of the population so that almost everybody felt a certain degree of improvement compared to their previous circumstances. Thus while the 1950s and 1960s witnessed various examples of political unrest among the workers and the intelligentsia and even among the military in Saudi Arabia (there were, for instance, arrests and imprisonments in 1953, 1956, 1963, 1964, 1976 and 1969), the 1970s were by contrast surprisingly quiet except for the events at Mecca at the end of 1979.

Yet the 1960s were not years of extreme poverty in Saudi Arabia, and what took place then should remind us that there is nothing peculiar to Saudi Arabia that should make her any more immune to coups, rebellions and revolutions than other Third World countries. In 1969 a number of military and civilian groups planned to launch a nationalist-oriented coup in the country's three main regions of Hijaz, Najd and the Eastern Province. The plan was pre-empted by the authorities and several hundred officers and civilians were arrested, their numbers serving to illustrate the dimensions of the scheme. If this could happen in the late 1960s, one should not exclude the theoretical possibility that something similar could happen some twenty-five or so years later, the 'blessings' bestowed by oil notwithstanding.

The oil boom – and the benefits that almost every Saudi derived from it – was indeed a pacifying factor. But again a major contradiction is involved: the more petro-dollars that Saudi Arabia acquires, the more the government can co-opt or appease larger sections of the population through financial handouts of one sort or another. On the other hand, the more that money is paid out to locals and foreigners and the more that activities are carried out, the more it becomes likely that complex social relations – including some ingredients for class conflict and political opposition – will develop within the society. The government has various means for appeasement and co-optation at its disposal. The main instruments it uses include appointments to key public offices (which is usually the way to build up contacts that will make private business more profitable), land grants and allocations (which can later be divided and sold at much higher prices, sometimes to the government itself), and the granting of permits and licences for importation and trading, are among the main instruments utilised.

The ideology of such regimes has been pejoratively labelled by some as 'petro-Islam'. This is mainly the ideology of Saudi Arabia but it is also echoed to one degree or another in most of the smaller Gulf countries. Petro-Islam proceeds from the premise that it is not merely an accident that oil is concentrated in the thinly populated Arabian countries rather than in the densely populated Nile Valley or the Fertile Crescent, and that this apparent irony of fate is indeed a grace and a blessing from God (ni'ma; baraka) that should be solemnly acknowledged and lived up to.

Khalil Ahmad Khalil speaks of Saudi Arabia combining an imaginary 'Islamic paradise' with a thriving 'petroleum kingdom' to produce a 'theo-petrocracy' [Khalil, 1984: 78–94]. An important function of petro-Islam, on the regional level, is to keep the oil wealth away from other Arabs. Hence petro-Islam is fiercely hostile to any Pan-Arabist idea or movement and strongly supportive of movements that use Islamic symbolism instead. On the other hand, and in spite of competition and bargaining (mainly via OPEC), the oil-exporting countries accept their role as part and parcel of the world capitalist order and are greatly in favour of its survival under its current American leadership. Capitalist (Western) countries are classified as 'people of the book', whereas socialists and socialism are identified with *kufr wa ilhad* (unbelief and atheism). Hence the appellation which is given to the current Arabian variety of Islam by the revolutionary Islamists in the Gulf area – "al-Islam al-Amriki li al-sultat al-Sa'udiyya" (the American Islam of the Saudi authorities) [cf. IRO/publications of Munazzamat al-thawra al-islamiyya fi al-jazira al-'arabiyya – the Islamic Revolution Organisation in the Arabian Peninsula].

In many ways the emphasis on Islam becomes the natural counterpart both to the Western-style consumerism of these countries and to their intimate political and strategic ties with the West. It is the gloss on their economic and cultural dependency *vis-à-vis* the Western capitalist powers, so that the asserted claim to Islamic authority may act to mask the real relationship of dependency and subservience.

Domestically, 'petro-Islam' emphasises an interpretation of religion that is both excessively ritualistic in style and conservative in socio-economic content (for example, sanctioning private property and the class system, etc.). The extensive building of mosques and religious centres, and the discreet financial support of various Islamic organisations and associations is typical of such regimes. Typical too is the technique of distracting people's attention towards trivial issues which are presented as serious dangers to Islam in the Gulf – these include things like Christian missionaries, masonic orders and the Indo-Muslim sect of Qadianism! [Ansar al-Dimuqratiyya, 1987: 42–8]. Fu'ad Zakariyya, who also uses the term petro-Islam, maintains that its objective is "to protect the petroleum wealth, or rather the type of social relations that exists in societies that have the largest share of oil, and which are characterised – as is known – by oligarchic control of the largest part of that wealth" [Zakariyya, 1986: 23–6].

In recent years petro-Islam has, in a rather defensive manner, been re-asserting itself in Arabia and the Gulf. Saudi Arabia (and more recently Kuwait) are the only Arab countries that restrict the granting of their nation-ality to Muslim individuals. The prohibition of alcohol is extended in scope and is more strictly enforced, and religio-political censorship over various cultural activities is becoming tighter. The king of Saudi Arabia has also changed his official title to that of *khadim al-haramain* (Servant of the Two Holy Sanctuaries – i.e. of Mecca and Medina).

So much for ideology. But what then about the political system at large? It is known that oligarchic regimes often resort to a defensive strategy of 'segmental incorporation' in order to preserve themselves. Having defeated, disarticulated or persecuted social forces, political organisations and/or ideological orientations that represent a serious challenge to the regime, they then co-opt their members (individually or in divided segments if possible) into the regime's own politico-organisational set-up. Segmental incorporation is particularly useful as a defensive strategy when coercion alone cannot sustain control over groups with competing interests, aspirations or socio-cultural agendas.[3]

Having assured themselves in power and having subsequently incorporated fractions of the traditional intelligentsia and the traditional merchants, oligarchic-authoritarian regimes often feel compelled to launch modernisation programmes via state initiatives. This is sometimes described as 'defensive modernisation' in that it represents a response by traditional regimes threatened by expanding Western power and culture. Historically this took place in countries as remote from each other as Russia, Mexico, Japan, the Ottoman Empire and Pahlavi Iran, and in the contemporary period it has taken place in most countries of Arabia and the Gulf. The intention is to emulate the apparent bases of Western superiority and particularly in economic, technological and organisational spheres. In order to create and staff a centralised administration and a good army, and to design and implement industrial, agricultural and social policies, such regimes encourage, through education and other means, the expansion and promotion of a 'New Middle Class' [Heller and Safran, 1985].

In contemporary Arabia and the Gulf, the inclination towards defensive modernisation has been sustained by the impetus of what one may call 'bonanza modernisation'.[4] The concept is connected to the nature of the *rentier* economies of such countries and to their modernisation policies. David Becker maintains that mineral export-based development with transnational corporate participation is a distinctive model or strategy of capitalist development that can be distinguished in both its economic mechanisms and its socio-political outcomes from other models: e.g. import-substitution industrialisation or export-promotion industrialisation. According to this 'model', the ruling class does not need to rely either on the favours of foreign interests or on raw coercion in order to maintain its power and privileges.

> The underlying mechanism is the production for exportation of mineral products, conducted such that a portion of the earned surplus is captured by the local state. The surplus share accruing to the state is distributed thus: to support the state apparatus financially; to develop other economic sectors related distantly

or not at all to mineral production; and to provide economic benefits to mobil-ized, vocal societal elements in hopes that they will refrain from challenging the existing structures of political domination and social control [Becker, 1987].

The distribution of largesse to mobilised societal groups takes place through increased state employment, public works construction and generous welfare services. It also 'trickles' sideways and a little downwards through various tax exemptions and various subsidies, both to individuals and also to 'private' enterprises, the latter in addition benefiting from government contracts and from the general promotion of trade and services in the society.

Bonanza modernisation allows a dominant strata to enjoy the advantages of quite a prosperous and relatively stable state, without paying for these out of its own pockets (in terms of higher taxes on personal income or company profits) and without having to squeeze the direct producers (cultivators, pastoralists, fishermen, etc.) for the purposes of 'primitive accumulation'. In consequence, opportunities for upward mobility are opened to ambitious societal elements, especially members of the middle classes who are capable of mounting serious threats to the status quo if frustrated by a situation of blocked ascent. The ruling stratum does not therefore have to be 'unpleasant' either to the owning classes by taxing their profits or to the working classes by extracting part of their surplus labour. This high degree of relative autonomy provides the state élite with a fair amount of freedom in choosing its class allies and in shifting and shuffling the alliances with greater ease.

To further ensure its continuing command of such an attractive state of affairs, the ruling stratum tries to 'depoliticise' social relations and to promote 'modernisation' or a certain variant of technicism or managerialism as a source of legitimacy for the regime. This kind of emphasis by necessity requires an expanding role to be assigned to the technocrats of the new middle class. By contrast, the interests of the traditional merchants with their family-based businesses may appear to be marginalised in favour of the modern types of large-scale corporation run by Western-style managers and technocrats, as part of an overall policy of indicative planning [cf. Field, 1984].

This new middle class, often heterogeneous and lacking the necessary solidarity to act as a class *for* itself, usually obliges and cooperates closely with the traditional ruling élites in the initial stages of modernisation. But as the modernisation process continues, there comes a time when the new middle class seems to be pushing hard for too much modernisation too fast; this occurs as the interests of the new middle class become closely linked to continuous modernisation. What is more dangerous is that rather than con-fining itself to the purely 'technical' areas assigned to it by the regime, demands by the new middle class now start to encroach on the more sensitive points in the formation of the regime: the privileges of the ruler, the basis of the regime's legitimacy, and the religious and cultural underpinnings of both [cf. Shaker, 1972]. The strained relationship between the new middle class and the traditional ruling élite may persist for lengthy periods without serious danger to the system. Yet

> if the state is confronted with a major crisis and found wanting, the alienated new middle class is often galvanized to act. In such circumstances, the middle class tends to abandon its creator, the traditional regime, and to transfer its allegiance to revolutionary forces who carry out a coup and promise a truly effective modernization program. [This] describes the experiences of many, though not all, defensive modernizers [Heller and Safran, 1985: 4–5].

Thus it should always be kept in mind that in Saudi Arabia, the oil prosperity notwithstanding, there are potential sources of contradiction and conflict that might very well be expressed politically at the right moment. Among the main ones are the following:

1. The Royal Family is so large (reportedly including nearly 3000 princes and 2000 princesses) that personal rivalries, differences of opinion, and so forth are bound inevitably to challenge – at least on the perimeter – the existing solidarity that is bound up by the common gains. This is nothing new. In the 1960s the 'Free Princes' disagreed with the rest of the family about matters of foreign and domestic policy, and in the 1970s, King Faisal was killed by a member of the Royal Family.
2. In spite of the symbolically egalitarian attitude of many leaders, the contradictions between the gargantuan Royal Family on the one hand and the rest of the population on the other are quite real. A particularly likely source of tension is the relationship between what one may call the traditional leaders (royal, tribal, etc.), and the 'new men' (mainly technocrats but also independent merchants and businessmen) who may favour a faster development of the merit system in the civilian and military sectors [Rugh, 1973: 12–16].
3. Regional differences continue to be significant. The Hijaz–Najd dichotomy is a historical one that is unlikely to disappear overnight since it still has an impact, especially on important and military appointments. Regional differences are reinforced by various economic, occupational and sometimes ethnic and religious factors. Tribal rivalries are also of significance and although bedouins are still neglected in many remote parts of the country, balancing tribes against each other is a useful control technique, while the role of the nomadic tribes as a whole in forming the National Guard is of the utmost importance in any potential conflict. People from the South who are more inclined towards farming (and who are claimed by Saudi Arabia's southern neighbours as brother Yemenis) are frequently regarded with some disdain, and people from the East (where most of the oil industry and hence the labour force is located, and where there are many Shi'is), are likewise often viewed with a certain degree of suspicion; and indeed,

since the late 1940s, the two regions have witnessed various events sparked by revolt or unrest.

4. Religious differences are important. Non-Muslims may work in Saudi Arabia, but Christian Arabs may not acquire Saudi nationality. More important politically is the status of the Shi'is. According to some sources they are very poorly represented in the higher official posts, their testimony as witnesses is not recognised in courts of law, and they are not allowed to take certain teaching positions. In 1979 and 1980 they organised some fairly violent demonstrations in the Eastern province in support of Khomeini's Islamic revolution in Iran.

5. Class distinctions to a large extent overlap with and are blurred by the distinctions that have already been explained. Class contradictions are unlikely to be violently manifested in the short run, since almost everybody seems to be benefiting to some extent from the oil boom and improving their conditions. The lack of rights for trade unionism and political expression also makes it extremely difficult for class interests to aggregate and for class consciousness to develop. Foreign labour, including the Palestinian workforce, is subjected to even stricter scrutiny. However, labour is not completely without a history of struggle (there were various protests especially by ARAMCO workers from the mid-1940s), and people are bound in the future to compare themselves with the more privileged members of the society, rather than to compare their own present condition with what they had themselves been like previously.

What then are the policies and/or ideologies that are likely to represent focal points for political action in Saudi Arabia? On a policy level, the most controversial areas are those of foreign policy and of oil policy. In the area of foreign policy there are subtle disagreements between those who prefer a more pro-American posture and those who would favour a more Pan-Arabist, non-aligned stand. In the area of oil policy there is a rather more outspoken disagreement between those who have been most anxious to please the United States and other industrial countries as much as possible (through, for instance, keeping oil supplies reasonably abundant and oil price increases gradual), and those who would like their country to follow a more independent policy with greater sensitivity to the needs of other OPEC members and to the problems of the developing countries at large [Lacey, 1982: 4–12, 7–8].

With the price of oil continuing to decline rapidly – especially from 1982 – without the Saudi government reacting quickly enough to cut production, questions increased and fierce criticisms escalated, as increasing numbers of people began to suspect that the 'oil glut' had in large part been engineered jointly by the United States and Saudi Arabia [cf. Alnasrawi, 1984]. An episode of confusion over oil policy resulted among other things in the dismissal of the famous Saudi Minister of Petroleum, Ahmad Zaki Yamani, in 1987.

On a more ideological level, one can say that the variety of radical national-ism (with Pan-Arabist and/or socialistic leanings) which manifested itself among numbers of intellectuals and officers in Saudi Arabia and the Gulf in the 1950s and 1960s, and which often had Nasserist or Ba'thist sympathies (such as, for example, the Arab National Liberation Front which was formed in 1963 and whose members included Prince Talal and his brothers) is less likely to find its way to the fore politically today. Some scattered sympathisers are still around, however, and although for the time being it is unlikely to happen, one cannot entirely rule out the future possibility of a 'radical-nationalist' coup in the Libyan style.

It seems that these days, rather than being Arab-Nationalist in orientation, most of the intelligentsia of Saudi Arabia incline more towards favouring a sort of Islamic reform (along lines similar to those set down by people such as Afghani and 'Abduh) in combination with certain manifestations of techno-logical modernisation. Such groups might want to see more open expression, more of a merit system, and possibly a more flexible interpretation of some Islamic precepts. Ideas of this sort, however, are unlikely to provoke their proponents into violent political action.

Other opposition groups involve a number of tiny underground organisa-tions that are unlikely to threaten the regime in the near future [cf. Lackner, 1978: Ch. 5; Salameh in *MERIP*, 1980: esp. 19–22; *Sawt al-Tali'a*, 1980: 1–22]. The Union of the People of the Arabian Peninsula has probably the longest continuous history of action since its formation in 1959. It is committed to socialism and unification of the Arabian Peninsula, and is Pan-Arabist in orientation. Its secretary-general, Nasir al-Sa'id, was kidnapped in Beirut in December 1979, presumably by Saudi agents, and is thought to have been assassinated. 'Voice of the Vanguard Supporters' is a small but vocal group with Iraqi Ba'thist connections and is mainly active outside Saudi Arabia, with some influence through its publications on Saudi students abroad. The Saudi branch of the Ba'th Party was formed in 1958. The Communist Party of Saudi Arabia had an earlier predecessor during the mid-1950s but an-nounced itself under its present name in 1974. It aims at a patriotic, democratic and republican regime, and is pro-Soviet in its international orientation. The 'Islamic Revolution Organisation' emerged after the riots in the Eastern region in 1979, and is probably still concentrated there. Its adherents believe in creating an Islamic republic in Arabia based in popular participation internally and full independence in foreign policy. There is also apparently a radical branch in Saudi Arabia of the Muslim Brothers (the Brotherhood having been formed initially in Egypt in 1928), whose members believe that *salafi* Islam is being used in Saudi Arabia today only to mask corruption and oppression, which the Brothers set themselves to resist. The existence of such Islamic groupings indicates that, like most other parts of the Middle East, Saudi Arabia too is witnessing certain, if sometimes distinct, aspects of the general phenomenon of the political revival of religion. This was made particularly clear by the dramatic takeover of Mecca's Great Mosque in November 1979 by a group ultimately descending from the Ikhwan movement of Arabia.

The abundant flow of oil money to Saudi Arabia and the Gulf states has been a major factor behind their relative stability and quiescence since the early 1970s, and has enabled the traditional tribal élites of these countries to maintain their rule and to counter most potential sources of opposition through an intricate disbursement of the revenues and a subtle policy of cooptation and incorporation. However, following the onset of the decline in oil revenues, some ten years after oil prices had quadrupled so remarkably in 1973, the functions of political control by the royal families over a populace with higher expectations and with appetites whetted for the 'good life', are likely to present the ruling élites of these countries with a very serious challenge as they begin to face their own version of the 'fiscal crisis of the state'. This is part of the irony of what Val Moghadam [1988] calls 'petroleum-based accumulation':

> With the rise of state oil companies, the contemporary peripheral oil states integrated themselves with international capital or became strong entrepreneurs in the world market. The entrepreneurial form of the peripheral state 'derives' from its access to international capital and its own revenues. This is the positive side of state autonomy. However, the centralization and concentration of political and economic power – as opposed to its diffusion – are also a liability. By becoming more visible and politicized, the state becomes vulnerable to blame for any crises of accumulation, when economic booms change to economic busts [228-9].

Saudi Arabia's external assets reached their peak in 1982, amounting to some $165 billion. From this peak there was a subsequent downturn in assets until 1986, when the reserve was estimated at only $90 billion, some $40 billion of which were committed loans to the World Bank, the International Monetary Fund, and other Gulf states [Khawajkiya, 1986]. In tandem with this decline in assets, an absolute decline in revenue and expenditure started to be reflected in the projections of the Saudi state budgets, beginning with that of 1982/83, although the drop since then has been bigger in revenue than it has been in expenditure. Given the extreme uncertainties concerning oil production and prices, the announcing of Saudi Arabia's state budget has had to be postponed several times, and there were forecasts of substantial budget spending cuts of up to 20 per cent annually that would most noticeably affect infrastructure, economic resource development and government lending institutions. Suggestions were made that further cuts in subsidies could be avoided by boosting non-oil revenues through a rise in import and income taxes.

A similar situation existed in other Gulf countries, so that in the United Arab Emirates for example, the 1986 budget, and subsequent budgets, was expected to be cut by 15 per cent or more per annum. Kuwait's budget expenditure for 1986 and the subsequent years was also to be cut by nearly 10 per cent per annum.

Until now, oil funds have cemented together the system of the various Gulf states so that, as long as funds have been sufficient to allow for almost everybody to benefit even after the needs of the Royal Family and the 'state' have been met, order and apparent socio-political peace have been maintained. With the growing decline in oil funds, cuts in the allocations directed to 'ordinary' citizens are likely to be made before there is any diminution of the allocations to the ruling families. It is quite possible that this will produce a political atmosphere similar to that of the 1950s and 1960s when smaller oil revenues – most of which were kept by the ruling élites – had created a situation within Arabia where dissident groups and attempted coups were recognised phenomena.

Some strains are already apparent. On the domestic front, for example, there were reports in the mid-1980s of increasing rivalry between branches of the Royal Family in Saudi Arabia and of a serious split, manifested in almost every policy issue or decision, that developed within government and the ruling circles over the increasing concentration of power within the Al-Fahd branch of the ruling family. Dissatisfaction and suspicion were expressed over the way in which the government was covering up for an understandable impotence in dealing with certain external economic and political matters (especially related to oil policy and to relations with the United States) that were adversely affecting the Kingdom. From the mid-1980s, the Saudis also introduced new and stricter rules for expatriate sponsorship, designed both to boost the drive towards 'Saudi-isation' and to reduce the possibility of blue-collar expatriate unemployment becoming a social issue.

The upshot of all these developments suggests that the citizens of the Gulf states, with their continuing high expectations, will be hurt economically on three fronts: (i) as a result of the decline in public expenditure, in particular on the infrastructure, subsidies and concessionary credits; (ii) as a result of possible growing levels of taxation; and (iii) as a result of a reduction in the availability of cheap expatriate labour. So far, the 'bedoucracies' of the Gulf have managed to maintain themselves domestically in large measure through the disbursement of 'petro-dollars'. With the decline in oil revenues, these 'bedoucracies-turned-petrocracies' will have increasingly to look for new bases for survival and legitimacy. In the meantime, alternative élites will not be standing idly by.

'POLITICAL TRIBALISM': OR CORPORATISM GULF-STYLE

We have seen earlier (in Chapter 5) that corporatism and consociationalism are two varieties of the same genre. If this contention is accepted, one can now see, partly in retrospect, that applying a corporatist/consociationalist paradigm to the study of the Arabian Gulf states can offer interesting insight into their workings.

In Saudi Arabia, because of its unique position in containing the sacred cities of Islam, and owing to the historical importance of the Wahhabi religious movement and the original coalition between Saudi tribalism and Shaikhly puritanism that had originally led to the formation of the state, religious ideology could play a particularly vital role in imparting cohesion to the state and in glossing over some of the contradictions involved. Ever since the formation of the state, the Al-Shaikh clan, originators of the Wahhabi movement/sect, has been closely coopted within the regime. Tribals are incorporated via a number of methods including subsidised sedentarisation projects, and recruitment into the National Guard, the country's parallel army.

In the other Arabian and Gulf states (e.g. the United Arab Emirates, Kuwait, Yemen, etc.), the lack of such a cohesive ideology has obliged the state to achieve such a coordination by resorting to consociational arrangements. Both inducement (enticement) and enforcement (coercion) were utilised to build up the tribal alliances that led to the emergence of the contemporary 'states'. A 'carrot and stick' policy has been (and is still being) used to ensure loyalty and compliance. In 'local' terminology this is the policy of what Muhammad al-Rumaihi calls combining the *saif* (sword = force) with the *mansaf* (the bedouin banquet = enticement) [Al-Rumaihi, 1989: 11–12]. Its devices include financial rewards and penalties, inter-familial and inter-tribal marriages, renewed recognition of certain remote tribal branches, or else 'forced' emigration of opponent groups and/or individuals, and the co-optation of religious institutions and local neighbourhoods.

Khaldun Al-Naqib's pioneering contribution has been in the application of a corporatist paradigm to the study of the contemporary states of Arabia and the Gulf. Corporatism according to him is a method of ensuring the domination of the authoritarian state over the society and the economy by controlling its major groupings, either in an implicit way as in Kuwait or in an explicit way as in Yemen [Al-Naqib, 1987: 171–4ff]. This strategy has often been presented as a mechanism for national integration and an alternative to despotic demagogy, or even as a revival of the traditions of tribal democracy. In Naqib's view, however, it is the exact opposite of democracy, as relationships within and among the tribal corps are unequal. Linking such traditional corps to the state only deepens patron–client relationships, as social promotion becomes contingent on finding a distinguished patron from among the ruling families or the tribal and commercial élites. This, in his view, weakens loyalty to the state as a whole and to the nation/people at large, since these groupings turn into pressure groups and lobbies that are intent on gaining special benefits and defending particularistic interests. This leads in turn to a re-traditionalisation of the society, the influence of mass communications notwithstanding, as illustrated for example by the revival of tribal names and connotations in many Gulf societies.

Corporatist practices, maintains Al-Naqib, enable the Gulf rulers to manipulate the social forces through new 'divisions of labour'. According to him, the main implicit corps in the Gulf are the following: the tribal groups that the state deals with via their shaikhs; the major commercial families; the religious Establishment (for Sunnis) and the 'sectarian' establishments (i.e. for communities such as the Shi'a, the Ibadis, the Zaidis, etc.). There are also the 'middle classes' which, lacking the right to form professional syndicates, have therefore to deal with the state on a family basis too; and finally the workers in the limited cases where there is an organised native working class. The army in North Yemen and the party in South Yemen may also be regarded, in Al-Naqib's view, as corporate organisations [Al-Naqib, 1987: 149].

These corps, of which the most important are probably the tribes, are only semi-formal since there are no corporate chambers in the classical pattern, but the key tribes are carefully represented in the state institutions centrally and locally, as well as in the army and the police. This is the basis of the system which he dubs 'political tribalism' (al-qabaliyya al-siyasiyya), and which is akin to the more familiar concept of 'asha'iriyya.[5] In the case of Kuwait they are also represented in the parliament. Shortly after independence in 1961 the ruling family followed an active policy of 'naturalising' the bedouins. The loyalty of these 'manufactured citizens' was much easier to gain than that of the established commercial élites. The impact of the tribes on politics and elections in Kuwait always remained strong thereafter, with the following tribes playing key political roles: Al-'Awazim, 'Utaiba, Shammar, Al-Fudul, 'Azman, Al-Rashayida and Mutair. These tribes act as semi-autonomous corps when preparing for elections, deciding internally on their candidates, in tribal primaries, before standing openly for elections [for full tables see Al-Nafisi, 1978: 28ff, 74–90].

In the 1981–84 Kuwaiti parliament (the last to have had a full term), they were represented as follows: (a) the tribal corps: twenty-seven deputies; (b) the merchants corps: fourteen deputies representing conservative and reformist trends; and (c) the religious establishment: four deputies (two Muslim Brothers and two Salafis). The middle classes were not represented separately from their tribal and religious communities (six members of the middle class gained seats as members of their traditional corps), and there was no representation for the workers [Al-Naqib, 1987: 149–50]. Likewise, the 1985 elections "produced a parliament reflective of the social structure as designed by the Kuwaiti authorities through their policies of tribal settlement, migration, labor and paternalism." Within it the tribals won some twenty-three out of the total of fifty seats [Gavrielides, 1987: 179–82 and refs cited].

All Arabian and Gulf countries attach very vital roles in their political structure to the tribal corps, which also represent the main reservoir for recruitment in the army, the police and the military militias (the national guard). [For a conceptual and historical background see our discussion on tribalism in Chapter 2.] The incorporation of tribes is achieved in various institutional ways, with Kuwait being the least institutionalised case with regard to its tribal corps, whereas in Saudi Arabia, Oman and Bahrain the tribal corps are semi-formal on the local level. The UAE and (North) Yemen are on the other end of the continuum, where the tribal corps is regarded as a state institution whose position in the political system is virtually stipulated by law.[6] This last Yemen case is particularly significant as Al-Naqib believes that it represents a *"potential future alternative for most countries in Arabia and the Gulf"* [Al-Naqib, 1987: 150–51].

The original incorporation of shaikhly leaders in Yemen took place soon after the revolution of 1962, by way of counteracting the Saudi strategy for co-opting the tribal leadership to the royalist camp. The situation was then institutionalised in 1963 with the establishment of a Higher Council for Tribes Affairs, which included leaders of the major tribes and was headed by the President of the Republic himself. Shaikhly councils were also organised within each tribe and in every province, and were provided with specific legal juris-diction and allowed to hold regular proportional elections. Tribal corps were thus adapted to modern conditions and institutionalised as part of the state apparatus.

Support of the Yemeni tribal corps to the state was to a large extent premised on the generous handouts that the chiefs received from the govern-ment. Their tribal overlappings with kin-communities in both Saudi Arabia and South Yemen enabled some of their leaders to gain arms or donations from these two countries, which they used as a bargaining device with their own government for more generous support. In return they have mobilised their folks for political or military support of the government against potential opposition and rebellion, as occurred, for example, during the war of Decem-ber 1967–February 1968, when the role played by tribal forces was more decisive than that played by the regular forces [Abu Ghanim, 1985: 329–36]. Some tribal chiefs did not formally withdraw their support for the 'royalists' until quite recently, and only did so in return for concrete promises from the state for construction works and services in their localities and/or in return for more than tacit condoning of their regional authority by the central government. As one observer explains, "The government of North Yemen since 1982 has been attempting to include particularism, to find it a subsidiary position, by building a nationwide system of political involvement in the form of local and regional committees that culminate in a General Popular Con-gress. It is so far succeeding well." Tribalism is also acquiring a symbolic (sentimental) value, and the president of the republic was quoted as saying that "the State is part of the tribes, and our Yemeni people is a collection of tribes" [Dresch, 1991: 279–8].

Anthropologists and historians have argued as to whether tribes and states are *sequential stages* in social development or whether they are *alternative answers* to the problem of security [cf. e.g. Gellner, 1991; Crone, 1986].[7] In Arabia and the Gulf, tribe and state complement rather than contradict each other – they are neither stages nor alternatives; they are *articulated* with each other in complex intricate ways via the quasi-corporatist form that Al-Naqib and others have dubbed 'political tribalism', *al-qabaliyya al-siyasiyya* [cf. e.g. Aarts, 1993].

Gulf corporatism is probably fairly akin to Albert Schäffle's concept of 'monarchical corporatism'. Because of the 'traditional' nature of the ruling élite, the way it achieved power and the manner in which it applies it, these systems are of a distinctly 'conservative' nature. This is basically a community-based (i.e. 'organic') corporatism premised on the primary tribal *gemeinschaft*, subsidised by a top layer derived from the traditional notion of the Islamic community (*umma*). But because of the sudden wealth and the concomitant policies of 'defensive modernisation' resulting in the emergence of semi-modern groups (mainly the merchants, but also increasingly the technocratic and military élites), some allowance is having to be made – with varying degrees from one case to another – for the interest-type associations (*gesellschaft-liche*) created through the modernisation process [cf. Black, 1984: 224ff; and Cantori, 1986].

The conservatism of the Gulf regimes can be observed in the frequent resort to 'organic' concepts such as family, kin, neighbourhood and community, in the attachment to custom and tradition, and in the nostalgia for the past. It can also be detected in the declared allegiance to collective morality and in the emphasis attached by these regimes to religion. However, as with most political conservatives, "religion for them [is] predominantly public and institutional, something to which loyalty and a decent regard for form [are] owing, a valuable pillar to both State and society, but not a profound and permeating doctrine, least of all a total experience". That latter kind of religion marks the 'Dissenters' who are deadly enemies of the Establishment [Nisbet, 1986: 69].

Power in small tribal communities was perhaps more 'hegemonic' than 'coercive' in the sense that it was more 'social' than 'political': 'nobody orders but everybody obeys', as Pierre Claster would have suggested [cf. Harb, 1985]. The transition from tribe to state was precarious in the Gulf, but once the new principalities got over their family feuds, they acted the way most conservative monarchies do: instinctively recognising society and its constitutive groups rather than constantly seeking to supplant them – which is what radicals try to do [see L. Bonald quoted in Nisbet, 1986: 44].

In the contemporary Gulf societies, kinship, oil and to some extent religion, seem to have coalesced to produce a 'tribal ideology' that is almost hegemonic, in the Gramscian sense of permeating all practices and institutions, in Arabia. Nicolas Gavrielides is basically right, if a little carried away, in suggesting that:

What makes tribal ideology even more powerful and pervasive besides being truly Arab, is the fact that it is never formally articulated, stated, written down or even openly criticized. It is just there, permeating every action, thought or process which is of sociopolitical significance. Only the States of the Arab Gulf, and maybe Jordan and Morocco, have such indigenous ideologies. No wonder they are the most stable countries in the Middle East in terms of the durability of their regimes [1987: 182].

Yet the conservative, kin-based monarchies are by no means highly organised systems, and there is indeed much to suggest that many of the Gulfian practices and arrangements are probably closer to a consociational model than they are to the more formal and highly institutionalised varieties of corporatism. To his credit, Muhammad Hafiz Diyab [1988: 164–8] has been almost unique in highlighting this conceptual point. Referring to the writings of such people as D. Apter, A. Lijphart and G. Lehmbruch, he suggested that what Khaldun Al-Naqib [1987] was talking about was not corporatism in the strict institutional sense but more of a 'clannish democracy' [*dimuqratiyya 'asha'iriyya*] similar to a consociational formula that forges élite solidarity at the top in an enforced vertically-ordered fashion, aiming at the erection of a modern state within a traditional society.

As in the traditional tribal confederacies where allied groups occupied different locations within a semi-hierarchical order, so in the newer forms of 'controlled-consociationalism' the various lineage, ethnic, regional and professional groups occupy differential positions both *around* and *underneath* the ruling family (as the power structure is both circular and pyramidal). The socio-political coalition is therefore composed of ruling families and tribal groupings as well as commercial and professional groupings, in complex vertically and horizontally differentiated ways [compare Khuri, 1980; Peterson, 1977].

Enver Koury [1978] has done some interesting work on the structure of power in Saudi Arabia, based on a concept of *halaqat* (concentric circles and élite-webs) which is compatible with our analysis. At the centre of it all is the House of Sa'ud and particularly the King and the Crown Prince, who are then surrounded by a middle and a number of outer concentric circles of power, which in turn are inter-webbed in very intricate ways:

> The ruling elite-web system is based on an assemblage of *halaqat* (i.e. rings, groupings, branches, clans) united by some form of interaction or interdependence ... The power flow has been much heavier from inner to outer circles; that is, fundamentally unidirectional. Yet, the ruling elite-web system has been also characterized by reciprocal power exchanges where the conflicting aggregates remain both hierarchically and horizontally balanced. Usually decisions are made by elite interaction-bargaining, accommodation and compromise ... The mechanism of the system encourages *halaqat* rivalry, but it also discourages detrimental confrontations ... [P]olicy formulation is not one of majority preference; rather,

it is an equilibrium of *halaqat* interaction which is a reasonable approximation of balanced societal preferences [Koury, 1978: 38–46].

Another example of such a system of constant balances and counter-balances, alliance-building and counter-pressuring is that of the United Arab Emirates. Mohammad Abdallah Al-Mahmoud has attempted with reasonable success, in a doctoral thesis written under my supervision [1992], to apply a consociational approach to the study of the UAE. As with several other consociationalisms, the UAE's experiment is replete with manipulation ploys and control techniques, and, as with a number of other cases, it does overlap with federalism [Lijphart, 1979: 499–515]. Al-Mahmoud makes use of the earlier concept of consociationalism as coined by David Apter, in which it is perceived as a continuum beginning at one end with a form of loose alliance where common ideological, political and economic benefits are sought; and finishing at the other end as a form of federal arrangement with a recognised structure where a greater consensus is achieved. Other quasi-consociational features of the UAE include the mutual veto secured by the two largest emirates in the federation of seven, Abu Dhabi and Dubai. By convention the presidency of the federation is with Abu Dhabi whereas the vice-presidency and the premiership go to Dubai. The appointment of ministers in the Cabinet then seeks some very tricky tribal balances and counterbalances. Likewise, most of the fifty members of the short-lived national consultative council of Abu Dhabi were tribal representatives. In the Federal National Council, Abu Dhabi and Dubai have eight representatives each, Sharjah and Ras al-Khaimah six each, and the remaining emirates four each. A certain element of proportionality and compromise is also attempted in most important state and administrative posts.

Although corporatism in the oil-exporting Gulf states is not formally and institutionally elaborate, it is generally more 'inclusionary' in its strategy than it is 'exclusionary' – even though its inclusionary methods are rather communally and ethnically based, and they do not (or only partly) involve non-citizens, 'less-authentic' citizens and, at least in the case of Saudi Arabia, Shi'is. The Gulf variety of inclusionary corporatism might have been helped by the existence of quasi-consociationalist traditions derived either from the Arabian practice of tribal confederations and/or from the Islamic tradition of the *milla*s (*millet*). Whether this was or was not the case, Gulf inclusionary corporatism was indeed made possible because of the oil bonanza and the abundance of funds accruing to the state. Others have related corporatism/consociationalism and the ability to hold tacit 'pacts' and alliances to the abundance of oil in Venezuela in South America: oil revenues paid the bill for the tacit political pact, subsidising both business and the popular sectors [Karl, 1986: 196ff; Gillespie, 1990: 58–9ff]. Likewise, but on an even larger scale, oil revenues accruing directly to the Gulf states have meant that the state does not have to depend on the domestic means of production for its revenues, thus affording it a high degree of economic and political autonomy from the local forces of production and the social classes and making the entire economic, social and political system closely dependent on state expenditure [cf. Katouzian, 1981]. As the sole recipient of oil rent, the state becomes directly involved in planning and managing on a large scale. Often too, "the state attempts to internalize social conflicts" [Moghadem, 1988: 228–30]. The abundance of oil revenues accruing directly to the state enables it to clientelise existing groups (e.g. the merchants in the Gulf) and to create new ones (e.g. the 'new entrepreneurs' in the Gulf) that may be functionally differentiated but structurally dependent on the state. As an acute observer of the Gulf region put it, "while the size of the client groups varied a great deal, oil states uniformly practiced corporatism on a grand scale, using distributive policies to create economic groups as a base of social support on the one hand and to ameliorate conflict between sectoral, occupational, economic and social groups on the other" [Chaudhry, 1992: 150].

If one is partly to apply Stepan's characterisation of the conditions conducive to the emergence of inclusionary corporatism [Stepan, 1978: Chs. 3, 4 and 5], the installation of co-optative corporatism was likewise relatively easy in the case of the oil-exporting countries because of the low degree of previous autonomous interest group organisation, the low degree of political and ideological polarisation, and the low degree of social welfare legislation. All these conditions have left the ruling élite substantial 'reform space' for incorporating 'available' constituencies by initiating distributive measures, and making the receipt of benefits conditional on the acceptance of new state-controlled arrangements. The relative 'demotion' in the socio-political status of the merchant classes in the smaller Gulf states could have caused trouble in normal circumstances, as these were previously activated groups. It could be achieved in the Gulf to the advantage of the interior-based social groups because it was part of what one may – with the Italians – call a *scambio politico*, that is, an act of political exchange whereby the merchant families accepted a certain measure of political 'exclusion' in return for enhanced economic and business opportunities.

Put differently, it seems that a situation of 'hegemonic corporatism' is more likely to be achieved (as indicated before) given a combination of late development (or in this case wealth), coupled with an early emergence of a welfare state [compare Cerny, 1987: 24–5]. The 'bonanza development' (as David Becker calls it) that is characteristic of mineral-export economies, especially if they also happen to be thinly populated, poses fewer difficulties for capital accumulation and even fewer problems with regard to consumption levels. Bonanza development is not therefore conducive, by virtue of its inner dynamic, to the 'bureaucratic authoritarianism' that G. O'Donnell thought was necessary for maintaining the developmental process in non-mineral exporting countries [cf. Becker, 1987: 337].

The 'easy phase' of modernisation in the oil-exporting countries (the equivalent to that of import-substitution in the relatively more industrially advanced countries) is that of economic *expansion*. Economic expansion should be distinguished from economic development or even economic growth [cf. Stauffer, 1981]. The main fields in which expansion takes place are construction, institution-building and social and commercial services, and the mechanism involved is not productive but distributive. The process does not contribute to the development of capitalism but is fuelled by a growth in consumption – public and private. The expansion is generated by the state, which penetrates the society just as it constructs streets and buildings, establishes organisations and furnishes services and benefits. Consumerism in this case is not based on a local consumer goods industry and therefore it does not (as was the case in Europe) enhance the autonomy of the society but, on the contrary, increases its dependency on the state. The policies are 'inclusionary', activating (even creating) a whole range of 'middle strata' for the first time (the lower strata in this case being mainly foreign).

One of the distinctive characteristics of Gulf corporatism is this activation (and indeed creation) of the 'new middle class' of salaried intelligentsia. It can be argued that given the limited production activities performed in these states and the fact that the working class in them is almost entirely expatriate, the new middle class comes functionally to play in these systems the role traditionally played by the working classes in conventional 'Latin-type' corporatism. The welfare services in the Gulf tend to benefit the new middle class most, providing it with education, employment and social opportunities. By the same token, it is the new middle class (rather than the working classes) which is most likely to cause difficulties to the regime, if the regime is unable to sustain its largesse (for example because of decline in oil revenues) or if the activated new middle class cannot be effectively absorbed into the political process owing to the narrowly based, conservatively oriented nature of the ruling élite. Thus, if populist corporatist regimes often find that it is easier to install an alliance which includes the lower classes than it is to sustain and consolidate such an alliance [Stepan, 1978: Chs. 3 and 4], conservative corporatist regimes may equally find it easier to initiate a co-optative formula that includes the middle classes than to sustain and consolidate it.

One of the main problems of 'bonanza development', however, is that it cannot impose its own limits on the expectations of various social groups:

> It suggests that development is, or can be made to be, a painless enterprise. It does not call for universal sacrifice to achieve its vaunted goals; does not delegitimate extremes of élite privileges; and does not activate enthusiastic, voluntary popular cooperation in a national development 'project'. In fact it exacerbates its own difficulties by raising the expectations of all groups sufficiently well organized to present claims against the 'bonanza' while providing no ideological mechanism for restraining these claims within the perimeter of what the 'bonanza' can

realistically supply. This is the core contradiction of bonanza development [Becker, 1987: 339].

The 'easy phase' of modernisation is bound to reach a certain ceiling at some point, both because of 'technical' limits to the 'expansionary' phase but more particularly as oil resources decline (while the aspirations remain high). The expansionary stage would then be 'exhausted', and these states will have to make some strategic choices. The most obvious would be to move increasingly away from the expansionist and consumerist policies with their emphasis on 'using' money towards a more productive emphasis on investment. Yet neither the pressures nor the inducements appear to be strong enough to usher in an immediate move in that direction. Some agricultural development is tried but there are serious limitations to it and the entire activity remains excessively dependent on the state. Industry also remains, in spite of some privatisation initiatives, basically an *étatiste* pursuit. One option tried rather successfully by the Kuwaitis is a kind of 'financial deepening'; by the time Kuwait was annexed by Iraq in 1990 Kuwaitis were earning more money from their financial investments than from selling their oil. Most of these investments, however, were overseas and did not help in a direct way in strengthening the economic base of the country. These countries could also try reducing foreign labour; but this also has its limits and could not be pursued beyond a certain point, although some reduction in wages (or increase in taxes) could be attempted.

In the long run, therefore, state policies are inevitably bound to become more 'exclusionary', especially with regard to the middle, technocratic and professional strata. Unless a democratic process has been set in train by then (which seems unlikely even after the Desert Storm shock), the state is more likely to become more authoritarian (although not necessarily bureaucratic: because industrial deepening is not required and because the pattern of authority is still oligarchic rather than technocratic). A little more detail may be required at this point.

In the case of Saudi Arabia, almost entirely new corps of businessmen and technocrats were built up, mainly from among the Najdi tribal élites which eventually took over the commercial and administrative lead from the traditionally prominent groups centred within the Hijazi community, though without completely dislodging these latter. As Kiren A. Chaudhry has acutely observed, the expanding bureaucracy was partly built along quasi-corporatist lines, the corps in this case being predominantly tribes:

> The powerful Ministry of Finance is dominated by the 'Aniza tribe from the Qasim area in the Nejd, a community that played an important role in the military campaigns of King 'Abd al-'Aziz during the wars of unification. Other ministries are similarly divided along tribal or corporate lines: Pilgrimage and Education for the religious elite; Industry and Commerce for the new Nejdi business elite; and Agriculture for the Al-Sheikh family [Chaudhry, 1989: 126].

During the boom years, state spending replicated the tribal and regional composition of the bureaucracy in the new business class, created new interest groups, and weakened the cohesion and competitiveness of the old Hijazi merchant class. "Under the umbrella of the state-subsidized Saudi Chambers of Commerce, Industry, and Agriculture, the new élite gained collective access to key ministries, which supplemented informal access through numerous joint projects with bureaucrats and members of the royal family" [ibid.: 129–30]. Yet the state's distributive measures that might have begun as informal, targeted spending were soon, with the sectoral development programmes, to become increasingly linked with market mechanisms, to involve broader segments of the population, and to generate their own direct income. The state appeared to possess tremendous autonomy and its policies appeared to be highly 'statising' during the boom years.

It was the bust years that revealed the strong 'privatising' influences of the civil society which were related in this case to the fact that the expansion of the state machine was not itself 'autonomous' from particularistic influences. When the global recession and the ensuing reduction in oil revenues required the Saudi government to cut down on expenditure, the Saudi austerity programme only succeeded in implementing policies that affected the general population and foreign workers and failed to carry through any reforms that would have targeted the merchant class:

> [The] category of measures aimed directly at the affluent commercial class drew stringent criticism and was unceremoniously withdrawn ... One by one, these were successfully opposed through the Riyadh Chamber of Commerce and informal lobbying ... In their opposition to regulation and tax, the Saudi private sector mobilised both primordial links and economic ties with bureaucrats and the Royal Family ... Consistently, legislation that was against the interests of business was passed, opposed, and withdrawn, upholding the interests of Nejdi businessmen, local banks, Islamic jurists, and the landed élite against those of Saudi labor, consumers, international banks and foreigners [Chaudhry, 1989: 139–40].

Thus we can see in the Saudi case that previously strong groups in the Hijaz were weakened or marginalised and new corporate groups were created directly through state spending. The deficiency of this system lay in the fact that group interests coalesced only as a result of group spending patterns. Rather than forming a loyal political base, continued financial support from the state was a prerequisite for the private sector's acquiescence. Despite the financial dependence of the Saudi merchant class on state patronage, primordial links with the bureaucracy actually strengthened its bargaining power in the recession and thereby enabled it to block austerity reforms. "Ironically, opposition to austerity measures was spearheaded not by the disenfranchised Hijazis, nor by the impoverished populations of Asir and Hassa, but by the two main beneficiaries of Saudi state spending: the state-sponsored landed elite and the new Nejdi merchant and industrial class" [Chaudhry, 1989: 142–5].

In Kuwait and the smaller Gulf states, the traditional commercial groups were relatively too powerful and too central to be dismantled – instead they were incorporated, in a subservient capacity, by the expanding rentier state.

> The historical transformation that has been most central to shaping Kuwaiti politics in the twentieth century has been the breakdown of the ruling coalition binding the ruler and the trading families and the relegation of the trading families to a bounded, primarily economic role in the private sector, leaving the political arena to the ruler, the ruling family, and shifting allies [Crystal, 1991: 109].

The Al Sabah family of Kuwait dominated all important political positions such as cabinet ministers, followed by members of other so-called *asil* ('authentic', tribally noble) clans and then by members of other clans: in the period from 1962 to 1986 the representation of the Al Sabah family in these cabinets was 24 per cent, 45.3 per cent and 30.7 per cent respectively [Assiri and Al-Monoufi, 1988: 49–50]. Almost half the ministerial positions were held by members of just nine families. The Al Sabah family continued to maintain a monopoly over the six most sensitive ministries, while other ministries were allocated to members of other leading families, including those of the merchants, old and new, and sometimes to the odd representative of the Shi'i community (since 1975 the regime has maintained the practice of appointing one Shi'i minister in the cabinet) [for details see ibid.: 48–57].

In all small, oil-exporting Gulf states the oil boom changed the nature of political struggle and alliance. As Jill Crystal has illustrated, the new revenues had snapped the link binding the rulers to the merchants. The external nature of oil rents, the enclave nature of the industry and the size of the boom spared rulers the need to extract resources through taxation and repression, thus freeing the rulers from their historical, economically-based dependence on the merchants.

> Yet the merchants, especially in Kuwait, maintained an unexpectedly strong corporate sense and continued to function, economically and socially, as a collective body. They did not simply disappear as a class ... [T]he merchants were bought off by the State, as a class. State distributive policies not only favored the historical economic elites, but favored them through mechanisms that perpetuated their group identity. Revenues were distributed not only through transfers, but indirectly through the market. Even as the state expanded its economic activities, it preserved an enclave private sector, a playground for the merchants [Crystal, 1989: 430–31].

The amirs extracted a price for their economic largesse: political quiescence. The transition to a rentier political economy was accomplished in the smaller Gulf states through a tacit deal (pact) between the amir and the merchant families in which power was traded for wealth. In return for receiving a sizeable share of oil rents,the merchants by and large conceded their historical claim to participation in decision-making. This is interesting, as we shall see later in the book, in that "the merchants' withdrawal from public politics suggests that demands for participation are tied to extraction and the ability of those who mediate the extraction to influence the distribution of extracted wealth" [Crystal, 1989: 431–3; 1991: 9ff].

A parallel measure followed by the ruling families was to re-define and resurrect the tribal corps. We have seen earlier on that 'political tribalism' ('asha'iriyya or qabaliyya siyasiyya) not only transcends the technical and environmental requirements of nomadism, but is also frequently invented or manufactured. It is true that the ruling families, such as the Sabahs in Kuwait, were given considerable power by the British under the protectorate in order to counter the influence of the merchants who were suspected of harbouring non-conservative political views, and there is no doubt that British policies have favoured the 'bedouin-Shaikhs' over the 'merchant-Shaikhs' [cf. e.g. Rush, 1987: 103–21]. Implicit in the 'cliency' arrangement under the British was a system that encouraged the establishment of an executive administration controlled by members of the ruling family – a pattern of government which persisted throughout the independent existence of Kuwait, for example [Tétreault, 1991: 573–5]. Yet the real expansion of the political role of the ruling family was basically a post-oil-boom phenomenon:

> Until oil, the ruling families were not cohesive political institutions; rather, family members were largely excluded from the amir's decisions. With oil, successive amirs strengthened family networks to provide more reliable elite recruitment pools for the increasingly large and bureaucratic governments catalyzed by oil ... The most distant family claimants were eliminated, the less distant received increased allowances, the nearer claimants sinecures, and the closest relatives high state posts [Crystal, 1989: 435].

Numerous 'centres of power' and various clientelistic and quasi-corporatist groupings started to form within the expanding bureaucracy and some of these were of trading family backgrounds, since the traders were the first to educate their sons abroad:

> Old family loyalties have not disappeared with the acquisition of these technocratic skills. Indeed with oil, traditional networks and institutions ... have been reworked to handle new demands ... An unintended consequence of the bureaucratic expansion is that merchants, taken out of decision-making at one end, may be gradually re-entering through the back door of the bureaucracy. They control administrative fiefs with no necessary loyalty to the amir or his policies [Crystal, 1991: 179].

At the same time, the continuation of the recessionary pressures may tempt governments in the Gulf to try to withdraw from their direct economic and political role, now that largesse has become less easy to extend, and to hide behind a denser and more complex web of institutional arrangements that would keep direct opposition and resistance at bay. Governments may therefore "step out of a direct mediating role, and replace the distributive bureaucracy with institutions that would provide a forum for the aggregation of interests and the resolution of conflicting claims" [Chaudhry, 1992: 150–51]. As we shall see in subsequent chapters, there are certain moves in this direction, but they are by no means sufficiently determined.

In sum, one may suggest with reason that although the oil-exporting Gulf societies are becoming increasingly complex, as 'states' these countries remain lamentably weak. Strategically they are among the most vulnerable and militarily dependent in the world [cf. Ayubi, 1982b; Snider, 1988; Tétreault, 1991]. Economically, they have, with the oil boom, increased their 'relational' power *vis-à-vis* certain regional and international actors, but their 'structural' power within the international political economy as a whole remains extremely constrained.[8] Politically, these states are weak because their structures have 'expanded' but did not develop:

> Historically, finance and defence, extraction and coercion, have played a central role in state formation throughout the world. States built on oil revenues are unusual in that their administrative structures grew originally from the imperative to expend rather than extract wealth. Oil enabled rulers to bypass this historic extractive process. But in bypassing this, rulers also bypassed the process of elite cooptation and coercion that elsewhere accompanied extraction ... The Gulf states are stable, not because they are able to handle opposition, to coopt and coerce, but because they have not yet faced the challenges that produce resistance [Crystal, 1991: 178, 1989: 440–41].

To conclude, it is possible to say, borrowing Hirschman's [1970] terminology, that if the 'modern' state with its new boundaries in the Gulf has made it impossible for the dissenters to 'exit' (as they used to do in the past), it can still secure people's 'loyalty' through the rulers' oil-derived largesse, even while allowing very little 'voice'. It should follow from this that once the largesse dries up (as oil revenues decline) and since 'exit' is no longer available, the 'voice' is bound to get louder in the countries of Arabia, and 'loyalty' will indeed be put to a severe test.

NOTES

1. Conservatism is a difficult concept to define but may be broadly identified with a set of notions such as 'tradition', 'custom', 'family', 'community', 'group', 'organism', 'tissue', etc. Conservatives are not particularly fond of change and they base their indictment of the present frankly and unabashedly on models supplied directly by the past. Generally they are apprehensive of the 'masses' and tend to be anti-populist (which contrasts with the type previously described in Chapter 6) [cf. Nisbet, 1986].

2. Until recently, and with the partial exception of Kuwait, power was personally concentrated and inner fighting within princely families was rife. The situation had been ameliorated as a result of more power- and wealth-sharing within the ruling dynasties. As Ghassan Salame explains, of the nine Amirs who ruled Abu Dhabi from 1818, five were murdered, two were deposed and only two died a natural death. Of the eight rulers who governed Sharjah from 1803, two were murdered, three were deposed and three died natural deaths. The present ruler of Qatar deposed his uncle in 1972 and the present Sultan of Oman had deposed his own father two years earlier. There is no formula for succession to the throne. In Abu Dhabi it is only since 1818 that the throne has gone to the son of the preceding ruler. Five times the ruler was succeeded by his brother including the current head of the UAE, Shaikh Zayid, who replaced his brother Shakhbut in 1966. Twice the throne went to a nephew and once to a cousin. In Sharjah only on two occasions since 1803 was a son able to succeed his father. The throne went to a nephew on two other occasions and to a cousin on the two last ones. Up to 1958, no ruler in Dubai was able to pass his position to his son [Salame, 1984].

3. Such a strategy was followed in bureaucratic-authoritarian Arab regimes with, for example, the intelligentsia and with members of leftist (especially Marxist) movements. In the oligarchic-authoritarian countries, such a strategy has been followed with the 'ulama' and with the Wahhabi-nomadic forces of the Ikhwan in Saudi Arabia, and with the merchants in the Gulf.

4. Cf. Becker, 1987. He uses the term 'bonanza development' and applies it to other types of mineral-export-based economies such as that of Peru. For traditional oligarchic regimes, where the drive is more defensive than motivated by a developmentalist ideology, the term 'bonanza modern-isation' would be more appropriate.

5. If the 'tribe' (qabila) is the symbol of social status, the 'clan' ('ashira) is its organisational instrument (based on solidarity, intermarriage, etc.), and represents therefore the nearest approximation to a political function in the tribal society. The conventional derivation of social and political clannishness ('asha'iriyya) from the word 'ashira was therefore more technically accurate. Al-Naqib's [1987] preference for qabaliyya (given that qabila is much broader than 'ashira) is probably meant to imply that the modern Gulfian phenomenon functions on the macro level (i.e. the whole political system) and not only on the micro-level as tends to be the case with 'asha'iriyya [for anthropological details see Khuri, 1980 and 1991].

6. Not all tribes are incorporated in equal measure, however. In most Gulf countries a distinction is made between members of asil (authentic) tribes on the one hand and the less 'established' baisaris or khudairis, on the other. According to Fu'ad al-Khuri [1991: 16–20] and to Muhammad al-Rumaihi [1983: 248, 279–91], the distinction has an 'economic' origin related to a hierarchy of attending to camels or to sheep and cattle, or to the agricultural or urban pursuits of the tribes. Tribalism therefore is not the same as nomadism and one can indeed speak of agricultural or even 'urban tribes'.

7. Patricia Crone [1986] defines a tribe as "a descent group which constitutes a political community" and maintains that: "Whatever else a tribe may be, it is a stateless society." She argues that "it is only when the autonomous and self-sufficient nature of the [tribal] building blocks has been undermined that we have a state as opposed to a tribe" [pp. 50–51; emphasis in original]. It should be clear that we do not accept such a view – our articulatory approach can conceive of a situation where tribalism and bureaucracy can coexist.

8. I have illustrated elsewhere [Ayubi, 1982b] how the oil boom, and contrary to simplistic impressions, exacerbated the dependency of the oil-exporting countries. Following to a large extent the model suggested by Raymond Duvall [1978], I found that Saudi Arabia and the Gulf states had become more dependent according to four criteria: (i) degree of reliance on importation (becoming in the region of 65–75 per cent of their needs); (ii) ratio of exports to GNP (becoming 78–87 per cent in the case of Kuwait and Saudi Arabia respectively); (iii) commodity concentration of exports (oil represented 96 per cent of the value of Saudi exports, 76 per cent of Kuwait's and 96 per cent of the UAE's); and (iv) number of trading partners (the major partner – almost invariably the United States, Japan or the United Kingdom – representing 20 per cent or more

of the total exports or imports respectively) What is more, the main importing partner is often (as in the case of Saudi Arabia) different from the main exporting partners – which is a situation lending itself to a higher level of vulnerability. In addition, whereas imports from the Middle East and Africa had fallen, Saudi Arabia was importing 67.8 per cent, or more than two thirds, of all its needs from the West (including Japan).

CHAPTER EIGHT

Civil–Military Relations

The growth in military personnel and expenditures in most Arab countries represents an important aspect of the growth in the 'body and muscle' of the state in the Arab World. In the Middle East at large, the military establishment is both larger and more costly than it is anywhere else in the Third World. Within the Arab World more specifically, Egypt, Syria and Iraq have had some of the most sizeable armed forces in relation to their populations and some of the most expensive in relation to their GDP (cf. Table 8.3 below). In the Gulf countries, even though the absolute numbers of native military personnel are quite small, these countries allocate very substantial proportions of their budgets to military expenditures and some of them, notably Saudi Arabia, are in possession of very large arsenals (cf. Table 8.4 below).

One of the more serious aspects of military expenditures is represented by the fact that these continued to be extremely high during the 1980s, both in absolute terms and in comparison with other (social and economic) expenditures even when, in cases such as that of Egypt, the immediate military threats had started to subside and even when, in cases such as the Gulf countries, the oil revenues had begun to decline. Even as declared officially (and thus, conservatively) by the Arab governments themselves, the percentage of the GDP allocated to military expenditures up to the mid-1980s had remained very high indeed (see Table 8.1).

This is partly due to the fact that Middle Eastern countries are the largest importers of arms within the Third World. Indeed five Arab countries are among the top 21 Third World importers of arms, viz.: Iraq (importing 21.1 per cent of all Third World imports); Egypt (9.8 per cent); Syria (8.5 per cent); Saudi Arabia (7.2 per cent); and Libya (4.5 per cent) [N.I. Ahmad, 1991: 40].

Although military expenditures as a proportion of GDP had started to fall off from the mid-1980s, in line with a general international trend, it is not clear whether this pattern will continue, and the Arab and Middle Eastern countries – in any case – remain relatively the highest spenders on arms in the entire Third World (see Table 8.2).

Table 8.1 Military expenditure as a percentage of GDP in the Arab countries

Countries	1984	1985	1986	1987	Average
Algeria	1.8	1.7	1.7	(1.7)	1.7
Bahrain	3.2	3.5	4.4	(4.6)	3.9
Egypt	6.9	5.8	(6.1)	(6.2)	6.3
Iraq	(29.1)	(27.5)	–	–	28.3
Jordan	(13.1)	13.6	14.8	(15.0)	14.1
Kuwait	7.1	(8.6)	(8.4)	(7.3)	7.9
Libya	(14.5)	–	12.7	–	13.6
Morocco	4.7	5.4	5.1	(5.0)	5.0
Oman	22.9	20.8	25.7	(24.2)	23.4
Saudi Arabia	(20.9)	(21.8)	(21.8)	(22.7)	21.8
Somalia	2.7	1.8	(1.8)	–	2.0
Sudan	(3.2)	(3.6)	–	–	3.4
Syria	16.7	15.6	13.8	(9.3)	13.9
Tunisia	4.7	5.2	5.9	5.4	5.3
United Arab Emirates	7.0	(7.5)	(8.8)	(6.8)	7.5
Yemen (North)	12.7	10.3	9.5	–	10.8
Yemen (South)	(17.7)	(16.7)	–	–	17.2
Average	1.0	10.6	10.0	9.8	9.0

Source: The Unified Arab Economic Reports, 1986, 1987.

Table 8.2 Military expenditures as a percentage of GDP in developing countries, 1985–90

Developing countries	1985	1986	1987	1988	1989	1990
Asian developing	4.4	4.3	4.1	3.8	3.7	5
Middle East	11.0	9.7	9.6	9.2	8.7	8.1
North Africa	5.8	5.4	4.7	4.6	4.4	3.9
Sub-Saharan Africa	3.1	3.4	3.6	3.5	3.4	3.2
Western hemisphere	2.0	2.2	2.0	1.9	1.8	1.8

Source: IMF/World Bank, *Finance and Development*, December 1993, pp. 24–5.

The expansion in the size and cost of the military establishment in most Arab countries has naturally reflected itself in a growing political role for the military. But whereas in the earlier, less institutionalised stages, this role had tended to take the form of coups d'état and of military or semi-military governments, there has since been a gradual shift away from direct and open 'interventions' and the military is now increasingly inclined to operate through more subtle, and sometimes structural, intertwinings between civil and military networks.

Up to the end of the 1960s or so, the Arab World was notorious for the frequency and scope of the intervention of its military in politics. In the three decades from the 1940s to the 1960s, there were at least three dozen actual and abortive coups observed in the region [Be'eri, 1970; Haddad, 1971, 1973].

CAUSES FOR MILITARY INTERVENTION

Why the military has interfered so often in the politics of the contemporary Middle Eastern countries is a controversial question. Some writers have looked at the political culture and have gone back into history to suggest that Islamic tradition lays the foundation for a close link between fighters and politicians [Hurewitz, 1969: Ch. 2]. This is not particularly helpful with regard to the Arab World, since from the time of the Abbasids onwards Arab governments have tended to recruit various types of slave or mercenary soldiers (Mamluks, janissaries, etc.), so that the military function has gradually become rather removed from the indigenous population – apart, perhaps, from certain tribal or mountain communities.

Others have looked at social developments and have suggested that the disintegration of the traditional (especially the patrimonial) system in the Arab World creates a number of political 'gaps' that – owing to a particular weakness in the polity – can only be filled by the bureaucracy, and especially its military wing; this is the phenomenon that is often discussed under the title of 'praetorianism' [Huntington, 1971: 192–263; Perlmutter, 1970: 275ff]. This is made easier because armies, often consolidated or reorganised by colonial powers, had represented the leading structure of the state even prior to the assimilation of that state into the imperialist system. Furthermore, as soon as they gain their independence most developing countries, Arab ones included, set about expanding their armies, installing a system for military service (often conscription), and establishing their own military colleges (e.g. in 1932 in Iraq, 1936 in Egypt, and 1946 in Syria) [Hammad, 1987: 182–3].

Other observers have emphasised that in the developing countries' search for 'modernity', the military are more equipped than many other groups to assume a leading role since they are among the relatively more educated, organised and technologically oriented sectors of the society. This fact has made the military a most important segment of 'the New Middle Class' of many Middle Eastern countries [Halpern, 1963]. The military themselves have tended to justify their intervention either by citing nationalistic reasons (fighting colonialism or confronting a foreign threat), the need for national unity above ethnic and tribal lines, the need for order, discipline and organisation, or the need for prompt socio-economic reform.

If one is to exclude the 'culturalist' explanation for military intervention, then the last two sets of reasons may be better conceptualised as a correlate for the absence of institutional and sociological hegemony in the society. Such an absence lends itself (if one is to borrow Gramsci's terminology) to 'wars of manoeuvre' (i.e. attempts at capturing the state machine) rather than to 'wars of position' (i.e. projects for 'surrounding the state' with an alternative 'counter hegemony') [cf. Buci-Glucksmann, 1980: 242–334]. As Aijaz Ahmad puts it:

> in the absence of a hegemonic bourgeoisie, and in conditions where the politics of the masses are essentially insurrectionary, the peripheral state is based on transparent coercion and repression. The repressive apparatus thus has an inherent tendency in this situation to subsume the political apparatus as well. In the process, the armed forces tend to appropriate the bulk of the national revenues [Ahmad, 1985: 55].

They usually effect this appropriation in the name of 'development', and indeed various 'military regimes' have increasingly adopted a number of radical socio-economic reforms, or 'revolutions from above' as Gramsci and Trimberger call them [cf. Trimberger 1978], with Turkey, Egypt, Algeria, Syria and Iraq representing some of the most notable cases [Bill and Leiden, 1984: Ch. 6].

Some of the possible reasons for this kind of development are the following:[1] (a) the need to safeguard and consolidate the military regime's power base by reducing the influence of the established classes of the *ancien régime* (e.g. the landed aristocracy). The fact that in several cases many officers came from village or small-town backgrounds might also have added to the attraction in their eyes of policies such as land reform and the nationalisation of big business; (b) the need to consolidate comprehensive national independence in all spheres has often brought the officers into conflict with the 'commercial minorities' and into confrontation with international business which, in turn, has led to wider nationalisations in trade, finance and industry; and (c) the need to pre-empt the platforms of their political opponents of some of their most attractive elements. In Egypt, Syria, Iraq, Algeria and Sudan the military regimes have to one extent or another adopted (or adapted) certain elements of the political programmes of the Marxist opposition, while usually persecuting the Marxists themselves.

Is the policy orientation of military regimes to any discernible degree governed by the nature of the social background of the officers who climb to power? Marxist writings tend to suggest that since younger army officers were inclined to come from middle- and lower middle-class backgrounds, (i) they appeared to be quite confused and hesitant when it came to class and ideological choices, and (ii) whenever they made a choice it tended to reflect their petit-bourgeois background [cf. e.g. A. Abdel Malek, 1968].

This type of class analysis may be useful in analysing some holistic and macro-social phenomena, but is quite limited in helping one to understand, for example, how the same Free Officers' Movement in Egypt would produce persons such as Nasser, Sadat and Khalid Mohyi al-Din with their very different policy choices and ideological underpinnings. Available empirical evidence does not suggest any clear correlation between the socio-economic background or military rank of the officers who launch coups, and their ideological orientation (nationalist, socialist, fascist, etc.). When analysing the role of the military élite, class analysis will not suffice unless it is related to a theory of the state, to an examination of military organisation and to a study of 'bureaucratic politics' within the society [Owen, 1978: 70–72].

The characteristics that are perhaps most shared among military regimes are the ones imported from their military organisations: an inclination towards "standardization and uniformity of actions, attitudes, outlooks and behaviors" [Khuri, 1982: 18]. On the whole, officers in government tend to prefer a rather artificially induced conformity and to incline towards organisational solutions and technical 'fixes', since they are somewhat disdainful of ideological differences and intellectual improvisations. Ideology may be embraced, however, if it fulfils an integrative function. Therefore, 'minority-cultural settings' render the military (as in Syria and Iraq) most receptive to modern secular-nationalistic concepts. At another level, the military élite in Syria and Iraq has, since the late 1960s, followed a policy – intended to put an end to further coups – of building 'ideologised armies' by politicising the army so that it is made unequivocally partisan to the ruling Ba'th Party [Khuri, 1982: 17–21].

EXPLAINING THE DECLINE IN COUPS

More puzzling perhaps than the question of why the military interfere in politics is the question concerning the relative scarcity of military coups in the Arab World since the beginning of the 1970s. Are Middle Eastern societies no longer 'praetorian', or are the Middle Eastern military no longer the 'agents of change' that they were believed (or that they thought themselves) to be? Several tentative explanations can be suggested here.

To start with, the days are gone when power could be seized by mobilising a few tanks. Armies are now larger, stronger and far more diversified, in a way that makes a coup a more difficult endeavour. This is the outcome of several factors. The Middle East is now the recipient of over half of all arms deliveries to the Third World and of more than a quarter of all world arms shipments. Military expenditure in general has escalated in Middle Eastern countries: it grew tenfold in value from $4.7 billion in 1962 to $46.7 billion in 1980 (nearly three times the world average), while military manpower increased by 64 per cent from 1972 to 1982, rising from 2.1 million to 3.5 million [Stork and Paul, 1983: 5].

Whereas the international average for expenditure on education is 95.4 per cent of military expenditure and on health 78.1 per cent of it, in the Middle East the figures are 33.0 per cent for education and 17.5 per cent for health.

In 1982 Iraq's military expenditure represented 29.7 per cent of its GDP and was 9.2 times higher than its expenditure on education. Syria's military expenditure represented 13.7 per cent of its GDP and was 2.1 times as high as its expenditure on education and 33.5 per cent as high as its expenditure on health. Jordan's military expenditure represented 11.3 per cent of GDP and was 1.8 per cent as high as expenditure on education and 6.5 per cent as high as that on health. In the same year and for each 10,000 citizens, Iraq had 243 soldiers, 5.5 doctors and 100 teachers; Syria had 235 soldiers, 10.8 doctors and 104 teachers; Jordan had 293 soldiers, 10.8 doctors and 112 teachers. This compares with an international average of 55.7 soldiers, 7 doctors and 72 teachers. Thus while the numbers for doctors and teachers are comparable or superior to international averages, the percentages for soldiers far exceed the international averages [R.L. Sevard, 1985, cited in Salama, 1987a].

In addition, contemporary rulers are more careful and calculating in taking precautions against possible coups. The methods here vary: in Egypt, for example, higher professionalism of the armed forces was encouraged, especially after the potential coup by the 'Amir group that followed the 1967 defeat. Illustrative of the impact of this development is the fact that power shifted smoothly from Nasser to Sadat and then from Sadat to Mubarak. Both successors, however, were ex-military men and the use of the army for security and political purposes has been acknowledged (as for example in the food riots of January 1977 when the armed forces were actually utilised in various Egyptian cities). Egypt's military establishment, like that of Turkey, has therefore a basically behind-the-scenes role in the political process [Dekmejian, 1982].

In Syria and Iraq, the consolidation of politicised Ba'th-dominated armed forces, and the very tight security and intelligence arrangements (which are characteristic of many other military regimes), must be responsible – at least partly – for the continuation of the present regimes. There are differences between the two countries, however, in that in Syria, the military wing of the Ba'th seems to have overpowered the civilian wing, while in Iraq the civilian wing appears to retain the upper hand. The situation in Iraq was particularly interesting, since the government launched its war against Iran shortly after the presidency had changed hands from the soldier Hasan al-Bakr to the civilian Saddam Husain, and with an army that almost certainly contained a Shi'ite majority, i.e. co-religionists with the enemy [Ayubi, 1983].

Another development that possibly affected Egypt, Syria and Iraq (among others) was the introduction of Soviet concepts of military organisation and tactics. Some suggest that this could have helped the regimes to maintain tighter control over their officer corps because of the limited scope for initiative allowed by Soviet practices to those who actually command troops [Owen, 1978: n. 5].

In Saudi Arabia, a policy of balancing powers within the armed forces is consolidated, especially between the regular army (about 50,000 active military personnel) and the National Guard (20,000 to 30,000 members), with the first being more modern in recruitment patterns and stronger in its air forces, while the second is based on tribal representation and is stronger in ground troops. Tribal and ethnic balances are also observed in the army of Oman and the smaller forces of the Gulf states.

The situation is rather similar in Jordan. Here, and in an exact reversal of the urban-biased Ottoman pattern, the alliance is between the throne and the tribes. Ghassan Salama puts it this way:

> As in Iraq, the Jordanian army was, in the early days of the kingdom, composed of a few dozen non-Jordanian pro-Hashemites, and as in Iraq, most of these were soon to enter into the civilian life of the land. It was no accident that the builder of the Jordanian army, John Glubb, had worked for years among Iraqi tribes before he moved to Jordan. The same 'British logic' was to move with the man from Iraq to Jordan, a logic of balancing the cities (where the various political currents exist) with a parallel rural 'asabiyya that is external [to the civil/politicised society]. This was done by attracting tribal chiefs, appeasing them, and consolidating their influence over their tribes. Thus, instead of giving the city dwellers the military means through which they could increase their authority over the countryside, according to the Ottoman logic of the latter decades of the Sultanate, the objective became to create a sort of balance between the countryside and the city, through an alliance between the 'state' (i.e. the throne and its British protectors) and the countryside which is poorer and less organised and influential but – more importantly – less politicised [Salama, 1987a: 159–61].

Another possible reason for the decline in coups is the poor performance record of the military in power; this may act as a discouragement to other military elements contemplating the taking of power, since there is not the same kind of confidence that they will be able to do the job. Israel is now stronger and more entrenched than it ever was, the record of socio-economic development under the military has not been very impressive, nor have military regimes succeeded in broadening the bases for legitimacy and participation in their societies.

At the same time, the military élite as a whole (and not only the group that made the revolution) have often managed to benefit in socio-economic terms. The new social opportunities created for all military people may help dissuade potential aspirants from indulging in political adventure again. In Egypt a winning stratiocracy [Vatikiotis, 1968] had merged itself under Nasser with the rising technocracy, and under Sadat with the prospering commercial oligarchy [Ayubi, 1980]. Although the situation in Syria has not developed in as dramatic a fashion as in Egypt, there are indications that it is going in the same direction. One of the main reasons for this development being slower in Syria is the ethnic division in that country between the state bourgeoisie and the commercial bourgeoisie (to which later reference will be made), which has no equivalent in Egypt. The Syrian state bureaucracy (which features a disproportionately high percentage of minority groups) is intent on effecting the policy of economic liberalisation in a measured fashion and under strict control, so that it can be sure that as great as possible a share of that policy's fruits will accrue to its members rather than reach the traditional (hence majority Sunni) commercial bourgeoisie.

In both Algeria and Iraq the situation is somewhat different. Oil resources have enabled the élite to continue with the same developmental strategy (popularly known as Arab socialism) that in Egypt and Syria has faced great difficulties, and to maintain therefore the alliance between the militocracy and the technocracy in the two countries.

In addition to controlling the army, the bureaucracy, the single party and the mass media, the military in government have, as Owen comments, set out in most Arab countries to

> obtain a firm grip over all the centres of power and eliminate or neutralize all the rivals. At the same time they strengthened their position by another major expansion of the size and persuasiveness of the state apparatus, appropriating a still larger share of the national resources, further reducing the scope of the private sector and either destroying or incorporating any of the remaining centres of independent political activity. This program was carried out in cooperation with a class of state functionaries whose interest in a policy of state-directed economic management ran parallel to their own [Owen, 1978: 76–7].

The fact that such military regimes have stayed in power, even that many of them have incorporated their officers into a wider state bourgeoisie does not, however, suggest that they must rest on a solid base or on widespread mass support. "Why should one assume that a regime is an extension of a society's dominant forces if neither a popular revolution occurs nor a representative system is in effect?" Iliya Harik asks the rhetorical question and then offers by way of an answer the concept of a "strategic political minority", which:

> consists of a small number of individuals or groups who are so located in society as to possess control over the means of coercion and the decision-making apparatus, that is the civil administration and security forces. By virtue of wresting such strategic positions, they are able to extend their control to other vital instruments of rule, like patronage and the mass media [Harik, 1981: 69–74].

In short, therefore, a possible explanation as to why there are not as many coups now as there used to be is that the military élite in many countries has consolidated itself in power (a) by using more sophisticated security techniques, and (b) by integrating itself with segments of the ascending classes and élites: the technocracy and/or the state/commercial bourgeoisie.

The implication of the foregoing analysis is that it has become both difficult and/or undesirable for elements within the military establishment (or the whole 'state bourgeoisie' for that matter) to rebel against the status quo. One result is that in recent years practically all potential challenges to the status quo have had to come from groups that are basically peripheral to the state establishment, expressing themselves in religious terminology in protest against the modern-secular state and its ruling military, technocratic and state-capitalist élites.

In Egypt, the militant Islamic movements derive their main personnel from people who were made socially mobile by Nasserist policies, but deprived of concrete opportunities for social promotion because of the regime's changing economic policies. They are recent immigrants into the hurriedly constructed belts of urban degradation around Cairo and other major cities, highly educated but alarmed about their career prospects, or recently given symbolic state employment with no real professional content and with abysmal financial and working conditions [Ayubi, 1982/83]. The team that assassinated Sadat in October 1981 was made up of active and reserve military personnel, and the act was performed during a military parade celebrating what is regarded as a military victory. The grave symbolism and the political implications of all this cannot easily be mistaken.

In Saudi Arabia those who attempted the Mecca takeover in November 1979 were also, in some sense, marginal, especially if one compares them with protest groups that were characteristic of the 1960s in that country (for example, the Free Princes movement in the mid-1960s and the attempted military coup in 1969). By contrast, the relative marginality of the leaders of the Mecca siege can be detected from the unmistakable tribal and regional dimension characterising their group (an indication, among other things, that the rewards of the oil boom had been unevenly spread among the various tribes and regions). Around 70 per cent of the forty-one Saudi citizens who were executed in January 1980 were from the relatively underprivileged Najd region, and 25 per cent were from the less than friendly 'Utaiba tribe alone [Ayubi, 1982/83]. The fact that the leader of the takeover, Juhaiman al-'Utaiba, had been a member of the National Guard for some eighteen years before resigning to dedicate his efforts to religious activism would not have gone unnoticed by the Saudi authorities.

In Syria the Islamic protest movement is somewhat different. It is more traditional, in that it represents the social movement of classes and groups who have been gradually deprived of their privileges. Traditionally, the socially eminent and politically influential class was composed mainly of Sunni land-owners and merchants (and economically, to some extent, Orthodox Christian merchants). With the consolidation of a state economy under successive Ba'thist governments and coups (land reform, nationalised industries, etc.), socio-political eminence shifted, relatively speaking, from the Sunni landowning and merchant groups to the state bourgeoisie, including the armed forces, where minorities (especially 'Alawites and to some extent Druzes and Isma'ilis) are more proportionately represented. (In the case of the Christian community, the 'economic losses' they suffered were probably roughly compensated for by the political gains that accrued to them from an ardently 'secularist' regime.) It is not easy therefore, in today's Syria, to separate the Sunni–'Alawi sectarian conflict from the 'class' conflict between the traditional commercial bourgeoisie on the one hand, and the dominant state bourgeoisie (with a growing mercantile sector of its own) on the other [cf. Drysdale, 1982; Batatu, 1982].

In another type of development, some military regimes have recently adopted at least the 'language' of the Islamic movement: most noticeably Sudan; to some extent Libya but also, at the periphery of the Middle East, Pakistan. It is also interesting to note that one of the main nationalist and socialist figures of the 1960s, Ahmad Bin Bella of Algeria has continued – even though outside power – to propagate an Islamic line as the real hope for the Arab World.

In some ways, therefore, the political revival of Islam can be seen as a reaction to a crisis of the modern secular state in the Middle East, especially under its 'modernising' military leaders. While the ruling classes and élites have been holding tightly to power and defending their interests extremely vigorously, the 'state' that they run has not only failed to live up to its professed goal of mobilising and assimilating the less privileged classes into a new socio-economic order, but has also been unable to solve several long-term problems and short-term crises, and has continually failed to uphold the national honour after at least a quarter of a century of military defeats by Israel [Khoury, 1983a: 214–24; Ayubi, 1991a].

The present state of the military in the Arab World is rather paradoxical. While military regimes seem to be lasting longer in power, there is no evidence that this phenomenon corresponds necessarily to greater legitimacy, higher participation or improved performance; it may simply be a function of a stronger and more sophisticated control and coercion mechanism applied by a benefiting 'strategic minority' or, at best, a 'state bourgeoisie', accompanied by a certain element of inertia or helplessness on the part of the secular élite in general.

So the apparent quiescence on the surface may conceal a serious potential for upheaval, since there are no alternative channels for expression and change available to the various social and political forces. Even in Egypt, where the process of constitutional democratisation has been the most active among Arab countries, the political leadership was prepared to reverse the process at the slightest sign of strain. By not doing a good job, while at the same time denying others the right to try, the 'bureaucratic bourgeoisie' of the Arab countries (with its important military core) is making it almost inevitable that whatever change may occur will quite possibly come from groups that are peripheral to the secular state establishment – and in today's conditions, this means almost inevitably the militant Islamic movements.

Having surveyed the main issues in general comparative terms, we now turn to a more detailed consideration of two sets of case studies: first of the radical, populist republics, then of the conservative, kin-based monarchies.

THE RADICAL REPUBLICS AND THE MILITARY–INDUSTRIAL COMPLEX

Egypt, Iraq, Syria, and – to some extent or another, at one point or another – Sudan, North Yemen, Algeria and Libya, have been ruled by governments whose leaders came from the armed forces. Even Tunisia, where the small army had been politically marginalised by President Habib Bourguiba, this leader was ultimately deposed by Zain al-'Abidin Bin-'Ali, a former head of military intelligence, in November 1987. Egypt, Iraq and Syria, in particular, have had one of the highest military profiles in the whole of the Third World, as measured by defence expenditure and by the numbers of armed and paramilitary forces recruited (see Table 8.3).

Iraq has one of the earliest histories of military regimes (although in Egypt both the dynasty of Muhammad 'Ali and the nationalist rebellion of 'Urabi in the nineteenth century were initiated by military men). Iraq's monarchy, which started to gain a certain measure of internal rule and political legitimacy in 1930, witnessed its first coup (some say the first in the Arab World) in 1936, under the leadership of Bakr Sidqi. The new government, still functioning under the monarchy and the constitution, declared a few reforms, but Sidqi was soon killed and confusion in military/civil relations ensued from 1937 to 1941. Although the civilian premier, Nuri al-Sa'id, had been the most influential politician from 1938 to 1958, the military, as represented by M. 'Abd al-Ilah, the Crown regent, exercised an unmistakeable influence on politics. The military impact reached a higher level in 1941 during Rashid 'Ali al-Gilani's short 'nationalistic' episode in power, which was brought to an end when British troops defeated the Iraqi army and paved the way for the return of Nuri al-Sa'id [cf. Be'eri, 1971; Batatu, 1978]. However, both he and King Faisal were to be swept aside in the fairly violent coup of July 1958.

'Abd al-Karim Qasim and 'Abd al-Salam 'Arif were the main leaders of the 1958 'revolution': initially Qasim, the populist orator, was uppermost but his over-reliance on the Communists encouraged the increasingly marginalised 'Arif to overthrow Qasim in favour of the establishment by him and his brother 'Abd al-Rahman (who succeeded him) of a more 'nationalist' (though not exclusively Ba'thist) orientation. Qasim's social reforms in favour of the middle and lower classes and against the landed classes were basically continued under the 'Arifs, but the Communist/Ba'thist rift that intensified during the Qasim/'Arif years had not really subsided.

Table 8.3 Military profile of Egypt, Iraq and Syria, 1989

Egypt

GDP	1986/87 £E44.05 bn ($62.94 bn)
Defence expenditure	1988/89 £E3.95 bn ($ 5.64 bn)
	1989/90 £E4.70 bn ($ 6.80 bn)
Total armed forces	
Active	448,000 (c. 250,000 conscripts)
Terms of service	3 years (selective)
Reserves	604,000; of which: Army 500,000
	Navy 14,000
	Airforce 20,000
	Air Defence 70,000
Paramilitary	
Coastguard	2,000
Central Security Forces	300,000
National Guard	60,000
Frontier Corps	12,000

Iraq

GDP	1987 est. ID12.144 bn ($39.061 bn)
	1988 est. ID14.000 bn ($45.000 bn)
Defence expenditure	1987 est. ID4.35 bn ($13.990 bn)
Total armed forces	
Active	100,000,000
Terms of service	21–24 months
Reserves	People's Army (paramilitary) est. 850,000
Paramilitary	
Frontier Guards	—
Security Forces	4,800

Syria

GDP	1987 £S126.33 bn ($32.19 bn)
	1988 est. £S203.39 bn ($18.12 bn) [devalued]
Defence Budget	1988 est. £S18.0 bn ($ 1.60 bn)
	1989 est. £S28.0 bn ($ 2.49 bn)
Total armed forces	
Active	404,000
Terms	conscription 30 months
Reserves	400,000; of which: Army 392,000 active
	Navy 8,000
Forces Abroad	30,000 (Lebanon)
Paramilitary	
Republican Guard	10,000
Desert Guard (Frontier)	1,800
Gendarmerie	8,000
Baath Party Workers' Militia (People's Army)	

Source: International Institute of Strategic Studies (IISS), *The Military Balance 1989–90*, London: Brassey's, 1989.

The Ba'thists went about reorganising themselves in a tightly disciplined manner, trying to ensure as much control over as many army officers as possible. When they took over power in 1968, the military and the civilian Ba'thists appeared to be in perfect coordination. They immediately set their sights on the task of political control and institution-building and, making use of the now more accessible oil revenues, on expanding social services to most middle and lower strata. At the same time, the process of purging the army of any suspected elements and of creating a purely 'ideological army' *(Al-Jaish al-'aqa'idi)* was all but completed [Abbas, 1986: 215ff]. By the time the second man, the civilian Saddam Husain, took over from the first man, General Hasan al-Bakr, in 1979, the army had been most thoroughly Ba'thised and the party most vigorously 'police-ised' so that no real threat to the new security-state could be expected either from the military or from the ideologues [for details see Al-Khalil, 1991: Ch. 1].

In Syria coups started to recur soon after the country had gained its in-dependence and had spent some time enjoying a pseudo-parliamentary system. In March 1949 Husni al-Za'im led a coup against the established regime of notables which had continued to rule after independence in 1946, but he was soon overthrown in another coup a few months later, led by Sami al-Hinnawi, himself to be overturned in the same year by Colonel Adib al-Shishakli, who then ruled until 1954. From then until 1958 there was another short semi-parliamentary spell under Shukri al-Quwwatli, a traditional leader who, aware of Syria's domestic and regional vulnerabilities, 'joined' Syria to Egypt in the United Arab Republic (1958–61). This in its turn was a period of Egyptian military domination that was ended by way of another military coup in alliance with the relatively powerful commercial bourgeoisie.

Eventually the Ba'thist officers assumed the upper hand and in 1963 in-itiated a period of party/military rule. By this time, and especially under the impact of 'Arabist' policies during the union with Egypt, the high representa-tion of minorities in the armed forces (which was a direct legacy from French Mandate policies) had declined for most communities, except for the Alawites whose numbers had actually grown. A more socially radical wing of the Ba'th (led by Salah Jadid and his party apparatchiks) came to the fore with yet another coup in 1966. But this group was eased aside in 1970 by another Ba'thist army officer, Hafiz al-Asad – who was more inclined towards the 'army side' – and he continues in power to the time of this writing, with the emphasis being placed on state-building and 'pragmatic' policies although the regime continues to count on the mobilised peasants and on minoritarian groups [Hinnebusch, 1982].

As Ghassan Salama explains:

> the defeat of the ideologues of the Ba'th, 'Aflaq, Bitar and their cohorts, from 1966 on, signalled a victory for the officers over the civilians, for pragmatism over utopia, for the countryside over the city, for a minority over a makeshift

army of majority and minorities, and for the military over the party which from that time on would become a means for propaganda and mobilisation in the hands of the military, or at least a group of them [Salama, 1987a: 162–6].

This became clear with the 1970 'corrective movement', which overcame the inclination to get carried away with rhetoric and focused attention on the concrete substance of power. From that time on, the military establishment was subjected to two more or less successful parallel policies: one aiming at improving its combative capability (which was manifested in the 1973 war and in Lebanon), and the other at preventing it from stepping outside the pre-scribed political line (by securing sensitive positions for relatives and friends and by creating parallel paramilitary forces such as the presidential guard and *saraya al-difa'*).

Egypt's coup of July 1952 under the symbolic patronage of General Nagib and the real leadership of Colonel Nasser has been the subject of so many studies that there is very little point in trying to recount the story here. The most important feature was the convergence between the purely professional grievances of the military combined with a broader social and political impasse (for example, the huge inequalities, especially with regard to land ownership, the futility of political parties, the presence of British troops, the corruption of the monarchy, etc.). The Free Officers were mainly middle ranking and of largely middle-class background (mostly urban with recent rural background), with a scattering of well-to-do as well as petty bourgeois elements. It has been suggested that they might have been acting as the spearhead of a nascent national bourgeoisie whose social ascent was blocked by the rigidity and corruption of the system. Once in power, however, the military were not always successful in reconciling the interests of the bourgeoisie with the objectives and 'logic' of the state as such [compare Hussein, 1973]. Increasingly they had to rely largely on the public bureaucracy as a control apparatus, on a populist base of support that hinged on the construction of modern industry and the provision of social welfare, and on a discourse of national liberation and enhanced international status.

The periods before and after the 1967 Arab–Israeli war offer striking con-trasts when we examine the impact of the military on policy-making in Egypt [the following discussion on Egypt draws upon Ayubi 1991b, Ch. 11]. Following the 1952 coup and until the Six Day War there were two power centres, not one, at the top level of the state: President Nasser, whose main sphere of influence was the civil administration and the 'masses'; and Field Marshal Amer, whose chief domain was the armed forces and a whole network of organisations and activities that were attached to them.

The military had managed in a number of ways to form a 'stratiocracy' whereby they occupied over one-third of all the top political posts during the Nasserist era, and had in addition managed to be highly represented within the higher echelons of the diplomatic service, security and local government, the Arab Socialist Union and the economic public sector. In addition, Amer acquired for himself a varied collection of posts ranging from that of being supervisor of the Sufi orders and head of the federation of football clubs to being in charge of the Nuclear Power Organisation, the National Research Centre, the Public Transportation Organisation and the 'Higher Commission for the Liquidation of Feudalism' [cf. Ayubi, 1989b: 113–19 and refs cited; Hammad, 1990: 29–50].

Although the relationship between the two leaders and their organisational networks appeared sufficiently cordial on the surface, it was only with the disaster of 1967 that the full measure of the discord between the two power and decision centres became publicly known. Many analysts now consider that this power duality was one of the major factors underlying several of the poor decisions that were made during those years; for example in the 1956 Suez crisis, during the 1958–61 period of unity with Syria, and particularly during the 1967 war with Israel [Imam, 1985]. Only after that crushing defeat and Amer's subsequent 'suicide' could the professionalism of the army be restored and a new cooperative relationship between the political and the military leadership be established. Consequently it was made possible for the launching of the 1973 war to be based on a most lengthy and extensive process of collective consultation and institutional decision-making that involved both the political and the military leadership [cf. Korany, 1984: 47–73].

Professionalisation of the armed forces does not, however, mean that their inclination towards certain types of foreign policy can be ignored. Thus it is generally believed that one of the reasons behind the expulsion of the Soviet experts from Egypt in 1972 was the officers' impatience with the patronising attitude of the Soviets, combined with the desire that any military success in the coming war with Israel should be attributed to the Egyptian army and not to its Soviet advisers. Following the October 1973 war, Sadat made sure that the military establishment was involved in all stages of the peace process with Israel; for example both General Gamasi and General Hasan-'Ali played particularly prominent roles in the disengagement negotiations and in the peace talks respectively [cf. 'Ali, 1986].

However, the foreign policy orientation of the armed forces had to be reversed under Sadat; in the process it acquired a decidedly pro-American slant in Middle Eastern and African affairs and, according to one specialist, "there exists considerable evidence that the new anti-communist role of the military was not well received either by the high command or by many lower echelon officers" [Dekmejian, 1983: 203]. Even after the peace moves of Camp David the Egyptian armed forces continued to grow. Active forces increased from 298,000 in 1975 to 460,000 in 1984, and dropped only marginally to 448,000 in 1988/89, while the defence budget consistently represented around 8.5 per cent of the country's GDP throughout the 1980s [IISS, 1989]. After President Mubarak came to power in 1981 the military establishment at large continued to expand its influence, and the armed forces are now financially semi-autonomous, possessing a significant 'economic wing' and a strong and rapidly developing arms industry. The political influence of the military, both domestically and externally, is also in the ascendant. However, there appear to be no obvious indications that the military would in the immediate future want to stage any direct takeover of power [cf. Ayubi, 1988b].

In spite of the 1979 peace treaty with Israel and the widely held expectation that the treaty would lead to a reduction in the country's military expenditure, Field Marshal 'Abd al-Halim Abu Ghazala, an ambitious and somewhat controversial figure, managed to persuade the politicians to keep the military budget at its high level. During this period, military expenditure became an issue for heated debate, although the discussions were lamentably lacking in supporting figures. The way the military have calculated it, there was a 'damaging reduction' in expenditure between 1975 and 1981, followed by another reduction in 1985/86; the prospect that this latter reduction was to be made even larger was, according to some reports, the reason behind the hasty resignation of the 'Ali Lutfi cabinet in 1986. The armed forces have succeeded in their aim of maintaining military expenditure at such high levels, and have justified such expenditure partly by choosing to play up the potential threat to Egypt's security from Libya, and the uncertain prospects caused by the turmoil in the Gulf, and partly by making frequent references to the 'success stories' of the expanding arms industry and of the growing economic and development-mental role that the armed forces have increasingly played in the society.

The political influence of the military has remained quite significant since the revolution of 1952 – Egypt's four presidents since that date have all been army officers. Sadat tried to reduce the political role of the military by civilian-ising the Egyptian cabinets and by excluding the military from its position as one of the components of the corporatist formula of Nasserism known as the 'alliance of the working forces of the people'. The military thus became prohibited from political and party activities. However, as Sadat had to call on the armed forces in 1977 to quell the extensive food riots it was inevitable that the army's role as a political actor would eventually be reasserted. Indeed, under Sadat – and constitutional prohibition notwithstanding – Field Marshal Abu Ghazala, who was commander of the armed forces until his downfall in spring 1989, was a member of the Politburo of the ruling National Democratic Party. Although President Mubarak removed him from this position in 1984, he continued to attend the general congress of the ruling party and to address it on military and security affairs. Mubarak, who has neither the charisma of Nasser nor the flamboyance of Sadat, has permitted only a minimum of structural freedom for the civilian opposition, and has thus, perhaps inadvert-ently, allowed a military which is no longer occupied with external hostilities to direct some of its attention to the civilian domain.

It was not always easy in the late 1980s to draw the line between the growing political role of the Egyptian army at large and the apparent political ambitions of its dynamic ex-commander Abu Ghazala, since both appeared to have been on the ascent simultaneously. The growing political clout of the military is demonstrated by the numerous appointments of army officers as provincial governors, the extensive jurisdiction of the military tribunal, and the military's pressure to merge the local motor industry with the American General Motors Company (against the advice of the Ministry of Industry) [for details see Springborg, 1987: 10–11]. In addition, the military establishment enjoys a considerable degree of autonomy from the rest of the state; its budgetary allocation, for example, is not itemised, nor is it subjected to the scrutiny of the Central Auditing Agency. It is also significant that the role of the army and the role of the police are regarded by the military command as complementing each other in the area of internal security, with the army assuming the upper hand. This was made very apparent, for instance, during and after the events of February 1986 when the security police staged a mutiny which was put down by the armed forces, and it has added tremendously to the clout of the military. The objectives of the Egyptian armed forces, as pronounced by its leaderships, included such things as 'the protection of constitutional legitimacy' and 'combating terrorism', which many people regard as being of a domestic political nature. Needless to say, the opposition has been very critical of all such objectives, particularly because of what they see as the almost complete absence of any mention of Israel as being a potential threat to the country's security.

Regionally and internationally, the army has on a general level also assumed a major role in defining the objectives and orientations of the country's 'national security' and the nature of its foreign alliances. Both areas remain controversial. In particular, the excessive dependence on the United States – and to a lesser extent on France and Britain – as suppliers of arms, and the continuation of the joint American–Egyptian military manoeuvres while the United States remained so closely wedded to the Israeli position, have been subject to serious criticisms. Nor was the Egyptian role in support of the Western alliance in the Gulf war of 1990/91 entirely immune to nationalist and Islamist criticism.

Given this strong influence of the army, is the military likely to take over political power in a direct way? A widespread Egyptian theory is that they need not take over power because they are already there – the top command, that is to say. As for lower-ranking officers, they would find such a proposition almost impossible in an army that is now so large and diffused both organisationally and geographically [Abdalla, 1988: 1464–6].

There is little at the present time to suggest that the top command is interested in, or that the middle ranks are capable of, taking over political power. However, should an Islamic-coloured popular uprising take place as a result of the accumulating economic and social difficulties, the likelihood of military intervention will become much greater. Such intervention might return power to the civilian government as it did in 1977 and 1986. Yet there are two other possibilities that cannot be excluded: one is that the high command would take over power under the pretence of restoring law and order (possibly adopting an Islamic stance in the Pakistan style), while alternatively, a deal could be struck between segments of the military and segments of the Islamic movement to run the country jointly. There is no doubt that the military is expanding both its economic domain and its political power. While this is a very significant development that could eventually bring about important political and strategic changes, current attitudes prevailing among the top command and the middle ranks indicate a low probability for direct intervention. Of course, an Islamic-oriented uprising might produce other outcomes altogether.

The military–industrial complex

The growth in military–industrial connections (sometimes including the development of a military industry) is noticeable in many countries of the Arab World. The military may no longer have to influence politics in a direct, 'raw' way by taking over power, but they remain influential, albeit in more subtle ways, as the society becomes institutionally and economically more complex. "With the development of military–industrial complexes, the military's influence over policy is becoming more diffuse, broadly based and substantive. Officers do not have to be in cabinets or parliaments nor stage coups d'etat to have significant influence over important economic and political decisions" [Bill and Springborg, 1990: 268ff].

Arms production in the Middle East at large has grown most obviously: whereas it was quite insignificant at the end of the Second World War, it amounted to some $4 billion in 1987 and continues to rise rapidly. As noted above, of the 23 Third World countries that produce significant quantities of arms, five are in the Middle East. In the Arab World Egypt is a major arms producer, Iraq, Algeria and Syria are significant producers, and Saudi Arabia, Jordan, Morocco, Sudan and Tunisia are manufacturers of munitions and small arms [cf. Stork, 1987: 12; Bill and Springborg, 1990: 269; N.I Ahmad, 1991: 46–8].

A parallel development is that of the 'economic wing' of the army, which has been growing in size and expanding into the civilian economy. In Egypt, Syria, Iraq and Sudan, army officers now perform a wide variety of economic, technical and social roles, either on their own or in collaboration with the local private sector or with multinational corporations. Indeed, in Syria the symbiosis between the military élite and the commercial bourgeoisie (traditional and new) has developed sufficiently strongly to justify talk of a 'military-commercial complex' in that country [Hinnebusch, 1993: 252 and refs cited].

The Egyptian arms industry was one of the earliest, having started up under Nasser in the 1950s. Even so, it was not until the 1970s that a major project was established in cooperation with Arab finance: created in 1975 with contributions from Saudi Arabia, Qatar and the UAE, this project was embodied as the Arab Industrialisation Authority [for details see Nasif, 1985: 36–60]. Following Egypt's separate peace treaty with Israel in 1979, these three countries withdrew their support, after which Egypt continued on her own, establishing a number of joint projects especially with European countries. Production was given a boost in the 1980s, not only in order to fill the gap in the country's own armament but also with the aim of creating a profitable export-oriented industry.

It is believed that between 50 and 60 per cent of the requirements of the Egyptian armed forces are now satisfied by local production. Where exports are concerned, Iraq was a major buyer, as to some extent was Sudan. Exports to these countries must have declined in recent years, however. Other Arab countries, including Jordan, Somalia, Morocco and Tunisia, are believed to be buying Egyptian arms, while there is considerable potential for arms purchases in the African continent, especially from countries such as Zaire and Kenya, as well as in some South East Asian countries [CPSS, 1986, 1987, 1988]. Total sales from the export of arms were estimated in the mid-1980s to be between $1 and $2 billion per annum. If the latter figure is taken as the more accurate, then it would place Egypt as the sixth largest arms exporter in the Third World. Following the re-establishing of diplomatic relations with most Arab countries in the late 1980s, the potential for increased sales, and even for a resumption of joint investment in military industries with countries in the Gulf, was considerably increased. This was enhanced by the activities of the various military delegations and military exhibitions that were sent from Egypt to various Gulf countries in 1987, and as a step in this direction it was reported that Egypt had already received financial aid from the Gulf countries to assist in the repayment of some of the country's large military debts (military imports are estimated at around $4 billion a year).

The Arab Industrialisation Authority was also reorganised in 1987, a new management was appointed, and discussions were held concerning the possibility that the Gulf countries would resume their contributions to it. The Authority is currently believed to employ some 15,000 Egyptian workers, out of a total number of 85,000 employees in the arms industry. The Egyptian arms exhibition mounted at the end of 1987 attracted considerable attention from various countries, including some Gulf states, and further strengthened the possibility of renewing the formal involvement of Gulf countries in financing Egypt's arms industry at large.

The 'economic wing' of the Egyptian army grew significantly throughout the 1980s. In 1978 a National Service Projects Organisation (NSPO) was created and in 1981 a Military Organisation for Civil Projects was established, engaging itself in various types of public works such as the construction of roads and bridges, telecommunications networks, and other engineering projects. The army is now involved in all kinds of civilian activities that include the building of railways, flyovers, irrigation canals and water pipelines, transport and communications networks, and a wide range of factories, laboratories, clinics and training centres. Other activities include the running of poultry batteries and a large set-up of bakeries and other projects for 'food security', and at one point even extended to the rather un-military task of organising opera performances! This expansion by the armed forces into civilian activities has been controversial, with strong arguments launched both in favour of and against it. Whatever its 'developmental' contribution may be, it has certainly benefited the military as a social stratum. One of the main vehicles for achieving this expansion has been through the selling, leasing or utilisation of the vast areas of land that fall under the control of the armed forces. Another is the extensive network of housing facilities, holiday complexes and consumer 'cooperatives' that cater exclusively for the military and their families. Such activities on the part of the army may have "engendered a class of military entrepreneurs whose loyalties are ambiguous, to say the least, and whose professional links are more likely to be with other entrepreneurs than with the army they serve" [Owen, 1987: 8].

Field Marshal 'Abd al-Halim Abu Ghazala was credited with a unique role in developing the new branch of the military industry, following his appointment in 1981 to the Defence Ministry (which, of course, has its own conventional military workshops). Even so, he was not the only active force behind military industrialisation, since there is a separate ministry for Military Production (also with its own military factories) [see interview with the Minister for Military Production, *Al-Siyasa*, 17 December 1987]. In addition there is also the semi-autonomous Arab Industrialisation Authority. In fact the plan to go for extensive military industrialisation preceded Abu Ghazala (and has continued after him), and most probably represented a strategic political decision of the Egyptian state. But Abu Ghazala was particularly assertive in pursuing this policy, even – according to some reports – to the extent of being personally involved in the attempt to smuggle materials out of the United States for use in arms manufacture (over which incident an Egyptian was arrested in the US in 1988). The removal of Abu Ghazala from the Defence Ministry in spring 1989 was not likely to curb the build-up of the Egyptian arms industry in any serious way, since this appeared by now to have become a long-term policy of the Egyptian regime.

By contrast there is likely to be increasing popular and political pressure on the government to contain the expanding role of the military establishment in the economic sphere, another of Abu Ghazala's policies. Various circles have criticised in particular the still large military budget over which there is no parliamentary scrutiny, and the involvement of the army in a whole range

of housing, construction, food and other industries. Because these are not
foreign currency-earning activities, the pressure aimed at curbing them may
eventually meet with more success.

Syria, Iraq and Sudan have also witnessed an expansion in the economic
role of their military establishments, represented in particular by the activities
of Mu'assasat al-Iskan al-'Askari (Milihouse) and its 'sisters' in Syria,[2] the
Military Industries Commission and its successor, the Ministry of Industry
and Military Production, in Iraq, and the Military Economic Corporations in
Sudan and in Yemen [cf. Picard, 1988: 136–9; M. Farouk-Sluglett and P.
Sluglett, 1990: 21; Bienen and Moore, 1987: 489–516]. Bill and Springborg
have succinctly summarised the situation as follows:

> In Syria, Iraq, and Sudan, as in Egypt, military officers now perform a wide
> variety of economic roles, many in association with local private sector firms or
> multinational corporations. Syria's military, although supporting a comparatively
> small arms industry, operates the largest construction business in the country,
> produces and processes large quantities of food, and manages a nationwide chain
> of retail outlets. The Iraqi military controls the Military Industries Commission,
> which 'runs a high-technology network making heavy equipment for military
> and civilian use – including Iraq's Al Hussein missile which it used to bombard
> Iran during the war of the cities'. Sudan's Military Economic Corporations,
> which operated in the final years of the Numairi era, became the largest business
> conglomerate in the country, concentrating particularly in importation and
> marketing. An estimated 80 percent of its trade was conducted with the private
> sector. In these and other Arab countries, officers are rapidly developing into a
> visible and powerful economic elite [Bill and Springborg, 1990: 272 and refs
> cited].

Prospects and comparisons

It can be seen from the previous discussion that somewhat similar developments have characterised civil–military relations in the populist republics in
recent years. The Egyptian pattern has been marked out by the following
factors. There has been progressive 'civilianisation' of cabinets and of other
political and administrative organisations, combined with increased emphasis
on professionalism within the armed forces and growing efforts aimed at
depoliticising the military, in addition to the enforcement of civilian control
over the army. At the same time, the large size and the substantial budget of
the armed forces have both been maintained, while – in addition to the
conventional 'combatant' forces – an 'economic wing' of the army has
emerged, which is involved not only in military industries but also in extensive
public works and various economic activities [for comparisons with other Arab
armies see Owen, 1987].

Similar developments, albeit on a smaller scale, have taken place in other
Arab countries such as Syria and Iraq [cf. Hammad, 1987: 177–200]. The
combative ability of the Syrian army in 1982 and of the Iraqi army in the

Iran–Iraq war and in the Gulf conflict of 1991 appear to attest to a reasonable level of operational effectiveness and possibly 'professionalism'. Yet the hostilities in which these two countries have continued to be engaged might to some extent have slowed the pace of such 'Egyptian-style' developments, especially with regard to the economic activity of the army. The Syrian, Iraqi and Sudanese armed forces have indeed been involved on a significant scale in military and civilian housing projects and in other general economic activities. The pattern of civil–military relations in such countries has become so complex in recent years that one should perhaps no longer speak simply of 'the role of the military in politics' but rather – as suggested by Roger Owen – of "the place of the army within the state" [Owen, 1987: 1].

What are the likely orientations for civil–military relations in Egypt? Studies from the 'Latin American school', especially those by Guillermo O'Donnell, suggest the existence in relatively diversified economies of a tendency towards 'bureaucratic-authoritarianism', with a major involvement by the military, as a response to the crisis that tends to coincide with the 'exhaustion' of the 'easy stage' of modernisation and industrialisation (which is usually based on import-substitution and populist policies). Evidence has been produced to substantiate this theory with regard to Argentina and Brazil [O'Donnell, 1973, 1977], and others have found the theory applicable to Chile, South Korea, Turkey and other countries [e.g. Clapham, 1985: Ch. 7]. Sometimes a military intervention of the type that S. Huntington terms a 'veto-type' coup [Huntington, 1971: Ch. 4] may initiate or consolidate this phase; as for example with the Chilean (1973) and the Argentinian (1976) coups.

Conditions within the post-populist system of Egypt seem to be indicating movement in a direction that does not preclude such a possibility, except that in this case the situation is being ameliorated by the availability of 'first-hand' but mainly of 'second-hand' oil money (by way of remittances from Egyptians working in the Gulf).[3] The availability of external 'rents' has also been an important ameliorating factor in Syria: from oil, remittances and aid, but also from the large quasi-illicit 'traders' with and or via a Lebanon that is closely subjected to Syrian supremacy.

During the 'easy stage' of (import-substitution) industrialisation, most regimes can follow 'populist' policies of one kind or another based on 'inclusionary' measures that tend to bring the 'popular classes' (mainly the intelligentsia and the skilled workers) into the economic and to some extent the political arena. When this phase reaches a certain 'ceiling' and exhausts its potential, a 'bureaucratic-authoritarian' regime may be expected to emerge that would follow basically 'exclusionary' policies towards the 'popular classes' in an attempt to constrain their demands. Such a regime is often based on an alliance between the military-technocracy and the upper bourgeoisie in co-operation with (subordination to) international capital. It is perhaps possible to detect some indications that such an alliance may be forming in Egypt.

One may also suspect that the Algerian military/party/technocracy compound had taken their policies of 'industrial deepening' seriously enough to start moving the regime from a populist towards a 'military-bureaucratic' direction. The popular reaction was particularly strong (with demonstrations, strikes, riots, etc.) temporarily forcing the regime to concede certain 'democratic' measures at the hands of Shazli Bin Jadid. But ultimately the conflict was to split the 'political bloc' into a bureaucratic-authoritarian wing, which is now in government, and a more populist wing that operates under the name of the Islamic movement.

Robert Springborg argues that Egypt has gone the farthest in the direction of developing a military/industry alliance. According to him the General Motors case and its component deals "embodied the alliance of the military and the bourgeoisie and its subordination to international capital". The military seem to perceive the public sector as being incompetent. They have developed an autonomous capability, its management concentrated in the NSPO, its manpower drawn from the ranks of conscripts and supplementary technical expertise solicited from various branches of the armed forces:

> The system now being established rests on the principle of farming out patronage to the private sector which, like its public sector predecessor, is to be the military's junior partner in these activities ... The military lets tenders to the private sector, domestic and foreign, worth hundreds of millions annually for its ventures into non-military areas. It actively seeks arrangements for military technicians to gain access to advanced technologies found in the private sector, such as food production and processing. These developments suggest the possible emergence of a Latin-American style corporate state based on an alliance of the military with the upper bourgeoisie [Springborg, 1987: 10, 14, 15].

Was President Mubarak endeavouring to arrest such a possible development when he removed Field Marshal Abu Ghazala in 1989? It may perhaps have been so, although it seems to me that the Egyptian upper bourgeoisie has not yet reached a level that is sufficiently high and sufficiently assertive to warrant such a direct intervention by the military on their behalf. Nor is the situation any riper for such a development in any of the other Arab populist republics with recent 'military interventions'.

THE CONSERVATIVE MONARCHIES AND THE MILITARY– TRIBAL COMPLEX

Although Saudi Arabia has had its tribal armed men from the early days of trying to consolidate the state, as well as a more professional army that was meant to keep at bay the republican thrust emanating from Yemen and Egypt in the 1960s, the real build-up of military capability was not to take shape in Saudi Arabia and the Gulf countries until after the oil boom in the 1970s and 1980s, when huge funds were allocated to that purpose. Yet even as the largest

Table 8.4 Military profile of Saudi Arabia, Kuwait and UAE, 1989

Saudi Arabia	
GDP	1987 SR267.6 bn ($71.146 bn)
	1988 est. SR274.8 bn ($73.385 bn)
Defence budget	1988 SR50.8 bn ($13.57 bn)
	1989 est. SR55.0 bn ($14.69 bn)
Paramilitary	
National Guard	56,000:
(Min. of Interior)	(10,000 active; 20,000 reserve; 26,000 tribal levies)
Frontier Force	8,500
Kuwait	
Armed forces	
Active	20,000–30,000 (conscription 2 years; university students 1 year)
United Arab Emirates	
Armed forces	
Active	43,000 (perhaps 30% expatriate)

Source: IISS, 1989, ibid.

of the Gulf states, Saudi Arabia is not really militarily powerful. All the more so, of course, for the smaller Gulf countries such as Kuwait or the United Arab Emirates (Table 8.4).

Saudi Arabia has a huge area (some 830,000 square miles) but a small population (of about 6 million to 8 million including 1.5 million to 2 million foreigners), and sits on top of some 26.6 per cent of the world's proven oil reserves. To protect these resources, the Saudis have been spending an estimated $20 billion annually on defence, which represents nearly one quarter of their annual GNP [Mansur, 1980: 48ff]. Yet the Saudis seem to have made only limited and slow progress in improving their military effectiveness. One reason is that until recently most defence expenditures have gone to developing the training capabilities, bases and infrastructure, rather than actual fighting power. About 50 per cent goes to construction, 30 per cent is spent on training, and only 20 per cent on hardware.

The territorial army is small by any standard, its effective active strength being probably equivalent to that of ex-South Yemen. It possesses advanced equipment, although it is not thought to have achieved adequate training performance. It also lacks modern mobile artillery and supporting fighting vehicles, which are definitely necessary because of the vastness of Saudi territory. Saudi naval capability is restricted, in spite of the long coastline of what is, after all, a huge peninsula. There are a mere 1,500 men, equipment is inadequate, and the force's patrol capabilities are limited. Thus, even on completion of the modernisation programme that is currently being undertaken, the Saudi naval forces will be insufficient for the country's maritime defence. The airforce is probably the most advanced branch of the country's armed forces. Although its total personnel is small, its equipment is very advanced. Initially dependent on British fighters they now employ American-made fighter-bombers, the transition from one to the other having been made with reasonable ease. The pilots are considered highly trained, and the air-to-air and air-to-surface munitions are relatively adequate. However, there is a shortage in numbers of ground crews and technicians, while other problems involve the air defences, which are quite simply inadequate.

After the start of the Iran–Iraq war the Saudis realised how weak their air control and warning systems were, and the United States was equally alarmed. In October 1981 the American government, with Senate approval, agreed to sell the 'AWACS package' at a cost to the Saudis of $8.5 billion. This equipment certainly improved Saudi deterrence capability against certain possible attacks on the oilfields, but on the other hand it also gave the United States forces more time in Saudi Arabia and the wherewithal to provide the Saudis with reinforcements, thus strengthening the military ties between the two countries. Indeed, the equipment is so highly complex that it was predicted that it might have to be maintained and operated by American personnel almost indefinitely [*Armed Forces Journal International*, September 1981: 56, 61, 78–80]. The sale and the package as a whole also gave the United States the opportunity to use many Saudi facilities, worth over $50 billion, with no further cost.

In short therefore the state of Saudi Arabia's military capability leaves much to be desired. The usual explanation given for the weakness of the Saudi armed forces is the shortage of personnel, and indeed this is an important factor. However, with an annual oil income of some $85 billion in the late 1970s and early 1980s, the Saudis should have been able to do better. Very close to their borders are two oil-poor countries whose armed forces are far better trained and equipped: Syria, whose population is not much larger, and Jordan, whose population is much smaller. It is not therefore beyond the bounds of possibility that the Saudi rulers themselves – for their own 'internal security' reasons – may not particularly welcome the idea of having a large and dynamic army. After all, their experiences with the Wahhabi movement and their struggle with the Ikhwan organisation make the Saudi Royal Family apprehensive about any fighting forces. This inclination was also fostered among the Saudis for decades by the British for their own purposes in the peninsula and the Gulf region at large. Then the coups that occurred in many countries around Arabia in the 1950s and 1960s also frightened the Saudi rulers and dissuaded them from further strengthening their own armed forces, so that, for example, unlike most other Middle Eastern countries, the Saudis have always failed to implement a system of military conscription (draft).

The Americans may also have had their own reasons for not accelerating the building of a large and capable army in Arabia. They are, of course, concerned that this area, so strategic for the West, is weakly defended. But as a number of American officials and commentators continue to repeat, the 'dangers' are as much likely to emanate from within as they are from 'without'. And given the nature of the American–Saudi alliance, many American policy-makers may share the same apprehensions as the Saudi Royal Family about the 'internal dangers' of a large and capable Arabian army. American policy-makers seem to favour direct strategic rights and/or facilities for the United States forces in and around Arabia. The Saudi rulers, however, realising just how much they depend in reality on American protection, have not been prepared to add to their political embarrassment by making the American presence so openly and officially obvious, and the issue therefore remained a source of disagreement between the countries – at least until the occupation of Kuwait by Iraq in 1990.

From the foregoing, one can conclude that owing to the richness of their resources combined with their limited military capability, Saudi Arabia and even more so the smaller city-states of the Arabian Gulf are susceptible to a number of external dangers that render them extremely vulnerable. At the same time, the security problem also has a domestic dimension, at least from the point of view of the ruling élites and that of all others, including foreign powers, whose interests are best served by the continuation of the existing political order.

Perceived external threats and strategic vulnerability prompted a remarkable expansion by the oil-exporting Gulf countries of their armed forces after the 1973–74 oil boom. Part of this expansion was guided by considerations of state-building as well as by the enforcement of socio-political security. "Security needs were redefined so as to protect the states not only from external threats but also from unadmitted potential internal challenges" [Chubin, Litwak and Plascov, 1982: 103–5]. Enormous quantities of advanced weapons were finding their way to the Gulf and the absorption of the new and sophisticated weapons required fundamental organisational and technical changes that created modern-looking formal armies. These were hard to staff, however, and foreign-ers such as Jordanians, Pakistanis (and Omanis) as well as some Yemenis, Egyptians, etc., had to be employed.

Nevertheless the issue of conscription has remained a thorny one for all Gulf states. Kuwait installed the system officially, mainly in an attempt to offset the numerical weight of its bedouin and Shi'i/Iraqi soldiers, and the United Arab Emirates was considering the enforcement of such a system too.[4]

In the early 1980s the military manpower of Saudi Arabia was slightly in excess of 88,000, of whom about 51,000 personnel were regular and 36,000 were paramilitary. In 1985 there were estimated to be from 52,000 to 56,000 regular forces personnel, and numbers in the National Guard were put at between 14,000 and 16,000. In 1988 the active armed forces numbered 65,700;

and the paramilitary personnel were put at 56,000 which included about 10,000 security forces with the Ministry of the Interior, 26,000 tribal levies, and 20,000 reserve forces [IISS, 1989].

The National Guard is crucial, and loyal, but "its reliability is not beyond question" [Heller and Safran, 1985: 25–6]; modernisation erodes the traditional (tribal) loyalties and strengthens the 'cash nexus'. The Guards dealt successfully with the Shi'a in 1979 and 1980, but were not successful in Mecca in 1979 (nor were the security forces, also in Mecca, in 1987). The number of military officers in Saudi Arabia increased from 5,600 in 1967, to 7,000 in 1975, to 11,100 in 1985 (i.e. an increase of 50 per cent in less than two decades), exceeding the percentage increase in any other sector of the 'new middle class' [ibid.: 10–16]. Until the early 1970s Hijazis were discriminated against in recruitment to the armed forces and in promotions to the officer corps because of doubts about their loyalty. This impaired modernisation, professionalism and efficiency. Since then, the regime has also tried to reduce the risks of discontent among officers by providing lavishly high pay and benefits. Yet at least one abortive coup attempt has been reported, in 1977, in addition to several cases of defections of individuals and small groups of officers.

Civil–military relations have not, of course, always been orderly and cordial. There were attempted coups in the 1950s and 1960s: in 1955 there was a plot 'to kill King Saud and Prince Faisal' and to establish a nationalistic military government. In 1963 nine pilots defected to Egypt, refusing to bomb Egyptian forces in Yemen. More serious attempts were witnessed in 1969: sixty-three officers, mainly from the air force, together with hundreds of civilian opponents, were arrested for attempting a coup; another attempted coup by senior officers took place in the same year, supported by elements of the Hijazi bourgeoisie, various reformist elements and some retired officers [Cordesman, 1984: 123–6]. In the early 1970s there were several reports of disgruntlement among certain elements of the military, who were said to have received support directly or indirectly from some sons of the deposed King Saud [Schechtermann, 1981–82: 15–25]. And although the salaries and living conditions of the officers improved markedly following the 1973–74 oil boom, several hundred military and civilian individuals were arrested following the abortive military coup which was discovered in 1977 (and which was reportedly sponsored by Libya). Two of the pilots involved escaped in their aircraft to Baghdad. Cordesman suggests that a dozen pilots from Tabuk air base had planned on that occasion to bomb the royal palaces in Riyad and Jiddah and "to proclaim an Islamic republic" [Cordesman, 1984: 227], but there is nothing to suggest that the coup would have been Islamic in any except the most symbolic of senses. Other minor aspects of military unrest were also reported from time to time.

Investigations following the attempted 1977 coup revealed that military pay had not kept pace with the increases in income in the civilian sector and that there was considerable dissatisfaction among the military with living and training conditions. Some of these problems were solved by doubling military salaries, though improvements in housing and other facilities were lacking or behind schedule. So, sources of grievance may not have been completely eradicated in relative terms.

The military–tribal complex

Realising that there is "a potential for the Saudi armed forces to intervene and overthrow the regime", the Saudi authorities have resorted to a variety of methods to curtail that potential. These include giving financial and material rewards, especially for senior officers, balancing the military and paramilitary forces against each other, spreading out the regular army in remote parts of the huge country, assigning crucial roles to foreign forces and advisors, and most particularly the entrusting of central command in the hands of officer-princes, [Al-Hamad, 1985: 295–304; Al-Faleh, 1987].

Efforts to modernise the National Guard to counterbalance the regular army and to deal with potential internal dissidence or sabotage gathered momentum from the mid-1970s. However, its deficiencies were revealed in the Mecca events of October 1979, when the Guard (tying up one third of Saudi Arabia's active military manpower) reacted to the incidents by seeking impractical increases in their equipment, such as tanks and anti-aircraft weapons (while simultaneously remaining the only force in over thirty Third World countries unable to maintain and service its own armoured vehicles!) [Cordesman, 1984: 179–86]. Controversy involving reported conflicts among members of the Royal Family continued over the future role of the National Guard and the method of its armament and organisation, and resulted in a distinct lack of coordination in operational as well as in financial and organisational terms. However, the Mecca events and Sadat's personal attacks on the Royal Family (when they failed to arrive at a consensus that might have condoned his Camp David settlement), had the effect of once again uniting the Royal Family over security and strategic matters.

With the exception of the harsh suppression of the Shi'is in the Eastern province, the Saudi regime has not so far needed to use its various military or paramilitary forces for direct oppression of the population. The regime has continued to rely mainly on the traditional 'tribal' structure of Arabian society, supplemented by calculated 'inclusionary' measures, and guarded co-optation of potential sources of opposition.

Although neither the insurgency at Mecca nor the Eastern province uprising revealed further instability in the Saudi armed forces, it is interesting to note that military pay rates were again doubled in 1981 and that fringe benefits – including land grants – were also increased in subsequent years. Yet the longer-term stability of the armed forces continues to be something of an unknown quantity [Cordesman, 1984: 242–4].

Of course the policy of co-optation and incorporation reaches its epitome with regard to the National Guard. The bulk of this is still a traditional tribal force. According to Anthony Cordesman

> It is more a means through which the Royal Family allocates funds to tribal and bedouin leaders than a modern combat or internal security force. The Guard helps key princes maintain close relations with the tribes in each region; it has not evolved into a force that can deal with urban disorders, oil field security problems, border security problems and ethnic or other internal divisions. The Guard is politically vital, but it has not found a clear military mission [Cordesman, 1984: 365].

The regime has been careful to limit the combat units in the capital city to the hand-picked 1,000–man Royal Guard and the 7,000 to 10,000 Security Forces within the Ministry of the Interior.

The 1980s saw a further expansion and upgrading of the armed forces, partly as a consequence of the long-running Iran–Iraq war. Short of skilled manpower, the regime increasingly went outside the conventional Najdi community in order to enlist educated Hijazis and Sunnis from Al-Hasa and elsewhere. Although the likelihood of the emergence of a Saudi version of the 'Young Turks' still seems relatively remote, given the system of checks and balances instituted in the country, the likelihood of such a military-led middle-class revolt are bound to increase if oil revenues continue to diminish. According to Mordechai Abir

> The newly-centred alliance of the royal house with the ulama for which the King opted, inter alia, to counter the growing power of the middle class, further exacerbates the latter's dissatisfaction, as does the 'Saudi-isation' of the central and provincial government at a time of growing unemployment among the new intelligentsia. In the present circumstances, the *ahl al-hal w'al-'aqd*, apprehensive of the ramifications of change in the kingdom's power structure, are even less likely to grant voluntarily the middle class participation in decision-making which, it fears, could lead to a rapid erosion of the Sauds' hegemony. Yet their continued exclusion from political participation further antagonises the new elites and militates the younger elements in this powerful and large component of the Saudi society [Abir, 1988: 204–5].

Thus it seems that one of the control strategies of the regime in the 1980s was to strengthen the regime's authority over the localities by applying a policy of Najdisation or, even preferably, Saudisation (i.e. from the Al Saud family) of provincial government. Young dynamic amirs were appointed as new governors in several provinces and with increased powers. More recently the resignation, dismissal or even virtual 'exile' of a number of mainly Hijazi technocrats was taken to signify a movement to enable power to revert to the hands of loyal 'Najdi' officials or technocrats from the Sudairi branch of the Al Sauds. Some Hijazi technocrats, merchants and entrepreneurs viewed the dismissal of the well-known oil minister Shaikh Yamani (and that of 'Abd al-Hadi Tahir) as another example of the decline of their position and the re-Najdisation of the regime as it moved in recent years towards a greater measure of conservatism. Yamani reportedly opposed the King's demands for higher oil prices and higher oil production simultaneously, and was also opposed to barter deals which – according to some sources – were often resorted to by the regime in order to secure arms supplies [Abir, 1988: 168–9, 173–4, 216–17]. The extent to which such a policy has affected the career prospects of 'commoner' officers (especially from Hijaz) is not clear yet, but combined with the relative economic squeeze, it is likely that the younger elements of the middle class would view such changes with concern, especially as the number of unemployed among the intelligentsia starts to grow.

The 'Iranian' disturbances in Mecca during the Hajj season of 1987 further strengthened the solidarity of the Royal Family and enhanced their internally conservative and externally pro-American inclinations. Although Prince Nayif's public security forces acted clumsily and heavy-handedly during these riots, he was given full support by the regime. Further assistance was sought from Western and Muslim countries for security purposes, and since then the holy city has been heavily infiltrated with armed troops.

It is also significant that although the Saudi budgets have been cut in total and in sectoral (including military) terms in recent years, the official defence and security budget has been trimmed in a proportionately less severe manner than the other components of the national budget [cf. e.g. EIU *Saudi Arabia Profile*, 1987]. Military spending has averaged about 44 per cent of total public expenditure in recent years, with defence expenditure appearing to be more immune to budgetary cuts than, for example, government investment [Looney, 1987–88: 698–700].

This is indicative of the importance that the regime attaches to security matters, and it renders it unlikely that the officer corps will have serious institutional concerns over the quantity and quality of their weapons. However, if the heightened sense of vulnerability is to continue to make the Saudi leaders more inclined to favour considerations of loyalty over those of meritocracy in placing and promoting military personnel, this can open the way for various personal, regional and political grievances to grow among the military. It is not unlikely, given the weakness of the civil, secular opposition forces in the country since the mid-1970s (although they seem to be gathering some momentum in recent years), that the informal forums (such as *shillas*, *jalsas* and *sahras*, etc.), and possibly including some military personnel, may increasingly become important focal points for opposition to the regime [Al-Faleh, 1987: 216–19].

According to Heller and Safran, the likelihood of the officers championing a new middle class in the future will depend on a number of internal variables which may include: professional and/or social grievances cast in relative terms;

negative repercussions of the decline in oil revenues; problems over employment and promotion opportunities for the new middle-class; failure to regulate the succession; major conflicts over oil policies and/or developmental options. Possible external 'triggers' of a new middle-class revolt may include: border disputes, regional challenges; or major disagreements with the United States [Heller and Safran, 1985: 17–24].

The Iraqi conquest of Kuwait in August 1990, the subsequent calling of American forces to Saudi Arabia, and the joint act of war against Iraq, can be expected to add further factors that may contribute to political instability and social unrest (including among the military) in Saudi Arabia. First, and above all, it has revealed the extreme strategic vulnerability not only of Kuwait and the smaller Gulf states but also of Saudi Arabia, the presumed leader of the Gulf Cooperation Council. It has illustrated that these countries could not (or would not) defend themselves on their own or with exclusively Arab help. After succeeding for many years in keeping the American presence formally out of its territory, Saudi Arabia can no longer do without massive United States (and Western) military aid – which the Saudis have to finance themselves.

On the eve of the war, the total number of American forces in the Gulf region had exceeded 400,000 men, or about half the size of the entire American army. Even though Iraqi forces were eventually expelled from Kuwait, some American personnel are likely to have stayed on in Arabia, Western naval presence continues on the horizon, and American strategic hegemony would thus be all but complete [*Sunday Times*, 28 October 1990; *Guardian*, 31 October 1990; Stork and Wenger, 1991: 22–6]. Indeed the Kuwaiti strategic bond with the United States has been formalised with the ten-year defence agreement between the two countries, announced in October 1991.

The crisis prompted the Saudi leadership to announce plans for expanding the armed and security forces, even to double them within five to seven years. Other Gulf states announced similar intentions, but all suffer from the same manpower constraints. Most of Kuwait's soldiers and policemen were people 'without citizenship' (*bidun*) whose situation is now problematic, and a conscription drive in 1991 reportedly drew only 2,000 new recruits. The UAE began recruiting women into the armed forces but, as with most GCC countries, continues to rely on mercenaries for much of their security requirements [Hardy, 1992: 28–9].

The shock of the war and its aftermath is likely to widen still further in the Gulf the gap between the conservatives and the modernists, the Islamists and the secularists, the pro-Arab and the pro-Western factions, those calling for more control and those calling for a measure of participation. These controversies are likely to make inroads among military personnel. As the presence of foreign personnel and foreign influence continues, one crucial element which contributed to the emergence of coups in other Middle Eastern countries and which has, at least until the beginning of the 1990s, been absent in Saudi Arabia, will be added to the picture. It will become virtually immaterial that foreign troops were called in by the governments of the Gulf countries themselves; the presence of foreign personnel on native soil and their countries' inevitable 'interference' with national policies will become a source of humiliation for the people in general, and for the military in particular. If this is added to a whole range of internal grievances that the new middle class may increasingly harbour, the possibility of military intervention in Saudi politics may become more likely with the passage of time. The establishment of an unquestionable *pax americana* over the Gulf region and much of the Arab East is not an event that will be particularly celebrated by nationalist, Islamist or 'leftist' forces in the region.

Prospects and comparisons

In the expansionary 'easy' stage of the modernisation of the Gulf states (characterised as it was by infrastructural construction and by institution-building), 'inclusionary' policies (not unlike those of more 'typical' populist regimes) were possible, whereby elements of an emerging 'new middle class' were increasingly brought into the economic and political arena in the 1970s and early 1980s [cf. Stauffer, 1981, and compare Becker, 1987]. This variety of regime differs from the typical 'populist' regimes, however, in that it does not consolidate or incorporate the 'working class' which, to all intents and purposes, remains expatriate by origin and therefore culturally and politically external to the system. But as this expansionary stage reaches its 'ceiling' (a process very much accelerated by the decline in oil revenues), various exclusionary measures can be expected to take place. The main target for exclusionary policies in this case is likely to be the technocrats (including managers and possibly some elements of the military) and to some extent merchants. The military, as prominent members of the new middle class, are not likely to take kindly to measures that are aimed at reducing their professional and financial privileges and at excluding them from the process of decision-making, and from the political arena in general.

Christopher Clapham has observed that "the traditional states of the Arabian peninsula provide the largest coup-free zone" in Asia [Clapham, 1985: 137]. There is no guarantee, however, that this situation will continue, especially with the withering away of the oil bonanza and the 'easy stage' of modernisation through construction works and institution-building. The possibility cannot be ruled out of hand, in such circumstances, of the military acting as champions of the beleaguered new middle classes in Saudi Arabia and other Gulf states in the not very remote future. If the presence of foreign troops and advisers in the Gulf is to continue, this may add a specifically 'nationalist' stimulus to the social grievances and political misgivings.

The type of coup that might take place is likely to be of the variety that S.P. Huntington terms "the breakthrough coup". This type takes place when the military – and especially the middle and lower ranks of the officer corps – is frustrated by the continued tenure of power by what it feels to be an outmoded and ineffective traditionalist élite [Huntington: 1971: Ch. 4].

Over a period of time, not only effective power but also the dominant concepts of legitimacy in a modernising society will come to favour the new bureau-technocratic élite. A claim to political power by the new middle class, which is often sparked by a professional, social or 'national' sense of grievance that is 'picked up' by the military, would normally be centred around demands for rationality, efficiency and modernity. There is really very little to prevent the sort of events that occurred in Libya in 1969 and in Ethiopia in 1974 from being repeated in Saudi Arabia [compare Clapham, 1985: 144]. Indeed this is all the more likely to occur as tensions and strains build up following the eclipse of the 'bonanza decade' of 1974–83 and the erosion of the 'pacifying' effects of the oil boom.

The fall in oil revenues, combined with a continuation of the 'traditional' patterns of resource allocation, is likely to arouse a heightened sense of social blockage as the rising expectations of the new middle classes become increasingly frustrated. A continued presence of foreign personnel would add a potent sense of national grievance. However, the maturation of this process is likely to take time. The expatriate labour force is likely to be a more immediate 'scapegoat' when it comes to financial and economic difficulties. Once the foreign labour force is reduced to a minimum, the Saudi and Gulfian intelligentsia is likely to become the main target for the exclusionary policies of the regimes. It is at this point that one may once again start to hear about attempted coups in Arabia.

NOTES

1. This analysis is derived in part from Ayubi, 1983.

2. Also affiliated to the Defence Ministry in Syria is the Constructions Organisation (MATA'), the Medical Industries Organisation, and the Military Social Organisation [Abu Shikha, 1983].

3. Robert Bianchi is too categorical in my view, however, when he generalises that "apart from Turkey and the Philippines there are very few prospective Argentinas or Chiles in the Middle East and Asia" [Bianchi, 1986: 507–39; see also Ayubi, 1991b: Ch. 12 for further elaboration of this point].

4. The United Arab Emirates has the highest ratio of defence forces to civil population in the world because each of the stronger emirates maintains a separate force and even purchases its own weapons. Saudi Arabia has not introduced a general conscription policy, since to embark on such a policy could tend to dilute the more reliable part of the dynasty's military forces and reduce the existing financial incentives which serve to encourage the army's loyalty [cf. Chubin, Litwak and Plascov, 1982: 105].

CHAPTER NINE

Bureaucratic Growth: Development Versus Control

The issue of bureaucratic growth has not attracted much attention in the Western literature until fairly recently. According to the Weberian thesis bureaucratic development was the sign of growing rationality, and according to the 'Open System' theories, it was the outcome of efforts by organisations to adapt to uncertain environments. Thus organisations were assumed to act rationally to accommodate the environment. It is only rather recently ('Parkinson's Law' notwithstanding) that bureaucratic growth has started to attract attention as being potentially unrational or inefficient (although Crozier [1964] had presented some earlier warning), and this theme has often come from economic theorists [e.g. Borcherding, 1977; Niskanen, 1971]. Bureaucrats were said to be 'budget-maximisers' who over-produce, or 'rent-maximisers' who overspend. In either case, growth seemed inevitable, although substantial empirical evidence was lacking [Meyer, 1985]. Organisational theorists then hypothesised that bureaucratic growth might also result from one or some of the following: (a) expansion of the state's role in society; (b) the tendency for bureaucratic organisations towards expansion, complexity and diversification; (c) inertia, or the unwillingness or inability to dissolve organisations or to cut them down once they have been established [Jackson, 1982].

This chapter sets out to test some of these broad hypotheses – derived from the general (but mainly Western) literature – against a number of Arab cases. My preliminary studies have indicated that indeed most Middle East managers and politicians seem to have accepted the proposition of 'bureaucratisation as development' [Ayubi, 1986]. In addition, I also hypothesised [Ayubi, 1988a] that other factors more specific to the developing countries and/or to the Middle East may also be at play. These include (a) the historical centralised traditions, reinforced by colonial rule, influence of the French monocratic model and by the Egyptians' 'transfer' of their own experience to the rest of the Arab World; (b) the huge expansion in formal education, with few other outlets for the employment of its graduates and with traditionally high status being attached to white collar and/or 'public' types of employment; and (c) the presence of weak entrepreneurial élites which, in capital-poor countries (where there was 'socialism') and in capital-rich countries (which are circulationist), led to an exceptionally important role for the state.

EXPANSION IN THE ECONOMIC ROLE
OF THE STATE

In the economic sphere the expansion of state roles has been most remarkable and has included practically all Middle Eastern countries regardless of size, politico-institutional history, wealth or socio-political doctrine. An explanation was needed as to why *all* the Arab countries had a very large public sector. Historically, of course, none of the Middle Eastern countries (Mount Lebanon excepted) had experienced 'feudalism' in its European form; rather they experienced various forms of basically state-controlled modes of production. This is not sufficient by itself, however, to explain the contemporary expansion of the state's economic role.

Dynamic theories of public enterprise expansion may be classified into three categories: cyclical, linear, and 'stochastic' [Wilson, 1985]. Theories assuming a linear pattern would show the scope of public enterprise expansion changing in a consistent direction, usually attributable to some underlying factors such as the existence of 'imperfect markets' or the rise of the 'professional classes'. Cyclical explanations relate changes in public enterprise expansion to broader changes in the political economy, especially things such as the supply of foreign exchange and investment capital. The explanation, in turn, may be cycle-matched (as in the famous Wagner's Law) or countercyclical [e.g. Wildansky, 1980]. 'Stochastic' explanations suggest that change is patternless or is so closely tied to historical, cultural and political factors that it cannot easily be generalised.

Indications gleaned so far suggest that although the 'linear' explanation may account for the initial stages of the *creation* of an economic public sector in several Arab countries, the *expansion* and *contraction* of that sector may be more successfully explained by a combination of cyclical and 'stochastic' factors. Cyclical explanations would illustrate that although the sources of income were different (e.g. nationalised assets and foreign aid for the radical republics; 'rentier' revenues for the oil-rich countries), and that although the scale of expenditure was also markedly different, public enterprise expansion in both the oil-poor and the oil-rich Middle Eastern countries has been cycle-related to a period of (relatively) high foreign exchange and relatively low 'entrepreneurial' investment.

But as public sector expansion, especially in industrialisation, has been one

Table 9.1 Government expenditure and revenue in Arab countries to 1990

	Total expenditure (% of GNP)	Total revenue (% of GNP)	Selected expenditures		Average annual inflation 1980–90
			Defence (% of total expenditure)	Education and health (% of total expenditure)	
Egypt	40.2	35.9	12.7	16.2	11.8
Jordan	39.4	22.3	23.1	20.0	–
Kuwait	31.0	23.6	19.9	21.4	-2.7
Libya	–	–	–	–	12.0
Morocco	26.2	23.8	15.7	22.9	7.2
Oman	48.6	38.2	41.0	15.3	–
Syria	28.0	25.5	40.7	9.9	14.4
Tunisia	37.2	31.8	6.5	22.4	7.4
United Arab Emirates	13.0	1.3	43.9	21.9	1.1

Source: World Bank, *The World Development Report 1992*, Washington DC, The International-al Bank for Reconstruction and Development (IBRD).

of the main vehicles used by the state élites for the purposes of 'state-building' [Chatelus and Schemeil, 1984], to what extent would these élites be prepared to reverse the pattern of public enterprise expansion (after a certain, under-standable, time lag) in response to external changes resulting in the relative decline in capital and foreign exchange? Furthermore, is the downwards trend (i.e. contraction of the public sector) likely to be slower in the 'socialist' than in the more capitalist-oriented Middle Eastern countries? Such questions will eventually be dealt with in this and in the following chapter. But for the moment let us concentrate on the expansionary phase.

It was natural for late industrialisers in the Third World, lacking the entrepreneurial skills that would have enabled them to start it all from the very beginning, to be attracted to the 'organisational model' of late capitalism with its big plants and enterprises and its accompanying 'managerial ideology'. Alexander Gerschenkron [1962: esp. 353–5] observed the propensity of élites in late-developing countries to adopt the latest organisational forms, modes of action, and ideologies that capitalism had to offer. Capitalist development in today's Third World countries therefore frequently takes the shape of local adaptation of late, or 'organisational', capitalism as it has developed since the Second World War. What are adapted to local needs are, principally, the corporate forms of economic organisation, some welfare-state redistribution-ism, and indicative planning [Becker, 1987].

Although I do not intend to dwell on this point here, careful empirical study indicates that the economic role of the state has grown remarkably since the 1950s in all Arab states, and in Iran, with the only exception of Lebanon where its particular circumstances may have caused the state to wither away altogether! More specifically, the direct role of the state in economic planning and management is not confined to the so-called radical (or socialist) regimes: countries like 'conservative' Saudi Arabia and 'Islamic' Iran possess planning mechanisms and public sectors that are easily comparable in size and in role with those of the 'socialist' states.

Examination of the recent public finance figures of the Arab state illustrates beyond any doubt the remarkable growth in the economic role of the state (see Table 9.1). The overall size of total budgets of the various Arab countries was very modest half a century or so ago. A comparison made by Yusif Sayigh in the case of some Arab countries between 1930 and 1980 in current prices showed that there had been a very steep rise in government expenditure for the eight countries for which data were available, the current budgets being more than 40 times larger than the 1930 budget at the minimum, and over 2,400 times at the maximum (at current prices) [Sayigh, 1982: 75–7].

Of particular importance has been the considerably enlarged role of government in the design, finance, control and execution of economic and developmental works. In the 1930s, the region's countries taken together allocated around 10 or 12 per cent of total budget expenditure to capital investment, with the then poorer countries allocating less than the lower of these two figures. The remainder of the budget went into recurrent expenditures. By comparison the Arab states were now involved much more directly and enormously in economic activity. The aggregate of planned investment in eighteen Arab states for the period 1975–80 totalled the equivalent of $326 billion. The total figure for the five years 1981–85 was – according to the published plans – going to be considerably larger. Even given the discrepancy between planned and actual investment (which can well be 30 per cent of investment plans), the volume involved is still very substantial. As the bulk of the investment is made by the government (including the public sector), an idea of the growing role of the state can be deduced from the indicator alone, not to speak of the corresponding growth of recurrent expenditures. Taken together, recurrent and capital expenditure for 1979 totalled about $160 billion for the Arab states excluding Djibouti. Capital investment allocations for 1979 amounted to 40 per cent of the aggregate combined budgets. Related to GDP, the overall budgets stood at 53 per cent, while budgeted investment stood at 23 per cent [Sayigh, 1982: 77–8].

The change has been qualitative also, and not simply quantitative. As Galal Amin explains, up to the 1940s public ownership rarely extended beyond irrigation works and public utilities. By the mid-1960s, the public sector in Egypt, Iraq and Syria had become predominant in all sectors outside agriculture (the Gezira project in Sudan was an exception to the regional pattern), retail trade, housing and small industry. In the rest of the Arab countries, the public sector has, since the 1960s, been fast-growing in all countries except Lebanon (where, in the mid-1960s, the share of public investment in total gross investment was less than one fifth). Apart from Lebanon (and at some point Jordan), the share of public investment in the mid-1960s was nowhere less than 50 per cent, and accounted in Egypt and Iraq for more than 75 per cent [G. Amin, 1980: 84–5].

Public expenditure, both recurrent and investment, grew even faster in the 1970s, as can be seen from the comparison between the period 1960–70 and 1970–75 [Sadiq, 1980: 118, 119]. Defence, education and health accounted for part of the growth in public expenditure. But public investments were growing rapidly too: in fact, while rates of growth of current expenditures were higher in 1960–70 than rates of growth in investment expenditure (with the exception of the petroleum-exporting countries), the situation was reversed in the period 1970–75 (again with the exception of the oil-exporting countries) [ibid.: 41–4]. Not only had public expenditure grown in absolute terms and as a percentage of GDP, but the share of public investment of total planned investments had become higher than the share of the private sector in all Arab countries, except Lebanon [Table 14 in Sadiq, 1980: 48; for some later details see Al-Mir, 1985].

The 'conservative' countries of the Gulf were no less enthusiastic for expanding the economic role of the state than were the 'socialist' ones, as Galal Amin noted in the early 1970s: "even 'traditional' Saudi Arabia has gone a long way *since the state itself was a private enterprise*" [G. Amin, 1980: 85 – emphasis added]. By 1979, there were some eighty-four public corporations working in the Gulf oil countries [Sadiq, 1980: 45 and Table 12]. The overall rates of growth in the public sector were no less impressive in the conservative Gulf countries than they were in the 'radical' Arab states. Without having to resort to socialist rhetoric, the oil-exporting Arab countries were enabled by the post-1973 oil boom to become distinguished members of the league of big government spenders, not only through social welfare services but also through ambitious industrialisation programmes. For as Chatelus and Schemeil [1984] have argued persuasively, the political imperative for expanding the public sector was similar: "Confronted with the major problem of building domestic order and regional stability, the Middle East Arab States tend to use economics as a way of solving strategic puzzles. It is the very industrialisation process which contributes to state-building rather than the state which helps to build a national industry" [257].

In Saudi Arabia (and to a lesser extent in its smaller oil-exporting neighbours) the oil boom led to a rather ironic situation whereby, although the state continued to adhere to the rhetoric of *laissez-faire* economics, its actual role – in terms of both expenditure and also organisation (such as the adoption of national planning) – was decidedly *dirigiste* in nature and comparable in many ways to the role of states that had declared more overtly 'socialistic' slogans. In 1978 the Saudi government was responsible for 60.3 per cent of gross fixed

Table 9.2 Government expenditure as percentage of GDP in Arab states, 1975–82

Country	1975	1976	1977	1978	1979	1980	1981	1982
Algeria	56.18	46.97	55.67	56.26	53.01	49.10	37.95	46.21
Bahrain	27.08	36.48	45.20	41.13	31.38	21.39	22.38	28.91
Egypt	59.61	52.26	54.82	62.57	43.40	53.62	59.14	53.23
Iraq	51.30	55.44	48.58	80.55	69.63	74.01	144.61	150.62
Jordan	72.16	62.55	68.57	55.66	74.78	56.40	54.22	28.13
Kuwait	26.35	28.33	32.39	39.32	26.13	45.33	44.31	21.94
Lebanon	13.61	43.09	20.26	25.68	25.16	33.57	32.05	33.85
Libya	42.73	54.94	51.19	57.00	54.24	48.24	48.22	60.01
Mauritania	36.70	50.67	45.45	45.07	41.95	31.59	30.40	29.60
Morocco	32.81	38.38	40.09	34.10	31.88	36.07	36.56	32.24
Oman	68.97	70.20	61.62	61.64	54.94	52.10	59.35	62.26
Qatar	46.26	50.34	76.16	59.75	55.90	37.62	42.61	79.15
Saudi Arabia	58.52	77.79	67.29	65.87	80.51	61.21	55.24	72.10
Somalia	14.98	15.95	21.92	31.86	32.73	35.98	36.77	27.63
Sudan	28.28	30.20	27.43	25.47	30.36	34.25	32.96	29.14
Syria	46.65	45.18	47.58	40.01	63.08	47.51	42.03	38.22
Tunisia	29.09	30.03	33.79	34.94	30.30	30.56	32.60	35.67
United Arab Emirates	41.37	37.61	37.12	40.63	39.27	32.96	36.32	39.53
Yemen (North)	18.87	19.13	24.58	33.35	30.14	57.66	54.12	76.41
Yemen (South)	44.71	38.96	65.11	67.34	59.18	73.89	92.50	99.77

Source: The Arab Monetary Fund, *The Unified Arab Economic Reports*, Abu Dhabi, 1981, 1982, 1983.

capital formation, for 61.7 per cent of expenditure in GDP, for 48 per cent of total consumption and (in 1976) for 33.3 per cent of all national purchases [El-Mallakh, 1982: 276]. But although the development plans have declared that the government would undertake capital investment only "where the size of investment is large and beyond the capacity of private individuals", and even though the policy of 'Saudisation' has entailed the offer of preferential incentives to Saudi rather than to expatriate contractors [ibid.: 403–8], private business has continued to a large extent to be contingent (and dependent) on public expenditure, and domestic producers seem unable to function without heavy subsidies.

Thus one sees that public expenditure as a percentage of GDP rose more or less steadily for *all Arab countries* in the period between 1975 and 1982: from 47.28 per cent in the former year to 62.16 per cent in the latter (see Table 9.2). If one classifies the Arab countries into various groups, it is indeed the oil-exporting states that stand above all others in terms of public spending as a percentage of GDP (with the exception of the former South Yemen which until recently had experienced the most 'East European' type of regime; and the special case of Iraq which had to overspend because of the prolonged war with

Table 9.3 Structure of public expenditure in Arab states in 1981 (%)

States	Recurrent expenditures	Development expenditures
United Arab Emirates	76.2	23.8
Saudi Arabia	28.7	71.3
Qatar	75.4	24.6
Kuwait	78.7	21.3
Libya	27.7	72.3
Group average	*39.5*	*60.5*
Algeria	60.6	39.4
Iraq	100.0	n/a*
Group average	*83.4*	*16.6*
Bahrain	57.4	42.6
Tunisia	53.1	46.9
Syria	54.8	45.2
Oman	73.0	27.0
Egypt	65.9	34.1
Group average	*63.1*	*36.9*
Jordan	58.1	41.9
Lebanon	67.2	32.8
Morocco	68.2	31.8
Group average	*65.8*	*34.2*
Djibouti	86.5	13.5
Sudan	80.4	19.6
Somalia	89.6	10.4
Mauritania	80.0	20.0
N. Yemen	53.3	46.7
S. Yemen	100.0	n/a*
Group average	*74.6*	*25.4*
Combined average	*52.7*	*47.3*

* All public expenditures for Iraq and South Yemen have been entered under 're-current' since no separate figure for investment is available.
Source: Arab Fund for Economic and Social Development, *Financial and Monetary Indicators for the Arab Countries* (Kuwait), 1971–81.

Iran). Public expenditure as a percentage of GNP is higher in most years in Saudi Arabia than it is in Tunisia, Syria or Egypt. Classified by groups, public expenditure represented nearly 60 per cent of GDP in the 'oil countries' compared to 45 per cent in the middle income Arab countries and 30 per cent in the poor Arab countries [Al-Mir, 1985]. The same generalisation is true with regard to the funds allocated to investment and development as a percentage of total outlays (see Table 9.3). Thus, for example in 1981, we find that the rich oil countries had spent 60.5 per cent of their total outlays on investment and development, compared to 34 per cent for Egypt, 45 per cent for Syria and 47 per cent for Tunisia (from among the 'populist' republics).

BUREAUCRATIC GROWTH IN THE ARAB COUNTRIES

The process of bureaucratisation that has swept through the Arab World since the 1950s is difficult to overlook. By 'bureaucratisation' I mean two things: (a) bureaucratic growth; that is, expansion in public bodies of the sort that can be measured by increases in the numbers of administrative units and personnel, as well the rise in public expenditure, including in particular wages and salaries; and (b) an orientation whereby the administrative and technical dominate over the social. Generally it is a tendency that goes very much in the direction of centralisation, hierarchy and control.

Bureaucratisation in both aspects has grown substantially in the Arab World in the last thirty years, and has happened in all states and regardless of the various differences: in the large and the small, the old and the new, and in the radical and the conservative. Thus we find heading in the same direction a country like Egypt, Weber's 'historical example' of a large developed bureaucracy, a country like Algeria, which started its statehood only thirty or so years ago with no bureaucracy worth mentioning and with what appeared to be a revolutionary distaste for things bureaucratic, and a country like Saudi Arabia – which is always speaking about 'free enterprise' even while possessing one of the largest public sectors in the region, and which, while suffering from manpower shortage, nevertheless complains at the same time of 'bureaucratic inflation'! [Othman, 1979: 34–41].

It is remarkable how extensively and rapidly the bureaucracy has expanded in almost all Arab states, the old and the new, the 'socialist' and the 'free-trade-ist',[1] even though the relative weight of the various causes of this expansion has differed from one type of country to another (see Table 9.4).

Four criteria are used to measure bureaucratic growth: increase in the number of administrative units, increase in the number of public employees, increase in current government expenditure, and, within this latter, increase in the wages and salaries of the employees. In considering the extent of bureaucratic growth, these four criteria should be taken together, in the sense that a relatively limited or slow increase in one at any particular stage should not distract us from observing the phenomenon of bureaucratic growth in its totality; i.e. as represented by all four factors combined.

It will become clear from the analysis that the role of the state and the size of public employment are not simplistically correlated to the ideological slogans of the state (e.g. 'socialist', 'free market', etc.) as some believe, but to more complex structural factors (see Table 9.5). Thus, for example, one finds (according to the World Bank estimates for the period from 1986 to 1990) that government employment represented 17 per cent of total employment in Jordan — only marginally lower than the 17.5 per cent obtaining in Egypt during the same period. Indeed, if one is to consider all public employment

Table 9.4 Central government apparatus in the Arab countries (late 1980s to early 1990s)

State	No. of ministries	No. of public organisations	Public organisations activities
Algeria	26	39	Industry, chemicals, petroleum, finance, commerce, transport, utilities, services, etc.
Bahrain	16	4	Monetary, insurance and pensions, municipal services
Egypt	29	96	Industry, agriculture, trade, petroleum, minerals, petrochemicals, housing, finance, banking and insurance, services, etc.
Iraq	21	75	Industry, petroleum, agriculture, construction, transport, finance, trade, education and culture, etc.
Jordan	23	42	Agriculture and natural resources, industry, electricity, transport and telecommunications, finance, trade, housing
Kuwait	17	21	Petrochemicals, investments, post and transport, food, social security, etc.
Lebanon	17	25	Water, electricity, public works, transport, agriculture, investment, social and educational
Libya	21	6	Petroleum, finance, transport, education
Mauritania	15	30	Commerce, industry, minerals, management, fisheries
Morocco	20	79	Finance, agriculture, commerce, industry, minerals, transport, water and electricity, tourism
Oman	19	6	Water, food, transport and telecommunications, commerce
Qatar	13	4	Petroleum, industry, finance, health
Saudi Arabia	20	32	Economic, financial, industrial, petroleum and chemicals, social services, construction, education and training, etc.
Somalia	25	49	Financial, agricultural, industrial and engineering, construction, transport, finance, trade, education and culture, etc.
Sudan	20	76	Economic, financial, agricultural, services, monetary and banking, etc.
Syria	24	78	Economic, industrial, agricultural, services, cultural, construction, etc.
Tunisia	19	300	Industry, finance, agriculture, transport and petroleum, etc.
United Arab Emirates	17	10	Economic, financial, services and management
Yemen	18	26	Agriculture, commerce and supplies, transport and telecommunications, water and electricity, education and services

Sources: Arab Organisation for Administrative Sciences (AOAS), *Al-Idara al-'amma* ... [Public Administration and Administrative Reform in the Arab World], Amman, 1986; author's research based on country reports and other official documents.

Table 9.5 Public service employment in the Arab countries

Country	No. of public servants	Year	Population (%)	Labour force (%)
Algeria	787,000	1986	3.5	15.0
Egypt	3,800,000	1990	7.3	25.3
Iraq	663,000	1978	5.0	22.3
Jordan	77,500	1986	2.0	8.6
Kuwait	146,600	1985	8.2	33.2
Libya	360,000	1990	8.4	40.0
Mauritania	16,000	1985	8.5	3.2
Morocco	296,500	1983	1.2	4.6
Oman	62,000	1984	5.9	25.8
Qatar	29,300	1984	10.7	43.2
Saudi Arabia	430,500	1985	4.4	13.9
Somalia	250,000	1990	5.2	16.1
Syria	343,000	1984	3.4	13.1
Tunisia	249,000	1984	3.5	11.6
United Arab Emirates	40,600	1983	4.0	10.1
Yemen	300,000	1986	3.3	9.9

Sources: Author's estimates, based on official country documents; records and publications of the Arab Organisation for Administrative Sciences (AOAS) and Arab Administrative Development Organisation (ARADO); *The Unified Arab Economic Reports*; and interviews with officials.

(i.e. in government and the public economic sector) Jordan comes higher, with 47 per cent of its manpower publicly employed compared to only 35 per cent for Egypt during the same period [Shihata, 1992: 9, and refs cited].

Bureaucratic growth in Egypt

Egypt has been home to one of the oldest bureaucracies in the world. The structure of the 'modern state' in Egypt dates back to the reign of Muhammad 'Ali, who came to power in 1805, and the first European-style cabinet to be formed in the Arab World was also organised in Egypt in 1878. The disproportionate growth of the country's public 'Establishment' is not a new phenomenon. However, with the 1952 Revolution, the public bureaucracy grew more rapidly and extensively under the impact of the regime's policies for expanding industrial activities, welfare services and free education [Ayubi, 1980: Ch. 3]. This growth was particularly striking after the 'socialist measures' of the early 1960s, which involved wide nationalisations of industry, trade and finance, worker participation, and also an extensive programme for social services and insurance. The size of the public bureaucracy, when measured by the four criteria established above, grew steadily between 1952 and 1970. The most notable changes followed the beginning of the 1960s and can be summarised thus: from 1962/63 Egypt's national income increased by 68 per cent, resting on an increase in the labour force of no more than 20 per cent. Yet at the same time, posts in the public bureaucracy had increased by 70 per cent and salaries by 123 per cent. Thus far the rate of bureaucratic growth had quite exceeded the rate of growth in population, employment and production.

The main irony, however, is that in the 1970s, and indeed following the adoption of the 'open door' economic policy (*infitah*) in 1974, the impetus of institutional growth continued under its own momentum even though the economic role of the government and the scope of the public sector were starting to diminish in importance [cf. Ayubi, 1992b].

In terms of manpower, the public bureaucracy – that is the civil service and the public sector excluding enterprise workers – employed in 1978 over 1,900,000 persons. If state companies are added, the public 'Establishment' was, at the beginning of 1978, employing about 3,200,000 officials and workers [CAOA and Ministry of Finance, 1978 and 1979]. The most detailed study of employment in the public sector indicates that in 1975 the Egyptian public sector employed over 868,000 people of whom about 573,000 worked in 170 industrial companies, about 266,000 in 160 service companies, and about 29,000 in agricultural companies [INP, 1975: 13].

At the beginning of the 1980s, the still expanding Egyptian bureaucracy looked even bigger. It employed 2,876,000 individuals in the central and local government as well as in the public sector, spent £E1,343,915 on salaries (excluding public companies) and £E5,394,699 on public expenditures (excluding companies). Public employment in general continued its phenomenal growth. In 1986/87 the state employed some five million people out of a labour force of some 13 million (of which about 500,000 were in the armed forces and about 2 million were working abroad). This means that at least 40 per cent, and probably more, of the civilian labour force resident in the country worked for the state. Of these, 3.4 million were in the civil service (more or less evenly divided between central and local government) and 1.6 million were in the public sector (just under half of them engaged in industry).

Bureaucratic expenses also remained very high. Out of a total public expenditure of some £E20 billion in the 1986/87 budget, £E3.865 million was earmarked for wages and salaries, and £E8.670 million was allocated for other current expenditures (including £E1.746 million for subsidies). This compares with £E7.467 million earmarked for investments and £E2.317 million for capital transfers (payments of domestic and external debts, financing deficits, etc.).

Analysis of the itemised figures that are available for the period 1977 to 1980/81 reveals some very interesting characteristics of the bureaucratic growth that was taking place. In these three years bureaucratic personnel grew noticeably, with employment in the bureaucratic machine increasing from about 1,911,000 to 2,474,000 – i.e. by 29.6 per cent or some 10 per cent per annum. This is about four times the population growth rate during the period (2.6 per cent) and actually surpasses the rate of bureaucratic growth even at the highest stage of 'socialist transformation' during the 1960s when it reached about 8.5 per cent annually [Ayubi, 1980: Ch. 3].

But bureaucratic growth did not take place in an even way across all sectors. In spite of the rhetoric about decentralisation and local government, employment in the central bureaucracy increased during the same period by 60.4 per cent whereas it increased only by 28.7 per cent in local government. (Many central government employees are located in branches all over the country and therefore count as 'local officials' although they are not strictly local government officers: in 1980 there were 1,218,000 'local officials' ['Umar and al-Shirbini, 1981: 96–111].) Within these general figures, specific employment in public welfare services grew by only 5.4 per cent and in public economic organisations by only 4.1 per cent, an indication that the 'conventional' rather than the 'developmental' bureaucracy had received the main bulk of the new recruits. The growth in public personnel also tended to be proportionately larger at the top echelons of each category of the bureaucracy: thus ministerial posts (to include governors) grew by 48.4 per cent, undersecretaries by 130.1 per cent and directors-general by 126.1 per cent. However, higher posts in general increased by 25.9 per cent. In the remaining categories, although middle management positions increased by 155.7 per cent, the lower executive and administrative posts had grown by only 114.5 per cent [Ghunaim, 1986: 232–3].

Looking at the expansion by sector we find that it was unfavourable to several 'developmental' sectors. With the exception of the industry and petroleum sector where personnel grew by 145.2 per cent (partly due to the expansion in the petroleum industry following the 'oil boom'), the largest expansion between 1977 and 1980/81 took place in law and order sectors (defence, police, and justice) by 212.6 per cent; in insurance by 162.1 per cent; in supplies and commerce by 142.1 per cent; and in the presidential (sovereignty) services by 140.3 per cent. The lowest growth rates were in electricity and energy (by 63.4 per cent); in culture and information (67.8 per cent); in tourism and aviation (113.1 per cent); in agriculture and irrigation (116.0 per cent); and in education, research, and youth (by 120.8 per cent). Growth in personnel had thus, on the whole, been more favourable to law and order, 'sovereignty' and other control and 'repressive' organs of the state bureaucracy than it had been to the 'developmental' and social welfare sectors (with the exception of oil and some industries).

Neither did public expenditure in general decline as a result of the adoption of *infitah*. If anything, the percentage of total public expenditure to GDP had increased – from 48.7 per cent in 1976 to 62.9 per cent in 1981/82 (at current prices) – indicating that the economic role of the state bureaucracy actually grew under *infitah*, especially with regard to income distribution.

In the four years following the announcement of *infitah* (1976 to 1980/81) total public consumption rose from £E3.2 billion to £E5.9 billion (that is to say, by 84 per cent). Not all of the increase was due to expansion in developmental activity but was caused rather by the huge growth of the 'law and order' and repressive organs of the state (e.g. Central Security Forces, State Security Investigation, State Security Courts and the so-called 'Morals Courts', the armed forces, etc.).

Expenditures on law and order grew from £E91.5 million in 1976 to £E241 million in 1980/81 (i.e. by 263 per cent at current prices, and by 139.6 per cent at fixed prices). Their share of total public consumption increased from 3.6 per cent in 1976 to 4.1 per cent in 1980/81. Expenditure on the armed forces increased by 152 per cent during the same period although its share of total public expenditure had decreased from 22.6 per cent in 1976 to 18.2 per cent in 1980/81. This remained a high percentage and military expenditure was, in any case, soon to resume its upwards climb.

By contrast expenditure on education remained unchanged and its share of total public consumption stayed almost the same: 10.9 per cent in 1976 and 11.0 per cent in 1980/81. Expenditure on public health decreased, however: its index number in fixed prices dropped from 340 in 1976 (1962/63 = 100) to 273 in 1980/81, while its share of total public consumption remained the same in 1980/81 as it had been in 1976 (i.e. 2.9 per cent of the total).

The general conclusion applicable to both 1976 and 1980/81 is that expenditure on law and order was in both years about double the expenditure on education and health (26.2 per cent : 12.9 per cent in 1976, and 22.2 per cent : 12.9 per cent in 1980/81). The political and developmental implications of this were significant, as the first type of expenditure represented the 'repressive' functions of the state whereas the second represented its role in reproducing the labour force and improving its productivity [Ghunaim, 1986: 240–41].

It can thus be seen that, the open door policy notwithstanding, the Egyptian bureaucracy was continuing to expand in terms of personnel and expenditure. However the expansion was more remarkable in areas related to the 'control' or repressive functions of the state than it was in areas related to its 'service' or socio-economic functions. As the figures surveyed above confirm, although the state bureaucracy had witnessed some important changes, its proportions had by no means declined.

Bureaucratic growth in the Mashriq

These countries also convey unmistakable features in terms of bureaucratic growth. The number of ministries often increases from a relatively limited number at the time of independence to upwards of two dozen or so by the

1980s. Public-sector organisations also emerge and increase in number, with noticeable speed. Employees and expenditures grow exponentially.

IRAQ The modern Iraqi bureaucracy dates back to 1920, at which time eight ministries were in existence, to which a separate Ministry of Education was subsequently added, while in 1953 a special Ministry for Development was created. By 1968 the number of ministries had increased to 18, then rose to the higher twenties during the mid-1970s before dropping back to the lower twenties in the mid-1980s [AOAS, 1986: 142, 209]. The pattern with regard to public organisations was more impressive. Four of these were established in 1964, but their number was to reach seventy-five in the mid-1980s [AOAS, 1986: 1209].

The number of government officials (excluding employees of the postal system and railways) scarcely exceeded 3,000 in 1920 but grew to nearly 10,000 in 1938 and to 20,000 in 1958 (in addition to nearly 4,000 in railways). Policemen also increased from 2,470 in 1920 to 12,000 in 1941 and over 23,000 in 1958. By 1960 the number of government officials and employees had reached nearly 208,000 and by 1967 the number had already jumped to 319,000 [Al-Maleh, 1990: 257–62]. The overall number of officials and employees, estimated at 85,000 at the time of the 1958 revolution had virtually quadrupled by 1967, i.e. during less than a decade.

Excluding defence, the bureaucracy in 1967 employed some 319,000 civil servants. By 1976 the number had again nearly doubled to 558,000 and then increased further, to 663,000 by 1978 [Al-Maleh, 1990: 265, 286; Al-Khafaji, 1983: 33–4]. Fifty-three out of each 1,000 of the population were therefore publicly employed, and the state had thus engaged 19 per cent of the workforce, excluding defence, and 26 per cent including the armed forces.

Because of the war with Iran, no figures were published for the period after 1978, but if the trends are extrapolated, there must have been some 835,000 public employees (or sixty-three for each 1,000 of the population) on the eve of the Iran–Iraq war [Al-Khalil, 1991: 41]. The number must therefore have multiplied nearly ten times since the revolution of 1958. Some other features of state employment were also becoming clear by the end of the 1970s, most notably the unrivalled growth in the personnel of the Ministry of the Interior (i.e. the security apparatus) to reach 22.8 per cent or nearly one out of each four publicly employed individuals, a fact that becomes more startling when compared, for example, to the decline in educational personnel: whereas security officials (Interior) had increased by 152 per cent between 1967 and 1976, educational personnel had decreased by -48 per cent. This might have been due not only to the new emphasis placed on security but also to the purging of the schools of all non-Ba'thist elements [Al-Maleh, 1990: 266–8].

In terms of public expenditure, and especially current expenditure on administration, detailed figures are even more scarce, but we know more generally that the expenditure of central government and public enterprise as a proportion of GDP had grown from 28.4 per cent in 1960 to 44.2 per cent in 1970 [quoted in Owen, 1992: 35]. This proportion had grown to 51.3 per cent in 1975, to 80.6 per cent in 1978, and to 74 per cent in 1980 from whence it started to exceed the 100 per cent mark since Iraq at war was beginning to live on borrowing and external donations (thus, for example, 155.6 per cent in 1981 and 150.6 per cent in 1982) [Arab Monetary Fund, 1981–83].

SYRIA At the time of independence Syria had fewer than ten ministries, a figure which had more than doubled by the 1980s to twenty-four. The number of public sector organisations also showed a similar increase, so that by the early 1980s there were some sixty public organisations (mu'assasat) and some twenty-five public corporations in Syria.

In terms of employment there were in Syria in 1982 some 440,000 public officials working in the civil service and the public sector (excluding the armed forces, police and security). Compared to total population for the same year (of 10,788,000) the ratio is one to 25, or four per cent [Minister of state, 1984]. Related to a total labour force of 2,174,000 in 1979, this means that civilian public employment represented 20 per cent of total employment [Syria, Central Statistical Office, 1981].

Current expenditure in Syria amounted to 23,438 million Lire out of total expenditures of 41,287 million Lire in 1983 (i.e. 56.8 per cent). Expenditure on wages and salaries in the same year amounted to 4,358 million Lire, or 18.6 per cent of current expenditures.

JORDAN In Jordan, organisational growth followed along the usual expansionary lines, with 22 ministries and around 38 public organisations of various descriptions [Abu Shikha, 1983] by the early 1980s.

According to the 1979 census, Jordan's population amounted to 2,152,000; the labour force was estimated at 398,000, or 18 per cent, of this figure. In 1982, 59,000 people worked for the government (excluding daily and project workers) [Public Statistics Department, 1982; Al-Khidma al-Madaniyya, June 1983]. Thus government officials represented 2.75 per cent of the population and 14.9 per cent of the labour force.

Looked at in terms of expenditure, one finds that in the Jordan state budget of 1981, current expenditures amounted to JD363 million (out of total outlays of JD638 million, i.e. about half the total). Current expenditures of the civilian sectors amounted to JD141 million, out of which figure wages and salaries accounted for JD77 million or 21 per cent [state Budget Department, 1981].

Bureaucratic growth in the Maghrib

Comparisons involving the Arab countries of North Africa do not always invoke the same variables. That region has been relatively less subject to Ottoman influences and to Egyptian 'two-steps transfer of administrative technology' and to Egyptian organisational improvisation. By contrast it has been more driven by *mimétisme* and by faithful imitation of the French model, with the result that even its administrative categories and terminology remain quite different from those prevalent in the Arab East [cf. Sbih, 1977; Benazzi, 1989: 26–37].

TUNISIA The number of ministries in Tunisia increased rather gently from thirteen to fifteen shortly after the country gained its independence in 1956, to eighteen in the mid-1970s and to nineteen in the mid-1980s [Moore, 1970: 340–43; AOAS, 1986: 142, 1208]. The number of public enterprises grew from a few public utilities (such as water and gas) on the eve of independence to 16 corporations (mainly in the areas of iron, and chemical, metallic and petroleum industries) in 1961, to more than 300 enterprises in the early 1980s, organised under various economic sectors: hotels, iron and steel, real estate, banking, insurance, agriculture, transport, electricity and gas, petroleum, etc. [Duwaji, 1967: 129–57; Midoun, 1985: 95–7].

The number of public functionaries grew from about 30 thousand at the time of independence to 52 thousand in 1964 [Ben Salem, 1976: 36–61 et passim]. By 1984 the number, including employees but not workers in the *Etablissements Public*, had jumped to 249,000, representing about thirty-seven public servants for each 1,000 of the population and 25 per cent of all waged employees outside the agricultural sector [Chekir, 1985; Ridha, 1989: 175–7]. Roughly half of this number worked in the civil service itself and the other half in the public sector. The percentage of public employment to all waged employees would reach 38 per cent if one were to add public enterprise workers [Al-Manubi, 1985: 111–13].

In 1982 public expenditure accounted for 42 per cent (and personnel and administrative expenses alone for 12.2 per cent) of GDP, and in the early 1980s the state sector was responsible for 59 per cent of all investments (17 per cent of the total government expenditure being spent on administration and 42 per cent spent on public enterprises [Ben Achour, 1985: 7–9; Al-Manubi, 1985: 106–7; AOAS, 1986: 1203]. The percentage of public salaries to overall wages continued to grow, reaching 28.7 per cent of the total in 1977 and 32.9 per cent of the total in 1984 [Cherif, 1985: 41–3]. If one is to add public enterprise workers the percentage would reach 60 per cent. Wages and salaries represented 28.3 per cent of all current expenditure in 1983, and 20 per cent of all public expenditure in the period 1978 to 1983 [Al-Manubi, 1985, 107–8, 117].

ALGERIA Algeria is also distinctive but in the opposite direction. Having been technically part of France, its regional administration was run by Europeans under French laws. The result was that when the country acquired its independence after a bitter war of liberation there were fewer than 30,000 minor employees and assistants (*adjoints indigènes*).

Finding themselves in somewhat of a legal and institutional vacuum the new nationalist government extended the validity of French laws and regulations, while issuing more of their own (some 35,000 laws to the mid-1980s), incorporated significant numbers of the FLN personnel, expanded education most radically (thus the number of higher education students was to increase from 1,000 in 1962 to 150,000, plus 5,000 in administrative and professional training, in 1984), and personnel were rushed to France for training, thereby allowing the number of functionaries in the bureaucracy to grow by about 30 per cent per annum during the early years of independence.

By the late 1980s the Algerian government had twenty-six ministries and about thirty-nine public organisations, and was employing over 800,000 functionaries (i.e. about 4 per cent of the population and nearly 20 per cent of the total labour force). The wages and salaries of these employees accounted by the early 1990s for 52 per cent of all current expenses [Muqaddam, 1993: 11–13].

Bureaucratic growth in the Gulf

Compared to Egypt's bureaucracy, which traces its origins back thousands of years and which in its 'modern' form dates from well over a century ago, the bureaucracies of the Gulf are both new and created from scratch. Their main expansion has been an outcome of oil wealth, which urged the state towards large-scale social welfare programmes and into very ambitious economic development plans. They are useful to consider at this point, by way of contrast with Egypt.

SAUDI ARABIA The Saudi bureaucracy was initiated in the 1950s and its growth during the first three decades of its life so far has been remarkable. The number of ministries has grown from four to twenty; thus, for example, the Council of Ministers formed in 1975 included sixteen 'operational' ministers and three ministers of state without portfolio [Al-Farsy, 1982: 98–9]. Over forty public authorities and corporations have been established (compared to none before 1950) [Othman, 1979: 234ff]. These include the General Petroleum and Mineral Organisation (Petromin), the Silos and Mills Organisation, the Hassa Irrigation and Drainage Authority, the Saline Water Conversion Corporation, the Saudi Basic Industries Corporation (SABIC), the Saudi Consulting House, and so on.

Civil service employees who numbered no more than a few hundred in

1950 increased to about 37,000 in 1962/63, to 85,000 in 1970/71, and to over 245,000 in 1979/80. The ratio of public employees to the total population in the early 1980s was approximately 3.5 per cent to 4 per cent, which is not in fact excessively high, but government civil servants represented 10 per cent of the total labour force and 13 per cent if one counted non-career personnel.

The 'oil boom' manifested itself in a massive increase in revenues which jumped most dramatically from $2,744.6 million in 1972 to $22,573.5 million in 1974. This was immediately followed by large increases in expenditure. Salaries and benefits grew remarkably, from SR3,122.8 million in 1972/73 to SR41,127.6 million in 1981/82. Current expenditure (Section Two) grew during the same period from SR1,365.1 million to SR18,656.5 million. In estimating bureaucratic outlays and expenditures in the Saudi case, one has also to look at some unusual categories such as those relating to local subsidies, municipal facilities, and 'Human Resources/Manpower Development'. If growth in public employment in Saudi Arabia has not been excessively exaggerated, then the expansion in public expenditure has definitely been most impressive.

KUWAIT A handful of administrations and directorates that existed in the early 1950s were developed into ten departments in 1959. These were turned into ministries in 1962 and three more were added, making a total of thirteen ministries. By 1976 the number of operating ministries had reached sixteen in addition to two ministers of state [Marouf, 1982: 32–9]. There were in addition a number of higher councils created (e.g. for Petroleum Affairs, for Housing Affairs, etc.), and over twenty-five public authorities and corporations have been brought into being, such as the Social Security Organisation, the Public Ports Organisation, the Public Investment Authority, the Petro-Chemical Corporation, the Flour Mills Corporation, etc.

The numbers of government employees grew remarkably. In 1963 they were 22,073, in 1965/66 they were 69,520, in 1970/71 had reached 70,922, in 1975/76 were 113,274, and in 1979/80 had risen to 145,451. By official accounts, government employees represented 12.5 per cent of the population and about 34 per cent of the total labour force of Kuwait in 1975.[2] The Kuwaiti bureaucracy is, by all accounts, overstaffed. In 1979 the Amir of Kuwait expressed the view that some 64,000 civil servants in Kuwait were redundant, and a World Bank report on Kuwaiti public administration suggested a total freeze on all new appointments.

Government expenditures have also grown remarkably. They increased from KD154.1 million in 1964/65 to KD271.6 million in 1967/68 to KD1,749.9 million in 1970/71. Wages and salaries followed suit, increasing from KD6.9 million in 1964/65, to KD98.6 million in 1967/68, and to KD119.8 million in 1970/71. As is to be expected, the most dramatic increases took place after the oil boom, thus raising current domestic expenditures from KD227 million in 1972/73 to KD658.4 million in 1975/76 to KD881.4 million in 1978/79, and to a budgeted KD1,196.4 million for 1979/80. Of these expenditures, the following amounts were spent on wages and salaries: KD188.9 million in 1972/73, KD353.5 million in 1975/76, KD456.6 million in 1978/79, and a budgeted KD485.8 million in 1979/80. Wages and salaries do indeed swallow up a large amount of public expenditure: in the 1978/79 budget, for example, they totalled KD485.8 million out of KD1,969.4 million, and ranked as the main item in the budget [Central Bank of Kuwait, *Economic Report for 1978*: 48].

It is estimated by some that nearly 39 per cent of all government expenditures can be classified as being of an 'organisational' nature. This includes items such as the 'head of state' and the 'Amiri Diwan', with their huge allocations, as well as more standard things such as expenses of the Employees' Bureau and of 'supplementary allocations'.

The invasion of Kuwait by Iraq in August 1990 and the subsequent intervention by the Western allies that in early 1991 led to their war against Iraq and to the almost total destruction of Kuwait, completely altered the picture of Kuwait's bureaucratic infrastructure. At the time of writing, it was impossible to say whether and how Kuwait was to return to the *status quo ante*, but the case still remains as a valid example for comparison here.

THE UNITED ARAB EMIRATES (UAE) The first federal government was formed immediately after the Union was declared in 1971, with Abu Dhabi being the main sponsor. In 1968 Abu Dhabi had some twenty government directorates which, by 1970, had increased to twenty-five in number. The first council of ministers of Abu Dhabi was formed in 1971 and included fifteen ministers, but was abolished in 1973; instead a federal cabinet that contained twenty-eight ministers was created, with Abu Dhabi establishing an executive council to run its own affairs. A number of public authorities and corporations have also been created in the UAE in recent years, such as the Abu Dhabi Steelworks, the General Industry Corporation, and the Abu Dhabi Investment Authority.

The number of government employees has grown appreciably. In 1968 the Abu Dhabi administration employed about 2,000 officials. By 1970 their number had already doubled, and by 1974 had reached 5,352, of which 37 per cent were UAE citizens, 42 per cent were other Arabs, and 21 per cent were foreign nationals [Rashid, 1975, and refs quoted]. Just eight years later (i.e. by 1982), the number of public employees in Abu Dhabi had jumped to 24,078 [AIPK and CAUS, 1983: 358].

Public employment on the federal level has also grown at an impressive rate: it had indeed quadrupled in size in just one decade, from 10,500 in 1972 to over 40,000 in 1982 [Arabian Government, 1983: 213]. The explosion in public employee numbers is, in fact, the most dramatic among the three Gulf countries studied, given the country's minute population base, its extremely recent state of independence, and the fact that the oil boom more or less immediately followed its formation. The UAE is representative – but in an extreme way – of what happened in other desert states where, because the local human base could not support the required expansion, heavy reliance was, as a result, placed upon expatriate labour. In the Abu Dhabi bureaucracy (which is the largest and most established within the UAE), a ridiculous 83.6 per cent of all officials are foreign nationals.

There are several indications that the state bureaucracy may have stretched itself far beyond its capabilities. In 1983, this country, which ranks among the highest in the world in terms of its per capita income, suffered a budgetary deficit of DH5,461 million and had, among other things, to delay the payment of salaries to its public employees for a number of months. As the budgetary deficit was expected to reach the even larger amount of DH6,635 million in 1984, the Ministry of Finance and Industry issued various ministries with memoranda forbidding the creation of any new public post for non-citizens during the following financial years.

A huge expansion in public finances has been taking place in the UAE, especially since the oil boom. Thus the federal budget (mainly financed by Abu Dhabi) had grown from BD21 million in 1971 to BD81 million in 1974, and to DH1.69 million in 1975. The various states continued, however, to maintain separate budgets and accounts. The state accounts of Abu Dhabi, for example, show most clearly how the revenues doubled and expenditures then more than doubled in just one year (from 1973 to 1974) as a result of the oil boom. Of these expenditures, outlays for Abu Dhabi and federal ministries accounted for nearly 40 per cent of the total ['Aziz, 1979: 55–70]. In the Abu Dhabi budget for 1976, current expenditures both for the emirate itself and for the federation as a whole had grown even further. In this year, Abu Dhabi contributed DH4 million to the federal budget of DH4.152 million (or about 96.3 per cent of the total). A high percentage of the federal budget also goes to current expenditures: in the 1977 federal budget, it was DH9,833 million out of DH13,150 million, or 74.8 per cent of the total.

In 1982, budgetary outlays in the federation were estimated at DH22,559.5 million, of which only DH3,539.5 million went to investments, while DH19,019.6 million represented current expenditures. Among these latter, Section I (mainly salaries and benefits) was responsible for DH3,893 million.

To conclude this section on bureaucratic growth, one can say that public administrations grow with the expansion and complexity of their societies and their economies, especially if the private sector happens to be historically and structurally weak. Politically, bureaucracies are expanded in order to provide the rulers with a 'stability platform', a control device and a space for extending patronage.

But then bureaucratic growth picks up its own momentum: the fast-growing numbers of educated people expect public jobs; and indeed scope for alternative (private) employment may also be 'historically' constrained or it may have been limited intentionally by the regime (for it is a potential base for competing politics) [cf. Ayubi, 1990a].

However the case may be, there comes a point in the history of the bureaucratic expansion of each country when the dysfunctions of institutional growth start to outweigh its positive functions. If one looks at the phenomenon historically, it is possible to see how at the initial period, many felt that expanding the public bureaucracy could be seen as an instrument of modernisation (and hence development); the bureaucracy was considered an agency of 'rationality', 'legality' and order/organisation in societies that were believed to lack these ingredients. Bureaucracies were also regarded as important vehicles for state- or nation-building in 'artificial' countries that lacked the social bases for a nation-state, while some considered them useful agencies for initiating infrastructural and/or industrial programmes in societies that were historically lacking in entrepreneurial traditions. American literature on modernisation during the 1960s featured several famous books on 'bureaucracy and development'.

Once a bureaucracy gets too large, not only does it absorb scarce resources that could better be directed towards more productive activities, but it also starts to 'get in the way': 'crowding out' private enterprise and pushing civil society to the margins. Internally such a bureaucracy would also suffer from quite a few pathologies: routine and red tape, rent-seeking attitudes, poor salaries and conditions, and quite possibly corruption. The point at which a bureaucracy becomes so dysfunctional can only be defined empirically for each country since it is contingent, among other things, upon the particular economic, entrepreneurial and organisational conditions of a particular society at a particular moment in time.

To stop bureaucratic expansion at this point needs not only the 'political will' that people like to talk about but also the political capacity to do so; it needs a strong regime just at a time when the regime would have exhausted most of its political credit and as its 'populist' policies reach their natural ceiling, beyond which they can go no further. But it is a job that has to be done, especially in the Arab World where the financial resources accruing, directly or indirectly, from oil resources are declining in absolute and in relative importance.

One thorny problem facing practically all Arab countries will be how to shed the huge number of publicly employed personnel, a problem that had reached extraordinary dimensions by 1990 in countries as different in their ideological orientations as Algeria (where 59 per cent of the labour force was publicly employed) and Jordan (where the figure was 47 per cent). Morocco is almost unique among the Arab countries in showing an employment structure that is more similar to that pertaining in 'standard' capitalist societies. During the same period (and according to some World Bank estimates) only 6.3 per cent of the labour force was working for the government and only 8 per cent was publicly employed (i.e. working for the government or the public sector) – thus making clear the extremely small percentage working in publicly owned enterprises [cf. Shihata, 1992: 9 and refs cited].

EXPLAINING THE EXPANSION

The reasons for bureaucratic inflation are multiple. Some of the expansion is due purely to demographic growth, and to the need to supply services for increasing populations. But as the percentage of public officials within the population in general and within the labour force at large tends to be higher than is found in many other societies, one has to examine other possible reasons for the bureaucratic expansion. Of these, the following seem to be of particular importance: the traditional prestige of public office (for long associated with the powerful foreign rulers); the strong belief in the developmental role of the bureaucracy; the importance of public office for building the contacts deemed necessary for pursuing private business; and possibly the impact of the Egyptian model both as an exemplar and also through the role of the large number of Egyptians working in many other Arab countries.

Some of the reasons for bureaucratic growth are quite entrenched in the social and political conditions of the society. Most important is the phenomenon of huge expansion in formal higher education that is in no way related to the economic needs and manpower requirements of the society. Under pressure from people aspiring to higher social prestige, and under the unproved belief that expanded 'qualification' produces economic development, the Middle East has witnessed a strong case of what has been termed "the diploma disease" [Dore, 1976].

Another major reason for the expansion in the size (and role) of the government bureaucracy in these countries is attributable to the growing 'rentier' nature of the state, mainly as a consequence of the oil boom. The rentier description is meant here to indicate that a dominant or significant proportion of the national income is derived from rents rather than from the returns of the productive (mainly commodity) sectors of the economy, and that these rent-type revenues do in a major part accrue to the state, which takes charge of their allocation and distribution. Some writers also maintain that " 'rentierism' is not merely an economic phenomenon ... rentier criteria ... also possess concomitant cultural/behavioral characteristics that make it difficult for the rentier state to increase its productive capacity and to maximise the economic and political advantages at its disposal" [Palmer, Alghofaily and Alnimir, 1984].

The rentier nature of the oil-rich states (Saudi Arabia, Kuwait, the UAE, etc.) is obvious enough. The percentage of oil to total exports in these countries has ranged between 90 and 99 per cent and the percentage of oil revenues to total state revenues between 85 and 99 per cent, and oil's contribution to

GDP is, in turn, to a large extent related to government expenditure which is almost totally dependent on oil revenues. The fact that oil revenues accrue to the state before they can be allocated and distributed has given the state in the oil-rich countries an extremely large and powerful economic and social role, in spite of all the 'anti-socialist' rhetoric of the governing élites.

For the rulers of the oil-rich states, the bureaucracy serves as a neat, 'respectable' and modern-looking tool for distributing part of the spoils. Instead of the traditional method of straightforward handouts, it offers a more dignified way for disbursing largesse, camouflaged in the language of meritocracy and national objectives. And sure enough, in spite of all its patrimonialism, the Gulf bureaucracy is a redistributive instrument, for it does provide people of lesser status and income with opportunities for social promotion through state education and bureaucratic careers.

The creation of jobs in the 'petrocracy' becomes almost an objective in its own right, with little regard for what these recruits should (or could) do. This explains, among other things, the high numbers of illiterate and other poorly educated nationals who tend to be employed by the bureaucracies of the oil-rich states. It may also partly explain why many officials are not in their offices for much of the time. Foreign and local advisers who recommend things like job description and classification, with possible reduction in job numbers, are often mistaken: the apparent inefficiency may be at least partly intentional Even before the oil bonanza, one analyst observed aptly enough that "Some of the inefficiency is deliberate, because civil service appointments are viewed as a vehicle for distributing oil wealth among the citizenry and as a means of giving idle Kuwaitis a job. Consequently most offices are grossly over-staffed; five people are commonly employed to do work that one could perform" [Al-Marayati, 1972: 290].

Even the growing number of foreigners in the bureaucracy of the oil-state, which is often regarded as a potential political risk, is not without its rewards. It gives locals the opportunity to command and supervise a respectable number of subordinates (who, furthermore, are frequently better qualified and experienced than the superior himself). This is bound to represent an element of satisfaction for the native officials and to lessen the possible antagonisms between them and their rulers, by emphasising instead the citizen–expatriate dichotomy. The assignment of technical tasks to 'outsiders' in the oil-states also happens to fit the established tradition, and therefore represents an element of continuity and does not interrupt existing patterns. Nomadic societies have traditionally assigned 'technical' jobs to slaves, minorities and outcasts, keeping for the insiders – in addition to the pastoral activities – the honour of carrying arms [cf. Gellner, 1981]. One might wonder, however, now that foreign troops are working for the Gulf states, whether the oil boom has moved the Arabian away even from this time-honoured function.

The deadlock in development administration

Marx has explained how bureaucracy survives by projecting the image of serving the general interest. In the Middle East the bureaucracy does the same, but it also projects the image of being the main 'vehicle for development'. Middle Eastern leaders called upon the bureaucracy not only to fulfil the conventional 'law and order' functions but also to involve itself in industry, trade, education, culture and so forth. The literature of the 1950s and 1960s was also replete with praise for the developmental potential of the public bureaucracy – to many people it represented an orderly alternative to the agonies of a social or a cultural revolution.

The direction of development administration was clear: expand and consolidate departmental-type administration, involve your bureaucracy in national comprehensive planning, in extensive industrialisation programmes, in urban construction, and in a fast-expanding system of conventional higher education.[3]

Discovering – usually half way along – that the bureaucracy was probably ill-equipped to deal with this heavy load, the authorities declared that in order to have successful 'development administration' there must first be effective 'administrative development'. Since administration was regarded as a science that had reached its maturity in the West, administrative development was to a large extent regarded as an exercise in the 'transfer of technology', and 'modernisation' of the administration was regarded as the solution to most of its problems [see Wickwar, 1963 for a historical review of this subject]. The 1950s and 1960s were also a high point for technical assistance (both national and international), concentrated first – in the Middle East – on Turkey, Egypt and Iran, and then proceeding to the rest of the Arab World.[4] A combination of the ideas of such people as Fayol, Taylor and Weber, with their underlying concepts of economy, efficiency and rationality were presented – sometimes in the simplified 'principles' form (such as in POSDCORB) – as the *passe-partout* 'science of administration'. This so-called 'scientific management' was indeed nothing other than what Gramsci called 'Fordism', which represented both a promise and a challenge to less advanced societies [cf. e.g. Buci-Glucksmann, 1980: 317–24].

One does not need to go out of one's way to illustrate the hold that the ideas of such authors, and particularly those of Max Weber, had and still have on experts on administration in the Arab World. All one has to do is to pick up any piece of writing by any reputable Arab expert on administration and there they will be. Of course, there is nothing wrong with referring to these writers; the problem is that the exercise very often not only begins with them but also ends up with them, making no reference at all to the relevance of their ideas to an Arab society.

With this 'science of administration' in mind, efforts for administrative reform adopted a variety of *approaches*, including the following:

— issuing new legislation or amending and supplementing the existing laws and regulations;
— organising and reorganising; wherever a problem is found, create or re-arrange an organisation to deal with it;
— personnel management; especially things like position description and classi-fication, merit systems and central personnel agencies;
— in the area of public finance and management of the economy; performance or programme budgeting, cost accounting techniques, 'management by objectives', etc.;
— training, especially institutionalised training, was very popular, but without adequate adaptation of the content or the methodology.

In attempting the various methods of administrative reform, the Arab countries tend to follow a set of distinctive *phases*:

— in an early phase the emphasis will usually be on new legislation, especially in the area of legalising, 'rationalising' and coordinating personnel laws and regulations in all sectors all over the country.
— in a following phase, a civil service bureau or commission will be formed and an institute for the training of public servants will be established. There is hardly an Arab country that has not followed this 'academy model', so that nearly every one of them by now has its own institute or institutes for administrative training.
— in a subsequent phase, calls for work simplification will inevitably lead to many attempts at reorganisation, organisation-and-methods units will be installed in various public organisations, and a central agency for organ-isation and administrative reform will sometimes be created. There are very few Arab countries that do not by now have at last one central commission or agency that is in general charge of its public service.
— in a later stage, it will be found that although the legal standardisation of personnel systems has had some undeniable benefits, it has not been par-ticularly conducive to raising efficiency. Calls are therefore heard for relating pay to the nature and requirements of every post rather than to the persons occupying the posts, or to the diplomas that they carry. Attempts are then made in the area of job description and job classification. These efforts, however, remain painfully slow, because of the many problems of implemen-tation and the considerable amount of social, and sometimes political, resistance that they encounter along the way.

By the 1970s it had become clear that, contrary to expectations, the strat-egies of development administration or policies of administrative develop–ment that were usually followed were unable to solve the various problems as had been hoped. First, concerning development administration, the following problems arose: a decline in agriculture and in the countryside; urban overcrowding, decay and a growing and frustrated lumpenproletariat; acute balance-of-payments difficulties, and dependence on the outside world for finance and technology; unemployment of the educated and a lopsided cultural development; domination by a bureau-technocratic élite, and so forth. A relative growth in gross national product (GNP) in the 1950s and 1960s was soon to decline from the early part of the 1970s in most of the non-oil-exporting countries, while many basic needs remained unsatisfied. Second, in the area of administrative reform, the changes introduced were never fully satisfactory, either to the clientele or to the political leadership, so that they had always to be repeated, each time with more vigorous rhetoric but with less effective performance.

A proposed explanation and a solution appeared here: the concepts were good but the application was bad (e.g. socialism was noble but its application – *tatbiq* – went wrong); the 'planning' was perfect, but the 'implementation' was defective. But this merely reflected a fallacy in which the process of planning was confused with the act of writing a plan, an approach succinctly described by Bernard Schaffer:

> This new version of an old fallacy seems to be arguing thus. Administrative reform (or urban policy, etc.) is the writing of reform plans and documents. Examples are the reports of reform committees. Then little enough seems to happen quickly or directly. The explanation, as quoted, is: there are two phases, writing and implementing, again. There is a weakness (an Achilles heel), but only in the second, separate phase (implementation). Why? Because in the second phase the 'reforms' encounter 'obstacles', including a 'lack of political will'. What can the reformers do about that? They can list these obstacles! (Someone else can then presumably remove them) ... the longer and tidier the list, the more advanced the literature and method: the more powerful an instrument of reform! So the lists quoted are now very long indeed. (Will they soon summarise the whole of life? After all, that is what they mean.) [Schaffer, 1980: 194]

Implementation cannot be separated from planning as a possible cause of failure. Implementation requires political support from the leadership, dedication from the lower administrative echelons, cooperation from the clientele or the public, and coordination at all levels. If mechanisms for ensuring these requirements cannot be incorporated in the planning process, there may very well be a case for considering this particular type of planning an 'inappropriate technology' for this type of society at this stage of its development [cf. Weinstein, 1981: 116–18].

Although the problem of implementation is not confined to the developing countries (indeed there has been much on the subject published in the United States since the 1970s), many observers believe that it is more of a complex 'problematique' in Third World countries [cf. Grindle's 'Introduction' and Cleave's 'Conclusion', in Grindle, 1980]. This may very well suggest that much of the failure in implementation in the Third World is probably due to the irrelevance of the policies or to the plans themselves, and not simply to some casual operational difficulties. An analysis that would confine itself only to 'obstacles to implementation' will not be sufficient in this case, and one's whole approach to policy and administration will have to be reconsidered if effectiveness is to be achieved.

This fallacy of 'obstacles to implementation' can be likened to the once dominant, and still influential, school of writing about 'obstacles to modern-isation', whereby any local differences from a presumed or North American model were so described [Schaffer, 1980: 192–3]. This same approach also characterised many attempts at administrative reform and practically all the ones where an element of 'technical assistance' was involved. The United Nations public administration teams of experts in the 1950s and 1960s are illustrative of this approach. One of their reports on administrative reform in Turkey tells the whole story. As Bernard Schaffer describes it: "the United Nations report was typical. The dominant features of the Turkish public service were seen as 'problems'. It followed that 'Turkey is ripe for the reform of its administration'" [Schaffer, 1974: 285–6]. This trend has always been part of modernisation theory. Very often aspects of the Egyptian, Syrian or Saudi society are *described*, then they are presented as the *cause* of the underdevelop-ment of these countries or of the inefficiency of their people. Middle Easterners are not advanced, or not efficient, because they grow moustaches, because they do not eat pork or – as Atatürk put it – because they wear the fez!

A slightly more articulate school, inspired by Orientalism and promoted by Weber and his disciples, would maintain that Middle Easterners are not advanced, or not efficient, because most of them are Muslims [cf. Turner, 1974]. A variety of latent Orientalism has characterised much technical assist-ance to the Middle East and has reflected itself in the thinking of most Western-educated élites in the Middle East itself. The following passage by an Arab (Jordanian) expert on administration is typical of the 'obstacles' approach expressed in behaviouralist terminology:

> the value dimension is most important. There are some values in our societies that sometimes obstruct the effective offering of service to the citizen ... Of these values it is obsequiousness and 'going along' in Arab societies which lead to waste of time and avoidance of the effective confrontation of problems. Other values include concern over appearance and formalities ... and the values of domination and authoritarianism ... and the scorning of manual labour which leads to inflation in the number of desk-type positions. Then there is the belittling of women which deprives the administration of half the society, and there is also the careless attitude to time [Ribhi al-Hasan in 'Ulwan, 1977: 142–3].

A more elaborate treatment of such behavioural 'obstacles' to development in the Arab World is to be found in the writings of an Egyptian psychiatrist and expert on administration [Girgis, 1974, 1975].

Such analyses, which simply attribute underdevelopment and inefficiency to cultural traits are interesting; but they are often misguided and are rarely useful. Most concepts and principles of organisation and management are derived from Western conceptions and norms. If that which is in reality no more than the organisational manifestation of Western norms and attitudes is taken to be '*the* science of management', then it is no wonder that any departure from this stereotype was considered an expression of a pre-scientific stage of development.

But this approach is faulty on at least two counts, first because there are few universal scientific principles about a great deal of administration and management as they are presented in the standard American textbooks. As Isaac Deutscher commented, was Weber really doing much more than para-phrasing the Prussian code of good official conduct? [Deutscher, 1969]. Most so-called 'principles' of management are little more than 'proverbs' and are therefore inherently culture-bound and often difficult to transfer to a different socio-cultural environment. Second, on a prescriptive level, this approach is futile (not to mention ethnocentric) since it seems to suggest that if the Middle Easterners want to improve, to develop, and to become more technologically advanced, they have to cease to be Egyptians, Tunisians, Syrians, and so forth. As William Siffin put it:

> This 'culture vs. technology' view can be pushed to the level of chauvinistic absurdity (just as the 'traditional vs. modern' dichotomy can be elevated into an absurd oversimplification). As an explanation of why technologies won't work, 'culture' is sometimes the refuge of the very pragmatic negativist [Siffin, 1977: 57].

The cultural and ecological school of public administration initiated by Gaus, enriched by Crozier, and brought to its full flowering by Riggs, has been useful in reminding people that administration is a social, and therefore a culturally bound activity. It is fortunate that this school has acquired a reasonable following in the Middle East [cf. Al-Kubaisy, 1974]. But the achieve-ments of this school can be easily negated if its findings are used merely to prove that certain people will continue to have certain insurmountable prob-lems simply because of the specific features of their culture. Among other things, the question should be asked: is the 'sala model' or the 'bazaar ap-proach' invoked by Riggs something more related to a stage of socio-economic development, or is it more related to a particular cultural sphere regardless of its stage of development? It would be useful here to bring in the historical discussion as to whether the 'Islamic city', or the 'Islamic guild', and so on, were so specifically *Islamic*, or whether they were medieval cities and medieval guilds but located in Muslim lands [Hourani, 1981]. Authors who write about Islam as an obstacle to development will also have to explain to us (a) how the same Muslim societies could be so scientifically and organisationally advanced in medieval times, and (b) why the whole of the Third World – and not only its Muslim component – is now underdeveloped [cf. Rodinson, 1978].

An analysis that would combine the ecological approach with the contingency view of organisation may prove more effective in dealing with the problems of administration and development in the Middle East.[5] Such an analysis would have to start by evaluating the achievements of the last three decades or so. As in most of the Third World, various improvements were introduced in the functions of personnel, budgeting, planning, organisation and training, usually at the central secretariat level and in the capital city. However, the line agencies, functional departments, sectoral units and operating levels of organisations – the real carriers of development – did not benefit as much from administrative development efforts [Islam and Henault, 1979: 259].

The cost, inefficiency and authoritarianism of the omnipotent bureaucracy is indeed a current problem that most Middle Eastern countries have to cope with. As in many other countries of the Third World, dependence upon the national bureaucracy as a vehicle for economic development has given rise to an ironic situation whereby societies which are lacking good administration establish the *most* comprehensive and complex array of administrative controls over every aspect of investment, production and trade [Weinstein, 1981: 120]. Egypt, under the open door economic policy – as I have illustrated elsewhere – is a very good case in point [Ayubi, 1991b].

Middle Eastern bureaucracies have not, on the whole, succeeded in solving most of the developmental problems of their societies that they had been called upon to solve. Poverty persists, although it has often been 'modernised' [Haq, 1976; Amin, 1980]. Technology-intensive industrialisation failed to create a sufficient number of jobs to absorb a rapidly expanding labour force, and the so-called 'trickle-down effect' from the modern industrial sector to the poor in general and to the countryside in particular remained negligible. In short, the 'quality of life' for the majority of the population continued to be abysmally low, with many of the basic needs for food, shelter, health and education still unsatisfied. Nor has the administration managed to reform itself and to improve upon its own performance as an instrument of service. Quite the contrary: in many Middle Eastern societies the bureaucracy has actually become a major instrument for political domination and bureaucrats have turned into an exploitative 'new class'.

Why has the record of development administration in the Arab states been so poor? A study by Palmer and Nakib enumerates an impressive array of "administrative problems besetting the Arab world". These have been classified into four main categories: problems related to structure and organisation; to bureaucratic attitudes and behaviour; to client attitudes and behaviour; and to political inputs into the bureaucracy [Palmer and Nakib, 1978].

Problems that are related to structure and organisation are the most technical in nature, and are also the most closely related to the bureaucrat's immediate training and experience. Dealing with these sorts of problems has therefore proved to be relatively more manageable than dealings with others has been.

Political problems can certainly be more tricky. No one can deny that there is a whole host of problems that relate to 'political inputs' into the bureaucracy. When the role of the politicians is not welcome, there is a tendency to speak of political intrusions in the work of the bureaucracy; when their intervention is desired but not obtained, there is a tendency to speak of the 'lack of political will'. The truth of the matter, however, is that no public bureaucracy is politically neutral and that in no situation is there a lack of political will – rather there is a conflict between various political wills. Quite often the complaint by the official of political interference is little more than yet another enlisting of a further 'obstacle' in an attempt to exempt himself from some of the blame for the poor performance of the administration. In practice there are in the Third World many poor performers among development programmes which apparently had significant political support and commitment behind them [Paul, 1982: 5–6].

The most interesting part of the essay by Palmer and Nakib [1978] is the section which deals with "behavioral and attitudinal" problems associated both with the officials and with the clientele, in which they quote delightful passages from Arab authors to illustrate all such problems. There is nothing more tempting than to make fun of the bureaucrats, and the temptation is always strong to blend their poor performance with aspects of their environment and habitat, or to attribute their bureaucratic behaviour to the general culture of the society to which they belong. It is one way of releasing our impatience with the irritations of bureaucracy and with the slow rate of change in the society at large [nor is the present writer altogether innocent of this practice! – see Ayubi, 1980, 1982a]. But what use can this be? The point here is not that culture is unimportant, nor are we denying that certain cultural traits may be unfavourable to certain aspects of development. It is that little is known about the exact impact of culture on efficiency and effectiveness, and that therefore there is always a risk of too easily offering 'culture' as the explanation for every drawback or failure. The dangerous practical outcome of this kind of explanation is that it tends to lead to passivity and inaction.

Palmer and Nakib are not alone in maintaining that quite a few problems of administration in the Arab World "find their roots in Arab culture" [1978: 11; see also Palmer, Al-Hegelan et al., 1989, and, at length, Palmer, Leila and Yassin, 1988]. Typically, they also emphasise that "many of the structural problems discussed are merely overt manifestations of deeper cultural, behavioral and political problems endemic to the area" [p. 20]. These two distinguished writers then arrive at the tempting but rather disconcerting conclusion that

> the Arab bureaucracies, after all, are a sub-set of the population as a whole.
> They originate from the general population and, by and large, they mirror the

values and behavior of the population at large. As the Arab public generally manifests low regard for civic responsibility, it is hard to expect bureaucrats to do otherwise. In much the same manner, the low skill and education levels which are characteristic of many Arab bureaucracies are also true of the population in general. A poorly educated population deeply endowed with traditional values and behavior patterns is less able to understand, appreciate and support the modernization projects which the bureaucracy is entrusted with implementing than are the populations of educated, technically skilled and modern oriented societies such as one is likely to find in the United States or Western Europe [Palmer and Nakib, 1978: 15].

This passage is reminiscent of a favourite theme in much of modernisation theory which laments the lack of understanding – on the part of the ignorant, traditional, fatalist public – of the brilliant ideas of the political or administrative modernizer; for example, the modernisation programmes of Muhammad Reza Shah were too sophisticated to be understood and occurred too rapidly to be assimilated by his people. This variety of modernisation theory, like its equivalent in administrative studies, often lacks explanatory power and almost always lacks prescriptive value. It is lacking in explanatory power because of its failure to explain how a country like Japan managed to industrialise and raise productivity while maintaining some of the norms that modernisation theory does not consider particularly favourable to development (e.g. reverence for age and seniority, consensus-building rather than democratic voting, near-life tenure, etc.). More importantly, even when such studies are factually accurate, they tend to be of little prescriptive value. Since all their expectations are hinged on the (vain) hope that the whole society will change its values and attitudes to enable the bureaucracy to function properly, it is no wonder that they usually conclude on a pessimistic and rather helpless note.

Let us consider for instance a good study on the Saudi Arabian bureaucracy [Al-Nimir and Palmer, 1982]. The authors eloquently elaborate the familiar theme that Saudi bureaucratic behaviour differs little from Saudi social behaviour in general – this being characterised by the lack of innovation and achievement motivation, by unwillingness to relocate away from the extended family, by disdain for rural or manual labour, and so on. Not only this, but there are no grounds for optimism about the future of the Saudi bureaucracy because "the bureaucratic behavior of the younger and more educated members of the bureaucracy does not differ significantly from that of their older, less educated colleagues" [p. 94]. The difficulty with this kind of analysis is not that it lacks accuracy – I do indeed believe that it is alarmingly true – but that it is not very helpful in policy terms. What should experts in, and practitioners of, administration actually do after attributing everything to culture? Does one simply sit and wait until the values and attitudes of the Saudi society have somehow been changed (by what means nobody is able to tell us) before something constructive is done about Saudi administration?

Cases of managerial, organisational and developmental success *do* occur in the Arab World, and the beginning of wisdom should partly revolve around a stock-taking of such cases. Even the cases that have not been a glowing success can be useful as a source of learning. This is not the occasion to elaborate on policy implications [for details see Ayubi, 1986] but I might in passing report my contention that a more effective approach towards administrative development might be to reverse the present order. Rather than attempting to test the efficiency and effectiveness of Middle Eastern organisations by measuring their proximity to an idealised version of organisation (or social relations) developed elsewhere, we should start from the existing situation and try – in light of the needs of the clientele and characteristics of the environment – to develop the best possible way of improving the capacity of the administration to deal with the challenge.

THE CONTROL FUNCTIONS OF ARAB BUREAUCRACIES

Part of the reason why central, monocratic types of administration are favoured and sustained in the Arab World is because this type of bureaucracy can be utilised for its useful 'control' functions. This is why other types of organisation and administration are not tried, and why, when they are adopted within various programmes of 'administrative reform' they are used only as techniques that are void of any power-sharing devices.

Rulers become impatient with the Weberian-style 'machine bureaucracy'[6] because of its narrow-minded, routine-bound, inflexible instrumentalism that seems incapable of meeting the innovative and mobilisational challenges of development [cf. Mintzberg, 1979: 314–47]. But these same rulers find the 'machine bureaucracy' with its elaborate hierarchy and strict chain of command an invaluable control device: they feel that the 'dysfunctions' of the monocratic-type bureaucracy that they inherited from the colonial period[7] can – indeed should – be criticised, but they know that its control qualities should never be eroded. Most leaders in Arab countries now want (or say they want) development; but many want power too, and in some cases this is the more immediate and pressing of the two objectives. Fathaly and Chackerian ask the question and offer an answer:

> Part of the superficial attractiveness of machine bureaucracies is that they do quite well in coping with hostile political environments. Power is centralized in the administrative apex, and this arrangement provides clear responsibility for administrative action and quick response to *political* threats. A large, older administrative system must decentralize if it is to deal with change effectively, but this will not happen unless it has legitimacy and acceptance (i.e. unless the political environment is sufficiently benign that the just-mentioned political defensive advantages of Weberian systems are not perceived by the organization as vital to its security) [Fathaly and Chackerian, 1983: 202–7].

So, the rulers continuously lament the inefficiency of the machine bureaucracy, while overlooking the fact that their obsession with control considerations is behind its survival and strength.[8] Arab rulers appear to prefer "a system of administrative authority in which all power emanates from a single political leader, and where the influence of others is derivative in rough proportion to their perceived access to him or their share in his largesse." They often subject their bureaucracies to "a policy of frequent and unpredictable transfers of administrators. Shifting people around is a continuous reminder of how those in superior positions can intervene on whim and will." In such a power-conscious sort of system it is predictable that "ministries are typically engaged in a competition for funds with other units of government, not so much as a means to pursue particular programs as an on-going test of their standing in the bureaucratic pecking-order." The often-criticised overlapping of juris-dictions may also be politically functional from the ruler's point of view. "To ensure a high level of competition among a leader's subordinates, they are endowed with roughly equal power and given overlapping areas of authority. An absence of defined responsibility fits well the system's informal modes and enhances the leader's flexibility to choose among personnel and policies" [Weinbaum, 1979: 3–7].

A certain element of 'tolerated' corruption would then go a reasonable way towards ensuring the official's loyalty. Not only does he benefit from the situation but he is always under the threat that the 'authorities' may decide to put a stop to that 'tolerance' and to start applying the law. Should it come as a surprise, after all these measures – and given the Arab rulers' obsession with the control functions of bureaucracy – that security organisations tend to be the most 'efficient' among public organisations in most Middle Eastern countries?

Nor are the top and middle administrators themselves – given their cultural and social background – likely to be less power-conscious. A study of fifty-two executives from six Arab countries (Egypt, Jordan, Kuwait, Lebanon, Saudi Arabia and the United Arab Emirates) showed that out of a range of decisions (seven in number) likely to be taken by these executives, 22 per cent were likely to be the individual executive's own decision, 55 per cent a consultative decision (i.e. discussion with a small 'selected' group followed by his own decision), 13 per cent a joint decision, and only 10 per cent a decision based on delegation. Furthermore, as one moved from personnel to departmental to organisational decisions, one noticed less power-sharing (more autocratic) behaviour from the executive [Muna, 1980: 47–60].

If the subordinates fail to comply with the Arab executive's decision he is most likely to rely on 'position power' to manage the conflict. In situations where the executive favours a decision and the subordinate opposes it, the power tactic most favoured by many executives is 'pulling rank' and going ahead with it in spite of the opposition. In situations where the executive opposes a decision that the subordinate favours, the power tactic most often used is non-decision-making (i.e. 'freeze it' or 'give it time to die'). Indeed, the Arab executive is so afraid of losing power if discussion is allowed and managerial conflict is tolerated that he will generally seek security in what appears to be complete subordinate compliance. As one Egyptian executive appropriately expressed it: "If a leader, whether on the national or organisational level, does not suppress opposition, then people (including my employees) would think he is weak [and he would] thereby lose respect"[9] [Muna, 1980: 63–8].

It is hard to imagine that anything but the monocratic, hierarchical machine bureaucracy could suit the inclinations of such a power-conscious executive. It is no wonder therefore that most administrative reform devices that are based on power-sharing, participation and delegation, tend to die a speedy death almost as soon as they are even tried in the Arab World.

Even when the rulers and the executives may be prepared, under popular pressure or expert advice, to consider some measures of reform that involve delegation or decentralisation, they will tend to apply them in such a way that they are robbed of their main participatory ethos. In Egypt the introduction of a system for 'management by objectives' (MBO) in the mid-1970s was unsuccessful since, among other things, the executives thought of it more as a means of increasing their managerial power than as a way of achieving a high level of consensus among the employees over the policies and programmes of the organisation [Ayubi, 1982a].

Likewise, the decentralisation measures announced by President Sadat in the 1970s were utilised more for control purposes than for purposes of development and democratisation. In spite of the rhetoric, most of the 'innovations' of the new local government system that was developed in the second half of the 1970s and announced as law in 1979 had represented reactions by the government to certain political developments that had occurred. The food riots of January 1977 in particular provoked a call for greater emphasis on agricultural and rural development in order to stimulate higher production of grain, meat, dairy products, etc., and to ensure 'food security'. Around 1977, and subsequently, various aspects of social violence were experienced throughout Egypt and especially in the countryside. From the government's point of view such manifestations of socio-political unrest warranted some control measures. Escalating political criticism was condemned as contrary to the 'morals of the village' which Sadat sought to reinstall. Criticism was considered 'aib (shameful), and morals' courts were formed to deal with it and to enforce 'ethical security' in various parts of the country.

By raising the status and privileges of the governor's post and by increasing its powers (while at the same time reducing the powers of the elected local councils), the immediate on-site powers of the governors were ensured and the official grip on local affairs strengthened. The link between local government and the Ministry of the Interior was particularly re-emphasised. Then the governor was made more directly accountable to (a) the president, (b) the Governors' Council, and (c) the ruling party (also headed by the president). While the explanation given for these changes was predominantly 'developmental' and partly related to 'democratisation', the main objective was security-related: the government felt its authority was being challenged not only in the capital but also in the regions, and therefore installed new ways and means of tightening its grip over the localities while promising them a measure of increased development [Ayubi, 1984a]. The results of the 1984 elections revealed that these measures must have been effective. For the 'government party' was far more successful in the countryside and the small towns than it was in the larger cities.

The dynamics of bureaucratisation are quite easy to comprehend in a 'hydraulic' society with old state traditions like Egypt. They are more difficult to understand in bedouin societies that are renowned for the autonomy and individualism of their tribal inhabitants. In other words, *'bedoucracy'* and bureaucracy seem to be completely at odds with each other. As Ernest Gellner explains, "bureaucracy is the antithesis of kinship" [Gellner, 1981: 77]. As organisational forms they have been developed to deal with completely different sets of problems. "Arid-zone tribalism is a technique of order-maintenance which dispenses with the specialised enforcement agencies that are associated with the state (and, in a way, *are* the state)" [Gellner, 1983: 439–40]. The two opposites can be partly reconciled if the logic of a *'petrocracy'* is understood.[10]

Through the creation, expansion and maintenance of a bureaucracy, the rulers of the oil-state are paying the citizen – by way of lucrative government employment – in return for a cessation of the old tribal wars, for tacit acceptance of the political supremacy of one tribe or fraction of a tribe (i.e. the royal or princely family) over the others. And what the central administration does for the 'modern' urban sector, the system of 'local subsidies' achieves for the rural and nomadic areas. In the 1982/83 Saudi budget, for example, SR11,705 million were allocated for this purpose. (This can be likened to a system of 'indirect administration' that recognises and utilises the traditional authority networks of the bedouin while co-opting and incorporating them into the state structure.)

The taxation function is thus reversed in the oil state: instead of the usual situation of the state taxing the citizen (in return for offering him services), here the citizen is taxing the state – by acquiring a government payment – in return for staying quiet, for not invoking tribal rivalries, and for not challenging the ruling family's position (i.e. acquiescence or support). The relationship that is being established between the official and the state is quite complex. On the one hand he knows that the state (or more specifically the ruling family) needs his acquiescence; on the other he knows that he needs a public post not only for the financial benefit it offers him but also for the contracts it provides him with (which are indispensable for the conducting of 'private' business). In the short run the official is tempted to feel that he is in the stronger position, that the 'state' needs him more than he needs the state, and that he can bargain with the state over the price of acquiescence. The secretary-general of the Saudi Civil Service Commission explained the situation thus:

> The employee does not like his job, but aims at using it for acquiring certain benefits, such as those of retirement, for example. The job and its privileges are not for him work but a security policy ... [And since he] has or thinks he has other competing interests outside his job (e.g. real estate deals) many officials follow in conducting their work a policy of *bargaining* [*Al-Yamama* magazine, 9–15 March 1982; italics added].

Given this feeling and given the abundant oil reserves accruing to the state, the official is bound to think that he is receiving a meagre price for his 'service' to the state. An empirical study conducted on 614 Saudi officials indicates that 79 per cent of the respondents were dissatisfied or "neutral" as far as their pay was concerned: the "petro-dollar flood" had obviously created "very high pay expectations" [Chackerian and Shadukhi, 1983: 321].

In the longer run, however, the individual is likely to be caught up in the web of organisational relations and eventually to submit to the grasping hand of the state. For he really has nothing to offer the state, in return for his salary and benefits, other than power over himself. This is the way that a bureaucratic culture may be making inroads in the 'inhospitable' bedouin environment with its individualistic and autonomous characteristics. The logic that governs such a process can be explained thus:

> A situation may arise when one needs the help of another but has nothing to exchange in return. The alternatives for the person who needs services are to seek help from another source, force another to give help, or get along without the help. If unwilling to choose any of these, the only remaining alternative is subordination to the giver, thereby rewarding him ... with power over oneself. This subordination may be 'cashed in' by the giver at a future time for undefined benefits. Rewarding others with power over oneself is the customary experience of many workers in large organisations. Workers are dependent on employers because the latter provide wages and benefits. This dependence is particularly great if workers are not willing to resort to force, if they have few alternatives to their current employment, or if they feel they cannot do without the wages and benefits supplied by the employer [Chackerian and Abcarian, 1983: 6].

There is much evidence to suggest that most Arabians either have no alternative to relying on the state bureaucracy or feel that they cannot do without the wages, benefits and subsidies with which it supplies them. Such 'unilateral services' offered by the state bureaucracy to meet the important needs of the populace provides those in control of the state apparatus with what Peter Blau calls "the penultimate source of power", its ultimate source, of course, being physical coercion [Blau, 1964]. This explains why the governments of the oil-rich states, although hardly liberal and democratic, have on the whole managed to rule with less physical coercion than do many governments of the oil-poor Arab states.

Hierarchy in organisation has two aspects. The first is as a channel for occupational mobility with related status and economic rewards; the second is as an instrument of control [Chackerian and Abcarian, 1983: 94]. When an Arabian takes a governmental job for the promise of mobility that it provides, he cannot escape, at least in part, the control effect that it will have on him. And the available empirical evidence tends to support this theoretical postulation: the Arabian *is* learning to obey, so that in Saudi Arabia, for example, "While government workers are not highly motivated, they do seem to be responsive to demands from superiors. Hierarchical information flows are quite effective, but decisions are made at the top of the hierarchies regardless of competence" [Chackerian and Shadukhi, 1983: 321].

Learning to obey indicates that the control functions of bureaucracy are working rather successfully. But to respect hierarchy is not the same as becoming an 'organisation man'. The *bedoucracy*, with its emphasis on family and kin relationships, has survived into the *petrocracy* with its superficially large, complex and 'modern' (i.e. formal-rational) arrangements, giving rise, in fact, to a new variety of state organisation that we may call a *petro-bedoucracy*.

The resulting conflict was graphically anticipated by Al-Awaji:

> As he seeks to maintain his position before his kin, friends and local folks, on the one hand, and his superior or superiors, on the other, he either evades the issue to avoid possible conflicts, or exploits the occasion to his best. While his loyalty to his particular group is largely an emotional one, his loyalty to his superior and his organizational mandate is for expediency. Therefore, in a situation where the conflict between his personal goal and that of his organization or superior is at ease, his opportunism remains unrevealed. This may occur when a bureaucrat is able to satisfy the demands of one interest without violently offending the other. In such a case, he is an exploitationist. He could be boldly corrupt when formal rules or the modes of control are flexible, but a legalist and moralist when this may best serve and enhance his personal interest. Nevertheless, in most cases, he is escapist, i.e. when the anticipated conflict is so sharp that it may endanger his position at the office and/or home or before his personal clique, he is most likely to evade the subject. The typical situation of this sort is when the interests involved are vital to both his particular group and his supervisor or formal regulations of his agency [1971: 187].

The existence of conflict, however, should not be taken to mean that bureaucratic organisations will not develop: bureaucracy can indeed coexist with

kinship, and bureaucratic organisations can be held together through patronage relationships. The case of Jordan does in fact illustrate that the two
apparent 'opposites' can be blended rather well. Concerning the Gulf region,
'Amir al-Kubaisi has coined the term *shaikhocracy* to describe the behavioural
outcome of such a juxtaposition between the attitudes of the shaikhs who act
the bureaucrat's role, and bureaucrats who act the shaikh's role [Al-Kubaisi,
1982: 152–4].

Third World rulers in general tend to use the bureaucracy as a 'political
maintenance' device that would help in incorporating the intelligentsia and
other aspiring groups while at the same time blurring ideological and class
issues, under the guise of the bureaucracy's universality and technicality. By
raising the slogan of 'meritocracy' and recruiting to the bureaucracy people
from a wider pool and through less ascriptive means, an impression is established in the society that social promotion is possible and attainable without
the need for conflict and struggle. This could take the heat off several potential
class conflicts and allow the state to control the situation. In populist regimes
(e.g. those applying a strategy of 'developmental nationalism', such as Egypt
under Nasser), a kind of 'Bonapartism' may emerge as the rulers declare that
'we are all workers', while trying at the same time to utilise the bureaucracy
as a means for 'creating their own class' [cf. Ayubi, 1980: Chs. 5 and 6]. In
a *petrocracy*, the bureaucracy seems to represent a good vehicle by means of
which the privileges of the royal entourage can become entrenched and given
a formal character, while confrontation of the issue of class is avoided altogether, sometimes in the name of the egalitarian ethos of the nomadic society
and sometimes in the name of the brotherhood of Islam. And sure enough,
Arab officials have proved to be politically docile. They have not on the whole
formed special trade unions of their own. And those among them who join as
individuals some professional (technically specialised) syndicate have usually
proved to be more of an asset to the government than to their fellow members
who have no government jobs – this can be illustrated in particular by the
case of professional syndicates in Egypt.

In situations like these, 'bureaucratic politics' is likely to assume a relatively
important role. When states are incapable of meeting the demands of their
citizens directly, their managers may try to limit participation. "In doing so,
they may inadvertently or purposely divert participatory impulses into the
administration itself. This not only makes independent political parties functionally redundant but 'politicizes' the bureaucracy" [Anderson, 1987: 8]. A
bureaucratic position for an individual (or for one of his relatives) will represent
useful access to sources of allocative and distributive power. Influence over
decision-making related to important national or local projects will represent
one of the few available channels for 'participation' in the public affairs of the
society. 'Networking' both within the bureaucracy and with the politicians
and interest groups outside it becomes one of the main 'political' practices in

the society. This subject, however, bordering as it is on 'political anthropology', is just as difficult to study as it is important to remark upon, because of the sensitive issues such as patronage and corruption that it inevitably invokes [cf. e.g. Waterbury, 1976; Moore, 1977; Springborg, 1982; Sullivan, 1990b].

In conclusion, one can say that the deficiencies of Arab bureaucracies in offering services and in promoting development are not simply due to the lack of knowledge by Arab officials and experts of modern theories of organisation and administration. As I have already suggested elsewhere [Ayubi, 1990a] the rigidity, formality and arbitrariness of the bureaucracy is in no small measure the outcome of its usages as an instrument of power: most Arab rulers find in the machine bureaucracy a useful control device, and most executives find in it a useful arena for acquiring authority and exercising influence. Most Arab rulers and executives are interested in a developmental role for their bureaucracies, but in their real order of priorities, power may indeed occupy a much higher rank than that occupied by 'development'.

NOTES

1. Morocco represents somewhat of an exception or at least the 'mildest' case in the Arab World. By the mid-1980s the Moroccan government was composed of twenty ministries and about eighty public organisations, but it only employed some 203,500 public servants (i.e. about 1.3 per cent of the population and 5 per cent of total employment) [Royaume du Maroc, 1985].

2. Three per cent of the population and 6 to 15 per cent of the labour force is considered the usual pattern for public employment in many countries.

3. The discussion on development administration that follows draws, with permission, upon Ayubi, 1986.

4. American technical assistance in Iran was by far the largest and closest. One of the earlier projects lasted from 1956 to 1961, cost over $2.3 billion and involved about twenty-six advisers to each of the Iranian ministries except for foreign affairs and war. The majority of such advisers, who remained in the country until 1978, had very little knowledge of the local environment or culture, and they expended most of their energy in trying to change local practices without even understanding why they existed. It is hardly surprising therefore that, with the exception of the police department, these advisers were not successful on the whole in transferring their techniques across cultural boundaries [cf. Seitz, 1980: 407–12].

5. While the ecological approach has achieved a fair degree of currency among administration experts in the Arab World, the contingency approach has hardly any following – a notable exception being Ahmad Saqr Ashur of Egypt.

6. The 'machine bureaucracy' is a term used by Henry Mintzberg [1979] to connote the type of bureaucracy first described by Max Weber. The operating work of such a bureaucracy is routine, the greatest part of it being rather simple and repetitive and hence easily standardised. However, if the tasks of the organisation require a high degree of innovation and necessitate flexible response to frequently occurring and not easily predictable changes (as is the case in developing countries), standardisation is not as easy, and other types of organisation would be needed to face the challenge.

7. Both the Ottomans and the European colonial powers were more concerned with control than with development, and relied on authoritarian administrations to achieve their goals. As Arab countries gained their independence they retained the ex-colonial administrations more or less intact, and whenever they introduced changes, they drew their inspiration mainly from the French or the Egyptian models, which are both strongly control-oriented [cf. Alderfer, 1967: 33–5, 59–62].

8. In the literature on organisation there are two orientations in studying control: one that views it mainly as a technical managerial device for ensuring efficiency in fulfilling organisational goals, another that views control mainly as the ability to use power *vis-à-vis* others within the organisation. Although the two are not mutually exclusive, we are more interested in the second, as it is more relevant to the subject of the state [compare Dunsire, 1978: 21–72].

9. It is interesting to note that this statement came from an Egyptian. Muna's study [1980: 56–7] found that executives from Egypt shared less of their decision-making powers with their subordinates than did executives from the other five countries. Among these, executives from Saudi Arabia showed more power-sharing in departmental decisions than the others. Could this be a reflection of the hierarchical traditions of the hydraulic society in the case of Egypt, and the egalitarian traditions of the bedouin society in the case of Saudi Arabia?

10. The term 'bedoucracy' is adapted from Muhammad al-Rumaihi. It is meant to imply that in spite of the acquired modern technology and equipment, the Arabian administrator is still predominantly a traditional nomad in his way of thinking and patterns of behaviour [Al-Rumaihi, 1977: 137]. The term 'petrocracy' is our own coinage, but inspired by the title of Usama 'Abd al-Rahman's book *The Petroleum Bureaucracy and the Development Dilemma* [1982]. It is meant to indicate a system whose politics as well as economics are dominated by the 'oil factor'.

CHAPTER TEN

Economic Liberalisation and Privatisation: Is the Arab State Contracting?

If the period of the 1960s and early 1970s was the era of *étatisme* and bureaucratic expansion in the Arab World, the late 1970s and the 1980s were to usher in a new discourse of 'opening up', liberalisation and privatisation. Privatisation programmes in the Middle East have not, however, followed from empirical evaluations of the performance of the public sector, nor have they resulted from pressures exerted by the native entrepreneurs. Rather, they represent mainly a *public* policy, carried out in response to the 'fiscal crisis of the state' and under pressure/temptation from globalised capitalism and from its international institutions.

The word 'privatisation' itself is of course relatively new, having first appeared in an English dictionary in 1983. Difficult to render in the Arabic language, the concept of privatisation was initially expressed, depending on the user's vantage point, either as encouraging the private sector or as selling the public sector. This, of course, is precisely what privatisation entails, although the points of emphasis vary from one case to another. It was only by the end of the 1980s that Arabic coinages for the concept started to emerge: *takhsisiyya, khawsasa, khaskhasa* (not to mention the more curious terms such as *tafwit* – literally 'passing on' from the public to the private sector – which is preferred in Tunisia).

The familiar argument in favour of privatisation in most of the literature is that public enterprises are less efficient than private ones: they are overstaffed and expensively maintained, and their profitability and factor productivity are low. It is claimed that part of the inefficiency is due to excessive political interference and/or bureaucratic regulation – but these, runs the argument, are necessary companions to any public sector. They delay decision, obscure expertise, and over-burden the firm with a number of extra-economic tasks that constrain its prospects for profitability [cf. e.g. Millward et al. in Cook and Kirkpatrick, 1988]. Some escalate the argument further by saying that the public sector is not only defective in terms of allocative efficiency on the micro (or managerial) level, but even in terms of productive efficiency on the macro (or economic) level. The choice of industries in which to invest may be faulty (or too 'political') to start with. The intensive engagement of the state in the production and delivery of goods and services may also 'crowd out' private investors from such areas [e.g. Hastings, 1983]. This may eventually lead to lower overall levels of investment, which would retard rather than enhance economic development.

The argument in favour of privatisation is usually presented as the logical counterpart to the argument against the public sector: i.e. if the public sector is inefficient, the private sector (existing or 'potential') *must* be efficient. Allocative efficiency is supposed to grow with competition [Hasan, 1987: 61ff], and productive capacity is supposed to accompany individual property rights more closely [Walters, 1989: 18ff]. Other attractions of privatisation may also be mentioned: 'rolling back the power of the state', opening up or widening share ownership for more people, and reducing costly government expenditure (while earning the government some money on the side from the sale of loss-making enterprises) [cf. Savas, 1982; Pirie, 1985]. This is, of course, mainly theory. In reality, a dynamic entrepreneurial community capable of running a leading private sector may not exist. Subsequently, as two authors have suggested: "Privatization in the Western context, including Japan, may mean denationalization ... In the Third World, however, since there is a lack of private investors, privatization may mean the internationalisation of important sectors of the national economy" [Haile-Mariam and Mengistu, 1988: 1581].

In general, the correlation between ownership and efficiency/profitability is also largely assumed, rather than empirically proven – particularly with reference to less developed countries. One difficulty with arguments for divestiture based on alleged superior allocative efficiency is that while main-stream micro-economic theory does point to the allocative superiority of *competition* it is actually silent on the *ownership* issue [Commander and Killick, 1988: 102]. Modern, large enterprises (public or private) do not ensure the same direct linkage between ownership and management that existed in older-style small businesses. And hardly any empirical studies exist that can confirm the freedom of the private sector in developing countries from the defects that are normally attributed to the public sector [cf. Al-'Isawi, 1989: 45–9]. As two World Bank experts acknowledge, many public enterprises in the developing world were originally failing private firms that were nationalised in order to prevent their closure and the consequent loss of employment and production [Nellis and Kikeri, 1989: 52–3]. Another leading World Bank official concerned with the Middle East region cautioned against general prescriptions of intervention based on the ownership classification of industries. It was true, he said, that in Turkey and elsewhere inefficiency and losses in public enterprises were a major part of the economic problem and certainly the largest single element in the overall public deficit. However, "it should also be borne in mind that private sector industries are often very good at masquerading as efficient, when the reality is that their profitability is frequently dependent on large-scale subsidy and a symbiotic relationship with bureaucracy" [Thalwitz in Roe et al., 1989: 16].

Any attempt to evaluate the role of the public sector, especially in the Third World, has to take into account the multiplicity of objectives (economic, social and political) that it has to pursue, as compared to the simple profitability objective that is characteristic of most private enterprises. Even so, there are recorded cases of efficient public enterprises, and there are known cases of private monopoly whose efficiency cannot be realistically measured [cf. cases in Cook and Kirkpatrick, 1988]. Some analysts accept the proposition that public enterprises were created to meet a mixed set of economic, financial and political objectives, but argue that "they have done poorly in fulfilling the first two goals and too well in fulfilling the last" [Nellis and Kikeri, 1989: 50ff].

The public/private, ownership-centred, dichotomy is not necessarily the key issue in discussing efficiency in less developed countries. Leadership and management may be more crucial factors. An empirical study by Robert Cunningham in which he observed a bank branch (private sector) and a tax bureau (public sector), of a similar size and both located in the same Jordanian town, has revealed interesting findings. The top managers in both organisations appeared in context not to live up to the pejorative image of the Arab manager. On the contrary: they delegate, assume responsibility, accept some participation, and 'stay out of the way'; they are in general 'tough on the issues and soft on the people', and they measure themselves against certain performance criteria. What is even more interesting, however, is that the public-sector organisation has turned out to be more flexible and rule-oriented than the private-sector organisation; which is of course a conclusion that challenges the conventional popular wisdom regarding the public/private dichotomy, in general and in the Arab World [Cunningham, 1989].

The privatisation drive in the Third World is not really the result of a careful evaluation either of the contribution of the public sector to development, or even of the managerial efficiency of the public enterprises. Rather it is a response/reaction to the fiscal crisis of the state, reinforced by pressure from agencies of the international capitalist order and encouraged, to some extent, by international fashion (which now envelopes both the West and the East – in 'Cold War' terms). The main factor, however, is the financial crisis; all the other arguments about development and efficiency are later additions and garnishes.

Very few developing countries have conducted their own empirical studies on the performance of their own public sectors. On this subject they have, on the whole, been prepared to take the word of 'experts' from the industrialised countries and their international organisations. Take this for a telling example: the director-general of the Arab Organisation for Administrative Sciences (who came from 'conservative' Saudi Arabia) and his director of training (who came from 'progressive' Libya) had apparently no doubts as to the desirability of privatisation in the Arab countries; all they were concerned about was "the circumvention of problems and difficulties and ... the liberalization of constraints and restrictions" in the way of the privatisation process [Al-Saigh and Buera, 1990: 125ff]. It is a measure of the intellectual dependency of these societies *vis-à-vis* the 'core' countries, that the former are prepared to buy what are frequently ideological statements sold as technical consultancies. For example, as a number of Arab economists have observed, the IMF-World Bank approach seems to be:

> based on a single model of development which fails to take into account the great variety of situations, structures and policy orientations in developing countries. Underlying that model is a set of value judgements in favour of market-oriented development and against government intervention in the economy. Adherence to a single model of development explains why Fund-supported programmes contain the same set of prescriptions for all countries. It also explains why programmes have not succeeded in achieving the objective of adjustment with growth [summarised by El-Naggar, 1987: 6–7].

In the core states, which are advanced capitalist countries, privatisation is in harmony with prevailing ideological norms. There is a relatively high level of correspondence in capitalist societies between the three 'instances' of the social structure: the economic base (involving forces of production and relations of production), the legal and political structure (i.e. the state), and the forms of social consciousness (including ideology). In the less-developed countries there is a much lower level of correspondence: several modes of production co-exist within the society, and as the reproduction function is usually weak, both the state and ideology seem to assume a higher degree of autonomy [cf. Cypher, 1979: 43–8]. Thus, in most less-developed societies, privatisation which harmonises comfortably with the hegemonic ideology of a really capitalist society (according to the principle of correspondence) would, ironically, often have to be adopted as an option by the *state*, and in the form of a *public* policy.

Not only that; but there are some indications that 'stronger' states may be better privatisers. Possessing the institutional network that is necessary for any economic restructuring, and enjoying sufficient 'self-confidence' to make raw violence and naked oppression less important, a 'strong' state is probably better qualified to privatise than a 'fierce' state (the 'fierce' state is often violent *because* it is weak). Thus Turkey, Egypt and Tunisia are probably more likely to succeed in privatisation than Syria, Iraq or Somalia.[1]

MODALITIES OF PRIVATISATION

There are three main approaches and seven main modalities for privatisation [my terminology and taxonomy here are similar but not identical to Eaton, 1989: 470–71].

(A) MANAGERIAL APPROACHES 'Managerialism' often represents a prelude to, or an early stage of, privatisation. There are two main methods here:

1. The government does not sell publicly owned assets but it allows the boards of directors of para-statal corporations (appointed by the government) to act fairly independently, thus privatising management and labour to a smaller or greater extent (e.g. Egypt Air, Royal Jordanian Airlines).

2. The government issues some of its assets to be managed by a private entrepreneur in return for a fee; i.e. 'contracting-out' (e.g. state-owned hotels and tourist organisations in Egypt). Privatisation in several Arab countries (e.g. Egypt, Tunisia, Algeria) was often initiated in this 'managerialist' manner, which makes it possible to aim for higher productivity while remaining under the banner of 'reforming' or 'improving' the public sector.

(B) POPULIST APPROACHES Populist-oriented methods, of which there are two main varieties, enable the move towards privatisation to take place without fears being aroused of an imminent 'capitalist takeover' of the economy:

3. Sale of a public service or enterprise to a cooperative association. It will be recalled that most 'socialist' and populist regimes in the Middle East have always stipulated the existence of a cooperative sector alongside the state sector and the private sector, and this has assumed a pronounced role in certain countries and at certain times, especially in agriculture. In most cases the cooperatives have been closely controlled by the state (e.g. Tunisia, Syria, Egypt), with Algeria's *secteur auto-géré* representing an important semi-revolutionary (but brief) exception. Populist privatisation often entails the transfer of real ownership to a cooperative association of workers, producers or consumers. Iran seems to have the most active scheme of this type in the Middle East at present. Several housing, trading and agricultural projects have been organised in Egypt in recent years along these lines, especially by the trade unions and professional associations.

4. Another method of populist privatisation is through an Employees Stock Ownership Plan (ESOP), with entitlements to purchase stock either equitably or in relation to each employee's wage level. An early, but unique, example of this took place under Nasser's rule in the late 1960s, when employees in the state-owned Al-Ahram publishing foundation were allowed to buy a certain quantity of 'shares' in that corporation. Turkey has applied such plans more recently, and there are calls for a more extensive application of this method in Egypt, Libya and elsewhere.

(C) CAPITALIST APPROACHES In all privatisation policies there is a shift of management from the government to non-governmental bodies. In capitalist privatisation, the *ownership* of what was once publicly owned is now openly transferred, in one proportion or another, to whoever is prepared to buy. This may take various forms:

5. Partial sale of publicly owned assets. This is a semi-private enterprise option and indeed the government may limit the sale of a public asset to 49 or 51 per cent. This procedure has been used widely in Britain and Italy. It is particularly appealing to developing countries because it avoids abrupt political shock and because it is often extremely difficult to secure much of the local capital needed to privatise. Major political debates continue, however, as to whether to confine sales to certain groups or to open them to all domestic investors, and whether to allow foreign multinational corporations to subscribe to such enterprises. Joint ventures between the Egyptian public sector and foreign multinational corporations were indeed the most favoured formula during the earlier phases of the open door policy (*infitah*) in Egypt. While it avoids a sudden reshuffling of the existing *formal* political coalitions at the domestic level, the government can claim that it is attracting new capital and management with modern know-how while retaining a degree of governmental and 'national' influence on the policies of the enterprise [compare Eaton, 1989: 475–7]. Tunisia and Iraq have also used this modality.

6. Total privatisation through the sale to the public or to an entrepreneur of all assets held. This option has taken place in only a few countries in the world, most notably in Chile, and to some extent Bangladesh, Sri Lanka and Malaysia, and it has often taken the form of restoring nationalised enterprises to their previous private owners. The process is usually highly political, done at least as much to settle scores as to improve productivity. In Chile, the action was so abrupt and disruptive that several Chilean firms had to be re-nationalised if they were to continue to exist [cf. Nankani, 1990: 43–5]. No such full and open privatisation of large firms has taken place yet in the Arab World (with the partial exception of Iraq), in the sense that *new* large private enterprises have been allowed to emerge, but large previously nationalised enterprises have not been fully restored to private owners. Lists of likely candidates for privatisation have been prepared in countries such as Egypt and Jordan.

7. A fully privatised system would see an end to all governmental monopolies and privileges in the field of economics and services. This is achieved either by closing down a government service and contracting out all its activities to the private sector, or by allowing private entrepreneurs to compete freely with an existing government service. It is hard to imagine fully privatised administration and courts without the entire concept of the state disappearing. But many of the activities conventionally perceived as being 'public' in some countries are privately owned and managed in others. This may include

security-sensitive scientific research, foreign aid activities, supplementary prison and detention services, railways, transportation, posts and telecommunications, etc. [Eaton, 1989: 479–81] In many countries, including Middle Eastern ones, the private sector is allowed increasing competition with the state in providing welfare services such as education, health and social insurance. Private schools are known in most Middle Eastern countries and private universities have started or may be on their way in Sudan, Jordan, Egypt (and Lebanon). The private sector is also becoming increasingly active in the area of public transportation in several Arab countries.

DOMESTIC VERSUS INTERNATIONAL STIMULI

To what extent was the move towards privatisation and economic liberalisation the outcome of domestic or external factors? This can represent an 'egg-and-chicken' type of question. To start with, there is no doubt that the world capitalist system as a whole is witnessing an economic crisis of recession and limited growth (combined with inflation; hence 'stagflation'). This crisis has reflected itself in many cases in the form of a 'fiscal crisis of the state'. However, and unlike the last major crisis of world capitalism in the 1930s which found in Keynsian theory the ingredients of a remedy based on economic intervention by the state, the current crisis has yet to discover an economic theory that can be brought to its rescue. Friedman's monetarism appeared as a partial theory that was embraced wholeheartedly by Thatcherism, and less literally by Reaganomics [cf. Strange, 1989: esp. Ch. 5]. Without a grand theory, however, the major economies seem to be moving away from the concept of the 'welfare state' and more towards a concept of the 'competitive state' [Cerney, 1990: esp. Ch. 8]. In this latter model the state is not expected to act as a direct entrepreneur or even as a provider of services: rather it is expected to set the scene for a more competitive business life, that includes the commercialisation of the state sector itself as well as the re-commodisation of capital and labour (i.e., it ceases to shelter them from the vagaries of market-defined supply and demand [cf. Bauman, 1982: Ch. 5]. 'Deregulation', a favourite slogan within this model, does not really imply a state that is retreating from the economic arena, but rather a process of *re-regulation* in the direction of increased international competitiveness, which frequently – but not always – includes an important privatisation component. States seem to compete within an almost totally globalised world economy, where capital is forever looking for more lucrative opportunities. The integrative tendency of capitalism in its current phase mitigates against national state boundaries, in its search for a more 'rational' and 'profitable' globalisation of the production process and the labour market [cf. Picciotto, 1990].

It is natural under these circumstances that small, late-industrialising economies, over-burdened with accumulating economic and financial problems, would find it difficult to resist the pressures and/or the temptations of contemporary world capitalism in its current globalising phase. Populist states with declining economic and financial resources are most vulnerable. In conditions of overall contraction, they find it extremely difficult to continue simultaneously with their twin developmentalist and welfarist roles. Once the technical and economic 'ceiling' of the relatively 'easy' phase of infrastructural expansion and import-substitution industrialisation is reached, and once the potential of this phase is exhausted, the state appears to be obliged to sacrifice one of its two pillars of legitimacy: welfarism or developmentalism. Continued industrialisation seems to be impossible without rearranging the existing broad populist coalitions and enforcing harsh austerity measures, and thus it encroaches on the welfarist achievements of the state, with serious social and political repercussions. Members of the ruling class of such a state (often composed predominantly of officers, technocrats and bureaucrats) are not really dedicated 'socialists', even if a socialistic terminology might have served their purposes or even caught their imagination in an earlier phase that was more characterised by economic planning and a relatively equitable income distribution. The apparently autarchic vision of a Maoist China or a Hoxha-ist Albania does not particularly attract them. The state leadership may therefore be inclined to think that a larger role for domestic and international capital might relieve it from some of its growing developmental burdens, and the state bourgeoisie may eventually find itself tempted, or even corrupted, by a domestic commercial bourgeoisie and an international corporate bourgeoisie both of which are anxious for 'partnerships' with its members and its organisations.

In the meantime, the concern of the state not to tamper with the welfarist pillar of its legitimacy, combined with the 'capitalist' consumerist inclinations of the state bourgeoisie, result in heavy financial burdens that force the state to live beyond its means, and eventually to over-borrow, both domestically and internationally. From the mid-1970s to the mid-1980s, the availability of large funds (mainly 'recycled' in the West from the oil-exporting countries) in conditions of relative recession in the capitalist core, encouraged the international banks to lend and the governments of the developing countries (especially those most affected by the rise in oil prices) to borrow. And it was not long before the debt situation was to get out of hand, forcing many of these countries to resort to the International Monetary Fund (IMF). The IMF came in turn with its 'conditionality' measures. These – in a nutshell – oblige the borrowers to comply with the current conventional wisdom of the monetarist 'core' if they are to receive any further credits.

Thus it can be seen that the picture is complex. The developmental and financial crisis of the Third World coincides with an economic and financial crisis in the world capitalist system at large. The developing countries are subjected simultaneously to the encroachment of a globalising world capitalism and to the temptations/pressures of a monetarist mini-theory that happens to be in vogue in the core countries and which is being propagated by the main international ambassadors of current economic wisdom; the IMF and the World Bank.

Yet the developing countries are not mere objects that lie passively at the receiving end of these external encroachments and pressures. The class nature and the consumer patterns of their bourgeoisies (and of other social groups to one degree or another) direct their states first towards extensive borrowing and subsequently towards accepting the rules and conditions of hegemonic capitalism.

The international signals (including pressures and temptations) have to be interpreted by local political leaders and élites. The leaders or élites may believe that the crisis is temporary and they will therefore procrastinate over reform or apply cosmetic, defensive reforms (e.g. Egypt in the early 1980s); or they may seek military or political solutions (e.g. aid and/or 'invasion' such as in the case of Iraq or Syria). It is also conceivable that the élites may be aware of the importance of restructuring, but they may not be prepared to take the political risks involved in a full privatisation which would lead to the rise of an alternative ethnic or sectarian community (e.g. Syria). states may also of course apply combinations of these and of other strategies in their constant attempt to mediate between the international and the domestic forces.

The idea of the Janus-faced state as a strategic actor, as a purposive body lodged between national and international systems, raises issues of the altern-ative political domains in which state goals are pursued, and of the trade-offs between them. The notion that there are *alternative* (although not mutually exclusive) 'external' and 'internal' arenas for state activity has been suggested by a number of analysts. Kenneth Waltz observed that stronger states (super-powers), because of their superior reliability and precision, depend on their own capabilities and the mobilisation of their domestic resources more than on the capabilities and resources of allies [Waltz, 1979: 168].

Historically, of course, it was the late industrialisers who were not as flexible and effective in restructuring their own societies for the purposes of capitalist development, and who, as in the case of Germany and Japan, engaged in more aggressive (external) wars aimed at territorial expansion within the lands of their neighbours. In the Middle East context, this brings to mind the case of Iraq's annexation of Kuwait in 1990. Iraq is not only a late developer but is also an impatient one, its sense of 'relative deprivation' being particularly exacerbated by the presence of less advanced but much richer neighbours, and its feelings of irritation being particularly heightened by a perceived lack of understanding and cooperation on the part of those on whose behalf it had fought for more than eight years. In any case, Iraq presents an interesting example of the use of alternative strategies. Whereas Algeria, another medium oil exporter, has resorted to the International Monetary Fund and to com-mensurate domestic restructuring in order to cope with its financial problems,

Iraq has refused to call in the IMF, choosing instead to play the external option to the fullest, in the form of annexation and war.

Stephen Krasner [1985] and Joel Migdal [1988a] have also distinguished, with particular reference to the Third World, between 'strong states' and 'weak states'. According to Migdal, strong 'developing' states are "just porous enough to allow military and economic world forces to weaken existing (traditional) social control", but sufficiently resilient to be able to counteract further external pressures beyond a certain point, while they are re-ordering their social structures. Krasner has adopted more closely the 'alternative domains' argument: developing countries with stronger state structures (e.g. newly industrialising countries – NICs) are less likely to want to challenge the existing economic world order than weaker – even if richer – states (e.g. OPEC countries).

John Ikenberry [1986] has developed the argument further, although his main concern has been the industrial countries. According to him, states manoeuvre within national and international arenas, using different strategies aimed at coping with adjustment problems. An adjustment strategy may be directed outward at international regimes, or inward at transforming domestic structures, or somewhere in between in order to maintain existing relationships. Which strategy is chosen will, in his view, depend on "the gross structural circumstances within which the State finds itself – defined in terms of state-society relations on the one hand, and position within the international system on the other" [Ikenberry, 1986: 57]. He advances three assumptions: (i) states seek to minimise the costs of governance and to maximise national competitiveness; (ii) International policies have "lower costs of governance" than domestic policies; and (iii) Offensive policies have higher competitive gains than defensive policies [60–64]. He then provides an empirical exploration of his model by illustrating how the United States, Germany and Japan have adjusted to the energy crisis (1973–79). Whereas the United States with its claims to international hegemonic leadership, tried several international strategies before scaling down its policy objectives, Germany and Japan, with their more reliable domestic institutions, moved more quickly towards a domestic offensive strategy of restructuring. So, countries respond differently according to their specific strengths and weaknesses. "States with less adaptability in domestic institutions, but with at least a glimmer of international influence are more likely to persist in trying to find international solutions to adjustment problems" [ibid.: 60–77].

The developments of the Gulf crisis of 1990–91 seem to lend credence to Ikenberry's proposition. The two states within the Western alliance, the United States and the United Kingdom, that chose to involve themselves most fully in a military solution to the Kuwait problem were the ones with the most difficult financial and economic problems at home, By contrast, Germany and Japan, even though they are more dependent on Middle East oil than the US or the UK, favoured a more political approach to solving the crisis – a reflection perhaps of their higher confidence with regard to their domestic economies.

In a Middle Eastern context, Egypt is an obvious example of Ikenberry's category of a country with lower domestic adaptability and higher regional/international influence. Although reluctantly accepting the IMF's recipe for economic restructuring, Egypt follows a basically 'defensive' domestic strategy of economic adjustment, while trying to use its diplomatic influence to persuade Western governments to ask their financial institutions (national, multinational and international) to be more lenient and understanding. Egypt's stand with the winning side in the Kuwait Campaign has resulted in the forgiving of various debts due to the USA and to other Western and Arabian debtors.

COUNTRY CASES

Before we proceed any further with the analysis, however, it would be useful to review at this point some of the actual cases of economic liberalisation and privatisation that have taken place in the Arab World in recent years.

Egypt

Egypt can be said in a certain sense to be the 'mother of Arab liberalisations'. Just as she was the first Arab country to champion a leading public sector during the 1950s and 1960s, she also became the first (with the partial exception of Tunisia) to experiment with economic liberalisation and privatisation, from the mid-1970s onwards. Yet it can perhaps be argued that Egypt did not press ahead seriously enough with this venture. After the country had initiated the 'open door policy' (or what one may call *glasnost*), it took almost two full decades for the process of restructuring and privatisation (or what one may call *perestroika*) to get under way [compare, in a different sense, Abdel-Khalek, 1992]. While this preference for *glasnost* weakened national industry by exposing it to sudden competition for which it was unprepared, it also distracted the available private funds, at their peak 'oil boom' period, away from industry and towards consumerist or generally commercial activities.

As for the process of privatisation in Egypt, it has proceeded in a piecemeal manner and at a slow though growing pace, as part of the open door economic policy (*infitah*) which was formally adopted in 1974. Very often it has been a function of changing emphases within the larger infitah policy. Initially the process implied a higher level of 'managerialism' within the public sector, allowing each firm to run its own affairs in a more autonomous and more economically oriented fashion. Subsequently the process involved a higher level of 'commercialisation' of the public enterprises, in the sense of making them more market-oriented and eventually more specifically profit-oriented.

Although there were several proposals during the 1980s to sell parts of the public sector to local investors, 'contracting out' to private companies has continued to be a more favoured form of privatisation. A specific organisational form that also became particularly important in the 1980s is that of joint ventures between the Egyptian public sector and foreign private capital. This has sometimes (for example in the hotel sector) included a separation of ownership from management, with the management function being delegated to a private – usually foreign – firm or with a certain project being leased to the private sector.

The privatisation policy reached its formal peak in 1987 with the approving in parliament of a new bill that made various types of divestiture possible. The new rules enable the government to 'hive off' any loss-making public company and to sell off all public companies functioning in the area of domestic trade and tourism. This was not put into practice, however, until the 1990s, when it became more politically feasible, in relative terms.

Privatisation in Egypt has followed a quiet, discreet approach rather than a 'big bang' strategy. Furthermore, although domestic capital has welcomed the new policies, and while international capital has encouraged it, privatisation in Egypt is still basically a public policy pursued by the state for its own purposes. The continued dominant role of the state has meant that privatisation has not necessarily involved deregulation but rather that it has become concerned with re-regulation. Thus a 'public policy for investment' was created in the 1970s and 'holding public corporations' were reintroduced in the 1980s. The continued dominant role of the state has also meant that the privatisation policy has not yet included any large-scale plans for de-manning of the public bureaucracy.

Egypt's open door policy has developed under the impact of the state bourgeoisie opting for alliance with international capital, more than it has under any pressure from the local industrial capitalists [parts of the following analysis draw upon Ayubi, 1990b and 1991b; for comparative evidence see Ayubi, 1993]. The state has become unable to continue with both a developmental function and a welfare function at the same time, but it continues to host an entrenched state bourgeoisie keen to preserve its distinction in power and wealth. This state is thus confronted by a dilemma which it tries to solve through disentangling the previously existing ideological and political link between its developmental and its welfare functions, by encouraging the public sector units to work for profit (even if this means that public industrial corporations will have to involve themselves in commerce), and by removing from the public companies their welfare functions (concerning wages, pensions, security of tenure, workers' representations, etc.). When these public companies appear to reach their maximum capacity in terms of productivity and profitability, the state then stretches out its hand to international capitalism to seek the latter's cooperation with the Egyptian public sector in 'joint ventures'.

This leaves domestic capital with available opportunities for investment only in the commercial and financial sectors (reinforcing its so-called 'parasitic' character), while a small domestic industrial capital is desperately trying to acquire the same advantages offered to foreign capital/public sector joint ventures. The main trend of the state bourgeoisie has indeed looked at domestic private capitalism with disdain, thus pushing it further into the area of commerce and finance where it has entrenched itself and shown itself ready to defend its interests against the state with great vociferousness.

There are various causes for the lack of foreign investment: the political instability of the region as well as Egypt's separation from the rest of the Arab World after the peace treaty with Israel is one reason. But there is also the notorious Egyptian bureaucracy with its ponderous weight and its slow, rigid and complicated procedures.

Another of the reasons for the reluctance of foreign capital is the additional fact that the regime was not solid and strong enough to be able completely to dismantle the state's inherited welfare functions and to float the Egyptian labour force as individual workers in a 'free' labour market, controlled and disciplined by the state in the Korean mould. There was considerable resistance from within the public sector itself to its being dismantled and sold to private investors, and to floating its labour force and nuclearising it. International capital was not prepared to take too many risks with what it regarded as still a 'spoilt' labour force.

On the other hand, the mainstream within the government and the bureaucratic élite was in favour of the public sector cooperating with foreign capital in the form of direct joint ventures. Some saw this as a way to rescue the public sector from its financial and production crisis; others saw in it an opportunity to improve their own careers and investment prospects. In fact, the public industrial sector was so keen on alliance with foreign capital that it often sold its own assets to the foreign partner in return for using the latter's commercial brand name (as happened between the Ideal Refrigerator Company and Thompson's Corporation); or it joined with foreign capital to form companies that actually competed with the existing public sector companies in marketing the same products (such as in the case of the Public Company for Batteries, Al-Nasr Company for Rubber Products and Tyres, the Public Company for Electric Products and Transformers, and the Public Company for Elevators and Air Conditioning).

For its part, international capital has cautiously welcomed cooperation with the public sector, which enjoys a dominant position over organisational and human resources in the country and which still possesses a number of monopolistic and preferential advantages within the economy as well as a number of important political and administrative capabilities [cf. Ghunaim, 1986, and compare S. Fawzi, 1992]. Partnership with the state sector is on the whole a safer bet for international capital in Egypt's current circumstances. Furthermore, foreign investors wanted to benefit from the significant amounts of aid that came to Egypt from foreign and international agencies after Camp David, and which accrued directly to the state. Indeed the USAID and the World Bank have sometimes, as a condition of offering credit to public sector companies, required that the latter should enter into joint ventures with the private sector, both foreign and domestic.

The adoption of the open door policy led to an end of public control over the 'commanding heights' of the economy by allowing private capital into the areas of finance, heavy industry and foreign trade [cf. Mursi, 1987]. It also led to the abolition of the 'public organisations' (mu'assasat 'amma) as general 'holding corporations' of planning and coordination, and while it permitted extensive managerial liberties to the various public sector units, it deprived them of the privileged position they had previously enjoyed in receiving finance from state banks. As the principle of comprehensive national planning was also abandoned, the public sector was no longer bound by the same political and social considerations to which it had previously been subject. As a result of all these developments, the share of the public sector's contribution to total GDP declined quite fast: from 54.5 per cent in 1974 to 49 per cent in 1979.

The Five Year Development Plan for 1987–92 stipulated an even higher contribution by the private sector and expects its investments to account for 50 per cent of total investment in the Plan (estimated at £E46.3 billion). This was meant to involve projects in medium industries, housing, land reclamation, banking and finance, and the private sector is expected to take on its own all investments in small-scale industry and in the agricultural sector [National Bank of Egypt, Economic Bulletin, 1986].

But although the intention was repeatedly expressed of wanting to sell parts of the public sector to local investors, the idea did not actually materialise until well into the 1990s – and very hesitantly at that. There are various views as to why this was the case: some have attributed it to the disinclination of Egyptian private capital to invest in productive activities, others to continuing resistance from public sector personnel towards this option. Although there is an element of truth in both, the main reason, in our view, is that the state and the bureaucratic bourgeoisie were not prepared to relinquish the control functions and the special privileges provided to them by a large, if transformed, public sector. Increasingly, too, a major fraction of the state bourgeoisie became more interested in allying the public sector with international capital than in forming and strengthening ties with domestic capital [on the political debates that surrounded privatisation, see Al-Sayyid, 1990].

Two major proposals in 1980 for selling the public sector to domestic capital therefore came to nothing. One was a proposal by 'Abd al-Razzaq 'Abd al-Majid, an ex-minister of economy, to turn public companies in the field of foreign trade and insurance into branches of mixed (public and private) holding companies. The aim of the other proposal, which was prepared by Taha Zaki, ex-minister of industry, was to involve local private capital in the existing and the new industrial public companies. A further proposal was announced in 1981, under the title of 'separating ownership from management', whereby the ownership of the public sector would remain governmental and would be entrusted to a new National Investment Bank, which would in turn establish holding companies that would manage the capital of mixed (public/private) companies. Around the same time a similar concept was applied in the tourism sector, where two public companies in that field became 'owning' but not managing companies when they leased their hotels and assets to six foreign investment companies (joint foreign and public shared). Yet another new proposal emerged in 1982 for the establishment of new agencies of coordination and control (similar to the previous 'public organisations' of the Nasserist era) to advise the ministers concerned on the activities of companies belonging to them. One further proposal then emerged in 1985 for 'rationalising' the public sector, whereby all 'loss-making' companies, as well as all public companies in domestic trade and tourism, would be liquidated and turned over to the private sector. The proposal was more or less accepted by parliament in 1987. According to this plan, the public sector would keep only the large companies in productive areas such as textiles and minerals. No specific mechanism for the divestiture of the public sector were spelled out officially, although some experts suggested following the experience of other countries and initiating 'employee stock ownership programmes' (ESOP), and the un-profitable Misr Dairy Company (public sector) was proposed as an early candidate for such a programme [cf. Sharif, 1987: 14].

None of these proposals for selling the public sector has been carried through, but there is no doubt that the overall shift in the state's economic policies has meant that an already overburdened public sector was receiving fewer resources for renewal of machinery, retention of qualified personnel, and so forth, at a time of growing competition resulting from the liberalisation of trade controls and the special exemptions and privileges given to infitah projects. Since the adoption of *infitah*, the ability of the public sector to generate surplus has certainly declined. Yet the public sector was not really so inefficient: in 1976 the number of public sector units making profits was 324, while only four units were making losses, amounting to no more than £E80 million (and their number was in any case on the decrease). Furthermore, during the ten years from 1975 to 1985, the state extracted an average 67.5 per cent of the distributable surplus of the public sector (27.2 per cent in the form of income tax and 40.3 per cent in the form of 'appropriation'), thus depriving public companies of the use of these funds for self-financing and for renovation and improvement [Mursi, 1987: 8, 49]. Even so, the public sector did not collapse completely: in 1984/85, eighty three profitable companies showed a combined profit of £E268 million, while thirty-four remaining companies showed a combined loss of £E142 million, for a net profit of £E126 million [American Embassy in Cairo, 1986: 13].

The application of infitah policies has no doubt helped in solving some of the technological (i.e. production) problems of the public sector, and in easing some of the liquidity bottlenecks (especially with regard to foreign currency). However, the basic problem of finance has not been solved. In addition, marketing has become an acute problem (because of opening up the local market to the severe competition of foreign products and because of disrupting the established trade with the Socialist countries). Furthermore, the retention of qualified and skilled personnel has also become quite problematic, as many such elements leave the public sector to work either in other Arab countries, or in the local private sector, native and foreign. Infitah has also harmed the public sector in another indirect way – by fuelling large-scale corruption. To a significant extent this has been a function of the emergence of a substantial private sector with better financial resources, alongside the existing public sector which is structurally exhausted and financially starved. Corruption had to a large extent been 'institutionalised' in the 1970s, partly as a safety valve for the badly paid bureaucracy, and partly as an accompanying symptom of the *laissez-faire* policy.

Although privatisation in the sense of denationalisation has not been an effective policy, at least to the end of the 1980s (and with the exception of tourism), privatisation in the broader sense of a growing role for the private sector within the economy has witnessed a fairly significant degree of success. Much of the growth in the Egyptian economy that took place between 1974 and 1980 (estimated at 9 per cent per annum) occurred in the private sector. The share of that sector in the total value added rose from 46 per cent in 1973 to 55 per cent in 1981/82 [cf. S. Ahmad, 1984]. The private sector (excluding foreign oil companies) accounted in 1985 for nearly 60 per cent of GDP, one-third of industrial output and perhaps as much as two-thirds of new industrial jobs.

Although some of this growth could be attributed to the changing political and business climate following *infitah*, most of it was really a function of the spill-over of the oil boom into Egypt, manifested in the growth of remittances and the expansion in Arab tourism and related services (the state has also benefited in terms of higher oil revenues, increased aid, etc.). The availability of liquid capital to the private sector resulted in many of its investments being capital-intensive. The continuation of various protection policies enabled the private sector to compete with state enterprises not only in trade, construction and services but even sometimes in industry.

As Egypt turned into an over-banked economy by the late 1970s, bankers were keen to lend and there was a tendency for the private sector to over-borrow, thus adding to its inclination towards capital-intensive investments – especially those with fairly high rates of return. To protect themselves against various risks, private investors have tended to hold large foreign exchange stocks, and to diversify their activities both vertically and horizontally. There are also some signs of a certain transition from importing to industrial activities, in response to declining financial revenues and declining importation of luxuries, although much of that 'industry' is still of a subsidiary nature and continues to be heavily dependent on semi-manufactured imports. Even the informal 'Islamic business' sector, for all its initial appetite for financial speculation, seems to have been diversifying – at least in certain cases – into some industrial and productive activities.

It is possible therefore to argue that the relationship of the private sector to the state sector has been in some ways contradictory. In the earlier phase of *infitah*, the state's preference for joint public sector/foreign capital ventures (to the exclusion of the domestic private sector) had tended to crowd the domestic private investors out of industry and to push them in the direction of commercial and financial activities. This had fitted in any case with the traditionally 'mercantile' inclinations of domestic capital, and was made easy by the availability to it of large financial windfalls ultimately traceable to the 'oil boom' in the neighbouring countries. However, since many of the state's policies of protection and subsidy had continued in spite of the liberalisation measures that were introduced, thus sustaining a partial import-substitution environment, the domestic private sector was gradually tempted to move into economic fields that were perhaps least subject to public pricing policies, but still subject to a certain degree of protection and subsidy from the state. Private investors who could 'link up' with the state were also presumably in a better position, making use of governmental licensing and often obtaining cheaper public sector inputs and supplying the government enterprises with 'favourably priced' inputs. In addition many investors combined their newly acquired financial assets with useful political and organisational assets brought about by attracting personnel with previous government, military or public-sector careers.

With the decline in foreign currencies available to the private sector (from the mid-1980s on, as a result of the relative dampening down of the oil boom) and the decline in importation opportunities (caused partly by the drop in demand for high-cost imported items and partly by new importation restrictions), the private sector was pulled further in the direction of supplementary industrial activity. A partial 'crowding-in' of private investment could thus be said to be taking place as businessmen gather to make use of the various 'rents' created both by state policies and by state failures. In size and in scope, however, this remains far more limited than the resources mustered by the state, as we will see.

Furthermore, expanding investment is not the same as raising productivity or enhancing development. Although local private investors had become accustomed in the earlier phase of *infitah* to expect rates of return on commercial activity as high as 50 to 100 per cent and to expect a rate of return on equity of some 20 to 50 per cent in other activities, profitability is not always the same as productivity. Most new investors continue to be risk-evasive, and to concentrate on immediately lucrative activities, and the factor productivity of their operations is not believed to be particularly high.

Although the treatment 'by shock' intended for the economy by Sadat and the IMF in the mid-1970s could not be carried out because of the food riots of January 1977, liberalisation nevertheless proceeded in a piecemeal way. Ten years later, in 1987, a new agreement was reached with the International Monetary Fund but implementation of structural reform was very slow and disagreements continued because of the government's apprehension over the political risks of radical restructuring. In the meantime, stagflation continued, investment dropped, unemployment increased. External debt grew to represent 46 per cent of all current revenues, debt servicing to represent 10 per cent of GDP, and arrears in payments accumulated to some $11.4 billion in 1990 [CPSS, *Report,* 1991].

The Gulf crisis of 1990/91, with both its negative and its positive aspects, represented a stimulus to go more radically for reform. On the negative side it exacerbated financial and economic problems and caused immediate direct losses conservatively estimated at over $4.5 billion. On the positive side external aid (mainly grants) worth about $3.9 billion was rushed to Egypt in 1990/91. The USA and the Gulf states cancelled some $12.9 billion worth of debts, including expensive American military ones. Debt servicing burdens were thus reduced by $1.3 billion. Such unusual forgiving of debts created a more favourable atmosphere among members of the political élite for accepting the 'conditionality' formula required by the IMF, and for selling it to the public [compare Hinnebusch, 1993a].

The Agreements with the IMF, starting in May 1991, were also part of a conditionality exercise applied by the Club of Paris countries towards the gradual cancellation of some 50 per cent of Egypt's public debt: 15 per cent on the implementation of the first agreement (May 1991–October 1992), another 15 per cent with the implementation of the second agreement (November 1992–April 1993), and the remaining 20 per cent with the implementation of the third agreement (May 1993–November 1994). The IMF in its turn agreed to offer Egypt credit amounting to 60 per cent of its contribution to the Fund but phased it, according to its conditionality rules, on six instalments corresponding to further Egyptian reforms based on meeting the requirements of the IMF and the World Bank. By November 1991 a unified market-determined exchange rate replaced the plethora of rates that had preceded it in other years.

At present there is agreement between the government of Egypt and the IMF over reducing import restrictions to 8–10 per cent of total products, a unified company law, further privatisations and further liberalisation of the banking sector and of the activities of the chambers of commerce and industry and of new businesses. The insurance sector would be modernised, energy prices increased and subsidies removed. Major bones of contention remain over customs duties, where the Egyptian government objected to the IMF's demand for reducing them to a maximum of 50 per cent by July 1993, 40 per cent by July 1994 and 30 per cent by July 1995. Another area of disagreement is the Fund's demand for more expansive and rigorous taxation arrangements, especially on sales and services, and a reduction in tax exemption (including that for industry).

Part of the structural reform revolves around privatisation policies, and several important prospective privatisations were announced at a high-profile symposium on privatisation held in September 1990 under the sponsorship of the Private Sector Commission in cooperation with the United States Agency for International Development (USAID). The symposium was attended by such high-powered personalities as the deputy prime minister and minister of agriculture, Yusif Wali, as well as by the ministers of industry, of manpower, of scientific research and of electricity, and by a good number of provincial governors. The new initiative that was announced included the sale of 100,000 *feddans* of 'agrarian reform' lands to their occupants, and the sale of shares that were owned by the Ministry of Industry in thirty-two public companies. Wali declared the government's intention to sell all public agricultural companies and to use the accruing funds in the financing of further programmes for land reclamation. Land owned by the Southern Tahrir public companies was released for ownership by the companies' own personnel, in return for them conceding their existing public employment with the government. Deputy premier Wali, one of the most influential personalities in government, maintained that President Mubarak supported full privatisation in agriculture. Wali expressed his own admiration of the Soviet plan to transfer 80 per cent of all large companies to the private sector within 800 days and expressed his belief that only defence, railways and postal services and energy activities should continue to be owned and managed by the state.

The minister of industry, Muhammad 'Abd al-Wahhab, did not go as far. He supported the concept of completely privatised 'cottage industries' but said that larger public sector companies would enjoy real managerial autonomy under a new amended public sector law that would narrow the differences between public and private enterprises. The need for a more flexible taxation system and a more dynamic stock exchange were acknowledged. On his part, the minister of transport and communications, Sulaiman Mutawalli, said that the private sector would be given priority in the field of transportation of passengers and commodities and in maritime transport.

A joint public-sector/private-sector committee was formed in 1990 under the name 'Partners in Development' to outline the preliminary framework for privatisation programmes, and to consider the prospective position of public sector and joint-venture companies. The committee agreed on dividing public enterprises into five categories:

—Joint ventures in which the public sector participates with private, domestic and foreign, capital. Of these companies 327 had registered losses for several years and their position had to be given speedy consideration.

—Partly nationalised companies, whose shares were already circulating in the stock market. The share of the private sector needed to be encouraged to grow in most of these companies.

—Companies owned exclusively by the government, which are functioning inside activities not compatible with, or complementary to, their main function. Such companies should be rationalised according to proper economic and technical criteria.

—Companies functioning in basically commercial activities, where the private sector should be the main actor.

—In addition there were organisations and authorities providing public services directly linked to private business and commercial activities (such as the General Authority for International Fairs and Markets) and these should be run as market units, and access to them should be given to the private sector.

An initial allocation of $300 million of American aid funds to Egypt was earmarked to finance the privatisation programme, including arrangements for Employee Stock Ownership Plans (ESOP) in the public sector. An American consultancy group was appointed to design a three-year programme in cooperation with an Egyptian team.

Egypt's privatisation programme, sluggish at best on the central level, was given a big boost in the early 1990s at the local level. Several projects were on offer for Egyptians returning from the Gulf and looking for small- to medium-sized opportunities for investment. Most of the single projects were below £E50,000 in value, but there were some valued at between £E100,000 and £E250,000, and a few valued at over £E250,000 each. The prime minister, 'Atif Sidqi, agreed with the provincial governors on the sale of 1,787 public projects to the private sector. Also considered was the sale of governorates' shares in 51 out of 78 existing public corporations

More than 2,000 small projects of the localities were to be sold during the period from 1991 to 1993. By the end of 1991 there were 1,673 such projects (each valued at under £E50,000) that had already been sold to the private or cooperative sectors, as well as 53 valued at over £E100,000 each, while 192 larger projects were prepared for sale. Local projects were easier to privatise first for a number of reasons. Many of them were of an agricultural nature and therefore came under the tutelage of the enthusiastic liberalist Yusif Wali, or they were more autonomous from the grip of central government, having been financed either through foreign aid and/or local initiative [on future prospects see Springborg, 1990]. Many of them were small to medium in size and suited the needs and inclinations of the new investor. In addition several were put out for sale just at the time when many Egyptian workers were returning because of the Gulf crisis of 1990/91 and these would have been appropriate for many returnees with rural backgrounds. Also agricultural projects did not employ large numbers of organised labour and did not therefore bear the same political risk that selling large public industrial firms in the cities would have carried [compare Pripstein-Posusney, 1994].

A radical restructuring of the public sector was initiated in 1991 under a new and rather interesting law. The main new feature of the Law No. 203 for 1991 concerning the so-called 'public business sector' (qita' al-a'mal al-'amm) is the separation of ownership and management. The new holding companies (sharikat qabida) and their affiliate companies (sharikat tabi'a) are no longer governmental bodies subject to public law but are among 'moral personalities' subject to private law and responsible to their own shareholders. Profits are to be distributed equally among private and governmental shareholders and the companies are no longer obliged to transfer to the state any of the previous disbursements for management, social insurance and welfare, etc. Companies would borrow from banks on commercial bases and would not be able to rely on the state budget for subsidies. Decisions on production and marketing are to be made by the directors and the boards of the affiliated companies. The law is applied to about 300 companies (of which about 117 are industrial), in addition to eighteen holding companies. The government also has significant shares in about 200 'mixed' companies subject to the investment law or to the companies' law. The book value of the companies subject to Law No. 203 for 1991 was estimated in the early 1990s at about £E77 billion (of which 35 per cent is in industry).

To realise the still dominant role of the state's economic sector it is sufficient to compare the value of its capital with that of the private sector. The capital of large private firms subject to the Companies' Law No. 159 for 1981 was estimated around the same time (the end of 1990) at no more than £E1.5 billion, whereas the capital of functioning private companies under the investment law No. 230 for 1987 was estimated at about £E5.9 billion, thus putting the total capital of all private companies at less than 10 per cent of the book value of the state sector.

However, the age of privatisation might have arrived at last in Egypt. The Technical Bureau for the Public Business Sector announced in spring 1993 that hundreds of companies would be put up for sale, which include some exclusively state-owned companies, some companies with no more than a 49 per cent share for the private sector (these two types are subject to Law No. 203 for 1991 concerning the 'public business sector'), and some 'mixed' companies (subject to Law No. 159 for 1981 or to Law No. 230 for 1987) in which public sector companies have shares of varying proportions. Joint ventures between the government sector and foreign capital under the investment Law No. 43 for 1974 are not on the whole being considered at this stage. (The multiplicity of laws is obviously confusing and there were proposals for unifying them into one law by the end of 1993.)

The timing and phasing out of these sales is still subject to deliberation, especially concerning the degree of reform to which these companies should be subjected before sale and whether all of them, or at least the loss-making companies, could be sold to one individual or only to collective share-holders, while what is particularly controversial is the proportion that might be sold to non-Egyptians.

Organisationally, the cabinet ends up overseeing the whole process, with ultimate responsibility in the hands of the President. The cabinet is believed to be divided, with regard to economic policy, into 'étatists' (e.g. the ministers of planning, industry and labour) and 'liberalists' (the ministers for tourism, agriculture and energy). The public business sector (p.b.s.) was meant to have a special minister but no agreement could be reached and the prime minister, 'Atif Sidqi is designated as supremo in charge of supervising the process.

The transition from state to market often lends itself to 'corporatist' arrangements [for further and comparative evidence see Bianchi, 1990; Ayubi, 1992b]. In a micro-corporatist formula, four cabinet ministers (including the most outspoken liberalists) were joined with four leading businessmen in the 'Partners in Development' Committee (PDC). In 1993 the ministers were Yusif Wali, secretary-general of the ruling National Party, deputy premier and minister of agriculture as leader for the PDC, the minister of tourism, Fu'ad Sultan, the minister of energy and electricity, Mahir Abaza, and the minister of social affairs, Amal 'Uthman. The private sector and the business community were represented by Husain Sabur, president of the Egyptian–American Businessmen's Association, 'Umar Muhanna, director-general of the Misr-Iran Bank, Tahir Hilmi, a law consultant, and Farid Khamis, a leading new-style businessman from the Tenth of Ramadan New City and a member of the Shura (Consultative) Council. The PDC receives external support by way of grants from the USAID and from the World Bank, aiming at the operationalising of the privatisation programme.

The executive aspect of privatisation is entrusted to the already mentioned Technical Bureau for the Public Business Sector. Holding companies would have a say about the desirability and/or necessity and about the timing and scope of privatisation within the affiliate companies, as their main function will be basically that of managing the financial portfolio of the holding company concerned and its affiliates.

The first batch of companies for sale in 1992/93 included twenty companies (worth £E9 billion), of which fifteen were fully owned and five partly owned by the state. Priority was given to companies that would not shed a lot of labour. By June 1993 assets and companies worth £E1.4 billion had been sold, including Misroub (for soft drinks) and Egypt Chemicals. In some cases an ESOP was introduced, as with the United Company for Housing and Construction with 50 per cent loans being provided by the Bank of Alexandria. Immediately available for sale by purchase tenders were eight leading hotels and four tourist vessels, and other lists were in preparation.

No holding companies would be sold, but over the following three years (1993–96) it was anticipated that up to 48 per cent of the number of affiliate companies, representing about 28 per cent of the total value of the public business sector, would be traded. Oil companies, railways and telecommunications, the national airlines and the Suez Canal (and possibly the state banks) would not be part of the privatisation drive. These corporations, whose book value is estimated at £E150 billion, are not part of the so-called public business sector and may therefore represent the main 'sacred cows' that should not, by the étatists' reckoning, be touched by privatisations.

From this one may conclude that the 'Mexicanisation' of Egypt is well under way: that is *de facto* one-party domination in a formally permitted multi-party system, with a relatively stagnant economy. The ruling coalition is stable, although its proportions are continually changing: the National Democratic Party (NDP) magnates, the politicians/bureaucrats-cum-businessmen, and the military (combatant plus 'economic' wing). The professional syndicates and the local élites are allowed increased freedom and decision-making scope in return for general allegiance to the national leadership/central government. Competing political parties are permitted to publish their opinions fairly freely but not to gain substantial numbers of seats in parliament. Indeed as their electoral defeat occurs, some of their members are appointed by presidential decree in parliament (from the Progressive-Tajammu' Party in the previous parliament; from the Wafd Party in the current parliament). The formula is loosely 'corporatist' but allows for broader segments to be incorporated via their associational or communal leaders.

Within the Public Establishment (the Civil Service and the public economic sector, which together employ nearly five million people), continuous balances and counterbalances take place, especially among the big patrons and their networks of clients [cf. Sullivan, 1990a]. However, no single patron is allowed to expand his fiefdom politically beyond a certain point. The President is still powerful enough to be able to put a stop to any expansionary attempts either by cutting the individuals concerned down to size (e.g. Wali, deputy premier, minister of agriculture and party chief), or by removing them altogether (Abu Ghazala, ex-defence minister; Qandil, ex-petroleum minister).

The national entrepreneurial bourgeoisie is not sufficiently strong to challenge the power of the statesmen-cum-businessmen class. The working class, although to some extent organised in (basically government-controlled) unions, has not revolted in an abrupt way for the following reasons: state welfarism is being removed only gradually; there is always the possibility (hope) of improving one's individual lot by temporary migration to an oil-exporting country; there has been no large-scale divestiture of the public sector [see also Pripstein-Posusney, 1994].

Economic reform and restructuring is being effected very gradually, which probably means that there will be no quick and effective economic improvement, but it has also meant that there have been no more repetitions of the January 1977 food riots. The latest batch of measures for economic reform initiated recently is probably the most daring so far; these seem to imply a more determined attempt at streamlining the public sector (more private investment may now take place as an alternative to saving in Gulf banks and/ or in Islamic investment companies), and they include the so-called 'sales tax' that is likely to curb consumption without reducing inflation substantially. These measures, combined with the continuing stealthy reduction of subsidies, are likely to hurt the lower and middle classes most. But as they are being implemented carefully and gradually, they have not resulted in immediate revolts. In the political arena, there were violent student demonstrations against the American destruction of Iraq's infrastructure in 1991, but they did not get out of hand and did not link up with any working-class discontent.

As regards privatisation, it is possible to conclude by saying that, apart from the special case of tourism (where the earliest privatisation started in the 1980s), and apart from the distinct case of local/agricultural projects (where privatisation was relatively easy to operationalise), industry will continue to be a much more difficult area for large-scale privatisation, mainly for political reasons. Although the business groups have become quite vocal, they continue to be rather 'junior' partners in the current informal coalition who cannot, and sometimes will not, push really hard for a completely liberalised industry. And although the technocrats and workers of state-owned industries are not as noisy nowadays as they could have been, they continue, objectively speaking, to be major partners in that coalition. The leadership has to play the game of balance and mediation quite carefully between the major, silent partners and the junior, vocal partners.

Tunisia

The Tunisian case is interesting, as some of that country's privatisation and liberalisation practices pre-date even those of Egypt. At the time that Tunisia acquired its independence in 1956, its petty bourgeoisie, formed mainly from among the intelligentsia, was quite limited in size since most economic activities were dominated by colonial monopoly companies or by private French entrepreneurs. The process of decolonisation enabled the state to acquire the facilities of the infrastructure (e.g. ports, railways, water and gas, some lands and mines), and most of the banking system was soon 'Tunisianised'.

As the native private sector was small, and since it was perceived as being interested only in real estate and commercial activities, the state was soon to adopt a decidedly interventionist policy, later to be known as *le dirigisme planifié*, that attached a central role to the public sector while forcing the private sector towards activities regarded as complementary to state action. An extensive cooperative sector was installed in agriculture, while a semi-corporatist organisational pattern emerged within which the Labour movement was co-opted and the relatively large traders were forced to direct their capital towards supporting the industrial and the tourist sectors [Al-Mahjub, 1989: 7–8].

One familiar pattern was for the state to initiate investments and activities in a particular area to indicate the feasibility of that area and its potential reward to the private sector. This was especially true of the tourist sector, where all investment was public from 1962 until 1966; the private sector was then encouraged to subscribe until, by 1970, its share in the tourist industry had reached 95 per cent of the total (75 per cent of this having originally come from the commercial sector). In industry, state investment was dominant, representing some four-fifths of the total during the first ten-year development plan (1962–71), although private industrial investment was increasing by 8 per cent per annum. The main governmental contribution was in areas such as fertilisers, oil refining, phosphates, and steel, with the government's share representing 75 per cent of all investments in such relatively 'large' industries [Ghurbal et al., 1989: 131].

By contrast, the earlier agricultural cooperatives, which had formed an important aspect of the single ruling Constitutional Socialist Party's socio-economic policies, were being phased out by the early 1970s, following the removal from power of Bin Salih and his mildly socialistic team and their subsequent replacement by a team that was more sympathetic to the private sector and to the liberalising of the economy. The main thrust of the second ten-year development plan (1972–81) revolved around dismantling the co-operative sector in agriculture, encouraging the private sector to open up to the international market, and persuading foreign capital to contribute to industrial, and especially to export-oriented, activities. Parallel to this was a state policy that encouraged investment in irrigation and agricultural technology and that placed particular emphasis on the regions that produced export crops. In consequence, the share of public investment in agriculture increased from 13 per cent in the period from 1971 to 1980 to 17 per cent in the period from 1981 to 1986. The 1987–91 development plan was to attach even more importance to the agricultural sector [Ait Amara, 1987: 141–51].

Between the end point of the first and the second development plans, the share of the private sector in capital formation grew from 20.6 per cent to 42.2 per cent, and the contribution of the private sector in production was to increase from 29.7 per cent to 74.1 per cent in agriculture and fisheries, from 20.7 per cent to 44.5 per cent in manufacturing industries, and from 65.6 per cent to 93.4 per cent in tourism. In certain industrial fields, the private sector became dominant, controlling 80.8 per cent of textile industries, 59 per cent of food industries, and 53 per cent of mechanical industries [Al-Mahjub, 1989: 9–11; Al-Manubi, 1986: 40–41].

Members of the emerging entrepreneurial class that was taking up these activities had come originally from the field of commerce, and were able to make great use of the state's protective economic policies; these policies favoured a certain degree of import-substitution, subsidised by the state through oil revenues which, although relatively modest, represented two-thirds of foreign currency earnings.

However, by the end of the second ten-year development plan, the early 1980s were witnessing serious social upheavals that drew attention to the fragility of Tunisia's economic system. The rate of growth of GNP (in fixed prices) declined from the previous levels of 5.2 per cent (during the first plan) and 6.3 per cent (during the second), to only 2.3 per cent during the four years from 1982 to 1986. The balance of payments deteriorated, commercial deficit grew, and by 1986, with the collapse in petroleum prices and a drop in tourism and agriculture, foreign currency reserves were nil and foreign debt amounted to $5 billion (representing 60 per cent of GDP), while an amount of $1.2 billion was due for debt servicing. It was at this juncture that the state had to resort to the International Monetary Fund (IMF) and the World Bank. These institutions duly came to the rescue, with their never-changing diagnosis and the set formula that accompanies it: suppressing demand, encouraging exports, and "reducing the weight of the State" [Ben Romdhane, 1990: 151–9; Ghurbal et al., 1989: 134ff].

At this point the state was still in control of two-thirds of GDP and responsible for about 60 per cent of all investments. In spite of the growing size of the private sector, many of the *dirigiste* policies of the state were still in place, with the government closely controlling prices, wages, interest rates and credit policy, and with many basic commodities heavily subsidised. The overall role of the state was still dominant: public expenditure represented 40.6 per cent of GDP (in 1983) and public consumption represented 45.6 per cent of this expenditure. Spending on the public administration represented 12–13 per cent of GDP and salaries in turn represented 28.3 per cent of all public expenditure [Al-Manubi, 1985].

Tunisia had at that time (i.e. in the mid-1980s) some 300 public enterprises (500 if the ones with the 'indirect' participation of the state are added), which seem to have been arranged in economic and technical sectors (such as metallic industries, petroleum, banks and insurance, transport, agriculture and so forth), rather than organised under public holding organisations (as is the case in many other Arab countries). The role of public enterprises was conceived of as being the following: the promotion of new techniques, the diffusion of development activities outside the traditionally favoured regions, the training of personnel and the enhancing of the private sector [Midoun, 1985: 95–6]. The last of these objectives is quite interesting and rather unusual.

As with all public sectors, however, the multitude of often contradictory objectives assigned to public companies was bound to have a distorting effect on their activities and to impose supplementary expenses that could not be tolerated in times of austerity. Economic profitability was modest from the outset, owing to high management costs and to the low selling prices necessitated both by the restricted purchasing power of the population at large and by the limits imposed by the government as part of its welfare policy. The financial situation of the public companies deteriorated steadily during the 1980s, which imposed increasingly heavy burdens on the state budget at a time when the state itself was unable to balance its public finances [Bouaouaja, 1989: 235–7].

Having called for the assistance of the IMF, the Tunisian government was asked to embark on a 'structural adjustment' programme in return for the availability from the Fund of a 'stand-by credit facility'. The programme required a curtailment on credit facilities, the floating of prices by 1991, liberalising interest rates, removing subsidies, liberalising imports and reducing protection by 1991, constraining domestic demand by freezing wages, and accelerating the rate of privatisation in areas that were felt to have the potential to benefit from increased competition. A national commission was formed to oversee the transfer of about a hundred public enterprises to the private sector.

Such activity paved the way for the signing of an agreement with the World Bank for the scheduling of the process of privatisation, and the new orientation was built into the new (seventh) development plan of 1987–91 through the stipulation that the private sector was to take a 65 per cent share of all investment in manufacturing industries [Al-Mahjub, 1989: 13–14]. In addition, foreign industrial investment was to be given a number of inducements, including tax exemptions, repatriation rights and improved infrastructural and exporting facilities. In 1986, 1987 and 1989 several pieces of legislation were enacted to govern the restructuring of public enterprises, a process which was to be carried out under the supervision of a specially formed committee with the assistance of the ministries of planning and finance as well as the ministries in charge of the specific enterprises concerned.

Although several difficulties were encountered in defining a strategy for privatisation, actual privatisations were eventually to take place in a much more significant way than has been the case in most other Arab countries. Three large public enterprises underwent large-scale restructuring that led to the privatisation of most of their assets: viz. the Société Générale des Industries Textiles (SOGITEX), the Société Tunisienne des Industries et Matériaux de Construction (SOTIMACO), and the Société Hotelière et Touristique de Tunisie (SHTT). Smaller privatised enterprises include marble factories (Thala), cinema houses (SATPEC), aluminium workshops (IMAL), print houses and disc and cassette manufacturers, fisheries organisations, and some trading companies (the latter being sometimes liquidated and sometimes merged with others) [Midoun, 1989: 10–12].

The outcome of restructuring has been quite mixed in Tunisia, with some observers maintaining that the overall attempt at liberalising the economy has made greater progress than the denationalising of public sector firms. This drive for liberalisation has earlier origins that date back, as we have seen to the appointment of a business-minded prime minister, Hadi Nuwaira (1970–80), who dominated the new endeavour to re-shape the country's economy up to the beginning of the 1980s. Denationalisation, on the other hand, has been more closely associated with the IMF's 'structural adjustment' plan of the second half of the 1980s, and although the government's efforts in this area have been lauded by the IMF as a good model for other countries, privatisation in Tunisia remains circumscribed within officially approved limits, due to the difficulties of transforming the nature of a 'patron state' within a limited span of time [cf. Harik, 1990].

As might be expected, resistance to privatisation does exist and can be difficult to overcome, although it tends to express itself in rather discreet ways: as in Egypt and Algeria it comes from some public sector managers but more particularly from workers and employees [cf. Bouaouaja, 1989: 242–6]. Indeed, workers' resistance might have been stronger had the regime not circumscribed the traditionally powerful trade union federation in 1986. But perhaps the main obstacles to privatisation have been the weakness of the entrepreneurial community and the limited financial capacity of the private sector. Among other things, Tunisia has one of the smallest stock markets in developing countries. The Tunisian capitalist class revolves primarily around a 'familial' network of those who seek easy profits and those who avoid business risks, none of whom are particularly tempted to take on many of the industrial concerns that are on offer [Midoun, 1989: 12–13; Harik, 1990: 11ff].

The private sector has in fact developed 'under the shadow' of the quasi-rentier Tunisian state and has become extremely dependent on government protection and subsidy. This was made very evident as soon as the 're-structuring' programme was put in motion, when in 1987 nearly four hundred private firms and in 1988 nearly seven hundred speedily went bankrupt or had to close down. This situation was made worse by the rapid and abrupt liberalisation of imports, and the concurrent rise in interest rates, the devaluation of the dinar by 60 per cent, and the rise in the cost of imported equipment. Voices were therefore heard once again calling for a reconsideration of the full-fledged privatisation drive and for a renewed emphasis on improving the capacity and productivity of the public enterprises [cf. Mahjoub, 1990: 305–10].

The Tunisian experiment represents an interesting case of applying the short-term teachings of the IMF and the middle-term strategies of the World Bank. "Instead of negotiating through the interminable meetings of the Paris Club like some of its neighbours, Tunisia took the initiative and deliberately set out to incorporate the thinking of its foreign creditors in its planning strategy. For Western bankers Tunisia is again a model country, demonstrating exemplary prudence in the management of its economic affairs" [Moore, 1988: 180]. However, Tunisia cannot yet speak of a privatisation 'success story' as long as its private entrepreneurs continue to shy away from industrial enterprises, which are still – in turn – partly coveted by the state bourgeoisie. Furthermore, Tunisian economic liberalisation is still fraught with political risks. Although the emasculation of their Federation has meant that direct workers' resistance was not particularly noteworthy, the political liquidation of the Habib Ashur group within the Federation has meant that the regime no longer has a safety valve among the workers [ibid., 1988: 187]. This, combined with the fact that political liberalisation has been only formalistic and superficial under the new leadership of President Zain al-'Abidin Bin 'Ali, must mean that the memories of the 'food riots' of 1984 and the spectre of the rising popularity of Islamic radicalism will continue to haunt the political leadership for quite some time to come.

Syria

Syria's small public sector, which emerged through nationalisation during the 1958–61 union with Egypt, was greatly expanded when a Ba'thist coup d'état in 1963 removed the anti-union junta from power, and when a more radical wing of the Ba'th seized the reins of government in 1966. By the mid-1960s the state owned all banks, most trade and much of commerce, controlled agricultural cooperatives, and possessed 80 per cent of all industry. A large number of public organisations and public companies were formed and the public sector's share in domestic production rose from 25 to 75 per cent. The legal position of the public sector was further regulated, following the Ba'thist 'corrective' coup of 1970, by various pieces of legislation, especially those issued in 1974 and 1980 [Sa'ud and 'Ali, 1986: 442–88]. As in most other populist regimes, industrial and agricultural projects are not viewed from a strictly technical or economic point of view. The mere installation of a project is a political objective in itself, providing 'modern' employment opportunities, disbursing wages and salaries and highlighting the presence of the state.

In addition to its control of the large public sector, the state acquires part of its relative autonomy from the social forces through the revenues that it derives directly from the country's small but still significant oil industry and from the fairly handsome aid that it receives from the Gulf countries.

> Syria is therefore in some ways an oil state by transference. But unlike countries with stable transfer economies, dependent only on market fluctuations ... Syria is influenced by fluctuations in the international political market, which in some way explains the strange variation of investment levels in the development plans [Leca, 1988: 184].

The first five-year plan (1961–65) was not really much more than a list of projects. The second five-year plan (1966–70) gave the state the decisive role in investment, especially in industry, allowing only 5 per cent of industrial investments for the private sector. Other development plans continued in a similar direction including the most recent (1986–90) development plan. The contribution of the public sector to investment in the various plans was as follows: 69.7 per cent of investments in the second plan, 80.6 per cent in the third plan, 82.7 per cent in the fourth, and 76.9 per cent in the fifth [Hilan, 1989: 8–14]. External sources of finance were expected to provide for 32.5 per cent of public sector investment in the second plan, 19 per cent in the third, 18 per cent in the fourth and 13.7 per cent in the fifth. External finance here was thought of in terms of foreign grants, aid and concessionary credits. It did not include oil revenues, which were counted as state revenues. If the two elements are added together, one can see that public sector expansion was to a significant extent dependent on, and vulnerable to, external economic and political considerations. This is perhaps one of the reasons why the *actual* contribution of the public sector investment has always been lower than the planned levels. It ranged between 57 per cent and 77 per cent, and amounted to only 62 per cent of the planned targets in 1981 and 1982. The actual percentage of external financing of investment (as officially defined) has also in reality exceeded the planned proportions, and was always on the ascent rather than on the descent. The percentage of domestic savings as part of expenditure on investment declined from 99.5 per cent in 1965 to 75.8 per cent in 1968, to 84.6 per cent in 1972, to 64.9 per cent in 1975, to 51.4 per cent in 1978, to 38.3 per cent in 1980, and to 40 per cent in both 1981 and 1982. By contrast, the percentage of external financing (aid) to actual expenditure in the state budget grew from 9.8 in 1971–72, to 24 in 1975–76, to 42 in 1979 (in current prices). The percentage of external finances within government expenditure on investment grew from 27.7 in 1970–71, to 48.3 in 1975–76, and to an alarming 85.8 in 1979 [Hilan, 1989: 14–16].

As in Iraq, although to a considerably lesser extent, industrial development escalated with the rise in oil revenues between 1973 and 1980, after which many projects started to face serious financing problems. Fixed capital formation saw a big jump in 1974 and 1975, slowed down again between 1975 and 1980, picked up gently until 1985, and then receded rapidly from 1986 on. It is not at all difficult to correlate these movements with fluctuations in foreign aid loans, and to realise the close dependence of domestic investment on foreign financing [Hilan, 1989: 32].

During the first half of the 1980s, several negative indicators were showing up. A declining growth rate started to dip into negative figures in 1984. Average levels of worker productivity within the economy were declining. In the meantime, imports had not declined, exports did not increase, and informal trade (imports smuggling) remained quite high. Such trends continued into the second half of the 1980s, further complicated by a proportional decline in the contribution of the commodity sector to GDP, and by growing budgetary and trade deficits [Dalila, 1989: 409–11].

In the rural/agricultural sector the picture was rather mixed. The consolidation of Ba'thist domination has corresponded with a period in Syrian development characterised by a gradual "ruralisation of political power", with a significant proportion of the new leadership of the party, the military and the civilian government coming from a rural or provincial town background [cf. Salama, 1987a: 228–35]. This new élite, which has also been rather disproportionately representative of religiously minoritarian communities, is therefore quite distinct from the older bourgeoisie that used to be composed of (mainly Sunni) merchants and landowners. Perhaps because of this background, and unlike many other populist authoritarian regimes which overemphasise industry and the urban centres, the Syrian regime has had a fairly active and rather successful policy in the countryside especially during the 1970s. This has helped in improving the socio-economic position of the peasants and in providing them with a certain element of political mobility, while ensuring ultimate political control for the central government, in an overall situation of fluid class relationships [cf. Hinnebusch, 1989].

Grand hydraulic projects such as in the Euphrates basin have helped to facilitate the state's penetration of society through public works but the civil society is not totally passive: a "retribalisation of social relations" takes place to some extent as various groups and families seek to secure the right contacts within the bureaucratic machine, the party and the cooperatives. Field administration as well as agricultural enterprises become an arena both for securing production and for building up clientelistic political networks [Hannoyer, 1985: 24–42]. State resources are transferred to the rural society partly through planned, 'rational' policies, and partly through the private farmers and peasants out-manoeuvring the state, by diversifying crops and activities [cf. Hopfinger, 1990], or by 'corrupting' the officials and resorting to family and clan solidarities. The coexistence of the public and the private sectors, added to the 'tolerance' or the complicity of the administration, gives the system a certain suppleness that allows for initiative and improvisation. "In certain respects the state plays the role of a springboard towards the private sector. An informal underground economy develops which allows for coming and going between the state sector and the so-called 'free' private sector" [Métral, 1985: 43–63].

Such complex interactions have become increasingly the norm since the guarded move towards a certain policy of relaxation (*infiraj*) in 1970 and towards a policy of limited opening-up (*infitah*) in 1974. These cautious reforms "are marked by a combination of more flexible market mechanisms and intense state planning, since the state controls both water and credit, and the private sector holds almost 80 per cent of the cultivated land" [Leca, 1988: 191–2]. Indeed this has become 'the name of the game' with regard to the political economy at large, including its commercial and industrial sectors: "restore the confidence of domestic capital and of the bourgeoisie and petit bourgeois Sunni merchants, without losing the support of the peasantry and the wage and salary earners" [ibid., 1988: 190].

A certain kind of 'specialisation and division of labour' seems to have established itself between a public sector that concentrates on modern technology, large-scale import-substituting industry and basic products, and a private sector that concentrates on commodity and service activities that are closer to the consumer, with fewer workers and higher profitability. On paper, the private sector appeared to be quite modest. In 1979, for example, there were 36,000 companies employing fewer than ten workers, and 300 companies employing more than ten workers. Their production was quite humble, but there were probably some statistical problems involved in accounting for their activities [Dalila 1990: 400–411; and compare the much larger estimates of Perthes, 1992a: 211–17]. There is no doubt, in any case, that the number of private projects has escalated most speedily since the late 1980s and that the value added is very much higher in the private than it is in the public sector.

The relationship between the state and the entrepreneurs of the private sector need no longer be antagonistic: indeed with *infitah* it is almost a relationship of alliance, provided that the entrepreneurs do not step severely out of line. The expansion of the various public enterprises under different ministries, and more recently of the activities of the military in various economic spheres (e.g. housing, construction and electric industries, food industries, etc.), benefits a significant stratum within the state apparatus just as it extends a certain system of clientelism that multiplies its effects within broader social sectors including the private sector [Longuenesse, 1985: 5–22]. Milihouse, the military housing establishment set up in 1975 as a public sector body to carry out construction projects for the military, is now, as we have already seen, very active in the civilian domain, which accounts for some 80 per cent of its activities; it has also been able to win some contracts in other countries such as Lebanon, Jordan and Yemen. To this should be added the effects of the Syrian involvement in Lebanon which allowed contraband traffic into Syria (amounting, in 1985 for example, to about 10 per cent of all its revenues), mainly to the benefit of the officers stationed in Lebanon [Leca, 1988: 183–4]. The clampdown on this illicit trade, as well as the periodic anti-corruption campaign, helps to remind the various forces of the presence of the 'state' and of the ruling clique, and to warn them not to overstep their limits.

One is therefore almost tempted by the foregoing analysis to think that the cohabitation of the public and the private sectors with a certain blurring, through clientelistic networks, of some of the boundaries between them, is a 'functional' policy in Syria. As Y. Sadowski puts it, perhaps in a rather exaggerated way:

Corporate boards are supposed to pursue profits, not popularity, and politicians are supposed to increase the public welfare, not their bank accounts. Patronage tends to violate this separation: it is the most 'economic' of political relationships ... It is the inequity not the inefficiency of patronage that offends Syrians. If every one had equal access to patronage few would complain ... Syrians, whatever their particular ideological orientation, believe that economic activities *require* the support of state power and that economic and political processes cannot be disentangled. In their historical experience, it is the effort to conduct business without political supports that has proven inefficient [Sadowski, 1988: 168–9].

Syria's reliance on external financing reached problematic dimensions by the mid-1980s, to the extent of seriously delaying the sixth development plan (1986–90), as state revenues were running short and external sources were not forthcoming in amounts that could cover the government's investment commitments. Such developments resulted in a situation where Syria's debt had reached $4.9 billion in 1988/89, representing 22.2 per cent of its GNP, with the debt service representing 16.2 per cent of the country's export of goods and services [ABC, 1990].

A retrenchment policy was adopted within the public sector, and domestic and joint private capital were encouraged, especially in the fields of agriculture, food industries and tourism, to relieve part of the financial responsibilities of the state. Various joint ventures were formed with a state contribution not exceeding 25 per cent of their capital, with 75 per cent of the capital owned by domestic, Arab or foreign investors. One such company was the Syrian Arab Company for the Development of Agricultural Products which was owned 75 per cent : 25 per cent by the private and the public sector respectively. Several financial, monetary and taxation facilities and organisational exemptions have been given to such companies to encourage their expansion. However, as with Iraq, the regime has not to date felt the need either to call in the IMF or to push towards full economic liberalisation (even though the Syrians could not count on the same large oil resources as in Iraq). But although the regime has not declared any impressive-sounding privatisation programmes, the Syrian private sector is both more dynamic and more structurally interlinked with the public sector than its Iraqi counterpart, and therefore a *de facto* privatisation process could be said to have been taking shape for a number of years. It is true that the share of the private sector in investments in 1987 (43 per cent) is not nominally much higher than it was in 1973 (41 per cent), but there are indications that the value added per each employee as well as capital productivity in general are on the increase in the private sector, whereas they are declining in the public sector [Longuenesse, 1985].

Thus a situation emerges of a very active private sector, but one that still has to work round the contours of the elaborate state requirements of authorisations, permits and licences. The bureaucratic bourgeoisie may not therefore entertain a full privatisation programme that would deprive it of such opportunities. The continuation of external revenues until very recently has enabled the state to continue to enjoy a certain degree of autonomy from the social classes; Syria's stand on the side of the winners in the Gulf drama of 1990/91 would ensure a continuation of some of these revenues.

Full privatisation, by contrast, carries with it the political risk of bringing back to full prominence the currently constrained Sunni/commercial bourgeoisie, with its subsidiary militant extension among the Muslim Brotherhood [cf. Al-Ahsan, 1984: 312, 315–518] – a prospect that the ruling élite would not at all entertain. It also carries with it the risk of antagonising the influential and fairly strong labour unions in which, with the intention of cultivating them as a supporting constituency, the regime has invested so much of its political energy [Lawson, 1990: 30–51]. A *de facto* privatisation appears to have served the interests of the regime for a number of years, but a more formalised, if still careful, approach towards the fostering of private investments is now in place, following the issue of Law No. 10 of May 1991 for the encouragement of 'productive investment'.

Iraq

The emergence of the public sector in Iraq, following the anti-monarchical coup of 1958, was basically motivated by political reasons such as the need to eradicate the economic base of the élite associated with the *ancien régime*, and was to a large extent influenced by the Nasserist model. Significant nationalisations in 1964 transferred to the state the ownership of about thirty important factories of cigarettes, building materials, food industries, textiles and leather, and nationalised all banks and insurance companies. However, up till 1973 the growth of the public sector remained rather slow and limited. It was the successive nationalisations of various processes of petroleum extraction (between 1972 and 1975), combined with the quadrupling of oil prices around the same time, that was to result in the great expansion of the Iraqi public sector, since the state was now in charge of over half, and eventually (in 1977), of 80 per cent of the national GDP, as well as being in possession of the main sources of economic surplus in the society. In this same year, 1977, there were about 400 public sector enterprises, employing 80,000 workers and absorbing 60 per cent of all industrial and commercial investment [Al-Khafaji, 1983: 25–33].

Iraqi industrialisation was therefore closely related to a 'mineral base' (oil), which gave the expansion of the economic role of the state features that are quite similar to those obtaining in other oil-exporting countries of the Gulf. More specifically, this industrialisation was very much related to a limited number of 'grand projects' in the area of 'industrialising industries' – i.e. heavy industries, closely tied to the almost free supply of oil and gas, rather externally oriented, and with "little connection with the overall economic and social life of the country" [S. Amin, 1982b: 86–7, 139–46]. Despite the seemingly high priority attached by the official development policy to import-substitution, the results remained rather modest as far as self-sufficiency is concerned. The industrialisation model of the oil boom period involved

> a combination of big capital-intensive and export-oriented industries, and the strategy tied the Iraqi development to the capitalist world market. Put differently, the Iraqi industrialisation of the 1970s meant growing dependency on the transnational companies because of their supplies of turn-key plants and numerous contracts within management, services and marketing [Olsen, 1986: 27].

By the early 1980s not only was the public sector predominant within these 'strategic' big industries, but it almost monopolised foreign trade and continued to play an important role in domestic trade and owned the banking, insurance and financial services [Al-Sayyid 'Ali, 1989: 27–31]. By 1987, as much as 96 per cent of the industrial work force was employed in state-owned factories, which produced more than 84 per cent of total industrial output [Chaudhry, 1991: 15–16]. This is not to suggest, however, that the private sector has been absent from the economic scene. An Iraqi *infitah* with regard to agriculture took place quite early on. The fairly extensive 'agrarian reform' implemented in the early 1970s was soon to be reversed, around 1978, with the liquidating of most collective farms and the phasing put of several agricultural cooperatives; and in 1983 a law was enacted that permitted the private rent of unlimited acreages of public land [cf. Springborg, 1986: 33–52]. Credit and infrastructural facilities were given to the private sector, Iraqi and Arab, to stimulate investment and mechanisation, and independent production and marketing activities were allowed.

The same pattern was to follow, but more slowly, in construction and in some commercial activities. According to 'Isam Al-Khafaji [1983, 1986a, 1986b], by the mid-1970s, a 'bourgeoisie of contractors', servicing and supplying the public sector, was already quite prosperous. This was, and has remained, the segment of the private sector most closely tied to direct political clientelism. Others maintain, however, that although the number of contractors has indeed been growing steadily, that group (apart from a core of some 200 wealthy individuals) is neither large enough nor stable and permanent enough to form a solid support base for the regime [Chaudhry, 1991: 16, 22]. Khafaji suggests that this group of contractors was soon followed by a new 'commercial bourgeoisie' engaged in trade and services, which continued to thrive in spite of the austerity enforced by the Iran–Iraq war. Gradually too a small 'industrial bourgeoisie' was also emerging, making use of generous credits, tax exemptions and subsidised state products, and eventually acquiring shares in the lucrative 'mixed sector' enterprises which had access to government foreign exchange and were used for political patronage.

These emerging business fractions (I do not agree with Al-Khafaji's use of the term 'bourgeoisie' in this respect) did not, however, represent a revival of the old 'houses' of businessmen that had been active before the revolution. They were on the whole newcomers, with good 'political' connections, either with the powerful 'bureaucratic bourgeoisie' and/or with the close circle of the ruling clique centred round the president and a small clientelistic minority of Sunni Arabs from the provincial towns of middle and north-western Iraq [cf. Al-Khafaji, 1983: Chs. 3, 4, 5 and 8]. This emerging class is distinctively of middle- or lower middle-class background, and represents a break, made possible through the development of state capitalism, with the older feudalist/colonial classes – except perhaps with regard to some established families of the industrial bourgeoisie, where some of the older surnames are still visible to this day [Al-Khafaji, 1983: 96–105, 179–80].

Al-Khafaji maintains that by 1986 the share of the private sector in GDP (excluding oil, defence and administration) had reached 64 per cent, its share in construction being 94 per cent, in transportation 76 per cent and in commerce 44 per cent [Al-Khafaji, 1986b]. Such figures may be somewhat exaggerated. Farhang Jalal, another Iraqi economist more sympathetic to the private sector, maintains that the only activities conceded by the state to the private sector prior to 1987 had only concerned very secondary fields such as excavating rubble and sand and manufacturing some refreshments [F. Jalal, 'Comment' in Al-Nasrawi et al., 1990: 365–6]. Based on a more comprehensive set of figures, yet another Iraqi economist, 'Abd al-Mun'im Al-Sayyid 'Ali, reports that in 1987 the share of the public sector in GDP (including oil) was 83.9 per cent compared to 16.1 per cent for the private sector. Excluding oil, the former's share amounted to 61 per cent of GDP and the latter's to 39 per cent thereof (being particularly high in areas such as transport: 77.7 per cent; and commerce: 60.1 per cent). In the same year, the public sector was responsible for 76 per cent of total fixed capital formation, compared to 24 per cent for the private sector [Al-Sayyid 'Ali, 1990: 350].

Whatever the case may be, such figures should not give one a false sense of the structural strength of the private sector, for the state has continued to maintain its grip on the economy and the society through its monopoly of the utilisation of the oil revenues (the petroleum industry accounting for 55–60 per cent of GDP), and through its control of the civil and military apparatus (one out of every three urban Iraqis is publicly employed) and most particularly the party/security machine. And although the oil revenues had more than halved during the war years with Iran (from their peak of $26.5 billion in 1980), they remained quite handsome indeed, and enabled the state to enjoy a considerable degree of autonomy from the domestic social classes. As in Algeria, this is a case of the private sector being *assigned* a role *by* the state. The government had no intention of relinquishing economic (much less political) power, but hopes to streamline the existing system:

The Ba'th wants the private sector to participate actively in achieving the *government's* goals. For example, if the State believes that urban markets lack eggs, it simply 'instructs' private poultry farmers to switch to egg production. It is unlikely that these instructions are ignored, but it is equally unlikely that such an *infitah* will effect many deep changes in the Iraqi political economy [Richards and Waterbury, 1990: 254–7].

This, one can perhaps say, is privatisation by *diktat*. Furthermore, the overwhelming proportion of the private sector has remained closely tied to the state and/or vulnerable to fluctuations in foreign trade and foreign politics. Lacking strong structural linkages with the rest of the economy, the private sector continued to be critically dependent on the state. After eradicating most segments of the older generation of shaikhly landlords, a 'modernised' agriculture could be safely handed over to a 'more efficient' private sector that would help to satisfy the growing appetites of the expanding urban populations. By the beginning of 1988 virtually all of Iraq's agricultural production and several food processing industries had been privatised. But the non-agricultural private sector was not particularly in a hurry at this stage to press for full autonomy from the state, nor was the state particularly anxious to push vigorously in that direction. Although some subsidies were reduced and benefits constrained, the state did not want to cut down severely on the levels of welfare, especially during the politically sensitive war years. Only a mild privatisation programme was therefore implemented during the years of war with Iran.

Serious privatisation began in 1987 and gained momentum in 1988, after the cease-fire with Iran. It involved consolidation of the privatisation drive in agriculture, the sale of very large poultry, dairy and fisheries enterprises, and divestiture to the private sector of a number of factories for food processing, textiles, construction materials, transport and services. It also included the elimination of state monopoly on the importation of consumer goods, an export earnings retention scheme for industrialists, and a new foreign investment law that provided greater incentives for Arab investment in Iraq (while still officially prohibiting exclusive non-Arab foreign investment). A second state-owned commercial bank, Al-Rashid Bank, was established in 1989 to introduce competition for Al-Rafidain Bank, though further liberalisation of the country's financial sector was still to be put into solid form. Tax exemptions and credit facilities were increased and several restrictions with regard to capital and employment were eased out.

As a Ba'th party document declared, there was no longer a need for Iraq to be a 'state of small shops and stores' (*dawlat dakakin*) [in Al-Sayyid 'Ali, 1989: 40]. The state was perceived to be more successful in the area of manufacturing industries, where cheap energy and the expanding technocratic élite were contributing to a more effective performance [ibid.: 58]. Rather than retreating, the state was actually endeavouring to free itself from what the leadership came to regard as minor economic pursuits in order to concentrate on larger, more strategic projects in iron and steel, engineering, arms and petrochemicals [cf. ABC, 1990: 42-5]. The same observer who was impressed by the scale and speed of privatisation had to admit that however dramatic they might appear, "the reforms of the 1980s did not signal a fundamental change in the balance between public and private shares in the economy outside agriculture. The state's share in manufacturing kept pace due to large investments in heavy industry ... At no point did [its] share of industry fall below 76 percent" [Chaudhry, 1991: 15].

The state had not retreated but had simply changed its order of priorities in the economic sphere. The private sector was being assigned a role *by* the state: this was divestiture without marketisation. If there were no industrial entrepreneurs to take on the role, some had to be manufactured by order, and fast, to fill in the 'entrepreneurial void' (from among contracting, commercial and political protégés). As one commentator put it: "a capitalist fraction (I refrain intentionally from describing it as a bourgeoisie) was created within weeks by a decree from above, and was then allowed to get its hands on the workers and on prices" [N. Firjani, 'Debate' in Al-Nasrawi et al., 1990: 897]. That prices have rocketed sky-high as a result is a fact (which contributed to the overall atmosphere of economic panic that led eventually to the invasion of Kuwait). As for the workers, they were certainly harmed, but the regime was careful to deprive an already emasculated labour movement of any channels through which collectively to express its grievances. In 1987, the labour union, which included public and private sector workers, was dissolved. Public enterprise workers became 'employees' in the public service, which was presumably undergoing an 'administrative revolution' and shedding some of its senior personnel. Private sector workers belonging to firms with over fifty workers each (only 8 per cent of the industrial workforce) could form unions but in reality they were too weak to do so, especially with available competition from 'less-demanding' Egyptian and other non-Iraqi workers and from nearly a quarter of a million soldiers returning from the war with Iran [cf. Lawson, 1990: 32-51; Chaudhry, 1991: 15-18; M. Farouk-Sluglett and P. Sluglett, 1990: 22-3].

The relatively significant debt to international banks and governments accumulated by the end of the Iran–Iraq war, (amounting to just under $15 billion and representing 29.2 per cent of GNP, with debt service representing 50 per cent of exports), was regarded as a serious but temporary condition that did not warrant resorting to the IMF [ABC, 1990: 40]. Additional unquantified liabilities due to Arab governments (estimated by some at $40 billion) included an obligation to Saudi Arabia and Kuwait to repay 'war relief' crude sold by these two countries on behalf of Iraq from 1983 to 1988. However, the continuation by the regime of its large-scale industrial and military investments (not to speak of war damage repairs and welfare expenditures) at a time of relatively low oil prices and at a juncture when several Western quarters were terminating their credits to Iraq, had combined to produce a rather desperate foreign exchange shortage. By the early months of 1990,the economy of Iraq had passed the stage of deterioration to reach that of collapse [Parisot, 1990; Picard, 1990: 26–7]. The Iraqi leadership was obviously still hoping that several debtor countries (Arab and foreign) would reschedule Iraq's debts under generous conditions and that the Gulf countries would forgive most of the debts due to them by way of a political reward for Iraq's performance in the war with Iran – and when Kuwait, the richest *and* the most vulnerable of the neighbours, was not particularly forthcoming in this respect, the chosen option was simply to take over its riches, by force!

Jordan

In spite of adopting a formally 'open' and 'liberal' economic policy, the government's involvement in the Jordanian economy has been very substantial. In addition to a highly controlled pricing and subsidisation policy, many economic activities, including those of the private sector, have been closely regulated by the state, and Jordanian industrial activity has been mainly initiated by the government. The 'imperative' for Jordanian industrialisation, however, has been somewhat different from that of the more populist Arab regimes that are often described as socialist or radical. The Jordanian royal family has had to impart 'substance' to an otherwise artificial state that lacks any really distinct geographical or human base, by emphasising in particular the process of institution-building. In a manner similar to that pertaining in the Gulf countries, Jordan illustrates the Chatelus-Schemeil dictum of a situation in which the observer is not so much witnessing a state that is embarking on an industrialisation programme just for the (economic and technical) sake of it, as he is witnessing an industrialisation programme that is intended primarily for the purposes of building a state [Chatelus and Schemeil, 1984]. Additional public expenditures have turned the population in a few decades (and in spite of extremely high population growth rates) from a predominantly illiterate into a largely literate one, and have raised the level of public utilities and general services (including housing, electricity, health, communications, etc.) to fairly high standards [Al-Sha'ir, 1990: 636–8].

Such a need to consolidate the socio-economic base of Jordan became more critical following the series of disruptions that were connected with the Israeli occupation of the (richer) West Bank and with the consequent rapid increase in Jordan's Palestinian population and all the social and political implications that this development was to bring about. The strengthening of a centralised management of the economy expressed itself in the adoption of a series of development plans. A three-year plan (1973–75) was launched with the specific aim of trying to revitalise the economy after the damage caused by the Six Day War and its aftermath, and this was followed by a series of five-year plans, starting in 1976–80, which had more ambitious objectives. In this and in the following (1981–85) plan the government favoured the commodity-producing sectors, especially in light and medium-scale industries such as timber processing, metal works, domestic appliances and building materials. The outcome of such a policy has been that in recent years budget expenditures have averaged 40–50 per cent of GDP annually, reflecting investments in industry and the infrastructure, price subsidies, and also large defence and security charges [ABC, 1990: 50–51]. Public expenditure as a percentage of GDP increased from less than 31 per cent in the 1950s and 1960s to around 55 per cent during the 1970s and early 1980s. Public investment as a percentage of total investment increased from about 35 per cent during the 1960s to almost 50 per cent during the 1970s and early 1980s. The share of planned public investment in total gross fixed-capital formation averaged 46 per cent in the period 1970 to 1990, reaching a peak of 55 per cent in the mid-1980s.

In institutional terms, such activities have resulted in the emergence of a significant public sector that includes some forty public organisations functioning in the areas of natural resources (mainly phosphates), industry, metallics and electricity, agriculture, electricity, transport and communications, housing and tourism, as well as trade, supplies and finance. Whereas some of these organisations were totally owned by the state, others had a government share of over 50 per cent of capital and therefore their management was government controlled [Abu Shikha, 1983; Abu Shikha and 'Assaf, 1985: Ch. 6]. Although agriculture has on the whole declined (owing to the loss of the fertile West Bank, population pressures and drought conditions), the government's involvement in agricultural affairs has increased through the role of the Jordan Valley Authority (which was subsequently merged with the Ministry of Water and Irrigation), and the role of the Jordan Cooperative Organisation, which was boosted after the mid-1970s [Adwan and Cunningham, 1989: 3; Gubster, 1988: 105].

The growth in the economic role of the state has been closely contingent upon the post-1973 oil boom in both direct and indirect ways, to the extent that some have described Jordan as the world's main "non-oil-producing oil economy" [ABC, 1990: 51]. During much of the 1970s and early 1980s, some four-fifths of gross domestic expenditure was estimated to have derived from direct grants and budget support loans from the neighbouring oil-exporting countries, from remittances from Jordanians working in the Gulf, and from Jordanian exports to the neighbouring oil-rich countries. Over one-third of the Jordanian labour force was employed in the Gulf and the remittances from these individuals were equivalent to almost two-thirds of Jordan's total revenues from exports of goods and non-factor services. Budget support by Gulf countries was usually equivalent to about half the government's revenues in the period from the late 1970s to 1983. And Jordan's exports to Arab countries represented on average about half of the country's total merchandise exports [Anani and Khalaf, 1989: 211]. Jordan is therefore highly vulnerable to economic and political developments in the Gulf, a fact that was made most tragically obvious during the Gulf war of 1990/91.

The momentum of economic activity during most of the 1980s was maintained by a much higher level of government expenditure, which was heavily financed by external and domestic borrowing, and which resulted in a net budget deficit that rose from 9 per cent of GDP in 1984 to 18 per cent in 1987. Although relatively buoyant tourism, a considerable expansion in the banking services resulting from the disruptions in Beirut, and the side-benefits of the re-export trade with Iraq during its war with Iran, had all somewhat ameliorated the situation, the overall decline in revenues as a consequence of the uncertain conditions in the Gulf had resulted in a rapid increase in Jordan's external indebtedness, from $2.5 billion in 1984 to an estimated $6–$7 billion in 1988. Debt represented 92 per cent of GDP and debt service represented 24.6 per cent of exports, while there were signs that GDP itself was declining in absolute terms. Foreign exchange reserves also declined during the same period from $515 million in 1984 to $110 million in 1988.

Jordan's financial situation reached crisis proportions in 1988, necessitating emergency austerity programmes and prompting the country to resort, rather desperately, to the International Monetary Fund. In spring 1989 the government entered into negotiations with the IMF for a 'stand-by credit facility' worth $125 million, conditional on a certain economic adjustment programme. This was followed by a $150 million loan agreement with the World Bank which was expected to be matched by a loan from the Japanese government. Jordan's debts to creditor governments that were members of the Paris Club were also rescheduled, and some aid from Arab countries was said to be forthcoming. The medium-term adjustment programme (1989–93) that formed the basis of Jordan's agreement with the IMF was essentially concerned with price stability, budget deficit reduction, and a tight credit policy. The abrupt removal of subsidies on several basic commodities that resulted from this arrangement led to violent and widespread rioting in April 1989 that seemed to challenge the legitimacy of the regime.

It is within the context of such a dramatic financial crisis, and in the absence of any indicators that its reversal was imminent, that the thinking on the subject of privatisation was to emerge. Government officials considered that revitalising the role of the private sector would be a way of relieving the state of some of its heavy financial commitments, and the argument in due course surfaced that the private sector was more rational and that privatisation and efficiency were two sides of the same coin [cf. Adwan and Cunningham, 1989].

The public sector's largest holding in absolute and relative terms is in mining, where total public investments amount to 58 per cent of the capital of mining companies and represent almost one half of total public shareholding in Jordanian corporations. The highly capital-intensive nature of mining companies and the perception that naturally occurring minerals are a national resource may not render this area particularly amenable to speedy privatisation. The second largest area of government participation is in the manufacturing sector, where the government contribution reaches 23.2 per cent of the sector's capital, with 87 per cent of public shares being held in the four largest companies: the Jordan Cement Factories, the Jordanian Petroleum Refinery, the Glass Industries, and the Engineering Industries. The subscribed capital of these four companies represents 56 per cent of the total capital of all 48 manufacturing companies in the country. In services, average public investment amounts to 20.8 per cent of the total capital of service companies [Anani and Khalaf, 1989: 211–17].

Pure public enterprises and public–private joint ventures vary widely in terms of productivity and efficiency, and it is not clear to what extent this criterion will be among the ones used for targeting projects for privatisation. Among the exclusively public institutions, the Telecommunications Corporation and the Electricity Authority are usually considered profitable, whereas the Water Authority incurs planned losses for 'equity' purposes. Within the mixed enterprises, some experts believe that "the higher the government participation, the higher the probability of having a loss-making industry. In fact, 58 percent or more of these companies were loss-makers in 1986. The comparable figure for enterprises with less than 35 percent public ownership was only 26 percent" [Anani and Khalaf, 1989: 215–17]. Privatisation proposals have been put forward for both profitable corporations (e.g. Telecommunications), and loss-making ones (e.g. Transportation) [Adwan and Cunningham, 1989: 5–8]. Since 1986, when privatisation was declared as a desirable objective, several studies and preparations have been carried out but no actual transfer of ownership from the public to the private sector has taken place. Three enterprises have in particular been identified as targets for privatisation: Royal Jordanian Airlines, the Public Transport Corporation, and the Telecommunications Corporation. But actual implementation has so far not progressed beyond focusing on the commercialisation of public enterprises as a preparatory step for the eventual transfer of ownership and control.

Differently from some other Middle Eastern countries, the pattern of government investment in Jordan did not cause a 'crowding-out' of the private sector. The state's concentration on services, utilities and the infrastructure and, within industry, on mining and mineral industries, as well as the widespread practice of joint public–private ventures in manufacturing and engineering industries, combined with the fact that the private sector and the state were both simultaneously receiving (in their different ways) 'surrogate oil revenues' – all these factors have helped in creating a situation where the public and the private sectors have complemented (rather than competed with) each other. This policy was also conducive to the political cohesion of Jordan, creating as it did common economic grounds between the predominantly Transjordanian bureaucratic bourgeoisie on the one hand and the predominantly Palestinian commercial bourgeoisie on the other.

Yet the equal reliance of the private sector on externally derived revenues as well as its close partnership with the state in many activities would also suggest that the private sector may not be capable of picking up the slack that is resulting from the decline in both official and private transfers to Jordan, and from the closely related reduction in the economic role of the state. It should also be remembered that many of the larger private sector enterprises (phosphates, oil-refining, potassium, cement, electricity and tobacco) are *régis* (*sharikat imtiyaz*), or companies by privileged appointment (i.e. private monopolies). In 1987 these companies realised 64.8 per cent of all value added in the industrial sector. They do receive much governmental protection and support, and are not subject to the usual business accounting and control procedures, and it is difficult therefore to predict the efficiency of their performance under more 'normal' market conditions [Al-Sha'ir, 1990: 640].

The Jordanian leadership has intelligently allowed a certain measure of political liberalisation to make up for the declining economic conditions. The elections held in November 1989 to usher in a return to the parliamentary life that had been suspended after the 1967 Arab–Israeli war have brought in some independent elements, including a significant number of Muslim Brothers. If such independent elements are permitted to function freely, this should signify a distinct move towards a process of democratisation in Jordan. However, the Jordanian leadership is likely to proceed very carefully along this path. From its inception, security considerations have constituted a vital core in the make-up of the Jordanian state. Of the 60 per cent or so of the local manpower that is publicly employed, nearly half work for security/defence organisations. Security/defence utilisations also represent about a quarter of the government budget, and armament expenses about half the external public debt [Al-Sha'ir, 1990: 643–5].

Over the years, the ethnic composition of the population and of the labour force has come to be considered a 'security-related' matter. As one commentator put it, if the 'state' (government and army) is Jordanian and the 'private sector' is Palestinian, it is conceivable (especially in view of some Israeli designs to regard Jordan as the Palestinian homeland) that the leadership will be reluctant about reducing the role of the state in Jordan or lowering government subsidies because of the political ramifications that are likely to result from such a policy [J. Al-'Anani, 'Comment' in Al-Nasrawi et al., 1990: 682–3].

With the eruption of the 1990/91 Gulf crisis, Jordan's economic and strategic vulnerability was made even more plain. Trapped between various conflicting parties, severely harmed by the blockade against Iraq, and then by the 'punishment' of the allies and the arrival of hundreds of thousands of

Palestinians, the country now faces a multitude of far more existential problems than the small matter of wondering which public enterprises to privatise first.

Algeria

With the coming of Algerian independence in 1962, Ahmad Bin Bella, the country's first president, introduced a system of self-management (*autogestion*) in agriculture and in industry as the basis of his country's economic policy. However, as a result of his removal from power through a military coup led by Houari Boumedienne in June 1965, Bin Bella's model did not last long. Under the regime of President Boumedienne, the country's economic policy was based on socialist planning and the setting up of large state enterprises – the *sociétés nationales*. The major enterprises included SONATRACH (in the field of hydrocarbons), and several companies in the fields of steel, engineering, electrics and building materials. There were also some smaller state enterprises such as those for metal-work, textiles, domestic gas and electricity supplies, leatherwork and footwear, and tourism. Complementary activities that remained under state control included a total monopoly on foreign trade and on banking and insurance. One may infer from this overall picture that the state was convinced of the need to have the Algerian economy firmly under its control [cf. Bouattia, 1993].

However, under the pressure of growing financial burdens Algeria, like other countries in the region, became part of the wave of economic liberalisation and privatisation that swept across the Arab World during the 1980s [cf. Sutton and Aghrout, 1990; Vandewalle, 1992]. After President Shadhli Bin Jadid took over in 1978, the country underwent a ten-year period of political and more particularly economic, reforms. These reforms reversed the earlier policies that had favoured a state capitalism based on a development strategy of heavy 'industrialising industries' and on *gigantisme*. In their place a rehabilitated version of the earlier and much constrained private sector of the economy was allowed to emerge, while a restructuring and subdividing of the dominant state industrial *sociétés nationales* was put in train [Osterkamp, 1982]. In the agricultural sector, the large self-managed or 'collective estate' farms and producer cooperatives that had emerged from two agrarian reform programmes were restructured and reduced in size.

Politically, the progressive replacement of members of Boumedienne's government by more 'pragmatic' FLN ministers during successive Bin Jadid administrations encouraged an increasing liberalisation that culminated in the introduction of a multi-party political system in 1989, and in the opening up of the Algerian economy to foreign investment in 1990.

Largely because of the constraints imposed by the 1966 *Code des Investissements*, the private industrial sector had stagnated throughout the 1970s. In 1982 a new investment code was issued that aimed to restore private initiative through mobilising savings and providing guarantees, credits and tax advantages. While heavy 'strategic' industry was retained within the state sector, private investment was encouraged in areas such as light manufacturing, craft industries and hotel infrastructure, and a third decentralised industrial sector that was supported and managed by the local *wilayat* authorities was also promoted. By the mid-1980s, this emerging private sector accounted for some 30 per cent of industrial workers who were distributed among 4,800 small and medium-sized enterprises, most of which employed between five and twenty workers only.

The creation in 1982 of the Office National pour l'Orientation, le Suivi, et la Coordination de l'Investissement Privé (OSCIP) also gave further encouragement to, as well as some control over, private industrial investment. Large private industrial projects whose investments exceeded 3 million dinars, required central approval from OSCIP's Commission Nationale d'Agrément (CNA), while smaller projects could be approved by local Commissions d'Agrément de Wilaya (CAW). In the period from 1983 to 1987 OSCIP approved 5,186 investment projects, of which 1,181 were in the larger-capital CNA sector. The private capital that was to be invested in this way averaged 2.6 billion dinars annually between 1983 and 1985, increasing to 3.7 billion dinars in 1986, and to 6.9 billion dinars in 1987. About 44 per cent of this was to go into industrial manufacturing projects from 1983 to 1986, with the transport, tourism and services sector ranking second and the construction materials sector ranking third during the same period, while all the projects approved by OSCIP up to the latter part of June 1987 would create 75,446 new jobs in this burgeoning private sector. By 1988/89, the regulations concerning private investment had been liberalised still further. At this point the regulatory role of OSCIP was done away with and with it went an interesting accumulation of investment statistics [Sutton and Aghrout, 1990: 6–7].

In the meantime, the public sector itself was being reorganised. From 1980 the Bin Jadid government had concluded that the state industrial sector was constrained both by vertical integration and by bureaucratic concentration deriving from the sixteen large industrial *sociétés nationales* that collectively accounted for some 80 per cent of industrial activity in Algeria and which employed 311,680 people. Accordingly a major reorganisation was undertaken with the aim of breaking up the unwieldy organisations into much smaller *entreprises nationales*, each one of which would be more specialised in clearly defined production activities that would usually separate the functions of production, distribution and marketing. The iron and steel complex (SNS) was therefore divided up into thirteen *entreprises*, and the wide-ranging SONACOME engineering corporation was split into eleven *entreprises*. Likewise the sixteen industrial *sociétés* were subdivided into 107 *entreprises*. It was estimated that the restructuring of the wider group of some thirty-five to thirty-nine

state *sociétés*, including commercial, financial and transport organisations, produced anything from 322 to 500 enterprises after subdividing had taken place.
While it was not a privatisation exercise as such, the restructuring involved a
great deal of decentralisation to regional units and resulted in a more flexible
and less concentrated state industrial sector with which private industry could
liaise and do business [Sutton and Aghrout, 1990 and refs cited].

In the early 1990s the Algerian public enterprise sector consisted of approximately 350 national and 2,500 provincial and communal enterprises. The
important provincial and communal state-owned enterprises sector was undergoing a process of consolidation (with World Bank support) as a first step
towards improving performance. More extensive and advanced reforms were
proceeding in the national state-owned enterprises sector, with the aim of
putting the public and the private sectors on an equal legal and regulatory
footing when engaged in the same field of activity, and in order to make the
state-owned enterprises conform to the requirements of the national commercial code (from which they had previously been exempt).

Whereas in the first phase of reform, a few of the largest and most concentrated state-owned enterprises, including the hydrocarbon giant SONA-
TRACH, were functionally and geographically decentralised, the second phase
of reform concentrated on sorting out the arrears (cross-debts) situation between parent companies and their subsidiaries. Enterprise restructuring was
not particularly successful initially, but it was claimed that the effectiveness of
future rehabilitation efforts would be improved by alterations to the system of
taxing the enterprises.

The extensive riots and disturbances that took place throughout the country
in October 1988 brought the magnitude of the problems sharply into focus,
not only in their economic but also in their social and political dimensions.
The country's fiscal crisis was now compounded by a huge food imports bill
and by the incessant demands of a highly 'mobilised' population for the
continuing provision of jobs, social services and subsidised commodities [Ben-
noune, 1990]. The regime responded by a dual action combining a high degree
of political liberalisation with an accelerated pace for economic restructuring
and managerial reform.

Further reforms in the area of economic management concentrated on
clarifying the relationship of the government with the national state-owned
enterprises, and on putting the management of the public companies at some
distance from the intervention of sectoral ministries. This was done through
eight *Fonds de Participation* – Participation or Shareholding Funds. These publicly
owned and operated Funds which were intended to act as holding companies,
would each hold shares in a diversified portfolio of state-owned enterprises,
and their mandate would be to buy or sell shares, and to invest or to disinvest
their holdings, with the aim of maximising their profits. Early in 1990 the
National Assembly authorised new joint ventures between state enterprises

and private capital, foreign or domestic. Each of the Funds would receive an initial allocation of a substantial minority of shares in a specific industrial sub-sector, but no single Fund would own more than 40 per cent of the shares of any one firm. In this way ownership of every enterprise would be spread among at least three Funds, which would monitor enterprise performance and enforce profitability standards. The aims of the Funds would be to stimulate competitive market forces, to reduce political and administrative interference in the day-to-day functioning of the firms, to provide enterprise management with profit-maximisation signals and the autonomy to achieve these goals, and generally to increase the operational efficiency of the enter-prise concerned [cf. Lee and Nellis, 1990: 6–7].

The Algerian Participation Funds came into existence officially in the middle of 1989, and the initial steps towards transformation involved the formation of an agency that advised on how each enterprise could be placed on a firmer financial footing. Each enterprise was assigned a value in terms of the number of shares that would be issued for each firm and at this point the enterprises were handed over to the Participation Funds, and Fund managers were then put in place. Operating procedures had still to be determined, however,, and it was not very clear how enterprise performance standards would be set, monitored and enforced [Lee and Nellis, 1990: 7]. The para-meters of managerial autonomy had also to be specified, though it was expected that managers would be able to hire and fire employees. Pricing was somewhat liberalised, but in view of the monopoly structure of the Algerian economy, margins were to remain controlled. Access to foreign currency remained severely constrained, but some progress was made in tightening up on the allocation of domestic credit as one of the moves towards the eventual imposing of a hard budget constraint.

At the beginning of the 1990s none of the national state-owned enterprises had been liquidated, despite the fact that they were now subject to the com-mercial code which allowed for closures. The country's growing political difficulties are further distracting the leadership from paying sufficient attention to the problems of economic management and reform.

Saudi Arabia, Kuwait and the United Arab Emirates

In spite of its liberal-economy rhetoric, Saudi Arabia is more typical, in organisational terms, of an etatist system than it is of a market-oriented one. This has, of course, been mainly a function of the oil boom. The country possesses an authoritative ministry of planning that prepares the all-important successive developmental plans. And it has extremely powerful ministries of Petroleum and of Industry that host dynamic technocratic teams which prepare general policies on the one hand and direct and control important public corporations on the other (e.g. in the areas of oil field development, petroleum engineering, refining, pipelines and gas, basic industries, petrochemicals, steel, fertilisers, etc.) [cf. Al-Farsy, 1982: 73–111].

The economic role of the state in Saudi Arabia is extremely important. In 1978, the government was responsible for 60.3 per cent of gross fixed capital formation, for 61.7 per cent of expenditure in GDP, for 48 per cent of total consumption and (in 1976) for 33.3 per cent of all national purchases [El-Mallakh, 1982: 276]. Although the development plans have declared that the government would undertake capital investment only "where the size of investment is large and beyond the capacity of private individuals", and even though the policy of 'Saudisation' has entailed preferential incentives to Saudi rather than expatriate and foreign contractors [ibid.: 403–8], private business is to a large extent contingent on public expenditure and domestic producers do not appear to be able to function without heavy subsidy from the government.

The development plan is the main vehicle through which the state reshapes the economy, largely through public spending. The first plan (1970–75) was a rather modest investment programme. Planning took off after the oil boom with the second development plan (1975–80) involving an expenditure of no less than SR498,230 million (about $142 billion) and with major features being the infrastructure and the Jubail and Yanbu' industrial cities. The third plan (1980–85) was intended to shift the emphasis from the infrastructure to the productive sectors, including agriculture. The fourth plan (1985–89) stressed operational efficiency and non-oil activities, and stipulated a larger role for the private sector, but it is generally believed to have fallen short of its objectives.

Saudi Arabia hosts a very large public sector that has been expanding tremendously since the oil boom. Several public organisations were established, especially during the 1970s, their number exceeding thirty by the mid-1980s. These included four public organisations in the area of services, ten in the area of education and training, as well as fifteen economic public corporations, most of which include several public companies and enterprises. The activities of the public corporations cover such varied areas as oil and minerals, silos, water and electricity, regional development, banking and investment funds, as well as a whole range of manufacturing, petrochemical, and construction industries [Al-Tawil, 1986: 379–84]. Heavy industry is almost entirely concentrated in the hands of the state-owned Saudi Arabian Basic Industries Corporation (SABIC), and oil refining in the hands of the Public Organisation for Petroleum and Minerals (PETROMIN).

It is no secret that the expansion of the public sector in Saudi Arabia was motivated not only by the need to expand industry and the infrastructure and to diversify the economy, but also by "the desire to redistribute part of the growing income in the form of services and public utilities" [Khawajkiya, 1990: 485]. Like other important oil-exporters in the Gulf, Saudi Arabia has been identified as an 'allocative state' that is actively involved in the circulation of petroleum rent. There are two main direct ways for circulating rent: by employing people to work for the government, and through the supply of goods and services at reduced costs. There are also at least five other mechanisms for redistributing wealth, identified by Giacomo Luciani. The first and best-known has been the distribution of lands, which has mostly benefited the élite but which has lost much of its 'clout' in recent years as a result of excessive speculation. Other distributive mechanisms include the licensing of commercial representatives and financial intermediaries, and the subsidisation of agricultural and of industrial development. The public sector has benefited from all such practices and has accumulated enormous liquid assets, much of them deposited abroad. The richest groups revolve around the royal family and a small number of often related or associated merchant families. They remain too dependent on the state, which continues to enjoy a high degree of budgetary autonomy, to be able to initiate really independent entrepreneurial activities or political demands [Luciani, 1990a: 84–93].

In the industrial field, the Saudi private sector is involved in the production of several items such as soft drinks, paper products, detergents, furniture, plastics and building products, and in textile manufactures and light metal industries. It makes good use of the Saudi Industrial Development Fund which was set up by the government in the 1970s to provide interest-free medium- and long-term loans to the private sector. In 1984 a private sector project, the National Industrialisation Enterprise, was established to help with the government's efforts to privatise industry and to promote plants using feedstock from the first generation projects of SABIC [EIU Saudi Arabia Country Profile, 1987/88]. By the mid-1980s the private sector was contributing 46 per cent of total fixed investments, producing 71 per cent of GDP (excluding oil) and employing 88 per cent of all manpower [Khawajkiya, 1990: 492–4].

Most private sector industrial companies are fairly small in size and more concentrated in the area of rather similar consumer products. Most are 'personal' private companies or partnerships, owned and managed by the individual and his family, and very few are limited companies. Saudi Arabia had 7,060 private companies in 1986, in addition to 297,000 registered individual 'establishments' (mu'assasat fardiyya) of one sort or another, mainly functioning as merchant stores or small workshops. Available empirical studies indicate that private manufacturing firms are not particularly efficient and many are run according to rather primitive managerial and accounting practices [Presley, 1991: 102–14]. There were only 22 limited companies active in the industrial field in the mid-1980s, with a total capital of SR12 billion, of which only SR5 billion were contributed by the private sector (and SR7 billion by SABIC and PETROMIN) [Khawajkiya, 1990: 501–2]. Private sector companies are also heavily dependent on subsidised borrowing from state financing bodies.

With the decline in the revenues of the oil-exporting countries from around 1982–83 on, as a result of lower oil prices and reduced interest rates, even such relatively rich countries as Saudi Arabia were beginning to feel the need to adjust their economic policies. Generally speaking, however, the rate of decline in public expenditure has not matched the rate of decline in public revenues and in some countries, such as Kuwait and Oman, the expenditures continued on their rising trend. In Saudi Arabia, budgeted expenditures declined from $82.2 billion in 1981 to $54.8 in 1985, but actual expenditure figures remained unknown to (or continued to be withheld from) even the country's public finance experts [U. 'Abd al-Rahman, 1988: 67–8]. It is believed, however, that new projects in Saudi Arabia were halted or at least slowed down, that imports were reduced and that attempts were made to constrain the expansion in public employment, especially of expatriates (although expenditure on salaries and on overall recurrent outlays has continued to grow) [ibid.: 110–26].

Faced with a substantial decline in foreign receipts, virtually all oil-exporting countries have sought to reduce aggregate demand in order to limit the loss of external reserves. To this end, they have tried to reduce public expenditure, which for them represents the primary source of liquidity creation and demand growth. Whereas certain cuts in development spending were made possible by the near completion of major infrastructural projects, the desire to continue to provide some support to private, non-oil sectors and the need to sustain a country's defence capability, have constrained the attempt at financial retrenchment, with budget deficits remaining high or continuing to rise [Shaalan, 1987: 26–8]. Despite reductions in imports, the fall in foreign exchange earnings has resulted in most oil-exporting countries experiencing deficits in their current external accounts, and several have resorted to external commercial borrowing. The situation has not been helped by the continuation of, or even escalation in, private capital outflow. "Typically, private sectors are contracting sharply rather than picking up the slack, as had been hoped" [ibid.: 28–9].

As with most other countries, the call for privatisation in the oil-exporting countries has been prompted by fiscal difficulties. With the drop in oil revenues and the difficulty of cutting down expenditure either on the infrastructure and defence or (more seriously from a socio-political point of view) on welfare services and the comprehensive employment of nationals, the idea has emerged that some of the financial burden may be removed from the government by transferring certain economic activities to the private sector. Ideologically, the regimes in Saudi Arabia and the Gulf do not have to resort to the same 'political acrobatics' which have been necessary in countries like Egypt, Algeria or Syria in order to justify radical reversals in economic and social policies. The line promoted by the Saudis, for example, is that of restoring things to their 'natural' order:

Following the completion of the infrastructure and other basic projects, the government felt that time was ripe to restore its priorities by returning to the principles of its economic philosophy of 'Laissez-faire' ... Privatization in the Kingdom is rather unique ... The application of such a concept has not been affected by the international acceptance of the concept, or by a failure on the part of the public sector, or by the introduction of new slogans and policies [Mansour, 1989: 15–16, 25].

In anticipation of such a transformation the Saudi Fourth Socio-Economic Development Plan (1984/85–1989/90) stipulated an annual growth rate of 10 per cent for the private sector, compared to -2.4 per cent for the government sector. Overall, the planners projected a rise in the share of the private (non-oil) sector in aggregate fixed capital formation from 25.4 per cent in 1979/80 to 47.8 per cent in 1989/90. The share of the government sector was projected to decline from 50.4 per cent in 1979/80 to 27.7 per cent in 1989/90 [Ministry of Planning, 1985].

Privatisation as a public policy in Saudi Arabia involves both the consolidation of private sector activities in the areas in which it has already shown initiative and vitality, such as commerce, finance and to some extent agriculture, as well as the actual transfer of ownership and/or management of public enterprises to the private sector [ibid.: 17ff]. The new development plan (1990–95) stipulates a number of measures that are pertinent to the privatisation objective, including the establishment of an organised stock market, incentives for new shareholding companies, and encouragement for the commercial banks to extend more credit for production projects [Ministry of Planning, 1989]. The management of certain public enterprises would be leased to the private sector, and the major state industries would be allowed to sell shares to the private sector. SABIC has already been selling some shares since 1987, and some of the holding companies of the main petrochemical complex, PETROMIN, are to be transferred to private ownership. Experts believe that though activities such as major construction works and large-scale agricultural projects will continue to depend on government subsidisation,[2] activities such as manufacturing, electricity, gas and water, telephones and airlines may be ready for privatisation [Ministry of Planning Workshop, 1989].

But is the Saudi private sector ready to step in and 'pick up the slack' resulting from the contraction in public investment? It should be remembered at this point that, the laissez-faire labels notwithstanding, public spending was indeed the principal engine of Saudi Arabia's boom decade, which ended in 1983. Interestingly enough, private consumption during that period "did not have a statistically significant impact on private investment, while direct government consumption provided a strong stimulus to increased private-sector capital formation". Furthermore, although the stimulus provided by government investment to private investors was rather slow in the short run, it represented in fact double the stimulus (provided by government consumption) in the long run [Looney, 1987/8: 65]. Despite vast amounts of public sector expenditure since 1973, Saudi Arabia's economic fortunes continue to be closely linked to continued government expenditures, which in turn continue to be heavily dependent on the world oil market. Given the projected state of these markets, it is believed unlikely that the private sector will be able to sustain positive overall rates of economic growth over the coming few years [ibid.: 66–7, 74].

One important factor deciding the likely contribution of the private sector in Saudi Arabia will be the degree to which the country will succeed in installing a process of 'financial deepening'. Given the size of the population and the infrastructure and the level of capital accumulation, the private sector has a potentially more important role to play in the domestic market in the smaller, neighbouring oil-exporting countries than it does in Saudi Arabia. Much will depend, however, on

> the ability and willingness of the commercial banks to divert assets from foreign to domestic lending ... [T]he country may be vulnerable to a serious liquidity crisis if significant increases in Euro-rates were to take place in an environment in which the government was unable, because of slack revenues, to significantly increase its expenditures [Looney, 1987/88: 66–7].[3]

In Kuwait and the UAE the pattern has been a little different since the business community was not overwhelmingly new as was the case in Saudi Arabia. In the UAE the state-engendered business community is very important but the 'continuing' commercial élite (mainly of Dubai) is still quite important. In Kuwait the business bourgeoisie is still more or less a continuation of the older commercial community.

Most private sector firms in Kuwait (98.8 per cent) are again 'personal' companies (not pubic shareholding ones), several being individual- or partnership-based and a few being limited companies. But one of the most peculiar aspects is that only 1.4 per cent of the labour force in all private companies is native Kuwaiti, whereas Kuwaitis represented 45.9 per cent of the labour force in the government bureaucracy in 1990. Also significant is the fact that the contribution of the private sector to GDP had declined from 34.5 per cent in 1982 to 23.7 per cent in 1985, and from 62.9 per cent to 48 per cent of the non-oil GDP [Al-Hamud, 1990: 544–7]. Whatever few studies were conducted also showed that the productivity of the private sector was generally poor [ibid.: 550–2].

The expansion in the public sector was mainly a function of the rise in oil rents, whereby the government not only expanded the services and the infrastructure but also contributed to the capital of many (formally private) companies with shares very often exceeding half the totals (e.g. banks, insurance companies, industrial companies and transport and service companies) [ibid.:

552–4]. Furthermore the government took over 33 companies whose owners could not finance or manage them, following the two stock exchange crises of 1976 and 1982.

It should therefore be obvious that the Kuwaiti private sector continues to depend on the state (especially with regard to provision of the infrastructure, no- or low-interest loans, exemptions on imports, subsidies and special prices, customs protection, and so on) while the government is prepared to step in to cushion the sometimes capricious private sector for reasons pertaining to political survival and expediency. That is why it has become government policy to continue to maintain companies that do not make a profit and not to sell too many government shares on the stock market to the public at any one time in order not to cause a downwards trend in the market price of shares [Al-Watan, 11 April 1990: 1, 22].

In the United Arab Emirates the main instrument of development policy is the federal budget which is essentially concerned with the implementation of infrastructure projects and social services. The state, of course, dominates the petroleum sector, although in 1983 the Emirates General Petroleum Corporation (EGPC), which markets the country's hydrocarbon output, announced plans to float 30 per cent of its share in a bid to encourage the private sector to invest in industry. Most of Abu Dhabi's heavy industry is centred in the Jabal Dhanna-Ruwais industrial zone (opened in 1982) which is mostly oil-related with refineries, petrochemicals and fertilisers. The General Industries Corporation was set up in 1979 to coordinate non-petroleum development enterprises and it is involved in activities such as brickworks, steel-rolling, animal feeds, etc. Dubai has taken the lead in non-petroleum industry with the Dubai Aluminium Company (DUBAL). There is also cable manufacturing and cement production, and the largest dry dock in the world. More private activity is obvious here with the Jabal 'Ali Free Zone Authority (inaugurated in 1985), to which various foreign companies are locating.

The promulgation of an agency law requiring all agencies to be held by UAE nationals has increased both indigenisation and government intervention in the economy. In the meantime a Companies Law was issued in 1989 to organise the business practice of local and foreign investors. The Abu Dhabi Investment Authority is responsible for coordinating the Emirate's public investment policy, but a special agency has been created with the object of providing finance for the private sector: the Abu Dhabi Development Finance Corporation.

In the UAE, as in Kuwait, the indigenous labour force has a stronger preference for public than for private employment, since the remuneration in the first is usually about double what it is in the latter. The private sector in turn prefers to employ Asians, who generally seek lower salaries than Emiratis or, for that matter, other Arabs [Elhussein, 1991]. Such factors are reflected in the fact that native Emiratis represent only 3 per cent of the manpower in the private sector whereas they represent 37 per cent in the government bureaucracy [*Al-Shuruq*, 23 April 1992]. In countries such as these, privatisation carries with it the political risks of even more foreign labour which the private sector finds cheaper (and which is already 90 per cent of the labour force in the UAE) in spite of the government's attempts at discouraging the expansion in foreign employment.

Government support in the UAE for the private sector took similar if sometimes more personally 'generous' forms: interest-free loans and mortgages for housing and for investment, subsidies and price controls and very generous social allowances including gifts for marriage dowries and a progressive 'child benefit' system (the more offspring you produce the higher the allowance per child!). Every citizen is also entitled to three virtually free pieces of land [Field, 1984].

Like other oil-exporting states the UAE responded to the recession by seeking to reduce aggregate demand, especially that generated through government expenditure, and following the mid-1980s no further expansion was to take place in public employment. Fiscal retrenchment has been tempered, however, by a desire to continue to provide support for the state-dependent private sector, and by defence priorities [cf. Shaalan, 1987: 29–129].

It is little wonder, given all these constraints, that although governments in the Gulf have declared some privatisation slogans, partly by way of following fashion and partly by way of coping with the constraints of the 'bust' years, the ability to implement any privatisation programme has been very limited indeed. One analyst found herself able to state categorically and in no uncertain terms that "Privatization and liberalization programs ... failed outright in the so-called market economy of Saudi Arabia and the United Arab Emirates" [Chaudhry, 1991: 145], a statement that is perhaps rather sweeping but not altogether far off the mark.

It can thus be seen that the private sector in Saudi Arabia and the other Gulf countries is not only financially and structurally dependent on the state sector, but that the two sectors are symbiotically linked in complex ways, including on the level of personnel. Members of the élite are often engaged in 'public' office and in 'private' business at the same time, thus making the distinction between the two domains extremely difficult [Al-Nasrawi, 'Discussion' in Al-Nasrawi et al., 1990: 529–30]. Given this situation, it is quite likely – paradoxical as this may seem – that it could be the private sector and the state's clients in the business sector who will constrain and slow down the move towards privatisation in Saudi Arabia and the Gulf.

ARAB LIBERALISATIONS IN COMPARATIVE PERSPECTIVE

It is suggested in this chapter that as liberalisation policies have been declared in both so-called 'socialist' and so-called 'conservative' states within the Arab

World, the move towards liberalisation cannot be correlated to the nature of regime ideology. Rather, it is related – domestically – to a worsening 'financial crisis of the state' and – externally – to the hegemonic emergence (in an age of globalising capitalism) of a fairly consistent body of diagnostic and prescriptive 'knowledge' pertaining to the economic problems of the developing countries that some have come to term the 'Washington Consensus'.

It would perhaps be useful at this point to outline the origins of the state economic sector in the Arab World. The establishment and expansion of public sectors has been motivated in all cases by a mixture of economic and political considerations. Economically it was regarded as a strategic (sometimes 'historical') necessity required by conditions of late development and the weakness of the domestic entrepreneurial class (accompanied sometimes by the prevalence of foreign or minoritarian groups) and/or the 'distorted' investment priorities of such a class. Politically, bureaucratic expansion, nationalisations and public industrialisation were part of a process of state-building. In newer, more 'artificial' states this process required the creation of symbols and institutions of boundary-specific allegiances, whereas in older societies with more established socio-cultural identities, the task was mainly one of forging new nationalistic and independence-oriented (anti-colonial) socio-political coalitions

In poorer countries with relatively significant oligarchic agrarian and commercial classes (which were often created by and/or linked to colonial interests), the public industrialising policies of the 'modernising' regimes were more likely to encounter resistance from the older classes, as these policies were inclined – at least initially – to 'crowd out' the older agrarian-commercial bourgeoisie and to appear to be depriving them of their 'natural' domain of activity. Such societies were therefore more likely to couch their policies of state expansion and public industrialisation in increasingly populist terms, in an attempt to build new coalitions around a nucleus led by the state technocracy and subscribed to by an 'incorporated' industrial proletariat [cf. Ayubi, 1992d]. In the newer, oil-exporting countries, such a 'socialistic' orientation was not necessary because no established agrarian/commercial bourgeoisie of the same magnitude was in place, and because the abundance of oil revenues had made it possible to expand expenditure and investment without apparently crowding out the private sector. I use the word 'apparently' here, because in the final analysis the private sector was not squeezed out completely, even in the so-called socialist economies. Through forward and backward linkages to the public sector, private sectors within 'socialist' regimes have managed not only to persevere, but often to consolidate, themselves side by side with state capitalism, and the private sectors of countries like Egypt and Syria may indeed be more entrepreneurially dynamic and politically significant than their equivalent in countries like Saudi Arabia and Qatar, for example. In fact it could be argued that it was the socialistically coloured state capitalism in countries such as Egypt, Syria, Iraq and Tunisia that has, in the final analysis, paved the way for the domestic entrepreneurial bourgeoisie by removing the foreign commercial and entrepreneurial élites, curtailing the landed oligarchy and creating a solid physical and industrial infrastructure conducive to the overall expansion of capitalism, public *and* private.

The exact extent and details of whether public investment has crowded out or crowded in the private sector in various countries remains unclear, however, and cannot be elaborated upon before detailed studies are made of the inter-linkages of public and private investments in each country.

It is often argued that several Arab countries have decided to privatise because they now realise that the private sector is more efficient and productive than the public sector. Yet this is another area in which information is also scant: just how productive *are* public *and* private enterprises in the Arab countries? Productivity and effectiveness for a public sector is not simply profitability; but even 'simple' profitability data for public enterprises are lacking or difficult to obtain (sometimes for understandable 'survivalist' political reasons!).

The move towards privatisation in both the oil-poor and the oil-rich Arab countries has been prompted more by a relative (and, in the case of the former group, severe) decline in revenues, than it has been motivated by any realisation of the inefficiency of the public enterprises and the efficiency of private ones in the various Arab countries. The developing countries were prepared to take on trust the word of the early privatisers in the 'centre' (the United Kingdom and the United States) on this issue, as well as the assurances of the international organisations of globalising capitalism (e.g. the International Monetary Fund and the International Bank for Reconstruction and Development), that reflected the thinking of the leading capitalist states and the multinationals. Although a few Arab writers have voiced some doubts and called for caution [e.g. Hafiz Mahmud, 1989; Hilan, 1989; Mahjoub, 1990], most Arab writings on privatisation have taken it for granted that private is more rational and efficient than public, and have proceeded *ipso facto* to suggest strategies and modalities for *implementing* such a policy [e.g. Abdel-Rahman and Abu Ali, 1989; Anani and Khalaf, 1989; Al-Saigh and Buera, 1990].

In most cases, the managerial argument over efficiency has been confused with (or else has tended to overshadow) the macro-economic argument over development. The most profitable enterprises are not always the most con-ducive to overall national development. Even some of the proponents of privatisation would concede that the state had acted in several Arab societies as a real 'agent of development' on the macro-economic level, and that several actual choices of projects for public investment cannot be described as ir-rational. Even now, the privatisation craze notwithstanding, few people who are familiar with conditions in the Arab countries would suggest a total withdrawal of the state from the economic arena; although several would perhaps argue that the state should have "a much more vital role to play as a promoter of business, *animateur*, than as a business entrepreneur" [cf. e.g. Harik, 1990].

What is it therefore that has made the slogan of economic liberalisation such a sweeping one in the Middle East in recent years? In our view it is the conjuncture of two sets of factors that has led to the almost universal drive towards economic liberalisation and privatisation: the escalation, domestically, of a fiscal crisis of the state and the emergence, internationally, of a hegemonic body of knowledge about the international economy (i.e. the 'Washington Consensus'.

The 'fiscal crisis of the state' was a concept first developed by James O'Connor, and started from the premise that the capitalist state must try to fulfil two basic and often naturally contradictory functions: accumulation *and* legitimisation, the first requiring the creation of the conditions for maximising profit, the second requiring the creation of the conditions for social harmony [O'Connor, 1973: 6–9, and Ch. 3]. The contradiction between the requirements of *étatisme* and the requirements of populism in many developing countries is somewhat similar to that identified by O'Connor and also by Claus Offé with regard to the welfare capitalist state. The state intervenes via control and discipline arrangements in order to secure capital accumulation – this is achieved through processes of 'commodification'. This commodification, however, stands in contradiction with the state's function of legitimation, which necessitates creating social relations in increasingly non-commodified forms, such as the provision of welfare services. The contemporary state is a system that functions to reconcile the demands of accumulation and legitimacy and to overcome the institutional contradictions resulting from them [Offé, 1984, 1985].

In the periphery (and to some extent in the semi-periphery) the financial crisis of the state has been even more acute in recent years. For the state in the periphery not only intervenes to secure capital accumulation in an indirect way but has often to act as a (frequently *the*) most important direct producer and entrepreneur. Economic growth and managerial efficiency therefore become in such countries a much more integral part of the concept of state legitimacy than is the case in advanced capitalist countries. This is what Samuel Huntington and others call 'performance legitimacy' [Huntington, 1991: 46–58]. In other words, the more a state is involved in the economic sphere, the more likely it is that an economic crisis will be regarded as '*state failure*' [cf. Jänicke, 1990].

In addition, states (and regimes) in the periphery and semi-periphery are less 'hegemonic' (in the socio-ideological, Gramscian sense) than they are in the core countries, and are therefore more concerned about reproducing 'themselves'. This they may try to achieve via populist, authoritarian or other methods [Mouzelis, 1986]. The peripheral state is therefore involved in several rather contradictory tasks. For simplification we will single out, as being particularly pertinent in this context, the contradiction between etatism and populism as guiding principles of state action: the first involves the state basically in production and the second basically in distribution, and the two cannot be easily reconciled except in unusual times of exceptional growth and/or availability of liquid capital. The period from the mid-1970s to the present has not been one of high growth and abundant capital for most countries of the periphery, for reasons that I have partly summarised elsewhere [Ayubi, 1993]. Thus the fiscal crisis in many peripheral countries may be summarised as a crisis resulting from a partly structural and partly conjunctural contradiction between the logic of etatism and the logic of populism.

Now, the 'Washington Consensus' is a specific diagnostic and prescriptive body of knowledge pertaining to the international economy in general and to the economic crisis of the Third World in particular. It is a favourite term among Latin American economists, following the expression used by the US economist John Williamson [cf. e.g. Fanelli et al., 1990: 1–16]. The word 'consensus' may be too strong but it is clear to many that a high level of agreement exists among the Washington think tanks, and more broadly within countries of the OECD, on the Third World economic crisis.

The intellectual origins of this consensus are to be found in the crisis of Keynsian economics and the demise of development economics [cf. e.g. Pilling, 1986]. It is characterised by the rise of a new (so-called neo-liberal) right inspired by the Austrian school (Hayek, Von Mises), the monetarists (Friedman), the new classicists (Lucas, Sargent), and the 'public choice' school (Buchanan, Olson, Tullock, Niskanen).

> These views, tempered with some degree of pragmatism, are officially shared by multilateral agencies in Washington, the Fed, the US Treasury, the finance ministries of G-7, and the chairmen of the 20 most important commercial banks. They form together the Washington consensus or the Washington approach – a dominant interpretation that, having Washington as [its] geographical origin, has a powerful influence over governments and élites in Latin America[4] [Bresser Pereira, 1991: 4–5].

On one level, the diagnosis of the crisis according to the Washington approach may not contradict an analysis based on the fiscal crisis of the state. The main causes of the Third Word crisis identified by the Washington approach are excessive state intervention (as manifested in protectionism, over-regulation and oversized public enterprises), and excessive social welfarism (manifested in extensive services and subsidies and in lax budgetary practices). In other words, these are our two contradictory policies of *étatisme* and populism. But the Washington approach is so sweeping in its current condemnation of these policies that it does not relate their efficacy or inefficiency to any time spans or specific conjunctures; that is, they are now being condemned almost on an ideological level, and with them, all policies of import substitution industrialisation and all involvement of the state in so-called 'market' (i.e. economic) matters. The reform recipe indicated in the Washington consensus is based on 'stabilisation' of the economy through strict fiscal and monetary policies, and on reducing the size and role of the state.

Such an analysis appears to ignore the fact that the currently discredited import-substitution industrialisation had fulfilled a role in its proper time, even though it was state-initiated, and that what is needed now in many countries is the redirection of some of that industry towards export promotion rather than the condemnation of any involvement by the state in the economy. The Washington consensus says very little about the structural and conjunctural causes leading to the foreign debt crisis that has occurred since the 1970s (and which induced or at least aggravated many of the economic problems in the periphery), and it assumes (against the actual experience of many Latin American countries, for example) that "growth will be automatically reinstated once macroeconomic stabilization, trade liberalization and privatization are completed" [Bresser Pereira, 1991: 7–9]. This is not borne out in reality because stabilisation is often achieved at the expense of public savings and investments, in a context where private savings and investments do not automatically substitute for state investment. Indeed, the available cases of successful adjustment and restructuring are all of countries that received a large and intensive infusion of capital while undergoing their reforms; for example, Korea, Chile and Turkey [cf. Fanelli et al., 1990; Wade, 1992; Öniş, 1991].

The expression 'the Washington Consensus' may also have a further meaning that goes beyond the mere fact that Washington 'happens' to host the main think tanks responsible for formulating this approach. Some analysts maintain that the hegemonic status of the United States within the international political economy and her position in the product cycle would be aided by foreign liberalisations or by

> a spread of responsibility and a sharing of misery, as bureaucratic-authoritarian regimes with economies in tatters are forced to compress; or an assault on exclusive markets insulated by strong States ... One cannot understand the 'opening' without consideration of the world system. If austerity is the programme, a bureaucratic-authoritarian regime only makes its costs worse for the target people, and raises the possibility of mercantilist default and withdrawal. In crises, democracy becomes a way of spreading and sharing responsibility, defusing the 'highly mobilized pueblo' and adapting to external realities [Cumings, 1989: 28–9].

Now, the important point – politically speaking – about the 'Washington Consensus' is not whether it is sound economics or not. What is more important is the powerful influence it has over governments and élites in the Third World. This is really an indication of the hegemonic (or ideological) power achieved by globalising capitalism [compare Ikenberry and Kupchan, 1990], through the transnational corporations (TNCs) and the international institutions of finance and development, a process in which Third World politicians and technocrats (both working 'at home' and in international organisations) play a crucial role.

> International institutions perform an ideological role as well. They help define policy guidelines for states and to legitimate certain institutions and practices at the national level. They reflect orientations favourable to the dominant social and economic forces ... Elite talent from peripheral countries is co-opted into international institutions in the manner of *trasformismo*[5] ... At best they will help transfer elements of 'modernisation' to the peripheries but only as these are consistent with the interests of established local powers ... *Trasformismo* also absorbs potentially counter-hegemonic ideas and makes these ideas consistent with hegemonic doctrine (the notion of self-reliance, for example) [Cox, 1983: 172–3].

We have suggested so far that it is the conjuncture between the escalating 'financial crisis of the state' on the one hand and the growing 'Washington Consensus' with regard to the Third World on the other, that has led to the recent shifts towards economic liberalisation. It should be observed, however, that the timing, scale and intensity of the transformation in economic policy will depend not only on the way international and domestic factors will combine, but also on the way the state élites will read and interpret both the changing factors themselves as well as the way they combine. In transforming their economic policies, the state élites will not only respond to what is taken to be real economic problems, pressures and opportunities; they will always be influenced (given their cultural and educational dependency) by the dominant themes in the economic thinking of the 'Centre', and they will also always be concerned about the political outcomes of whatever changes they may consider adopting. Not only will they be wary of such things as possible popular discontent (and even uprising) but also – and more fundamentally – of the possible ways in which 'alternative' élites may benefit from certain changes in economic policies. A change of policy towards privatisation would be more easily conceivable, for example, if previous state policies would have sufficiently paved the way, intentionally or inadvertently, for the emergence of a 'cooperative' private sector that is eager to engage in business, and if the 'human' (ethnic, religious, tribal, etc.) core of this sector is not perceived to belong to a seriously antagonistic social force.

Nor are *all* state élites necessarily and completely 'sold' on the idea or the practicality of liberalisation and privatisation. Tough negotiations do take place between economists and technocrats of the developing countries on the one hand and officers of the international financial organisations on the other. Some of these, as one indignant and badly paid 'nationalist' economist once told me, may not only be citizens of the same country but also graduates of the same (American) university. The background may be similar but the role is different. Part of the Egyptian press, for example, carried some pointed criticism of the ideas of Abd al-Shakour Shaalan, the senior IMF official of

Egyptian nationality who was a member of the Fund's team in its tough negotiations with Egypt in the late 1980s. The officials of the peripheral state may try to wriggle off the hook but there is little doubt as to who has more clout within the bargaining exercise.

THE POLITICS OF ECONOMIC ADJUSTMENT

Peripheral states facing structural dependency and vulnerability have followed a number of possible approaches in the last two decades or so in order to cope with this situation:

A. de-linking, or cutting themselves off from the global market as much as possible, in a few autarchic regimes (e.g. Albania and at one time Cambodia).
B. refusing to de-link, but seeking to change 'the rules of the game' and to install a 'new international economic order' (NIEO). This was the case of most developing countries, including for a period even the rich oil-exporting Middle East countries.
C. accepting the international rules of the game but using a 'developmental state' model (and bureaucratic authoritarianism) to enhance export-oriented production. The level of success varied depending on cultural and institutional factors (solidaristic cultures and 'hard states' being more successful), and this led to the eventual emergence of the NICs [cf. Krasner, 1985: 49ff et passim]. Countries with 'socialist' or populist regimes have found it hardest to meet the requirements of the 'competition state' model. Partly autarchic, fairly centrally planned, and heavily dependent on a large welfare package for their legitimation, they have experienced extreme difficulty in embarking on the required 'adjustment'.

The newly industrialising countries reacted by following a strategy that G. O'Donnell has termed 'industrial deepening' [O'Donnell, 1977: 48], arrived at through a policy of both solidifying the developmental states (bureaucratic-authoritarian) *and* encouraging the native private sector (by allowing joint ventures but within a tightly defined nationalist strategy). Let us call this bunch of policies *perestroika* or restructuring. Most other countries, on the other hand, went for policies that were quite the opposite: they opted for *glasnost, abertura* and *infitah*. This has usually involved a kind of 'commercial widening', sometimes accompanied by an element of 'financial deepening' [compare Ayubi, 1991b: Ch. 1; Moore Henry, 1986], i.e. heavy reliance on financial rents and over-banking, a relative softening of an already weak (if despotic) state [Migdal, 1988a], and the encouragement of joint ventures between the public sector and international capital (rather than the native private sector). Privatisation within such regimes usually entails three processes, which are sometimes achieved in successive stages as follows: (a) managerialism within the public sector; (b) commercialisation of the state economic sector; and (c) concessions to, and partnerships with, international capital.

Partly in anticipation of the analysis that will follow, one may suggest in passing that, ironically, it is the first model, for all its authoritarianism, that may in the long run be more conducive to democratic development (rather than chaos). By encouraging the native private sector, it lays the foundation for the emergence not only of a national industry but also of a native bourgeoisie: this latter, even if not totally autonomous from the state, will assert its political rights (and indeed is already doing so in countries such as Korea). Second, by preserving the solidity of the state it is more likely in the long run to guarantee order and the 'rule of law', without which no democratic development can be real. By contrast, 'capitalism' in the second group is often represented by a parallel (underground) economy where the rights of the consumer and the poor cannot be protected (e.g. the 'money utilisation companies' in Egypt).

Policies of economic adjustment are not purely technical or financial in nature, but by necessity carry with them important social outcomes and therefore require significant shifts in political coalitions. A familiar pattern of political coalition in industrialising Third World societies has been represented by a 'populist' coalition centred around the military, the techno-managerial élite of the public sector, and organised labour. This is the political corollary of the famous import-substitution strategy, with its strongly industrial and urban bias and its elaborate 'social welfare' policy. Once in serious crisis, a state that is dominated by such a coalition may either attach top priority to the imperative of 'industrial deepening' and thus opt for an open bureaucratic-authoritarian model, as has been explained by G. O'Donnell [1973, 1977], or it may follow a less radical and more incremental set of measures in an attempt to respond to a developmental crisis that often represents itself most severely in the financial sphere.

An initial response to the fiscal crisis of the state will often make itself felt through a number of 'belt-tightening' and 'economising' measures that are usually followed on an *ad hoc* basis and that sometimes include 'more of the same' remedies. This may involve an intensification of import controls, increased reliance on administrative allocation of resources, and the application of a number of interventionist policies designed to widen the gap between domestic prices and world prices. It is usually only when such countries discover that the consequences of such an approach are ultimately unsustainable, that they delve into the short-term 'stabilisation programmes' (sponsored by the IMF), and the longer-term 'structural adjustment' programmes (sponsored by the World Bank) [cf. Da Silva Lopes, 1989].

Short-term stabilisation programmes, typified by the IMF 'stand-by arrangements' are oriented primarily to the quick reduction of deficit, by cutting domestic demand or controlling its expansion. They involve expenditure-

reducing policies and expenditure-switching policies (i.e. stimulating the production of exportable and importable goods and changing the demand patterns
in favour of goods that do not enter into international trade). These programmes are usually based on a small number of instruments: ceilings to the
expansion of domestic credit and to public-sector borrowing, rises in interest
rates, exchange rate depreciation, and sometimes wage controls and the adjustment of some key prices [Da Silva Lopes, 1989: 22–30]. The potential
social beneficiaries in this stage would be agricultural exporters, private and
perhaps public exporters of manufactured goods, the tourist sector and migrant
workers who can convert their earnings at the new devalued exchange rates.
Among the main potential losers would be public-sector enterprises which
will suffer from reduced investment and expenditure and from the restrictions
on imports [Waterbury, 1989: 56–7].

Programmes of structural adjustment are more ambitious in that they do
not rely merely on demand management but are oriented more towards
improving the conditions of supply and the allocation of domestic resources,
and towards "institutional transformations which may contribute to reinforcing
the growth potential and to reduce the vulnerability to external shocks by
reducing external payments imbalances" [Da Silva Lopes, 1989: 22–3]. The
measures involved in this phase are more varied and profound but they
certainly include reduction in consumers' subsidies, deregulation of agricultural
producers' prices and of some industrial prices, as well as the liberalisation of
trade and of the exchange rates. Very often they also include a certain
'privatisation' drive; i.e. a move towards increased private management and/
or ownership of enterprises and a general encouragement of private investment
within the economy, especially in the export-oriented sectors.

The likely social beneficiaries of this phase are the agricultural sector in
general and exporters in particular, along with some public enterprises that
sell mainly to the domestic market, after all of them have benefited from the
'streamlining' necessitated by the reduction in public investment flows. This
phase is likely to have a "moderate or intermediate impact" on public or
private import-substituting industries, since they will experience rising costs of
domestic inputs, and probably of wage bills, which may or may not be offset
by easier borrowing and deregulation of prices. Those engaged in the export
of manufactured goods will also experience a rise in the cost of labour and
domestic inputs [Waterbury, 1989: 56–7].

What are the coalition shifts that are likely to result from such changes?

First and perhaps most consistently, organised labour cannot expect a
continuation of the symbolically favoured, if institutionally incorporated, status
that it enjoyed in earlier, more populist times. Unprecedented workers' strikes
may start to take place as happened, for example, in Egypt and Tunisia. Even
the professional syndicates and associations may show signs of resistance (as
occurred in Sudan) or of defiance and restlessness (as took place in Egypt).

More spectacular protests against the declining standard of living and the removal of basic subsidies tend to come from the urban sub-proletariat and lumpenproletariat, as has been seen in Egypt, Tunisia, Algeria and elsewhere. Organised labour can be drawn into some of the protest actions that are best expressed by the urban sub-proletariat and lumpenproletariat: this is illustrated by the 1978 events in Tunisia that resulted in the creation of an ambivalent relationship between the government and the once organically incorporated trade union federation, the UGTT [Waterbury, 1989: 57–60]. The possibility of more militant labour action might have been higher in several countries, had the safety valve of work opportunities in the oil-exporting countries not existed. Migrant labour constitutes an important financial factor which has no formal organised representation in the emerging coalitions but which is potentially of great economic and social (and subsequently political) impact.

By contrast, relations between the ruling élite and the private bourgeoisie seem on the whole to improve, although they are often fraught with contradictions and complications. The native businessmen may initially welcome the role of foreign capital as offering a means to pave the investment way for them; however, they soon complain that without continued government support they cannot cope with the more open competition or with a more advanced and sophisticated capitalism. Importers of foreign commodities, especially if they enjoy the benefit of large foreign exchange reserves, may even challenge the state's attempts to regulate the trade and finance sectors, as happened on more than one occasion in Egypt. Although capitalist farmers and agricultural exporters almost always stand to benefit from liberalisation policies, they are not entirely free of complaints, since they may lose some of the indirect subsidies on energy, fertilisers and the infrastructure that they might previously have utilised. The peasantry, by contrast, continues to be absent from practically all coalitions.

In most countries, the military retain their membership of the new coalitions, although often in a somewhat adjusted capacity. Armies continue to acquire the lion's share of public expenditure, and in some cases to have exclusive control of their own financial affairs. Some armies have also expanded in 'civilian' economic activities (e.g. in Egypt, Syria, etc.). Even in Tunisia, where the military were previously subordinate to the civilian government, the arrival of General Zain al-'Abidin Bin 'Ali to power signals a likely enhancement of the political status, if not of the political role, of the military. While the conventional civil service continues, despite its huge size, to be of limited political importance, the same cannot be said of the public sector management. The managers and technocrats of the state enterprises and economic organisations continue to carry significant political weight in countries such as Egypt, Algeria, Iraq, and elsewhere. Although part of the technocracy has gone private, there continue to be many technocrats who still regard their life careers as being closely tied to the future of the public sector.

What conclusions can be drawn from the foregoing analysis and case studies? One general conclusion is that both the expansion *and* the contraction of the public economic sector have been correlated with the availability of liquid capital. The availability of capital may be domestically based (e.g. nationalisations or 'agricultural squeeze') or externally based (e.g. oil rents, aid and remittances). The tightening of finance also corresponds with domestic signals (such as declining revenues in the public enterprises and growing deficits in the state budget), and/or with external signals coming from creditors, international financial organisations, trade partners and potential investors. These are the two sets of factors that we have labelled the 'financial crisis of the state' and the 'Washington Consensus' respectively.

Such signals have to be 'interpreted' and 'acted upon' by the local – political and technocratic – élites in a certain way, and hence we see the variety of policies and methods even though there is apparent general agreement on the desirability of some measure of economic liberalisation. Global economic changes and international 'fashions' are not reflected on to states in a uniform manner – they have to be filtered through the 'interpretive apparatuses' of the political regime and its élites, who may prefer to think that the problems are temporary or transitional or who may weigh up the anticipated political risks involved in an economic reform and conclude that they are higher than the potential economic gains.

In most cases the move towards privatisation as a way of overcoming the 'financial crisis of the state' takes the form of a *public* policy; i.e. one that is initiated by the state (sometimes in collaboration with international capital) for its own reasons, rather than under pressure from the private sector. If it is in a state of readiness to do so, the private sector may, of course, pick up on the process and push ahead with it. The pace and intensity of privatisation will, however, depend (a) on the degree to which capital accumulation has been both *extensive* and *internally oriented*; and (b) on the degree to which both the state bourgeoisie and the private bourgeoisie find it useful (safe) to seek further autonomy from each other. The following are some examples:

— in situations where the state bourgeoisie can invest privately without having to sacrifice its political positions, it may not press ahead with full privatisation;
— in situations where the private bourgeoisie is still too dependent on the state it may not press for full-fledged economic liberalisation;
— in situations where full privatisation carries with it a high likelihood of a competing ethnic or primordial community assuming economic predominance or disproportionate ascent, it may be resisted or constrained by the ruling élite.

It is surmised from the case studies that privatisation slogans and appearances notwithstanding, actual privatisation remains rather limited and that the Arab state is not really about to withdraw from the economy. Privatisation is still basically a public policy that is pursued by the state with reluctance and caution largely for its own purposes; it has not yet become a dynamic process whose initiative is taken by the private sector itself. If the private sector is gaining it is not because of its initiative, drive and organisation, nor is it because the ruling élites have decided sincerely to hand the economy over to it; rather it is mainly because the state can no longer, given its chronic 'fiscal crisis', continue with its *étatiste* and its welfarist policies at the same time. In other words, the private sector may end up growing 'by default', so to speak, although the proportions, timings and modalities vary depending on a number of key factors. These include the solidity and coherence of the state machinery; the strength and autonomy of the labour movement; the attitude of the public sector managers and party *apparatchiks*; the vitality and capabilities of the domestic business community; the degree to which the government's intervention might or might not have 'crowded out' the private sector; and last but not least the levels and patterns of external pressures/temptations exercised on the state by international organisations and by globalising capitalism.

We have also seen that as they adopt various liberalisation and privatisation measures, ruling élites will normally weigh the likely political risks against the potential economic gains. Most ruling élites will be wary of one particular 'risk' above all others. To sharpen the often blurred distinction between the public and the private economic sectors (i.e. between the state and the market) would highlight the boundaries between the state and the civil society, would make any exploitative (economic) relationship 'transparent' by robbing it of its political (nationalist or populist) mask, and could eventually result in a consolidation of the concept of citizenship and in an enlivening of the public (political) space. Not all regimes in the Arab World are prepared – structurally and psychologically – for this eventuality.

NOTES

1. The strong state is hegemonic in the Gramscian sense: power penetrates everything to the extent – as explained by Foucault – that it ceases to be noticeable except, perhaps, at the political–legal peak. A strong state may, but does not necessarily have to be 'hard' (France is a strong/hard state; Britain is strong without being hard). The 'fierce' state is almost always structurally weak and therefore has repeatedly to use (rather than to threaten to use) open violence and force (as well as intrigue and conspiracy) in order to ensure *direct* control and domination (and not simply hegemony).

2. Until the early 1980s, most recipients of government land grants were individual farmers and small projects. The policy was then changed in the 1980s to allow the granting of large acreages to a few sizeable agricultural companies. These companies have benefited from very extensive government programmes for the development of the infrastructure and have enjoyed a high level of state protection and subsidisation for their products. Consequently, Saudi Arabia was the only country within the Gulf Cooperation Council (GCC) to be able to meet most of its cereal needs and to be self-sufficient in eggs and dairy products by 1984, and even to export a certain

amount of wheat in subsequent years. This policy has been founded on the encouragement of private investment in agriculture based on high levels of modernisation and intensive technology and mechanisation, with generous support from the government. Despite these efforts, the King-dom remains one of the world's largest importers of foodstuffs, and whatever is being produced locally is produced at exorbitant costs (an estimated $18 billion up to the mid-1980s) that cannot be sustained for long [cf. Al-Rawaf, 1987].

3. An ominous development in the 1980s has been the deceleration in expansion of assets and liabilities of the commercial banking system. Much of the private business in Saudi Arabia continued to be financed by the government-subsidised specialised banks; but the previous levels of subsidy could not be maintained for long. Recent moves towards incorporating aspects of the interest rate concept into the financial system have met with some Islamically-based opposition, and this has sometimes led to a situation of near standstill.

4. And in the rest of the periphery, one may add.

5. *Trasformismo* is a Gramscian term that connotes a (superficially and artificially) modernising strategy whereby personnel from other camps and coalitions are coopted, and whereby potentially dangerous ideas are assimilated and domesticated by adjusting them to the policies of the dominant coalition. It is a component of the concept of 'passive revolution' which is the counterpart of the Gramscian (socio-ideological) concept of hegemony. According to Robert Cox, reforms inspired by the "superstructure of international institutions" could achieve very little because they have no "popular political base" in the host country: "They are connected with the national hegemonic classes in the core countries and, through the intermediacy of these classes, have a broader base in these countries. In the peripheries, they connect only with the passive revolution" [Cox, 1983: 166–7, 173].

CHAPTER ELEVEN

Prospects for Democracy: Is the Civil Society Striking Back?

Transitions to democracy have become so widespread all over the world since the mid-1980s that they have left their mark even on the apparently impervious Middle East region. The signs and indications are in the early 1990s still so nebulous and uncertain that many predict that they can be easily reversed, and some believe that they will never be able to become self-sustaining. Therefore the question may justifiably be asked as to whether democracy is possible in the Middle East?

To start with there are certainly significant, if still limited, signs that some formal manifestations of democracy, notably elections, are becoming a more normal feature of the Middle East political scene. Turkey, of course, returned to the formally democratic fold in 1983. More remarkable is the fact that seven Arab countries accounting for over half the population of the Arab World have recently experienced electoral competition and/or multi-party activity. These include Egypt (latest elections held in 1990), Tunisia (1989), Jordan (1989, 1993), Morocco (1993), Yemen (1988 in the North; 1993 in the unified country), Kuwait (1992), and Lebanon (1992). In addition to these seven, Syria held elections in 1990 although many would consider these as having been of little democratic significance. Even Iraq held elections in 1989 that were a landslide for the Ba'th and its allies and that would be ranked by many as 'elections without choice'. Algeria had looked highly promising, holding important municipal elections in June 1990 and parliamentary elections in December 1991. But the process went disastrously wrong since the impressive victory of the Islamists alarmed the military and state apparatchiks and prompted them to launch a pre-emptive court *coup* to rescue the regime in February 1992 (see further details below in this chapter).

In the case of Lebanon the process has revolved to some extent around a modified return to the country's own variety of 'consociational democracy' that existed before the civil war (of 1975–91). The civil war may not have produced a 'civilianising effect' as such, but at least it brought about a state of mutual exhaustion that made most factions ready to accept an application of the Ta'if agreement of 1991 under a now unchallenged *pax Syriana* that was made possible by Iraq's defeat in Operation Desert Storm. The Ta'if agreement was basically a somewhat ameliorated edition of the tacit 'national pact' that had governed Lebanese politics since independence. One hundred and twenty-eight parliamentary seats have been divided equally among Christians and Muslims, the president continues to be a Maronite, the prime minister a Sunni Muslim and the speaker a Shi'i Muslim, but the two latter positions have now a politically enhanced role, whereas the president has been deprived of his previous all-important vote in the Council of Ministers [Norton, 1991]. Lebanon's consociational democracy has, of course, had several drawbacks in the past, not least of which was the limitation of the efficacy of political parties and the constraints on the development of a concept of citizenship (for example, no one was allowed to vote on a non-sectarian basis). It is indeed a conservative system based on preserving the status quo, but many would consider it a better alternative to a sixteen-year-long civil war and some regard it as the only available pathway towards rebuilding the shattered Lebanese state.

Nor should one forget the less orthodox cases: the Palestinians who managed to maintain a measure of their democratic process against all the odds; the Libyan 'mass-ocracy' (*jamahiriyya*) which is going further with its experiment in direct democracy by dividing the country into communes or little 'mass-ocracies'; even contemporary Iran which, although infringing on many a human right, is certainly experiencing more political debate and competition than it did under the shah.

The analysis becomes more rewarding if one does not look for 'democracy' as a final product and end result, but rather considers democratisation, or better still liberalisation, as an ongoing process pointing in the direction of pluralism and polyarchy (or *ta'addudiyya*, as it is called in Arabic) [cf. Dahl, 1971].

CULTURAL AND INTELLECTUAL REQUISITES FOR DEMOCRACY

Democracy is not simply a form of government; it is also a cultural and intellectual tradition. Western civilisation, in its celebration of its supremacy over the rest of the world, has developed a distinct literature that traces its liberal traditions back into history while contrasting them with the allegedly despotic traditions of the 'East'.

The Greeks of Aristotle's time are said to have been familiar with an alternative image of the Athenian *polis* – that of Babylon, the world-city defined by the interconnected facts that it was enormous, heterogeneous and unfree (i.e. not self-governing). This was *not* a political community; the Middle Eastern city, both ancient and mediaeval, is said to have represented *urbs*, a physical agglomeration, rather than *civitas*, a space for collective debate and action. Its heterogeneous multitudes could remain in a political coexistence without an occasion to deliberate with their neighbours [Weintraub, 1990]. Cosmopolitan Middle Eastern cities, from the Baghdad of Harun al-Rashid to Istanbul, Alexandria and Beirut in this century, have exercised a certain charm of diversity, colour and 'street life', sometimes of tolerable coexistence of groups that mingle without joining – but such cities are not usually blessed with active citizenship.

It is also claimed that the Middle East lacks a 'contractual tradition' (owing perhaps to the missing 'feudal' link in its social history) and a tradition of institutional autonomy, as both the *'ulama* and the guilds were often subservient to the ruler. Montesquieu, Weber, Marx and many others have much to say – not always justifiably – about all this [cf. e.g. Turner, 1974; also Bernal, 1987; and P. Springborg, 1992].

Some would also argue that the Arabo-Islamic tradition was not conventionally familiar with the concept of 'liberty', nor did it develop a concept of individualism. The word *ahzab*, currently used for political parties, certainly has pejorative connotations in Islam. On the contrary, the Arabo-Islamic culture has remained communal, collectivist and 'organic' [compare Dumont, 1986]. In modern times it has been more readily admitting of solidaristic and corporatist rather than of liberal intellectual influences from Europe (some of the notable figures in this respect being Herder, Fichte, Plessner, Durkheim, Carrel and Duguit).

There are indeed those who argue that democracy is culturally specific to a certain geographic zone encompassing the English Channel and the North Sea, with some extension in Central Europe (and with offshoots of this zone in the New World). These are the regions that historically had experienced feudalism, the Renaissance, the Reformation, the Enlightenment and the French Revolution, and liberalism/individualism, whereas the rest of Europe had been subject to the Czarist or Ottoman empires and to the influences of Islam or Orthodox Christianity [cf. Parekh, 1992]. Others maintain that democracy is potentially universalist, but with some cultures being especially averse to it – Confucianism and Islam often being singled out as prominent among these [cf. Huntington, 1991: 298–307]. Bernard Lewis, for example, has argued that Islam is inclined towards totalitarianism/authoritarianism which, he maintains, is why several Muslim countries were attracted to the Communist model in the 1950s and 1960s [Lewis, 1958]. Several Muslim authors have contributed to the debate and some of them agree that the dominant tradition of the Islamic heritage as it has reached us today is not liberal or 'democratic' even though many contemporary writers would like to see it in this light for their own contemporary purposes. The contemporary Islamic philosopher Hasan Hanafi [e.g., 1983; Hanafi and Al-Jabiri, 1990: Ch. 5] has argued along similar lines in some of his writings, and so has the Tunisian sociologist Al-Tahir Labib, who asks rhetorically: "Is democracy really a social demand in the Arab World?" [Labib, 1992b: 339ff]. The Moroccan historian 'Ali Umlil [1991] has also argued that although difference and disagreement were known in the historical Arabo-Islamic state, they were never accepted on the ideological level by the jurists and the thinkers who always believed that it was only one idea and one group holding to that idea who were right. I would argue myself that Islamic culture contains elements that may be both congenial and un-congenial to democracy, depending on the particular society and on the historical conjuncture. Whatever the case may be, between 1981 and 1990, only two of the thirty-seven countries in the world with Muslim majorities were ever rated 'free' by Freedom House in its annual survey (the Gambia for two years and Northern Cyprus for four) [cf. also Nelson, 1991].

The really important point to emphasise is that whereas opposition move-ments in other regions almost universally espoused – or at least declared – Western-style democratic values, movements that campaigned explicitly for democratic politics were relatively weak in authoritarian Muslim societies in the 1980s. By contrast, the most powerful opposition came from so-called 'Islamic fundamentalists'. Many of these groups are openly anti-democratic, and it is impossible, with regard to those who are not, to know whether they would relinquish power voluntarily once they had achieved it. It is ironic that the Algerian Islamists who nearly made it to government via democratic elections, had first condemned democracy and then reluctantly accepted it, threatening that if elections did not result in a 'natural outcome' (i.e. their victory) then the natural order of affairs would have to be restored by other means. In the meantime, the strongly Islamic character of the opposition has forced many Middle Eastern countries to adopt, by way of self-defence, some of the policies or the slogans of the opposition (even when these were anti-liberal or anti-secular), and, as the commitment of the Islamic radicals to democracy remained questionable, to become more wary of the liberalisation process in general.[1]

SOCIO-ECONOMIC REQUISITES FOR DEMOCRACY

It could also be argued that the prerequisites for a democratic transformation are not available in most Middle Eastern countries because these are not advanced capitalist societies. Traditionally, most of these countries had pos-sessed control-based modes of production. Currently, the articulated nature of their modes of production has not allowed for the emergence of a hegemonic class or ideology that can ensure political order in the society. In consequence the state in such societies is 'fierce' (rather than strong) precisely because it is structurally and ideologically weak. In such a situation the expression of interests is bound to be direct, not mediated, and relations between state and society are contradictory, not complementary.

There have been attempts to decide upon a certain economic or developmental threshold beyond which democracy becomes possible or likely, though not necessary. The main measurement has usually been GNP per capita, although glaring exceptions – most notably India – may also emerge, sometimes through political engineering [compare Sørensen, 1991]. The idea is that processes of economic development involving significant industrialisation lead to a more diverse and a more complex class structure which becomes increasingly difficult for authoritarian regimes to control, especially with regard to new sources of wealth and power outside the state. Involvement of a country in the world economy creates non-governmental sources of wealth and influence and opens the society to the impact of the democratic ideas prevailing in the industrialised world [Huntington, 1991: 65–7].

> Oil-based economies, however, represent a different case: The implication is that broad-based economic development involving significant industrialization may contribute to democratization but wealth resulting from the sale of oil (and, probably, other natural resources) does not. Oil revenues accrue to the State: they therefore increase the power of the State bureaucracy and, because they reduce or eliminate the need for taxation, they also reduce the need for the government to solicit the acquiescence of its subjects to taxation. The lower the level of taxation, the less reason for publics to demand representation. 'No taxation without representation' was a political demand; 'no representation without taxation' is a political reality [Huntington, 1991: 65].

Dependence on oil revenues develops a 'rentier state' with weakened extractive, regulatory and distributive powers which appears superficially strong and autonomous but which is not really able effectively to mediate and arbitrate among the various 'raw' interests developing in the society [cf. Chaudhry, 1989].

Democratic development might be expected in countries reaching levels of economic development in what the World Bank calls the 'upper-middle-income' zone or above. In 1990, some Middle East countries were in this zone, such as Algeria, Iran and Iraq. These are oil-exporters with substantial populations and some industrial development but serious democratisation has not yet occurred in them. Lebanon is at a slightly lower level of wealth, i.e. in the lower-middle-income category (with incomes ranging between $500 and $2,200) but with improving democratic prospects. Countries in the category in which income levels ranged between $1,000 and $2,000 included Syria, Jordan and Tunisia. If they continue to sustain the same good rate of growth and if Syria grows a little faster than previously, they will in principle be moving to levels of economic development that are supportive of democratisation.

The zone in which income levels ranged between $500 and $1,000 included

Morocco, Egypt and Yemen. If they can maintain the substantial rate of growth that they enjoyed during the 1980s, they will be moving into the economic zone favourable to democratisation by the early part of the twenty-first century. However, the sequence does not always match the theory: for example, Egypt, Yemen (and Morocco) are better democratisers than Iraq and Syria, not to speak of Oman and Saudi Arabia who are all richer to one degree or another.

It is very significant that the overwhelming majority of those countries worldwide where economic conditions supportive of democratisation were emerging during the 1990s were in the Middle East and North Africa [Huntington, 1991: 312–13]. But much will depend on what will happen to the state bureaucracies of the oil-exporting countries, and on the possible outcomes of the economic crises in the other countries.

Further studies by Letterie and Puyenbroek [1991] of developments over the past three decades (the 1960s, 1970s and 1980s) corroborate the evidence concerning the impact of national economic development on political democratisation, but they add the almost equally important factor of 'position in the world system' (i.e. the more 'peripheral' a country, the less likely it is to democratise). The idea is that it is not simply economic status that matters but rather the dependency/autonomy situation. K.A. Bollen summarised the argument as follows:

> the traditional development/democracy arguments view socio-economic development as giving rise to a number of powerful groups in the bourgeoisie, a skilled and organized labour force, etc. – which successfully challenge the traditional élites to obtain a more democratic political system. World-system and dependency theorists argue that these groups do not play the same role in the non-core as they do in the core. One dependency perspective argues that these groups are extremely weak in the non-core because of the alliance between non-core and core élites. A second argument is that these new groups resulting from development are still strong but rather than challenging the autocratic political system, they help to maintain it. In either perspective the hypothesised effect is the same. Outside the core democracy is a rarity [quoted in Letterie and Puyenbroek, 1991: 5].

Middle East countries are among the most dependent and vulnerable countries in the world, and this may explain at least partly why democracy has not, except till very recently, been a prominent objective among the middle classes: nationalism, economic growth and socialism have been far more prominent since the 1950s.

Whatever limited democratisation might have occurred in the Middle East was the indirect outcome of two factors: the financial crisis of the state and globalisation. The fiscal and structural exhaustion of the state has led to regimes permitting a certain degree of plurality, partly by way of reducing the financial and organisational overload, and partly by way of increasing the numbers of those who would share the blame for the expected austerity measures. Democratisation can thus be seen, at least partly, as a mechanism for system maintenance [cf. MERIP Editors, 1992].

However, the connection between economic crisis and political liberalisation is not inevitable. In other historical circumstances economic crisis led either to Fascism or to bureaucratic-authoritarianism. Even recently, instances of economic crisis leading to authoritarianism rather than democratisation have been observed, for example in Turkey, Nigeria, Ghana and Korea [cf. Haggard and Kaufman, 1991]. What has tilted the balance more towards democracy in recent years has been the growing globalisation and the undisputed ideological hegemony of the 'West' following the collapse of socialist regimes in Eastern Europe. But, again, the connection is not automatic here either. The hegemonic discourse sometimes described as the 'Washington Consensus' [cf. Ayubi, 1993] is much less ambiguous about economic neo-liberalism while remaining quite vague on democracy. Thus, for example, the USAID's 'Democracy Initiative' for the Middle East puts much emphasis on small businesses and entrepreneurship rather than on democratic representation or participation as such. Nor has American policy in the Middle East been historically pro-democratic: in Iran in 1951 and in Jordan in 1957 the US sided against democratic forces in favour of despotic but friendly monarchs, and following the Gulf crisis of 1990/91 it did not side with the democratic forces in Iraq (or against despotic powers in Saudi Arabia or in Kuwait) [MERIP Editors, 1992: 47]. Even its, and the West's, human rights policy is so selective that it has often been described as being a new 'imperialist' device.

Although Arab rulers may indeed derive from the events in East Europe (and from the decline in Soviet aid) the lesson that a capitalist transformation is desirable, they would not necessarily draw the conclusion that a democratic transition is due. President Hafiz al-Asad of Syria has openly declared that the events in East Europe are not pertinent to developments in Syria, and rumour has it that President Saddam Husain of Iraq showed his party and security cadres a video of the trial and execution of Ceauşescu of Romania and his entourage by way of alerting them to their likely fate once they start to 'go soft'.

POLITICAL CORRELATES OF ECONOMIC LIBERALISATION

But if Arab rulers would interpret the global situation to mean that 'capitalisation' rather than democratisation is in order, could one not wonder, with Claus Offé [1991], whether it may be possible to have "democracy by capitalist design" – that is, that they will opt for capitalist development but will end up getting democracy by default so to speak? In answering this question one should remember that not all capitalism is a liberalising force: in historical perspective it is only bourgeois capitalism that has been so. The middle classes in the Third World, the Middle East included, have not always preferred democracy, and most capitalists in the contemporary Middle East continue, in spite of the liberalisation slogans, to seek state protection, and are far from being a really autonomous social force. Under the existing globalising pressures, maintains Adam Przeworski [1991], governments will only be able to pursue the required 'adjustment' either through 'concertation' (i.e. consultation and negotiation with groups, especially unions, that will be hurt by reforms) – which he sees as unlikely in developing countries; or else through the 'insulation' of policy-makers from affected groups – which he sees as undermining democracy. The latter strategy was followed in countries such as Turkey, Egypt and Tunisia with regard to the labour unions, although these regimes have tried to maintain political support by appealing to the relatively unorganised 'masses' while marginalising all better-organised groups (including political parties) that may be opposed to the adjustment policies. Privatisation, as a possible component of such adjustment policies, does not automatically create a free economic market, even less a political market. As one can already observe in a number of Middle Eastern countries, the transition may not necessarily be 'from plan to market' but rather may be from 'plan to clan': both in the sense of favouritism towards one's own kith and kin, and in the sense of mafia-type cliques that 'enclose' segments of the market as their own exclusive domain.

Initially, a state bourgeoisie pushed towards, or tempted by, economic liberalisation, finds that a certain measure of political liberalisation would serve its purposes. Some rulers think that an appearance of political liberalisation is more reassuring to foreign investors and aid-giving Western governments. If they are the successors to regimes that were perceived to be authoritarian, they may use a 'democratisation' terminology as a banner under which to rally support for the new regime from previous opposition groups. In any case, they will probably want to involve as many forces as possible in the political campaign to support the (unpopular) reduction in the welfare benefits available to the popular classes that is bound to accompany privatisation and liberalisation policies.

Eventually the new emphasis on the importance of private investment, both foreign and domestic, is bound to produce what O'Donnell terms 'privatising' effects on the state [O'Donnell, 1977]; in the sense that the entrepreneurs and their business associations will start to make inroads within the state apparatus, and to build alliances and establish pressure groups that will defend their interests within the networks of 'bureaucratic politics'. This phenomenon has developed quite significantly in Egypt in recent years. Another phenomenon, known to have manifestations in Egypt, Iraq, Tunisia, Syria and other countries, shows itself in the development of what Joseph La Palombara terms *clientela* and *parantela* relationships [quoted in Peters, 1978:

148–55]. These concepts are obviously inspired by the Italian experience, but Japan is also known to harbour similar practices [cf. Shimizu, 1988: 10–12]. A *clientela* relationship is said to exist when an interest group succeeds in becoming – in the eyes of a given administrative agency – the 'natural' representative of a given social sector which comes under the jurisdiction of that administrative agency. A *parantela* relationship describes a situation of 'kinship' or close fraternal ties between a pressure group and the government, which enjoys the added linkage of a political party – usually a hegemonic one. Even after multi-partism is formally permitted, the hegemonic National Democratic Party in Egypt and the New Destourian Party in Tunisia continue to 'intermediate' with government departments to make sure that certain contractors are favoured with certain business deals. Both during the phase of cohabitation between the public and the private sector, and more par-ticularly during the transition towards privatisation, government departments and hegemonic parties have their 'favourite' (and favoured) associations and entrepreneurs.

An important question has to be asked as to the extent to which completely independent business interests will be allowed to function under more or less purely market-directed conditions. This question also has its political con-sequences, because a really autonomous business bourgeoisie will act dif-ferently, in political terms, from one that is closely tied to the state. John Waterbury has noted the emergence in the Middle East of some interesting proto-*zaibatsu* arrangements, i.e. "the consolidation of large diversified private economic groups, dependent on the state business, credit and protection". Koç in Turkey, 'Uthman in Egypt and Omnium in Morocco are good cases in point [Waterbury, 1988]. These are particularly outstanding examples, but the Egyptian, Iraqi, Tunisian, Syrian and other cases indicate that the sym-biotic relationship between the public and the private sector involves also smaller and less conspicuous examples. Nor can it be a mere coincidence that many of the directors of 'privatised' banks and companies tend to be ministers and higher bureaucrats. Private businesses cream off public resources, and public officials 'parachute' on private companies. There is a fairly grey area lying in between what can be termed 'public' and what can be termed 'private'. In the Middle East, it is perhaps only the traditional artisan-com-mercial sector in some countries and the emerging so-called 'Islamic business' sector in other countries that can claim a relative (but by no means absolute) degree of autonomy from the state.

The public/private distinction is an issue not only of economics and management, but also of politics. If one is to judge by the Western experience, political liberalism can only emerge in situations where public and private interests are clearly defined, thus allowing for the development of a 'political sphere', or an *espace public* as the French call it, that mediates between the two. Bourgeois society is often viewed as one in which economic and social relation-

ships are functionally differentiated on the one hand, mediated through citizenship and represented by political relationships in the public arena on the
other. This notion, as Jean Leca observes, may or may not be true of the
industrial societies, but is it at all likely to apply in the Middle East? [Leca,
1988: 198].

In some ways the difficulty of distinguishing between the state and civil
society, between the public and the private is derived from the characteristics
of the welfare state or *l'Etat-Providence* as such. For, as Michel Camau puts it,
the large public sector characteristic of such states in some respects blurs the
boundaries between the public and the private by 'socialising the state' and
'etatising the society', and it thus contributes to the emergence of a third,
mixed sector that is partly social and partly statist (*un mixte social-étatique*)
[Camau, 1990: 68, 76]. He maintains that one of the important manifestations
of the growth in the size and impact of the public sector is the 'clientelisation'
of society, whereby allegiance to the state will not acquire any moral justifi-
cation but will simply be a function of the resource allocation process, which
will turn social groups into mere satellites of the producer-distributer state.
Camau argues that it is only through the emergence of a political arena or
espace public where *citizenship* is at work, that a social counterweight to the
state's intervention in the fields of labour and exchange (taking the form of an
economic private sector) can thrive [ibid.: 70–75]. By 'citizenship' we mean of
course "something more than merely being subject to the laws of a state ...
It must be a social role which is partly, but not wholly, defined in terms of
rights" [Miller, 1989: 245–6].

We may not agree with Camau's entire thesis, but there can be little doubt
that unless the clientelisation of the society *vis-à-vis* the state is curtailed, the
emergence of a proper political sphere or public space will be handicapped,
and the prospects for political liberalisation will be restricted. We have seen
that, with the exception of the traditional artisan-commercial sectors in some
countries (for even this is penetrated by the state in countries such as Tunisia
and Morocco) and the emerging 'Islamic business' sector in others (where it
is often persecuted by the authorities), the emerging private sectors in most
Arab countries are still largely 'clientelised' by the state, or else they remain
'informal' or underground. The move towards genuine political liberalisation
is therefore seriously constrained.

What are the prospects for the future? The situation varies from country to
country [cf. Waterbury, 1988]. In states where the public sector is mainly of
the 'grand projects' variety (especially if these are also externally oriented
with fewer linkages to the society and to the private sector), such as Iraq,
Algeria and Saudi Arabia, the state will probably continue to control the
'commanding heights' of the economy and to subordinate the private sector
to its own priorities. In countries where the state's policies, intentionally or
inadvertently, have not 'crowded out' the private sector, and where a reason-

able number of public/private linkages exist, such as in Egypt and Tunisia, and perhaps in Syria and Jordan, the public sector is likely to retain its preponderant position, but will grow more slowly than the private sector which will concentrate on the most profitable activities (e.g. trade, tourism, contracting and services), and will rely on the state to absorb risks. The 'balance' in such an arrangement will always remain delicate, so that a serious crisis experienced by the private sector will always be likely to prompt a return to a more comprehensive etatist policy, as happens periodically in Turkey.

In the near to medium term very few economies indeed are likely to end up being predominantly private, the recommendations and conditions advanced by the International Monetary Fund notwithstanding. Morocco is a possible, though unlikely, exception where private sector growth combined with public sector divestiture may eventually lead to a privately dominated economy. Other cases of much weaker economies, such as the Sudan, may witness a situation whereby the private sector could, by default, end up being in preponderance owing to the almost total collapse of the state sector.

Thus we may be able to generalise by saying, especially with regard to countries with substantial public sectors (mostly the ones that used to be called 'socialist'), that the state bourgeoisie is likely to encourage the growth of a private sector but is unlikely to want to do away with the public sector. In other words, the state bourgeoisie is unlikely to migrate *en masse* to the world of private business. It will want to keep its options open, and to have as much as possible the best of both worlds. Many of its members do still believe, in any case, in the developmental and 'modernizing' role of the state, although they may be increasingly aware of its managerial limitations. In many of these countries (as indeed in the oil-rich countries of the Gulf), public officials are likely to continue to engage themselves in private business (formal restrictions notwithstanding), while or after being in public office. As John Waterbury rather colourfully remarks:

> For those at the top of the state structure, there was the challenge of pioneering in new production techniques, engaging in vast schemes of social engineering, altering the very structure of one's economy, and living well at the same time. Why would any of those at the top or within reach of the top trade this in for a small shoe factory, a travel agency, or a chicken farm? Very few would, especially in that they learned with time that they could have their small private enterprise *and* their public position [Waterbury, 1988: 20].

The continuation of a large public sector alongside a substantial and expanding private sector, with a broad 'grey' area in between, is also a suitable political match for the authoritarian post-populist regimes: it removes from the state part of the blame for economic and managerial problems, but does not lead to a full autonomy of the civil society that would require a genuine political liberalisation. As Jean Leca puts it:

Secular patrimonial authoritarianism is more easily supported by a mixed structure which combines public and private sectors than it would be by a purely
state economy (whose inefficiency would dissatisfy the emerging classes) or by a
strictly private economy (which, by rendering visible the social structure of the
groups, would exacerbate social conflicts and make them less easy to handle)
[Leca, 1988: 197].

Clement Henry Moore argues along similar lines, but wonders whether such
half-way house arrangements have the strength to endure:

Changing patterns of allocation rather than ownership may produce the kinds of
political economies that will give an exhausted statist regime a new lease of life.
Instead of managing economic exchanges directly, such a regime may manage
them indirectly, while still continuing in principle to own the means of production. Supporting client groups then becomes less expensive because some of the
costs are farmed out ... But how long can a regime have it both ways, conserving its power and autonomy while selectively unloading economic decision-
making onto a protected marketplace? [Moore, 1986: 637].

The picture therefore is not simple and the relationship is quite complex.
The state bourgeoisie wants some expansion in the private sector but not the
disappearance of the public sector. The private sector calls for economic
liberalisation but wants to continue to make use of state patronage and asks
for state support and protection. This prevents politico-economic relations
from becoming transparent: only 'transparency' would delineate the political
from the economic, the public from the private, the employer from the employee – thus expanding the political arena in which politics of individuals,
groups, parties and classes can take place.

The state bourgeoisie tends to act in a rather contradictory manner. Certain individuals and groups, with more immediate business gains in sight and/
or with original or recently-acquired attraction to the merits of liberalisation,
would push for speedy commercialisation and privatisation. The *overall* movement of the state bourgeoisie would, however, be more cautious. For many
there are opportunities (which should not be missed) for deriving financial
gains from the expanding private sector, gains that may be accrued only
through the control of public office (and therefore the allocation of permits
and licences as well as technical advice and expertise). More broadly, a full
liberalisation and privatisation of the economy would simply lead to an erosion
of the state bourgeoisie's ability to extract economic surplus and rent via non-
economic (political and administrative) means, and would eventually reveal a
more sharply defined class map characterised by a higher degree of
transparency of economic and socio-political relations. Such an outcome is
not in the interest of the state bourgeoisie and its authoritarian leadership,
which would most probably prefer a more blurred class map.

The private sector, on the other hand, will also assume a contradictory posture. Although always pushing for increased privatisation, the business community may not necessarily opt either for full economic liberalisation or for ultimate autonomy from the state. To start with, its members will always ask for as much state subsidy, protection and support as possible. Many of them may prefer to remain close to the state. As Jean Leca says:

> The private sector growing up in the shadow of the state (and thanks to the public sector) certainly has an interest in gaining freedom of economic action, more access to credit and fiscal facilities, the freedom of cross-border traffic, but why should it have to undertake open political action when it can try to obtain all this at less cost to itself by remaining entrenched in bureaucratic or palace politics where the informal network of family, regional and factional solidarity is at the heart of the game? [Leca, 1988: 197].

The main mobilisation against the state bourgeoisie and its authoritarian apparatus has so far not come from the economic private sector but rather from the 'socio-cultural' private sector, so to speak – from the radical Islamic movements and from the informal so-called 'Islamic business' groups with their alternative network of schools, hospitals and social services. In some, though not in all, cases the latter may also be joined with the traditional artisan/commercial sector which has not developed the same organic links with the state as did the more recent commercial bourgeoisie. In Egypt, where the Islamic business sector has become particularly active in recent years, it came into serious confrontation with the state. The apparent conflict was over the 'legality' of the status and practices of these companies, but it is also likely that the state saw in the development of this group (as distinct from the 'privatising' state bureaucrats), the movement of a civil society that was seeking genuine autonomy from the state. This was 'real' capitalism in the making, believes one commentator, but it was promptly aborted by a state that was, in spite of all its slogans, unable to divest itself from its Nasserite *étatiste* mantle. Unlike the hybrid 'private' sector that linked itself to the state:

> The fault of the [Islamic] Companies was not in seeking power [as claimed by the authorities] but in paying insufficient attention to the issue of power. They [mistakenly] thought that they could start by building a capitalist economy, that they could establish industry in a society ruled by Mamluks – and they paid dearly for it [Kishk, 1989: 160 et passim].

The overall picture, therefore, is one in which the transition towards an economic market will not automatically translate itself into the creation of a political market, characterised by open bidding from classes, groups and parties. Economic liberalisation will not immediately lead to political liberal-isation, but to a more complex picture of multiplicity of interests and organisations in a state of competition, bargaining and intermediation. More specifically, the etatist scene of earlier decades will probably give way to something similar to what Robert Bianchi calls a "corporatist-associative" model [Bianchi, 1988: 5ff]. Within this model, 'state', 'market' and 'community' are likely to engage in elaborate processes of 'political exchange' with each other. For these processes to take place the state élite must be sufficiently weakened by the protracted financial and legitimacy crisis to accept groups and associations as junior partners, but must still be strong enough to extract cooperation as the price for group privileges [compare Bianchi, 1988: 6–7]. There is evidence to suggest that such a situation is already obtaining in countries like Turkey, Egypt and Tunisia. Other countries, such as Syria, Algeria and possibly Sudan, may be on their way. The trends may be similar but the pertinent groups will vary from one country to another: for example, the business community (part private and fully private) in Egypt, Syria and possibly Tunisia; the professional and labour syndicates in Egypt, Tunisia and Sudan; the rural 'kulaks' and 'second strata' in Egypt, Syria and possibly Iraq; and so forth.

Egypt is of course the most 'advanced' case in this respect and can offer an interesting 'preview' of what may follow in several other Arab countries. The state continues to 'incorporate' the professional syndicates, the labour unions and the agricultural cooperatives [cf. Bianchi, 1989]. The growing private sector, however, is developing 'privatising' inroads within the political and bureaucratic apparatuses of the state. For this it uses the semi-official (partly incorporated or 'hybrid' – to use Bianchi's term) Federation of Egyptian Industries and Federation of Chambers of Commerce, and increasingly the more recent Egyptian Businessmen's Association and the American–Egyptian Chamber of Commerce [Qandil, 1988: 59–123]. In the countryside, the state has been prepared to allow higher economic and financial freedoms for the emerging alliances of agrarian entrepreneurs, field bureaucrats and local businessmen, provided that they are able to reduce their demands for government funds and services and also to secure overall allegiance to the national/central leadership and to the ruling National Democratic Party [cf. Auda, 1989].

Even with the informal business sector, represented most dramatically by the Islamic Investment Companies which added a certain element of ideological (religious) challenge to their economic and financial challenge to the state, the state has been either unwilling or unable to follow an all-or-nothing confrontational approach. Long negotiations took place, and attempts were made to fit at least some of the maverick businesses into the overall legal framework of the country's economy [see Ayubi, 1991a: Ch. 8].

In general, the Egyptian state has been striving to trade the expansion of certain political freedoms for the moderation of certain economic demands [Bianchi, 1988: 11]. In Egypt, and in similar regimes, the state-centred variety of corporatism which was more typical of earlier stages may be giving way to a more variegated and flexible form of corporatism that will perhaps allow more play both to modern-type organised social interests – such as those of the professional and the business associations — as well as to the more 'traditional' community-centred groups that are formed around familial, factional or local nuclei [see on the Tunisian scene the chapters in Zartman, ed., 1991].

This latter variety is reminiscent of what Pearl Robinson [1991] calls 'neo-traditional corporatism'. Populist corporatism (as we have seen in Chapter 6) is typically associated with the early stages of import-substitution industrialisation, when economic expansion is rapid and when "projections of increased state resources provide the rationale for a broad range of distribution policies that enable ruling élites to control the demand side of politics. But absent is an efficient industrial infrastructure, a lucrative mining industry or profitable agro-industries, [and] populist corporatism is not a viable governing option." What you may get instead is bureaucratic-authoritarian corporatism (for which, as we have seen, the conditions have not been conducive in most Arab countries), or else a variety of neotraditional corporatism:

> In contrast to the distributive policies promoted under populist corporatism and the exclusionary practices of bureaucratic-authoritarian corporations, neotraditional corporatism is geared toward deflecting consumption demands away from central government authority and on to local level jurisdictions or the private sector, while simultaneously broadening the base of participation in policy ratification and implementation [Robinson, 1991: 2–5].

Thus one can see that in the expansionary phase, the state used to take political rights away in exchange for granting socio-economic ones; in the 'contractory' phase the state concedes political rights for groups and individuals in return for being relieved from some of its financial and welfarist commitments.

Such arrangements enable authoritarian regimes to court favoured groups as coalition partners, while tolerating some protest and quasi-opposition from aggrieved groups. Under such circumstances:

> political liberalization need not appear to authoritarian elites as a risky and radical departure from the past. Rather, they might be able to assure themselves by viewing 'corporatist democracy' as a useful defence mechanism in which the state redistributes authority from one set of publicly accountable organs to another, while retaining clear responsibility for overall coordination and concertation [Bianchi, 1988: 13].

A formula such as this will not, of course, resolve class conflicts; its function will be partly to disguise and partly to manipulate class antagonisms [compare Shimizu, 1988: 22–31]. Such an arrangement can perhaps survive for a reasonable length of time – but it cannot continue indefinitely, and regimes may eventually find themselves obliged to democratise to one degree or another.

MANIFESTATIONS OF POLITICAL LIBERALISATION

If one is to speak of broadly defined political liberalisation rather than tightly defined democratisation (in the sense of institutionalised representation, participation and opposition), what then are the manifestations that one can currently enumerate within the Arab World?

Cosmetic democratisation: 'for the Yankees to see'

First, and as already hinted, there is the type of superficial, formalistic democratisation to which regimes may resort for the sake of appearances – this is really 'cosmetic democracy' (*shakliyya* in Arabic) or, probably more to the point, 'defensive democracy'. Sometimes this is resorted to because of the (usually mistaken) belief that super- and big powers will be impressed and that they would subsequently increase the flow of trade, investment and aid. In Portugal and Brazil in the late 19th century, this consideration was expressed via the phrase *para os ingleses ver*: for the English to see [Whitehead, 1992: 150]. The contemporary alternative is more likely to be: 'for the Yankees to see'!

The possibility should not, however, be ruled out that a certain measure of such 'opportunistic democratisation' may eventually take root and develop a life of its own. The pluralisation measures introduced by people such as Atatürk and Sadat survived their initiators, even though Sadat had not intended these measures to represent a relinquishment of his own powers – one of his famous sayings was that "democracy has fangs"!

Therefore one should not think in dichotomous terms of dictatorship and democracy but rather in terms of a process (of liberalisation and pluralisation) and of the various shades that may exist along the continuum between the two ideal types. Thus if one is to use the terminology coined by O'Donnell and Schmitter, Sadat's regime may be described as a *dictablanda* (i.e. a liberalised autocracy), while Mubarak's regime may be closer to a *democradura* (i.e., a system of limited political democracy) [O'Donnell and Schmitter, "Tentative conclusion", 1986].

Street politics: or 'setting the state dancing to the beat of civil society'

One manifestation of growing dynamism and pluralisation is manifested by what one may call 'street politics'. A familiar pattern of street politics in Egypt and in Turkey used to show itself in the series of strikes/demonstrations/riots that would be initiated by the workers and/or students and that would then spill over into the streets, engaging other social classes and fractions [compare Öncü, 1991].

In recent years street politics has often been activated via 'food riots' or 'austerity protests'. Widespread street riots took place in Egypt in January 1977 and in the remaining few years of the 1970s four other countries (Morocco, Tunisia, Turkey and Iran) were to experience massive urban protests, leading in the last two cases to a military coup and a revolution respectively [Seddon, 1993: 88ff]. In the 1980s numerous states (Sudan, Tunisia, Morocco, Egypt, Algeria and Jordan) were shaken by outbreaks of popular protest against austerity measures, and even in Lebanon, which was in the midst of its civil war, there were protests in 1987 against the effects of currency devaluation [cf. also Ibrahim, ed., 1993: 26–30].

At the beginning of the 1990s it was clear that austerity protests would continue to accompany the process of economic restructuring: demonstrations took place in Morocco, Algeria and Turkey in 1990. During the Gulf War of 1990/91 the massive demonstrations in the Maghrib countries were closely linked to protests over the effects of government economic policies and to demands for political liberalisation.

'Street politics' can lead to important political outcomes including immediate concessions (for example the overthrow of the Numairi regime in Sudan) or to various political reforms, such as in Tunisia, Jordan and Algeria. Their main potential importance is derived from the fact that they often join the sub-proletariat and the lumpenproletariat on the one hand, with the students and with parts of the working class and parts of the intelligentsia on the other.

However, unless street politics are a spill-over of other organised (e.g. political party or trade union) politics, they are usually 'praetorian' and unmediated, and they often, as noted by O'Donnell [1979], set the state dancing to the beat of civil society (thus, for example, the usually hurried, panicky withdrawal of price and subsidy reforms). They are usually more protest-centred than demand-based, and are often easy to quell after a few days. They may reflect a yearning for participation, but they are often used by authoritarian regimes as an excuse to clamp down on liberties and to slow down any existing democratisation processes.[2]

An invigorated role for the judiciary

The late 1980s and the early 1990s witnessed a surge in the political significance of law and the political status of the judiciary. As the regimes have had to concede the principle of the 'rule of law' or even the 'state of law' (*Rechtstaat*, *Etat de droit*, *dawlat al-qanun*), judges and lawyers have been trying to push the logic of laws and institutions (and by implication the concept of natural law or *jusnaturaliste*) to its maximum possible limits [cf. Al-Ahnaf, Botiveau and Cesari, 1993]. To be sure, both the authoritarian state and the Islamist movements (whose democratic intentions are suspect) are also manipulating law for their own purposes, and even sometimes taking the initiative (as, for example, with the Moroccan government in regard to the opposition parties or to the human rights discourse). But here is at least a platform upon which some contested ideas can be aired, and a once-again proud profession that has managed on more than one occasion to safeguard human rights, to cancel elections and allow the formation of parties, and even to protect the (arguably anti-state, anti-positive law) Islamists from unlawful punishment by the state. Examples for such acts exist in Tunisia, Morocco, Algeria and elsewhere, but the Egypt-ian case is the one that has advanced most. The Egyptian high constitutional court was able in 1990 to declare the elections law unconstitutional and to call for dissolving the parliament. The higher administrative court has also, and against government directions, pronounced legal the formation of three political parties, while the Egyptian judiciary has shown growing autonomy and remarkable innovation in interpreting the laws in several cases involving elections and political rights and has also formulated a number of useful rules and standards for guaranteeing the judges' supervision over the electoral process [cf. Zahran, 1988; CPSS, 1991].

Interest group politics: 'privatising the state'

Another aspect of relative pluralisation and liberalisation may represent itself in the growing influence of interest groups. This often accompanies a relative structural weakening in the *étatiste* regimes that urges them, through acts of *scambio politico*, to recognise a certain degree of autonomy for professional syndicates, trade unions and the like in return for these conceding some of their welfarist demands and for supporting the *overall* orientation of state policies. This is not necessarily openly democratic, as it may express itself mainly in making 'privatising' inroads into the state machine, or even in the 'capture of the state' on behalf of very specific interests. But again it is potentially a force for pluralisation if nothing else.

Interest group politics have grown noticeably in countries such as Turkey, Egypt and Tunisia, but they are also of significance in other countries such as Morocco and Sudan [cf. the various studies by Bianchi, M.K. Al-Sayyid, Qandil and Faris 'Abd al-Mun'im].

Loosely related to this point is the growing political role, in countries where neither political parties nor professional unions are active, of social and cultural associations. Such associations have become more vocal in discussing national issues and in formulating alternatives to public policies, and have sometimes even acted as pressure groups. Their own elections, if available, are usually both even-handed and highly competitive, and they generally receive a great deal of public attention. Examples are the University Graduate Association in Kuwait, the Social Professions Association in the UAE, and the Jasra Cultural Forum in Qatar [Ibrahim, ed., 1993: 25–6].

Pacts: 'pluralisation by non-democratic means'

Pacts are characteristic of the coalition shifts that either follow or else pave the way for important policy and structural transitions. They generally represent a move towards democracy by un-democratic means [O'Donnell and Schmitter, 1986: 38]. Such pacts should be distinguished from 'charters' (a task made somewhat difficult by the fact that the Arabic word *mithaq* is used to describe both, although words such as *wifaq* and *'ahd* are also sometimes used for pacts).

National charters are more typical of the periods during which single-party or popular-front regimes are being consolidated (e.g. the Egyptian Charter of 1962, the Algerian of 1976, the Yemeni of 1982). National pacts, on the other hand, are more characteristic of periods of transition towards national conciliation and of a more serious acceptance of the principle of plurality, and may sometimes convey a semi-consociational orientation. The Lebanese National Pact of 1943 among the Christian and Muslim leaders (modified and renewed in Ta'if in 1991 after years of bitter fighting) is a classic example [Norton, 1991]. Other 'pacts' have emerged in recent years in Tunisia in 1988 [cf. Anderson, 1991] and in Jordan in 1989/90 [cf. Brand, 1992]. A pact of sorts appeared in unified Yemen, and although the level of violence remained significant, it may be developing into a more distinct consociational formula.

The main point about these modalities of liberalisation is that even though the regime may intend the democratisation measures to remain mainly cosmetic, the state in most Arab countries is now so structurally exhausted (as a result of its financial crisis), and the society so much more complex, that real social plurality is developing and will almost inevitably feed into the democratisation process. The marginalisation and subsequent radicalisation of various social fractions, the spread of a sizeable informal economy, and the emergence of various semi-autonomous professional and cultural groups means that social differentiation is becoming more elaborate and that plurality – at least in its pre-political form – is becoming a matter of daily life. These changes, taken together with actual democratisation measures – however limited – point in the direction of polyarchy and away from the familiar monocracies [cf. Dahl, 1971].

Proper democratisation, of course, is more likely to take place at a conjuncture where a common denominator emerges between the interests of the rulers and those of the ascending social classes: that is, when negative, reactive or 'defensive' democratisation on the part of the rulers happens also to coincide with the need for positive and pro-active democratic transition, as part of a longer-term project of the ascending social classes. This is a picture that does not apply to many Arab countries at the present time – although the possibility of some approximations emerging in the future should not be completely ruled out of hand.

COUNTRY CASES

Existing cases of democratisation are taking place mainly within two types of systems: one of these is in societies in which industrialisation and structural differentiation has allowed some element of class and interest differentiation to emerge, notably in Turkey, Egypt and Tunisia; and the second is in highly 'articulated' societies where consociational and/or corporatist arrangements may allow for a less conflictual, and rather pluralistic formula, notably Lebanon and Yemen. Before proceeding with further analysis, let us first consider some country cases.

Egypt

Egypt has pioneered the transition towards democracy within the Arab World [cf. Ayubi, 1991b]. Since the late 1960s and early 1970s, demands for increasing political participation have been building up. In response to such calls, 'platforms' (*manabir*) were eventually allowed to emerge and to adopt distinctive programmes and produce lists for parliamentary elections in 1976. Shortly afterwards, the 'platform' organisations were allowed to turn themselves into legal political parties. However, both the 1976 and the 1979 parliamentary elections gave the 'government party' a very substantial majority in the legislative branch.

The first parliamentary elections under Mubarak were held in May 1984 under a rather curious new electoral law based on proportional representation. According to this law no parties were allowed representation in parliament unless they obtained at least 8 per cent of all national votes (i.e. some 423,000 votes in the 1984 elections). All the votes and seats acquired by those political parties that failed to reach the required percentage were added automatically to those of the winning party, which also monopolised the 30 seats allocated exclusively for women in the People's Assembly. (This provision concerning women's representation was cancelled in the 1987 elections.) The ruling National Democratic Party achieved 72.9 per cent of the votes and 87 per cent of the seats in the People's Assembly (total number of seats 448), the right-wing Wafd Party 15 per cent of the votes and 13 per cent of the seats, the Labour Socialist Party 7.73 per cent of the votes and no seats, the left-wing Progressive Tajammu' Party 4.1 per cent of the votes and no seats, and the Liberals' Party 0.65 per cent of the votes and no seats.

The elections made it clear, therefore, that the ruling party, headed by Mubarak himself, was well in control. But the extent to which this 'control' was actually responsible for the results of the elections remained controversial for quite some time. One obvious result was that the ruling party fared much better in the countryside, where the government's grip over local government and the security machine is tighter. The opposition, by contrast, registered impressive victories in the large cities, gaining 38.4 per cent of all votes in Cairo, 32.7 per cent in Alexandria, 36 per cent in Suez, and as much as 53.3 per cent of all votes in Port Said.

All in all, however, it appeared that the government had managed to marginalise the existing opposition parties, with the possible exception of the pre-revolutionary Wafd Party (which succeeded not only in legalising itself as a result of winning a judicial case against the government, but also in winning a reasonable number of seats in a tight election through alliance with the Muslim Brothers). It is possible that the country might indeed have been settling for a *de facto* one-party system (similar to that in Mexico), especially since it remains extremely difficult for new parties to be formed under the existing 'Parties Law'. Yet, by persecuting small parties, the government might inadvertently have helped to promote the idea of electoral alliances: first between the Muslim Brothers and the Wafd, and then between the Muslim Brothers and Labour.

As expected, the April 1987 elections again saw victory for the National Democratic Party (NDP), although with fewer seats than it had gained in 1984. Of the 14 million registered voters, less than half actually voted. According to the rules, any party failing in these elections to win some 546,000 votes nationally would lose any seats gained locally. The NDP received about 4,752,000 votes (69.6 per cent); all opposition parties together obtained about 2,073,000 votes of which about 1,164,000 (17 per cent) went to the Alliance of Labour/Liberal with the Ikhwan (Muslim Brothers), about 746,000 (10.9 per cent) went to the Wafd, 151,000 to the Progressive Tajammu', and about 13,000 (0.19 per cent) to the minor religious party al-Umma. These party votes translated into the following seats (excluding the forty-eight seats specifically allocated for 'independents'): the NDP acquired 309 seats, the Alliance with the Ikhwan took fifty-six seats, the Wafd gained thirty-five seats and the Tajammu' and the Umma parties won no seats. Of the seats reserved for the 'independents', forty also went to candidates sponsored by the NDP.

It should be noted, however, that in this election the NDP's share of seats was some sixty fewer than it had acquired in the previous elections, while the opposition's share increased by some thirty seats. But instead of the Wafd, which formed the main opposition party in the 1984 parliament, the main opposition bloc was now represented by the Alliance between the Nationalistic-Islamic Labour, the Right-Wing Liberal, and the 'fundamentalist' Ikhwan. This meant that the Ikhwan, although technically still an illegal organisation, would now be substantially represented in the parliament (and by some of its most distinguished leaders) for the first time since the 1952 revolution. The Wafd's ageing and paternalistic leadership, its wavering over secularism and its temporary alliance with the Ikhwan, and its obsessive hatred of Nasser had possibly reduced its popularity.

The government party thus won again, even though there were repeated accusations, most notably from the leader of the Wafd party, of rigging and corruption. But even without much overt rigging and corruption (although in this case there were violent skirmishes involving governmental and security authorities in the working class town of Kafr al-Dawwar and elsewhere), the NDP has access to a whole organisational network, especially in the country-side, which ensures that there are proportionately more votes cast in the countryside and that these votes 'go in the right direction'. As with the 1984 elections the highest turnout was in the countryside, while in Cairo the turnout was estimated at only 20 per cent. Presumably those who were not inclined to support the government party found it easier to 'vote with their feet' in Cairo than did their counterparts living in smaller towns and villages under the tight grip of the control-oriented local government system introduced by Sadat in 1979.

The government does operate a patronage system in the localities whereby public services and economic privileges are identified with the NDP. At the same time most local public officials, including regional governors, tend to identify themselves with the ruling party. As one governor bluntly remarked: "I support the NDP; for the governor is, in the first and last resort, partisan. A success for the NDP signifies a people that is behind its leader and which supports his steps" [in Hilal et al., 1982: 83].

Another round of elections was held in 1990, and was the second to be organised two years in advance of its due date. Once again this was the outcome of a ruling by the increasingly politically influential Egyptian judiciary. The Higher Constitutional Court had declared unconstitutional the electoral law under which the People's Assembly had been elected in 1987. The parliament was dissolved and new elections were held under a new electoral system based on two-member constituencies and with fewer con-straints on independent candidates. However, the continuation of the em-ergency laws which restricted the activities of the opposition during election campaigns had led to disagreements with the government and to the boycott of the election by most of the major political parties except for the Tajammu', which acquired five seats and ended up representing the opposition in parlia-ment. The Nasserists participated in the electoral campaign for the first time, under several organisational labels, and gained five seats altogether.

It is clear, however, that the influence of the 'government party', although still dominant, has been significantly reduced. The National Democratic Party gained only 253 seats, with its successful candidates now representing only 57 per cent of all successful candidates as compared to 75 per cent in the previous (1987) elections. But since ninety-five ex-members of the NDP were elected as independents, the Party succeeded in re-incorporating several of them into its ranks, by this means raising its parliamentary representation to about 80 per cent of the seats [CPSS, 1991: 415–50]. And so the 'Mexican' scenario con-tinues.

Tunisia

If a coup d'état had not removed President Habib Bourguiba from power (after he had held it for just over thirty years) in November 1987, Tunisia would perhaps have been one of the Third World countries most vulnerable to prolonged political agony. Not only had the country been experiencing a succession crisis during the two previous decades, but it had also suffered "a crisis of regulation" resulting from a style of leadership that enabled Bourguiba to break "political clans" before their alliances could acquire enough bases of real power to cause him any bother [Moore, 1988: 176–7].

The constitution of 1959 had stipulated an elected national assembly, but the seats were overwhelmingly dominated by members of the single party: the Parti Socialiste Destourien. In 1975 Bourguiba was designated president for life and although he announced that the National Assembly elections of 1981 would be freely contested, his men still dominated all important positions, both legislative and executive. By then, however, the country's problems were escalating. 'Growth by expansion' had reached a ceiling, and the necessary economic restructuring that had to be resorted to had its own social and political pains. Furthermore, "as the original elite aged, the economy became more differentiated and society correspondingly more complex. The ability of the party leaders to represent all of the increasingly divergent interests within society diminished" [Anderson, 1991: 247–9]. Failure by the President's lieu-tenants to cope with the country's problems, combined with their jockeying for position in anticipation of presidential succession to their increasingly senile boss, had created a general atmosphere of uncertainty and apprehension. This paved the way for the Interior minister, former brigadier-general Zain al-'Abidin Bin 'Ali, to oust the ailing president in what was half way between a palace coup and a military coup. Bin 'Ali "presented himself as a man of 'renewal' and called for political pluralism and respect for human rights. He opened a dialogue with the opposition forces, socialist and Islamist. An am-nesty released hundreds of political prisoners and allowed thousands to return home. The media reflected the more open atmosphere" [Halliday, 1990b: 25].

Bin 'Ali set about a rejuvenation of the ruling party, now renamed the Rassemblement Constitutionnel Democratique (RCD). By then the party had a membership of more than one million (out of a total population of 7.3 million) organised in 4,404 cells, but was lacking both in discipline and in spirit [Moore, 1988: 186–7]. By the end of Bin 'Ali's first year in office the party claimed that 40 per cent of the cadres had been replaced and that the average age of membership had dropped to the mid-30s.

The new president and party boss also proposed a National Pact *(mithaq)* that was to be discussed with a view to enabling a broad national consensus to emerge over the issues of national identity, the political system, economic development and foreign policy. Lisa Anderson was not alone in interpreting these developments optimistically and in regarding the proposed pact not as an attempt to pre-empt moves towards political pluralism but rather, like the Spanish Pact of Moncloa, as a general agreement on principles among political and social élites, which would symbolise, summarise and perhaps extend popular consensus [Anderson, 1991: 251–7]. The eventual signatories to the pact included representatives of the six recognised political parties, including the Mouvement des Democrats Socialistes (RCD), the Parti Communiste Tunisien (PCT) and the Parti de l'Unité Populaire (PUP), as well as representatives of some interest organisations such as the national labour commission, the Union of Industry and Commerce, the National Union of Farmers, the National Union of Women, the Human Rights Association and the national unions of engineers, lawyers, doctors and pharmacists. This indeed looked like a preparatory forum for a more elaborate corporatist formula with a growing pluralist potential.

Yet optimism in many quarters was to be dampened, because of the pact's failure to steer itself towards the direction of democratic development. The reasons were partly related to the nature of the Tunisian political élite and partly to the continuation of Tunisia's socio-economic problems and the way these problems appeared to be fuelling the increasingly vocal Islamic movement. The presidential elections of April 1989 saw Bin 'Ali as the only candidate, elected with a familiar 99.27 per cent of the votes. And in the parliamentary elections held in the same month not a single candidate (from six opposition parties) was to win any of the 141 seats in the assembly. The RCD finds it difficult, for historical reasons, to disentangle the Nation, the state and the Party, as the country has developed into a kind of *partitocrazia* that sees the cadres, political as well as technocratic, fiercely defending their vested interests everywhere.

The Parti de la Renaissance (*Nahda*), formerly the Mouvement de la Tendance Islamique (MTI), was prohibited from contesting the elections, although the opposition figures, including some with Islamic tendencies, managed to gain nearly 20 per cent of the votes. Islamist candidates won 14.5 per cent of the vote nationwide and an impressive 30 per cent or so in important cities like Tunis, Gabes and Sousse [Esposito and Piscatori, 1991: 431–2]. The opposition subsequently boycotted the local elections of June 1990 (although thirty-four independents were to win) and the Nahda militants decided to go even further in the direction of demonstrations and protests. There is no doubt that Ben 'Ali's attitude towards the Islamists had hardened with the passage of time, influenced perhaps by what was seen as the dangerous march of the Islamists in Algeria towards political power. In October 1991 three Islamic activists were executed for an alleged attack on the RCD offices. Many arrests, detentions and trials followed after that and in summer 1992 penalties were imposed on members of a splinter organisation from the Nahda known as the Vanguards of Sacrifice (*Tala'i' al-fida'*), and prison sentences were handed to certain accused among a group of forty-eight members of al-Nahda who were being tried for political corruption and endangering security [*Al-Hayat*, 14, 15 and 16 May 1993].

Although a Higher Assembly for the National Pact continues to exist, the opposition has repeatedly been denied their request for the 1988 elections law to be reformed so as not to allow the RCD such an automatic majority in the assembly. The interest associations continue, in a semi-corporatist way, to participate in the elections on the RCD's list (the labour federation, the farmers' union, the women's association, etc.). The regime also resorted to constraining the activities of the Tunisian League of Human Rights by making it illegal to combine its membership with membership in any political party. The League found it impossible to function and dissolved itself in July 1992. In short, I would generally agree with Fred Halliday's observation that "Bin Ali's post-Bourguibist regime remains as committed to a monopoly of power and to its secular program as did *le combattant suprême* himself" [Halliday, 1990b: 27].[3]

Though the Tunisian regime, like other Middle Eastern regimes, has been prepared to experiment, and to re-experiment with corporatist formulae, there appears still to be (even in the post-populist era) a continuing apprehension about recognising and institutionalising differential interests in an openly corporatist form. Rather, it seems as though there is a distinct inclination to deny the existence of differences and then, as these become stronger, to repress them [cf. Anderson, 1991: 250–51, 257–60].

Jordan

In November 1989 the Jordanians held their first parliamentary elections since the electoral process had, as a result of the Six Day War, been suspended in 1967. In April of that year Jordan had witnessed 'food riots' against the structural readjustment policies required by the International Monetary Fund (IMF), and the riots, which also condemned corruption and asked for greater participation, resulted in a change of government and in a number of liberalising measures. These were aimed partly at compensating for the worsening economic situation and partly at apportioning the prospective burden of blame more widely.

The 1989 elections saw a high rate of electoral registration although in the end the actual turnout was less than 55 per cent of the registered voters. But what came as a surprise to many was the scale of the Islamists' victory in winning thirty-four seats, although a warning had already been signalled in the 1984 supplementary elections in which three vacant seats were won by candidates with Islamic tendencies. This result was an indication of the emergence of the Islamic trend as a serious competitor that would need to be added to the conventional 'tribal' and 'notables' elements which had dominated in previous elections [cf. Al-Sha'ir, 1989: 181–2]. Four candidates from the left, including one Communist, were also elected in 1989, and so were three Ba'thists, and a representative of the Jordan branch of respectively the Popular Front for the Liberation of Palestine and the Democratic Front for the Liberation of Palestine. Seats were reserved, in the conventional micro-consociational manner, for the Christian and the Circassian minorities [*Al-Muntada*, November,1989: 22].

Further liberalisation measures followed the elections. Political parties, hitherto not legal, were allowed to function, the anti-Communist legislation was abolished, and many political prisoners were freed. A sixty-member Royal Commission was formed by the king in April 1990 to draft a 'National Charter' that would regulate political life and represent a common denominator among the various parties and ideologies [Amawi, 1992: 26–7]. A draft Charter was completed in December 1990: it speaks of the State-of-Law and of political pluralism [see on the Charter and the emerging political parties, 'Ayyad, 1991]. The Charter allows the formation of political parties with the proviso that they should function democratically, should not organise within the armed or security forces, and should not be linked to any external organisation – a requirement that is certain eventually to prove quite controversial [Hudson, 1991: 418–20]. Restrictions on travel and employment were removed and most other martial law provisions were lifted in July 1991. With the country's economic difficulties exacerbated by the Gulf crisis of 1990/91, and the suspension of much Arab and Western aid as well as the unplanned return of many Palestinians from the Gulf, the regime has obviously chosen to broaden, rather than to contract the democratisation process. This policy would relieve the regime from having directly to shoulder the full blame for all problems, but the process remains quite precarious because it links the democratisation issue to external factors such as the situation in the Gulf, relations with the Western powers, and prospects for a Palestinian settlement.

The role of the Islamists is also starting to be rather unsettling for the regime. The Muslim Brothers form the largest bloc and the real opposition in parliament – with their allies they control over one third of the legislative body. They disagree with the government over important policies such as the 'limited' settlement of the Palestine problem through the on-going peace negotiations and have boycotted the government of Tahir al-Misri over this issue. Islamists also won the presidency of the medical association, the engineering association and the pharmacists' association and are therefore making their presence felt at the level of associative activity too.

Syria

The Syrian regime would like to count itself among the early liberalisations in the Arab World. The 'corrective movement' initiated in 1970 by the pragmatic faction within the Ba'th (led by Hafiz al-Asad) against the more doctrinaire leftist faction of Salah Jadid, is seen in that light. Asad's virtually uncontested coup of November 1970 was carried out in the name of 'relaxation' of state restrictions and of a partly 'ajar' door (*infiraj*). A limited degree of deregulation followed, first in the commercial sector and then to some extent in the industrial sector.

This did not mean the end of state control over the economy, however, and indeed some further expansion in state-run heavy industry and in import/export and banking had taken place in the late 1970s and early 1980s. Such policy equivocations might have been partly responsible for many dislocations, especially in the regions around Hamah and Homs. Fred Lawson has illustrated how differences in economic organisation between Syria's north central provinces and those in the southern and western parts of the country came to be associated with marked differences in the scale and frequency of political violence in the 1970s and early 1908s. Whereas the regime's policies have encouraged the emergence of a new urban bourgeoisie in the capital and to a lesser extent in Aleppo and Latakia, in the areas around Hamah large landholders provided a focus for rural discontent. Moreover, the considerable number of artisans and merchants associated with small industry in the province provided rural dissidents with potential allies capable of supporting organised political action, with the Muslim Brotherhood providing the overall ideological guidance. Such is the context in which one can understand the Hamah revolt of February 1982 which pitted small-scale merchants, resurgent private landholders, and local Islamic militants against provincial authorities and the managers of state-run factories in a last-ditch struggle against the regime's economic programmes [Lawson, 1989: 20–8]. Its suppression by the regime was made easier through the refusal of small merchants in Damascus and Aleppo, who had closer ties with the public sector, to participate in the revolt on a national level. The Damascus Chamber of Commerce, headed by Badr al-Din al-Shallah, had kept the Damascene bourgeoisie from joining the uprising [Hinnebusch, 1993b: 225]. Eventually it became apparent that the country was ruled by an alliance (which some have called the 'military-commercial complex') where visible power was with a group centred around the top of the state apparatus (including military, party and 'communal' elements), whereas a more diffuse 'invisible sort of power was increasingly being enjoyed by a growing mercantile capitalist class [cf. Kienle, 1991: 214ff]. It is clear therefore that the regime has succeeded in transforming itself from a heterogeneous collection of poor farmers, trade unionists and military officers into a fairly coherent coalition of state administrators and commercial and industrial sponsors, overseeing a hierarchically ordered system of 'popular front organisations' [Lawson, 1989: 22–8].

For the guarded economic liberalisation of the 1970s had involved, among other things, an extension and broadening of the patronage net of the regime from a few cliques and families to a larger proportion of the population. Once the external resources of the regime (mainly Arab aid but also oil revenues and remittances) started to decline and established consumer levels could no longer be sustained, a certain controlled measure of political liberalisation was required to compensate for the austerity measures of the later 1980s and the early 1990s, which were made even more urgent by the decline in East European aid and trade. Although the eclipse of socialism in Eastern Europe had also represented an ideological shock, 'socialist residues' are still defended by a powerful array of interests: party *apparatchiki*, public sector managers, trade unionists, the cooperatives, all of whom would do their utmost to ensure that the liberalisation remains incremental, and firmly under state control [Hinnebusch, 1993c: 185–90].

Thus in May 1990 Syrian voters were asked to elect a new parliament (*Majlis al-Sha'b*, or People's Assembly). The number of seats was expanded from 195 to 250 to encourage 'independent' candidates, for whom about one third of all seats was now reserved, as against two thirds for the Ba'th Party and its allies in the National Progressive Front. In practice, the Front's lists were fully elected, giving about 137 seats to the Ba'th, thirty-one to its allies and eighty-two to independent candidates [Perthes, 1992b: 15–16]. While voters had little choice with regard to the Front's list they could choose from among some 9,000 independent candidates nationwide. Perthes identifies three dominant groups among the independents who won: respected urban upper-middle-class professionals, traditional (including religious) leaders, and merchants and members of the 'new commercial bourgeoisie' [ibid.: 17]. Otherwise, the Ba'th Party bloc has changed little from previous parliaments.

> Syria's parliamentary reform and the elections of 1990 did not intend to develop the *majlis al-sha'b* into a parliament which would regard itself as a counterweight to the executive. The concept of a separation of powers does not correspond with the regime's political and ideological approach. Rather, the Syrian parliament in its present – as in its previous – composition resembles a *majlis al-shura* in the traditional Islamic sense. In terms of modern political science, it is a consultative, quasi-corporatist body ... Syria's parliamentary reform can be understood as a corporatist strategy to respond both to political demands for participation and to the technical demands of organizing an increasingly complex society [Perthes, 1992b: 17–18].

Although various independent businessmen and even Ikhwan-associated figures have been coopted into parliament, as Hinnebusch, who also imparts a corporatist description to these measures [1993b: 256–7], remarks, their permitted role is "to gain access to the State, not to organize as a social force and to check it". And although the incorporation of elements of the bourgeoisie, old and new, into the regime coalition has greatly diluted its populist character, the salaried middle class and the peasantry have not been excluded. If decision-makers reject recommendations for further liberalisation and continue to deploy (expensive) patronage to satisfy key constituents, this may not be explainable solely as a neo-patrimonial capture of the state, but to a certain extent may also reflect a certain *raison d'état* [Hinnebusch, 1993c: 197–201]. The expansion of the Syrian parliament to include a significant number of people from outside the conventional sources of the Ba'th, the Front, the mass organisations and the bureaucracy helps to incorporate new groups into the institutions of the state while serving to diversify the regime's support base to include, in particular, the new commercial class [Perthes, 1992b: 18].

Iraq

To speak about democratisation in relation to Iraq, and however much one may stretch the meaning of this term, seems almost to border on the ridiculous. However, the lack of any serious movement towards democracy and the occasional appearance of false liberalisation signals in the country still warrant explanation.

Samir al-Khalil [1991] has given a vivid, if nightmarish, picture of the reign of terror in Iraq. The Ba'th Party is meant to epitomise democracy within the system and, as Saddam Husain claimed soon after he became supreme, more than one million organised persons practised democracy inside the party on a wide and profound scale [cf. Iskander, 1980: 381–9], a figure that was to reach a million and a half by the mid-1980s, including 25,000 full party cadres. And the party was in principle in alliance with various other national and 'progressive' parties that, theoretically, shared power with it.

The regime has managed to pacify the once important Iraqi Communist Party (ICP) by persecuting its radical wing (the Central Command) and extending a tentative truce to its 'milder' wing (the Central Committee) – that is to say, by virtually dividing the party. In July 1970 the regime announced conditions which, if accepted, would enable certain political forces (the Communist Central Committee included) to join a 'Progressive National Front'. Foremost among these conditions was the recognition of the Ba'th as "a revolutionary, unionist, socialist and democratic party", as well as recognition of its "commanding role in the government, the mass organisations and the front", and also the restriction of political activity within the armed forces exclusively to the Ba'th [Al-Khalil, 1991: 232–3]. In July 1973 a National Charter was framed as a blueprint for the Progressive National Front, and the cabinet symbolically enlisted members of other parties, including most notably two from the ICP for the very first time.

De facto economic liberalisations during the war with Iran were followed, in the aftermath of the conflict, by a series of more formal and ostensibly serious privatisation programmes. To a war-weary society these sounded radical enough because they were also accompanied by significant changes in the official political discourse of the regime. In 1988 President Saddam Husain announced a general pardon of all political prisoners and promised a demo-cratic multi-party system. A month later he started to float the idea of a new constitution that would arrange for direct elections to the presidency, allow formation of opposition parties and a free press, and provide for the dis-mantling of the Revolutionary Command Council. He got this latter group to endorse his proposals in January 1989 and set up a special committee to draft a working memorandum for a new constitution [Karsh and Rautsi, 1991: 197]. In April 1989 the Iraqis went to the polls, for the third time since Husain had attained his supreme position in 1980, to elect a new National Assembly. Non-Ba'thists were allowed to stand for election and half the elected candidates were described as 'independent'. Further manifestation of a more 'liberal' atmosphere also appeared as the state-controlled media began to publish some rather critical items and claims were made about the end of censorship.

It is not entirely clear why Saddam had decided to take this much vaunted democratisation detour during that episode. Like other Machiavellian rulers, he was known for his tactic of periodically enticing his potential critics to come out into the open so that he could measure (and prove) the exact extent of their disagreement with him before condemning them to be purged or executed. Was this an application of the same technique but on the macro level, at the end of a very bitter war when he needed to know how its outcome had affected people's attitudes towards him? Or was the liberalisation process simply a safety valve, to let off steam at a time when he knew that people's expectations of greater prosperity by the end of the war were not going to be realised because of the serious debt with which the economy was now burdened? Either or both of these are possible explanations, as is the suggestion that this liberalisation gesture was targeted at the West in an attempt to improve the image of the country's human rights record in the aftermath of the horrendous atrocities committed by the Iraqi regime in Halabja and elsewhere as the Iran–Iraq war was coming to an end. If this last criterion was the most important then it would also explain why it was unnecessary for Saddam's democratic proclamations to be put into practice. Like several Third World leaders he must quickly have realised that in spite of the indignation of Western public opinion at the slaughter of the Kurds, Western governments and multinationals were more inclined to overlook his domestic excesses in return for lucrative contracts for military and civilian supplies to Iraq [Karsh and Rautsi, 1991: 198–200]. In the meantime, Saddam's real concern was not about his system of government but about how to replenish his financial resources in order to deal with the aftermath of the Iran–Iraq war.

Another 'opportunity' to liberalise appeared to follow on the heels of the 1991 defeat. A regime that has barely survived a humiliating blow by its foreign adversaries and a huge popular revolt against it in the Kurdish north and the Shi'i south might be expected to relax its political constraints or at least to introduce new elements into its government especially from among the less represented communities. On the contrary, power has become even more exclusionary and more tightly consolidated, except in one area represented by a return to the pre-republican practice of relying on tribal chiefs to guarantee the loyalty of their followers [Al-Khafaji, 1992: 20–21].

The 'external factor' was of tremendous importance in constraining the potential for any democratisation process to develop out of the military defeat. It soon became clear that the Western allies were only interested in destroying the military capabilities of Iraq. They would have liked, of course, to see Saddam disappear but what President Bush had in mind when he called on the Iraqis to take things into their own hands was not a popular revolt but a military coup that would keep the country intact and ensure the stability and continuity of Western interests. What the allies got instead was a genuine popular uprising which – although having a democratic potential – was too radical and unpredictable for Western comfort. Furthermore the Kurdish uprising in the north threatened serious regional repercussions for friendly countries like Turkey and the Shi'i uprising in the south carried some un-settling (Islamist) revolutionary implications, whereas the sporadic protests in Baghdad – where things really matter – were late and indeterminate. The relative ease with which the remnants of the Iraqi army were able to save the regime shocked the opposition leaders but it also awakened them to the fact the United States was interested in reducing the Iraqi military threat solely in regional terms, hence the concentration of bombing on the retreating units, which were to play a vital role in the uprising. As Faleh 'Abd al-Jabbar argues:

> The quantitative approach pursued by the US helped rather than weakened the regime's calculations. If the Iraqi military defeat helped detonate the popular revolt, the manner in which this defeat was inflicted undermined the uprising itself. The rout relieved Saddam of the most troublesome part of his army and preserved the most loyal divisions ['Abd Al-Jabbar, 1992: 12–13].

In addition, the Shi'i characterisation given to the uprising by the Western and Arab media, combined with some overstatements by some Shi'i leaders had led to apprehension and robbed the movement of potential regional and international sympathy. The 'Islamist nightmare' changed attitudes towards the uprising and was perhaps responsible for the reports that the rebels were denied access to the Iraqi weaponry and ammunition dumps that were under US control [ibid.: 13].

For the meantime the only opposition to the regime that one hears of is that of the loosely coordinated and inevitably divergent opponents in exile. They managed, with great symbolic effect, to hold a 'national' conference for the opposition in Kurdistan, but their real potential is still subject to many doubts.

Arabia and the Gulf

SAUDI ARABIA Is the Kingdom of Saudi Arabia, as an absolute monarchy with no legislature, political parties or written constitution, in any way affected by the recent tremor of democratisation?

Promises of a 'basic law' of government and of a consultative council (*majlis shura*) are almost as old as the kingdom itself, and they are renewed from time to time – especially at critical moments such as the seizure of the great mosque in Mecca in 1979. The Gulf War of 1990/91 seems, however, to have given embarrassing impetus to the process, and in March 1992 a 'basic law' was issued and it was announced that the formation of a consultative council was due within six months. Although the members of this *majlis* would be chosen by the king and would only be able to propose laws but not to pass them, the formation of such an entirely appointed and purely advisory council was still pending well over a year after it had been promised. Although every attempt was made to emphasise that the Council would have a basically technocratic character, the delay in its formation was perhaps due to the inevitable significance that would be attached to its regional and tribal composition [Al-Hasan, 1993: 2–3]. The Council was at last formed in August 1993 in a manner seeking to 'represent' and balance the various social forces, however symbolically. Over half the members are technocrats (mainly PhDs), and although most members are Najdis the main other regional and tribal communities seem also to be included, while the Shi'is of the east are represented by two members. A number of *'ulama'* is also involved, mostly of mild orientation with the exception of the Head of the Council, Muhammad Ibrahim ibn Juhair, who is a known *'salafi'* [cf. Ghazi al-Qusaibi in *Al-Hayat*, 25 August 1993; and Riyad al-Rayyis in *Al-Dustur*, 27 September 1993]. The king was always anxious to underline the strict limits of political liberalisation in Saudi Arabia: "The prevailing democratic system in the world is not suitable for us in this region", he asserted, further remarking that "elections do not fall within the sphere of the Muslim religion" [quoted in Hardy, 1992: 12–13].

Even before Desert Storm, severe signs of social restlessness and demands for freedom were starting to emerge, as manifested, for example, in the controversy and eventual confrontation over women's right to drive cars, and the need to curtail the growing power of the moral police (*mutawwi's*). Operation Desert Storm and the close involvement of Saudi Arabia on the 'Western' side has meant that potential critics and opponents would include, in addition to liberal and nationalist elements, a growing number of *'ulama'* not happy with the regime's moral and political outlook [Al-'Alawi, 1993: 20–23]. The anxiety of the *'ulama'* was manifested not only in critical sermons and cassette recordings but even more openly in a 'memorandum of advice' signed and circulated by about one hundred of them in 1992, and calling for a greater role for the *shari'a* [*Mudhakkirat al-Nasiha*, 1992]. This was also partly motivated by the fear that increased reliance by the regime on 'positive' laws and techno-political organisations might erode the traditional influence of the *'ulama* on policy-making [Hardy, 1992: 9–15; *Al-Watan al-'Arabi*, no. 203, 7 February 1992]. To counteract the challenge of the clerics' pressure group, a cabinet reshuffle in August 1993 saw the Ministry of Waqf and Hajj Affairs split to form two distinct ministries headed by a 'non-cleric'. At the same time the strict and rather inflexible cleric, Shaikh 'Abd al-'Aziz Ibn Baz, was made the country's *Mufti* (religious authority/counsellor) and the 'moral police' functions (with their annual budget of a billion dollars) taken away from him and given to the new minister of Awqaf [Al-Rayyis, 1993: *loc.cit.*].

Not long afterwards another confrontation – this time involving an odd mixture of Islamists and liberals – was to take place, when an Islamically coloured human rights committee of sorts (*Lajnat al-difa' 'an al-huquq al-mashru'a*) formed by a number of professionals and scholars was banned as 'un-Islamic' and its members dismissed from their jobs [*Al-Watan al-'Arabi*, 28 May 1993; *Guardian*, 14 May 1993; *Observer*, 16 May 1993; *Sunday Times*, 16 May 1993].

It is quite clear from these two examples that the most effective opposition to the regime is most likely to emerge if not from people to the 'right' of the regime, then at least from people who use an Islamically flavoured language in an attempt to outdo the regime at its own game.

KUWAIT Not only was Kuwait the only Gulf country with some experience with elections and 'political life', but it was also the country where Desert Storm generated the highest expectations of democratisation.

Kuwait had a national assembly (*majlis al-umma*) and a relatively free press, and although it had no political parties, it knew fairly organised opposition groupings that often participated in the elections, which ran regularly between 1963 and 1975. The whole thing is, of course, relative in comparison to other Gulf countries, since the franchise is severely restricted to literate Kuwaiti males over the age of 21 who can trace their indigenous lineage back to 1920 or beyond. This excludes not only long-term resident immigrants but all women as well as many Kuwaitis deemed not authentic and deeply rooted *(asil)* enough, and also several thousands who are without Kuwaiti or any other nationality *(bidun)*. So one is talking about a mere 62,000 individuals who, in the early 1990s, had full political rights. Furthermore the Amir dissolved the national assembly twice, in August 1976 and in July 1986, because of criticism of the government and of individual ministers, and on the second occasion some of the constitution's provisions were suspended [Al-Munufi, 1985; 'Assiri and Al-Manoufi, 1988; Gavrielides, 1987; Peterson, 1988; Hardy, 1992]. In the absence of open political life, the *diwaniyya*s (native social and literary salons) as well as voluntary clubs and associations came to play an increasing political role, although they were also frowned upon by the government [Al-Duwaila, 1992; Ghabra, 1991].

Another round of elections was held in June 1990 after negotiations with the opposition groups and partly in response to the pro-democracy street rallies in December 1989 and January 1990. The invasion of Kuwait by Iraq took place in August 1990 and lasted until February 1991. The opposition became more critical of the royal family, the adroit way they had fled the country without any show of defiance, their poor management of the crisis, and their excessive reliance on Western might. The civil society at large strengthened its sinews through subtle acts of mutual assistance and resistance to the Iraqi occupation that were carried out by spontaneously formed organisations such as *harakat al-murabitin* [Al-Shahin, 1992: 32ff]. Expectations for a serious democratic transition after liberation were high, and the liberal-nationalist opposition reorganised itself into a quasi-political party, the Democratic Front, led by 'Abdallah al-Naibari and Ahmad al-Khatib.

But the disappointment was as acute as the expectations had been high. Many factors helped to restore the situation to the *status quo ante*. The escape of the royal family meant that it remained intact, while Saddam Husain failed to recruit an alternative government from among known Kuwaitis. With the invasion and the flight, Kuwait turned from an 'oilfield-state' to a 'treasury-state' and the royal family continued to pay allowances and emoluments to all its citizens abroad (of which there was a large number – since the invasion had occurred in summer and the number of Kuwaitis estimated to have remained during the occupation was no more than 300,000).[4] The policy was continued once the rulers returned, and the 'state' offered to pay all lost salaries and to compensate for most lost possessions and savings of Kuwaiti people. Bad debts worth $20 billion were also bought by the government from banks. This was a continuation of the well-established practice of "Take and shut up!" [Ansar, 1978: 35]. The royal family continued therefore to lay claim not only over the territory of Kuwait but also over the citizens of Kuwait. The 'continued threat' from Iraq could also be evoked, and many people felt that "Better the thief than the murderer" [Hardy, 1992: 20]. The Saudi conservative/authoritarian influence was becoming stronger as a result of her role in hosting the Kuwaiti rulers and in helping with the war effort. The bottled-up emotions of most Kuwaitis were soon to be directed away from the pursuit of 'taking the rulers to task' and towards a brutal, individual and collective settling of scores with Palestinians, Sudanese, Yemenis and all those accused of sympathy with Iraq, an act of diversion that might have been at least partly aided by members of the royal family. Things gradually went back to normal, including the heavy reliance on poorly treated foreign labour.

The promised elections were postponed until October 1992. Women were not given the vote (in spite of the possibility having been hinted at in Jiddah in October 1990) and the franchise remained restrictive, covering only 81,000 voters out of the total population. The turnout was estimated by the authorities at 85 per cent. The results, however, were not completely favourable to the royal family, since more than thirty of the fifty assembly seats were taken by critics or independent-minded candidates, including in particular the Islamists. The winners were distributed as follows: the Democratic Platform two seats; the Constitutional and National Rally ten seats; 'Muslim Brothers' three seats; 'Salafi' Islamists three seats; Shiʻi Islamists three seats; the Islamic Tendency nine seats; Independents ten seats; 'tribalists' ten seats [Al-Amal, October 1992; Al-Muslimun, 20 November 1992]. "It was in effect a vote of no confidence in the postwar government led by Crown Prince Sheikh Saad, who in response introduced a new and more broadly based government but the risk of confrontation, as in 1986, between the parliament and the ruling family remained considerable" [Hardy, 1992: 22]. In spring 1993 the relationship became particularly strained as certain members of parliament tried in vain to find out the names of those whose debts (of some $20 billion) to the banks had been 'bought' by the government during 1992 [Al-Hayat, 29 April 1993].

UNITED ARAB EMIRATES In the UAE things were not as heated – it seemed to be even less open to liberalising than its other small neighbours, Bahrain and Qatar. In Bahrain, which had had a brief experience with an elected assembly between 1973 and 1975, many liberals were disappointed when it was announced in December 1992 that a promised new consultative council would be exclusively appointed by the Amir [Al-Amal, December 1992, January 1993]. In Qatar a petition calling for political reform was presented to the ruler in December 1991, although little has changed in consequence and the country continues to have a purely advisory council (first formed in 1972), currently consisting of thirty members.

In the UAE no important political changes were to follow from the Gulf War. The country continues to have an advisory federal assembly (set up first in 1972) with forty members proportionately selected by the rulers of the various emirates, and political change continues to be to a large extent a function of balancing acts between the various emirates and the various key personalities. Abu Dhabi also has its own fifty-member consultative council based on a largely tribal membership [Peterson, 1988: 91–102].

In the Gulf region as a whole the war against the invasion of Kuwait by Iraq, a country ruled by a regime notorious for its despotism, authoritarianism and infringement of human rights, had raised hopes that the traditional Gulf states might engage in some measure of democratisation, either by way of putting themselves in stark contrast with the Iraqi system, or under pressure from their Western allies who would not want to appear to be the protectors of openly despotic regimes. Most of these hopes have been dashed and the Gulf states are back to 'business as usual', being if anything more prepared to use regional 'threats' as an excuse for not speeding up with the process of political change. They continue with the same remedy: price cuts and financial concessions such as took place in Kuwait, Saudi Arabia and Bahrain. With declining oil prices and growing military spending such policies of 'financial largesse' cannot be continued for ever. What is more, with democratisation now clearly an item on the political agenda, internationally and regionally, the 'compensatory' role of giving financial largesse in return for keeping away political freedom will cease – as it did in the Iran of the 1970s – to be as effective a stratagem as it had been formerly. Rather it will sound like saying to the thirsty: 'Please drink some bread'!

THE YEMENI ADVENTURE

In April 1992 Yemen, the least economically fortunate state in Arabia, held the first comprehensive free elections ever to have been organised in the entire Arabian Peninsula. The singularity of this needs some explanation, and makes one wonder if *Arabia Felix* can act as a happy exemplar or whether this precedent was indeed the exception that proves the rule!

The two Yemens, which united in May 1990, are among the four poorest Arab countries and their unification process was fraught with difficulties. To make things worse, Yemen's independent position during the Gulf War of 1990/91 resulted not only in the expulsion of Yemenis from Saudi Arabia and the suspension of their indispensable remittances but also in the severe and abrupt cutting off of almost all Gulfian and Western aid. And all this was taking place in what is also one of the most densely armed societies in the Arab World.

Yet Yemen is a land of 'articulations' *par excellence* and of a fairly significant consociational/corporatist experience. Even its *qat* sessions[5] where most issues are discussed and many a business or political decision is taken, are set in a status order that assigns the most dignified seating positions to an intricate mixture of political ranking, tribal distinction and modern learning [see Weir, 1985]. We have already seen (in Chapter 7) that sympathetic tribal chiefs were incorporated into the (military) state machine from the early days of the Republic [Stookey, 1984: 253–5]. The incorporation of most tribal leaderships became more extensive in the 1970s and 1980s, and this became part of a much more elaborate corporatist formula under President 'Ali 'Abdallah Salih. Such a formula applied in a relatively strong civil society with a relatively small state machine seems to have partly compensated for the unfavourable factors that disfavour democratisation.

In the 1980s the government gradually extended its control and penetrated the tribal areas in the North and East. This was no longer achieved by force as during the civil war but through the construction of roads, schools and hospitals, relying on oil money and Arab aid. Tribal personnel were offered services and positions in exchange for acquiescence to a slowly growing presence of the state.[6] Although the Constitution of 1970 forbade all political parties, attempts were made by 'Ali 'Abdallah Salih from the time of his

coming to power in 1978 to bring together the political as well as the 'primordial' forces and groups that continued to play a significant role in the life of
the country. Committees were formed in a semi-corporatist fashion from
among various 'nationalist', 'revolutionary' and 'popular' forces, which discussed and ratified the National Charter of 1982 [*Al-Thawra*, 30 December
1986]. A Council aggregating these committees in 1982 included political and
intellectual leaders, tribal chiefs, higher officers and businessmen and was
engaged in long discussions for two years, followed by a referendum and the
formation of the General People's Congress (3,000 members including some
women). In addition, about four hundred syndicates, cooperatives and societies
as well as various tribal and rural consultative councils were organised, and
some of them affiliated to the GPC. The regime has been keen to secure
stability through:

> balancing the various influences present in the Yemeni arena (for example, the
> various intellectual currents and the various tribal formations). Thus, for instance,
> one finds in the *shura* Council that the Speaker is from Bakil (the main tribal
> confederation in Yemen), the deputy-speaker from the Hajariyya region (which
> represents the commercial and administrative sector); the secretary-general is
> from Hashid (the second main tribal confederation) and his deputy from the
> Tihama region [Al-Saqqaf, 1989: 137–8].

Whereas the tribal system (with its own firearms) was allowed to thrive in
the countryside, efforts towards creating a melting-pot and a new national
identity were widespread in the cities. Positions in the government and within
the economic organisations were also used for the purpose of gaining allegiance (although sometimes at the cost of lowering efficiency) and of creating
common interests among the most influential groups: the military, the tribals
and the officials. The whole picture has been complemented by a touch of
'direct democracy' whereby political leaders arrange for a weekly open day
with citizens; the president too runs semi-open functions but allocates in
particular all evenings during the month of Ramadan for meetings with the
'various categories of the society' [Al-Saqqaf, 1989: 138–9]. Fred Halliday has
described this regime as Bonapartist and hybrid:

> The 18th Brumaire of 'Ali 'Abd Allah Salih has created a Yemeni Bonapartism
> ... Their calculation on government consolidation and a prudent Yemeni
> nationalism has led many Yemenis to support this hybrid regime ... a fusion of
> tribal faction, military apparatus, and civilian recruitment [Halliday, 1985: 4–5].

In the meantime, Yemeni civil society continued to be fairly strong. This
was mainly a function of the huge remittances transferred to the country
every year by about a million and a half Yemenis working abroad (mainly in
Saudi Arabia). Excellent work has been done on this subject by Kiren A.
Chaudhry [1989] and some of the following passages will rely a great deal on

that work. One of the most pertinent points is represented by the fact that labour remittances in Yemen almost completely bypassed both the state institutions and the formal banking system. They invigorated an independent and affluent private sector but also provided opportunities for the government to tap remitted funds indirectly through import duties. The bureaucracy grew, but not as much as it did in other Arab countries, and its extractive power did not grow accordingly. The number of personnel employed by the state (excluding education and the public sector) had grown from 91,000 in 1968 to 210,000 in 1979, to 280,000 in 1984 and to a projected 300,000 in 1986 [Ministry of the Civil Service, 1984]. In addition to these being fairly reasonable numbers for a country of Yemen's size, the public service manpower had only trebled in about two decades. This compares to a tenfold increase in Syria in two decades, to eightfold growth in Iraq over a similar period, and to ninefold growth in Egypt in twenty-five years [Batatu, 1983].

Ironically enough, the fiscal crisis precipitated by the fall in oil prices in 1983–84 found the Yemeni government more able to institute a thoroughgoing reform package than was its more prosperous and strong neighbouring state, Saudi Arabia. Unlike oil revenues, labour remittances concentrated economic opportunity in the private sector, where the traditional southern Sunni merchant class not only maintained its dominance but expanded dramatically, as migrants from the south entered the lower echelons of the business community. The northern Shi'i (*Zaydi*) tribal areas, which were not centres for labour export, continued to staff the army and the bureaucracy. "The Yemeni bureaucracy, lacking the financial means to create a system of distribution under conditions of wide-based prosperity, actually augmented its political and social independence from the private sector", while sectarian and regional polarisation between business and the bureaucracy made gains in centralisation and institutional entrenchment possible [Chaudhry, 1989: 103–4, 117].

Between 1971 and 1983 Yemen was the recipient of massive inflows of economic and military aid which averaged 43 per cent of the total state budget. Until the early 1980s Gulf countries paid the total current expenditure encountered by the government, and helped with various services and projects. During the same period labour remittance grew greatly to reach an estimated $3.8 billion to $4 billion, or 126 per cent of the official GNP for the peak year of 1981. Spent largely on consumption of imported goods, remittances indirectly helped with the government's reliance on customs duties, to the increasing exclusion of the previously important agricultural taxes. At the same time, development aid encouraged the centralisation of planning and spending institutions in the Central Planning Organisation. At the level of the society, informal money exchangers provided better rates and costs and more speedy and personal service [ibid.: 130–32].

The most striking effect of remittances was the emergence of over two hundred democratically elected grassroots organisations in the southern part of the country. These cooperatives were funded by local donations from a surplus created by labour remittances. As the central administration withdrew from the countryside, local populations formed development cooperatives that undertook the development of infrastructure, education and health. Development expenditure by these cooperatives outstripped government project spending by over 300 per cent in the period from 1973 to 1980. The cooperatives eventually took on an overtly political character and recognising both the potential and the threat of the independent cooperatives, the government aggregated them under the central umbrella of the Confederation of Yemeni Cooperatives in 1978. Although the central government largely abrogated control over local revenues (taking only 25 per cent of local *zakat* dues),

> it gained a political infrastructure, buttressing its administrative weaknesses by legitimizing and co-opting local power. In the recession, the expression of demands suddenly changed direction: the local development cooperatives were to undergo yet another transformation in the service of expanding the administrative authority of the central state [Chaudhry, 1989: 134].

After the recession, the regional/sectarian composition of the bureaucracy that had kept it autonomous from the business community became entwined with the economic interests of the state as the latter struggled, from 1983, to replace diminishing aid revenues with local taxes. In 1986/87, following a decline in the market exchange rate of the Yemeni *riyal*, the state moved in swiftly and by curbing the speculative market, closing down money-changers and regulating the activities of commercial banks, ensured that all foreign currency was immediately transferred to the Central Bank – a job, incidentally, that the presumably 'strong' Egyptian state was unable successfully to fulfil around the same time [cf. Ayubi, 1991b: 230ff], but one that was achieved in Yemen "through a series of measures that are astonishing in their simplicity and in the impunity with which they were enforced" [Chaudhry, 1989: 137–41]. The state also stepped into the area of importing and strictly regulated retailing prices. Taxes were collected from the commercial class on a retroactive basis covering the previous six years. Important reorganisation reforms were introduced in the taxation, land registry and other branches, and the government used the local development cooperatives to extend administration into the countryside by merging the *Zakat* Department with the Local Councils and thereby transforming existing institutions into the local administration of the country. Locally elected officials of the cooperatives were named the mayors, tax collectors and assessors. "The experience of Yemen illustrates the importance of strong civil groups for effective state action, and lays bare the danger of regarding state and civil strength as a zero-sum relationship. In Yemen, strong local groups organized along democratic lines were aggregated at the center" [ibid.: 141–2, 145].

The overall picture that one gains of North Yemen just before the unification is therefore that of a country with many economic problems but one that, socially and politically, is full of 'articulations' and balances and counter-balances. The society has its lively social groupings, and the state apparatus – although small in size – is fairly 'autonomous' and increasingly penetrating the society and regulating it. The state in many ways 'complements' rather than 'contradicts' the society.

The picture in South Yemen on the eve of the union was not as flowery, but not really much simpler. In spite of the regime's achievements in the area of education and family and social affairs, the economy was in a critical situation because of the decline both in Soviet-bloc aid and in workers' remittances. Politically the bloodbath of January 1986, in which President 'Ali Nasir Muhammad's pre-emptive strike at a rival and reputedly more radical faction led to his own defeat, set in motion a process of soul-searching among the survivors and to a decision within the Yemeni Socialist Party to liberalise prior to the launching of the unity movement [Hudson, 1991: 423]. The bloody street fighting of 1986 was itself the result of unresolved contradictions and unmediated 'articulatory' realities. As the single openly Marxist regime in the Arab World, installed in one of the most tribally-conscious parts of that world, the regime had formally regarded 'de-tribalisation' as one of its prime policies. Because the army had been tribally based prior to independence, the new conscription system was instituted in a way that would, through training, placements and promotion, de-tribalise the institution. Furthermore, all licences of clubs, societies and organisations of a tribal character were cancelled and their branches closed. The regime tried instead to regroup the population, in a semi-corporatist fashion, into modern-type 'progressive' organisations: mainly the General Union of Yemeni Workers, but also the Peasants' Union, the Youth Union and the Women's Union. In the residential areas, People's Defence Committees were set up according to the Cuban model, as neighbour-hood groups with wide responsibilities. A popular militia was also established and could mobilise up to 100,000 members. However, the de-tribalisation efforts were not fully and thoroughly successful [Lackner, 1985: 99–102, 110–12]. This was made dramatically clear in the 1986 events in which, in the brutal struggle for power, ideological and foreign-policy issues became confusingly overlapped with personal and tribal impulses and resulted in the tragic street fighting in Aden and elsewhere [cf. Halliday, 1990a: 41–53; Al-Azmina al-'Arabiyya, October 1986: 8–10].

In retrospect these events were so shattering to anyone who witnessed them that in a curious way they inspired a certain sense of the futility of violence and prompted a quest for a measure of mutual understanding. Bordering as it did on civil war, this trauma, like many wars in history, might actually have had a certain 'civilising' effect on the population. The regime began slowly but surely to open up, and even in April 1990, weeks before the ratification of the unification agreement, the South Yemeni parliament was expanded from

III to 133 members and, in addition to representatives of the conventional 'toiling forces', was to have a quota of 20 per cent of the seats allotted to "representatives of patriotic forces, independent personalities and representatives of national capitalism" [Naba, 1990: 104].

Following the unification of the two Yemens in 1990, government was held jointly by the General People's Congress (GPC) of the North and the Yemeni Socialist Party (YSP) of the South. The unification heralded an extraordinary wave of political activity and openness involving the formation of new political parties and a fairly free media exchange and criticism. The Gulf crisis of 1990/91 only enhanced the public debate, and Yemen's independent position instilled a distinct sense of pride, even though the sudden suspension of Saudi, Kuwaiti and Iraqi aid, the embargo on Iraqi oil shipments, the collapse of tourism and the decline in regional commerce collectively cost Yemen nearly $2 billion in 1990 [cf. Carapico, 1991: 26].

A new Constitution was approved in May 1991, stipulating an independent legislature and guaranteeing basic rights as well as rights of political expression and association. Parliamentary elections were meant to take place in November 1992 but were postponed to April 1993 amid fears that the two governing parties would continue to share power indefinitely. Nearly forty political parties were announced, but the important ones, in addition to the governing two, were the Yemeni Reform Rally (*Al-Islah*) representing a certain tribal/Islamist mix under the leadership of Shaikh 'Abdallah al-Ahmar, chief of the Hashid tribal confederation, the Ba'th (Iraq line), the Nasserists, and Al-Haqq (a mildly Islamic party) [*Al-Majalla*, 24 June 1992; *Al-Wasat*, 2 November 1992].

Against all the odds, the elections were eventually held and by all accounts were conducted fairly, thus vanquishing the fears either of a suffocating Egyptian or Tunisian model (that would ensure by all possible means that the ruling party was the only one that could win significantly), or of a tragic 'Algeria syndrome' (that would arrest the process at the half way point once it was anticipated that the results would be unfavourable to the ruling party). This latter fear was markedly present and indeed some maintained that the hurried act of unification was itself largely an attempt by the two ruling groups to form an alliance that would be able to face the growing influence of the Islamists in the two Yemens [cf. Naba, 1990: 106]. Following the unification, there were many assassinations, especially of cadres of the YSP, most of which were blamed on the Islamist Al-Islah, a party that had formed a junior ally to the governing party in North Yemen in recent years and which was therefore politically, not to mention ideologically, unhappy about the new partnership with the Socialists.

In the elections the General People's Congress won 123 seats out of 301 (140 seats if its 'independent' supporters are added), including the only two successful women; the YSP won sixty-nine seats (eight-two if its supporters are added); and the Yemeni Reform Rally – more its tribal than its fundamentalist wing – won sixty-eight seats. The Ba'th took seven seats, the Nasserists three and Al-Haqq took two [*Al-Hayat*, 1, 5 and 9 May 1993; *Al-Majalla*, 26 May 1993].

Democracy had thus triumphed. But this was no Western-style liberal democracy. It was a kind of *democradura pactada*, but with distinct consociational dimensions. This is clear, first, from the fact that from the time of unification in May 1990 to May 1993 the GPC and the YSP had jointly ruled in a power-sharing arrangement. Their tacit pact was declared in written form in March 1993 (*mithaq al-'amal al-siyasi*) and was open for other parties and associations that support the principle and objectives of the two Yemeni revolutions, democracy and national integrity. An intermediation organ was to be formed to coordinate among the signatories. A special appendix was prepared after the election results on coalition with Al-Islah.

When the results of the elections were declared, the secretary-general of the YSP, 'Ali Salim Al-Bid (subsequently to become the deputy-president), spoke in a conciliatory tone and in distinctly Gramscian terms of the need to forge a 'historic bloc' inside the new house of deputies and to form a coalition government of the three parties with the largest votes [*Al-Hayat*, 5 May 1993]. In an unmistakeably power-sharing formula (rather reminiscent of Lebanon) it was agreed that while 'Ali 'Abdallah Salih, the leader of the GPC, would continue as president, Haydar al-'Attas of the YSP would continue as prime minister, while Al-Ahmar, leader of Al-Islah, was elected as speaker of the house. Ministries were also distributed in a proportionate way: fifteen for the GPC, nine for the YSP and four for Al-Islah.[7]

Yet the optimism could not last for long. From the beginning the experiment was extremely fragile, as within it the process of unification and the process of democratisation were so intricately intertwined. In a certain sense the two processes were also contradictory to each other and the end result of enforcing unity on the South by arms, in July 1994, was achieved at the expense of democratic transformation. Thus for example the idea of merging the two ruling parties in May 1993 might have enhanced the unification process but would almost certainly have constrained the democratisation drive. In any case, the election results themselves were indicative of the entanglement between the two processes, since the GPC (and the Islah) had won over-whelmingly in the Northern and Western provinces whereas the YSP had won overwhelmingly in the Southern and Eastern provinces. Neither of the two leading parties had thus managed to attract a substantial constituency in the previous geographic domain of the other.

Although the elections were followed by various steps ostensibly aiming at power-sharing, most of these were regarded by the ex-'Southern' leadership as being unfair. Whereas President Salih was apparently trying to cut the YSP down to a size that perhaps corresponded to the South's demographic weight (20 per cent of all Yemeni population), the Southern leadership were thinking in different terms. The YSP, they reckoned at the meeting of their Central Committee in November 1993, had contributed a whole state and two thirds of all land, all wealth and all cadres to the Union, and accordingly its contribution ought to be rewarded in the power-sharing process [cf. W. 'Abd al-Majid, 1994]. 'Ali al-Bid went several times into a state of *i'tikaf* (i.e. retreating to his home region, though without resigning, to express his displeasure), the most serious episode of which started in August 1993. From that date he and several other leaders of the YSP started to accuse Salih of authoritarianism and to hint that his 'apparatus' was responsible for repeatedly assassinating many of their cadres. In the meantime the YSP put in several proposals for 'concrete' power-sharing. Some, such as a more flexible local government system, were accepted and some, such as the election of both the president and his deputy (rather than the existing system of the former selecting the latter) were not. The Socialists then came up with their most daring proposal, which was an alternative federal or even confederal formula for the Union. In the meantime the 'civil society' seemed to be moving ahead of the state institutions towards advancing the cause of both unity and pluralism. Political debate multiplied at all levels, while a 'dialogue committee' of thirty distinguished political and intellectual personalities (in and outside government) was formed to discuss ways out of the impasse. In early 1994 they came up with the draft of a 'pact' (*wathiqt al-'ahd w'al-wifaq*) spelling out comprehensive reforms. The pact was positively received by an overwhelming majority of the public and the intellectuals, and even though it was basically accepted and signed by the two leaders in Jordan in February 1994, the two sides continued to stall with regard to implementation, thus failing to live up to the momentum created by the civil society [compare Carapico, 1994: 24–7].

Several regional and international attempts at reconciling the positions of the two leaderships were also unsuccessful, and, given that the armies of the North and the South were never seriously unified, it became increasingly clear that war was going to be the final arbiter. A battle was launched by the president against the 'forces opposed to legitimacy and union'. Lasting for just over two months, from May to July 1994, it ended in the imposing of unity by arms but at the expense of sacrificing further democratisation. Although a general amnesty (excluding sixteen of the top Southern leaders) was declared, and the YSP was not liquidated but requested to 'reconsider its position with regard to unity', there are serious fears that the democratisation process may indeed end up being the victim of a unification process that could only be achieved by force.

PUBLIC/PRIVATE; CIVIL/CIVIC

It should be clear by now that although the process of democratic transformation still leaves much to be desired, there can be no denying that practically all Arab societies are now far more complex and pluralistic than they were three or four decades ago. Not only is the public economic sector in desperate straits, but the various interest groups are making their presence increasingly noticeable, and the radical Islamic movements are increasingly challenging the moral legitimacy of the state.

Is the 'civil society' striking back at last, and is the emerging private sector managing in any way to counterbalance the dominant Statal sector? Such questions lie behind a number of current and on-going debates in the Arab World, including, for example, the one that concerns the 'democratic potential' of the Islamic movements. There are those who believe that these movements with their alternative network of schools, clinics and banks represent a revival of the forces of the civil society (or at least of the private sector) vis-à-vis the omnipotent state [cf. Ayubi, 1991a: Ch. 8]. On the other hand there are those who prefer to distinguish between the 'civil' (ahli) and the 'civic' (madani) and imply that the Islamist revival would not benefit the latter because of its anti-secularist and often anti-modernist (including anti-nationalist) inclinations.

The specific characteristics of culture and society in the Muslim world add some unusual complexities to this already intricate debate. First, the 'private' in the Arabo-Islamic society is not only understood in contrast to what is public in the modern sense of being 'statal' but may also be construed as part of a dichotomy between 'domesticity' and 'sociability' (i.e. between the hidden, covered, withdrawn; and the open, revealed, expressed). In Muslim as in some Mediterranean societies, life is often 'lived in public', and all things in life acquire a certain cruel publicity. Matters of personal conduct, sex and the family are often regarded as public morals that should be enforced collectively [Ayubi, 1991a: Ch. 2]. The family has not (yet?) developed into an island of privacy and intense intimacy in the way it has on the whole done in North European and North American societies. The 'public' realm is a realm of sociability mediated by conventions that allow social distance to be maintained despite physical proximity – this world is in some ways less intimate, but it is also less impersonal [compare Weintraub, 1990]. The private here is that narrow behavioural sphere subject to personal or individual control, whereas the public is that (wider) behavioural sphere subject to social or collective control [compare also Kaminski, 1991: 263, 337ff].

In the Middle East the breakdown of the older 'public' realm of poly-morphous sociability (the market-place, the public bath, the coffee house) has not yet been accompanied by a sharp polarisation of social life between an increasingly 'public' realm (of the market and the state) and a 'private' realm of intense intimacy and emotionality ('modern' family and love, etc). The word 'privacy' does not exist in Arabic and the concept is difficult to explain to the average Arab (although the concept of a formalised 'sanctuary' or a secluded zone forbidden to strangers, haram, is known). The inward-looking traditional Arab house centred around the courtyard insulated the house partly from the harsh weather conditions and partly from the unrelenting public gaze [cf. Fathy, 1973; Ezaki, 1991]. The 'public space' here is a space of symbolic display, of interaction rituals and personal ties, of physical proximity coexisting with social distance. It is not conventionally a space for collective political action and is only rarely a space for a discourse that addresses common concerns. This latter type of space I prefer to describe as *civic*: it is the realm of public debate and conscious collective action or, in a word, of citizenship.

As explained by Julien Freund, Jürgen Habermas and others [cf. Sales, 1991], the civic culture cannot be imagined in the absence of the state. Although it is the area of the public sphere that is closest to the state, it is still basically part of the civil society. The mediating function between the state and society is vested in special interest associations and unions (private sphere) and in political parties (public sphere) that together constitute the civic domain. In other words, the civic realm is that part of the public sphere that is not colonised by the state bureaucracy and the system of public administration. In short therefore, civic society is the more political and more institutionalised boundary of civil society. To paraphrase some of the tenets of Arnand Sales, the civil society is a place of association and social integration where mediations take place between individuals and groups, groups and social institutions, social institutions and political and economic institutions; a place where social identities and new lifestyles are formed, which is diversified but not divided. The more 'civic' end of that civil society is the locus of public opinion formation and resulting struggles. It is a domain that is primarily linked to the state, a domain possessing fundamental ties with democratic systems as a condition for its existence and development [Sales, 1991: 208–9]. The relationship between state and society should be viewed as both conflictual and complementary. "Democratization is neither the outright enemy nor the unconditional friend of State power. It requires the State to govern civil society neither too much nor too little, [because] while a more democratic order cannot be built *through* state power, it cannot be built *without* State power" [Keane, 1988: 23].

In light of all this, what are the roots of the civil society and the civic culture in the Arab World, to what extent can one regard the rise of Islamicist movements as a sign of revival of the civil society, and what are the implications of such a rise for the potential development of a civic culture in the Arab World?

Let us begin first by taking stock of the fact that Islamists now form the main opposition groups in most Arab societies and the largest opposition group in most parliaments that allow opposition representation [cf. Esposito and Piscatori, 1991]. Since democracy is not only about representation and participation but also about opposition or formal contestation [Dahl, 1971], the Islamists have become in practice and in objective terms part of the democratisation process in many Arab countries. A brief review should make this factually clear.

In Egypt, the Muslim Brothers, in alliance with the Wafd Party, won twelve seats in 1984, and in 1987, in alliance with Labour, won thirty-six seats, but they boycotted the November 1990 elections as a way of protesting against government restrictions. In Jordan, the Muslim Brothers won twenty-two seats in the November 1989 elections, and twelve more seats went to other Islamists. Subsequently they also gained in several local elections. The speaker of parliament was a member of the Muslim Brothers and in January 1991 the Brothers were given five cabinet posts (although some were excluded later on). The 1993 elections reduced the number of Islamists in the parliament but not significantly: it brought in sixteen 'organised' and ten independent Islamists – together representing near enough to a quarter of the total of deputies.

In Tunisia the MTI (Mouvement de la Tendance Islamique, later called Al-Nahda) participated in the parliamentary elections of April 1989. Islamist candidates won 14.4 per cent of the country's vote and about 30 per cent in important cities such as Tunis, Sousse and Gabes, but failed to win any seats in parliament. In the Kuwait elections of November 1992 Islamists won at least nineteen of the seats (compared to four seats in the 1981 Assembly), thus making big strides even in this recently liberated 'traditional' principality. Even in Lebanon, the 1992 elections brought to parliament eleven Islamists of various orientations plus three more elected on the 'Islamic list'.

In Algeria the events were, of course, particularly dramatic [cf. Mortimer, 1991]. In the June 1990 municipal elections the FIS (Front Islamique du Salut) won an incisive victory, taking 54 per cent of the vote (against 34 per cent for the ruling FLN) and predominating in thirty-two out of the forty-eight governorates, including Algiers, and in 853 out of 1,539 local councils (with the FLN taking only 487). Intoxicated with such an unexpected triumph, which was perhaps more a vote against the FLN than a vote for the FIS, the Islamists demanded that the general parliamentary elections should be brought forward and that the election laws were to be amended. Taking to the streets, their slogans were often openly anti-democratic and they subsequently engaged with the police in violent skirmishes. The regime appears to have assumed that such a show of violence and destruction would have illustrated to the public the anti-democratic inclinations of the Islamists and that their popularity with the electorate would thus have been reduced. The parliamentary elections went ahead in December 1991. The level of apathy was high: the majority of potential FLN supporters or FIS opposers did not vote, with the stunning result that the FIS won 188 out of 231 seats, with twenty-eight seats left for a second round of voting that was to have been held on 1 January 1992 but did not take place, due to a military-backed 'palace coup' having taken over power.

It is possible, broadly speaking, to interpret the rise of Islamism as a contest with the state over public space. The post-independence Arab state has tended to impart to public space a distinctly *economic* meaning (hence the indigenisation and nationalisation of firms and the creation of many 'public' enterprises). Politics was turned into economics, and the state encroached on the civil society via the public economic sector. The failure or exhaustion of this model, and the exclusion and marginalisation of some of the upwardly mobile segments of the society that ensued, have resulted in the rise of radical Islamic movements in many Arab societies [for details see Ayubi, 1991a]. The Islamists struck back at the state by imparting to the public space a distinctly *moralist* colouring. They invoked ethics as the substance of politics and lashed out at the state with the whip of public morality.[8]

The point is that neither the state nor the Islamists have been willing to address politics head-on as the main concern of the public space: the state has emphasised economics and the Islamists have emphasised morals, while the distinctly political 'civic realm' continues to be impoverished.

Partly because Arab regimes have resisted public/private 'transparency' and partly because the *economic* private sector remains subservient to the state, it is the *'cultural'* private sector – so to speak – that currently represents the main challenge to the state, in the form of the Islamist organisations. And these organisations are of course partly formal and declared, and partly illegal and underground, which rather complicates the issue of whether the Islamic trend can help in constructing a veritable civic culture and a viable democratic process.

A review of some of the recent Arab discourse on the subject may help in arriving at some answers. We start with Al-Tahir Labib, the Tunisian sociologist, who argues that although differing opinions and movements were known in Islamic history, they had no cumulative effect that would have resulted in the emergence of a recognisable 'civil society'. The concepts and demands resulting from these movements have "only reached us as rejected deviance or strife. They did not reach us as 'liberal' or revolutionary concerns, but we imparted such a colouring to them in an attempt to Arabise or Islamise our current concerns" [Labib, 1992b: 339–49]. He agrees with 'Abd al-Rahman al-Kawakibi that in the 'East' man might have rebelled but his rebellion was against the despot, not against despotism as such [Al-Kawakibi, 1984: 107–8]. The *political* concept of liberty was an importation from Europe, and its adoption was often forced on the Arabs by the big powers for their own colonial and capitalistic reasons and usually as a prelude to or an accompaniment for occupying these countries [Labib, 1992b: 351–6].

Colonialism did, of course, activate the civil society against the colonial power. But this activation was mainly for the purpose of *national* independence and not as a search for civic freedoms. Such a context had created a cleavage between the state and civil society: resistance against the former by the latter has continued to this day to be its main inclination. 'Mutual exclusion' between the state and society is still characteristic of the relationship, rather than complementarity through dialectical conflict. What lies between the state and society in the Arab World is not a 'space' but a 'vacuum' [Labib, 1992b: 356]. Whatever democratic procedures were applied under colonialism were manifestations of a 'subjugational democracy' (*dimuqratiyya ikhda'iyya*) in the sense of forcing the 'bastards' to be free in spite of themselves [ibid.: 358]. And many of these semi-democratic measures were in any case suppressed after independence in the name of nationalism and development. The current revival of interest in society and more specifically in the still vague and controversial concept of civil society is important but it is still confined, for understandable reasons, to the level of pre-civic democratisation (*dimuqratiyya qabl madaniyya*). It is manifested in charitable associations and in popular 'uprisings'; it is perhaps more of a post-totalitarian transition than it is a definite democratic transition [ibid.: 361–6].

But how would the Islamic movements fit within such a post-totalitarian transition? It is important to observe here that although the term 'civil society' (*mujtama' madani*) is used frequently in the Arab debate, its connotations are not always specified. The secularists in particular usually use the term in the sense of the *civic* society, and tend to exclude the Islamic movements from its compass. Thus one is told, for example, that the concept of 'civil society' is used in the Arab Maghrib, and especially in Tunisia, as a weapon against the Islamists [Al-Zaghal, 1992: 438].

The Syrian political scientist Burhan Ghalyun has also detected a distinct attempt to contrast the concept of the civic society (*al-mujtama' al-madani*) with that of the civil society (*al-mujtama' al-ahli*). This attempt springs, in his view, from a political utilisation of the concept as a means of confronting the trends and the movements regarded by the modernists as 'carriers of traditional values'. In this case, 'civic society' is equivalent to modern organisations and structures such as political parties, trade unions and women's associations, and such a concept is to be used as an instrument of war against the old structures of society that are of a religious, tribal or regional nature. In the current discourse of Arab political thought, such a division represents, in Ghalyun's view, a recent attempt at reviving the doctrine of modernity, after the eclipse that it suffered as a result of the failure of leftist and socialist projects. This revival is attempted, this time in the name of democracy, through a new alliance between the modern élites that are scared of social demotion and the monopolistic state which is regarded as the only guarantor for the continuation of modernity and rationalisation [Ghalyun, 1992: 733–5].

Yet the civil society is not (as some present it) a reservoir of liberty and democracy as such, but is rather one of diversity, contradictions and partial solidarities, maintains Ghalyun. The state develops not by obliterating, but by surpassing these divisions and confrontations in an innovative way. He argues that our definition of the civil society should therefore include both the primordial and the associative groups and that there is no point in distinguishing between them without running the risk of depriving the society of its natural dynamism and creative capabilities [ibid.: 736–9]. The state in the Arab World, not having grown organically and structurally out of its own society, has aspired to 'develop' that society by interpolating 'politics' in lieu of social, cultural and economic affairs, and by extending bureaucracy everywhere. Yet this state has not succeeded in tackling the problems of its hybrid, cross-bred society (mujtama' hajin) but has gradually killed off the whole creature instead:

> For the socially alien State has feared its own society and regarded every move, signal or whisper emanating from the civil society as political opposition, a rejection of the authority of the State, and a direct threat to the existence of the Community, the Nation and the Revolution. This has driven the State to turn inwards, towards its own coercive forces, which are developed at great expense – not to provide for the needs of the society but to maximise the means for crushing it [Ghalyun, 1992: 744–5].

Since the state has managed to encircle the society to this extent, the only way to go around the encirclement is to revive and re-engage all sub-political structures of the civil society by way of pumping in new blood and reviving the various social forces so that they can participate in due course in the process of political change. These include the mosques, zawiyas, religious orders and brotherly solidarities that have been re-embraced by the popular forces, at a time when nationalist and leftist élites are still struggling (partly because they are unable to abandon their gamble on the state) to turn their civilian associations and societies (including human rights organisations) into viable structures for rejuvenating the civil society. Muhammad 'Imara would also add the awqaf institution as a major bastion of the civil society and an organisation that has helped the 'nation' historically in surmounting the lapses of the 'state' ['Imara, 1993]. To exclude the new Islamic social forces from any perception of the civil society, Ghalyun maintains, would be nothing more than an attempt by the dominant élite to re-legitimise its own authoritarianism in the name of protecting the integrity of society and the unity of the state. It is no longer possible to reconstruct civil society in the Arab World on the basis of forming a few small associations here and there. It is crucial to think strategically and at the level of politics – but not necessarily through a fixation on the state or on state policies. Politics should be perceived beyond and above the state, preferably in terms of 'civilisational' spheres [Ghalyun, 1992: 745–55].

This brief explanation should give us an idea of some of the debates that surround this issue in the Arab World. But to return more specifically to our earlier question, can one regard the Islamic movements not only as part of a reviving civil society but also as part of an emerging civic culture? And is it at all possible that radical Islamism may eventually become a force for longer-term pluralisation?

Most 'fundamentalist' groupings act, in the immediate instance, as a counter-democratic force: they frighten regimes off initiating further liberalisation while pushing them increasingly towards adopting parts of the Islamists' (anti-secularist and anti-humanist) platform. But is it completely beyond the bounds of the possible that radical Islamism may eventually become a force for long-term democratisation [compare Binder, 1988], by virtue of the fact that it currently acts as one of the few effective anti-state forces in Arab societies?

If one is to think in terms of historic parallels, it is perhaps possible to see Protestantism, especially in its Calvinist form, as having been just as much of a discourse against the state's absolute authority in society as it was a force for capitalist development. Could the radical Islamic movement likewise come eventually to form the basis for a post-absolutist political order in a country like Egypt, for example? And even though the Islamist groups themselves may remain rather authoritarian and fairly anti-democratic, could the whole process nonetheless be heading in a democratic direction?

Proceeding from earlier suggestions by E. Gellner, C.H. Moore and N. Ayubi, Ellis Goldberg has argued, in an extremely interesting article, that this is a conceivable possibility:

> Both Calvinism and the contemporary Islamist Sunni movements in Egypt are discourses on the nature of authority in society. Historically, both movements arose as central state authorities made absolutist claims to political power and in the process sought to dominate transformed agrarian societies in new ways. Ideologically, both movements asserted that the claims of sweeping power by nominally religious secular authorities were blasphemous egotism when contrasted with the claims of God on the consciences of believers. Socially, both movements transferred religious authority away from officially sanctioned individuals who interpret texts to ordinary citizens. Institutionally both movements create communities of voluntary, highly motivated and self-policing believers that yield greater degrees of internal cohesion and compliance than the absolutist authority can achieve and they therefore can become the basis for postabsolutist political authority in an authoritarian and antidemocratic fashion [Goldberg, 1991: 3–4].

This is an interesting theoretical possibility indeed – but many in the Middle East (especially among those subjected to the violence of the 'fundamentalists') would doubt its practical probability in the foreseeable future.

NOTES

1. Two other factors about 'culture' should also be mentioned in passing in order to complement the picture. One is the noticeable impact of the 'British factor': i.e. the more likely tendency of ex-British settler societies or colonies to opt for democracy [Ware, 1992: 140–41]. The second is what one may call the 'addiction factor': although in the 1990s the wave of democratisation has started to affect countries without significant previous democratic experience, twenty-three out of

the twenty-nine countries that democratised between 1974 and 1990 had in fact had previous experiences with democracy [Huntington, 1991: 44].

2. The most colourful description of praetorianism is that given by G. O'Donnell [1973]. "In a praetorian system, social forces confront each other nakedly ... Each group employs means which reflect its peculiar nature and capabilities. The wealthy bribe; students riot; workers strike; and the military coup" [76–7].

3. This was symbolically illustrated by a televised token visit to Bourguiba by Bin 'Ali in May 1993 in which he described him as "our father, from whom we learned everything".

4. Even more cynically Sa'd al-Din Ibrahim has termed Kuwait a 'hotel-state' where the 'guest-citizen' is used to five-star service provided by hordes of servants and maids from all over the world. All that happened was that Kuwaitis who were abroad during the invasion "replaced their familiar luxury hotel with other temporary hotels for seven months"! [Ibrahim, 1992: 292, 297] It remains to be seen whether the stark difference between the experience of those who were inside and those who were out of the country might have any longer-term political implications.

5. *Qat* is a mildly narcotic leaf widely chewed in Yemen and to a lesser extent in parts of East Africa.

6. A poem by 'Abd al-Dayim al-Malakhi published in December 1987 symbolises this process exquisitely. In it he addresses his telephone, silenced by a fault in the system, and begs it to resume its dialogue with him. Acknowledging that installing it was an achievement of the Revolution of no less significance than the postal service, the irrigation canals, the highways and the petroleum oil fields, he nevertheless complains that until this remarkable equipment, so lamentably out of order, is working again he will remain cut off, deprived of the means to ring up to greet his cousin and the great 'Ali (i.e. 'Ali 'Abdallah Salih, the president).

7. The passages on the Yemeni adventure as it developed during 1994 were written a year after the main body of the case study had been completed, and hence the far less optimistic tone.

8. An underlying assumption behind this statement is that whereas *exploitation* seems often to give rise to class struggles, *exclusion* seems often to give rise to cultural struggles. Because the Arab *state* (and not an autonomous *class*) has been the main entrepreneur within the society, the issue of exploitation seems to be overshadowed by those of control, domination and exclusion. In response, cultural struggles (as spearheaded by the Islamic movements of the marginalised urban youth) take precedence over class struggles and often mask them, but without completely covering them.

CHAPTER TWELVE

Conclusion: the 'Strong', the 'Hard' and the 'Fierce'

That the Arab state is an authoritarian state, and that it is so averse to democracy and resistant to its pressures should not, of course, be taken as a measure of the strength of that state – indeed, quite the reverse.

We have seen earlier that two types of regime, expressed by two similar-sounding Arabic words, predominate in the Arab World: one relying for its survival mostly on political capital revolving around categories such as nationalism, populism, radicalism and *revolution* (*thawra*); the other relying for its survival on kin-based relations, but above all else on financial capital, or *wealth* (*tharwa*). However, on closer scrutiny it transpires that neither of these systems is as politically strong as it first appears. Both could grow bureaucratically and expand economically. But *expansion* is of course the 'easy phase' in economic development. The real powers of regulation of these states are less impressive. Their capabilities for law enforcing are much weaker than their ability to enact laws, their implementation capabilities are much weaker than their ability to issue development plans.[1] These states have 'annexed' parts of the society and the economy 'from the outside', without penetrating the society at large. Waddah Sharara expresses it most powerfully:

There is nothing new about the State (i.e., the apparatus of domination) trying to confront social disintegration and to consolidate the society. What is historically special [in the case of the Arab State] is that this State has not emerged as a result of an internal conflict that had divided the society and its blocs, enabling one of them to establish its dominance through a long process involving the actual condensation of contradictions in society ... The State in our societies was, by contrast, born as an 'external' power, thus rendering it – together with its personnel, apparatuses and intellectuals – marginal in the literal sense. It has not succeeded in overcoming its marginality even at the peak of its dominance when it held the reins of government, political organisation, the means of production and the official ideology. It has, therefore, faltered at the first shock, and the carefully erected facade has cracked open to reveal all manner of horrid monsters that many thought History had long since laid to rest [1980: 228].

The 'radical' (*thawri*) systems (with the apparently self-imposed exception of Tunisia in this respect) could also recruit large armies and sustain them for lengthy periods and through several wars or conflicts (Iraq was claimed to possess the fourth largest army in the world). They could mobilise the populace (via education, the media and social welfare programmes), but they could not as effectively *integrate* the newly mobilised social forces (partly because their economic and industrial plans had not yielded the required accelerated development). They suffer from a 'hegemony crisis': a mildly prolonged fiscal crisis (often resulting from the very contradictory nature of their economic policies) is sufficient to tear away the thin veneer of their populist ideology and to reveal that it is more of an eclectic blueprint than it is of a genuine self-sustaining 'world-view'. Once their powers of (coercive) expropriation are exhausted, it becomes clear that their powers of (politico-economic) extraction, via direct taxation, are seriously impaired.

The 'wealthy' (*tharwi*) regimes of the oil-exporting countries, on the other hand, are excessively vulnerable and extremely and *structurally* dependent on the outside world (even if they are *relationally* strong *vis-à-vis* certain other countries or groups thereof). Being overwhelmingly allocative or distributive states they have lost most of their extractive powers, due to the fact that they do not need to appropriate revenue from the local population but rather circulate revenue that is directly accruing to the state from the outside world. Their ideology, blending tribalism and Islam with a concept of the welfare state, has not been as severely challenged as that of the radical, populist regimes, but apart from Saudi Arabia, it is difficult to test the real hegemonic nature of that ideology if stripped of its 'oil' lubrication. Furthermore, although the state is fairly autonomous from the prospective (consumer) taxpayer (due to the abundance hitherto of oil rents), it is familially and tribally entwined with the business-type prospective taxpayer in so many ways that the state is deprived of any ability to adjust its 'generous' allocative and distributive policies in times of depression.

Although both the *thawri* and the *tharwi* states have been good and ambitious 'economic expansionists', neither of them has been a particularly good and efficient 'economic developer'. As, under the impact of fiscal crisis or at least fiscal constraints, they now feel the need somewhat to reduce the economic role of the state, they find it difficult – owing again to their structural weakness – to 'impose the market'.[2] The end result may well be weaker, if still repressive, states lording it over stagnating economies.

But if the Arab states are really so feeble, what was it that induced much of the earlier literature to over-state their strength? [for a further discussion of the literature see Sadowski, 1993]. In trying to answer this question let us suggest, with regard to state power, a distinction between the 'strong', the 'hard' and the 'fierce' aspects of that power.

Observers have often mistakenly taken a hard or a fierce state to mean a strong state. In reality a strong state may or may not be a hard state. France is a classic example of a hard/strong state. Britain is classified by Badie and Birnbaum [1983: 121ff] as a soft state. According to our analysis, however, Britain is a strong but not a hard state. Badie and Birnbaum arrive at their conclusion because they draw too sharp a contrast between state and civil society. If one adopts, on the contrary, the Gramscian concept of *lo stato integrale* whereby the civil society is a basic component/ingredient in defining the state (i.e. the state = the armour of coercion + the apparatus of hegemony), then one is likely to arrive at different conclusions.[3]

Hard states are often relatively late-industrialisers, with strong executives and higher levels of centralisation, that try to enforce a detailed, standardised regulation of the economy and the society, and favour intervention aimed at long-term goals centred around accumulation [compare Katzenstein, 1978]. Such hard states (adopting *dirigiste* domestic policies and Listian, mercantile foreign-trade policies) were often assumed to be strong states, whereas states adopting liberal economic policies, domestically and internationally, were assumed to be weak. Such an approach also lent too much credence to the declared objectives of the state and to its own claims about 'achievements' rather than to actual implementation outcomes in the various sectors and sub-sectors. A hard, regulatory/interventionist state is not the same as a strong state since what may be required is flexibility and the capacity to break with past patterns of behaviour. In such circumstances, the state's ability to reduce or redirect its regulatory involvement in the economy may be as powerful an expression of state capacity as direct intervention [cf. Cammack, 1992, referring to J. Ikenberry, S. Krasner and others].

One can perhaps also suggest that whereas hard states tend, in penetrating their society, to rely heavily on administrative means and instruments, less hard states will tend to rely more prominently, in penetrating their societies, on ideological (Gramscian hegemonic) means. Unlike many African countries, where local socio-political structures have been able to elude the penetrative reach of central authorities, the Arab states have, with only a few exceptions, managed to penetrate their societies, at least administratively, and to break up many rural systems of production and networks of exchange. The informal economy and the so-called Islamic economy are partial exceptions to this generalisation.

A strong state should also be distinguished from the 'fierce' state, which is so opposed to society that it can only deal with it via coercion and raw force (hence the 'police state', the 'security state' and the '*mukhabarat* state'). The strong state is complementary, not contradictory, to society, and its strength is not demonstrated by its subjugation of the society but by its ability to work with and through other centres of power in society. Michael Mann [1986] has suggested a distinction, that is quite reminiscent of Gramsci [Castiglione, 1994], between 'despotic' and 'infrastructural' power, which Hall and Ikenberry [1989: 12–14] have found useful in studying the state. The fierce state excels in the first type, the strong state in the second. The despotic power of the state is great when the state (or its ruling incumbents) can act arbitrarily, free from constitutional constraint. The practice of such an arbitrary power, as is still possessed by many an Arab ruler, can be cruel, but quite often the sound and fury of command would mean little when it comes to translating these orders into a sound political or social reality. The Arab state is therefore often violent *because* it is weak [Ju'ait, 1984: 172–81, 213ff; Al-'Arawi, 1981: 145ff].[4] After surveying a whole range of authoritarian Arab experiences one Lebanese writer advised his readers to distinguish between *quwwat al-dawla* and *dawlat al-quwwa*; i.e. the 'strong state' and the 'state of force' (*l'État-Force*) [Khalil, 1984: passim and 169]. For as a Syrian writer correctly points out, the Arab state is not on the whole a modern 'solidarity' (*'asabiyya*) that penetrates, synthesises and surpasses other solidarities, but one that simply overpowers, then dissolves and replaces all other solidarities. And once in government the ruling caste strives to derive its legitimacy from references to other things: national independence, economic development, socialist transformation, etc., but never from the act of (good) governing itself [cf. Safadi, 1986: Ch. 5].

By contrast, the infrastructural dimension of state power is manifested above all in the ability to penetrate society and to organise social relations. State power is thus very much related to state capacity, and one has to be sceptical about states conventionally believed to be strong, before putting their capacity to the test. For example, the French absolutist state in the nineteenth century was not, again, nearly as powerful as its constitutional British rival. It had a lesser infrastructural capacity to penetrate its society than did its British counterpart, despite its formally greater despotic power, and this was particularly obvious with regard to the ability to tax the aristocracy. "The conclusion to be emphasized is that the strength of a state depends greatly upon its ability to penetrate and organise society; the pretensions of despotism must not be taken at face value" [Hall and Ikenberry, 1989: 13].

Two kinds of approach have been attempted in trying to measure state strength. The first is aggregate and the second is analytical. An example of the former would be Joel Migdal's contention that strong states are those more capable of achieving, through state planning, policies and actions, the kinds of changes in society that their leaders have sought [Migdal, 1988a: esp. Preface and Ch. 1]. In the Third World, one familiar test for measuring state strength has been to examine the extent to which such a state would have succeeded in achieving its declared developmental goals. Obviously on this front, as we have seen in previous chapters, none of the Arab countries has been a glaring success story although the degree, and the areas, of success and failure have varied from one case to another.

In adopting effective implementation as an aggregate measure for state strength care should be taken not to assume a monistic character of the state's goals or to assume a complete autonomy of the state from social forces and interests. Instruments of policy implementation should then always be related to the specific goals at hand and to the socio-political context in general. Migdal [1988b] maintains, for example, that Nasser failed in transforming Egyptian society through agrarian reform, and he regards this as indicative of his failure in building a dominant state capable of social control. But whether the reform was successful or not obviously depends on what we take to be its main objectives. If we take at face value the claim that it was basically meant for the betterment of the poor peasants' lot, and overlook any possible 'hidden agenda', then obviously it was not a total success. If one is to concentrate on its possible 'political' objectives, such as the undermining of the landowners' power base, the improvement of agricultural productivity, and the diversion of capital to urban development, then the reform must be regarded as a success [cf. Ayubi, 1989b: Ch. 4]. Similar questions may also be raised in relation to the Syrian and the Algerian agrarian reforms [cf. Hinnebusch, 1986; Pfeifer, 1985]. As Paul Cammack argues, there is no paradox in Nasser's "undermining his own agencies", as Migdal says he did when he demobilised the Arab Socialist Union (ASU). "It was mobilised in the middle 1960s to act as a counter to the army, and to prevent the emergence of new layers of rich peasants outside State control, then demobilised when the threat had been countered, and the same groups could be trusted to operate in harmony with the goals of the State." Cammack concludes [1992: 4–12] by suggesting that intervention and withdrawal on the part of the state cannot therefore be mechanically correlated to the strength of the state.

> Ikenberry celebrates a decision to withdraw or not to intervene as evidence of state strength, while Migdal presents withdrawal from intervention as evidence that the purposes of the State have been corrupted from within, therefore demonstrating the defeat of the weak state by a 'strong' society. Each gives a one-sided picture. Ikenberry glosses over the possibility that a decision to withdraw may come at the end of a long sequence of policy failure indicative of weakness. Migdal, in contrast, fails to consider that a decision to dissolve a particular state institution may reflect precisely that flexibility which Ikenberry sees as essential to the preservation of State capacity over time ... The particular interpretations offered by Ikenberry and Migdal appear arbitrary, then, because each fails to explore either the content of the goals of the State, or the links between the State and social actors [ibid.: 10, 12].

Confusion arises from the treatment of the state as an independent actor. The appearance of failure, as in Migdal's analysis of Nasser's Egypt, may be a direct consequence of the initial assumption that the state is an independent actor rising above society, and completely autonomous from capital and from social forces and interests, and that its intention was indeed to benefit the poor peasantry.

We know now, in retrospect, that the achievements of the agrarian reform in Egypt were mixed: it was quite effective in terms of eradicating the political and economic power base of the old landowning class in the countryside, it was partly effective in raising productivity and transferring capital towards urban and industrial development, but it was hardly effective in building an alternative political power base or in sustaining a long-term political coalition between the urban and the rural sectors. The Egyptian state, as restructured by Nasser, has not therefore been as strong as many observers had thought it was at an earlier 'socialistic' stage, when it appeared to own everything and to control everything [for a further discussion on the 'softness' of the Egyptian state see Waterbury, 1985]. As Jalal (G.) Amin explained recently, "When we read what Professor Myrdal wrote about the 'soft state' in the late sixties [i.e. 1968] it did not occur to us at all that his analysis applied to Egypt ... We had several problems at the time but this was not one of them." Then gradually it became clear in the 1970s and 1980s that the Egyptian state was too soft to manage the economy, too feeble to stand up to its external antagonists and too incapacitated even to maintain law and order within the society [Jalal Amin, 1993: 7–10].

This limited strength is further illustrated, currently, by the state's inability to 'impose the market' even after political intentions to that effect have been declared. As suggested in a recent study by Yahya Sadowski [1991: 1–14], it is not for lack of 'political will' for market-oriented reform that Egypt's restruc-turing policies are faltering, but rather for the lack of 'political capacity' to introduce and implement the required reforms.[5] In other words, the Egyptian state is, in a sense and despite all appearances, a 'soft state' whose power is greatly overestimated by, among others, the 'Washington development com-munity':

> Too often people assume that because a country has a flag and an army, it must have an effective State. They infer that because a government is not restrained by a democratic constitution or a representative assembly, state power must be autocratic and unlimited. Westerners in particular tend to see Middle Eastern dictatorships like those of Nasser and Sadat as modernized versions of 'Oriental despotism'. They presume that in Egypt the State is strong and society is weak. The reality is almost exactly the opposite [ibid.: 90].

Now, if this is the description of Egypt, the presumably archetypal case of state strength within the Arab World, then little persuasion should be needed to realise the real weakness of the others [see e.g. Rida 1992: 78–92, where he invokes G. Myrdal in connection with the 'softness' and other weaknesses of the Gulf states].

The second approach to measuring state strength is analytical. State power is disaggregated into a number of capabilities and each of them is examined both separately and in conjunction with the others. Among the most important to be examined are the extractive, regulatory and allocative/re-allocative capacities of the state. We have already implied that the regulatory power of the state has advanced considerably in many Arab countries, particularly those of the populist-corporatist regime type. So much so, as we have seen in the chapter on administration, that this function might repeatedly have defeated the allocative activities of the state in the area of industrialisation and the attempt to create a modern, diversified economy.

The allocative function, by contrast, has been so overwhelmingly important in the rentier oil-exporting countries that they have been dubbed 'allocative states' [e.g. Luciani, 1987]. The allocative function involves, in the economic sphere, both the apportioning of funds for investment (including infrastructural) purposes as well as the reallocative or redistributive function related to income distribution and to services and benefits of the 'welfare state'.

All such activities have been very dependent, in the populist states, on the initial appropriation by the state of private (foreign, then native) businesses, supported by aid and external 'rents' both from the West and from the 'East', and from the Arab World. It should be clear therefore that both the oil-rich and the oil-poor countries in the Arab World have, in fulfilling their allocative functions, depended too heavily and too recklessly on ultimately 'non-renewable' resources.

It is often forgotten, however, that the state allocates *all* kinds of value in society: it allocates not only (economic) resources but also (moral) values [compare Easton, 1953]. The Arab state has often not only nationalised industry but has also tried to nationalise 'class struggle' [Sayyid-Ahmad, 1984: Ch. 2] and 'moral capital' [Etienne, 1987]. This has been particularly prominent in the case of the radical, populist regimes. If such states fail – as did most Arab countries – in achieving their developmental promises, for which they claim they have allocated the society's resources, then the society's response is likely to present itself either in an attempt to appropriate from the state part of its enlarged economic domain (i.e. via privatisations) and/or in an attempt to regain part of the 'moral capital' for the direct benefit of the civil society (as represented, for example, by the Islamist groupings).

It is perhaps the extractive capacity of the state that is most important in the long run because, once external rents dry up, it is the state's capacity to extract surplus from its local population that would enable it to allocate and to regulate, to distribute and to redistribute. States extract surplus differently and this is usually a good way both to identify the nature of the state itself and to anticipate the type of relationship it has with its civil society. Thus one would find, for example, that whereas the 'fierce' state often expropriates the economic surplus from society by semi-coercive methods, the strong state is capable of extracting the surplus through direct taxation practices based on known and approved legal, economic and accounting principles.

In the Arab World, the radical, populist regimes have tended to expropriate the surplus via political means (including the 'nationalisation' of industry) and to supplement that by the receiving of foreign aid. In the oil-exporting 'rentier states' the need for the state to extract resources from their society has been avoided altogether, thus resulting in a rather feeble capacity of the state, apart from the purely allocative functions [cf. Krasner, 1985; Chaudhry, 1989; Snider, 1988]. The 'relative autonomy' that rentier or semi-rentier states may derive from external revenues directly accruing to the state (whether in the form of petro-dollars or aid monies) may eventually be translated into weakness, if it leads to an avoidance of internal state-building activities of the kind which linked taxation, participation and legitimacy in Europe [Anderson, 1987: 1–18].

Not only is the advanced extractive capacity of the state, via direct taxation, indicative of its own strength and institutional sophistication, but it may also suggest that matters are on the move towards some kind of democracy. European experience indicates that parliaments emerged as arenas in which monarchs bargained with citizens over taxes, and that it was the costs of warfare that propelled them as supplicants into these forums [cf. Bates, 1991: 24–5]. It is therefore a measure both of the limited real strength of the Arab state as well as of the constrained prospects for democratic transformation that the Arab states in general are not efficient tax collectors. Joel Migdal has suggested this with regard to three 'populist' states: Egypt, Syria and Iraq [Migdal, 1988b]. These countries have succeeded in recruiting people, in comparatively high numbers and percentages, into their armed forces and their nationwide school systems. They have thus demonstrated relatively high capabilities with regard to their ability to pluck people from the society and deploy them according to the state's mobilisational purposes. These countries, however, have done much less well with regard to more indirect measures of state strength such as the capacity to tax their citizens. For countries that are not oil exporters, Egypt and Syria had in the years 1978 to 1985 some of the lowest scores in the world of domestic tax revenues as a percentage of total revenues.

More comprehensive work has been done recently on this subject by Giacomo Luciani [1993], who has tried to investigate how the various Arab countries have responded, in terms of their taxation policies, to the recent 'fiscal crisis of the state', and how this kind of response is likely to influence democratisation prospects. The theoretical base of the argument is, again, that if the state needs to tax in order to support its activities, taxation (especially modern direct taxation) in its turn requires compliance and is therefore unlikely in the longer run to co-exist with authoritarian rule. A state resorting to increased taxation, especially if direct income taxation is involved, is thus bound to meet with growing demands for popular participation, and for control through democratic institutions. Taxes on foreign trade require little legitimation, and not even full control of the national territory; hence they have historically been imposed by bandits and non-governmental actors, as well as weak governments. Yet these and other relatively simple forms of taxation soon reach a limit and do not grow as rapidly as national income. Once the state really needs to encroach on people's own incomes, goes the argument, then a process of democratisation is likely to be in the offing. This process presumably involves both an increasing sophistication of the workings of the state machine and at the same time a flourishing of the forces of civil society, including the private economic sector. Direct taxes on individuals are much more difficult to collect than indirect taxes because they require more infrastructural power. The greater the proportion of tax revenue that comes from direct taxes on individuals, the greater the government's penetration of society – regardless of the degree of government intervention in the economy as such [Snider, 1988: 466–72]. Although mainly derived from the European historical experience, this proposition appears to have potential universal applicability. A 'cultural' note of caution has to be inserted, however, with regard to Muslim societies, although its implications may not alter the real situation in any drastic way.[6]

Another important factor is the degree to which the state controls the economy. The less market-based an economy is (which is the case with most Arab economies), the less elastic the tax base. This in turn shapes the terms of the possible bargain between state and society. Historical experience suggests again that:

> The more elastic the tax base, the greater the degree to which the sovereign had to give control over public policy to those whose money he sought to appropriate for public purposes ... The more completely economic activities are organized by the markets, the greater the ease of tax avoidance, the greater the elasticity of tax payment, and thus the greater the need for governments to bargain when in search of revenue [Bates, 1991: 25–6].

The tax base in most Arab countries is probably still on the 'inelastic' side, thus reducing the real need for governments to supplicate and to bargain even when they are suffering from serious fiscal crises. And this in turn must act as a constraint on the prospects for democratic transformation.

In analysing tax revenue as a percentage of total revenue (and grants) for a group of Middle Eastern countries, Luciani has come to the remarkable conclusion that tax revenue appears to account for more than 50 per cent of total revenue in only five Middle Eastern countries: i.e. Morocco, Tunisia, Egypt, Syria and Iraq. In the case of Syria, tax income must include taxes on foreign oil companies and is therefore most likely exaggerated. It is notable that taxes play only a limited role in Jordan. The most significant figures are

Table 12.1 Income taxes as a share of total revenue in selected Middle East countries

	1982	1983	1984	1985	1986	1987	1988	1989	1990	1991
Algeria	n.a.	n.a.	n.a.	16.35	21.39	20.96	22.4	18.85	13.73	15.1
Bahrain	2.18	2.81	3.56	3.73	4.15	4.61	3.82	3.79	5.01	5.04
Egypt	16.53	17.72	13.24	14.46	15.69	17.86	18.79	21.25	15.95	14.00
Iran	7.30	7.75	9.50	13.43	21.42	18.24	19.27	11.96	9.91	11.48
Jordan	7.90	8.01	9.82	9.00	7.82	7.63	6.83	6.56	13.06	11.56
Morocco	15.55	17.48	18.58	18.46	18.86	18.93	n.a.	n.a.	n.a.	n.a.
Tunisia	14.67	13.54	12.17	14.28	15.60	13.29	11.82	12.31	12.25	14.30
Yemen	n.a.	9.37	10.28	11.38	9.73	11.10	18.44	19.26	20.06	n.a.

Source: Luciani [1993] and refs therein.

those concerning income taxes (see Table 12.1), and the limited importance of these by international standards is clear, except for the cases of Algeria, Morocco, Tunisia and Egypt (and for Yemen after 1987) [for a possible explanation of the Yemeni surprise see the section on the 'Yemeni Adventure' in Chapter 11 above]. In 1990 the comparative ratios were 52 per cent in the USA, 39 per cent in the UK, 36 per cent in Italy, 17 per cent in France and 16 per cent in Germany. It should be noted, however, that in the case of Egypt and Yemen income taxes are almost entirely (90 per cent in the first and 65 per cent in the latter) paid by corporations. Morocco is the only Arab country in which taxes on individual incomes have exceeded taxes on corporate income ever since 1982. Is it a mere coincidence that these countries with the highest ratios of income tax to overall state revenue are actually the most state-like in the Arab World (Egypt, Tunisia and Morocco), or at least (as in the case of Algeria and Yemen) are among the Arab countries that have held genuine democratic elections in recent years?

The ability of Arab countries to respond to a fiscal crisis of the state will of course vary from one country to another but the major difference will be that between the major oil-exporters and the rest. The members of the Gulf Cooperation Council (GCC) have on the whole been able to respond to reduced oil revenues by cutting down some public expenditure and by resorting to some of their accumulated reserves. The main attempt to raise non-oil revenue represented itself in Saudi Arabia in the introduction of some users' fees and in the raising of rates on key utilities including electricity and water – but these were reduced again after Operation Desert Storm. A clumsy attempt at imposing an income tax on foreign workers was made in 1988 and had hurriedly to be withdrawn shortly afterwards, as we have seen earlier on. As development remains dependent on oil revenue the (normal) link between economic growth and government revenue is severed, thus reducing the *necessity* for the state to promote non-oil economic growth as such. The mismanagement of funds that causes temporary bottlenecks should not be mistaken for a serious fiscal crisis and most of these oil-exporting countries are still in possession of sufficient 'appeasement funds' to keep the dissatisfaction and occasional protests from turning into an organised movement for democracy.

In non-oil countries, democratisation is more likely to correspond to the decline in exogenous revenue sources and the need to increase direct local taxation. This was clear in the case of Jordan [cf. Brand, 1992: 186]. It was 'analytically' clear in the case of Algeria except that things went 'politically' wrong in a rather unfortunate way. Egypt, that key Arab exemplar, could, on the one hand, be said to "have faced a fiscal crisis throughout its modern existence" [see Luciani, 1993 for details]. In this particular case, could this be said to have blunted the possible link between the fiscal crisis and the democratisation process? Although some political liberalisation has been achieved, the more recent economic liberalisation wave of the 1990s does not promise to be matched with serious democratisation moves. The situation is similar, if not as financially acute, in Tunisia. The infusion of foreign official transfers to Egypt in the aftermath of Desert Storm might briefly have given the country some precious breathing space but the transfers are unlikely to continue at a high level for long, thus making the limited tax reforms announced so far (including a general sales tax) appear quite insufficient. More will need to be done with respect to personal income taxes, but would that necessarily deepen the democratisation process, given Egypt's circumstances of an omnipotent military, an illusive business community and a threatening Islamic opposition? Similar constraints on democratisation apply to other Arab countries suffering from fiscal crises. For a while rulers may try to 'have their cake and to eat at the same time': i.e. to enlarge taxes without increasing participation. But if states attempt to expand the tax base (a process that usually leads to a rise in political awareness) without expanding citizens' access to policy-making and without the use of the tax system to reduce social and political inequalities, the new demands by the state will not be perceived as legitimate, and increased political turmoil may be in the offing [Snider, 1988: 481].

The problem is compounded by the fact that the Arab state, already drained by its financial crisis, is also suffering from a serious 'hegemonic' crisis. The 'interpellatory' power of ideologies such as nationalism and socialism is practically exhausted, and the regimes are on the whole unable to formulate alternative interpellatory ideologies and to assemble new power blocs. Very little 'political credit' is left, and political demands are now almost wholly required 'in cash'.[7] This is a crisis that pits the state against the civil society, or as Islamic sympathisers would prefer to put it, the state against the *umma* [cf. Ghalyun, 1993]. The neo-populist Islamic movements appear currently to hold the higher moral ground with their incessant calls for a *stato etico* in more than one country in the Arab World. What is more, whereas most regimes are relying primarily on tactics and manoeuvres, the Islamic movement may be preparing, to use Gramsci's terms, for a 'war of position' that aims at 'surrounding' the state with an entire counter-hegemony [cf. Buci-Glucksmann, 1980: 242–334].[8] The real question now is not whether, but how, to include the Islamic groups in the political process, together with other groupings and associations of the civil society. We have conceded, perhaps for too long, the historical necessity of 'developmental dictatorship' for coping with the causes and consequences of economic underdevelopment. Is it now possible to hope, with Richard Sklar [1987] for the emergence of a 'developmental democracy' in which democratic participation would be conducive (rather than constrictive) to economic efficiency?

One conclusion should become clear from all this analysis: state/society relations do not resemble a zero-sum game – both State and Society can prosper together, indeed both *must* prosper together. The current vicious coupling of political despotism and economic stagnation is unlikely to be checked unless Arab political élites will grasp this 'lesson' – and the sooner the better.

NOTES

1. Nor is the prospective Palestinian state likely to be more fortunate. Indeed, quite the reverse: destined to be extremely small in size and split in its physical conformation, it still lacks most of the 'basics'. It has been sardonically described by Salim Nassar as "a Palestinian State whose airport is in Egypt, whose seaport is in Israel, whose central bank is in Jordan and whose people is scattered over more than four countries" [*Al-Hayat*, 4 December 1993].

2. We might as well remember that there are two possible ways for the state to 'impose the market': "State power is needed to create legitimacy (hegemony) for ideologies of market competition or, in the absence of hegemony, to coerce those who actively resist competitive practices; and State power is needed either to legitimise, or to enforce by more brutal means, the redistributive consequences of competitive struggles" [Moran and Wright, 1991: 246].

3. The debate is rich on the nature of the French state and the British state and the contrasts between them, and reference may be made, among others, to the writings of Birnbaum and Badie, Anderson, Gamble, Cerny, Hall, Leys, Jessop and many more. For the purposes of this analysis, this quote from Laclau [1979] will have to suffice: "The particularism and *ad hoc* nature of dominant institutions and ideology in Great Britain does not reflect an inadequate bourgeois development but exactly the opposite: the supreme articulating power of the bourgeoisie" [p. 162].

4. The subjects of political cruelty and of state violence and counter (social) violence are important but poorly researched ones in the Arab World. The reader is referred in particular to the following: for an interesting if schematic survey of torture in the historical Muslim states see Al-'Alawi [c. 1985]. For an updating in relation to the contemporary Arab countries (particularly Iraq) see Makiya [1993]. And for a good analytical and quantitative study on political violence (state and anti-state) in the contemporary Arab World see Hasanain T. Ibrahim [1992].

5. As I have indicated elsewhere in the book (e.g. in Chapter 9) I do not like the phrase 'lack of political will' as an explanation for slow or inefficient action, because what we normally have is not *a* political will that is present or absent but a multiplicity of political *wills* that are in a state of conflict, concordance or compromise.

6. Because of the specific nature of the 'tributary' historical Islamic state, whereby most 'taxes' (*fay'*, *jizya*, *'ushur*, even *zakat*) were religiously sanctioned by generations of religious jurists, non-

religious taxes (*mukus*) have very frequently been resisted by the society as illegitimate [Shalaq, 1989: 39–42]. This happened, for example, under the Fatimids, the Ayyubids and the Mamluks, and more recently during Ibn Sa'ud's attempts to subject Arabia to his dominance. The *Mudhakkirat al-nasiha* (Memorandum of Advice) [1992: 34] of the Saudi *'ulama* and Islamists also condemns the imposition of various taxes and charges that are not religiously based (*dun istidlal shar'i*). Most of the contemporary radical Islamic movements encourage their members not to pay taxes to the 'infidel state' and call for the restoration of 'religious' taxes, including the *jizya* on non-Muslims. Finally, of course, if the state is despotic enough it may be able to increase income tax without necessarily conceding much political power – at least for a time.

7. This economic metaphor is somewhat similar to the language used by W.F. Ilchman [1969]. According to him, 'legitimacy' in more developed polities is considered as 'political infrastructure' (which is reminiscent of Gramsci and Mann) whereas in less developed polities it is more of a political resource, in the sense that it has "productive and scarce characteristics. The statesman needs or wants legitimacy because to the extent he has it, he needs to expend fewer other resources to secure compliance" [73ff].

8. On the possibilities of religious discourse becoming national-popular, and therefore hegemonic in the Gramscian sense, see: 'I. Fawzi [1992: 128ff]; Labib [1992a: 68, 74 and refs cited], and Farah [1992: 194ff].

Bibliography

AARTS, Paul, G. Isenloeffel and A.J. Termeulen (1991), 'Oil, Money and Participation: Kuwait's *Sonderweg* as a Rentier State', Orient, Vol. 32, no. 2, June.

— (1993), 'Les limites du "tribalisme politique": Le Koweït d'après-guerre et le processus de démocratisation', *Maghreb-Machrek*, no. 142, octobre–décembre 1993.

ABBAS, A.A. (1986), 'The Iraqi Armed Forces, Past and Present', in Committee Against Repression and for Democratic Rights in Iraq (CARDRI), *Saddam's Iraq: Revolution or Reaction?*, London: Zed Books.

'ABD AL-FADIL, Mahmud (1988), *Al-Tashkilat al-ijtima'iyya wa al-takwinat al-tabaqiyya* ... [Social Constellations and Class Formations in the Arab World], Beirut: Centre for Arab Unity Studies (CAUS) and UN University.

— (1989), *Al-Khadi'a al-maliyya al-kubra* ... [The Great Financial Confidence Trick: the Political Economy of the Money Utilisation Companies], Cairo: Dar al-Mustaqbal al-'Arabi.

'ABD AL-HAKIM, Shawqi (1986), *Al-Shakhsiyya al-wataniyya al-misriyya* [The Egyptian National Character], Cairo: Dar al-Fikr.

'ABD AL-JABBER, Faleh (1992), 'Why the Uprisings Failed', *Middle East Report* (MERIP), May–June 1992.

ABDALLA, Ahmed (1988), 'The Armed Forces and the Democratic Process in Egypt', *Third World Quarterly*, Vol. 10, no. 4, October 1988.

'ABD AL-MAJID, Wahid (1994), 'Limadha 'ajazat al-dimuqratiyya' [Why Has Democracy Failed to Avert the Yemeni War?], *Al-Hayat*, 9 June 1994.

'ABD AL-MUN'IM, Ahmad Faris (1983), 'Jama'at al-masalih' [Interest Groups], in Aliy al-Din Hilal, ed., *Al-Nizam al-siyasi* [The Political System], Cairo: Al- Markaz al-'Arabi.

'ABD AL-RAHMAN, Usama (1982), *Al-Biruqratiyya al-naftiyya wa mu'adilat al-tanmiya* [Petroleum Bureaucracy and the Dilemma of Development], Kuwait: National Council for Culture and Arts.

— (1988), *Al-Mawrid al-wahid wa al-tawajjuh al-infaqi al-sa'id* [The Preponderant Spending Trend of the Single Resource Economy], Beirut: CAUS.

'ABD AL-SALAM, Ahmad (1985), *Mustalah al-siyasa 'ind al-'arab* [The Term 'Politics' among the Arabs], Tunis: Société Tunisienne de Diffusion.

ABDEL-KHALEK, Gouda (1992), *Perestroika Without Glasnost? Economic Liberalization and Democratization in the Middle East*, Amsterdam: Middle East Research Associates, Occasional Paper no. 16, December.

ABDEL-MALEK, Anouar (1968), *Egypt: Military Society*, New York: Random House.

— (1979), 'The Occultation of Egypt', *Arab Studies Quarterly*, Vol. 1, no. 3, Summer.

— (1981), *Nation and Revolution*, Albany: SUNY Press.

— (1983), *Contemporary Arab Political Thought* (trans.), London: Zed Press.

ABDEL-RAHMAN, I.H. and M.S. Abu Ali (1989), 'Role of the Public and Private Sectors with

In a number of instances, information was obtained in typed or mimeographed form from government departments or organisations. Such unpublished material is referred to in the text but has no bibliographic entry.

special reference to Privatisation; the Case of Egypt', in Said El-Naggar, ed., *Privatization and Structural Adjustment in the Arab Countries*, Washington, DC: International Monetary Fund.

ABIR, Mordechai (1988), *Saudi Arabia in the Oil Era: Regime and Elites, Conflict and Collaboration*, London: Croom Helm.

ABOU-EL-HAJ, Rifaat (1982), 'The Social Uses of the Past: Recent Arab Historiography of Ottoman Rule', *International Journal of Middle East Studies*, Vol. 14, no. 2, May.

ABRAHAMIAN, Ervard (1974), 'Oriental Despotism: the Case of Qajar Iran', *International Journal of Middle East Studies*, Vol. 5, no. 1.

— (1991), 'Khomeini: Fundamentalist or Populist?', *New Left Review*, 186, March/April.

ABU 'ALAM, 'Abd al-Ra'uf (1968), 'Al-Wisaya al-idariyya 'alaal-haraka al-niqabiyya' [Administrative Tutelage over the Trade Union Movement], *Al-Tali'a*, Vol. 4, no. 1, January.

ABU GHANIM, Fadl A. (1985), *Al-Bunya al-qabaliyya fi al-Yaman* [The Tribal Structure in Yemen], Damascus: Al-Katib al-'Arabi.

ABU SHIKHA, Nadir (1983), *Al-Tanzim al-idari ...* [Administrative Organisation in Thirteen Arab States], Amman: Arab Organisation for Administrative Sciences (AOAS).

— , and 'Abd al-Mu'ti 'Assaf (1985). *Al-Idara al-'amma ...* [Public Administration in Jordan], Amman: Al-Mu'assasa al-Sahafiyya.

ADWAN, Yasir and R. Cunningham (1989), 'Privatisation in Jordan', paper presented to the 21st International Congress of Administrative Sciences, Marrakech, 24–28 July 1989.

'AFLAQ, Michel (1970), *Fi Sabil al-Ba'th* [In the Cause of the Rebirth], Beirut: Dar al-Tali'a, 4th edn.

AGNUSH, 'Abd al-Latif (1987), *Tarikh al-mu'assasat wa al-waqa'i' al-ijtima'iyya bi al-Maghrib* [History of Social Institutions and Events in Morocco], Casablanca: Ifriqiya al-Sharq.

AHMAD, 'Abd al-'Ati Muhammad (1979), *Al-Diblumasiyya al-sa'udiyya fi al-khalij* [Saudi Diplomacy in the Gulf], Cairo: Al-Ahram/CPSS.

AHMAD, Aijaz (1985), 'Class, Nation and State: Intermediate Classes in Peripheral Societies', in Dale L. Johnson, ed., *Middle Classes in Dependent Countries*, Beverly Hills and London: Sage Publications.

AHMAD, Nabil I. (1991), 'Al-Infaq al-'askari ... ' [Military Expenditure and its Impact on Development], *Al-Bahith al-'Arabi*, no. 27, July–September.

AHMAD, Sadiq (1984), *Public Finance in Egypt: its Structure and Trends*, Washington, DC: World Bank Staff Working Papers, no. 639.

AHMED, Jamal Mohammed (1960), *The Intellectual Origins of Egyptian Nationalism*, London: Oxford University Press.

AL-AHNAF, M., B. Botiveau and J. Cesari (1993), 'Sur les usages politiques du droit: Egypte, Maroc, Algérie', *Maghreb-Machrek*, No. 143, octobre–décembre.

AHSAN, Syed Aziz (1984), 'Economic Policy and Class Structure in Syria, 1958–1980', *International Journal of Middle East Studies*, Vol. 16, no. 3, August.

AIT AMARA, Hamid (1987), 'The State, Social Classes and Agricultural Politics in the Arab World', in H. Beblawi and G. Luciani, eds, *The Rentier State*, London: Croom Helm.

AJAMI, Fouad (1978/79), 'The End of Pan-Arabism', *Foreign Affairs*, Winter.

AKE, Claude (1985), 'The Future of the State in Africa' *International Political Science Review*, Vol. 6, no. 1.

AKLIMANDUS, Tawfiq (1988), 'Al-Shilal wa 'alaqat al-mahsubiyya ... ' [Cliques and Clientelistic Relations in the Egyptian Political System], in 'Aliy al-Din Hilal Disuqi, ed., *Al-Nizam al-Siyasi al-misri* [The Egyptian Political System], Cairo: Al-Nahda al-Misriyya.

ALAVI, Hamza (1979), 'The State in Post-Colonial Societies: Pakistan and Bangladesh', in Harry Goulbourne, ed., *Politics and the Third World*, London: Macmillan.

AL- 'ALAWI, Ghalib (1993), 'Al-Mu'assasa al-diniyya al-sa'udiyya tatahawwal ila al-muwajaha' [The Saudi Religious Establishment Turns to Confrontation], *Al-Azmina al-'Arabiyya*, no. 245, Winter.

AL-'ALAWI, Hadi (c. 1985), *Min tarikh al-ta'dhib ...* [On the History of Torture in Islam], Damascus: Markaz al-Abhath al-Ishtirakiyya.

ALDERFER, Harold H. (1967), *Public Administration in Newer Nations*, New York: Praeger.

'ALI, Kamal Hasan (1986), *Muharibun wa mufawidun* [Fighters and Negotiators], Cairo: Dar Al-Ahram.

AL-'ALLAM, 'Izz al-Din (1994), 'Mulahazat hawl al-ra'iyya ... ' [Observations on the Concept of the 'Flock' in Sultanic Political Literature], *Al-Ijtihad*, Vol. 6, no. 22, Winter.

ALNASRAWI, Abbas (1979), 'Arab Oil and the Industrial Economies: the Paradox of Oil Dependency', *Arab Studies Quarterly*, Vol. 1, no. 1, Winter.

— (1984), 'The Rise and Fall of Arab Oil Power', *Arab Studies Quarterly*, Vol. 6, nos. 1 and 2, Winter/Spring.

AMAWI, Abla (1992), 'Democracy Dilemmas in Jordan', *Middle East Report* (MERIP) January–February 1992.

AMERICAN EMBASSY IN CAIRO (1986), *Egypt: Economic Trends*, Cairo.

'AMIL, Mahdi (1979), *Bahth fi asbab al-harb* ... [An Inquiry Into the Causes of the Civil War in Lebanon], Beirut: Dar al-Farabi.

— (1987), *Azmat al-hadara al-'arabiyya* ... [A Crisis of Arab Civilisation or the Crisis of the Arab Bourgeoisies?], Beirut: Dar Al-Farabi.

AMIN, Galal (1980), *The Modernization of Poverty: A Study in the Political Economy of Growth in Nine Arab Countries 1945–1970*, Leiden: Brill.

AMIN, Jalal (G.) (1993), *Al-Dawla al-rakhwa* [The Soft State in Egypt], Cairo: Sina.

AMIN, Samir (1974), *Accumulation on a World Scale; A Critique of the Theory of Underdevelopment* (2 vols), Sussex: Harvester Press.

— (1976), *Unequal Development: An Essay on the Social Formations of Peripheral Capitalism*, Sussex: Harvester.

— (1978), *The Arab Nation: Nationalism and Class Struggles*, trans., London: Zed Press.

— (1982a), *The Arab Economy Today*, trans., London: Zed Press.

— (1982b), *Iraq and Syria*, London: Penguin Books.

— (1985), *Azmat al-mujtama' al-'arabi* [The Crisis of Arab Society], Cairo: Dar al-Mustaqbal al-'Arabi.

— (1986), 'Hawl al-taba'iyya wa al-tawassu' al-'alami li al-ra'similiyya' [On Dependency and the Global Expansion of Capitalism], in Centre for Arab Unity Studies (CAUS) Seminar on *Al-Tanmiyya al-mustaqilla* [Independent Development in the Arab Fatherland], Amman, April 1986.

'AMMAR, Hamid (1964), *Fi Bina' al-bashar* ... [On Constructing Human Beings: Studies in Cultural Change and Educational Thought], Sirs al-Layyan: MTM.

ANANI, Jawad and Rima Khalaf (1989), 'Privatization in Jordan', in Said El-Naggar, ed., *Privatization and Structural Adjustment in the Arab Countries*, Washington, DC: International Monetary Fund.

ANDERSON, Benedict (1983), *Imagined Communities: Reflections on the Origins and Spread of Nationalism*, London: Verso.

ANDERSON, Lisa (1986), *The State and Social Transformation in Tunisia and Libya, 1830–1980*, Princeton, NJ: Princeton University Press.

— (1987), 'The State in the Middle East and North Africa', *Comparative Politics*, Vol. 20, no. 1, October.

— (1991), 'Political Pacts, Liberalism and Democracy: the Tunisian National Pact of 1988', *Government and Opposition*, Vol. 26, no. 2, Spring.

ANDERSON, Perry (1974/79), *Lineages of the Absolutist State*, London: New Left Books/Verso Editions.

ANSAR AL-DIMUQRATIYYA (1987), *Al-Ta'amur* ... [Conspiring Against Democracy in Kuwait], Kuwait: n.p.

AL-ANSARI, Muhammad Jabir (1980), *Tahawwulat al-fikr wa al-siyasa fi al-sharq al-'arabi* [Intellectual and political Transformations in the Arab East, 1930–1970], Kuwait: Al-Majlis al-Watani li al-Thaqafa.

— (1993), 'Limadha tadakhkhamat al-qabila ... ' [Why Has the Tribe so Expanded Within the Arab Political Formation?], *Al-Hayat*, 6 April 1993.

— (1994), *Takwin al-'arab al-siyasi* ... [The Political Formation of the Arabs and the Significance of the Territorial State], Beirut: CAUS.

ANTHONY, John Duke (1982), 'The Gulf Cooperation Council', *Journal of South Asian and Middle Eastern Studies*, Vol. 5, no. 4, Summer.

APTER, David (1987), *Rethinking Development: Modernization, Dependency, and Postmodern Politics*, California and London: Sage Publications.

ARAB ADMINSTRATIVE DEVELOPMENT ORGANISATION (ARADO) (1992), 'Al-Islah wa al-tanmiya al-iddariyya ... ' [Administrative Reform and Development in the Arab States; A Summary and Comparison], paper prepared by Jamil Jreisat for the First Ministerial Conference on Administrative Development, Cairo, December 1992.

ARAB BANKING CORPORATION (1990), *The Arab Economies: Structure and Outlook*, 3rd rev. edn, London: ABC.

ARABIAN GOVERNMENT AND PUBLIC SERVICES 1983, directory, London: Beacon.

ARAB INSTITUTE OF PLANNING IN KUWAIT (AIPK) and Centre for Arab Unity Studies (CAUS) (1983), *Al-'Amala al-ajnabiyya fi aqtar al-khalif al-'arabi* [Foreign Employment in Countries of the Arabian Gulf], Beirut: CAUS.

ARAB MONETARY FUND (1981, 1982, 1983, 1989, 1990), *Al-Taqrir al-iqtisadi al-'arabi al-muwahhad* [The Unified Arab Economic Report – various years], Abu Dhabi: League of Arab States/ Arab Monetary Fund.

ARAB ORGANISATION FOR ADMINSTRATIVE SCIENCES (AOAS) (1984), 'Liqa' khubara' hawla al-juzur al-mutamayyiza' [Experts' Meeting on Islands of Excellence in the Management of Public Sector Organisation], *mimeo*, Amman: AOAS, July.

— (1986), *Public Administration and Administrative Reform in the Arab World* (in Arabic), Amman: AOAS.

AL-'ARAWI, 'Abdallah (1981), *Mafhum al-dawla* [Concept of the State], Casablanca: Al-Markaz al-Thaqafa al-'Arabi.

— (1983), *Mafhum al-huriyya* [The Concept of Liberty], Casablanca: Al-Markaz al-Thaqafi al-'Arabi.

ARKOUN, Muhammad (1990), *Al-Islam: al-akhlaq wa al-siyasa* [Islam: Ethics and Politics], trans., Beirut: Markaz al-Inma' al-Qawmi.

ASAD, Talal (1980), 'Mansha' al-dawla al-'arabiyya al-islamiyya' [Arabic translation of 'Ideology, Class and the Origin of the Arab State'], *Al-Mustaqbal al-'Arabi*, Vol. 3, no. 22, December.

ASSIRI, Abdul-Reda and Kamal Al-Monoufi (1988), 'Kuwait's Political Elite: the Cabinet', *Middle East Journal*, Vol. 42, no. 1, Winter.

AUDA, Gehad (1989), 'Local Government/Administration and Development: Political Context and Dynamics in the Post-Nasser Era', in Takeji Ino et al., *Local Administration and Center–Local Relations in Egypt*, Middle East Studies Series no. 25, Tokyo: Institute of Developing Economies.

'AWAD, Louis (1969), *Tarikh al-fikr al-misri al-hadith* [History of Modern Egyptian Thought]: Vols I and II: *From the French Expedition to Ismail's Era*, Cairo: Dar al-Hilal.

— (1975), *Aqni'at al-Nasiriyya al-sab'a* [The Seven Masks of Nasserism], Beirut: Dar Al-Qadaya.

— (1978), 'Ma'na al-qawmiyya' [The Meaning of Nationalism], in Sa'd al-Din Ibrahim, ed., *'Urubat Misr* [Egypt's Arabness], Cairo: Centre for Political and Strategic Studies (CPSS).

— (1980), *Tarikh al-fikr al-misri al-hadith* [History of Modern Egyptian Thought], Vol. III: *From Ismail's Era to the 1919 Revolution: Historical Background*, Cairo: al-Hay'a al-'Amma li al-kitab.

— (1986), *Tarikh al-fikr al-misri al-hadith* [History of Modern Egyptian Thought], Vol. IV: *From Ismail's Era to the 1919 Revolution: Political and Social Thought*, Cairo: Madbuli.

AL-AWAJI, Ibrahim M. (1971), *Bureaucracy and Society in Saudi Arabia*, unpublished PhD thesis, University of Virginia, USA.

'AWDA, Jihad (1988), 'Al-Mu'ayyanun bi majlis al-sha'b ... ' [Appointees at the People's Assembly: Continuity and Change], in 'Aliy al-Din Hilal, ed., *Intikhabat Majlis al-Sha'b ...* [The People's Assembly Elections of 1987], Cairo: CPSS.

'AWDA, Mahmud (1979), *Al-Fallahun wa al-dawla ...* [Peasants and the State: A Study in Modes of Production and the Social Formation of the Egyptian Village], Cairo: Dar al-Thaqafa.

AYUBI, Nazih N. (Al-Ayyubi) (1978), *Istratijiyyat al-tanmiya fi al-'alam al-thalith ...* [Development Strategies in the Third World], Cairo: CPSS.

— (1980), *Bureaucracy and Politics in Contemporary Egypt*, London: Ithaca Press.

— (1982a), 'Bureaucratic Inflation and Administrative Inefficiency: The Deadlock in Egyptian Administration', in *Middle Eastern Studies*, Vol. 18, no. 3, July.

AYUBI, Nazih N. (Al-Ayubbi) (1982b), 'Vulnerability of the Rich: the Political Economy of Defense and Development in Saudi Arabia and the Gulf', *Gulf Project Monograph*, Washington, DC: Georgetown University Center for Strategic and International Studies (CSIS).

— (1982/83), 'The Politics of Militant Islamic Movements in the Middle East', *Journal of International Affairs*, Vol. 36, no. 2, Fall/Winter.

— (1983), 'The Military Elite in the Contemporary Middle East', in Philip H. Stoddard, ed., *The Middle East in the 1980s: Problems and Prospects*, Washington, DC: Middle East Institute.

— (1984a), 'Local Government and Rural Development in Egypt in the 1970s', *Cahiers Africains d'Administration Publique*, no. 23.

— (1984b), 'OPEC and the Third World: the Case of Arab Aid', in Robert W. Stookey, ed., *The Arabian Peninsula: Contemporary Politics, Economics and International Relations*, Stanford, CA: The Hoover Institution.

— (1986), 'Bureaucracy as Development: Administrative Development and Development Administration in the Arab World', *International Review of Administrative Sciences*, Vol. 56.

— (1988a), 'Arab Bureaucracies: Expanding Size, Changing Roles', in A. Dawisha and W. Zartman, eds, *Beyond Coercion: Durability of the Arab State*, London: Croom Helm.

— (1988b), 'Domestic Policies', in L.C. Harris, ed., *Egypt: Internal Challenges and Regional Stability*, London: Routledge for The Royal Institute of International Affairs.

— (1989a), 'Bureaucracy and Development in Egypt Today', *Journal of Asian and African Studies*, nos. 1–2, January–April.

— (1989b), *Al-Dawla al-markaziyya fi misr* [The Centralised State Tradition in Egypt], Beirut: CAUS.

— (1990a), 'Arab Bureaucracies: Expanding Size, Changing Roles', in Giacomo Luciani, ed., *The Arab State*, London: Routledge.

— (1990b), 'Etatism vs Privatisation: the Case of the Public Sector in Egypt', *International Review of Administrative Sciences*, Vol. 56, no. 1, March.

— (1991a), *Political Islam: Religion and Politics in the Arab World*, London and NY: Routledge.

— (1991b), *The State and Public Policies in Egypt Since Sadat*, Reading: Ithaca Press.

— (1992a), *Al-'Arab wa mushkilat al-dawla* [The Arabs and the Problem of the State], London: Al-Saqi.

— (1992b), 'Political Correlates of Privatization Programs in the Middle East', *Arab Studies Quarterly*, Vol. 14, nos. 2–3, Spring–Summer.

— (1992c), 'State Islam and Communal Plurality', *Annals of the American Academy of Political and Social Science*, Vol. 524, November.

— (1992d), 'Withered Socialism or Whether Socialism: the Radical Arab States as Populist-Corporatist Regimes', *Third World Quarterly*, Vol. 13, no. 1.

— (1993), 'The "Fiscal Crisis" and the "Washington Consensus": Towards an Explanation of Middle East Liberalisations', in L. Blin (dir.), *L'Economie Egyptienne: Libéralisme et Insertion dans le Marché Mondial*, Paris: L'Harmattan.

— (1994), 'Pan-Arabism', in Michael Foley, ed., *Ideas That Shape Politics*, Manchester: Manchester University Press.

'AYYAD, Ranad al-Khatib (1991), *Al-Tayyarat al-siyasiyya* ... [Political Trends in Jordan and Text of the Jordanian National Charter], Amman: Al-Matba'a al-Wataniyya.

'AZIZ, Khairi (1983), *Qadaya al-tanmiya wa al-tahdith* ... [Issues of Development and Modernisation in the Arab Fatherland], Beirut: Dar al-Aflaq al-Jadida.

'AZIZ, Muhammad (1979), *Anmat al-infaq w'al-istithmar fi aqtar al-khalij al-'arabi* [Expenditure and Investment Patterns in Countries of the Arabian Gulf], Cairo: Institute of Arab Research and Studies.

AL-'AZM, Sadiq Jalal (1969), 'Al-Naqd al-dhati ba'd al-hazima' [Self-Criticism after the Defeat], *Mawaqif*, Vol. 1, no. 4, May–June.

AL-'AZMA, 'Aziz (1992), *Al-'Ilmaniyya min manzur mukhtalif* [Secularism: A Different Perspective], Beirut: CAUS.

AL-AZMEH, Aziz (1988), 'Arab Nationalism and Islamism', *Review of Middle Eastern Studies* (London: Ithaca Press), no. 4.

— (1993), *Islams and Modernities*, London: Verso.

BAALI, Fuad and Ali Wardi (1981), *Ibn Khaldun and Islamic Thought Styles: A Social Perspective*, Boston, Mass.: G.H. Hall.

BADIE, Bertrand and Pierre Birnbaum (1983), *The Sociology of the State*, trans., Chicago: Chicago University Press.

— (1986), *Les Deux Etats: pouvoir et société en Occident et en terre d'Islam*, Paris: Fayard.

AL-BADRAWI, 'Abd al-Mun'im (1960), *Al-Madkhal li al-'ulum al-qanuniyya* [Introduction to Legal Sciences: the General Theory of Law], Cairo: Dar al-Kitab al-'Arabi.

BAER, Gabriel (1964), *Egyptian Guilds in Modern Times*, Jerusalem: The Oriental Society.

BARAKAT, 'Ali (1982), *Ru'yat 'Ali Mubarak li tarikh misr al-ijtima'i 1982* [Ali Mubarak's Perspective on Egypt's Social History], Cairo: CPSS.

BARAKAT, Halim (1984), *Al-mujtama' al-'arabi al-mu'asir* [Contemporary Arab Society], Beirut: CAUS.

BARQAWI, Samih Mas'ud (1988), *Al-Mashru'at al-'arabiyya al-mushtaraka* [Arab Joint Ventures], Beirut: CAUS.

BATATU, Hanna (1978), *The Old Social Classes and the Revolutionary Movements of Iraq*, Princeton, NJ: Princeton University Press.

— (1982), 'Syria's Muyslim Brethren', *MERIP Reports*, 12, no. 9.

— (1983), 'The Egyptian, Syrian and Iraqi Revolutions: some observations on their underlying causes and social character', *Inaugural lecture*, Georgetown University, Washington, DC.

BATES, Robert H. (1991), 'The Economics of Transitions to Democracy', *Political Science and Politics*, Vol. XXIV, no. 1, March.

BAUMAN, Zygmunt (1982), *Memories of Class: the Pre-History and After-Life of Class*, London: Routledge and Kegan Paul.

BAYDUN, Ibrahim (1983), *Al-Hijaz wa al-dawla al-islamiyya* [The Hijaz and the Islamic State: a Study in the Problematic of Relationship with the Central Authority in the first Hijri Century], Beirut: Al-Mu'assasa al-jami'iyya.

BEBLAWI, Hazem (1987), 'The Rentier State in the Arab World', in H. Beblawi and G. Luciani, eds, *The Rentier State*, London: Croom Helm.

— and Giacomo Luciani, eds (1987), *The Rentier State*, London: Croom Helm (Vol. II of *Nation, State and Integration in the Arab World*, ed. G. Luciani).

BECKER, David (1983), *The New Bourgeoisie and the Limits of Dependency: Mining, Class, and Power in 'Revolutionary' Peru*, Princeton, NJ: Princeton University Press.

— (1987), 'Bonanza Development and the New Bourgeoisie', in D. Becker et al., eds, *Postimperialism*, Boulder, CO: Lynne Reinner.

BE'ERI, Eliezer (1970), *Army Officers in Arab Politics and Society*, New York and London: Praeger and Pall Mall Press.

BEININ, Joel (1987), 'The Communist Movement and Nationalist Political Discourse in Nasirist Egypt', *Middle East Journal*, Vol. 41, no. 4, Autumn.

— and Zachary Lockman (1987), *Workers on the Nile: Nationalism, Communism, Islam, and the Egyptian Working Class, 1882–1954*, Princeton, NJ: Princeton University Press.

BELLAMY, Richard (1987), *Modern Italian Social Theory: Ideology and Politics from Pareto to the Present*, Cambridge: Polity Press/Blackwell.

BEN ACHOUR, Yadh (1980), *L'Etat Nouveau et la Philosophie et Juridique Occidentale*, Tunis: Imp. de la République Tunisienne.

— (1985), 'Administration publique et crise de développement', in Institut International des Sciences Administratives (IISA) and Association Tunisienne des Sciences Administratives (ATSA), *Administration et Développement en Tunisie*, Bruxelles et Tunis: IISA and ATSA.

BENAZZI, Lakhdar (1989), 'L'Administration publique et le changement: des préjugés à combattre', in L'Association Marocaine des Sciences Administratives (AMSA), *L'Administration Publique et le Changement*, Casablanca: Afrique Orient/AMSA.

BENNOUNE, Mahfoud (1988), *The Making of Contemporary Algeria, 1830–1987; Colonial Upheavals and Post-Independence Development*, Cambridge: Cambridge University Press.

— (1990), 'Algeria's Façade Democracy', in *Middle East Report*, March–April 1990.

BEN ROMDHANE, Mahmoud (1990), 'Fondements et contenu des restructurations face à la crise économique en Tunisie: une analyse critique', in J.-C. Santucci et H. El Malki, eds, *Etat et Développement dans le Monde Arabe: Crises et Mutations au Maghreb*, Paris: Editions du CNRS.

BEN SALEM, Lilia (1976), *Développement et Problème de Cadres: le Cas de la Tunisie*, Tunos: Cahiers de Centre d'Etudes et de Recherches Economiques et Sociales (CERES).

BERNAL, Martin (1987), *Black Athena*, (London: Free Association Books).

BERQUE, Jacques (1972), *Egypt: Imperialism and Revolution*, London: Faber and Faber.

BERTRAND, Michèle (1979), *Le Statut de la religion chez Marx et Engels*, Paris: Editions Sociales.

BEZIRGAN, Najm A. (1978/79), 'Islam and Arab Nationalism', *Middle East Review*, Vol. XI, no. 2, Winter.

BIANCHI, Robert (1984), *Interest Groups and Political Development in Turkey*, Princeton, NJ: Princeton University Press.

— (1986), 'Interest Group Politics in the Third World', *Third World Quarterly*, Vol. 8, no. 2, April.

— (1988), 'The Strengthening of Associational Life and its Potential Contributions to Political Reform', paper for JCNME/SSRC Conference on Retreating States and Expanding Societies: the State Autonomy/Civil Society Dialectic in the Middle East and North Africa, Aix-en-Provence, March 1988.

— (1989), *Unruly Corporatism: Associational Life in Twentieth Century Egypt*, New York and Oxford: Oxford University Press.

— (1990), 'Interest Groups and Politics in Mubarak's Egypt', in Ibrahim M. Oweiss, ed., *The Political Economy of Contemporary Egypt*, Washington, DC: Georgetown University Center for Contemporary Arab Studies.

BIENEN, Henry and Jonathan Moore (1987), 'The Sudan: Military Economic Corporations', *Armed Forces and Society*, 13, Summer.

BILL, James A. (1972), 'Class Analysis and the Dialectics of Modernisation in the Middle East' *International Journal of Middle East Studies*, Vol. 3, no. 4, October.

— and Carl Leiden (1984), *Politics in the Middle East*, 2nd edn, Boston: Little, Brown.

— and Robert Springborg (1990), *Politics in the Middle East*, 3rd edn, NY: HarperCollins.

BILQAZIZ, 'Abd al-Ilah (1991), *Ishkaliyyat al-wahda al-'arabiyya ...* [The Problematique of Arab Unity: Discourse of the Desirable, Discourse of the Possible], Casablanca: Ifriqia al-Sharq.

BIN 'ABD AL-'ALI, 'Abd al-Salam (1992), 'Hawas al-Hawiyya' [Identity-Mania], *Al-Hayat*, 23 November 1992.

BIN 'ASHUR, 'Iyad (1990), 'Ta'ammulat fi al-shar'iyya ... ' [Reflections on Legitimacy, Culture and the 'Populist' State], *Al-Fikr al-'Arabi al-Mu'asir*, No. 72/73, January/February.

BINDER , Leonard, (1978), *In a Moment of Enthusiasm: Political Power and the Second Stratum in Egypt*, Chicago and London: Chicago University Press.

— (1988), *Islamic Liberalism: a Critique of Development Ideologies*, Chicago and London: Chicago University Press.

BISHARA, 'Abdallah (1985), *Tajrubat majlis al-ta'awun al-khaliji* [The GCC Experiment: A Step Towards Arab Unity or a Barrier in its Path?], Amman: Arab Thought Forum.

AL-BISHRI, Tariq (1980), *Al-Muslimun wa al-aqbat ...* [Muslims and Copts in the Context of the National Community], Cairo: Hay'at al-Kitab.

— (1983), *Al-Haraka al-siyasiyya ...* [The Political Movement in Egypt 1945–1952], rev. edn, Cairo: Dar Al-Shuruq.

BLACK, Anthony (1984), *Guilds and Civil Society in European Political Thought from the Twelfth Century to the Present*, London: Methuen.

— (1985), 'Lorenzo Ornaghi: Stato e Corporazione', book review in *History of Political Thought*, Vol. VI, no. 3, Winter.

— (1988), *State, Community and Human Desire: A Group-centred Account of Political Values*, New York: Harvester-Wheatsheaf/St Martin's Press.

BLAU, Peter M. (1964), *Exchange and Power in Social Life*, New York: Wiley.

BOGGS, Carl (1976), *Gramsci's Marxism*, London: Pluto Press.

BONNÉ, Alfred (1973), *State and Economics in the Middle East; A Society in Transition*, 2nd edn, Westport, CT: Greenwood Press.

BORCHERDING, T. (1977), *Budgets and Bureaucrats: The Sources of Goverment Growth*, Durham, NC: Duke University Press.

BOUAOUAJA, Mohammed (1989), 'Privatization in Tunisia', in Said El-Naggar, ed., *Privatization and Structural Adjustment in the Arab Countries*, Washington, DC; International Monetary Fund.

BOUATTIA, Brahim (1993), 'From Central Planning to Market Economy: a Study in the Political Economy of Changes in Algerian Industrial Development', paper presented to Conference on *Liberalisation*, University of Exeter, UK, March 1993.

BRAND, Laurie A. (1992), 'Economic and Political Liberalization in a Rentier Economy; the Case of the Hashemite Kingdom of Jordan', in I. Harik and D. Sullivan, eds, *Privatization and Liberalization in the Middle East*, Bloomington: Indiana University Press.

BRECHT, Arnold (1959), *Political Theory; the Foundations of Twentieth-Century Political Thought*, Princeton, NJ: Princeton University Press.

BRESSER PEREIRA, Luiz Carlos (1991), 'Economic Crisis in Latin America', *East South Systems Transformations*, Working Paper, No. 6, January 1991, Dept. of Political Science, University of Chicago, Illinois.

BREWER, Anthony (1980), *Marxist Theories of Imperialism; a critical survey*, London, Routledge and Kegan Paul.

BROMLEY, Simon (1994), *Rethinking Middle East Politics*, London: Polity Press.

BROWN, L. Carl (1984), *International Politics and the Middle East: Old Rules, Dangerous Games*, London: I.B.Tauris.

BUCI-GLUCKSMANN, Christine (1980), *Gramsci and the State*, trans., London: Lawrence and Wishart.

BULL, Martin J. (1992), 'The Corporatist Ideal-Type and Political Exchange', Political Studies, Vol. 40, no. 2.

BURAQIYYA, Rahma (1991), *Al-Dawla wa al-sulta wa al-mujtama'* ... [State, Authority and Society in Morocco], Beirut: Dar al-Tali'a.

BURDEAU, Georges (1970), *L'Etat*, Paris: Editions du Seuil.

BUTSHIT, Ibrahim al-Qadri (1989), 'Hal 'araf al-mujtama' al-'arabi al-iqta'?' [Has Arab Society Known Feudalism?], *Al-Wahda*, June.

BYRES, T. J. (1985), 'Modes of Production and Non-European Pre-Colonial Societies', in T.J. Byres and H. Mukhia, eds, *Feudalism and Non-European Societies*, London: Frank Cass.

— and Harbans Mukhia, eds (1985), *Feudalism and Non-European Societies*, London: Frank Cass.

CAMAU, Michel (1990), 'Etat, espace public et développement: le cas tunisien', in J.-C. Santucci et H. El Malki, eds, *Etat et Développement dans le Monde Arabe: Crises et Mutations au Maghreb*, Paris: Editions du CNRS.

CAMMACK, Paul (1992), 'Strong States, Weak States, and Third World Development', *Manchester Papers in Politics*, Department of Government, Manchester University, Manchester, UK.

CANOVAN, Margaret (1981), *Populism*, London: Junction Books.

CANTORI, Louis J. (1986), 'Corporatism, Conservatism and Political Development in the Middle East', paper presented to APSA Conference, Washington, DC, 14 August 1986.

CAPORASO, James A. (1978), 'Dependence, Dependency and Power in the Global System', *International Organization*, Vol. 32, no. 1. Winter.

CARAPICO, Sheila (1991), 'Yemen: Unification and the Gulf War', *MERIP*, Vol. 21, no. 3, May/June.

— (1994), 'From Ballot Box to Battlefield: the War of the Two 'Alis', *Middle East Report*, September–October 1994.

CARNOY, Martin (1984), *The State and Political Theory*, Princeton, NJ: Princeton University Press.

CASTIGLIONE, Dario (1994), 'History and Theories of Civil Society' in D. Lovell and N. Rupke, eds, *Ideas and Ideologies*, special issue of *Australian Journal of Politics and History*, Vol. 40, 1994.

CAWSON, Alan (1986), *Corporatism and Political Theory*, Oxford and NY: Basil Blackwell.

CENTRAL BANK OF KUWAIT (1978), *Economic Report for 1978* .

CENTRE D'ETUDES ET DE RECHERCHES MARXISTES (CERM) (1969), *Sur le 'Mode de production Asiatique'*, Paris: Editions Sociales.

CENTRE FOR ARAB UNITIY STUDIES (1981), *Al-Qawmiyya al-'arabiyya wa al-Islam* [Arab Nationalism and Islam], Beirut: CAUS.

CENTRE FOR POLITICAL AND STRATEGIC STUDIES [Markaz al-Dirasat al-Siyasiyya wa al-Istırajiyya] (CPSS) (1986, 1987, 1988, 1991, 1992), *Al-Taqrir al-istiratiji al-'arabi* [The Arab Strategic Report], pub. annually, Cairo: Al-Ahram Foundation/CPSS.

CERNY, Philip G. (1987), 'Reconceptualising Corporatism: State Structures and Patterns of Interest Intermediation', paper presented to Political Studies Association Annual Conference, 7–9 April 1987.

— (1990), *The Changing Architecture of Politics: Structure, Agency, and the Future of the State*, London: Sage Publications.

CHACKERIAN, Richard and Gilbert Abcarian (1988), *Bureaucratic Power in Society*, Chicago: Nelson Hall.

— and Suliman M. Shadukhi (1983), 'Public Bureaucracy in Saudi Arabia: An Empirical Assessment of Work Behavior', *International Review of Administrative Sciences*, Vol. 69, no. 3.

CHALIAND, Gérard (1964), *L'Algérie est-elle socialiste?* Paris: Maspéro.

CHALMERS, Douglas A. (1977), 'The Politicized State in Latin America', in James M. Malloy, ed., *Authoritarianism and Corporatism in Latin America*, Pittsburgh: University of Pittsburgh Press.

— (1985), 'Corporatism and Comparative Politics', in Howard Wiarda, ed., *New Directions in Comparative Politics*, Boulder, CO: Westview Press.

CHATELUS, Michel and Yves Schemeil (1984), 'Towards a New Political Economy of State Industrialization in the Arab Middle East', *International Journal of Middle East Studies*, Vol. 16.

— (1987), 'Politics for Development: Attitudes Toward Industry and Services', in H. Beblawi and G. Luciani, eds, *The Rentier State*, London: Croom Helm.

CHAUDHRY, Kiren Aziz (1989), 'The Price of Wealth: Business and State in Labor Remittance and Oil Economies', *International Organization*, Vol. 43, no. 1, Winter.

— (1991), 'On the Way to Market: Economic Liberalisation and Iraq's Invasion of Kuwait', *Middle East Report* (MERIP), no. 171, May–June.

— (1992), 'Economic Liberalization in Oil-Exporting Countries: Iraq and Saudi Arabia', in Iliya Harik and Denis J. Sullivan, eds, *Privatization and Liberalization in the Middle East*, Bloomington: Indiana University Press.

CHEKIR, Mohamed (1985), 'La Fonction publique et la réforme administrative en Tunisie', *mimeo*, Tunis, 1985.

CHERIF, Slaheddine (1985) 'Fonction Publique et Développement', in IISA and ATSA, *Administration et Développement en Tunisie*, Bruxelles and Tunis: IISA and ATSA.

CHODAK, Szymon (1989), *The New State: Etatization of Western Societies*, Boulder and London: Lynne Rienner.

CHOUEIRI, Youssef (1990), *Islamic Fundamentalism*, London: Pinter Publishers.

CHUBIN, Shahram, Robert Litwak and Avi Plascov (1982), *Security in the Gulf*, Aldershot, UK: Gower for the International Institute for Strategic Studies.

CLAPHAM, Christopher (1985), *Third World Politics, An Introduction*, London: Croom Helm.

— (1992), 'The Collapse of Socialist Development in the Third World', *Third World Quarterly*, special issue on *Rethinking Socialism*, Vol. 13, no. 1.

CLARKE, Simon, (1991), 'The State Debate', in S. Clarke, ed., *The State Debate*, Basingstoke and London: Macmillan.

CLEGG, Ian (1971), *Workers' Self-Management in Algeria*, New York: Monthly Review Press.

CLEVELAND, William L. (1971), *The Making of An Arab Nationalist: Ottomanism and Arabism in the Life and Thought of Sati' al-Husri*, Princeton, NJ: Princeton University Press.

COLE, Donald P. (1975), *Nomads of the Nomads: the Al Murrah Bedouin of the Empty Quarter*, Arlington Heights, Ill: Harlan Davidson.

COLLIER, David and Ruth B. Collier (1977), 'Who Does What, To Whom, and How; Toward a Comparative Analysis of Latin American Corporatism', in James M. Malloy, ed., *Authoritarianism and Corporatism in Latin America*, Pittsburgh: University of Pittsburgh Press.

COMBS-SCHILLING, M.E. (1989), *Sacred Performances: Islam, Sexuality, and Sacrifice*, New York: Columbia University Press.

COMMANDER, Simon and Tony Killick (1988), 'Privatisation in Developing Countries: A Survey of the Issues', in P. Cook and C. Kirkpatrick, eds, *Privatisation in Less Developed Countries*, Sussex: Wheatsheaf Books.

COOK, Paul and Colin Kirkpatrick, eds (1988), *Privatisation in Less Developed Countries*, Sussex: Wheatsheaf Books.

COOPER, Mark (1982), *The Transformation of Egypt*, London: Croom Helm.

CORDESMAN, Anthony H. (1984), *The Gulf and the Search for Strategic Stability*, Boulder and London: Westview and Mansell.

COURY, R.M. (1982), 'Who Invented Egyptian Arab Nationalism?', *International Journal of Middle East Studies*, Vol. 14, nos. 3–4, August–November.

COX, Robert W. (1983), 'Gramsci, Hegemony and International Relations: An Essay in Method', *Millenium: Journal of International Studies*, Vol. 12, no. 2.

CRANE, Robert D. (1978), *Planning the Future of Saudi Arabia*, New York: Praeger.

CRONE, Patricia and Michael Cook (1977), *Hagarism: the Making of the Islamic World*, Cambridge: Cambridge University Press.

— (1986), 'The Tribe and the State', in John A. Hall, ed., *States in History*, Oxford and NY: Basil Blackwell.

CROZIER, M. (1964), *The Bureaucratic Phenomenon*, Chicago: Chicago University Press.

CRYSTAL, Jill (1989), 'Coalitions in Oil Monarchies: Kuwait and Qatar', *Comparative Politics*, Vol. 21, no. 4, July.

— (1991), *Oil and Politics in the Gulf: Rulers and Merchants in Kuwait and Qatar*, New York: Cambridge University Press (2nd printing of 1990 edn.).

CUMINGS, Bruce (1989), 'The Abortive Abertura: South Korea in the Light of Latin American Experience', *New Left Review*, no. 173, Jan/Feb.

CUNNINGHAM, Robert (1989), *The Bank and the Bureau: Organizational Development in the Middle East*, New York: Praeger.

CYPHER, James M. (1979), 'The Internationalization of Capital and the Transformation of Social Formations', *The Review of Radical Political Economics*, Vol. 11, no. 4, Winter.

DAHIR, Mas'ud (1986), *Al-Mashriq al-'arabi al-mu'asir min al-badawa ila al-dawla al-haditha* [the Contemporary Arab Levant from Nomadism to the Modern State], Beirut: Ma'had al-Inma' al-'Arabi.

DAHL, Robert A. (1971), *Polyarchy: Participation and Opposition* (New Haven and London: Yale University Press).

DALE, Roger (1984), 'Nation State and International Systems: the World-system Perspective', in Gregor McLennan, David Held and Stuart Hall, eds, *The Idea of the Modern State*, Milton Keynes, UK: Open University Press.

DALILA, 'Arif (1989), 'Al-Islah al-iqtisadi fi al-qutr al-suri' [Economic Reform in the Syrian State], in Ramzi Zaki, ed., *Al-Siyasat al-tashihiyya wa al-tanmiyya* ... [Corrective Policies and Development in the Arab Fatherland], Beirut and Kuwait: Dar al-Razi.

— (1990), 'Tajrubat al-suriya ma' al-qita 'ain al-'amm w'al khas' [Syria's Experience with the Public and Private Sectors] in 'A. Al-Nasrawi et al., *Al-Qita' al-'amm* ... [The Public and the Private Sectors in the Arab Fatherland], Beirut: CAUS.

DALLU, Burhan al-Din (1985), *Musahama fi i'adat kitabat al-tarikh al-'arabi al-islami* [A Contribution to a Re-writing of Arab-Islamic History], Beirut: Dar al-Farabi.

DARIF, Muhammad (1988), *Mu'assasat al-sultan 'al-sharif' bi al-Maghrib* [The 'Sharifian' Sultanic Institution in Morocco], Casablanca: Ifriqiyya al-Sharq.

— (1991), *Al-Nasaq al-siyasi* ... [The Contemporary Political System of Morocco], Casablanca: Afriqiya al-Sharq.

DA SILVA LOPES, Jose (1989), 'Policies of Economic Adjustment to Correct External Imbalances', in Alan Roe et al., *Economic Adjustment in Algeria, Egypt, Jordan, Morocco, Pakistan, Tunisia, and Turkey*, Economic Development Institute Policy Seminar report, no. 15, Washington, DC: World Bank.

DAVIDSON, Alastair (1977), *Antonio Gramsci: Towards an Intellectual Biography*, London and New Jersey: Merlin Press and Humanities Press.

DAVIS-WILLARD, Eric (1978), 'Theory and Method in the Study of Arab Nationalism', *Review of Middle East Studies*, London: Ithaca Press, no. 3.

DAVIS, Eric (1983), *Challenging Colonialism: Bank Misr and Egyptian Industrialization 1920–1941*, Princeton, NJ: Princeton University Press.

DAVIS, Eric (1994), 'History for the Many or History for the Few? The Historiography of the Iraqi Working Class', in Zachary Lockman, ed., *Workers and Working Classes in the Middle East*, New York: SUNY Press.

DAWISHA, Adeed and William Zartman, eds (1988), *Beyond Coercion: Durability of the Arab State*, London: Croom Helm.

DEEB, Marius (1979), *Party Politics in Egypt: the Wafd and its Rivals, 1919–1939*, London: Ithaca Press.

DE JASAY, Anthony (1985), *The State*, Oxford: Basil Blackwell.

DEKMEJIAN, Richard H. (1982), 'Egypt and Turkey: the Military in the Background', in R. Kolkowicz and A. Korbonski, eds, *Soldiers. Peasants and Bureaucrats: Civil–Military Relations in Communist and Modernizing Societies*, London: George Allen and Unwin.

— (1983). 'Government and Politics', in R.F. Nyrop, *Egypt; A Country Study*, Washington, DC: The American University.

DENOEUX, Guilain (1993), *Urban Unrest in the Middle East; A Comparative Study of Informal Networks in Egypt, Iran and Lebanon*, Albany, NY: SUNY Press.

DEUTSCHER, Isaac (1969), 'Roots of Bureaucracy', *The Socialist Register 1969*, London: Merlin.

DI PALMA, Giuseppe (1991), 'Legitimation from the Top to Civil Society: Politico-Cultural Change in Eastern Europe', *World Politics*, Vol. 44, no. 1, October.

AL-DISUQI, 'Asim A. (1975), *Kibar mullak al-aradi ...* [Large Owners of Agricultural Land and their Role in Egyptian Society 1914–1952], Cairo: Dar al-Thaqafa al-Jadida.

— (1981), *Nahwa fahm tarikh Misr* [Towards an Understanding of Egypt's Socio-Economic History], Cairo: Dar al-Kitab al-Jami'i.

DI TELLA, Torcuato (1965), 'Populism and Reform in Latin America', in C. Veliz, ed., *Obstacles to Change in Latin America*, London: Oxford University Press.

DIYAB, Muhammad Hafiz (1988), 'Al-Mujtama' wa al-dawla ... ' [A Review of Kh. Al-Naqib's 'Society and State in Arabia and the Gulf'], *Al-Mustaqbal al-'Arabi*, no. 115, September.

DORE, Ronald (1976), *The Diploma Disease: Education, Qualifications and Development*, Berkeley and Los Angeles: University of California Press.

DRAPER, Hal (1977), *Karl Marx's Theory of Revolution: Vol. I, State and Bureaucracy*, New York: Monthly Review Press.

DRESCH, Paul (1991), 'Imams and Tribes: the Writing and Acting of History in Upper Yemen', in Philip. S. Khoury and Joseph Kostiner, eds, *Tribes and State Formation in the Middle East*, London and New York: I.B. Tauris.

DRYSDALE, Alasdair (1982), 'The Syrian Armed Forces and National Politics', in R. Kolkowicz and A. Korbonski, eds, *Soldiers, Peasants and Bureaucracy: Civil–Military Relations in Communist and Modernizing Societies*, London: Allen and Unwin.

DUBAR, Claude and Salim Nasr (1976), *Les Classes sociales au Liban*, Paris: Presses de la Fondation Nationale des Sciences Politiques.

DUMONT, Louis (1986), *Essays on Individualism: Modern Ideology in Anthropological Perspective*, Chicago and London: Chicago University Press.

DUMPER, Michael (1994), *Islam and Israel: Religious Endowments and the Jewish State*, Washington, DC: Institute for Palestinian Studies.

DUNSHIRE, Andrew (1978), *Control in a Bureaucracy*, Oxford: Martin Robertson.

DUPRÉ, Georges and Pierre-Philippe Rey (1980) 'Reflections on the Pertinence of a Theory of the History of Exchange', in Harold Wolpe, ed., *The Articulation of Modes of Production*, London: Routledge and Kegan Paul.

AL-DURI, 'Abd al-'Aziz (1982), *Muqaddima fi al-tarikh al-iqtisadi al-'arabi* [An Introduction to Arab Economic Theory], Beirut: Dar al-Tali'a.

— (1984), *Al-Takwin al-tarikhi li al-umma al-'arabiyya* [Historical Formation of the Arab Nation], Beirut: CAUS.

DUVAL, R.D. (1978), 'Dependence and Dependency Theory: Notes towards Precision of Concept and Argument', *International Organization*, Winter.

DUWAIDAR, Muhammad (1978), *Istratijiyyat al-tatwir al-'arabi ...* [Arab Development Strategy and the New International Economic Order], Cairo: Dar al-Thaqafa al-Jadida.

AL-DUWAILA, Mubarak (1992), 'Taqyim al-tajruba al-barlamaniyya' [The Evaluation of the

Parliamentary Experiment], in Ahmad Al-Khaja et al., *Al-Kuwait wa tahaddiyat ...* [Kuwait and the Challenges of the Era for Reconstruction], Cairo: Markaz al-Buhuth al-Siyasiyya.

DUWAJI, Ghazi (1967), *Economic Development in Tunisia: The Impact and Course of Government Planning*, New York: Praeger.

EASTON, David (1953), *The Political System*, New York: Alfred A. Knopf.

EATON, Joseph W. (1989), 'Bureaucratic, Capitalist and Populist Privatization Strategies', *International review of Administrative Sciences*, Vol. 55, no. 3, September.

ECONOMIST INTELLIGENCE UNIT (EIU) (1987/88), *Saudi Arabia: Country Profile 1987/88*, London: EIU.

EGYPT, Central Agency for Organisation and Administration (CAOA) (1978), 'Internal Memoranda', Cairo: CAOA.

— Institute of National Planning (1975), *Bahth hasr wa taqdir al-ihtiyajat min al-'amala bu al-qita' al-'am* [Employment in the Public Sector ...], ed. Md. 'Abd al-Fattah Munki, Cairo: INP.

— Ministry of Finance (1979), *Al-Bayan al-ihsa'i ...* [The Statistical Statement for the 1979 Budget], Cairo.

EICKELMAN, Dale F. (1981), *The Middle East: An Anthropological Approach*, Englewood Cliffs, NJ: Prentice-Hall.

ELHUSSEIN, Ahmed Mustafa (1991), 'Manpower Nationalization in the United Arab Emirates: The Case of the Banking Sector', *Journal of Developing Societies*, Vol. VII, no. 2, July–October.

ENTELIS, John P. (1982), 'Algeria: Technocratic Rule, Military Power', in I. William Zartman et al., *Political Elites in Arab North Africa: Morocco, Algeria, Tunisia, Libya and Egypt*, New York and London: Longman.

ESMAN, Milton J. and Itamar Rabinovich, eds (1988), *Ethnicity, Pluralism and the State in the Middle East*, New York: Cornell University Press.

ESPOSITO, John L. and James Piscatori (1991), 'Democratization and Islam', *Middle East Journal*, Vol. 45, no. 3, Summer.

ETIENNE, Bruno (1987), *L'Islamisme radical*, Paris: Hachette.

EVANS, Peter B., D. Rueschmeyer and T. Skocpol, eds (1985), *Bringing the State Back In*, London and New York: Cambridge University Press

EZAKI, Masahiro (1991), *The Ideal Notion and its Embodiment: the Courtyard House of the Arab-Islamic World*, Institute of Middle Eastern Studies, Working Papers Series, no. 26, The International University of Japan, Niigata.

AL-FALEH, Matrook (1987), *The Impact of the Processes of Modernization and Social Mobilization on the Social and Political Structures of the Arab Countries with special emphasis on Saudi Arabia*, PhD dissertation, University of Kansas, 1987.

FANELLI, José Maria, R. Frenkel and G. Rozenwurcel (1990), *Growth and Structural Reform in Latin America*, Buenos Aires: CEDES.

FARAH, Nadia Ramsis (1985), 'Al-Tanmiya wa azmat al-tahawwul al-siyasi' [Development and the Crisis of Political Transition], *Al-Manar*, Vol. 1, no. 6, June.

— (1992), 'Al-Muthaqqafun wa al-dawla ... ' [Intellectuals, the State and Civil Society], in Amina Rashid, ed., *Qadaya al-mujtama' al-madani al-'Arabi fi daw' utruhat Gramshi* [Issues of the Arab Civil Society in Light of Gramsci's Theses], Cairo: Markaz al-Buhuth al-'Arabiyya.

FARAH, Tawfic E., ed. (1987), *Pan-Arabism and Arabic Nationalism: the Continuing Debate*, Boulder and London: Westview Press.

FARAHAT, Muhammad Nur (1987), 'Al-'unf al-siyasi wa al-jama'at al-hamishiyya' [Political Violence and Marginal Groupings ... in the Social History of Egypt], in U. Al-Ghazali Harb, *Al-'Unf wa al-siyasa ...* [Violence and Politics in the Arab Fatherland], Amman: Arab Thought Forum.

FARNSWORTH, Lee W. (1989), "Clan Politics' and Japan's Changing Policy-Making Structure', *The World Economy*, Vol. 12, no. 2, June.

FAROUK-SLUGLETT, Marion and Peter Sluglett (1990), 'Iraq Since 1986: the Strengthening of Saddam', *Middle East Report* (MERIP), no. 167, November/December.

AL-FARSY, Fouad (1982), *Saudi Arabia: a Case Study in Development*, London and Boston: Kegan Paul International.

EL-FATHALY, Omar and Richard Chackerian (1983), 'Administration: the Forgotten issue in Arab Development', in I. Ibrahim, ed., *Arab Resources: the Transformation of a Society*, Washington, DC and London: Georgetown University Center for Contemporary Arab Studies and Croom Helm.

FATHY, Hassan (1973), *Architecture for the Poor: An Experiment in Rural Egypt*, Chicago: Chicago University Press (first published in 1969 as *Gourna: A Tale of Two Villages*, by the Ministry of Culture, Cairo).

AL-FAWWAL, Salah (1983), *Dirasat 'ilm al-ijtima' al-badawi* [The Study of Nomadic Sociology], Cairo: Maktabat Gharib.

FAWZI, 'Isam (1992), 'Aliyyat al-haymana wa al-muqawama ... ' [The Dynamics of Hegemony and Resistance in Popular Discourse], in Amina Rashid et al., *Qadaya al-mujtama' al-madani ...* [Issues of the Arab Civil Society in Light of Gramsci's Theses], Cairo: Markaz al-Buhuth al-'Arabiyya.

FAWZI, Samiha (1992), 'Al-Iqtisad al-misri wa al-sharikat muta'addiyat al-jinsiyya' [The Egyptian Economy and Supranational Corporations', paper presented to Conference organised by Centre d'études et de documentation économique et juridque (CEDEJ) and Center for Economic and Financial Research and Studies (CEFRS) on *Liberalisation of the Egyptian Economy*, Cairo University, 2–3 May 1992.

FEMIA, Joseph (1975), 'Hegemony and Consciousness', *Political Studies*, Vol. 23, no. 1, March.

FIELD, Michael (1984), *The Merchants: the Big Business Families of Arabia*, London: John Murray.

AL-FIQI, Mustafa (1985), *Al-Aqbat fi al-siyasa al-misriyya* [The Copts in Egyptian Politics], Cairo and Beirut: Al-Shuruq.

FISHMAN, Robert M. (1990), 'Rethinking State and Regime: Southern Europe's Transition to Democracy', *World Politics*, Vol. 42, no. 3, April.

FORAN, John (1988), 'The Modes of Production Approach to Seventeenth Century Iran', *International Journal of Middle East Studies*, Vol. 20, no. 3, August.

FOSTER-CARTER, Aidan (1978), 'The Modes of Production Controversy', *New Left Review*, no. 107, Jan.–Feb.

FOUCAULT, Michel (1984), *The History of Sexuality*, Middlesex: Penguin Books.

GAVRIELIDES, Nicolas (1987), 'Tribal Democracy: the Anatomy of Parliamentary Elections in Kuwait', in Linda Layne, ed., *Elections in the Middle East; Implications of Recent Trends*, Boulder, CO: Westview Press.

GELLNER, Ernest (1981), *Muslim Society*, London: Cambridge University Press.

— (1983), 'The Tribal Society and its Enemies', in Richard Tapper, ed., *The Conflict of Tribe and State*, London: Croom Helm.

— (1991), 'Tribalism and the State in the Middle East', in Philip S. Khoury and Joseph Kostiner, eds, *Tribes and State Formation in the Middle East*, London and New York: I.B. Tauris.

GERMANI, Gino (1978), *Authoritarianism, Fascism, and National Populism*, New Brunswick, NJ: Transaction Books.

— (1980), *Marginality*, New Brunswick, NJ: Transaction Books.

GERSCHENKRON, Alexander (1962), *Economic Backwardness in Historical Perspective*, Cambridge, MA: Harvard University Press.

GERSHONI, Israel (1981), *The Emergence of Pan-Arabism in Egypt*, Tel Aviv: Shiloah Centre for Middle Eastern Studies.

GERTH, H.M. and C. Wright Mills, eds (1970), *From Max Weber*, London: Routledge and Kegan Paul.

AL-GHABRA, Shafiq (1988), 'Al-Ithniyya al-musayyasa' [Politicized Ethnicity], *Majallat al-'Ulum al-Ijtima'iyya*, Vol. 16, no. 3, Autumn.

GHABRA, Shafeeq (1991), 'Voluntary Associations in Kuwait: the Foundation of a New System?', *Middle East Journal*, Vol. 45, no. 2, Spring.

GHALYUN, Burhan (1992), 'Bina' al-mujtama' al-madani al-'arabi' [Constructing the Arab Civil Society], in Sa'id B. Al-'Alawi et al., *Al-Mujtama' al-madani fi al-watan al-'arabi. ...* [The Civil Society and its Role in Realising Democracy in the 'Arab Fatherland'], Beirut: CAUS.

— (1993), *Al-Mihna al-'Arabiyya: al-dawla didd al-umma* [The Arab Malaise: The State Against the Nation], Beirut: CAUS.

AL-GHAZALI HARB, Usama (1987), 'Thawrat yulyu wa i'adat tashkil ... ' [The July 1952 Revolution and the Reconstitution of the Political Elite in Egypt], in A. Saqr et al., *Thawrat 23 Julyu* [The July 1952 Revolution], Cairo: Dar al- Mustaqbal al-'Arabi.

— (1988), 'Sahwat al-mujtama' al-madani fi misr' [Awakening of the Civil Society in Egypt], *Al-Ahram*, 8 April 1988.

GHAZUL, Firyal J. (1992), 'Manzur Gramshi fi al-naqd al-adabi' [Gramsci's Perspective on Literary Criticism], in Amina Rashid et al., *Qadaya al-mujtama' al-madani al-'arabi fi daw' utruhat Gramshi* [Issues of the Arab Civil Society in Light of Gramsci's Theses], Cairo: Markaz al-Buhuth al-'Arabi.

GHUNAIM, 'Adil (1986), *Al-Namudhaj al-misri li ra'smaliyyat al-dawla al-tabi'a* [The Egyptian Model of Dependent State Capitalism], Cairo: Dar al-Mustaqbal al-'Arabi.

GHURBAL, 'Abd al-Fattah, 'A. Al-'Amus and 'A. Sha'ban (1989), 'Al-Siyasat al-tashihiyya fi al-iqtisad al-tunisi' [Adjustment Policies in the Tunisian Economy], in Ramzi Zaki, ed., *Al-Siyasat al-tashihiyya wa al-tanmiyya* ... [Corrective Policies and Development in the Arab Fatherland], Beirut and Kuwait: Dar al-Razi.

GILLESPIE, Charles G. (1990), 'Models of Democratic Transition in South America: Negotiated Reform versus Democratic Rupture', in Diane Ethier, ed., *Democratic Transition and Consolidation in Southern Europe, Latin America and Southeast Asia*, London: Macmillan.

GILSENAN, Michael (1991), 'The Grand Illusion', *Marxism Today*, March 1991.

GIRGIS, Fawzi (1958), *Dirasat fi tarikh misr* ... [Studies in the Political History of Egypt Since the Mamluke Era], Cairo: Al-Dar al-Misriyya.

GIRGIS, Malak (1974), *Saykulujiyyat al-shakhsiyya al-misriyya* ... [Psychology of the Egpytian Character and Obstacles to Development], Cairo: Rose al-Yusuf Press.

GLAVANIS, Kathleen and Pandelis Glavanis (1983), *The Rural Middle East: Peasant Lives and Modes of Production*, London: Zed Books.

GODELIER, Maurice (1978), 'Infrastructures, Societies and History', *New Left Review*, 112, November–December.

GOLDBERG, Ellis (1991), 'Smashing Idols and the State: the Protestant Ethic and Egyptian Sunni Radicalism', *Comparative Studies in Society and History*, Vol. 33.

— (1992), 'The Foundations of State–Labor Relations in Contemporary Egypt', *Comparative Politics*, Vol. 24, no. 2.

GOMAA, Ahmad M. (1977), *The Foundation of the League of Arab States*, London: Longman.

GOURDAN, Hubert (1989), 'A propos de l'Islam étatique', in Mostafa K. El Sayed (dir.), *Récentes Transformations Politiques dans le Monde Arabe*, Cairo University, Centre for Political Research and Studies.

GRAMSCI, Antonio (1971), *Selections from the Prison Notebooks*, trans., London: Lawrence and Wishart (reprinted 1986).

— (1978), *Selections from Political Writings 1921–1926*, trans., London: Lawrence and Wishart.

— (1987), *The Modern Prince and Other Writings*, trans., New York: International Publishers.

GRAN, Peter (1979), *Islamic Roots of Capitalism: Egypt, 1760–1840*, Austin: University of Texas Press.

— (1980), 'Political Economy as a Paradigm for the Study of Islamic History', *International Journal of Middle East Studies*, Vol. 11, no. 4, July.

— (1987), 'Reflections on Contemporary Arab Society: the Political Economy School of the 1970s', *Arab Studies Quarterly*, Vol. 9, no. 1.

GRAZIANO, Luigi (1983), 'Political Clientelism and Comparative Perspectives', *International Political Science Review*, Vol. 4, no. 4.

GREEN, Jerrold D. (1986), 'Are Arab Politics Still Arab?', *World Politics*, Vol. 38, no. 4, July.

GRINDLE, Merilee S., ed. (1980), *Politics and Policy Implementation in the Third World*, Princeton, NJ: Princeton University Press.

GUBSTER, Peter (1988), 'Jordan: Balancing Pluralism and Authoritarianism', in Peter J. Chelkowski and Robert J. Pranger, eds, *Ideology and Power in the Middle East*, Durham, NC and London: Duke University Press.

GURR, Ted Robert (1970), *Why Men Rebel*, Princeton, NJ: Princeton University Press.

— (1989), 'War, Revolution, and the Growth of the Coercive State', in James A. Caporaso, *The Elusive State*, London: Sage Publications.

HAARMANN, Ulrich W. (1988), 'Ideology and History, Identity and Alterity: The Arab Image of the Turk from the 'Abbasids to Modern Egypt', *International Journal of Middle East Studies*, Vol. 20, no. 2, May.

HABIB, Kazim (1991), 'Hawl ba'd khasa'is ... ' [Some Distinguishing Characteristics of the Arab Bourgeoisie], in 'Isam al-Khafaji, ed., *Al-Burjuwaziyya al-'arabiyya al-mu'asira* [The Contemporary Arab Bourgeoisie], Damascus and Cyprus: Mu'assasat 'Ibal.

HADDAD, George M. (1971, 1973), *Revolution and Military Rule in the Middle East*, parts 1 and 2, New York: R. Spiller.

HAFIZ MAHMUD, Sa'd (1989), 'Maqal fi al-qita' al-'amm' [An Essay on the Public Sector and its Developmental Role], in the Arab Planning Institute, Kuwait, Seminar on *Dawr al-Dawla ...* [The Role of the State in Economic Activity in the Arab Fatherland], Kuwait, May.

HAGGARD, Stephan and Robert Kaufman (1991), 'Economic Adjustment and the Prospects for Democracy', paper presented at the International Political Science Association's 15th World Congress, Buenos Aires, July 1991.

HAILE-MARIAM, Yacob and Bernhanu Mengistu (1988), 'Public Enterprises and the Privatisation Thesis on the Third World', *Third World Quarterly*, Vol. 10, no. 4, October.

HAIM, Sylvia G., ed. (1974), *Arab Nationalism: An Anthology*, Berkeley, CA: University of California Press.

HAJRAH, Hassan Hamza (1982), *Public Land Distribution in Saudi Arabia*, London and New York: Longman.

AL-HAKIM, Tawfiq et al. (1975), *Malaf 'Abd al-Nasir* [The Nasser File], Cairo: Dar Al-Ahram.

HALL, John A. and G. John Ikenberry (1989), *The State*, Milton Keynes: Open University Press.

HALLIDAY, Fred (1974), *Arabia Without Sultans*, Harmondsworth: Penguin Books.

— (1985), 'North Yemen Today', *MERIP Reports*, no. 130, Vol. 15, no. 2, February.

— and H. Alavi, eds (1988), *State and Ideology in the Middle East and Pakistan*, Basingstoke and London: Macmillan Education.

— (1989), *Cold War, Third World: an Essay on Soviet–American Relations*, London: Hutchinson Radius.

— (1990a), *Revolution and Foreign Policy: the Case of South Yemen, 1967–1987*, Cambridge: Cambridge University Press.

— (1990b), 'Tunisia's Uncertain Future', *MERIP Reports*, no. 163, March–April.

— (1993), ''Orientalism' and its Critics', *British Journal of Middle Eastern Studies*, Vol. 20, no. 2, 1993.

HALPERN, Manfred (1963), *The Politics of Social Change in the Middle East and North Africa*, Princeton, NJ: Princeton University Press.

AL-HAMAD, Turki H. (1985), *Political Order in Changing Societies: Saudi Arabia; Modernization in a Traditional Context*, PhD dissertation, University of Southern California, 1985.

HAMMAD, Majdi (1987), *Al-'Askariyyun al-'arab wa qadiyyat al-wahda* [The Arab Military and the Issue of Unity], Beirut: CAUS.

— (1990), 'Al-Mu'assasa al-'askariyya wa al-nizam al-siyasi' [The Military Establishment and the Egyptian Political System 1952–1980], in Ahmad 'Abdallah, ed., *Al-Jaish wa al-dimuqratiyya fi misr* [The Army and Democracy in Egypt], Cairo: Sina.

AL-HAMUD, Mudi (1990), 'Tajrubat al-kuwayt ... ' [Kuwait's Experience with the Public and the Private Sectors], in 'A. Al-Nasrawi et al., *Al-Qita' al-'amm ...* [The Public and the Private Sectors in the Arab Fatherland], Beirut: CAUS.

HANAFI, Hasan (1983), 'Al-Judhur at-tarikhiyya li azmat al-huriyya ... ' [Historical Roots of the Crisis of Liberty and Democracy in our Contemporary Conscience], in Centre for Arab Unity Studies, *Al-Dimuqratiyya wa huquq al-insan* [Democracy and Human Rights in the Arab Fatherland], Beirut: CAUS.

— (1986), *Al-Harakat al-Islamiyya fi misr* [The Islamic Movement in Egypt], Beirut: Al-Huda.

— and Muhammad 'Abid al-Jabiri (1990), *Hiwar al-mashriq wa al-maghrib* [A Mashreq/Maghreb Dialogue], Casablanca: Dar Tubqal.

HANNA, 'Abdallah (1987), *Min al-ittijahat al-fikriyya ...* [Some Intellectual Currents in Syria and Lebanon in the First Half of the Twentieth Century], Damascus: Al-Ahali.

HANNOYER, Jean (1985), 'Grands projets hydrauliques en Syrie', *Maghreb-Machrek*, no. 109, juillet–septembre.

HAQ, Mahbub ul- (1976), *The Poverty Curtain: Choices for the Third World*, New York: Columbia University Press.

HARB, 'Ali (1985), *Asl al-'unf wa al-dawla* [The Origin of Violence and the State], Beirut: Dar al-Hadatha.

HARDY, Roger (1992), *Arabia After the Storm: Internal Stability of the Gulf Arab States*, London: Royal Institute of International Affairs.

HARIK, Iliya (1968), *Politics and Change in a Traditional Society: Lebanon 1711–1845*, Princeton, NJ: Princeton University Press.

— (1981), 'The Political Elite as a Strategic Minority', in Fuad J. Khuri, ed., *Leadership and Development in Arab Society*, Beirut: American University in Beirut Press.

— (1982), 'The Economic and Social Factors in the Lebanese Crisis', *Journal of Arab Affairs*, Vol. 1, no. 2, April.

— (1987), 'The Origins of the Arab State System', in Ghassan Salame, ed., *The Foundations of the Arab State*, London: Croom Helm.

— (1990), 'Privatisation et développement en Tunisie', *Maghreb-Machrek*, no. 128, avril–juin.

— (1992), 'Privatization: the Issue, the Prospects and the Fears', in Iliya Harik and Denis Sullivan, eds, *Privatization and Liberalization in the Middle East*, Bloomington, IN.: Indiana University Press.

AL-HASAN, Hamza (1993), 'Limadha fashal al-malik fi tashkil majlis al-shura?' [Why has the King Failed in Forming the Consultation Council?], editorial in *Al-Jazira al-'Arabiyya*, no. 28, May.

HASAN, Parvez (1987), 'Structural Adjustment in Selected Arab Countries: Need, Challenge and Approaches', in Said El-Naggar, ed., *Adjustment Policies and Development Strategies in the Arab World*, Washington, DC: International Monetary Fund.

AL-HASAN, Ribhi (1977), 'Discussion', in Muhammad Yusuf 'Ulwan et al., 'Hiwar hawl al-nazariyya wa al-tatbiq ... ' [A Dialogue on Theory and Practice in Administration and Bureaucracy], *Majallat al-'Ulum al-Ijtima'iyya*, Vol. 4, no. 4, January.

HASTINGS, Samuel (1982), 'Privatisation', in S. Hastings and H. Levie, eds, *Privatisation 1979–1982*, Nottingham: Spokesman.

HEINE, Peter (1993), 'Political Parties, Institutions and Administrative Structures', in D. Hopwood, H. Ishow and T. Koszinowski, eds, *Iraq: Power and Society*, Reading, UK: Ithaca Press.

HELD, David (1983), 'Introduction: Central Perspectives on the Modern State', in David Held et al., eds, *States and Societies*, Oxford: Martin Robertson for the Open University.

HELLER, Mark and Nadav Safran (1985), *The New Middle Class and Regime Stability in Saudi Arabia*, Cambridge, MA: Harvard University Center for Middle Eastern Studies.

HELMS, Christine Moss (1981), *The Cohesion of Saudi Arabia*, London: Croom Helm.

HEPER, Metin (1985), *The State Tradition in Turkey*, Beverley, Yorkshire: Eothen Press.

HILAL, 'Aliy al-Din (1977), *Al-Siyasa wa al-hukm ...* [Politics and Government in Egypt: the Parliamentary Era 1923–1952], Cairo: Nahdat al-Sharq.

— (1980), 'Al-Wahda al-misriyya/al-suriyya ...' [The Egyptian/Syrian Union 1958–1961], *Al-Mustaqbal al-'Arabi*, Vol. II, no. 13, March.

— et al. (1982), *Tajribat al-dimuqratiyya fi misr* [The Democratic Experience in Egypt 1970–1981], Cairo: Al-Markaz al-'Arabi.

HILAN, Rizqallah (1989), 'Mithal al-qutr al-'arabi al-suri' [The Case of the Syrian Arab State], in The Arab Planning Institute, Kuwait, Seminar on *Dawr al-Dawla ...* [The Role of the State in Economic Activity in the Arab Fatherland], Kuwait, May 1989.

AL-HIMSI, Mahmud (1990), 'Dawr al-qita' al-'amm w'al-qita' al-khas fi tahqiq al-takamul al-iqtisadi al-'arabi' [The Role of the Public and the Private Sectors in Realising Arab Economic Integration], in 'Abbas Al-Nasrawi et al., *Al-Qita' al-'amm ...* [The Public and the Private Sectors in the Arab Fatherland], Beirut: CAUS.

HINNEBUSCH, Raymond A. (1982), 'The Islamic Movement in Syria', in A. Dessouki, ed., *Islamic Resurgence in the Arab World*, New York: Praeger.

— (1985), *Egyptian Politics Under Sadat*, New York: Cambridge University Press.

— (1986), 'Syria under the Ba'th: Social Ideology, Policy and Practice', in W. Michalak and J. Salacuse, eds, *Law and Social Policy in the Middle East*, Berkeley, CA: IIS.

HINNEBUSCH, Raymond A. (1989), *Peasant and Bureaucracy in Ba'thist Syria: The Political Economy of Rural Development*, Boulder, CO: Westview Press.

— (1990), *Authoritarian Power and State Formation in Ba'thist Syria: Army, Party and Peasant*, Boulder, CO: Westview Press.

— (1993a), 'The Politics of Economic Reform in Egypt', *Third World Quarterly*, Vol. 14, no. 1.

— (1993b), 'State and Civil Society in Syria', *Middle East Journal*, Vol. 47, no. 2, Spring.

— (1993c), 'Syria', in T. Niblock and E. Murphy, eds, *Economic and Political Liberalization in the Middle East*, London: British Academic Press.

AL-HIRMASI, 'Abd al-Baqi (1987), *Al-Mujtama' wa al-dawla fi al-Maghrib al-'arabi* [Society and State in the Arab Maghreb], Beirut: CAUS.

AL-HIRMASI, Muhammad Salih (1990), *Tunis: Al-Haraka al-'ummaliyya ...* [Tunisia: The Labour Movement in a Dependent, One-Party System, 1956–1986], Beirut: Al- Farabi.

HIRSCHMAN, Albert O. (1970), *Exit, Voice, and Loyalty: Responses to Decline in Firms, Organizations, and States*, Cambridge, MA: Harvard University Press.

HOBSBAWM, E.J. (1959), *Primitive Rebels: Studies in Archaic Forms of Social Movement in the 19th and 20th Centuries*, Manchester: Manchester University Press.

— (1990), *Nations and Nationalism Since 1780*, Cambridge: Cambridge University Press.

HOPFINGER, Hans (1990), 'Capitalist Agro-Business in a Socialist Country? Syria's New Share-holding Corporations as an Example', in *Bulletin* (British Society for Middle Eastern Studies), Vol. 17, no. 2.

HOURANI, Albert (1970), *Arabic Thought in the Liberal Age 1798–1939*, London: Oxford University Press.

— (1981), *The Emergence of the Modern Middle East*, Berkeley and Los Angeles: University of California Press.

HROCH, Miroslav (1985), *Social Preconditions of National Revival in Europe*, trans., Cambridge: Cambridge University Press.

HUDSON, Michael C. (1968), *The Precarious Republic: Political Modernization in Lebanon*, New York: Random House.

— (1977), *Arab Politics: the Search for Legitimacy*, New Haven and London: Yale University Press.

— (1991), 'After the Gulf War: Prospects for Democratization in the Arab World', *Middle East Journal*, Vol. 45, no. 3, Summer.

HUNTINGTON, Samuel P. (1971), *Political Order in Changing Societies*, New Haven and London: Yale University Press (reprint of 1968 edition).

— (1991), *The Third Wave: Democratization in the Late Twentieth Century*, Norman and London: University of Oklahoma Press.

HUREWITZ, J.C. (1969), *Middle East Politics: the Military Dimension*, New York: Praeger.

HUSAIN, 'Adil (1985), *Nahwa fikr 'arabi jadid* [Towards a New Arab Thought], Cairo: Dar al-Mustaqbal al-'Arabi.

HUSAINI, Mawlawi (c. 1958), *Al-Idara al-'arabiyya* [Arab Administration], Cairo: Maktabat al-Adab.

AL-HUSRI, Sati' (1984/85), *Al-A'mal al-qawmiyya: Abhath mukhtara* [The Nationalist Oeuvres: Selected Investigations], Beirut: CAUS.

HUSSEIN, Mahmoud (1973), *Class Conflict in Egypt: 1945–1970*, New York: Monthly Review Press.

IBRAHIM, Hasanain Tawfiq (1992), *Zahirat al-'unf al-siyasi ...* [The Phenomenon of Political Violence in Arab Systems], Beirut: CAUS.

IBRAHIM, Saad E. (1982), *The New Arab Social Order: A Study in the Impact of Oil and Manpower Movement*, Boulder, CO: Westview Press.

IBRAHIM, Sa'd al-Din (1978), 'Urubat Misr [Egypt's Arabness], Cairo: CPSS.

— (1980), *Ittijihat al-ra'y al-'amm ...* [The Attitudes of Arab Public Opinion towards the Issue of Unity], Beirut: CAUS.

— (1984), *Mashru' bahth istihraf ...* [Research Project on Forecasting the Future of the Arab Fatherland], mimeo, Beirut: CAUS.

— (1992), *Ta'ammulat fi mas'alat al-aqaliyyat* [Reflections on the Issue of Minorities], Cairo: Markaz Ibn Khaldun.

—, ed. (1993), *Al-Mujtama' al-madani* ... [Civil Society and Democratic Transformation in the Arab Fatherland: the Annual Report], Cairo: Markaz Ibn Khaldun.

IKENBERRY, G. John (1986), 'The State and Strategies of International Adjustment', *World Politics*, Vol. 39, no. 1, October.

— and Charles A. Kupchan (1990), 'Socialization and Hegemonic Power', *International Organization*, Vol. 44, no. 3, Summer.

ILCHMAN, W.F. and N.T. Uphof (1969), *The Political Economy of Change*, Berkeley, CA: University of California Press.

IMAM, 'Abdallah (1985), *Nasir wa 'Amir* [Nasser and Amer], Cairo: Rose al-Yusuf.

'IMARA, Muhammad (1993), 'Dawr al-awqaf fi sina'at al-hadara al-islamiyya' [The Role of Awqaf in the Making of the Islamic Civilisation], *Al-Hayat*, 4 June 1993.

INTERNATIONAL INSTITUTE FOR STRATEGIC STUDIES (IISS) (1989), *The Military Balance 1989–1990*, London: Brasseys.

IONESCU, Ghita and Ernest Gellner, eds (1969), *Populism: its Meaning and National Characteristics*, London: Weidenfeld and Nicholson.

'ISA, Salah (1986), *Muthaqqafun wa 'askar* [Intellectuals and Soldiers], Cairo: Madbuli.

AL-'ISAWI, Ibrahim (1989), *Al-Masar al-iqtisadi fi misr wa siyasat al-islah* [The Economic Path and Reform Policies in Egypt], Cairo: Markaz al-Buhuth al-'Arabiyya.

ISKANDER, Amir (1980), *Saddam Hussein: the Fighter, the Thinker and the Man*, Paris: Hachette Réalités.

ISLAM, Nasir and Georges Henault (1979), 'From GNP to Basic Needs: A Critical Review of Development and Development Administration', *International Review of Administrative Sciences*, Vol. 45, no. 3.

ISLAMOGLU-INAN, Huri, ed. (1987), *The Ottoman Empire and the World Economy*, Cambridge: Cambridge University Press.

ISMA'IL, Mahmud (1980), *Susyulujiya al-fikr al-islami* [Sociology of Islamic Thought], 2 vols, Casablanca: Dar al-Thaqafa.

ISSAWI, Charles (1982), *An Economic History of the Middle East and North Africa*, New York: Columbia University Press.

JABBUR, George (1976), *Al-'Uruba wa mazahir al-intima'* ... [Arabism and other Aspects of Belonging in Current Constitutions of the Arab Countries], Damascus: Ministry of Culture.

AL-JABIRI, Muhammad 'Abid (1982a), *Al-'Asabiyy wa al-dawla* [Group Solidarity and the State: Khaldunian Theoretical Features of Islamic History], Casablanca: Dar al-Nashr al-Maghribiyya.

— (1982b), *Nahn wa al-turath* [Ourselves and the Cultural Heritage], Casablanca and Beirut: Dar al-Tali'a.

— (1985), *Takwin al-'aql al-'arabi* [Formation of the Arab Mind], Beirut: Dar al-Tali'a.

— (1989), *Ishkaliyyat al-fikr al-'arabi al-mu'asir* [Problematics in Contemporary Arab Thought], Beirut: CAUS.

— (1990), *Al-'Aql al-siyasi al-'arabi* [The Arab Political Mind], Beirut: CAUS.

JACKSON, P.M. (1982), *The Political Economy of Bureaucracy*, Oxford; Philip Allan.

JACKSON, Robert H. and Carl G. Rosenberg (1985), 'Juridical Statehood in the Crisis of Tropical African States', paper presented at the International Political Science Association's 13th World Congress, Paris, 1985.

— (1993), *Quasi-States: Sovereignty, International Relations and the Third World*, Cambridge: Cambridge University Press.

JAGHLUL, 'Abd al-Qadir (1987), *Al-Ishkaliyyat al-tarikhiyya* ... [Historical Problematics in Ibn Khaldun's Political Sociology], Beirut: Dar al-Hadatha.

AL-JAMAL, Yahya (1984), 'Anzimat al-hukm ...' [Government Systems in the Arab Fatherland], in Sa'd al-Din Ibrahim et al., *Azmat al-dimuqratiyya* ... [The Crisis of Democracy in the Arab Fatherland], Beirut: CAUS.

JÄNICKE, Martin (1990), *State Failure: the Impotence of Politics in Industrial Society*, Cambridge: Polity Press.

AL-JARF, Tu'aima (1960), *Mujaz al-qanun al-dusturi* [Concise Constitutional Law], Cairo: Maktabat al-Qahira al-Haditha.

JESSOP, Bob (1982), *The Capitalist State*, Oxford: Martin Robertson.

— (1990), *State Theory: Putting the Capitalist State in its Place*, Cambridge: Polity Press.

— (1991), 'Accumulation Strategies, State Forms and Hegemonic Projects', in Simon Clarke, ed., *The State Debate*, Basingstoke and London: Macmillan.

JOHNSON, Dale L., ed. (1985), 'Class and Social Development: Toward a Comparative and Historical Social Science', in Dale L. Johnson, ed., *Middle Classes in Dependent Countries*, Beverly Hills and London: Sage Publications.

JOHNSON, Michael (1986), *Class, Client in Beirut: The Sunni Muslim Community and the Lebanese State 1840–1985*, London: Ithaca Press.

JORDAN, GOVERNMENT OF (1983), *Al-Khidma al-madaniyya* [The Civil Service], Amman.

JU'AIT, Hisham (1984), *Al-Shakhsiyya al-'arabiyya al-islamiyya* ... [The Arab-Islamic Personality and the Arab Destiny], trans., Beirut: Dar al-Tali'a.

JUREIDINI, Paul and R.D. McLaurin (1984), *Jordan: The Impact of Social Change on the Role of the Tribes* (The Washington Papers, Vol. 12, no. 108), New York: Praeger.

KAMINSKI, Antoni Z. ed. (1991), 'The Public and the Private: Introduction', and 'Res Publica, Res Privata', *International Political Science Review*, Vol. 12, no. 4, October (special issue on *The Public and the Private*).

AL-KANZ 'Ali (1992), 'Min al-i'jab bi al-dawla ...' [From Fascination with the State to the Discovery of Social Praxis], in S. Al-'Alawi et al., *Al-Mujtama' al-madani fi al-watan al-'arabi* [The Civil Society and its Role in Realising Democracy in the Arab Fatherland], Beirut: CAUS.

KARL, Terry Lynn (1986), 'Petroleum and Political Pacts: the Transition to Democracy in Venezuela', in G. O'Donnell, P. Schmitter and L. Whitehead, eds, *Transitions from Authoritarian Rule: Prospects for Democracy*, Baltimore: Johns Hopkins University Press.

KARPAT, Kemal (1988), 'The Ottoman Ethic and Confessional Legacy in the Middle East', in Milton J. Esman and Ithamar Rabinovich, eds, *Ethnicity, Pluralism, and the State in the Middle East*, Ithaca and London: Cornell University Press.

KARSH, Efraim and Inari Rautsi (1991), *Saddam Hussein; a Political Biography*, London: Futura Publications.

KATOUZIAN, Homa (1981), *The Political Economy of Modern Iran*, London and NY: Macmillan/ New York University Press.

KATZENSTEIN, Peter (1978), *Between Power and Plenty*, Madison, WI: University of Wisconsin Press.

AL-KAWAKIBI, 'Abd al-Rahman (1984), *Taba'i' al-istibdad* [On the Nature of Despotism], new edn, Beirut: Dar al-Nafa'is.

KAWTHARANI, Wajih (1988), *Al Sulta wa al-mujtama' wa al-'amal al-siyasi* [Authority, Society and Political Action], Beirut: CAUS.

KAZANCIGIL, Ali, ed. (1986), 'Paradigms of Modern State Formation in the Periphery', in Ali Kazancigil, ed., *The State in Global Perspective*, London: Gower/UNESCO.

KAZZIHA, Walid (1975), *Revolutionary Transformation in the Arab World: Habash and his Comrades from Nationalism to Marxism*, London: Charles Knight and Co.

KEANE, John (1988), *Democracy and Civil Society*, London: Verso.

KEDOURIE, Elie, ed. (1970), 'Introduction', in *Nationalism in Asia and Africa*, London, n.p.

— (1985), *Nationalism*, rev. edn, London: Hutchinson.

KEOHANE, Robert O. and Joseph S. Nye (1977), *Power and Independence*, Boston: Little, Brown.

KERR, Malcolm (1971), *The Arab Cold War*, London: Oxford University Press.

— and El Sayed Yassin, eds (1982), *Rich and Poor States in the Middle East*, Boulder, CO: Westview Press.

KEYDER, Çaglar (1987), *State and Class in Turkey*, London and NY: Verso.

AL-KHAFAJI, 'Isam (1983), *Al-Dawla wa al-tatawwur al-ra'simali fi al-'iraq* [The State and Capitalist Transformation in Iraq, 1968–1978], Cairo: Dar al-Mustaqbal al-'arabi.

— (1986a), 'The Parasitic Base of the Ba'thist Regime', in Committee Against Repression and for Democratic Rights in Iraq (CARDRI), *Saddam's Iraq: Revolution or Reaction?*, London: Zed Books.

— (1986b), 'State Incubation of Iraqi Capitalism', *MERIP Reports*, no. 142, September.

— (1992), 'State Terror and the Degradation of Politics in Iraq', *Middle East Report* (MERIP), May–June.

KHALAF, Samir (1987), *Lebanon's Predicament*, New York: Columbia University Press.

KHALIL, Khalil Ahmad (1984), *Al-'Arab wa al-dimuqratiyya* [The Arabs and Democracy], Beirut: Dar al-Hadatha.

AL-KHALIL, Samir (1991), *Republic of Fear: Saddam's Iraq*, London: Hutchinson Radius (new edn).

KHATRAWI, Mohammed F. (1989), 'Privatization and the Regional Public Joint Ventures in the Gulf Cooperation Council', in Said El-Naggar, ed., *Privatization and Structural Adjustment in the Arab Countries*, Washington, DC: International Monetary Fund.

KHAWAJKIYA, Muhammad Hisham (1986), 'Al-Tajruba al-sa'udiyya ...' [The Saudi Experience of Economic Development], in Centre for Arab Unity Studies (CAUS), *Symposium on Independent Development in the Arab World*, Amman, Jordan, 26–29 April.

— (1990), Tajrubat al-sa'udiyya ...' [The Saudi Experience with the Public and the Private Sector], in 'Abbas Al-Nasrawi et al., *Al-Qita' al-'amm ...* [The Public and the Private Sectors in the Arab Fatherland], Beirut: CAUS.

KHOROS, V.G. (1986), *Populism: Its Past, Present and Future*, trans., Beirut: Al-Farabi.

KHOURY, Philip S. (1983a), 'Islamic Revivalism and the Crisis of the Secular State in the Arab World: an Historical Appraisal', in I. Ibrahim, ed., *Arab Resources: the Transformation of a Society*, London: Croom Helm.

— (1983b), *Urban Notables and Arab Nationalism*, Cambridge: Cambridge University Press.

— (1987), *Syria and the French Mandate: the Politics of Arab Nationalism 1920–1945*, London: I.B. Tauris.

KHURI, Fuad (1980), *Tribe and State in Bahrain: The Transformation of Social and Political Authority in an Arab State*, Chicago: Chicago University Press.

— (1982), 'The Study of Civil–Military Relations in Modernizing Societies in the Middle East: A Critical Assessment', in R. Kolkowicz and A. Korbonski, eds, *Soldiers, Peasants and Bureaucrats: Civil–Military Relations in Communist and Modernizing Societies*, London: George Allen and Unwin.

AL-KHURI, Fu'ad (1988), *Imamat al-shahid wa imamat al-batal* [Leadership of the Martyr and Leadership of the Hero], Beirut: Markaz Dar al-Jami'a.

— (1991), *Al-Sulta lada al-qaba'il al-'arabiyya* [Authority Among the Arab Tribes], London and Beirut: Al-Saqi.

— (1993), *Al-Dhihniyya al-'arabiyya* [The Arab Mentality], Beirut and London: Dar al-Saqi.

KHURI, Ra'if (1983), *Modern Arab Thought: Channels of the French Revolution to the Arab East* (trans. Ihsan Abbas from Arabic original, 1943), Princeton, NJ; Princeton University Press.

KIENLE, Eberhard (1990), *Ba'th versus Ba'th*, London: I.B. Tauris.

— (1991), 'Entre Jama'a et Classe: le Pouvoir Politique en Syrie Contemporaine', *Revue de Monde Musulman et de la Méditerranée*, 59–60, 1991/1–2.

KISHK, Muhammad Jalal (1989), *Al-Nasiriyyun qadimun ...* [The Nasserists are Coming! the Massacre of Money Utilisation Companies], Cairo: Al-Zahra' li al-I'lam al-'Arabi.

KITCHING, Gavin (1989), *Development and Underdevelopment in Historical Perspective: Populism, Nationalism and Industrialization*, rev. edn, London: Routledge.

KORANY, Bahgat (1984), 'The Glory that Was? The Pan-Arab, Pan-Islamic Alliance Decisions October 1973', *International Political Science Review*, Vol. 5, no. 1.

— (1987), 'Alien and Besieged Yet Here to Stay: the Contradictions of the Arab Territorial State', in G. Salamé, ed., *The Foundations of the Arab State*, London: Croom Helm.

— et al. (1991), *The Foreign Policies of Arab States: the Challenge of Change*, Boulder, CO: Westview Press.

KOURY, Enver M. (1978), *The Saudi Decision-Making Body*, Maryland: Institute of Middle Eastern Affairs.

KRASNER, Stephen D. (1984), 'Approaches to the State: Alternative Conceptions and Historical Dynamics', *Comparative Politics*, Vol. 16, no. 2, January.

— (1985), *Structural Conflict: the Third World Against Global Liberalism*, Berkeley and London: University of California Press.

AL-KUBAISI, 'Amir (1982), *Al-Idara al-'amma w'al-tanmiya bi dawlat al-imarat al-arabiyya al-muttahida* [Public Administration and Development in the UAE], Al-Shariqa: Dar al-Khalij.

AL-KUBAISY, Amer K. (1974), *Administrative Development in New Nations with Reference to the Case of Iraq*, Baghdad: Al-Jumhuriyah Press.

KUMAIR, Al-Wathiq (1989), 'Tajrubat al-sudan ...' [Sudan's Experience with Political Pluralism], in S. Ibrahim, ed., *Al-Ta'addudiyya al-siyasiyya wa al-dimuqratiyya fi al-watan al-'arabi* [Political Pluralism and Democracy in the Arab Fatherland], Amman: Arab Thought Forum.

LABIB, Al-Tahir (1992a), 'Gramshi fi al-fikr al-'arabi' [Gramsci in Arabic Thought], in Amina Rashid et al., *Qadaya al-mujtama' al-madani al-'arabi fi daw' utruhat Gramshi* [Issues of the Arab Civil Society in Light of Gramsci's Theses], Cairo: Markaz al-Buhuth al-'Arabi.

— (1992b), 'Hal al-dimuqratiyya matlab ijtima'?' [Is Democracy a Social Demand?], in Sa'id Al-'Alawi, *Al-Mujtama' al-madani fi al-watan al-'arabi* ... [The Civil Society and its Role in Realising Democracy in the 'Arab Fatherland'], Beirut: Centre for Arab Unity Studies.

LACEY, Robert (1982), 'Saudi Arabia: A More Visible Role in the Middle East', *The World Today*, January 1992.

LACKNER, Helen (1978), *A House Built on Sand: A Political Economy of Saudi Arabia*, London: Ithaca Press.

— (1985), *P.D.R. Yemen: Outpost of Socialist Development in Arabia*, London: Ithaca Press.

LACLAU, Ernesto (1979), *Politics and Ideology in Marxist Theory: Capitalism, Fascism, Populism*, London: Verso (2nd impression 1982).

— and Chantal Mouffe (1985), *Hegemony and Socialist Strategy*, London: Verso.

LACOSTE, Yves (1984), *Ibn Khaldun: the Birth of History and the Past of the Third World*, trans., London: Verso.

LAMBTON, Ann K.S. (1980), 'Reflections on the Iqta'', in *Theory and Practice in Mediaeval Persian Government*, London: Variorum Reprints (1st printing 1968).

LANDES, David (1985), *Bankers and Pashas*, Arabic trans. and preface by 'Abd al-'Azim Anis, Cairo: Kitab al-Ahali.

LA PALOMBARA, Joseph (1963), *Interest Groups in Italian Politics*, Princeton, NJ: Princeton University Press.

LAPIDUS, Ira M. (1984), *Muslim Cities in the Later Middle Ages*, Cambridge: Cambridge University Press.

LARIF-BEATRIX, Asma (1987), 'L'état tutélaire, système politique et espace éthique', in Michel Camau et al., *Tunisie au présent: une modernité au-dessus de tout soupçon?*, Paris, Editions du CNRS.

LAROUI, Abdallah (1976), *The Crisis of the Arab Intellectual*, trans., Berkeley, CA: University of California Press.

LAWSON, Fred H. (1989), 'Class Politics and State Power in Ba'thi Syria', in Berch Beberoglu, ed., *Power and Stability in the Middle East*, London and New Jersey: Zed Books Ltd.

— (1990), 'Liberalisation économique en Syrie et en Irak', *Maghreb-Machrek*, no. 128, avril–juin.

LAZREQ, Marnia (1976), *The Emergence of Classes in Algeria*, Boulder, CO: Westview Press.

LECA, Jean and Yves Schemeil (1983), 'Clientèlisme et patrimonialisme dans le monde arabe', *International Political Science Review*, Vol. 4, no. 4.

— (1988), 'Social Structure and Political Stability: Comparative Evidence from the Algerian, Syrian and Iraqi Cases', in Adeed Dawisha and William Zartman, eds, *Beyond Coercion: Durability of the Arab State*, London: Croom Helm.

LEE, Barbara and John Nellis (1990), *Enterprise Reform and Privatization in Socialist Economics*, Washington, DC: The World Bank.

LEFEBVRE, Henri (1978), *De l'Etat-III le Mode de Production Etatique*, 10/18, Paris: Inédit, Editions Ouvrier.

LETTERIE, Jacobus W. and Rob van Puyenbroek (1991), 'Position in the World System and Political Democracy: New Evidence from the Seventies and Eighties', paper for the International Political Science Association's 15th World Congress, Buenos Aires, July 1991 .

LEWIS, Bernard (1958), 'Communism and Islam', in Walter Z. Laqueur, ed., *The Middle East in Transition*, New York: Frederick Praeger.

— (1988), *The Political Language of Islam*, Chicago and London: University of Chicago Press.

LICHTHEIM, G. (1963), *Marx and the 'Asiatic mode of Production'*, St Antony's Papers no. 14, London: Chatto and Windus.

LIJPHART, Arend (1977), *Democracy in Plural Societies: a Comparative Exploration*, New Haven: Yale University Press.

— (1979), 'Consociation and Federation: Conceptual and Empirical Links', *Canadian Journal of Political Science*, Vol. 12, no. 3, September.

LINDBERG, Leon N., J.l. Campbell and J.R. Hollingsworth (1991), 'Economic Governance and the Analysis of Structural Change in the American Economy', in John L. Campbell et al., eds, *Governance of the American Economy*, Cambridge: Cambridge University Press.

LONG, David E. (1976), *Saudi Arabia*, The Washington Papers 39, Beverly Hills, CA: Sage Publications.

LONGUENESSE, Elisabeth (1979), 'The Class Nature of the State in Syria', *MERIP Reports*, Vol. 9, no. 4, May.

— (1985), 'Syrie: Secteur public industriel', *Maghreb-Machrek*, no. 109, juillet–septembre.

— (1987), 'Etat et nouvelles couches moyennes en Syrie: à propos de la place des ingénieurs dans la structure sociale', *mimeo*, IRMAC-UA 913, Lyons, mai 1987.

LOONEY, Robert E. (1987/88), 'Growth Prospects of the Saudi Arabian Private Sector', *Arab–American Affairs*, no. 23, Winter.

LUCIANI, Giacomo (1987), 'Allocation vs. Production States; A Theoretical Framework', in H. Beblawi and G. Luciani, eds, *The Rentier State*, London: Croom Helm.

— and G. Salamé, eds, (1988), *The Politics of Arab Integration*, London: Croom Helm.

— (1990a), 'Arabie Saoudite: l'industrialisation d'un état allocataire', *Maghreb-Machrek*, no. 129, juillet–septembre.

— ed. (1990b), *The Arab State*, London: Routledge.

— (1993), 'The Oil Rent, the Fiscal Crisis of the State and Democratisation', *mimeo*, Rome.

LUHMAN, Niklas (1990), *Political Theory in the Welfare State*, Berlin and NY: Walter de Gruyter.

LUSTICK, Ian (1979), 'Stability in Deeply Divided Societies: Consociationalism versus Control', *World Politics*, Vol. 31, no. 3, April.

MAHDAVI, Hossein (1970), 'The Pattern and Problems of Economic Development in Rentier States: the Case of Iran', in Michael Cook, ed., *Studies in the Economic History of the Middle East*, London: Oxford University Press.

MAHJOUB, Azzam (1990), 'Etat, secteur public et privatisation en Tunisie', in J.-C. Santucci and H. El Malki, eds, *Etat et Développement dans le Monde Arabe: Crises et Mutations au Maghreb*, Paris: Editions du CNRS.

AL-MAHJUB, Azzam (1989), 'Tunis', in the Arab Planning Institute, Kuwait, Seminar on *Dawr al-Dawla* ... [The Role of the State in Economic Activity in the Arab Fatherland], Kuwait, May 1989.

MAHJUB, Muhammad 'Abduh (c. 1974), *Muqaddima li dirasat al-mujtama'at al-badawiyya* [An Introduction to the Study of Nomadic Societies], Kuwait: Wikalat al-Matbu'at.

AL-MAHMOUD, Mohammad 'Abdullah (1992), *Harmony and Conflict in the Political Systems of the UAE*, unpublished PhD thesis, University of Exeter, UK.

AL-MAJID, Majid (1986), *Majlis al-ta'awun* ... [The GCC: The Crisis of Policy and Legitimacy], London: Taha Publishers.

MAKHZUM, Muhammad (1986), *Azmat al-fikr* ... [The Crisis of Thought and the Problems of Political Authority in the Arab Levant in the Renaissance Era], Beirut: Ma'had al-Inma' al-'Arabi.

MAKIYA, Kanan (1993), *Cruelty and Silence*, London: Jonathan Cape.

AL-MALEH, Sabah Y.T. (1990), *Qualified Manpower in the Developmental Process: A Study of the Role of Public Administration in Iraq 1950–1980*, unpublished PhD thesis, University of Liverpool, UK.

AL-MALIKI, Habib (1989), *Trakumat* ... [Accumulations: Views on Economy and Society], Rabat: Al-Nashr al-'Arabi al-Ifriqi.

EL-MALLAKH, Ragaei (1982), *Saudi Arabia: Rush to Development*, Baltimore and London: Johns Hopkins University Press.

MALLOY, James, ed. (1977), *Authoritarianism and Corporatism in Latin America*, Pittsburgh: University of Pittsburgh Press.

MALONE, Joseph T. (1981), 'The Politics of Social Change in the Arabian Peninsula: Observations in Kuwait and Saudi Arabia', *International Seminar on the Arabian Peninsula*, University of Arizona Near East Center, Tucson, 4–5 December 1981.

MANN, Michael (1986a), 'The Autonomous Power of the State: Its Origins, Mechanisms and Results', in John A. Hall, ed., *States in History*, Oxford and New York: Basil Blackwell.

— (1986b), *The Sources of Social Power, Vol. I: A History of Power from the Beginning to AD 1760*, Cambridge: Cambridge University Press.

MANSOUR, Hussein Omar (1989), 'Reflections on Preparations for Privatisation in the Kingdom of Saudi Arabia', paper presented to 21st International Congress of Administrative Sciences, Marrakech, 24–28 July.

MANSUR, Abdul Kasim (1980), 'The Military Balance in the Persian Gulf: Who Will Guard the Gulf States from their Guardians?', *Armed Forces Journal International*, November.

AL-MANUBI, Khalid (1985), 'Infaq al-dawla ...' [Public Expenditure in the Maghreb: Tunisia, Algeria, Morocco], paper presented to the Istituto Affari Internazionali's Second International Conference on *Nation, State and Integration in the Arab World*, Corfu, September 1985 (Vol. 5, Rome).

— (1986), 'Ishkaliyyat al-tanmiyya ...' [The Problematique of Independent Development in Tunisia], in *Al-Tanmiya al-mustaqilla ...* [Independent Development in the Arab Fatherland], Centre for Arab Unity Studies Symposium, Amman, Jordan, 1986.

AL-MARAYATI, Abid A. (1972), *The Middle East: Its Government and Politics*, Belmont, CA: Duxbury.

MARDIN, Şerif (1969), 'Power, Civil Society and Culture in the Ottoman Empire', *Contemporary Studies in Society and History*, 11, June 1969.

— (1973), 'Center–Periphery Relations: A Key to Turkish Politics?' *Daedalus*, 102, Winter.

MARIN, Bernd (1987), 'From Consociationalism to Technocorporatism', in I. Scholten, ed., *Political Stability and Neo-Corporatism*, London: Sage.

MAROUF, Nawal (1982), 'Administrative Development in Kuwait', *Arab Journal of Administration*, April 1992.

MARSOT, Afaf L. Al-Sayyid (1984), *Egypt in the Reign of Muhammad Ali*, New York: Cambridge University Press.

MASARRA, Antoine N. (1986), 'Al-I'tiraf bi al-wala'at al-tahtiyya wa shar'anatiha ...' [The Recognition and Legitimation of Sub-Loyalties: A Factor for Integration or for Division?], *Al-Majalla al-'Arabiyya li al-'Ulum al-Siyasiyya*, Vol. 1, no. 1.

MATHIAS, Gilberto and Pierre Salama (1983), *L'Etat surdéveloppé; des métropoles au tiers monde*, Paris: La Découverte/Maspéro.

MERIP EDITORS (1992), 'The Democracy Agenda in the Arab World', *Middle East Report* (pub. by Middle East Research and Information Project — MERIP), January–February 1992.

METRAL, Françoise (1985), 'Etat et paysans dans le Ghab en Syrie', *Maghreb-Machrek*, no. 109, juillet–septembre.

MEYER, Marshall W. (1985), *Limits to Bureaucratic Growth*, Berlin and New York: W. de Gruyter.

MIAILLE, Michel (1982), *L'Etat juridique* [Arabic trans. *Dawlat al-qanun*], Algiers: University Publications.

MIDOUN, Mohamed (1985), 'Entreprises publiques et développement économique', in Association Tunisienne des Sciences Administratives, *Administration et développement en Tunisie*, Tunis: ATSA and Institut International des Sciences Administratives.

— (1989), 'Privatisation en Tunisie', paper presented to the 21st International Congress of Administrative Sciences, Marrakech, 24–28 July 1989.

MIGDAL, Joel S. (1988a), *Strong Societies and Weak States: State–Society Relations and State Capabilities in the Third World*, Princeton, NJ: Princeton University Press.

— (1988b), 'The Transmission of the State to Society', paper presented to JCNME/SSRC Conference on *Retreating States and Expanding Societies: the State Autonomy/Civil Society Dialectic in the Middle East and North Africa*, Aix-en-Provence, 25–27 March, 1988.

MILANOVIC, Branko (1989), *Liberalization and Entrepreneurship: Dynamics of Reform in Socialism and Capitalism*, NY and London: M.E. Sharpe.

MILIBAND, Ralph (1983), *Class Power and State Power*, London: Verso.

MILLER, David (1989), *Market, State and Community: Theoretical Foundations of Market Socialism*, Oxford: Clarendon Press.

MILLWARD, Robert (1988), 'Measured Sources of Inefficiency in the Performance of Private and

Public Enterprises in LDCs', in P. Cook and C. Kirkpatrick, eds, *Privatization in Less Developed Countries*, Sussex: Wheatsheaf.

MINTZBERG, Henry (1979), *The Structuring of Organizations*, Englewood Cliffs, NJ: Prentice-Hall.

AL-MIR, 'Ali, ed. (1985) *Al-Idara wa al-tahlil al-mali* ... [Financial Analysis and Administration in the Governmental Sector in Arab Countries], report on experts' meeting of the UNDP and the Arab Organisation for Administrative Sciences, *mimeo*, Amman, 1985.

MIREL, Pierre (1982), *L'Egypte des ruptures: l'ère Sadat, de Nasser à Moubarak*, Paris: Sindbad.

MITCHELL, Timothy (1988), *Colonising Egypt*, Cambridge: Cambridge University Press.

— (1991), 'The Limits of the State: Beyond Statist Approaches and their Critics', *American Political Science Review*, Vol. 85, no. 1, March.

MOGHADAM, Val (1988), 'Oil, the State, and Limits to Autonomy: the Iranian Case', *Arab Studies Quarterly*, Vol. 10, no. 2.

MONROE, Elizabeth (1963), *Britain's Moment in the Middle East, 1914–1956*, London: Chatto and Windus.

MOORE, Barrington Jr. (1969), *Social Origins of Dictatorship and Democracy: Lord and Peasant in the Making of the Modern World*, Harmondsworth, UK: Penguin/Peregrine Books.

MOORE, Clement Henry (1970), *Politics in North Africa: Algeria, Morocco and Tunisia*, Boston: Little, Brown.

— (1974), 'Authoritarian Politics in Unincorporated Society: the Case of Nasser's Egypt', *Comparative Politics*, Vol. 6, no. 2, January.

— (1977), 'Clientelist Ideology and Political Change: Fictive Networkers in Egypt and Tunisia', in E. Gellner and J. Waterbury, eds, *Patrons and Clients in Mediterranean Societies*, London: Duckworth.

— (1980), *Images of Development: Egyptian Engineers in Search of Industry*, Cambridge, MA: MIT Press.

— (1986), 'Money and Power: the Dilemma of the Egyptian Infitah', *Middle East Journal*, 40, 1986.

— (1988), 'Tunisia and Bourguibisme: Twenty Years of Crisis', *Third World Quarterly*, Vol. 10, no. 1, January.

— (1986), 'Financial "Deepening" and Political Mediation: Counterpart to Bureaucratic-Authoritarianism', paper presented at the American Political Science Association annual meeting, Washington, DC, August 1986.

MORAN, Michael and Maurice Wright, eds (1991), *The Market and the State: Studies in Interdependence*, London: Macmillan.

MORTIMER, Robert (1991), 'Islam and Multiparty Politics in Algeria', *Middle East Journal*, Vol. 45, no. 4, Autumn.

MOUZELIS, Nicos P. (1986), *Politics in the Semi-Periphery: Early Parliamentarianism and Late Industrialisation in the Balkans and Latin America*, Basingstoke and London: Macmillan.

MUDHAKKIRAT AL-NASIHA (1992), [A Memorandum of Advice], by *'Ulama'* and Islamists to King Fahd of Saudi Arabia: n.p..

MUHYI AL-DIN, Khalid (1992), *Wa'l-an atakallam* [And Now I Speak], Cairo: Markaz al-Ahram.

MUMJIAN, Khatshik (1981), *Marahil al-tarikh* ... [Stages of History: Marxist Principles on Socio-Economic Formations], trans., Tashkent: Progress Publishers.

MUNA, Farid (1980), *The Arab Executive*, London: Macmillan.

AL-MUNUFI, Kamal (1985), *Al-Hukumat al-kuwaitiyya* [Kuwaiti Cabinets], Kuwait: Sharikat al-Rubai'an.

MUQADDAM, Said (1993), 'Réalités et exigences du développement de l'administration publique algérienne' [in Arabic], *Idara* (revue semestrielle, Algeria), Vol. 3, no. 2.

MURSI, Fu'ad (1969), 'Al-Bu'd al-ijtima'i li al-shakhsiyya al-misriyya al-hadira' [Social Dimension of the Present Egyptian Character], *Al-Fikr al-Mu'asir*, no. 50, April.

— (1987), *Masir al-qita' al-'amm* ... [Fate of the Public Sector in Egypt], Cairo: Markaz al-Buhuth al-'Arabiyya.

MURUWWA, Husain (1981), *Al-Naza'at al-madiyya fi al-falsafa al-'arabiyya al-islamiyya* [Materialist Tendencies in Arab-Islamic Philosophy], 2 vols, Beirut: Dar al-Farabi.

MUSHAKOJI, Kinhide (1985), 'Comparative Political Development and the Development of Comparative Politics', paper presented at the International Political Science Association's 13th World Congress, Paris, 1985.

NABA, René (1990), 'Le Yémen à l'heure de l'unification', *Maghreb-Machrek*, no. 128, avril–juin.

AL-NAFISI, 'Abdallah F. (1978), *Al-Kuwait: al-ra'y al-akhar* [Kuwait: Another View], London: Taha.

— (1982), *Majlis al-ta'awun* ... [The GCC: the Politico-Strategic Framework], London: Taha.

EL-NAGGAR, Said, ed. (1987), *Adjustment Policies and Development Strategies in the Arab World*, Washington, DC: International Monetary Fund.

—, ed. (1989), *Privatization and Structural Adjustment in the Arab Countries*, Washington, DC: International Monetary Fund.

NAJJAR, George K. (1978), 'Social Systems, Delineation and Allocative Mechanising: Perspectives on Budgeting for Development', *Administration and Society*, Vol. 9, no. 4, February.

AL-NAJJAR, Ghanim H. (1984), *The Decision-Making Process in Kuwait: The Land Acquisition Policy as a Case Study*, unpublished PhD thesis, University of Exeter, UK.

AL-NAKU', Mahmud M. (1991), *Al-Sulta wa al-istibdad* [Authority and Despotism in the Arab Fatherland], Beirut and London: Dar Ibn Qudama.

NANKANI, Helen B. (1990), 'Lessons of Privatisation in Developing Counties', *Finance and Development* (IMF and World Bank), March.

AL-NAQIB, Khaldun Hasan (1985), 'Bina' al-mujtama' al-'arabi ...' [The Structure of Arab society: some Research Hypotheses], *Al-Mustaqbal al-'Arabi*, Vol. 8, no. 79, July–September.

— (1986), 'Bina' al-mujtama' al-'arabi ...' [The Structure of Arab Society: Some Research Hypotheses], in Muhammad 'Izzat Hijazi et al., *Nahwa 'ilm ijtima' 'arabi* [Towards an Arab Sociology], Beirut: CAUS.

— (1987), *Al-Mujtama' wa al-dawla fi al-khalij wa al-jazira al-'arabiyya* [Society and the State in the Gulf and the Arabian Peninsula], Beirut: CAUS.

— (1991), *Al-Dawla al-tasallutiyya* ... [The Authoritarian State in the Contemporary Arab East], Beirut: CAUS.

NASIF, Munir (1985), 'Sina'at al-silah al-'arabi' [The Arab Arms Industry], *Al-'Arabi*, no. 314, January.

NASR, Marlène (1981), *Al-Tasawwur al-qawmi al-'arabi fi fikr Jamal 'Abd al-Nasir* [The Arab Nationalist Perception in the Thought of Nasser], Beirut: CAUS.

NASR, Muhammad 'Abd al-Mu'izz (1963), *Fi al-dawla wa al-mujtama'* [On State and Society], Alexandria: Alexandria University Press.

AL-NASRAWI, 'Abbas (1990), 'Nushu' al-qita' al-'amm wa tatawurihi' [Emergence and Evolution of the Public Sector in the Arab Fatherland], in 'Abbas Al- Nasrawi et al., *Al-Qita' al-'amm* ... [The Public and the Private Sectors in the Arab Fatherland], Beirut: CAUS.

— et al. (1990), *Al-Qita' al-'amm w'al-qita' al-khas fi al-watan al-'arabi* [The Public and the Private Sectors in the Arab Fatherland], Beirut: CAUS (and see also 'Comments' and 'Discussions' by J. Al-'Anani, N. Firjani, F. Jalal, 'A. Al-Nasrawi and 'A. Zalzala).

NASSAR, Nasif (1986), *Tasawwurat al-'umma al-mu'asira* ... [Perceptions of the Contemporary Nation in Modern Arabic Thought], Mu'assasat al-Taqaddum al-'Ilmi.

NATIONAL BANK OF EGYPT (1986), 'The Role of the Private Sector in the Five Year Plan 1987–1992', *Economic Bulletin*, Vol. 39, no. 3.

AL-NAYFAR, Mustafa (1992), 'Khayr al-Din al-Tunisi ...' [Khair al-Din the Tunisian: Good Leadership or Modern State], *Al-Ijtihad*, Vol. 5.

NELLIS, John and Sumita Kikori (1989), 'The Privatisation of Public Enterprises', in Said El-Naggar, ed., *Privatization and Structural Adjustment in the Arab Countries*, Washington, DC: IMF.

NELSON, Joan M. (1991), 'The Politics of Stabilization and Structural Change: Is Third World Experience Relevant in Post-Communist Nations?', Instituto de Estudos Avançados, Universidade de São Paulo, Serie Especial, *Politica e Economia*, No. 2, July 1991.

NETTL, J.P. (1968), 'The State as a Conceptual Variable', *World Politics*, Vol. 20, no. 4, July.

AL-NIMIR, Saud and Monte Palmer (1982), 'Bureaucracy and Development in Saudi Arabia: A Behavioral Analysis', *Public Administration and Development*, Vol. 2, no. 2.

NISBET, Robert (1986), *Conservatism: Dream and Reality*, Milton Keynes, UK: Open University Press.

NISKANEN, W.A. (1971), *Bureaucracy and Representative Government*, Chicago: Aldine.

NORDLINGER, Eric A. (1972), *Conflict Regulation in Divided Societies*, Boston, MA: Harvard University Center for International Affairs.

NORTON, Augustus R. (1991), 'Lebanon After Ta'if: is the Civil War Over?', *Middle East Journal*, Vol. 45, no. 3, Summer 1991.

NYE, Roger P. (1978), 'Political and Economic Integration in the Arab States of the Gulf', *Journal of South Asian and Middle Eastern Studies*, Vol. 2, no. 1, Fall 1978.

O'CONNOR, James (1973), *The Fiscal Crisis of the State*, New York: St Martin's Press.

O'DONNELL, Guillermo (1973), *Modernization and Bureaucratic Authoritarianism: Studies in South American Politics*, Berkeley, CA: IIS.

— (1977), 'Corporatism and the Question of the State', in James M. Malloy, ed., *Authoritarianism and Corporatism in Latin America*, Pittsburgh: Pittsburgh University Press.

— (1979), 'Tensions in the Bureaucratic-Authoritarian State and the Question of Democracy', in David L. Collier, ed., *The New Authoritarianism in Latin America*, Princeton, NJ: Princeton University Press.

— and Philippe G. Schmitter (1986), 'Negotiating (and Renegotiating) Pacts', and 'Tentative Conclusions about Uncertain Democracies', in G. O'Donnell, P. Schmitter and L. Whitehead, eds, *Transitions from Authoritarian Rule: Prospects for Democracy*, Baltimore: Johns Hopkins University Press.

OFFE, Claus (1984), *Contradictions of the Welfare State*, ed. J. Keane, London: Hutchinson.

— (1985), *Disorganized Capitalism*, Cambridge: Polity Press.

— (1991), 'Capitalism by Democratic Design? Democratic Theory Facing the Triple Transition in East Central Europe', paper presented to International Political Science Association's 15th World Congress, Buenos Aires, July 1991.

OLSEN, Gorm Rye (1986), *Economy and Politics in the Arab World: A Comparative Analysis of the Development of Egypt, Iraq and Saudi Arabia since the 1950s*, University of Aarhus, Denmark, Institute of Political Science.

ÖNCÜ, Ayşe (1991), 'Street Politics in Egypt and Turkey', mimeo., Istanbul.

ÖNIŞ, Ziya (1991), 'Political Economy of Turkey in the 1980s: Anatomy of Unorthodox Liberalism', in Metin Heper, ed., *Strong State and Economic Interest Groups: the Post-1980 Turkish Experience*, Berlin and NY: de Gruyter.

OSTERKAMP, Rigmar (1982), 'L'Algérie entre le Plan and le Marché: points de vue récents sur la politique économique de l'Algérie' *Canadian Journal of African Studies*, Vol. 16, no. 1.

O'SULLIVAN, Noel (1983), *Fascism*, London: Dent and Sons.

OTHMAN, Osama A. (1979), 'Saudi Arabia: An Unprecedented Growth of Wealth with an Unparalleled Growth of Bureacracy', in *International Review of Administrative Sciences*, Vol. 45, no. 3.

OWEN, Roger (1969), *Cotton and the Egyptian Economy 1820–1914: a Study in Trade and Development*, Oxford: Clarendon Press.

— (1978), 'The Role of the Army in Middle Eastern Politics', *Review of Middle Eastern Studies*, no. 3, London: Ithaca Press.

— (1981), *The Middle East in the World Economy 1800–1914*, London and NY: Methuen.

— (1987), 'Arab Armies Today', paper presented at British Society for Middle Eastern Studies Annual Conference, Exeter University, July 1987.

— (1992), *State, Power and Politics in the Making of the Modern Middle East*, London: Routledge

PALMER, Monte and Khalil Naqib (1978), 'Bureaucracy and Development in the Arab World: an Outline for Future Research', paper presented to International Conference on *Strategies of Development in the Arab World*, Louvain, 11–14 December 1978.

—, Ibrahim Alghofaily and Saud Alnimir (1984), 'The Behavioral Correlates of Rentier Economies: A Case Study of Saudi Arabia', in Robert W. Stookey, ed., *The Arabian Peninsula: Contemporary Politics, Economics and International Relations*, Stanford, CA: Hoover Institution.

—, Ali Leila and El Sayed Yassin (1988), *The Egyptian Bureaucracy*, New York: Syracuse University Press.

—, Abdelrahman Al-Hegelan et al. (1989), 'Bureaucratic Innovation and Economic Development in the Middle East: A Study of Egypt, Saudi Arabia and the Sudan', in Joseph G. Jabbra, ed., *Bureaucracy and Development in the Arab World*, London: E.J. Brill.

PAREKH, Bhikhu (1992), 'The Cultural Particularity of Liberal Democracy', *Political Studies*, Vol. 40, 1992, special issue on *Prospects for Democracy*, ed. David Held.

PARISOT, Benoit (1990), 'La situation économique et financière de l'Irak à la mi-1990: quelle influence sur la décision d'envahir le Koweït?', *Maghreb-Machrek*, no. 130, octobre.

PAUL, Samuel (1982), *Managing Development Programs; the Lessons of Success*, Boulder, CO: Westview Press.

PERLMUTTER, Amos (1970), 'The Arab Military Elite', *World Politics*, no. 22.

PERTHES, Volker (1992a), 'The Syrian Private Industrial and Commerical Sectors and the State', *International Journal of Middle East Studies*, Vol. 24, no. 2.

— (1992b), 'Syria's Parliamentary Elections: Remodelling Asad's Political Base', *Middle East Report* (MERIP), January–February 1992.

PETERS, B. Guy (1978), *The Politics of Bureaucracy; A Comparative Perspective*, New York and London: Longman.

PETERSON, Erik R. (1977), 'Tribal Components in the Development of Modern States', *Middle East Journal*, Vol. 31, no. 3, Summer.

— (1988), *The Gulf Cooperation Council: Search for Unity in a Dynamic Region*, Boulder, CO: Westview Press.

PFEIFER, Karen (1985), *Agrarian Reform Under State Capitalism in Algeria*, Boulder, CO: Westview Press.

PICARD, Elizabeth (1988), 'Arab Military in Politics: from Revolutionary Plot to Authoritarian State', in A. Dawisha and W. Zartman, eds, *Beyond Coercion: the Durability of the Arab State*, London: Croom Helm.

— (1990), 'Le régime Irakien et la crise: les ressorts d'une politique', *Maghreb-Machrek*, no. 130, octobre–décembre.

PICCIOTTO, Sol (1990), 'The Internationalization of the State', *Review of Radical Political Economies*, Vol. 22, no. 1.

PIKE, Frederick B. (1974), 'The New Corporatism in Franco's Spain and Some Latin-American Perspectives', in Frederick B. Pike and Thomas Strich, eds, *The New Corporatism: Social–Political Structures in the Iberian World*, Notre Dame, Ind: Univeristy of Notre Dame Press.

PILLING, Geoffrey (1986), *The Crisis of Keynesian Economics*, London: Croom Helm.

PIRIE, M.M. (1985), *Dismantling the State: the Theory and Practice of Privatization*, Dallas, TX: National Center for Policy Analysis.

PISCATORI, James P. (1980), 'The Role of Islam in Saudi Arabia's Political Development', in John Esposito, ed., *Islam and Development: Religion and Socio-political Change*, Syracuse: Syracuse University Press.

POGGI, Gianfranco (1978), *The Development of the Modern State: A Sociological Introduction*, London: Hutchinson.

POULANTZAS, Nicos (1971), *Pouvoir Politique et Classes Sociales*, Paris: Maspéro (English edn, London 1973).

PRESLEY, J.R. (1991), 'Managerial Inefficiency in Small Manufacturing Businesses in Saudi Arabia: A Constraint upon Economic Development', in *Proceedings of the Annual Conference of the British Society for Middle Eastern Studies*, London, July 1991.

PRIMAKOV, E.M. (1985), *Al-Sharq ba'd inhiyar al-nizam al-isti'mari* [The East after the Collapse of the Colonial System], trans., Moscow: Progress Publishers.

PRIPSTEIN-POSUSNEY, Marsha (1992), 'Labor as an Obstacle to Privatization: the Case of Egypt', in I. Harik and D. Sullivan, eds, *Privatization and Liberalization in the Middle East*, Bloomington, IN.: Indiana University Press.

PRZEWORSKI, Adam (1991), *Democracy and the Market: Political and Economic Reforms in Eastern Europe and Latin America*, New York: Cambridge University Press.

PUHLE, H.J. (1992), 'The Nationalism of the Small Nations in the 20th Century', Lecture at the European University Institute, Florence, January 1992.

AL-QAHTANI, Fahd (1985), *Al-Islam wa al-wathaniyya al-sa'udiyya* [Islam and Saudi Paganism], London: Al-Safar Publishing.

QANDIL, Amany (1988), 'Interest Groups and Economic Policy in Egypt', in Manabu Shimizu et al., *Pressure Groups and Economic Policies in Egypt*, Middle East Series no. 21, Tokyo: Institute of Developing Economies.

AL-QASIMI, 'Abdallah (1977), *Al-'Arab zahira sawtiyya* [The Arabs as a Phonetic Phenomenon], Paris: n.p.

QATAR NEWS AGENCY (1981, 1982), *Watha'iq* ... [Documents of the Gulf Cooperation Council], Qatar.

QAZZIHA, Wahid (1979), 'Al-Usus al-ijtima'iyya al-siyasiyya li numuw al-haraka al-qawmiyya al-mu'asira fi al-mashriq al-'Arabi' [The Socio-political Bases for the Development of the Contemporary Nationalist Movement in the Arab Levant], *Al-Mustaqbal al-'Arabi*, Vol. 6, no. 3.

QURBAN, Milhim (1984), *Khalduniyyat: al-siyasa al-'umraniyya* [Khaldunian Issues: the Politics of Urbanity and Civilisation], Beirut: Al-Mu'assasa al-Jami'iyya.

RABI', Hamid A. (1980, 1983), *Suluk al-malik fi tadbir al-mamalik: ta'lif al-'allamma shihab al-Din ibn Abi al-Rubayyi'* [Suluk al-malik fi tadbir al-mamalik: by the scholar Shihab al-Din ibn Abi al-Rubayyi'], Vol. I (1980), and Vol. II (1983), Cairo: Dar al-Sha'b.

— (1985), 'Al-Khibra al-Islamiyya ...' [The Islamic Experience and the Process of Political Theorization], *Al-Iqtisadi*, no. 848, 15 April.

AL-RAFI'I, 'Abd al-Rahman (1982), *'Asr Muhammad 'Ali* [The Era of Muhammad Ali], 4th edn, Cairo: Dar al-Ma'arif.

RAMADAN, 'Abd al-'Azim (1981), *Dirasat fi tarikh misr al-mu'asir* [Studies in the Contemporary History of Egypt], Cairo: Al-Markaz al-'Arabi.

RASHAD, 'Abd al-Ghaffar (1984), *Al-Taqlidiyya wa al-hadatha* ... [Tradition and Modernity in the Japanese Experience], Beirut: Arab Research Foundation.

RASHID, Ahmad (1975), 'Government and Administration in the UAE', *Bulletin of Arab Research and Studies*, Vol. 6.

RASHID, Amina et al., (1992), *Qadaya al-mujtama' al-madani al-'arabi fi daw' utruhat Gramshi* [Issues of the Arab Civil Society in Light of Gramsci's Theses], Cairo: Markaz al-Buhuth al-'Arabiyya.

AL-RAWAF, Othman Y. (1987), *Policies and Programs of Rural Development in Saudi Arabia; a Presentation and Evaluation*, Riyadh, King Saud University Press.

RAYMOND, André (1974), *Fusul min al-tarikh al-ijtima'i li al-qahira al-'uthmaniyya* [Chronicles from the Social History of Ottoman Cairo], trans., Cairo: Rose al-Yusuf.

AL-RAYYIS, Muhammad Diya' al-Din (1985), *Al-Kharaj wa al-nuzum al-maliyya* ['Tax' and the Financial Systems of the Islamic State], Cairo: Dar al-Turath.

RICHARDS, Alan and John Waterbury (1990), *A Political Economy of the Middle East: State, Class and Economic Development*, Boulder, CO: Westview Press.

RIDA, Muhammad Jawwad (1992), *Sira' al-dawla wa al-qabila* ... [The State/Tribe Conflict in the Arabian Gulf], Beirut: CAUS.

RIDHA, Benyoussef (1989), 'La Fonction publique et le changement: le cas tunisien', in L'Association Marocaine des Sciences Admininstratives (AMSA), *L'Administration Publique et le Changement*, Casablanca: Afrique Orient for AMSA.

RIGGS, Fred W. (1964), *Administration in Developing Countries: the Theory of Prismatic Society*, Boston: Houghton Mifflin.

RIZQ, Yunan Labib (1975), *Tarikh al-wazarat al-misriyya* [History of Egyptian Ministries], Cairo: CPSS.

— (1977), *Al-Ahzab al-misriyya qabla thawrat 1952* [Egyptian Political Parties Before the 1952 Revolution], Cairo: CPSS.

ROBINS, Philip (1988), *The Consolidation of Hashemite Power in Jordan, 1921–1946*, unpublished PhD thesis, Exeter University, Politics Department.

ROBINSON, Pearl T. (1991), 'Niger: Anatomy of a Neotraditional Corporatist State', *Comparative Politics*, Vol. 24, no. 1, October.

RODINSON, Maxime (1978), *Islam and Capitalism*, trans., Austin: University of Texas Press.

— (1981), *The Arabs*, trans., Chicago and London: Chicago University Press and Croom Helm.

ROE, Alan, Jayanta Roy and Jayshree Sengupta (1989), *Economic Adjustment in Algeria, Egypt, Jordan, Morocco, Pakistan, Tunisia, and Turkey*, Economic Development Institute Policy Seminar report, no. 15, Washington, DC: World Bank.

ROULEAU, Eric (1967), 'The Syrian Enigma: What is the Ba'th?', *New Left Review*, no. 45.

ROYAUME DU MAROC (1985), *Receuil statistique des fonctionnaires de l'état*, Rabat: Secrétariat d'Etat aux Affaires Administratives, janvier.

RUF, Werner (1984), 'Tunisia: Contemporary Politics', in R. Lawless and A. Findlay, eds, *North Africa: Contemporary Politics and Economic Development*, London: Croom Helm.

RUGH, Willliam (1973), 'Emergence of a New Middle Class in Saudi Arabia', *Middle East Journal*, Vol. 27, no. 1.

AL-RUMAIHI, Muhammad Ghanim (1975), *Al-bitrul wa al-taghayyur al-ijtima'i ...* [Oil and Social Change in the Arabian Gulf], Kuwait: Mu'assasat al-Wahda.

— (1977), *Mu'awwiqat al-tanmiya ...* [Obstacles to Socio-Economic Development in Contemporary Gulf Societies], Kuwait: Kazima.

— (1980), 'Al-Sira' wa al-ta'awun ... ' [Conflict and Cooperation among the States of the Arabian Gulf], *Al-Mustaqbal al-'Arabi*, Vol. 2, no. 13, March 1980.

— (1983), *Al-Khalij laisa naftan* [The Gulf is not Simply Oil], Kuwait: Kazima.

— (1989), 'Al-Siyagh al-taqlidiyya al-mu'asira' [Neo-Traditional Forms for Expressing Plurality], in S. Ibrahim, ed., *Al-Ta'addudiyya al-siyasiyya wa al-dimuqratiyya fi al-watan al-'arabi* [Political Pluralism and Democracy in the Arab Fatherland], Amman: Arab Thought Forum.

RUNCIMAN, W.G. (1989), *A Treatise on Social Theory*, Cambridge: Cambridge University Press.

RUSH, Alan (1987), *Al-Sabah: History and Genealogy of Kuwait's Ruling Family 1752–1987*, London: Ithaca Press.

AL-SA'ATI, Hasan (1985), 'Al-Fi'at al-murasmala ...' [Capitalised Categories in Contemporary Egypt], *mimeo*, Cairo: 'Ain Shams University.

SABAGH, Georges (1988), 'Immigrants in the Arab Gulf Countries: "Sojourners" or "Settlers"?', in G. Luciani and G. Salamé, eds, *The Politics of Arab Integration*, London: Croom Helm.

SABIR, Muhyi al-Din and Louis Kamil Mulaika (1986), *Al-Badu wa al-badawa* [Nomads and Nomadism], Beirut: Al-Maktaba al-'Asriyya.

SA'D, Ahmad Sadiq (1981), *Tahawwul al-takwin al-misri* [Transition of the Egyptian Formation from the Asiatic Mode to the Capitalist Mode], Beirut: Dar al-Hadatha.

— (1988), *Dirasa fi al-mafahim al-iqtisadiyya lada al-mufakirin al-islamiyyin: Kitab al-Kharaj li Abi Yusuf* [Studies on Economic Concepts Among Islamic Thinkers: Al-Kharaj Book of Abu Yusuf], Cairo: Dar al-Thaqafa al-Jadida.

SADIQ, Muhammad (1980), *Idarat al-tanmiya ...* [Development Administration for Social and Economic Development in the Arab World in the Year 2000], Amman: Arab Organisation for Administrative Sciences.

SADOWSKI, Yahya M. (1988), 'Ba'thist Ethics and the Spirit of State Capitalism: Patronage and the Party in Contemporary Syria', in P. Chelkowski and R.J. Pranger, eds, *Ideology and Power in the Middle East*, Durham, NC and London: Duke University Press.

— (1991), *Political Vegetables? Businessman and Bureaucrat in the Development of Egyptian Agriculture*, Washington, DC: The Brookings Institution.

— (1993), 'The New Orientalism and the Democracy Debate', *Middle East Report*, no. 183, July–August.

SAFADI, Muta' (1986), *Istratijiyyat al-tasmiya* [The Strategy of Nomenclature], Beirut: Markaz al-Inma' al-'Arabi.

SAID, Mohamed (1982), 'The Rise and Decline of Bureaucratic Bourgeoisie in Egypt', paper for Conference of the African Studies Association (USA), 1982.

SAIF AL-DAWLA, 'Ismat (1983), 'Tatawwur mafhum al-dimuqratiyya fi misr' [Evolution of the Concept of Democracy in Egypt], *Al-Mustaqbal al-'Arabi*, Vol. 56, no. 10.

— (1984), 'Al-Dimuqratiyya ...' [Democracy and the 23 July 1952 Revolution: A Comment], in Centre for Arab Unity Studies, *Azmat al-dimuqratiyya ...* [The Crisis of Democracy in the Arab Fatherland], Beirut: CAUS.

— (1991), *Al-Nizam al-niyabi ...* [The Representative System and the Problem of Democracy], Cairo: Dar al-Mawqif al-'Arabi.

AL-SA'IGH, Nabil (1980), *Al-Ahkam al-dusturiyya li al-bilad al-'arabiyya* [Constitutional Rulings of the Arab Countries], Beirut.

AL-SAIGH, Nassir M. and AbuBaker M. Buera (1990), 'Privatization in the Arab World: Pre-requisites for success', *International Review of Administrative Sciences*, Vol. 56, no. 1, March.

SALAMA, Ghassan (1980), *Al-Siyasa al-kharijiya al-sa'udiyya* [Saudi Foreign Policy Since 1945], Beirut: Ma'had al-Inma' al-'Arabi.

— (1987a), *Al-Mujtama' wa al-dawla fi al-mashriq al-'arabi* [Society and State in the Arab Levant], Beirut: CAUS.

— (1987b), *Nahwa 'aqd ijtima'i 'arabi jadid* [Towards a New Arab Social Contract], Beirut: CAUS.

SALAMÉ, Ghassan (1984), 'Aspects of Political Decision-Making in the Gulf', paper presented to the Oxford Institute for Energy Studies seminar on *The Gulf: Economics, Politics and Security*, Oxford, 5–6 April 1984.

—, ed. (1987), *The Foundations of the Arab State*, London: Croom Helm.

— (1987), '"Strong" and "Weak" States, a Qualified Return to the Muqaddimah', in G. Salamé, ed., *The Foundations of the Arab State*, London: Croom Helm.

— (1988), 'Integration in the Arab World: the Institutional Framework', in G. Luciani and G. Salamé, eds, *The Politics of Arab Integration*, London: Croom Helm.

SALAMEH, Ghassane (1980), 'Political Power and the Saudi State', *MERIP Reports*, no. 91, October.

SALES, Arnaud (1991), 'The Private, the Public and Civil Society: Social Realms and Power Structures', in A.Z. Kaminski, ed., *International Political Science Review*, Vol. 12, no. 4, October (special issue on *The Public and the Private*).

SALIM, Jamal (1982), *Al-Tanzimat al-siriyya* ... [Secret Organisations of the 23 July (1952) Revolution], Cairo: Madbuli.

SALIM, Al-Sayyid 'Abd al-'Aziz (c. 1983), *Tarikh al-dawla al-'arabiyya* [History of the Arab State], Vol. 2, Alexandria: Mu'assasat Shabab al-Jami'a.

SANTUCCI, Jean-Claude and Habib El Malki, eds (1990), *Etat et Développement dans le Monde Arabe: Crises et Mutations au Maghreb*, Paris: Editions du CNRS.

AL-SAQQAF, 'Abd al-'Aziz (1989), 'Sigha yamaniyya jadida li al-dimuqratiyya' [A New Yemeni Formula for Democracy], in S. Ibrahim, ed., *Al-Ta' addidiyya al-siyasiyya* ... [Political Pluralism and Democracy in the Arab Fatherland], Amman: Arab Thought Forum.

AL-SARRAF, 'Ali (1992), 'Al-Wahda al-qawmiyya naqadat al-ishtirakiyya [Arab Unity vs. Socialism], *Al-Hayat*, 20 July 1992.

SA'UD, Dalal Barakat and Mohammad Salih 'Ali (1986), 'Al-Idara al-'amma w'al-islah al-idari fi al-watan al-'arabi' [Public Administration in Syria], in AOAS, *Al-Idara al-'amma w'al islah al-idari fi al-watan al-'arabi* [Public Administration and Administrative Reform in the Arab Fatherland], Amman: Arab Organisation for Administrative Sciences.

SAUDI ARABIA, Ministry of Planning (1985), *Report, 1985*, Riyad.

— (1989), *Workshop, 1989*, Riyad.

SAUDI ARABIA YEARBOOK (1980/81).

SAVAS, E.S. (1982), *Privatizing the Public Sector: How to Shrink Government*, Chatham, NJ: Chatham House Publishing.

SAYIGH, Yusif A. (1982), *The Arab Economy: Past Performance and Future Prospects*, London: Oxford University Press.

AL-SAYYID, Mustafa Kamil (1983), *Al-Mujtama' wa al-siyasa* ... [Society and Politics in Egypt: Interest Groups in the Egyptian Political System], Cairo: Dar al-Mustaqbal al-'Arabi.

— (1990), *Privatization: the Egyptian Debate*, The Cairo Papers in Social Science, Vol. 13, Monograph 4, The American University in Cairo Press.

— (1991), 'Dirasat jama'at al-masalih ...' [The Study of Interest groups in Egypt], in Nivin A. Mus'ad, ed., *Al-'Alamiyya wa al-khususiyya* ... [Universalism and Specificity in the Study of the Arab Region], Cairo University: Centre for Political Research and Studies.

AL-SAYYID, Radwan (1984), *Mafahim al-jama'at fi al-islam* [The Concept of Groups in Islam], Beirut: Dar al-Tanwir.

— (1988), 'Al-Haraka al-islamiyya wa al-thaqafa al-mu'asira' [The Islamic Movement and Contemporary Culture], in Sa'd al-Din Ibrahim, ed., *Al-Sahwa al-islamiyya wa humum al-watan al-'arabi* [The Islamic Revival and Concerns of the Arab Homeland], Amman: Arab Thought Forum/Mu'assasat Al-al-Bait.

SAYYID-AHMAD, Muhammad (1984), *Mustaqbal al-nizam al-hizbi fi misr* [The Future of the Party System in Egypt], Cairo: Dar al-Mustaqbal al-'Arabi.

AL-SAYYID 'ALI, 'Abd al-Mun'im (1989), 'Taqwim wa istishraf dawr al-dawla ...' [An Evaluation and a Projection of the Role of the State in Economic Activity in Arab Countries with special

Orientations regarding Justice and the Redistribution of Income], in the Arab Planning Institute, Kuwait, Seminar on *Dawr al-Dawla* ... [The Role of the State in Economic Activity in the Arab Fatherland], Kuwait, May.

— (1990), 'Tajrubat al-'iraq ...' [The Iraq Experience with the Public and Private Sectors], in 'A. Al-Nasrawi, *Al-Qita' al-'amm* ... [The Public and the Private Sectors in the Arab Fatherland], Beirut: CAUS.

SBIH, Missoum (1977), *Les Institutions Administratives du Maghreb* (thèse, Droit public, Univ. Paris I), Paris: Ed. Hachette. (An Arabic trans. is also available from the Arab Organisation for Administrative Sciences, Amman 1985.)

SCHAFFER, Bernard (1974), *Political Integration*, University of Sussex, Institute of Development Studies, Discussion Paper no. 53, June.

— (1980), 'Insiders and Outsiders', *Development and Change*, Vol. 11.

SCHECTERMAN, Bernard (1981/82), 'Political Instability in Saudi Arabia and its Implications', *Middle East Review*, Vol. 14, nos. 1 and 2, Fall–Winter.

SCHMITTER, Philippe G. (1974), 'Still the Century of Corporatism?', in Fredrick B. Pike and Thomas Strich, eds, *The New Corporatism: Social–Political Structures in the Iberian World*, Notre Dame: University of Notre Dame Press.

— (1985), 'Neo-Corporatism and the State', in Wynn Grant, ed., *The Political Economy of Corporatism*, London: Macmillan.

SCHOLTEN, Ilja (1987), 'Corporatist and Consociational Arrangements', in I. Scholten, ed., *Political Stability and Neo-Corporatism*, London: Sage.

SEDDON, David (1986), 'A "New Paradigm" for the Analysis of Agrarian Relations in the Middle East', *Current Sociology*, Vol. 34, no. 2.

— (1993), 'Austerity Protests in Response to Economic Liberalization in the Middle East' in T. Niblock and E. Murphy, eds, *Economic and Political Liberalization in the Middle East*, London and New York: British Academic Press.

SEITZ, John (1980), 'The Failure of U.S. Technical Assistance in Public Administration', *Public Administration Review*, Vol. 40, no. 5, September–October.

SHAALAN, A. Shakour (1987), 'Adjustment Challenges and Strategies Facing Arab Countries', in Said El-Naggar, ed., *Adjustment Policies and Development Strategies in the Arab World*, Washington, DC: IMF.

SHAFIR, Muhammad (1988), 'Azmat al-usus al-majaliyya ...' [Crisis in the Spatial Bases of the Moroccan State], *Al-Majalla al-Maghribiyya li 'Ilm al-Ijtima' al-Siyasi*, Vol. 2, Summer/Autumn.

AL-SHAHIN, 'Isa (1992), 'Kalimat al-iftitah' [Prelude], in Ahmad Al-Khaja et al., *Al-Kuwait wa tahaddiyat* ... [Kuwait and the Challenges of the Era for Reconstruction], Cairo University: Markaz al-Buhuth al-Siyasiyya.

AL-SHAIKH, Tawfiq (1988), *Al-Bitrul wa al-siyasa* ... [Petroleum and Politics in the Kingdom of Saudi Arabia], London: Al-Safa Publishing.

AL-SHA'IR, Jamal (1989), 'Al-Mumarasat al-'arabiyya al-hizbiyya al-mu'asira' [Contemporary Arab Practices with regard to (Political) Parties], in Sa'd al-Din Ibrahim, ed., *Al-Ta'addudiya al-siyasiyya wa al-dimuqratiyya* ... [Political Pluralism and Democracy in the Arab Fatherland], Amman: Arab Thought Forum.

AL-SHA'IR, Wahib (1990), 'Tajribat al-'urdun ...' [Jordan's Experience with the Public and Private Sectors], in 'A. Al-Nasrawi et al., *Al-Qita' al-'amm* ... [The Public and the Private Sectors in the Arab Fatherland], Beirut: CAUS.

SHAKER, Fatima Amin (1972), *Modernization of the Developing Nations; the Case of Saudi Arabia*, unpublished PhD thesis, Purdue University.

SHALAQ, Al-Fadl (1988), 'Al-Kharaj wa al-iqta' wa al-dawla' [Tribute, Eastern Feudalism and the State], in *Al-Ijtihad*, special issue, Vol. 1, no. 1, July–September.

— (1989), 'Al-Hisba ...' [Al-Hisba; A Study in Legitimacy of Society and State], *Al-Ijtihad*, Vol. 1, no. 2.

SHARABI, Hisham (1987), *Al-Binya al-batrakiyya* ... [The Patriarchal Structure: a Study in Contemporary Arab Society], Beirut: Dar al-Tali'a.

SHARARA, Waddah (1977), *Al-Mas'ala al-tarikhiyya* ... [The Historical Question in Contemporary Arab Thought], Beirut: Ma'had al-Inma' al-'Arabi.

— (1980), *Hawl ba'd mushkilat al-dawla* ... [On Some Problems of the State in Arab Culture and Society], Beirut: Dar Al-Hadatha.

— (1981a), *Al-Ahl wa al-ghanima* [Kin and the Booty: The Foundations of Politics in the Kingdom of Saudi Arabia], Beirut: Dar al-Tali'a.

— (1981b), *Isti'naf al-bad'* ... [Resuming the Start: Essays on the Relationship Between Philosophy and History], Beirut: Dar al-Hadatha.

SHARIF, Khalid (1987), 'Tajarub al-duwal al-namiya ...' [The Experience of Developing Counties in Liquidating Losing Public Sector Companies], *Al-Ahram al-Iqtisadi*, 30 November 1987.

SHAW, Stanford J. (1962), *The Financial and Administrative Organization and Development of Ottoman Egypt*, Princeton, NJ: Princeton University Press.

SHIHATA, Ibrahim (1992), 'Al-Islah al-idari fi al-duwal al-'arabiyya ...' [Administrative Reform in the Arab Countries: General Observations and Comparative Solutions], paper for Arab Administrative Development Organisation (ARADO), First Ministerial Conference on Administrative Development, Cairo December 1992.

SHIMIZU, Manabu (1988), 'Introductory Notes for the Study of Pressure Groups in Egypt', in Manabu Shimizu, Amany Qandil and Samia Said Imam, *Pressure Groups and Economic Policies in Egypt*, Middle East Series no. 21, Tokyo: Institute of Developing Economies.

AL-SHINNAWI, 'Abd al-'Aziz (1980), *Al-Dawla al-'uthmaniyya* [The Ottoman State], 2 vols, Cairo: Anglo-Egyptian.

SIFFIN, William J. (1977), 'Two Decades of Public Administration in Developing Countries', in Lawrence W. Stifel et al., eds, *Education and Training for Public Sector Management in Developing Countries*, New York: Rockefeller Foundation.

SIVERS, Peter von (1988), 'Retreating States and Expanding Societies: the State Autonomy/Civil Society Dialectic in the Middle East and North Africa', paper for JCNME/SSRC Conference on Retreating States and Expanding Societies ..., Aix-en-Provence, 25–27 March 1988.

SKLAR, Richard L. (1976), 'Post imperialism: A Class Analysis of Multinational Corporate Expansion', *Comparative Politics*, Vol. 9, no. 1, October.

— (1987), 'Developmental Democracy', *Comparative Studies in Society and History*, Vol. 29, no. 4, October.

SMITH, Anthony D. (1991), *National Identity*, London: Penguin Books.

SMITH, M.G. (1986), 'Pluralism, Violence and the Modern State', in Ali Kazancigil, ed., *The State in Global Perspective*, London: Gower/UNESCO.

SNIDER, Lewis (1988), 'Comparing the Strength of Nations: the Arab Gulf States and Political Change', *Comparative Politics*, Vol. 20, no. 4.

SØRENSEN, Georg (1991), 'Third World Democratic Experiences and Development Theory', paper at International Political Science Association's 15th World Congress, Buenos Aires, July 1991.

SPRINGBORG, Patricia (1992), *Western Republicanism and the Oriental Prince*, Cambridge: Polity Press.

SPRINGBORG, Robert D. (1974), *The Ties that Bind: Political Association and Policy-Making in Egypt*, unpublished PhD dissertation, Stanford University, California.

— (1982), *Family, Power and Politics in Egypt: Sayed Bey Marei; His Clan, Clients and Cohorts*, Philadelphia: University of Pennsylvania Press.

— (1986), 'Infitah, Agrarian Transformation, and Elite Consolidation in Contemporary Iraq', *Middle East Journal*, Vol. 40, no. 1, Winter.

— (1987), 'The President and the Field Marshal: Civil–Military Relations in Egypt Today', *Middle East Report*, no. 147, July–August.

— (1990), 'Agrarian Bourgeoisie, Semiproletarians, and the Egyptian State: Lessons for Liberalization', *International Journal of Middle East Studies*, Vol. 22, no. 4, November.

STAUFFER, Thomas (1981), 'Dynamics of Petroleum Dependency Growth in an Oil Rentier State', *Finance and Industry* (Kuwait), Vol. 1, no. 2.

STEPAN, Alfred (1978), *The State and Society: Peru in Comparative Perspective*, Princeton, NJ: Princeton University Press.

STEWART, Angus (1969), 'The Social Roots', in G. Ionescu and E. Gellner, eds, *Populism: its Meaning and National Characteristics*, London: Weidenfeld and Nicholson.

STOOKEY, Robert W., ed. (1984), *The Arabian Peninsula: Contemporary Politics, Economics and International Relations*, Stanford, CA: The Hoover Institution.

STORK, Joe and Jim Paul (1983), 'Arms Sales and the Militarization of the Middle East', *MERIP Reports*, Vol. 13, no. 2, February.

— (1987), 'Arms Industries of the Middle East', *MERIP: Middle East Report*, no. 144, January–February.

— and Martha Wenger (1991), 'From Rapid Deployment to Massive Deployment', *Middle East Report* (MERIP), no. 168, January/February.

STRANGE, Susan (1989), *States and Markets: An Introduction to International Political Economy*, London: Pinter Publishing.

SULEIMAN, Michael W. (1967), *Political Parties in Lebanon: the Challenge of a Fragmented Political Culture*, Ithaca, NY: Cornell University Press.

SULLIVAN, Denis J. (1990a), 'Bureaucracy and Foreign Aid in Egypt: the Primacy of Politics', in Ibrahim M. Oweiss, ed., *The Political Economy of Contemporary Egypt*, Washington, DC: Georgetown University Center for Contemporary Arab Studies.

— (1990b), 'The Political Economy of Reform in Egypt', *International Journal of Middle East Studies*, Vol. 22, no. 3, August.

SUNAR, Ilkay (1993), 'The Politics of State Interventionism in "Populist" Egypt and Turkey', research paper, Boğaziçi University, Istanbul.

SUTTON, Keith and Ahmed Aghrout (1990), 'Agricultural Policy in Algeria in the 1980s: Progress Towards Liberalisation', paper presented at AFEMAM-BRISMES Conference, Paris, 9–11 July 1990.

SYRIA, Central Statistical Office (1981), *The Statistical Collection for 1981* (in Arabic), Damascus.

TABLIYYA, Al-Qutb Muhammad (1985), *Nizam al-idara fi al-islam* [The System of Administration in Islam], Cairo: Dar al-Fikr al-'Arabi.

TAGUCHI, Fukuji and Tetsuro Kato (1985), 'Marxist Debates on the State in Post-War Japan', *Hosei Ronsyu* [Journal of Law and Political Science], no. 105.

TAPPER, Richard, ed. (1983), *The Conflict of Tribe and State*, London: Croom Helm.

— (1991), 'Anthropologists, Historians, and Tribespeople on Tribe and State Formation in the Middle East', in Philip S. Khoury and Joseph Kostiner, eds, *Tribes and State Formation in the Middle East*, London and NY: I.B. Tauris.

TARKHAN, Ibrahim 'Ali (1968), *Al-Nuzum al-iqta'iyya* [Feudal Systems in the Middle East in the Middle Ages], Cairo: Al-Katib al-'Arabi.

AL-TAWATI, Mustafa (c. 1985), *Al-ta'bir al-dini 'an al-sira' al-ijtima'i fi al-islam* [Religious Expression of Social Conflict in Islam], Tunis: Dar al-Nashr li al-Maghrib.

AL-TAWIL, Muhammad (1986), *Al-Idara al-'amma fi al-mamlaka al-'arabiyya al-sa'udiyya* [Public Administration in the Kingdom of Saudi Arabia], Riyad: IPA.

TAYLOR, John G. (1979), *From Modernization to Modes of Production: A Critique of the Sociologies of Development and Underdevelopment*, London: Macmillan.

AL-TAYYIB, Hasan Abashar (1984), *Mu'assasat al-tanmiya al-idariyya al-'arabiyya* [Arab Administrative Development Institutions], Amman: AOAS.

TETREAULT, Mary Ann (1991), 'Autonomy, Necessity, and the Small State: Ruling Kuwait in the Twentieth Century', *International Organisation*, Vol. 45, no. 4, Autumn.

THALWITZ, Wilfred P. (1989), 'Introduction', in Alan Roe et al., *Economic Adjustment in Algeria, Egypt, Jordan, Morocco, Pakistan, Tunisia, and Turkey*, Economic Development Institute Policy Seminar Report no. 15, Washington, DC: World Bank.

AL-THAQIB, Fahd (1985), 'Jara'im dhawi al-nufudh ...' [Crimes by People of Influence: A Definition with Cases from Societies of Arabia and the Gulf], *Majallat, Dirasat al-Khalij wa al-Jazira al-'Arabiyya*, Vol. 11, no. 44, October 1985.

TIBI, Bassam (1981), *Arab Nationalism: A Critical Enquiry*, trans., M. and P. Sluglett, London: Macmillan.

TIGNOR, Robert L. (1984), *State, Private Enterprise, and Economic Change in Egypt, 1918–1952*, Princeton, NJ: Princeton University Press.

TIZINI, Tayyib (1981), *Mashru' ru'ya jadida li al-fikr al-'arabi* [A Project for a New Perspective Towards Arabic Thought in the Medieval Era], Damascus: Dar Dimashq (first pub. 1971).

TLEMCANI, Rachid (1986), *State and Revolution in Algeria*, London and Boulder: Zed Books and Westview Press.

TRIMBERGER, Ellen Kay (1978), *Revolution from Above: Military Bureaucrats and Development in Japan, Turkey, Egypt and Peru*, New Brunswick, NJ: Transactions.

TURNER, Bryan S. (1974), *Weber and Islam* (London: Routledge and Kegan Paul).

— (1978), *Marx and the End of Orientalism*, London and Boston: Allen and Unwin.

— (1984), *Capitalism and Class in the Middle East: Theories of Social Change and Economic Development*, London: Heinemann.

'ULWAN, Muhammad Yusuf, et al. (1977), 'Hiwar hawl al-nazariyya wa al-tatbiq ...' [A Dialogue on Theory and Practice in Administration and Bureaucracy], *Majallat al-'Ulum al-Ijtima'iyya*, Vol. 4, no. 4, January.

'UMAR, Ibrahim A. and M. Saif Al-Shirbini (1981), 'Idarat al-mawarid al-bashiriyya ...' [Manpower Management in the Egyptian Administration], *Al-Idara*, Vol. 14, no. 1, July.

UMLIL, 'Ali (1985), *Al-Islahiyya al-'arabiyya wa al-dawla al-wataniyya* [Arab Reformism and the National State], Casablanca: Al-Markaz al-Thaqafi al-'Arab.

— (1991), *Fi shar'iyyat al-ikhtilaf* [On the Legitimacy of Difference], Rabat: Al-Majlis al-Qawmi li al-Thaqafa.

VANDEWALLE, Dirk (1992), 'Breaking with Socialism: Economic Liberalization and Privatization in Algeria', in I. Harik and D. Sullivan, eds, *Privatization and Liberalization in the Middle East*, Bloomington: Indiana University Press.

VAN NIEKIRK, A.E. (1974), *Populism and Political Development in Latin America*, Rotterdam: Rotterdam University Press.

VATIKIOTIS, P.J. (1968), 'Some Political Consequences of the 1952 Revolution in Egypt', in P.M. Holt, ed., *Political and Social Change in Modern Egypt*, London: Oxford University Press.

— (1969), *The Modern History of Egypt*, London: Weidenfeld and Nicolson.

VERGOPOULOS, Kostas (1990), 'The Political Economy of Democratic Consolidation in Southern Europe', in Diane Ethier, ed., *Democratic Transition and Consolidation in Southern Europe, Latin America and Southeast Asia*, London: Macmillan.

VIROLI, Maurizio (1992), *From Politics to Reason of State*, Cambridge: Cambridge University Press.

WADE, Robert (1992), 'East Asia's Economic Success: Conflicting Perspectives, Partial Insights, Shaky Evidence', *World Politics*, Vol. 44, no. 2, January.

WAHIDA, Subhi (1950), *Fi usul al-mas'ala al-misriyya* [On the Origins of the Egyptian Question], Cairo: Matba'at Misr.

WALLERSTEIN, Immanuel (1974), *The Modern World System*, New York: Academic Press.

WALTERS, Alan (1989), 'Liberalisation and Privatisation: An Overview', in Said El-Naggar, ed., *Privatization and Structural Adjustment in the Arab Countries*, Washington, DC: IMF.

WALTZ, Kenneth (1979), *Theory of International Politics*, New York: Wiley.

WARE, Alan (1992), 'Liberal Democracy: One Form or Many?', *Political Studies*, Vol. 40, special issue on *Prospects for Democracy*, ed., David Held.

WATERBURY, John (1976), 'Corruption, Political Stability and Development: Comparative Evidence from Egypt and Morocco', *Government and Opposition*, Vol. 11.

— (1983), *The Egypt of Nasser and Sadat: the Political Economy of Two Regimes*, Princeton, NJ: Princeton University Press.

— (1985), 'The "Soft State" and the Open Door: Egypt's Experience with Economic Liberalization', *Comparative Politics*, October.

— (1988), 'Twilight of the State Bourgeoisie?', paper for JCNME/SSRC Conference on Retreating States and Expanding Societies ..., Aix-en-Provence, 25–27 March.

— (1989), 'The Political Management of Economic Adjustment and Reform', in Alan Roe et al., *Economic Adjustment in Algeria, Egypt, Jordan, Morocco, Pakistan, Tunisia, and Turkey*, Washington, DC: World Bank.

WEBER, Max (1947), *The Theory of Social and Economic Organization*, trans., London: William Hodge.

WEINBAUM, Marvin G. (1979), 'Bureaucratic Norms, Structures and Strategies in Agricultural Development Policies in the Middle East', paper presented to Middle East Studies Association Annual Conference, Salt Lake City, November 1979.

WEINSTEIN, John M. (1981), 'A Structural Analysis of the Modernizer's Dilemma', *Comparative International Development*, Vol. 16, nos. 3 and 4.

WEINTRAUB, Jeff (1990), 'The Theory and Politics of the Public/Private Distinction', paper for the American Political Science Association's annual meeting, San Francisco, August 1990.

WEIR, Shelagh (1985), *Qat in Yemen: Consumption and Social Change*, London: British Museum Publications.

WENNER, Manfred W. (1975), 'Saudi Arabia: Survival of Traditional Elites', in Frank Tachau, ed., *Political Elites and Political Development in the Middle East*, New York: John Wiley.

WHITEHEAD, Laurence (1992), 'The Alternatives to "Liberal Democracy": a Latin American Perspective', *Political Studies*, Vol. 40, special issue on *Prospects for Democracy*, ed., David Held.

WICKWAR, W. Hardy (1963), *The Modernization of Administration in the Near East*, Beirut: Khayat.

WILDANSKY, Aaron (1980), *How to Limit Government Spending*, Berkeley, CA: University of California Press.

WILLIAMSON, Peter J. (1989), *Corporatism in Perspective: An Introductory Guide to Corporatist Theory*, London: Sage Publications.

WILSON, Ernest J. (1985), 'State, Growth and Contraction in the Third World: Models of Analysis', paper presented to Annual Congress of the International Political Science Association, Paris, July 1985.

WITTFOGEL, Karl A. (1957), *Oriental Despotism*, New Haven: Yale University Press.

WOLF, Eric R. (1982), *Europe and the People Without History*, Berkeley, CA: University of California Press.

WOLPE, Harold, ed. (1980), *The Articulation of Modes of Production*, London: Routledge and Kegan Paul.

WORLD BANK (1992), *The World Development Report 1992*, Washington, DC: International Bank for Reconstruction and Development/World Bank.

YAPP, M. E. (1987), *The Making of the Modern Near East 1792–1923*, London: Longman.

YASIN, Al-Sayyid (1983), *Al-Shakhsiyya al-'arabiyya* ... [The Arab Character: Between Self-Image and Perception by Others], Beirut: Dar al-Tanwir.

AL-YASINI, Ayman (1987), *Al-Din wa al-dawla* ... [Religion and State in the Kingdom of Saudi Arabia], London: Al-Saqi.

ZAGHAL, 'Abd al-Qadir (1982/83), 'Al-Madaris al-fikriyya ...' [Western Intellectual Schools and Social Structures in the Middle East], *Al-Mustaqbal al-'Arabi*, no. 37.

— (1992), 'Al-Mujtama' al-madani wa al-sira' ...' [The Civil Society and the Struggle for Ideological Hegemony], in S. Al-'Alawi et al., *Al-Mujtama' al-madani fi al-watan al-'arabi* [The Civil Society and its Role in Realising the Arab Fatherland], Beirut: CAUS.

ZAHLAN, Rosemarie Said (1989), *The Making of the Modern Gulf States*, London: Unwin Hyman.

ZAHRAN, Jamal (1988), 'Al-Dawr al-siyasi li al-qada' ...' [The Political Role of the Egyptian Judiciary], in A. Hilal, ed., *Al-Nizam al-Siyasi al-misri* [The Egyptian Political System], Cairo: Al-Markaz al-'Arabi.

AL-ZAIN, 'Ali (1977), *Al-'Adat wa al-taqalid fi al-'uhud al-iqta'iyya* [Customs and Traditions in the Feudal Eras], Beirut and Cairo: Dar al-Kitab.

ZAI'UR, 'Ali (1982), *Qita' al-butula* ... [The Heroism and Narcissism Sector in the Arab Self], Beirut: Dar al-Tali'a.

ZAKARIYYA, Fu'ad (1986), *Al-Haqiqa wa al-wahm fi al-haraka al-islamiyya al-mu'asira* [Fact and Fiction in the Contemporary Islamic Movement], Cairo: Dar al-Fikr li al-Dirasat.

ZAKI, Ramzi, ed. (1989), *Al-Siyasat al-tashihiyya wa al-tanmiyya* ... [Corrective Policies and Development in the Arab Fatherland], Beirut and Kuwait: Dar al-Razi.

ZARTMANN, I. William, ed. (1991), *Tunisia, the Political Economy of Reform*, Boulder and London: Lynne Rienner.

ZIYADA, Niqula (1962), *Al-Hisba wa al-muhtasib* ... [Market Control and Market Controllers in Islam], Beirut: Al-Matba' al-Kathuliqiyya.

ZUBAIDA, Sami (1989), *Islam, the People and the State*, London: Routledge.

ZUREIK, Elia (1981), 'Theoretical Considerations for a Sociological Study of the Arab State', *Arab Studies Quarterly*, Vol. 3, no. 3, Autumn.

NEWSPAPERS AND MAGAZINES

Al-Ahram, Al-Ahram Al-Iqtisadi, Al-'Amal, Al-Anba', Arab Perspectives, Al-'Arabi, Arabia, Al-Azmina Al-'Arabiyya, Al-Dustur, Guardian, Al-Hawadith, Al-Hayat, Al-Khalij, Al-Majalla, Le Monde, Al-Muntada, Al-Muslimun, Al-Mustaqbal, Observer, Al-Ra'Y Al-'Am, Saudi Report, Sawt Al-Tali'A, Al-Sharq Al-Awsat, Al-Shuruq, Al-Siyasa, Sunday Times, Al-Thawra, Al-Watan, Al-Watan Al-'Arabi, Al-Wasat

Index

496

147; Marxism 142; North Africa 142n.5; public sector 151; Saudi Arabia 233; state capitalism 158–9

parliaments 454; Bahrain 430; Egypt 209–11, 413, 415–17, 441; Iraq 425; Islamism 440–1; Jordan 371, 421–2, 441; Kuwait 231, 242, 428–30, 441; Lebanon 441; Qatar 430; Saudi Arabia 231, 427; Syria 423; Tunisia 418–20, 441; United Arab Emirates 430; Yemen 435–6; see also constitutions, democracy, elections, political participation, political parties

participation, political see political participation

parties, political see political parties

partitocrazia 203, 419

Partners in Development Committee (Egypt) 347–50

party (general) 141

party system 203–4

patriarchy 166–7, 224; see also neo-patriarchy

patrimonial states 164, 258

patronage see clientelism

pearling industry 227

peasants 61, 63, 74, 76, 78, 83, 118, 179, 392; Egypt 81, 101, 103, 451–2; Iraq 95; Syria 359–60; see also farmers, village communities

penal law 52

peripheral capitalism 92, 96, 103, 131, 172

peripheral states 13–14, 177–8, 385–6

Peronism 189, 192

Perpetual Maritime Truce (1853) 132

Persia 47, 56, 111; see also Iran

Perthes, Volker 423

Peterson, Erik 231

petrocracy 323, 325

petro-Islam 232–3

Phalange Libanaise see Kata'ib Party

pharaohs 99

philosophy 64–5

Phoenicians 115–16

phosphates 172

planning, economic see economic planning

police 242–3, 272, 286, 302; see also police states, security forces

police states 203, 449; see also police, security forces, violence

policy, economic see economic policy

polis 397

political exchange 220, 247, 409

political integration 1, 135, 143–4, 152, 158, 183, 436–8, 448; see also Pan-Arabism

political participation 32–3, 35, 181, 197–8, 262, 265, 284, 415, 454, 458; see also constitutions, democracy, elections, parliaments, political parties

political parties 413–40; Algeria 372; Egypt

106–7, 150, 198, 210–11, 351, 415–17; Iraq 113, 201, 424–5; Jordan 421; Kuwait 429–30; Lebanon 116; Morocco 121; Saudi Arabia 427; Syria 17, 93–4, 116; Tunisia 120, 212, 418–20; Yemen 436; see also constitutions, democracy, elections, opposition groups, parliaments, political participation and under the names of individual parties

politics of the street see street politics

polyarchy 397, 414

lo popular 204–5

Popular Front for the Liberation of Palestine 142, 421

population 159, 279–80, 300, 303, 367–8, 380

populism 35, 182–3, 185, 188–9, 193, 199, 205–14, 217–21, 277, 386, 410, 448, 453

ports 91

post-colonial states 12–13

post-industrial mode of production 187

Poulantzas, Nicos 8

power 27, 38, 98, 244, 324–6, 332n.1

praetorianism 34, 93, 258, 260, 412

presidency 203–4, 213, 261

press 227, 231, 425, 428

principle of compensation 29, 33

prisons ix

privacy 439–40

private capital see capital, domestic

private companies 330–1, 334–5, 348–9, 356, 360–1, 371, 377, 380

private ownership 15, 42, 44, 46–8, 66, 70, 73–5, 114, 128, 201; see also landlords, private sector

private sector 159–60, 171, 273, 293, 308, 383–90, 393–4; Algeria 372–5; competition 330, 334–5; efficiency 330–1; Egypt 200, 278, 340–52, 383, 409; Iraq 200–1, 362–7; Jordan 367–72; Kuwait 251, 380–1; Lebanon 293; Morocco 406; public sector 404–8, 439, 442; Qatar 383; Saudi Arabia 250, 375–80, 382–3; Sudan 406; Syria 200, 357–62, 383; Tunisia 352–7; United Arab Emirates 380–2; Yemen 433

private space see haram

privatisation 4, 30, 35, 159, 200, 221, 384–9, 393–4, 403–4, 407–8; Algeria 372–5; competition 330, 334–5; contracting-out 333; cooperatives 333; developmentalism 336–9; efficiency 329–31; Egypt 200, 339–52; ideology 332; Iraq 362–7, 424; Jordan 367–72; Kuwait 380–1; Saudi Arabia 375–80; share ownership 330, 333; Syria 357–62; Tunisia 352–7; United Arab Emirates 380–2

production see forces of production, means of production, modes of production, relations of production